BARRON'S

PSAT/NMSQT®

Study Guide

WITH 4 PRACTICE TESTS

Brian W. Stewart, M.Ed.

Founder and President

BWS Education Consulting, Inc.

Dedication

Dedicated to Caitlin, Andrew, and Eloise—without your love and support, this book would not have been possible. I would like to especially thank my mom, my dad, Andy, Pam, Hannah, Mitchell, Michal, Julia, and Lydia for their invaluable help with this undertaking. I am grateful to all the support from my publisher, especially Annie Bernberg and Allison Harm.

Thanks so much to all of my students over the years—I have learned far more from you than you have learned from me.

About the Author

Brian W. Stewart is the founder and President of BWS Education Consulting, Inc., a boutique tutoring and test preparation company based in Columbus, Ohio. He has worked with thousands of students to help them improve their test scores and earn admission to selective schools. Brian is a graduate of Princeton University (A.B.) and The Ohio State University (M.Ed.). You can connect with Brian at *www.bwseducationconsulting.com*.

© Copyright 2020 by Kaplan, Inc., d/b/a Barron's Educational Series

Published by Kaplan, Inc., d/b/a Barron's Educational Series
750 Third Avenue
New York, NY 10017
www.barronseduc.com

ISBN: 978-1-4380-1296-4

10 9 8 7 6 5 4 3 2 1

Kaplan, Inc., d/b/a Barron's Educational Series print books are available at special quantity discounts to use for sales promotions, employee premiums, or educational purposes. For more information or to purchase books, please call the Simon & Schuster special sales department at 866-506-1949.

Contents

MATH

Introduction to the PSAT/NMSQT

What Is the PSAT and How Is It Organized?

The PSAT is a preliminary SAT exam that is used both for assessing student academic progress and for determining eligibility for the National Merit Scholarship competition. Over 4,000,000 high school students take the PSAT or PSAT 10 each year. It is such a popular test because the PSAT helps students gauge their college readiness as well as prepare for the SAT exam. There are different PSAT exams, including PSAT 8/9, PSAT 10, and PSAT/NMSQT, which are typically based on a student's grade level.

The PSAT/NMSQT exam is 2 hours and 45 minutes long. It is broken into two sections:

- **Evidence-based Reading and Writing:** The first half of this section, Reading Comprehension, consists of reading passages and questions that test your reading abilities. The second half, Writing and Language, features passages and questions that test your grammar and editing skills
- **Math:** The first part of this section is non-calculator, and the second part allows you to use a calculator.

The two sections are each scored between 160 (minimum) and 760 (maximum) points, for a total possible score between 320 and 1520. There is no penalty for guessing, so be sure to answer every question.

TIP

The PSAT is very similar to the SAT. However, the SAT is slightly longer, has a bit more advanced math, and includes an essay. This book will not only prepare you for the PSAT but also includes most of what you will find on the SAT.

PSAT Structure		
1. Reading	60 minutes	47 questions and 5 passages
5-Minute Break		
2. Writing and Language	35 minutes	44 questions and 4 passages
3. Math—No Calculator	25 minutes	17 questions (13 multiple-choice and 4 grid-in)
5-Minute Break		
4. Math—Calculator	45 minutes	31 questions (27 multiple-choice and 4 grid-in)

What Does the PSAT Test?

The PSAT tests the skills and general knowledge you will need to be successful in college and beyond.

- **Reading Comprehension Skills**
  - Determining what you can infer from a reading passage
  - Finding what evidence in a passage supports a claim
  - Establishing the meaning of words in context
  - Analyzing graphs as they relate to a reading passage

- **Writing and Language Skills**
  - Knowledge of English grammar fundamentals (punctuation, subject-verb agreement, verb tense, etc.)
  - Understanding how best to organize writing to help the flow of ideas
  - Awareness of proper English language use (idioms, words in context, essay tone, etc.)

- **Math Problem-Solving Skills**
  - Solving questions with an emphasis on Algebra 1 and Algebra 2 (just a handful of questions may relate to geometry and precalculus)
  - Analyzing and problem solving using charts and graphs
  - Understanding and solving real-world applications

What Should I Take to the Test?

Be certain to bring the following on test day:

- Several number 2 pencils.
- A permitted calculator (see *https://www.collegeboard.org/psat-nmsqt/approved-calculators* for a complete list).
- A watch to monitor your pacing. (Be sure it doesn't make noise and cannot connect to the Internet.)
- A photo ID. (If you are taking the exam at your own school, you will likely not need one.)
- An e-mail address so colleges can contact you and you can access your scores online.
- A snack or drink for your break. Be sure you do not place these on your desk.
- Do NOT bring a cell phone. You don't want to risk it going off accidentally. Also, you won't be able to check it during a break.

If you are taking a digital version of the test, which is identical in content and format to a paper version of the PSAT, you will be provided with scrap paper.

What Should I Do in the Days Leading Up to the PSAT?

If the PSAT were a test for which you could cram, it would make sense to stay up late studying the night before. Since it is more of a critical thinking test, you need to be as relaxed and as well rested as possible to do your best. Here are some things you must do before the PSAT.

- Go to bed at a reasonable hour starting a week before the test. If you wait until the night before the test to get a good night's sleep, you may not be rested enough on test day. After all, calming down and relaxing the night before a major assessment can be extremely difficult.
- Know the test directions—you do not want to waste time reading the directions on each section. At a minimum, know that you SHOULD INCLUDE AN ANSWER for every question since there is no guessing penalty.

- Become comfortable with timing. Do at least some practice with timing so you will not work too quickly or too slowly on test day.
- Know your strategic approach ahead of time—this way you can devote your full attention to solving problems instead of experimenting with strategies during the test.

What Is a National Merit Scholarship and How Do I Qualify?

The National Merit Scholarship is a prestigious award administered by the National Merit Scholarship Corporation that recognizes students based on their academic merit, using PSAT scores as the principle eligibility factor. The scores are used to compute the Selection Index. Your section scores from the Reading, Writing and Language, and Math sections are each doubled to give you a selection index between 48 and 228. (So even though the Reading and the Writing and Language sections comprise *half* of the PSAT, they make up *two-thirds* of your selection index calculation.) Depending on which state you live in, a selection index between 212 and 223 may qualify you for some type of National Merit recognition.

National Merit Scholarships range from single-payment $2,500 scholarships to college-sponsored scholarships that provide a full ride for tuition, room/board, plus a stipend for all four years of school. Out of the roughly 1.6 million high school juniors who take the PSAT/NMSQT, about 50,000 receive some sort of National Merit recognition, such as being named a Commended Scholar or a Semi-Finalist. Only about 7,500 students nationwide receive a National Merit Scholarship. In order to be a National Merit Scholar, you must typically perform in the top 0.5 percent of students. To learn more about the National Merit program, go to *www.nationalmerit.org*.

In addition to the National Merit Scholarship program, PSAT scores are now used to determine eligibility for other academic recognition programs. If you are African American, Hispanic American or Latino, Indigenous, and/or live in a rural area, you may be eligible to apply for academic recognition by the College Board. You can go to *www.psat.org/recognition* for the latest information on these programs.

What are the Requirements to Participate in the National Merit Scholarship Program?

- Take the PSAT/NMSQT no later than the third year of high school—typically this is the junior year for students who take the full four years to graduate.
- Be a high school student in the United States or its territories, or be a U.S. citizen or resident attending high school abroad.
- Be on track for high school graduation and college admission the fall after high school graduation.

What If I Miss the PSAT/NMSQT Because of an Emergency?

You or a school official should write to the National Merit Scholarship Corporation as soon as possible (at the latest, April 1 after the PSAT) to request information about alternate entry into the scholarship program. The mailing address is:

National Merit Scholarship Corporation
1560 Sherman Avenue, Suite 200
Evanston, IL 60201-4897

Go to *www.nationalmerit.org* for more details.

What About PSAT Accommodations and Extended Time?

If you are a student who has special learning needs and you have an IEP or 504 plan with your school, you may be eligible for accommodations on the PSAT. Some of the different types of accommodations offered include 50 percent or 100 percent extended time, extra breaks, and large-print and audio test formats. Applying for accommodations on the PSAT is easiest and fastest if you do so through your school. Keep in mind that you should allow at least seven weeks for the College Board to review your request. You can find more information about PSAT testing with accommodations at *https://accommodations.collegeboard.org/*.

What If English Is Not My Native Language?

The College Board offers testing options to students who have English language support in school and are considered to be an "English learner" by the state or federal government. Students with English learner support may be able to use 50 percent extra time, an approved bilingual dictionary, and translated test directions. Unlike special needs accommodations, extended time for English learners is available only on the test date for which you register. Speak to your school counselor, ESL teacher, or administrator for help on PSAT English learner testing support.

What Is the PSAT 10? How Will This Book Help Me Prepare for It?

The PSAT 10 is the same test as the PSAT/NMSQT. Thus, if you would like to prepare for the PSAT 10, this book is exactly what you need. Although the tests themselves are identical, there are three important differences between the PSAT 10 and the PSAT/NMSQT.

- The PSAT 10 is offered in the spring, while the PSAT/NMSQT is offered in the fall.
- The PSAT 10 is for tenth-grade students, while the PSAT/NMSQT is for eleventh-grade students. (Although many underclassmen take the PSAT/NMSQT.)
- The PSAT 10 will not enter students in the National Merit Scholarship competition, while juniors who take the PSAT/NMSQT can enter this competition. Students who take either exam will be considered for other scholarship programs through the Student Search Service®.

If your school does not offer the PSAT 10 and you would like to try the PSAT as a tenth grader, talk to your guidance counselor about taking the PSAT/NMSQT in the fall of your tenth-grade year.

How Can I Manage My Test Anxiety?

The PSAT will be scored on a curve. So if it seems more difficult or easier than you thought it would be, don't worry. Everyone is taking the same test, and the curve will reflect how people did.

With only one shot to perform well on the PSAT for National Merit consideration, taking the PSAT can be a very stressful process. Being nervous is completely normal. Here are a few things to keep in mind if you find anxiety interfering with your ability to perform your best.

- When it comes to college admissions, how you perform on the actual SAT and/or ACT will be much more important than your PSAT performance. You will have many opportunities to take the SAT and/or ACT.
- Colleges will receive your scores only if you opt-in to the informational services.
- Mentally rehearse *ahead of time* to think about how you can best respond to the pressure of the PSAT. Are you someone who tends to rush through the test? Instead, are you someone who tends to get stuck on questions? Knowing your tendencies will help you recognize if your

thought process is off track, enabling you to make adjustments to your test-taking strategies for test day.

- Realize that if the PSAT doesn't go well even after quite a bit of preparation, you will have built skills that will help you on both the SAT and ACT since those two tests have very similar questions to much of what you will find on the PSAT.

How Can I Use This Book to Prepare?

This book allows you to focus on your areas of weakness. It also helps you customize your strategies and mindset depending on your particular situation. Not only can you spend your time practicing math, for example, but you can spend your time practicing the types of math questions that are most challenging for you, be they algebra or data analysis. The practice exercises are designed to give you comprehensive coverage of all the types of questions you will face. If you work through everything in this book, it is unlikely that you will encounter surprises on test day.

If you are unsure what areas of the test are most difficult for you, start by taking the full-length PSAT diagnostic test. Evaluate your performance to see what types of passages and questions give you the most difficulty. Then review the strategies and materials from the different chapters to sharpen your skills. When you are done with the chapters, do more practice with the two full-length PSAT practice tests at the end of the book and the additional one online. To really push yourself, try the advanced practice drills and online resources for extra-challenging questions.

If you wish to do even more long-term preparation, you should read a wide variety of well-written texts. At a minimum, install an e-reading app on your phone and use it to spend a few minutes each day reading, no matter where you are. If you want to go all out, seek the types of reading that you find most difficult. Read more material from those genres so that your weaknesses turn into strengths. Reading books will help improve your reading comprehension skills, your ability to pick up the meaning of vocabulary in context, and your feel for English grammar.

TIP

Remember that the strategy that works for one student may not work for another student. This book is designed to help you customize your strategy and practice.

What If I Have a Limited Amount of Time to Prepare?

Here are some suggested plans depending on how long you have to prepare.

- *If you have one day*, read through the strategies in the chapters for each test section: Reading, Writing and Language, and Math. Look through the full-length diagnostic test to become familiar with the directions, time requirements, and structure of the PSAT. Try a few practice questions.
- *If you have one week*, take the full-length diagnostic test under timed conditions to determine your strengths and weaknesses. Then review the strategies in the chapters for each of the test sections. Target your areas of weakness based on the diagnostic test by working through selected review drills. The drills are broken down by categories, so it will be easy to pick out where you should focus.
- *If you have one month*, systematically work through everything in this book. The strategies, content review, drills, and practice tests will give you the best possible preparation to achieve a top score on the PSAT/NMSQT.

If you have even more time available to prepare, you may want to take the SAT once before you take the PSAT—there is a test offered in October shortly before the PSAT administration. If you are a sophomore or freshman, you may want to take the PSAT when it is offered at your school even though it will not count toward National Merit consideration. The pressures of these actual tests will prepare you for when it is most important for you to do well on the PSAT—in October of your junior year. The better prepared you are, the less nervous you will feel on test day.

Let's get to work!

> Be sure to check out the appendix in this book—"After the PSAT"—once your scores come back to help you understand how to use your PSAT results to help plan future testing.

Diagnostic Test

Diagnostic Test

A full-length PSAT diagnostic test is on the pages that follow. Allow roughly 3 hours of uninterrupted time to complete the entire test. Find a spot to take the test where you will not be distracted. You can take a 5-minute break after the Reading Test and another 5-minute break after the Math (No Calculator) Test.

Completing this diagnostic test will help you determine your PSAT strengths and weaknesses. Think about the following after you take the test.

- How are you with timing?
- Do you find certain types of reading questions to be challenging?
- Do particular reading passages give you more difficulty than others?
- Do you need to review English grammar concepts?
- Do some types of writing and language questions give you more trouble than others?
- Do you need to review or learn some math concepts?
- What kinds of math questions are toughest for you?

After completing the test, review your answers with the "Diagnostic Test Analysis Guide" to determine what types of passages and questions you most need to study.

Good luck!

ANSWER SHEET
Diagnostic Test

Reading Test

1. Ⓐ Ⓑ Ⓒ Ⓓ	13. Ⓐ Ⓑ Ⓒ Ⓓ	25. Ⓐ Ⓑ Ⓒ Ⓓ	37. Ⓐ Ⓑ Ⓒ Ⓓ
2. Ⓐ Ⓑ Ⓒ Ⓓ	14. Ⓐ Ⓑ Ⓒ Ⓓ	26. Ⓐ Ⓑ Ⓒ Ⓓ	38. Ⓐ Ⓑ Ⓒ Ⓓ
3. Ⓐ Ⓑ Ⓒ Ⓓ	15. Ⓐ Ⓑ Ⓒ Ⓓ	27. Ⓐ Ⓑ Ⓒ Ⓓ	39. Ⓐ Ⓑ Ⓒ Ⓓ
4. Ⓐ Ⓑ Ⓒ Ⓓ	16. Ⓐ Ⓑ Ⓒ Ⓓ	28. Ⓐ Ⓑ Ⓒ Ⓓ	40. Ⓐ Ⓑ Ⓒ Ⓓ
5. Ⓐ Ⓑ Ⓒ Ⓓ	17. Ⓐ Ⓑ Ⓒ Ⓓ	29. Ⓐ Ⓑ Ⓒ Ⓓ	41. Ⓐ Ⓑ Ⓒ Ⓓ
6. Ⓐ Ⓑ Ⓒ Ⓓ	18. Ⓐ Ⓑ Ⓒ Ⓓ	30. Ⓐ Ⓑ Ⓒ Ⓓ	42. Ⓐ Ⓑ Ⓒ Ⓓ
7. Ⓐ Ⓑ Ⓒ Ⓓ	19. Ⓐ Ⓑ Ⓒ Ⓓ	31. Ⓐ Ⓑ Ⓒ Ⓓ	43. Ⓐ Ⓑ Ⓒ Ⓓ
8. Ⓐ Ⓑ Ⓒ Ⓓ	20. Ⓐ Ⓑ Ⓒ Ⓓ	32. Ⓐ Ⓑ Ⓒ Ⓓ	44. Ⓐ Ⓑ Ⓒ Ⓓ
9. Ⓐ Ⓑ Ⓒ Ⓓ	21. Ⓐ Ⓑ Ⓒ Ⓓ	33. Ⓐ Ⓑ Ⓒ Ⓓ	45. Ⓐ Ⓑ Ⓒ Ⓓ
10. Ⓐ Ⓑ Ⓒ Ⓓ	22. Ⓐ Ⓑ Ⓒ Ⓓ	34. Ⓐ Ⓑ Ⓒ Ⓓ	46. Ⓐ Ⓑ Ⓒ Ⓓ
11. Ⓐ Ⓑ Ⓒ Ⓓ	23. Ⓐ Ⓑ Ⓒ Ⓓ	35. Ⓐ Ⓑ Ⓒ Ⓓ	47. Ⓐ Ⓑ Ⓒ Ⓓ
12. Ⓐ Ⓑ Ⓒ Ⓓ	24. Ⓐ Ⓑ Ⓒ Ⓓ	36. Ⓐ Ⓑ Ⓒ Ⓓ	

Writing and Language Test

1. Ⓐ Ⓑ Ⓒ Ⓓ	12. Ⓐ Ⓑ Ⓒ Ⓓ	23. Ⓐ Ⓑ Ⓒ Ⓓ	34. Ⓐ Ⓑ Ⓒ Ⓓ
2. Ⓐ Ⓑ Ⓒ Ⓓ	13. Ⓐ Ⓑ Ⓒ Ⓓ	24. Ⓐ Ⓑ Ⓒ Ⓓ	35. Ⓐ Ⓑ Ⓒ Ⓓ
3. Ⓐ Ⓑ Ⓒ Ⓓ	14. Ⓐ Ⓑ Ⓒ Ⓓ	25. Ⓐ Ⓑ Ⓒ Ⓓ	36. Ⓐ Ⓑ Ⓒ Ⓓ
4. Ⓐ Ⓑ Ⓒ Ⓓ	15. Ⓐ Ⓑ Ⓒ Ⓓ	26. Ⓐ Ⓑ Ⓒ Ⓓ	37. Ⓐ Ⓑ Ⓒ Ⓓ
5. Ⓐ Ⓑ Ⓒ Ⓓ	16. Ⓐ Ⓑ Ⓒ Ⓓ	27. Ⓐ Ⓑ Ⓒ Ⓓ	38. Ⓐ Ⓑ Ⓒ Ⓓ
6. Ⓐ Ⓑ Ⓒ Ⓓ	17. Ⓐ Ⓑ Ⓒ Ⓓ	28. Ⓐ Ⓑ Ⓒ Ⓓ	39. Ⓐ Ⓑ Ⓒ Ⓓ
7. Ⓐ Ⓑ Ⓒ Ⓓ	18. Ⓐ Ⓑ Ⓒ Ⓓ	29. Ⓐ Ⓑ Ⓒ Ⓓ	40. Ⓐ Ⓑ Ⓒ Ⓓ
8. Ⓐ Ⓑ Ⓒ Ⓓ	19. Ⓐ Ⓑ Ⓒ Ⓓ	30. Ⓐ Ⓑ Ⓒ Ⓓ	41. Ⓐ Ⓑ Ⓒ Ⓓ
9. Ⓐ Ⓑ Ⓒ Ⓓ	20. Ⓐ Ⓑ Ⓒ Ⓓ	31. Ⓐ Ⓑ Ⓒ Ⓓ	42. Ⓐ Ⓑ Ⓒ Ⓓ
10. Ⓐ Ⓑ Ⓒ Ⓓ	21. Ⓐ Ⓑ Ⓒ Ⓓ	32. Ⓐ Ⓑ Ⓒ Ⓓ	43. Ⓐ Ⓑ Ⓒ Ⓓ
11. Ⓐ Ⓑ Ⓒ Ⓓ	22. Ⓐ Ⓑ Ⓒ Ⓓ	33. Ⓐ Ⓑ Ⓒ Ⓓ	44. Ⓐ Ⓑ Ⓒ Ⓓ

Math Test (No Calculator)

1. Ⓐ Ⓑ Ⓒ Ⓓ 5. Ⓐ Ⓑ Ⓒ Ⓓ 9. Ⓐ Ⓑ Ⓒ Ⓓ 13. Ⓐ Ⓑ Ⓒ Ⓓ
2. Ⓐ Ⓑ Ⓒ Ⓓ 6. Ⓐ Ⓑ Ⓒ Ⓓ 10. Ⓐ Ⓑ Ⓒ Ⓓ
3. Ⓐ Ⓑ Ⓒ Ⓓ 7. Ⓐ Ⓑ Ⓒ Ⓓ 11. Ⓐ Ⓑ Ⓒ Ⓓ
4. Ⓐ Ⓑ Ⓒ Ⓓ 8. Ⓐ Ⓑ Ⓒ Ⓓ 12. Ⓐ Ⓑ Ⓒ Ⓓ

14. 15. 16. 17.

Math Test (With Calculator)

1. Ⓐ Ⓑ Ⓒ Ⓓ 8. Ⓐ Ⓑ Ⓒ Ⓓ 15. Ⓐ Ⓑ Ⓒ Ⓓ 22. Ⓐ Ⓑ Ⓒ Ⓓ
2. Ⓐ Ⓑ Ⓒ Ⓓ 9. Ⓐ Ⓑ Ⓒ Ⓓ 16. Ⓐ Ⓑ Ⓒ Ⓓ 23. Ⓐ Ⓑ Ⓒ Ⓓ
3. Ⓐ Ⓑ Ⓒ Ⓓ 10. Ⓐ Ⓑ Ⓒ Ⓓ 17. Ⓐ Ⓑ Ⓒ Ⓓ 24. Ⓐ Ⓑ Ⓒ Ⓓ
4. Ⓐ Ⓑ Ⓒ Ⓓ 11. Ⓐ Ⓑ Ⓒ Ⓓ 18. Ⓐ Ⓑ Ⓒ Ⓓ 25. Ⓐ Ⓑ Ⓒ Ⓓ
5. Ⓐ Ⓑ Ⓒ Ⓓ 12. Ⓐ Ⓑ Ⓒ Ⓓ 19. Ⓐ Ⓑ Ⓒ Ⓓ 26. Ⓐ Ⓑ Ⓒ Ⓓ
6. Ⓐ Ⓑ Ⓒ Ⓓ 13. Ⓐ Ⓑ Ⓒ Ⓓ 20. Ⓐ Ⓑ Ⓒ Ⓓ 27. Ⓐ Ⓑ Ⓒ Ⓓ
7. Ⓐ Ⓑ Ⓒ Ⓓ 14. Ⓐ Ⓑ Ⓒ Ⓓ 21. Ⓐ Ⓑ Ⓒ Ⓓ

28. 29. 30. 31.

Diagnostic Test

READING TEST

60 MINUTES, 47 QUESTIONS

Directions: Each passage or pair of passages is accompanied by several questions. After reading the passage(s), choose the best answer to each question based on what is indicated explicitly or implicitly in the passage(s) or in the associated graphics.

Questions 1–9 are based on the following excerpt.

The following passage is an excerpt from the 1912 French novel "The Gods Will Have Blood." Citizen Brotteaux, an elderly humanist, is visiting Citizeness Gamelin, a widowed artist, for lunch. They are briefly interrupted by Gamelin's son, Évariste, a young artist and recently appointed magistrate in the French Revolution.

That morning, very early, the Citizen Brotteaux had made the Citizeness Gamelin the magnificent gift of a capon.* It would
Line have been imprudent on his part to say how
(5) he had come by it: for he had been given it by a certain lady of the market at Pointe Eustache, whose letters he occasionally wrote for her, and it was well known that the ladies of the market cherished Royalist sympathies
(10) and were in touch by correspondence with the émigrés. The Citizeness Gamelin had accepted the capon with deep gratitude. Such things were scarcely ever seen now; food of all kinds became more expensive every day. The
(15) people feared a famine: everybody said that that was what the aristocrats wanted, and that the food-grabbers were preparing for it.

Invited to eat his share of the capon at the midday meal, the Citizen Brotteaux duly
(20) appeared and congratulated his hostess on the rich aroma of her cooking. For indeed the artist's studio was filled with the smell of savory meat soup.

"You are a true gentleman, monsieur,"
(25) replied the good lady. "As an appetizer for your capon, I've made some vegetable soup with a slice of bacon and a big beef bone. There's nothing gives soup a flavor better than a marrow bone."

(30) "A praiseworthy maxim, Citizeness," replied old Brotteaux. "And you will do wisely, if tomorrow, and the next day, and all the rest of the week, you put this precious bone back into the pot, so that it will
(35) continue to flavor it. The wise woman of Panzoust used to do that: she made a soup of green cabbages with a rind of bacon and an old *savorados*. That is what they call the tasty and succulent medullary bone in her coun-
(40) try, which is also my country."

"This lady you speak of, monsieur," the Citizeness Gamelin put in, "wasn't she a little on the careful side, making the same bone last so long?"

(45) "She did not live on a grand scale," Brotteaux replied. "She was poor, even though she was a prophetess."

GO ON TO THE NEXT PAGE

At that moment Évariste Gamelin came in,
still deeply affected by the confession he had
(50) just heard and promising himself he would
discover the identity of Élodie's seducer, so
that he might wreak on him the vengeance of
the Republic and of himself.

After the usual politenesses, the Citizen
(55) Brotteaux resumed the thread of his discourse:

"Those who make a trade out of foretelling
the future rarely grow rich. Their attempts to
deceive are too easily found out and arouse
(60) detestation. And yet it would be necessary
to detest them much, much more if they
foretold the future correctly. For a man's life
would become intolerable, if he knew what
was going to happen to him. He would be
(65) made aware of future evils, and would suffer
their agonies in advance, while he would get
no joy of present blessings since he would
know how they would end. Ignorance is the
necessary condition of human happiness,
(70) and it has to be admitted that on the whole
mankind observes that condition well. We
are almost entirely ignorant of ourselves;
absolutely of others. In ignorance, we find
our bliss; in illusions, our happiness."
(75)   The Citizeness Gamelin put the soup on
the table, said the *Benedicite*, seated her son
and her guest, and began to eat standing up,
declining the chair which Brotteaux offered
her next to him, since, she said, she knew
(80) what courtesy required of her.

*A *capon* is a domesticated rooster.

1. The passage is best representative of what
    genre of world literature?

    (A) Magical realism
    (B) Short story
    (C) Historical fiction
    (D) Fantasy

2. The characters in the passage use the terms
    "citizen" and "citizeness" to distinguish
    between

    (A) different genders.
    (B) different social classes.
    (C) different ages.
    (D) different ethnicities.

3. It can reasonably be inferred that the
    "people" believe the "aristocrats" and
    "food-grabbers" in lines 14–17 are likely
    planning to

    (A) poison the food of the peasants.
    (B) save food to give away to the needy.
    (C) hoard food to profit at a later time.
    (D) develop better agricultural technology.

4. Which choice provides the best evidence for
    the answer to the previous question?

    (A) Lines 1–3 ("That morning . . . capon")
    (B) Lines 5–8 ("for he . . . for her")
    (C) Lines 8–11 ("it was . . . émigrés")
    (D) Lines 12–14 ("Such . . . every day")

5. As used in line 45, "grand" most nearly
    means

    (A) vast.
    (B) imposing.
    (C) lavish.
    (D) prime.

6. We can reasonably infer from the passage
    that Évariste's approach to the treatment of
    lawbreakers is

    (A) tolerant and patient.
    (B) unforgiving and relentless.
    (C) ignorant and illusory.
    (D) generous and gentlemanly.

GO ON TO THE NEXT PAGE

7. Which choice provides the best evidence for the answer to the previous question?

(A) Lines 48–53 ("At that . . . himself")
(B) Lines 62–68 ("For a . . . would end")
(C) Lines 71–74 ("We . . . happiness")
(D) Lines 75–80 ("The Citizeness . . . of her")

8. The main idea conveyed in Brotteaux's monologue in lines 57–74 can best be summarized as

(A) let bygones be bygones.
(B) the truth will set you free.
(C) focus on the moment.
(D) do unto others as you would have them do unto you.

9. As used in line 78, "declining" most nearly means

(A) repulsing.
(B) decreasing.
(C) turning down.
(D) plummeting.

Questions 10–19 are based on the following passage and table.

This passage is adapted from a 2014 article about Canada and the War of 1812.

Spanning a distance of more than 1,500 miles, the border between Canada and the United States has been called the longest
Line undefended international boundary in the
(5) world. This is true to some extent in that neither the U.S. nor Canada maintains a military presence at the border. But as anyone who has crossed from one side of Niagara Falls to the other knows, civilian law enforcement is
(10) present and accounted for at checkpoints on both sides of the boundary, where entrants are monitored and customs laws administered. Partly because of our cultural similarities and partly because of the remarkable
(15) amiability of our diplomatic relations over the past 150 years, it can sometimes seem almost as though the distinction between Canada and the United States is more one of policy than one of practice. But this has not
(20) always been the case. There was a time when the kinship between these two nations was far more dubious, particularly in the years prior to 1867, when Canada was granted its dominion status and thus its independence
(25) from the British parliament.

In 1812, U.S. president James Madison declared war on the British Empire. There were a variety of reasons for the declaration: British-U.S. relations were strained by
(30) England's attempts to thwart international trade between the U.S. and France—with whom the British were already at war—and on several occasions, the Royal Navy had endeavored to conscript American sailors
(35) by force. However, perhaps no cause for war was more compelling in the U.S. than the desire to expand the nation into the northern territories of modern-day Ontario and modern-day Quebec, which were still British
(40) colonies at the time.

With the United States paralyzed by partisan infighting and confused about its federal military policies, and Canada's meager militias practically unaided by the British
(45) army—which was largely embroiled in fighting against Napoleon's forces in Spain— neither side was well-prepared for a war. Nonetheless, in July of that year, Congress launched its untrained 35,000-man army
(50) into the first stage of a four-pronged offensive starting at Detroit, then Niagara, then Kingston, and finally at Montreal. Madison— who anticipated the conflict's resolution in

GO ON TO THE NEXT PAGE

a matter of weeks—had as grossly overesti-
(55) mated the efficacy of the American military
as he had underestimated the tenacity of
New England Federalists' opposition to the
war. By adopting a cautious, defensive strategy, Native-American and Canadian militias
(60) led by British officers successfully rebuffed
the invaders and eventually—following the
surrender of General William Hull to British
Major General Isaac Brock and Shawnee
Leader Tecumseh—captured not only Detroit
(65) but most of the Michigan territory as well.

The war dragged on for two years with
little progress on either side. By concentrat-
ing their defenses in Ontario, the Canadians
left Quebec vulnerable to invasion along the
(70) St. Lawrence River. Consequently, the U.S.
seized portions of Upper Canada but because
of a combination of poor military leadership,
logistical obstacles, and inadequate funding, never managed to take the key posi-
(75) tions of Montreal or Quebec City. By April
of 1814, Napoleon was defeated in Europe
and a greater brunt of the British military fell
upon the United States. The primary theaters
of war, in turn, shifted from the Canadian
(80) frontier to coastal American cities such
as Baltimore, Washington D.C., and New
Orleans. Canada's role in the conflict was by
that time essentially at an end, though fighting continued intermittently in the North
(85) until the signing of the Treaty of Ghent in
December of that year.

Since the War of 1812, Canada and the
U.S. have maintained a warm and neigh-
borly diplomatic relationship; the two
(90) nations fought as allies in both World Wars and
collaborated closely throughout the
Cold War with NORAD. More recently, the
Canada-United States Free Trade Agreement
implemented at the beginning of 1988 ushered
(95) in a tremendous increase in commerce and
business between the two. A shared British

colonial heritage and the English language
have provided all the common ground necessary to make our two neighboring nations
(100) fast friends, but the now-antique batteries
and ramparts that still line the St. Lawrence
River stand as testament to a time when our
international intercourse was far less friendly
than it is today.

Canadian-American Trade

Year*	Total Annual Exports from the U.S. to Canada (Billions of U.S. Dollars)	Total Annual Imports from Canada to the U.S. (Billions of U.S. Dollars)
1986	45.3	68.3
1987	59.8	71.0
1988	71.6	81.4
1989	78.8	87.9
1990	83.7	91.4
1991	85.1	91.0
1992	90.6	98.6

*Data obtained from *https://www.census.gov/foreign-trade/balance/c1220.html#1985*

10. It can be inferred from the passage as a
whole that the author believes that many
present-day readers of this piece are

(A) knowledgeable about the history of the
major battles in the different military
theaters in the War of 1812.

(B) well-informed about the difficult early
relations that the U.S. and Canada had in
the early 1800s.

(C) eager to use the information in this
reading to advocate the increased
militarization of the undefended
U.S.-Canada border.

(D) generally unaware of the past hostility
between the U.S. and Canada given the
present-day friendliness between the
two countries.

GO ON TO THE NEXT PAGE

11. Which of the following does the author argue was the most significant motivation for U.S. citizens who wanted to go to war with Canada in the early 1800s?

(A) Vengeance toward the British
(B) Territorial ambitions
(C) The continued capture of American sailors
(D) Defense against Native-American incursions

12. Which choice provides the best evidence for the answer to the previous question?

(A) Lines 20–25 ("There was . . . parliament")
(B) Lines 33–35 ("on several . . . force")
(C) Lines 35–40 ("However . . . the time")
(D) Lines 59–64 ("Native-American . . . Tecumseh")

13. As it is used in line 22, "dubious" most nearly means

(A) congenial.
(B) suspect.
(C) familial.
(D) loathsome.

14. As it is used in line 56, "tenacity" most nearly means

(A) determination.
(B) anger.
(C) existence.
(D) function.

15. Based on the fourth paragraph, lines 66–86, which of the following was NOT an obstacle to a lasting U.S. victory in Quebec?

(A) The quality of the U.S. generals
(B) The lack of good transportation and supplies
(C) A lack of funding
(D) A strong Canadian defense

16. According to the passage, the North American battles in the War of 1812 gradually shifted from

(A) being fought and led by great generals to being fought and led by elected representatives.
(B) decisive victories by the British to decisive victories by the United States.
(C) being fought in the wilderness to being fought in urban areas.
(D) French to British military involvement.

17. Which choice provides the best evidence for the answer to the previous question?

(A) Lines 61–64 ("following . . . Tecumseh")
(B) Lines 75–78 ("By April . . . States")
(C) Lines 78–82 ("The primary . . . Orleans")
(D) Lines 83–86 ("fighting . . . year")

18. The table after the passage is most helpful when quantifying the qualitative description given by which word in the passage?

(A) "Collaborated," line 91
(B) "Tremendous," line 95
(C) "Neighboring," line 99
(D) "Intercourse," line 103

19. According to lines 92–96, a free trade agreement between the U.S. and Canada was implemented in 1988. Based on the data provided in the table, what type of business can we reasonably conclude would most likely have had the greatest immediate benefit in the first year of the treaty becoming law?

(A) A company that manufactures cars in the United States and sells them to Canadians
(B) A company that purchases raw materials from Canada to manufacture products in its U.S. factories
(C) A Canadian company that manufactures products exclusively for the Canadian government
(D) A U.S. company that provides retail services to customers in the continental United States

GO ON TO THE NEXT PAGE

Questions 20–28 are based on the following passage.

This passage is adapted from the article "Woman Suffrage Must Be Non-Partisan," by Susan B. Anthony, August 1896.

The different woman suffrage committees of Southern California, it is understood, are planning to do some very effective campaign
Line   work on behalf of the eleventh amendment
(5)   by forming allied women's clubs to the old parties. The plan, it is argued, will be perfectly consistent, owing to the fact that the Republicans, Populists and Prohibitionists all put a woman-suffrage plank in their State
(10)   platforms, and that while the Democracy refused this, many of the delegates from this end of the State favored it and are staunch supporters of the movement. It is considered "good politics" to work in connection with
(15)   instead of independent of the present organized political parties.

The plan of action proposed in the above item from Los Angeles in yesterday's Call would be most disastrous to the woman's
(20)   suffrage amendment. Every one must see that for a part of the suffrage women to thus ally themselves with the Republican party, another portion with the Democratic party, another with the Populist, another with the
(25)   Prohibition, another with the Nationalist, and yet another with the Socialist Labor party, would be to divide and distract public thought from women as suffragists to women as Republicans, Populists, etc. To do this may
(30)   be "good politics," for the different political parties, but it would surely be very "bad politics" for amendment No. XI. It doesn't need a prophet to see that "allied clubs to the old parties" will turn the thought of the women
(35)   themselves to proselyting for members to their respective political party clubs instead of each and every one holding herself non-partisan, or

better all-partisan, pleading with every man of every party to stamp "yes" at amendment No.
(40)   XI, not for the purpose of insuring success to his party at the coming election, or to win the good will of the women of the State for future partisan ends, but instead, pleading with every one to thus vote that he may help to secure
(45)   to all the women of California who can "read the constitution in the English language" their citizen's right to vote to help the political party of their choice in all elections in the good times to come.

(50)   Of course each of the political parties, old and new, would be glad of the help of the women throughout this fall campaign, but who can fail to see that the women who should join one alliance would thereby lose their
(55)   influence with the men of each of the other parties. They would at once be adjudged partisans, working for the interest of the party with which or to which they were allied. Women of California, you cannot keep the
(60)   good will and win the good votes of all the good men of all the good parties of the State by allying yourselves with one or the other or all of them! You must stand as disfranchised citizens—outlaws—shut out of "the body
(65)   politic," humble supplicants, veriest beggars at the feet of all men of all parties alike.

The vote of the humblest man of the humblest party is of equal value to that of the proudest millionaire of the largest party. And
(70)   every woman must see that if a vast majority of the women of the State should, under the Los Angeles plan, ally themselves to either one of the parties, the men of all the others might well take alarm lest their party's chances
(75)   of success would be vastly lessened if women were allowed to vote and so from mere party interest, be influenced to stamp "no" at amendment No. XI.

It is very clear to every student of politics
(80)   that what is "good politics" for political parties

GO ON TO THE NEXT PAGE

is "mighty poor politics" for a reform measure dependent upon the votes of the members of all parties. It will be time enough for the women of California to enroll themselves as

(85) Republicans, Democrats, Populists, etc., after they have the right to vote secured to them by the elimination of the word "male" from the suffrage clause of the constitution. And to work most efficiently to get the right to become a

(90) voting member of one or another of the parties of the State women must now hold themselves aloof from affiliation with each and all of them.

20. The primary purpose of this passage is to

(A) confront a geographical region.
(B) dispute a historical recollection.
(C) attack a gender identity.
(D) make a tactical argument.

21. In order to ratify the eleventh amendment, the author most directly encourages women to focus on winning over which group of men?

(A) Leaders of major political parties
(B) Men who are less fortunate
(C) Literate, educated men
(D) Men from all walks of life

22. Which option gives the best evidence for the answer to the previous question?

(A) Lines 1–6 ("The different . . . parties")
(B) Lines 17–20 ("The plan . . . amendment")
(C) Lines 45–49 ("all the . . . come")
(D) Lines 63–66 ("You must . . . alike")

23. The author most strongly suggests that the interests of the political parties and of women are

(A) aligned.
(B) uniform.
(C) divergent.
(D) belligerent.

24. Which option gives the best evidence for the answer to the previous question?

(A) Lines 6–10 ("The plan . . . platforms")
(B) Lines 13–16 ("It is . . . parties")
(C) Lines 29–32 ("To do . . . XI")
(D) Lines 67–69 ("The vote . . . party")

25. As used in line 12, "staunch" most closely means

(A) strong.
(B) democratic.
(C) disloyal.
(D) mistaken.

26. The author uses quotation marks around the phrase "good politics" in line 14 primarily to

(A) properly cite her past writings.
(B) distance herself from a point of view.
(C) predict a likely course of events.
(D) explain a controversial position.

27. As used in line 43, "ends" most closely means

(A) completions.
(B) objectives.
(C) sorrows.
(D) casualties.

28. The sentence in lines 83–88 ("It will be . . . constitution") serves mainly to

(A) encourage women to be patient in fighting for their ultimate political goal.
(B) underscore the importance of identifying oneself with a political party.
(C) demonstrate how a historical precedent applies to a modern situation.
(D) explain how women will achieve elected positions.

GO ON TO THE NEXT PAGE

Questions 29–38 are based on the following passages and table.

The following passages are adapted from 2013 articles about microwaves.

Passage 1

It's a common fixture in household kitchens all across the United States, but remarkably few of us who use them have any
Line   real idea of how our microwave ovens work.
(5)   Contrary to most other food-heating appliances—the toaster, the convection oven, and the stove for instance—the microwave itself has no internal heating element: flame, coil, or otherwise. Instead, the microwave oven
(10)   uses the principle of dipole rotation to generate heat from the molecules within the food itself.

Polar molecules, like a bar magnet, possess an electrical dipole moment, and, when
(15)   introduced to a strong enough electromagnetic field, will align their positive and negative ends appropriately. The microwave oven produces a strong electromagnetic field, but this is not enough to generate heat from
(20)   within the food.

As anyone who has watched a bag of instant popcorn expand knows, the tray inside of a microwave oven rotates as the food cooks. This rotation has the interesting
(25)   effect of increasing the kinetic energy of the food's polar molecules as they too must constantly rotate in order to remain aligned with the field. As they do so, these molecules rub and grind against their neighbors, converting
(30)   their kinetic energy into intermolecular friction, thus evolving heat. In fact, the motion of molecules is so directly related to internal heat that one can actually calculate a material's exact temperature by averaging the
(35)   kinetic energy of the atoms and molecules that comprise it.

Passage 2

It is probable that humans have been cooking since not long after our ancestors harnessed the power of fire some several
(40)   hundred thousand years ago. Since that time, the sophistication of our technology has increased more or less exponentially, and the technology of cooking is no exception. Insofar as it pertains to heat, the nature
(45)   of culinary innovation has fallen primarily into one of two categories common to many technology arcs: speed and precision.

The first great breakthrough in cooking had to be the division of fires into their
(50)   component functions. That is, a campfire used to produce light or to heat a large area is not typically the ideal fire for cooking. Once a fire ring was designated specifically for the preparation of food, the earliest
(55)   earthen stoves almost certainly began to evolve shortly afterward and would have significantly increased the degree to which primitive cooks could distribute heat evenly. Discovered in the Ukraine, the oldest known
(60)   stoves appear to date from about 30,000 years ago and were used primarily to bake mammoth meat.

The stove and the oven remain to this day our most commonly used cooking tech-
(65)   nologies. Innovations in the field of heating elements have frequently ameliorated the mechanism without much change to the principle design. The commercialization of natural gas in late 17th-century England
(70)   eventually gave cooks the ability to manipulate their cooking flame precisely as well as the convenience of instantaneous ignition. To this day, gas ranges are preferred by many professional chefs.
(75)   The electric oven is an anomaly in the cooking technology arc, as it developed nearly one hundred years after the gas oven

GO ON TO THE NEXT PAGE

but is markedly slower and often less precise. Nonetheless, advancements in conductive
(80) materials, convection technology, and electromagnetic induction have tremendously improved on the efficacy of the original resistive-coil ranges.

Electricity in the kitchen, of course, ush-
(85) ered in a new age of powered cooking appliances. Perhaps none is more curious, clever, and common than the microwave oven. The epitome of speed cooking, the microwave uses a wholly different approach to heating
(90) food than any of its predecessors—however, its remarkable swiftness comes at the expense of precision, particularly when dealing with physically dense foodstuffs. In consequence, the microwave is a fantastic device for thawing
(95) stored vegetables but should hardly be relied upon to properly prepare, say, a Thanksgiving turkey or perhaps a mammoth steak.

Polar Substances	Nonpolar Substances
Ethanol	Methane
Water	Carbon dioxide
Glucose	Ethylene
Ethyl alcohol	Gasoline
Acetic acid	Hexane

29. As it is used in line 31, "evolving" most nearly means

(A) advancing.
(B) reproducing.
(C) selecting.
(D) generating.

30. According to Passage 1, what is the aspect of microwaves that most distinguishes it from other types of cooking devices?

(A) Its capacity to increase the kinetic energy of food
(B) The precision with which it can cook food
(C) Its lack of an internal heating element
(D) The presence of intermolecular friction in its cooking process

31. Which choice provides the best evidence for the answer to the previous question?

(A) Lines 6–8 ("the . . . element")
(B) Lines 13–17 ("Polar . . . appropriately")
(C) Lines 24–28 ("This . . . field")
(D) Lines 31–36 ("In . . . it")

32. What is the overall structure of Passage 2?

(A) A persuasive argument in favor of the use of older cooking methods
(B) A technical explanation of the workings of cooking devices
(C) A survey of the gradual developments in cooking technology
(D) An evaluation of which cooking technology is most effective in the modern kitchen

33. As it is used in line 47, "arcs" most nearly means

(A) discharges of energy.
(B) curvatures of machinery.
(C) portions of circles.
(D) lines of development.

34. Which of the following does the author of Passage 2 state is a step backward in the progression of cooking technology?

(A) The electric oven
(B) The microwave
(C) The Ukrainian earthen stove
(D) The gas oven

GO ON TO THE NEXT PAGE

35. It is reasonable to infer that the primary scholarly fields of the two authors of Passage 1 and Passage 2 are respectively

(A) cooking and history.
(B) physics and paleontology.
(C) science and anthropology.
(D) chemistry and biology.

36. Unlike Passage 1, Passage 2 discusses what about the microwave?

(A) Its popularity
(B) Its shortcomings
(C) Its methodology
(D) Its possible applications

37. Based on the table and the passages, the molecular behavior of an acetic acid molecule introduced to a strong electromagnetic field will most likely resemble that of

(A) a stove.
(B) a gas range.
(C) a fire.
(D) a magnet.

38. Based on the information in the passages and the table, which combination of substances can it reasonably be inferred would be most likely to be heated by a microwave oven?

(A) Ethylene and acetic acid
(B) Glucose and water
(C) Carbon dioxide and methane
(D) Ethyl alcohol and gasoline

Questions 39–47 are based on the following passage.

This passage is adapted from a 2013 article about Halley's Comet.

Much like Old Faithful at Yellowstone National Park—by far the most well-known of the American geysers—Halley's Comet
Line is neither the most visually brilliant nor the
(5) largest of its kind; its renown derives from the dependable frequency with which it can be observed. Halley's falls into a category called Great Comets, which are those that become bright enough during their passage
(10) near Earth to be observed by the naked eye. Predicting whether or not a comet will be "great" has proven to be a treacherous task even for the most talented of astronomers and astrophysicists. The comet must pass
(15) through a relatively small expanse of space near enough to the Sun to reflect a large amount of light but remain close enough to Earth for the light to reach and penetrate our atmosphere. Moreover, it is thought
(20) that a Great Comet must possess a large and active nucleus, though the exact physics of comet nuclei—which consist of dust, ice, and perhaps particulate minerals—are still poorly understood. Even so, comets meeting these
(25) criteria have on occasion failed to achieve "greatness." To date, the most recent Great Comet was C/2006 P1, which appeared in January 2007 and was the brightest in more than 40 years.
(30)   The intrinsic difficulty of predicting a comet's greatness makes the consistency of Halley's visibility all the more remark-able. Most Great Comets will pass near Earth only once every several thousand years,
(35) while Halley's does so on a cycle of about 75 years—making it the only Great Comet with the potential to appear twice in a human

GO ON TO THE NEXT PAGE

lifetime. With an eccentricity of 0.967, the orbit
of Halley's Comet is extremely elliptical; at
(40) one end of its major axis, Halley's is roughly
the same distance from the Sun as Pluto. At
the other end, it passes between the orbits
of Mercury and Venus. The highly elliptic
character of Halley's orbit means that, apart
(45) from having one of the highest velocities of
any body in our solar system, it passes near
Earth both during its approach and its return
from the Sun. Though becoming visible during only one of these passes, the two near
(50) points of the orbit make Halley's the parent
body of two annual meteor showers: the Eta
Aquariids in early May and Orionids of late
October.

Though humans have likely marveled at
(55) the spectacle of Halley's Comet for thousands of years (the Talmudic astronomers of
the 1st century describe a star that appears
once every 70 years to wreak havoc on nauti-
cal navigation), it was little more than 300
(60) years ago that Edmond Halley—a friend of Sir
Isaac Newton's—used Newton's newly conceived laws of gravity to explain the motion
and predict the periodicity of comets. By
using these equations in tandem with histori-
(65) cal records, Halley surmised that the comets observed in 1531 by German Humanist
Petrus Apianus, in 1607 by Johannes Kepler,
and by himself and Newton in 1683 were one
and the same. Moreover, he predicted its
(70) return in 1758. Halley passed away in January
1742 at the age of 85, nearly 16 years to the
day short of seeing his prediction confirmed
firsthand. Yet, in an almost poetic cyclicity,
Halley's Comet—the periodicity of which
(75) Halley had derived from the observations of
two German astronomers—was observed
and documented by German farmer and
amateur astronomer Johann Palitzsch on

Christmas Day, 1758. The confirmation of
(80) Halley's theory constituted the first occasion
in which Western science had proven that
any bodies apart from planets orbit the Sun.
Halley's Comet has been visible in our sky
just three times since Palistzch's observation,
(85) but it will return again sometime in the summer of 2061.

39. The overall tone of the passage is best
characterized as one of

(A) solemn pessimism.
(B) playful whimsy.
(C) analytical curiosity.
(D) religious fervor.

40. As it is used in line 4, "brilliant" most nearly
means

(A) luminous.
(B) showy.
(C) intellectual.
(D) august.

41. It can reasonably be inferred that "Old Faithful"
(line 1) and Halley's Comet share what aspect
that primarily contributes to their fame?

(A) Presence of water
(B) High eccentricity
(C) Nuclear particulates
(D) Periodic observability

42. Which choice provides the best evidence for the
answer to the previous question?

(A) Lines 5–7 ("its . . . observed")
(B) Lines 14–19 ("The . . . atmosphere")
(C) Lines 20–23 ("large . . . minerals")
(D) Lines 38–39 ("With . . . elliptical")

GO ON TO THE NEXT PAGE

43. According to the passage, which characteristic of a comet is most essential to its being categorized as a "Great Comet"?

(A) Whether it has a significant proportion of dust and ice in its core
(B) Whether it has an orbital eccentricity greater than zero
(C) Whether humans can observe it without a telescope
(D) Whether it contributes to meteor activity visible by astronomers

44. Which choice provides the best evidence for the answer to the previous question?

(A) Lines 7–10 ("Halley's . . . eye")
(B) Lines 21–23 ("though . . . minerals")
(C) Lines 38–39 ("With . . . elliptical")
(D) Lines 48–53 ("Though . . . October")

45. The primary purpose of the second paragraph (lines 30–53) in the passage as a whole is to

(A) discuss the physical definition of elliptical eccentricity.
(B) provide scientific justification for the rarity of Halley's predictable visibility.
(C) give historical evidence of human observation of Halley's velocity.
(D) differentiate Halley from other celestial bodies, such as planets and meteors.

46. The statement in 63–65 ("By using . . . records") mainly serves to

(A) provide a key biographical detail.
(B) explain how a hypothesis was created.
(C) demonstrate a contradiction in a memory.
(D) show a mathematical calculation.

47. The scientist Halley's relationship to the ideas of Newton most resembles the relationship between

(A) a musician who uses music theory to enable creative compositions.
(B) a politician who uses philosophical maxims to predict societal outcomes.
(C) a mathematician who uses scientific data to justify algebraic theories.
(D) an engineer who uses the laws of physics to build long-lasting constructions.

If there is still time remaining, you may review your answers.

WRITING AND LANGUAGE TEST

35 MINUTES, 44 QUESTIONS

> **Directions:** The passages below are each accompanied by several questions, some of which refer to an underlined portion in the passage and some of which refer to the passage as a whole. For some questions, determine how the expression of ideas can be improved. For other questions, determine the best sentence structure, usage, or punctuation given the context. A passage or question may have an accompanying graphic that you will need to consider as you choose the best answer.
>
> Choose the best answer to each question, considering what will optimize the writing quality and make the writing follow the conventions of standard written English. Some questions have a "NO CHANGE" option that you can pick if you believe the best choice is to leave the underlined portion as is.

Questions 1–11 are based on the following passage and supplementary material.

Occupational Therapy

When a child with developmental delay ties his shoes independently, an adult recovering from stroke returns to driving, **❶** a teenager learns to use a power wheelchair following spinal cord injury, and an older adult stays in her home longer, an occupational therapist was part of **❷** our care.

Occupational therapy began in the United States in 1917 with the establishment of the Society for the Promotion of Occupational **❸** Therapy, now named, the American Occupational Therapy Association (AOTA). Historically, AOTA stood for restorative properties of everyday, meaningful

1. Which choice is most consistent with the listing pattern of the sentence as a whole?

   (A) NO CHANGE
   (B) a spinal cord injury is suffered by a teenager learning to use a power wheelchair,
   (C) a power wheelchair is used by a teenager after a spinal cord injury,
   (D) a spinal cord injury causes a teenager to suffer which a power wheelchair helps her overcome,

2. (A) NO CHANGE
   (B) his or her
   (C) their
   (D) her

3. (A) NO CHANGE
   (B) Therapy, now named the
   (C) Therapy now name the
   (D) Therapy now named, the

GO ON TO THE NEXT PAGE

activity and occupational therapy ❹ today is one of the fastest growing occupational categories in the United States.

Today, occupational therapy has grown into a science-driven and evidence-based practice that serves people across the lifespan. According to AOTA, occupation refers to the activities that people, populations, and organizations engage in, not necessarily a job. The areas of ❺ occupations—or categories of ways people use their time—that an occupational therapist considers when working with clients include activities of daily living, instrumental activities of daily living, rest and sleep, education, work, play, leisure, and social participation.

Newly licensed occupational therapists have a minimum of a four-year undergraduate degree and a two-year master's degree. ❻ Many occupational therapists also have a doctorate. Occupational therapy assistants have a two-year associate's degree and work under the supervision of an occupational therapist. Occupational therapists and occupational therapy assistants work in a wide variety of settings, like hospitals, skilled nursing facilities, schools, home health, outpatient clinics, sports medicine, and private practice ❼ alongside all types of healthcare practitioners.

In these settings, occupational therapists work with clients to help them better participate ❽ in all the any of the areas of occupation. For example, in a school, an occupational therapist may help children learn to write. In hospitals, occupational therapists may make splints to prevent contracture in patients with burns. At an outpatient clinic, an occupational therapist might work with families to develop better sleep habits for their children. In sports medicine, occupational therapists often help golfers return to the links after rotator cuff surgery. In skilled nursing facilities,

4. Which choice maintains the focus of and appropriate ending to the paragraph?

   (A) NO CHANGE
   (B) will one day be recognized for its contributions to modern medical science.
   (C) has extensive requirements for the educational background of its practitioners.
   (D) was widely used in large mental health facilities and with veterans returning from World War I.

5. (A) NO CHANGE
   (B) occupations: categories
   (C) occupations; or categories
   (D) occupations, or categories

6. The writer is considering deleting the underlined sentence. Should the sentence be kept or deleted?

   (A) Kept, because it gives the first mention of the educational qualifications to become an occupational therapist.
   (B) Kept, because it further elaborates on the educational possibilities for occupational therapists.
   (C) Deleted, because it repeats information stated elsewhere in the passage.
   (D) Deleted, because it contradicts information found later in the paragraph.

7. (A) NO CHANGE
   (B) conjoined to
   (C) what with
   (D) in addition to

8. (A) NO CHANGE
   (B) in any all of
   (C) in any or all of
   (D) in all of and any of

GO ON TO THE NEXT PAGE

occupational therapists **❾** taught older adults how to prevent falls and safely ambulate through their morning routines. If an activity occupies **❿** their clients' time, it's something an occupational therapist can treat.

Fortunately for students considering careers, the job prospects for both occupational therapists and occupational therapy assistants are excellent. In 2012, 113,200 people were employed as occupational therapists and 38,600 as occupational therapy assistants. **⓫** The Bureau of Labor Statistics estimates that the employment for occupational therapists will increase 43% between 2012 and 2022. The estimate for the increase in all jobs is 29%.

9. (A) NO CHANGE
   (B) has taught
   (C) teached
   (D) teach

10. (A) NO CHANGE
    (B) they're clients
    (C) there client's
    (D) their clients

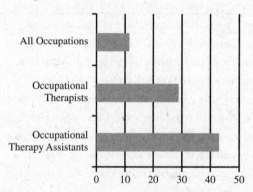

Percent Change in Employment, Projected 2012–2022

■ Percent Change in Employment, Projected 2012–2022

Adapted from the Bureau of Labor Statistics

11. Which choice offers an accurate interpretation of the data in the chart above?

   (A) NO CHANGE
   (B) The Bureau of Labor Statistics estimates that the employment for occupational therapists will increase 29% between 2012 and 2022. The estimate for the increase in all jobs is 11%.
   (C) The Bureau of Labor Statistics estimates that the employment for occupational therapists will increase 43% between 2012 and 2022. The estimate for the increase in all jobs is 11%.
   (D) The Bureau of Labor Statistics estimates that the employment for occupational therapists will increase 11% between 2012 and 2022. The estimate for the increase in all jobs is 29%.

GO ON TO THE NEXT PAGE

Questions 12–22 are based on the following passage.

Frick

{1}

Of all the legacies left behind by American industrialists of the 19th century, Henry Clay Frick's is perhaps the most **⓬** interesting. Frick is most remembered for his role in precipitating the violent outcome of the 1892 Homestead Steel labor strike.

{2}

In an effort to oust the Amalgamated Association of Iron and Steel Workers, or AA, from the Homestead Works in Pennsylvania, Frick—after **⓭** fortifying the factory with fences water cannons, barbed wire, and sniper towers—locked union workers out of the plant one day prior to the expiration of its contract. A renegotiation of the contract had failed recently when AA workers—citing a steady rise in the price of steel—requested an 8% wage increase and were met by Frick with a 22% decrease. **⓮** Incensed by Frick's actions, AA workers alongside townspeople and several other labor unions began picketing the factory two days after the lockout.

{3}

After about one week in which strikers successfully prevented new laborers and supervisors from entering the plant, Frick contracted 300 Pinkerton Detectives to break the strike by **⓯** working quite hard. Hoping to catch the picketers off guard, the Pinkertons—armed with Winchester rifles—boarded two shielded barges around 4 A.M. and were towed two miles upriver to the plant.

{4}

Conflicting testimonies exist as to **⓰** whom fired the first shot. The strikers, having been tipped off about the assault, **⓱** were laying in wait and prevented the barges from coming ashore. For more than twenty-four hours, the strikers and

12. Which of these words would be most consistent with the characterization of Frick that follows in the passage?

   (A) NO CHANGE
   (B) well-known.
   (C) infamous.
   (D) unusual.

13. (A) NO CHANGE
   (B) fortifying the factory with fences, water, cannons barbed wire,
   (C) fortifying, the factory with fences, water cannons, barbed wire,
   (D) fortifying the factory with fences, water cannons, barbed wire,

14. (A) NO CHANGE
   (B) Encouraged by
   (C) Inspired by
   (D) Dispirited by

15. Which choice would best express the firm determination of Frick to accomplish his goal?

   (A) NO CHANGE
   (B) using force only rarely.
   (C) any means necessary.
   (D) focusing energetically.

16. (A) NO CHANGE
   (B) who
   (C) what
   (D) that

17. (A) NO CHANGE
   (B) was lying
   (C) was laying
   (D) were lying

GO ON TO THE NEXT PAGE

Pinkertons were embroiled in **18** an intermittent exchange of gunfire and makeshift incendiaries that left several dead and many wounded. At the earliest escalations of the situation, AA leaders sought to contact Frick in order that the skirmish might be quelled and further bloodshed avoided. Frick, however, refused to speak with the leaders. He realized that the more dangerous and lawless conditions grew, **19** the more likely it was that the strikers would eventually emerge victorious.

{5}

He was correct. Not long after the Pinkertons surrendered, Pennsylvania Governor Robert Pattison authorized the militia to advance and placed the town of Homestead under martial law. In the days that followed, steel production at the plant resumed with strikebreakers living on the **20** mills grounds: it was still too dangerous for them to cross the picket.

{6}

21 Initially, the events at Homestead galvanized sympathy and support for labor unions nation-wide, **22** and public fervor quickly dissipated following a failed attempt on Frick's life by the notorious anarchist Alexander Berkman. Though Frick survived the assassination attempt and ultimately won the conflict when it entered the courts, his relationship with Carnegie* was irrevocably blemished, and his reputation as "America's most hated man" was solidified for years to come.

*Carnegie refers to Andrew Carnegie, the American industrialist and philanthropist.

18. (A) NO CHANGE
    (B) some rather intense combat that was rather harmful to the participants
    (C) a rough fight
    (D) a really deadly exchange

19. Which choice would give the most logical explanation for what comes earlier in the sentence while providing a good transition to the next paragraph?

    (A) NO CHANGE
    (B) the less likely it was his company would be in a position to negotiate a long-lasting end to the work stoppage.
    (C) the more likely it became that the governor would call in the state militia and put the strike down for good.
    (D) the less likely it was that Frick's end goal of securing high-paying positions for his workers would be accomplished.

20. (A) NO CHANGE
    (B) mills' grounds—it was still
    (C) mill's grounds, it was still
    (D) mill's grounds; it was still

21. Where would paragraph 6 most logically be placed?

    (A) Where it currently is.
    (B) Before paragraph 1
    (C) Before paragraph 3
    (D) Before paragraph 4

22. (A) NO CHANGE
    (B) consequently
    (C) but
    (D) in fact

GO ON TO THE NEXT PAGE

Questions 23–33 are based on the following passage.

Dali and Surrealism

23 The use of discrete symbolism is essential to the surrealist movement. One of the most highly regarded surrealist artists, Salvador Dali, often drew on symbols that he saw in his dreams and incorporated them into his paintings. Dali's formal art education began in 1921 at the School of Fine Arts in Madrid, where he studied for several years. However, Dali was expelled shortly before graduating because he claimed **24** for his teachers were insufficiently competent to examine him. In this same year, he painted *Basket of Bread,* which features four slices of buttered bread in a basket with one set off from the others and missing a bite. **25** Dali was recognized for the great skill that his uniquely crafted paintings demonstrated.

By 1931, Dali had officially joined the surrealist group in Paris and **26** completes perhaps his most famous work, *The Persistence of Memory,* which depicts several pocket watches melting away in an immense landscape that includes a mountain and

23. Which choice provides the best introduction to the paragraph?

(A) NO CHANGE
(B) Art has been appreciated by millions of museumgoers the world over.
(C) Salvador Dali was born in Spain in the city of Figueres.
(D) It is rare to find artistic works that have truly stood the test of time.

24. (A) NO CHANGE
(B) in
(C) on
(D) that

25. Which choice would most specifically support Dali's beliefs about his abilities?

(A) NO CHANGE
(B) The painting uses a dematerializing lighting technique that shows just how far Dali's skill had already developed when he was only 22.
(C) This work focuses on the outstanding by-products of Dali's culinary ingenuity— freshly baked, flawlessly crafted bread.
(D) Dali was publicly recognized for his revolutionary abilities, yet he retained a noteworthy internal modesty.

26. (A) NO CHANGE
(B) has completed
(C) completed
(D) have complete

GO ON TO THE NEXT PAGE

seascape. **27** There are [1] several symbols [2] in this painting [3] that Dali used in many other paintings from the same [4] period—one of which is ants that cover the watch in the lower left of the piece. Dali used ants as a symbol for death in several of his other paintings. Supposedly, *The Persistence of Memory* is partially **28** inspired by a dream sequence while sleeping that Dali experienced, where the clocks represented the passage of time as felt by the dreamer.

In 1940, Dali and his wife Gala moved to the United States, and he **29** reclaimed his Catholic faith. Following their return to Spain in the late 1940s, Dali began drawing inspiration from his faith for his work. During this period of Dali's life, he produced *La Gare de Perpignan,* which contains several religious symbols and references. **30** In contrast, there is the shadow of Christ on the cross bearing his thorny crown near the center of the painting. Additionally, there is a boat passing **31** to a calm sea, which is an ancient depiction symbolizing the passage of death to life and which strengthens the symbol of Christ in reference to the Resurrection.

Dali's interests weren't limited to painting; **32** he had an intense interest in great literary works. One of his most prominent sculptural pieces is the *Lobster Telephone,* also called the *Aphrodisiac Phone.* In his book *The Secret Life*, Dali inquired as to why in a restaurant when he requested a grilled lobster, he was never **33** brung a boiled telephone. The lobster phone is a prime example of surrealist sculpture since it evokes immense introspection.

27. What would be the most logical place to insert the word "present" in this sentence?

(A) [1]
(B) [2]
(C) [3]
(D) [4]

28. (A) NO CHANGE
(B) encouraged by a subconscious night time mental event
(C) constructed from the brain that
(D) based on a dream

29. (A) NO CHANGE
(B) reproduced
(C) rejected
(D) redomesticated

30. (A) NO CHANGE
(B) Surprisingly,
(C) For instance,
(D) As an example of what can be seen,

31. (A) NO CHANGE
(B) over
(C) and journeying throughout
(D) sequencing

32. Which choice would best support and elaborate on the first part of the sentence?

(A) NO CHANGE.
(B) his artistic skill was well-regarded worldwide.
(C) he also explored film, literature, and sculpture.
(D) he was devoted to the mastery of sculptural techniques.

33. (A) NO CHANGE
(B) brought
(C) bring
(D) brang

GO ON TO THE NEXT PAGE

Questions 34–44 are based on the following passage.

Unmanned Space Exploration

We must ask ourselves as a society, what is it that we most value? **34** Do we seek out knowledge and wisdom or are we only concerned with chest-thumping and braggadocio? If the former, we should shift away from an obsession with manned space flight and invest resources in robotic exploration. **35** One should be focused on what will enable us to learn the most about our universe in the most cost-effective manner.

Most people would cite Neil Armstrong's first steps on the Moon as the most exciting moment in space exploration. Seeing a human walk on another heavenly body for the first time sends chills down your spine. **36** But why should it be this way? I would argue that the exploration of the *Voyager 2* unmanned spacecraft has given us far more momentous accomplishments. Among many discoveries, it **37** found that Io a moon of Jupiter has volcanic activity—the first time another astronomical body was found to have this Earthlike characteristic. *Voyager* gave us evidence that the Great Red Spot of Jupiter was an enormous storm,

34. Which choice would best connect the preceding and following sentences?

   (A) NO CHANGE
   (B) Are we interested in focusing on exploring the moon, nearby planets, and even faraway star systems?
   (C) Do we want only to save money so that we can use it for domestic research programs to fight disease here on Earth?
   (D) Are we focused on making the world a better place for our children, or do we want to leave them a legacy of environmental devastation?

35. (A) NO CHANGE
   (B) They should have been focused
   (C) He or she needs to focus
   (D) We should focus

36. Should the underlined sentence be kept or removed?

   (A) Kept, because it provides a key transition to the following sentence.
   (B) Kept, because it provides details on the emotional reaction to space flight.
   (C) Removed, because it provides irrelevant details.
   (D) Removed, because it does not logically connect the preceding and following sentences.

37. (A) NO CHANGE
   (B) found that Io, a moon of Jupiter has
   (C) found that Io, a moon of Jupiter, has
   (D) found that Io a moon, of Jupiter has

GO ON TO THE NEXT PAGE

that distant planets have rings, and ㊳ which undiscovered moons are had by many outer planets. It also left the solar system and is now on an interstellar mission. If we had insisted that humans be a part of the *Voyager* craft, it wouldn't have been able to accomplish nearly as much.

    Sure, there ㊴ isn't a made-for-television moment like disembarking a spacecraft onto the Moon's surface for the first time. However, ㊵ isn't it time we realize that space exploration needs to be a top priority of our country, instead of merely being given lip service?

    One possible justification for involving humans in the actual exploration is that ㊶ they do increase interest in funding space exploration projects. Humans are naturally drawn to want to explore space vicariously by seeing astronauts do it on television. It is much like how humans would rather hear about someone's trip to a foreign country ㊷ then to look merely at photographs of the country on the Internet. An interesting approach is the one taken by the new Mars One project. In an effort to spur interest in exploration and minimize costs, the project managers

38. Which choice is most consistent with the structure of the previous part of the sentence?

(A) NO CHANGE
(B) outer planets have moons that are undiscovered.
(C) where we find the unprecedented discovery of the outer planet moons.
(D) that outer planets have many undiscovered moons.

39. (A) NO CHANGE
(B) isn't a television made
(C) isn't a television that is made for
(D) isn't a made-for-the-television

40. Which choice would provide a rhetorical question that provides a fitting conclusion to the paragraph?

(A) NO CHANGE
(B) are we more interested in the theater of science or the actuality of improving our understanding of the universe?
(C) why should we spend valuable money on advanced robotic space exploration when there are better Earth-bound investments we can make?
(D) who is to say what will have more of an impact a century from now—a man on the Moon or a manned mission to Mars?

41. (A) NO CHANGE
(B) it does
(C) one do
(D) OMIT the underlined portion

42. (A) NO CHANGE
(B) then to merely look
(C) than too look merely
(D) than merely look

GO ON TO THE NEXT PAGE

have recruited volunteers who will be the first **43** to go to Mars, and won't be able to return to Earth. If only we could be satisfied with acquiring knowledge instead of treating space exploration like some kind of competitive sport, **44** there would be no thought of people needing to die on a foreign world in order to promote interest in space.

43. (A) NO CHANGE
(B) to go to Mars, however won't
(C) to go to Mars but won't
(D) to go to Mars, and, won't

44. Which choice most logically concludes the paragraph?

(A) NO CHANGE
(B) we should focus on space exploration using the most efficient means possible to maximize our understanding of the universe.
(C) we wouldn't have to waste money on pointless projects like the Mars One mission.
(D) there wouldn't be the slow, lonely death of astronauts on a distant world.

STOP

MATH TEST (NO CALCULATOR)

25 MINUTES, 17 QUESTIONS

Directions: For questions 1–13, solve each problem and choose the best answer from the given options. Fill in the corresponding oval on the answer sheet. For questions 14–17, solve the problem and fill in the answer on the answer sheet grid. Please use any space in the test booklet to work out your answers.

Notes:
- You **CANNOT** use a calculator on this section.
- All variables and expressions represent real numbers unless indicated otherwise.
- All figures are drawn to scale unless indicated otherwise.
- All figures are in a plane unless indicated otherwise.
- Unless indicated otherwise, the domain of a given function is the set of all real numbers x for which the function has real values.

Radius of a circle = r

Area of a circle = πr^2

Circumference of a circle = $2\pi r$

Area of a rectangle = length × width = lw

Area of a triangle = $\dfrac{1}{2}$ × base × height = $\dfrac{1}{2}bh$

Pythagorean theorem: $a^2 + b^2 = c^2$

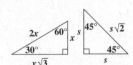

Special right triangles: 30-60-90 and 45-45-90

Volume of a box = length × width × height = lwh

Volume of a cylinder = $\pi r^2 h$

Volume of a sphere = $\dfrac{4}{3}\pi r^3$

Volume of a cone = $\dfrac{1}{3}\pi r^2 h$

Volume of a pyramid =

$\dfrac{1}{3}$ × length × width × height = $\dfrac{1}{3}lwh$

GO ON TO THE NEXT PAGE

DIAGNOSTIC TEST

KEY FACTS:

- **A circle has 360 degrees.**
- **There are 2π radians in a circle.**
- **There are 180 degrees in a triangle.**

1. If $x^2 > y^2$ which statement must be correct?

   (A) $x > y$
   (B) $x < y$
   (C) $x \neq y$
   (D) $x^3 > y^3$

2. What values of y satisfy this system of equations?

   $$x = y^2 - 3y + 1$$
   $$2x = 10$$

   (A) −4 and 2
   (B) −1 and 4
   (C) 3 and 4
   (D) 6 and 10

3. Which of the following operations could be performed on both sides of the inequality $-2x > 4$ to require the direction of the inequality sign be changed while keeping x on the left-hand side of the inequality?

   (A) Add 4
   (B) Subtract 7
   (C) Divide by −2
   (D) Multiply by 12

4. What are the values of a in this equation?

   $$3a^2 - 27a - 108 = 0$$

   (A) −9, −3
   (B) 6, −4
   (C) 9, 6
   (D) 12, −3

5. When Andrew does his homework, he always takes 10 minutes to set up his desk and get totally ready to begin. Once he starts working, he is able to complete 1 homework problem every 5 minutes. Assuming that Andrew studies for over 10 minutes, which of the following represents the total number of homework problems, p, Andrew is able to complete in m minutes?

   (A) $p = 5m + 10$
   (B) $p = 5m - 1$
   (C) $p = \frac{1}{5}(m - 10)$
   (D) $p = \frac{1}{10}(m - 5)$

6.

x	y
−1	−6
1	2
5	18
7	26

   The variables x and y have a linear relationship; the table above contains several corresponding x-y values for the line. What is the equation of the line made up of x-y values?

   (A) $y = 4x - 2$
   (B) $y = 2x$
   (C) $y = -2x + 4$
   (D) $y = -4x + 2$

7. How many solutions does the equation below have?

   $$3x - 4y = 73$$

   (A) None
   (B) Exactly 1
   (C) Exactly 2
   (D) Infinite

GO ON TO THE NEXT PAGE

8. What is the product of xy given the system of equations below?

$$4 + y = 32x$$
$$y = 2x + 2$$

(A) $\dfrac{6}{25}$

(B) $\dfrac{12}{25}$

(C) 12

(D) 15

9. Maria currently has \$10,000 in her retirement fund. She wants to see how much money she will have in her fund for several different years in the future, assuming that her portfolio has a steady annual growth rate of 10%. What function $f(n)$ would model the amount she should have in her portfolio in n years?

(A) $f(n) = 10{,}000^n$

(B) $f(n) = 10{,}000 \times 0.1^n$

(C) $f(n) = 10{,}000 \times 1.1^n$

(D) $f(n) = 10{,}000 \times 1.11^n$

10. The amount of money (A) in a bank account after a principal amount (P) is on deposit for t years at an annual interest rate r compounded n times per year is given by this equation:

$$A = P\left(1 + \frac{r}{n}\right)^{nt}$$

Suppose that a banker would like to determine how changes in these variables would cause the bank to pay *less* interest to its clients. Which of the variables— $P, r, n,$ and t—if minimized, would cause less interest paid to clients?

(A) P only

(B) r and t only

(C) n and t only

(D) $P, r, n,$ and t

11. Which of these equations, when combined into a set of equations with $4x = 2y - 6$, will result in no solutions to the set?

(A) $y = x - 4$

(B) $y = 2x + 10$

(C) $y = 4x - 1$

(D) $y = \dfrac{1}{4}x - 6$

12. A dry cleaner has a computer program to determine the price it will charge an individual customer to clean a bag full of shirts (S) and pants (P). The total cost in dollars (C) is given by the following expression:

$$C = 10S + 6P + 5$$

What does the constant 5 most likely represent in the above expression?

(A) A set fee the cleaner assesses to do any amount of cleaning

(B) The cost to clean a shirt

(C) The cost to clean a pair of pants

(D) The total minimum cost to clean either one shirt or one pair of pants

13. What will happen to the graph of the function $f(x) = 4x^2 - 18$ if it is transformed into the function $g(x) = 4(x - 2)^2 - 15$?

(A) It will shift down 2 units and shift to the left 3 units.

(B) It will shift up 3 units and shift to the right 2 units.

(C) It will shift up 2 units and shift to the left 3 units.

(D) It will shift down 3 units and shift to the right 2 units.

GO ON TO THE NEXT PAGE

Grid-in Response Directions

In questions 14–17, first solve the problem, and then enter your answer on the grid provided on the answer sheet. The instructions for entering your answers follow.

- First, write your answer in the boxes at the top of the grid.
- Second, grid your answer in the columns below the boxes.
- Use the fraction bar in the first row or the decimal point in the second row to enter fractions and decimals.

Answer: $\frac{8}{15}$ Answer: 1.75   Answer: 100

Write your answer in the boxes

Grid in your answer

Either position is acceptable

- Grid only one space in each column.
- Entering the answer in the boxes is recommended as an aid in gridding but is not required.
- The machine scoring your exam can read only what you grid, so you **must grid-in your answers correctly to get credit**.
- If a question has more than one correct answer, grid-in only one of them.
- The grid does not have a minus sign; so no answer can be negative.
- A mixed number *must* be converted to an improper fraction or a decimal before it is gridded.

  Enter $1\frac{1}{4}$ as $\frac{5}{4}$ or 1.25; the machine will interpret 11/4 as $\frac{11}{4}$ and mark it wrong.

- **All decimals must be entered as accurately as possible.** Here are three acceptable ways of gridding

$$\frac{3}{11} = 0.272727\ldots$$

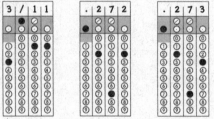

- Note that rounding to .273 is acceptable because you are using the full grid, but you would receive **no credit** for .3 or .27, because they are less accurate.

GO ON TO THE NEXT PAGE

14. If $2x + 3 = 4$, what is the value of $6x + 9$?

16. The function $f(x) = (x-3)(x+2)((x-1)^2)$ will intersect the x-axis how many times?

15. If $x > 0$ and $x^2 + 10x = 11$, what is the value of $x + 5$?

17. In a certain right triangle, the sine of angle A is $\frac{5}{13}$ and the cosine of angle A is $\frac{12}{13}$. What is the ratio of the smallest side of the triangle to the median side of the triangle?

STOP

If there is still time remaining, you may review your answers.

MATH TEST (WITH CALCULATOR)

45 MINUTES, 31 QUESTIONS

Directions: For questions 1–27, solve each problem and choose the best answer from the given options. Fill in the corresponding oval on the answer sheet. For questions 28–31, solve the problem and fill in the answer on the answer sheet grid. Please use any space in the test booklet to work out your answers.

Notes:
- You CAN use a calculator on this section.
- All variables and expressions represent real numbers unless indicated otherwise.
- All figures are drawn to scale unless indicated otherwise.
- All figures are in a plane unless indicated otherwise.
- Unless indicated otherwise, the domain of a given function is the set of all real numbers x for which the function has real values.

Radius of a circle $= r$
Area of a circle $= \pi r^2$
Circumference of a circle $= 2\pi r$

Area of a rectangle $=$ length $\times$ width $= lw$

Area of a triangle $= \dfrac{1}{2} \times$ base $\times$ height $= \dfrac{1}{2} bh$

Pythagorean theorem: $a^2 + b^2 = c^2$

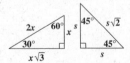

Special right triangles: 30-60-90 and 45-45-90

Volume of a box $=$ length $\times$ width $\times$ height $= lwh$

Volume of a cylinder $= \pi r^2 h$

Volume of a sphere $= \dfrac{4}{3}\pi r^3$

Volume of a cone $= \dfrac{1}{3}\pi r^2 h$

Volume of a pyramid $=$
$\dfrac{1}{3} \times$ length $\times$ width $\times$ height $= \dfrac{1}{3} lwh$

GO ON TO THE NEXT PAGE

KEY FACTS:

- **A circle has 360 degrees.**
- **There are 2π radians in a circle.**
- **There are 180 degrees in a triangle.**

1. What is the difference between $7a^2 + 3ab - 8b$ and $-2a^2 + ab - 2b$?

   (A) $5a^2 + 4ab - 10b$
   (B) $9a^2 + 4ab - 8b$
   (C) $9a^2 + 2ab - 6b$
   (D) $7a + 3ab - 10$

2. $(2x^2 + 4xy + 2y^2) \times \dfrac{1}{2x + 2y} =$

   (A) $y + x$
   (B) $\dfrac{2x + 4y + 2}{x + y}$
   (C) $2x + 4xy + 2y$
   (D) 2

3. A professor will cancel his sociology class if the number of students in attendance is less than or equal to 10. Which of the following expressions would give the possible values of students, S, necessary for the professor to conduct class, given that S is an integer?

   (A) $S < 10$
   (B) $S > 10$
   (C) $S \le 10$
   (D) $S \ge 10$

4. What is a possible value for x in the expression below?

   $$-6 < \frac{8}{3}\,x < -\frac{1}{4}$$

   (A) 8
   (B) 1
   (C) -2
   (D) -5

Questions 5–7 refer to the following information and table.

The data are collected from a survey of 500 randomly selected people in the United States. The researcher asked participants their ages and what type of social media they use the most frequently: video sharing, photo sharing, text sharing, or none. The goal of the researcher was to determine the general characteristics of social media use by different age groups throughout the United States.

Type of Social Media Use by Numbers of People in Different Age Groups					
Age Group	Video Sharing	Photo Sharing	Text Sharing	No Social Media	Total
12–18	40	32	20	2	94
19–30	31	51	43	6	131
31–45	20	20	40	24	104
46–60	9	8	36	35	88
61–up	2	3	29	49	83

5. If one were to create a graph with age groupings (from younger to older) as the variable along the x-axis and percentage of group members who use video sharing (from smaller to larger) along the y-axis, what would be the relationship portrayed by the data?

   (A) Positive correlation
   (B) Negative correlation
   (C) Equivalence
   (D) Exponentially inverse

GO ON TO THE NEXT PAGE

6. The researcher is going to pick two of his research subjects from this survey to speak anecdotally about their experiences with social media so that he may have qualitative data to supplement his quantitative data. The first person who will speak will be from the 12–18-year-old group. The second person will be from the 31–45-year-old group. What is the probability (to the nearest hundredth) that the first speaker will primarily use photo sharing and that the second speaker will primarily use text sharing?

(A) 0.02
(B) 0.06
(C) 0.11
(D) 0.13

7. The survey summary states that the researcher collected the data "randomly." Which of these methods of finding survey participants would likely provide the most accurate results given the researcher's goal?

(A) Ask for volunteer responses through television advertising and give a number for interested subjects to call in, ensuring a high level of motivation among survey participants

(B) Have a survey booth at a local shopping mall where only every 5th person is selected to share his or her individual thoughts about social media use, ensuring that each participant provides photo ID to verify his or her identity

(C) Post a survey advertisement on a variety of websites that appeal to a great number of demographic groupings, including income, gender, and ethnicity

(D) Call randomly selected phone numbers from across the country, both cellular and landlines, and ask for household members of a particular random age group to share their thoughts

8. A politician proposes a new federal tax bracket system for single tax payers with the following tax rates for the given ranges of income:

Taxable Income Range	Tax Rate
$0 up to $9,000	15%
Greater than $9,000 up to $50,000	20%
Greater than $50,000	30%

If Julian has $62,000 in taxable income, what is the total amount of federal tax he would pay under the proposed system?

(A) $9,300
(B) $12,400
(C) $13,150
(D) $15,000

9. If the line given by the equation $y = 4x + 7$ is reflected about the x-axis, what will be the graph of the resulting function?

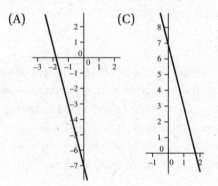

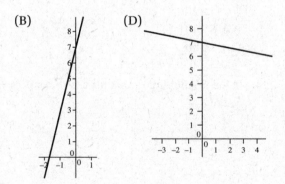

GO ON TO THE NEXT PAGE

10. What is the solution(s) for x in this equation?

$$\frac{12}{\sqrt[3]{x}} = 4$$

(A) −3 and 81

(B) −27 and 27

(C) 9 only

(D) 27 only

Questions 11–12 refer to the following information and graph.

A new business uses a crowdfunding website to raise money for its expansion. The graph below plots the number of new investment pledges per week, collecting the data once at the end of each week after the crowdfunding has begun. For example, "Week 1" gives the total number of new pledges at the very end of Week 1.

Number of New Investment Pledges Per Week

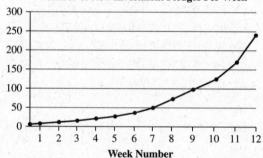

Week Number

11. A marketing professional defines the point at which something goes "viral" as the point at which the item shifts from linear to exponential growth. During which week does the value of the new investment pledges become viral?

(A) 2

(B) 3

(C) 6

(D) 10

12. Given that the function increases at the same geometric rate as it does in weeks 9–12, what would most likely come closest to the number of new investment pledges in week 14?

(A) 450

(B) 650

(C) 800

(D) 1,000

13. How many solution(s) does this system of equations have?

$$m + 2n = 1$$
$$6n + 3m = 9$$

(A) None

(B) 1

(C) 2

(D) 3

14. A convenience store has a "change bowl" on its counter in which there can be 5-cent nickels and/or 1-cent pennies. The store manager insists that whenever there is a dollar (100 cents) or more in the bowl, some change must be removed. What expression gives range of P pennies and N nickels that could be in the change bowl at any given time without the cashier needing to remove any coins?

(A) $100P - N > 5$

(B) $6(P + N) < 100$

(C) $0.01P + 0.05N < 100$

(D) $P + 5N < 100$

GO ON TO THE NEXT PAGE

Questions 15–18 refer to the following tables.

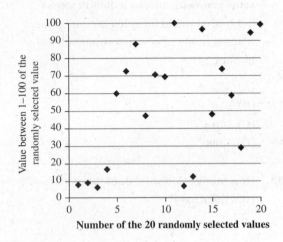

Number of the 20 randomly selected values

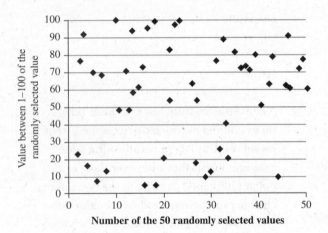

Number of the 50 randomly selected values

15. If a third graph of 1,000 randomly selected values were created, what would most likely be the average of the randomly selected values?

   (A) 35
   (B) 50
   (C) 60
   (D) 75

16. Out of the following options, what is the most unexpected result of the collection of the random sets of numbers?

   (A) The values in both sets of data have a range of roughly between 1 and 100.
   (B) The selection of 50 random numbers has a significantly higher percentage of values above 50 than does the selection of 20 random numbers.
   (C) The selection of 20 random numbers has a much greater range among its values than does the selection of 50 random numbers.
   (D) The sets of both data are portrayed as scatter plots rather than as best-fit lines.

17. Suppose that the random selection process of numbers between 1 and 100 was conducted for a group of 100 values and for a group of 1,000 values. After the selection process is completed, the range of each group is determined. What would most likely be closest to the difference between each group's range of values?

   (A) 0
   (B) 20
   (C) 50
   (D) 100

18. What would most likely be the average of the slopes of the best-fit lines of the data if the researcher collects and plots the 50 randomly selected values 100 times?

   (A) –2
   (B) 0
   (C) 1
   (D) 3.5

GO ON TO THE NEXT PAGE

19. In the equation $y = 2x^n$, in which x is an integer greater than 1, what is a possible value of n that will ensure that the expression has exponential growth?

    (A) 0
    (B) 1
    (C) 4
    (D) Not sufficient information

20. Assume that a scientist is able to measure the average weight of lobsters within a 50-mile radius of an island with a confidence level of 90% by collecting data from 100 random spots around the island. If he wishes to increase the confidence level in his results to 95%, what would best help him achieve his goal?

    (A) Compare the results to those from another island 300 miles away.
    (B) Expand the radius of sampling to 100 miles and redistribute his 100 random spots within the larger range.
    (C) Increase the number of data samples.
    (D) Use a scale with 5% more accuracy.

21. How many more kilograms (to the nearest hundredth) will a 2 cubic meter balloon that is filled with air weigh than an identical balloon that is filled with helium, given that helium has a density of 0.179 $\dfrac{\text{kg}}{\text{m}^3}$ and air has a density of 1.2 $\dfrac{\text{kg}}{\text{m}^3}$?

    (A) 0.21
    (B) 1.02
    (C) 1.38
    (D) 2.04

22. If a set of 20 different numbers has its smallest and largest values removed, how will that affect the standard deviation of the set?

    (A) The standard deviation will increase.
    (B) The standard deviation will decrease.
    (C) The standard deviation will remain the same.
    (D) Not enough information is provided.

23. Jay is purchasing gifts for his four friends' high school graduation. He has a budget of at most $150. He is purchasing a restaurant gift card of $25 for one friend, a tool set that costs $40 for another friend, and a $35 college sweatshirt for a third friend. For his fourth friend, he wants to see how many $0.25 quarters ($Q$) he can give for the friend to use for laundry money. What expression gives the range of quarters Jay can acquire given his budgetary restrictions?

    (A) $1 \le Q \le 300$
    (B) $1 \le Q \le 200$
    (C) $10 \le Q \le 120$
    (D) $40 \le Q \le 60$

GO ON TO THE NEXT PAGE

24. A pretzel stand has fixed costs for the facility and cooking supplies of $500. The cost for the labor and supplies to cook one pretzel after the pretzel stand has been set up is $2 per pretzel. What is the graph of the cost function $c(x)$ given x pretzels?

(A)

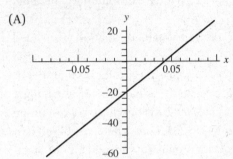

(B)

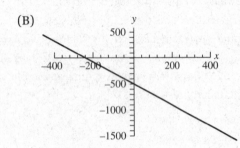

(C)

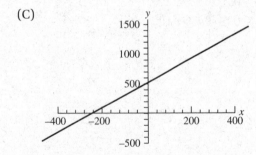

(D)

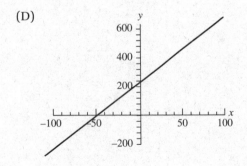

25. Which of the following could be a value of x in this equation?

$$8x^2 = -16x - 2$$

I. $-1 - \dfrac{\sqrt{3}}{2}$

II. $\dfrac{1}{2}\left(-2 - \sqrt{6}\right)$

III. $\dfrac{1}{2}(\sqrt{3} - 2)$

(A) I only
(B) II only
(C) I and III only
(D) II and III only

26. An interior designer is selling wood flooring to be used by his client for a new room. The client has already purchased a set length of trim, which goes between the edge of the wood flooring and the wall. The trim is straight and cannot be curved, yet it can be joined to make right angle corners. The client does not wish to purchase any more trim and would like to use all of the trim when building the new room. If the interior designer wants to maximize the amount of wood flooring that the client purchases while satisfying the client's requirements, what should be the relationship between the length (L) and width (W) of the room's dimensions?

(A) $L = W$
(B) $L = 2W$
(C) $W = L^2$
(D) $L = W^3$

27. Given that $i = \sqrt{-1}$, what is the value of $i^4 + i^{12}$?

(A) $\sqrt{-1}$
(B) -1
(C) 1
(D) 2

GO ON TO THE NEXT PAGE

Grid-in Response Directions

In questions 28–31, first solve the problem, and then enter your answer on the grid provided on the answer sheet. The instructions for entering your answers follow.

- First, write your answer in the boxes at the top of the grid.
- Second, grid your answer in the columns below the boxes.
- Use the fraction bar in the first row or the decimal point in the second row to enter fractions and decimals.

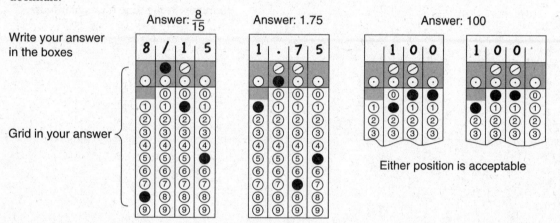

Write your answer in the boxes

Grid in your answer

Either position is acceptable

- Grid only one space in each column.
- Entering the answer in the boxes is recommended as an aid in gridding but is not required.
- The machine scoring your exam can read only what you grid, so you **must grid-in your answers correctly to get credit**.
- If a question has more than one correct answer, grid-in only one of them.
- The grid does not have a minus sign; so no answer can be negative.
- A mixed number *must* be converted to an improper fraction or a decimal before it is gridded.

  Enter $1\frac{1}{4}$ as $\frac{5}{4}$ or 1.25; the machine will interpret 11/4 as $\frac{11}{4}$ and mark it wrong.

- **All decimals must be entered as accurately as possible.** Here are three acceptable ways of gridding

  $$\frac{3}{11} = 0.272727\ldots$$

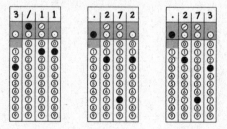

- Note that rounding to .273 is acceptable because you are using the full grid, but you would receive **no credit** for .3 or .27, because they are less accurate.

GO ON TO THE NEXT PAGE

28. Eloise is told by her doctor that she should try to average 9 hours of sleep a night because that is what a typical teenager needs for optimal mental and physical health. If Eloise was awake for 126 hours in a given week, how many additional hours of sleep should she have had in order to follow her doctor's advice?

29. The variables m and n have a directly proportional relationship given by the equation $m = kn,$ where k is a constant of proportionality. When $m = 10, n = 2$. What will be the value of n if m equals 38?

30. A botanist plants a small ivy plant and evaluates its growth function. She finds that 2 months after planting, the plant is 5 inches tall; at 4 months after planting, the plant is 8 inches tall. Additionally, the botanist has noticed that the plant has grown at a constant rate since its initial planting. Given this information, what was the plant's height in inches at the time it was planted?

GO ON TO THE NEXT PAGE

31. The table below shows the number of applications and the number of admissions to a particular college at the end of each calendar year.

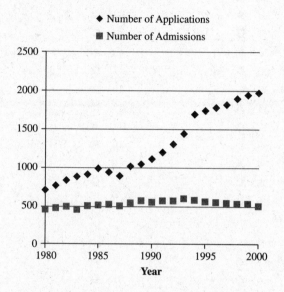

During one year between 1980 and 2000, the college started to accept the Common Application and also began offering early decision to its applicants. The Common Application allows students to use the same application to apply to multiple schools,

making applying easier. Early decision gives students the opportunity to apply early for admission. If accepted, though, students must commit to go to the school. The college made these two changes to encourage more students to apply and to enable the school to admit only students who were really committed to attending, thus helping the college's application yield (i.e., the number of students admitted who actually attend). These factors resulted in an overall increase in the selectivity of the college. In what year did the college most likely first implement these policies?

If there is still time remaining, you may review your answers.

ANSWER KEY
Diagnostic Test

Reading Test

1. **C**	13. **B**	25. **A**	37. **D**
2. **A**	14. **A**	26. **B**	38. **B**
3. **C**	15. **D**	27. **B**	39. **C**
4. **D**	16. **C**	28. **A**	40. **A**
5. **C**	17. **C**	29. **D**	41. **D**
6. **B**	18. **B**	30. **C**	42. **A**
7. **A**	19. **A**	31. **A**	43. **C**
8. **C**	20. **D**	32. **C**	44. **A**
9. **C**	21. **D**	33. **D**	45. **B**
10. **D**	22. **D**	34. **A**	46. **B**
11. **B**	23. **C**	35. **C**	47. **B**
12. **C**	24. **C**	36. **B**	

Writing and Language Test

1. **A**	12. **C**	23. **A**	34. **A**
2. **C**	13. **D**	24. **D**	35. **D**
3. **B**	14. **A**	25. **B**	36. **A**
4. **D**	15. **C**	26. **C**	37. **C**
5. **A**	16. **B**	27. **B**	38. **D**
6. **B**	17. **D**	28. **D**	39. **A**
7. **A**	18. **A**	29. **A**	40. **B**
8. **C**	19. **C**	30. **C**	41. **B**
9. **D**	20. **D**	31. **B**	42. **D**
10. **A**	21. **A**	32. **C**	43. **C**
11. **B**	22. **C**	33. **B**	44. **A**

Math Test (No Calculator)

1. **C**	6. **A**	11. **B**	16. **3**
2. **B**	7. **D**	12. **A**	17. **5/12**
3. **C**	8. **B**	13. **B**	
4. **D**	9. **C**	14. **12**	
5. **C**	10. **D**	15. **6**	

ANSWER KEY
Diagnostic Test

Math Test (With Calculator)

1. **C**	9. **A**	17. **A**	25. **C**
2. **A**	10. **D**	18. **B**	26. **A**
3. **B**	11. **C**	19. **C**	27. **D**
4. **C**	12. **A**	20. **C**	28. **21**
5. **B**	13. **A**	21. **D**	29. **7.6 or 38/5**
6. **D**	14. **D**	22. **B**	30. **2**
7. **D**	15. **B**	23. **B**	31. **1994**
8. **C**	16. **B**	24. **C**	

Note: This table represents an estimate of how many questions you will need to answer correctly to achieve a certain score on the PSAT. Each section on the PSAT has a score range of 160 and 760, making your total score range between 320 and 1520.

PSAT Section Score	PSAT Math (48 Total Questions)	PSAT Evidence-Based Reading and Writing (91 Total Questions)	PSAT Section Score
760	48	91	760
710	45	86	710
660	43	79	660
610	38	71	610
560	34	63	560
510	28	53	510
460	24	43	460
410	18	30	410
360	13	19	360
310	8	12	310
260	4	6	260
210	2	3	210
160	0	0	160

DIAGNOSTIC TEST ANALYSIS GUIDE

Use this guide to determine which skills you should focus on when you review the chapters. As you go through the test, circle the questions you missed. This will let you easily identify the areas in which you need to improve. The test questions that correspond to different skills are organized below.

Reading

Question Type	Evidence	Words in Context	Graph Analysis	Passage Analysis
Fiction	4, 7	5, 9		1, 2, 3, 6, 8
Social Science	12, 17	13, 14	18, 19	10, 11, 15, 16
Historical Document	22, 24	25, 27		20, 21, 23, 26, 28
Science	31, 42, 44	29, 33, 40	37, 38	30, 32, 34, 35, 36, 39, 41, 43, 45, 46, 47

Writing and Language

Question Type	
Idea Development	4, 11, 12, 15, 23, 25, 32, 40, 44
Organization	1, 6, 19, 21, 22, 27, 34, 38
Language Use	7, 14, 18, 24, 29, 30, 36
Sentence Structure	9, 28, 31, 33, 35, 39, 43
Usage Rules	2, 8, 16, 17, 26, 41, 42
Punctuation	3, 5, 10, 13, 20, 37

Math

Question Type	Non-calculator Questions	Calculator Questions
Heart of Algebra	1, 2, 3, 5, 6, 7, 11, 14	3, 4, 9, 13, 14, 21, 23, 28, 30
Passport to Advanced Math	4, 8, 9, 10, 12, 13, 15, 16	1, 2, 10, 19, 25, 26, 29
Problem Solving and Data Analysis		5, 6, 7, 8, 11, 12, 15, 16, 17, 18, 20, 22, 24, 31
Additional Topics in Math	17	27

Diagnostic Self-Assessment

Check any areas you feel you need to work on.

READING

☐ Reading timing

☐ Overthinking Reading questions

☐ Not sure how to think through Reading questions

☐ Careless errors on Reading questions

☐ Other issues?

WRITING AND LANGUAGE

☐ Writing and Language timing

☐ Writing and Language grammar review

☐ Overthinking Writing and Language questions

☐ Not sure how to think through Writing and Language questions

☐ Careless errors on Writing and Language questions

☐ Other issues?

MATH

☐ Math timing

☐ Math formula and concept review

☐ Overthinking Math questions

☐ Not sure how to think through Math questions

☐ Careless errors on Math questions

☐ Other issues?

GENERAL

☐ Test anxiety and testing mindset issues?

ANSWER EXPLANATIONS

Reading Test

1. **(C)** As indicated by the introduction, this excerpt is from a novel about the French Revolution. Further, the descriptions of events in the story are realistic. Thus, this passage is best characterized as historical fiction. Magical realism and fantasy would involve more fantastic elements. A short story would be self-contained, while this is an excerpt.

2. **(A)** "Citizen" is consistently used to refer to Brotteaux, who is a man; "citizeness" is consistently used to refer to Gamelin, a woman. There is no clear indication that Gamelin and Brotteaux are of different social classes, age groupings, or ethnicities. After all, they both refer to the aristocracy with an outside perspective. In addition, they are both elderly. Finally, they are both most likely French.

3. **(C)** The sentence before the one in lines 14–17 refers to how the food is becoming more expensive every day. This gives a logical justification to the motives of the food-grabbers. If the food became more expensive, the food-grabbers would profit more from selling it to needy consumers. Choice (A) would be too grotesquely negative. Choices (B) and (D) are the opposite of the purported aristocratic goal of starving and controlling the lower classes.

4. **(D)** Lines 12–14 give evidence in support of the answer to the previous question because they state that food was becoming increasingly expensive, making it more likely that people would want to hoard food. The other options provide no such evidence.

5. **(C)** The sentence that follows indicates that she was "poor." Therefore, it makes the most sense that she did not live in a luxurious or "lavish" way. "Vast" relates to size, "imposing" relates to intimidation, and "prime" relates to high quality but not necessarily luxury.

6. **(B)** Lines 48–53 give evidence of Évariste Gamelin being unforgiving and relentless. He resolved to discover the identity of Élodie's seducer and further resolved to seek out vengeance on the person. None of the adjectives in the other choices are applicable to his treatment of lawbreakers.

7. **(A)** Lines 48–53 give the most direct evidence about Évariste's unforgiving and relentless attitude. Choices (B) and (C) support an attitude of ignorance, and choice (D) supports a polite attitude.

8. **(C)** Brotteaux discusses the futility of spending time trying to predict the future. Additionally, he discusses how knowing the future would take away one's enjoyment in the present. Hence, he would advise people to "focus on the moment." Choice (A) means to be forgiving, choice (B) advocates seeking knowledge, and choice (D) advocates reciprocal kindness.

9. **(C)** Gamelin politely refuses to sit in the chair that is offered to her, so she is best described as "turning down" the chair. "Repulsing" is too negative, and "decreasing" and "plummeting" generally relate to amounts of things.

10. **(D)** This is best seen from the first paragraph, in which the author thoroughly acknowledges how surprising it must be to modern readers that hostility once existed between the U.S. and Canada. The first paragraph contradicts the supposed knowledge described in choices (A) and (B). The passage does support the notion that people are eager to militarize the U.S.-Canada border as mentioned in choice (C).

11. **(B)** Lines 35–38 provide the evidence for this answer, saying that "no cause for war was more compelling in the U.S. than the desire to expand the nation into the northern territories." Although the other options would motivate U.S. citizens to fight against the British, they do not represent the "most significant" motivation to do so.

12. **(C)** Lines 35–40 state that the most compelling cause for war with Canada was the desire to expand the boundaries of the United States. The other line selections do not provide direct evidence in support of the answer to the previous question.

13. **(B)** Based on the surrounding context, the relations between the U.S. and Canada were not very positive in the past. So it would be appropriate to say that these relations were "suspect," which means "mistrustful." "Congenial" means "friendly," "familial" means "family-like," and "loathsome" means "repulsive," which is too negative in this context.

14. **(A)** "Tenacity" refers to the attitude held by the New England Federalists who were strongly determined not to enter the war. Although their attitude was likely angry, existed, and had a function, these words do not best capture the overall attitude.

15. **(D)** A strong Canadian defense was NOT an obstacle to U.S. victory in Quebec. Line 69 indicates that the Canadians left "Quebec vulnerable to invasion" by moving their defenses elsewhere. The other choices give reported obstacles to a lasting U.S. victory. Be sure you did not miss the "not" in the question.

16. **(C)** Lines 78–82 discuss how the "theaters of war," i.e., the places where the battles were fought, shifted from the frontier to cities. The passage does not mention a shift to elected representatives leading the armies as described in choice (A). The war was not marked by decisive victories by either side as listed in choice (B). The British were involved throughout the war in contrast to choice (D).

17. **(C)** Lines 78–82 best demonstrate that the battles shifted from being fought in the wilderness to being fought in urban areas. Choice (A) focuses on a singular event in the war. Choice (B) focuses on foreign affairs. Choice (D) focuses on the end of the war.

18. **(B)** Line 95 discusses how a free trade agreement in 1988 caused a "tremendous" increase in trade between the U.S. and Canada. The data in this table show just how large that increase in trade was between the countries. The other options do not focus on quantitative changes but just on the overall relations between the two countries.

19. **(A)** A significant increase in exports from the U.S. to Canada occurred after the treaty's passage, so a U.S. company that manufactures cars to be sold in Canada benefited most from the free trade agreement. The answer is not choice (B), because there is not as significant an increase in imports from Canada to the U.S. No information is provided about how this treaty impacted commerce within each country, making choices (C) and (D) incorrect.

20. **(D)** Susan B. Anthony is arguing that the major goal of passing women's suffrage would more likely be accomplished if women maintain a united front and avoid attaching themselves to individual political parties. Hence, the primary purpose of the passage is to make a tactical argument, i.e., to explain how this goal can best be attained. The other options refer to much more specific elements of the passage, and all misinterpret the general meaning of the passage.

21. **(D)** This can most clearly be seen in lines 63–66, in which Anthony states, "you must stand as disfranchised citizens—outlaws—shut out of 'the body politic,' humble supplicants, veriest beggars at the feet of all men of all parties alike." The phrase "all walks of life" refers to people from all sorts of backgrounds. Therefore, choice (D) is correct. There is no evidence that Anthony is directly encouraging women to win over the other groups of men mentioned.

22. **(D)** Lines 63–66 give the best evidence in support of the idea that Anthony encouraged women to focus on winning the support of men from all different backgrounds. The other line selections do not give such evidence.

23. **(C)** This can be seen most directly in lines 29–32, in which Anthony argues that dividing women into political parties is in the interest of the political parties but not in the interest of women's ultimate political goal, which is passage of women's suffrage. Since the interests of the political parties and of women differ, they can be described as "divergent." Choices (A) and (B) express the opposite of the intended meaning, and choice (D) is too extreme since there is no evidence in the essay that political parties and women will violently fight with one another.

24. **(C)** Lines 29-32 give the best evidence that Anthony believed the goals of political parties and of women diverged. The other lines do not provide direct evidence in support of the answer to the previous question.

25. **(A)** The first paragraph of the essay presents the viewpoint with which Anthony disagrees, namely that it is a good idea to have women identify with political parties rather than maintain a united front. The word "staunch" means "strong" in this context because the delegates are strongly supporting dividing female political efforts among different political parties. The other options fail to capture the intended meaning of the word and do not use commonly understood definitions of the word "staunch."

26. **(B)** Based on the passage as a whole, Anthony disagrees with the main idea presented in the first paragraph—she believes that women should remain united in their quest for voting rights and avoid dividing themselves by declaring loyalty for individual political parties. Putting quotation marks around a phrase is a common stylistic device that one can use to express distance from a point of view. Choice (A) is incorrect because there is no evidence that she said any such thing. Choice (C) is incorrect because she is not making a prediction. Choice (D) is incorrect because such a short phrase cannot offer much in the way of an explanation.

27. **(B)** Based on the context of the sentence, Anthony is referring to future goals of the political party, which could be expressed as "objectives." Choice (A) mistakenly uses an alternative meaning of "ends," and choices (C) and (D) skew the meaning in an overly negative direction.

28. **(A)** For this question, be sure to focus on the primary function of the sentence. Anthony uses this sentence to express that there will be plenty of time to focus on other political goals once the major goal of earning the right to vote is achieved. Choice (B) expresses the opposite of the intended purpose. Choices (C) and (D) do not relate to the intended purpose of this sentence.

29. **(D)** "Evolving" is used to describe the process by which molecules gradually give off heat in the microwave, so "generating" best captures this meaning. Although the other options do give possible definitions of "evolving," they do not reflect the process of giving off heat.

30. **(C)** The first paragraph gives evidence of this, stating that other types of cooking devices have internal heating elements while the microwave uses dipole rotation to heat food. Choices (A) and (D) are incorrect because all types of cooking increase the kinetic energy and intermolecular friction of food molecules, albeit by different methods. Choice (B) is not correct because this is a focus of Passage 2, not Passage 1.

31. **(A)** Lines 6–8 give the most direct support to the fact that microwaves lack an internal heating element. Choices (B), (C), and (D) give technical explanations of dipole rotation but do not clarify how the microwave is distinct from other forms of cooking.

32. **(C)** A "survey" best represents the structure of this passage since the author gives general facts and analysis about human cooking techniques over time. Choice (A) is not correct because the author is not attempting to persuade readers in favor of using older cooking methods. Choice (B) is incorrect because Passage 2 is more of a historical survey than a technical explanation, as found in Passage 1. Choice (D) is incorrect because the author does not take sides as to what type of cooking method is best overall.

33. **(D)** "Lines of development" is correct because in the context of the first paragraph of Passage 2, the "arcs" are referring to gradual trends in cooking innovation. The other options provide valid definitions of "arc" but not appropriate definitions in this context.

34. **(A)** Lines 75–83 discuss how the electric oven is an anomaly in the development of cooking. Even though the electric oven developed later, the electric oven is technologically inferior to the technology that preceded it. The other options are presented chronologically and demonstrate the gradual improvement in cooking technology.

35. **(C)** The first passage focuses on the scientific aspects of microwave cooking, such as the microwave's use of electromagnetic properties to heat food. The second passage discusses changes to the human practice of cooking over time, which fits under the umbrella of anthropology, which is the holistic study of humans and their ancestors. Choice (A) is incorrect because although history might be correct for Passage 2, the technical analysis in Passage 1 is beyond what would be needed to study cooking. Choice (B) is incorrect since paleontology involves the excavation of ancient remains. Choice (D) is incorrect because Passage 2 does not focus on biology.

36. **(B)** Passage 1 does not discuss problems with the microwave. In contrast, Passage 2 does mention how the speed of microwave cooking comes at the expense of precision (lines 90–93). Both passages mention the widespread popularity, cooking methodology, and possible cooking applications of the microwave.

37. **(D)** Based on the table, acetic acid is a polar substance. Lines 13–17 of the passage state, "Polar molecules, like a bar magnet, possess an electrical dipole moment, and, when introduced to a strong enough electromagnetic field, will align their positive and negative ends appropriately." Although the other choices are mentioned in the passage, they are not cited as models for the molecular behavior of a polar molecule.

38. **(B)** The second and third paragraphs of Passage 1 discuss how microwaves use the rotation of the polar molecules within food to heat up the food. Therefore, glucose and water would be heated within a microwave because they are both polar molecules according to the table. The other options each include at least one nonpolar substance.

39. **(C)** The author gives an in-depth analysis of the history and science of Halley's Comet, using words like "remarkable" and "poetic." The tone of the passage is best described as "analytical curiosity," because the author is clearly interested in understanding Halley's comet. Choice (A) is not correct because it is too negative. Choice (B) is incorrect because the passage gives quite a bit of scientific detail and stays focused on the topic. Choice (D) is wrong because although the author is clearly interested in Halley's Comet, he does not worship the comet.

40. **(A)** The first paragraph discusses the fact that Halley's Comet is a rare "Great Comet," i.e., one that is bright enough for humans on Earth to see without the aid of a telescope. Therefore, the brilliance referred to in line 4 describes the light-giving aspect of the comet, which is luminance. The other options are meanings of "brilliant" but are not correct in this context.

41. **(D)** Lines 1–7 assert that Halley's Comet and Old Faithful are renowned because of the dependable frequency with which they can be observed. Other ways of phrasing this idea are to say "periodic observability" or regular observability. Both the comet and the geyser contain water and nuclear particulates as listed in choices (A) and (C), but these factors do not contribute to their fame because water and nuclear particulates are relatively commonplace. Choice (B) is not correct because high eccentricity applies only to the comet, not to the geyser.

42. **(A)** Lines 5–7 most directly support the idea that Halley's Comet and Old Faithful are famous because of the regularity with which they can be seen. The other choices focus on aspects of the comet only.

43. **(C)** Lines 8–10 define a Great Comet as one that is bright enough to be observed by people on Earth with the naked eye. Although the other options may be attributes of a Great Comet, they are not, by definition, necessarily attributes.

44. **(A)** Lines 7–10 provide the best evidence for the idea that a Great Comet is one that can be observed without a telescope. The other options do not provide a definition of this term.

45. **(B)** The author uses this paragraph to give scientific reasons, such as Halley's unusually elliptical orbit, as to why Halley's Comet is a uniquely observable comet. The other options do not give the "primary" purpose of the paragraph, just minor things that are mentioned.

46. **(B)** Immediately after this selection, the narrator states that "Halley surmised that the comets observed . . . were one and the same." So the statement in lines 63–65 mainly serves to show how Halley's hypothesis was created. Choice (A) is incorrect because this statement does not provide any key biographical information and, instead, focuses more on an intellectual approach. Choice (C) is incorrect because no memories were discussed, and choice (D) is incorrect because there is no demonstration of a mathematical calculation in this statement, just a reference to some.

47. **(B)** Newton's theories gave Halley a general structure he could use to make better predictions about the behavior of comets. Out of the options, this is most similar to a politician who uses philosophical maxims to predict societal outcomes because the philosophical maxims give the theoretical structure that the politician would use to predict what would come next. Choice (A) is incorrect because the musician is not making predictions. Choice (C) is wrong because the mathematician is using the data to create theories, while Halley was using the theory to make experimental predictions as to what the data would be. Choice (D) is not correct because the engineer is not focused on making predictions about data but, instead, on using established laws of physics for construction.

Writing and Language Test

1. **(A)** The other parts of the sentence list things by placing the subject followed by the verb and by using the active voice. This is the only choice that maintains parallelism with the rest of the sentence.

2. **(C)** The pronoun is referring to the "child," "adult," and "teenager," and so needs to be "their" in order to be plural. The other options do not match with a third-person plural subject.

3. **(B)** One comma is necessary to separate the independent clause that comes before "now" and the dependent clause that begins with the "now." Choice (A) is too choppy, choice (C) lacks any pauses, and choice (D) puts the pause in the incorrect place.

4. **(D)** The paragraph is focused on the origins and early history of occupational therapy. Choice (D) is the only answer that focuses on the profession's past. Although the other choices do discuss topics related to occupational therapy, they do not connect to the paragraph's focus on this history of occupational therapy.

5. **(A)** A dash is needed to set off the parenthetical phrase in the same way the parenthetical phrase is ended, namely with another dash. Choices (B) and (C) are incorrect because a complete sentence must come before a semicolon or a colon. Choice (D) would start the parenthetical phrase with a comma even though it ends with a dash. This would be fine if the phrase instead ended with a comma.

6. **(B)** The previous sentence discusses some of the educational degree possibilities for occupational therapists, and the underlined sentence continues that focus. The underlined sentence is not redundant. It provides information that is helpful in understanding the full range of educational options for occupational therapists. So the underlined sentence should be left as is.

7. **(A)** Occupational therapists work "along with" doctors, nurses, and other health professionals. So "alongside" is the best option. Choice (B) means more of a literal, physical joining. Choices (C) and (D) give illogical and disconnected transitions.

8. **(C)** This answer works because the occupational therapist could potentially help with "any" of the areas or with "all" of the areas. Choices (A) and (B) do not use prepositions correctly. Choice (D) uses "and," which would not make sense because it links "all of" and "any of."

9. **(D)** This is the only choice consistent with the present tense used elsewhere in the nearby context of the paragraph. Choice (A) is in the past tense, choice (B) is in the present perfect, and choice (C) is not a proper form of the verb.

10. **(A)** "Their" shows possession by the occupational therapists, and "clients'" shows that the time belongs to the plural clients. "They're" is the same as "they are," and "there" refers to a place.

11. **(B)** Based on the first bar at the top of the graph, all occupations will experience an 11% increase from 2012–2022. Based on the middle bar of the graph, occupational therapists will experience a 29% increase in employment in the same time period. The other options give incorrect information based on the graph.

12. **(C)** Frick is described as helping bring about violence during a labor strike, which would be generally considered an "infamous" accomplishment. "Infamous" means "famous for doing something bad." The other options could be applicable. However, they are far too vague to give the most consistent characterization of Frick.

13. **(D)** This is the only option that clearly separates all of the unique items listed. Choice (A) does not include commas to separate "fences" and "water cannons." Choice (B) puts a comma between "water" and "cannons," changing the intended meaning since a water cannon is a type of crowd-control device. Choice (C) breaks up the complete expression "fortifying the factory."

14. **(A)** Based on the context, the union workers would have been angered by Frick's actions— "incensed" means "to anger greatly." Choices (B) and (C) are too positive. Choice (D) implies a lack of energy, although the workers were actually quite energetic in their response.

15. **(C)** "Firm determination" involves not letting anything get in one's way of accomplishing a goal. Saying that one will use "any means necessary" best conveys this desire to do what one wants, no matter the consequences. The other options do not express the strength of will that choice (C) does.

16. **(B)** The clause that matters is "who/whom fired the first shot." What occurs beforehand does not affect the choice between who and whom. In the phrase "he fired the first shot," the "he" is acting as a subject. Therefore, the relative pronoun comes in the place of the subject and should be "who." Choices (C) and (D) are incorrect because these refer to non-persons.

17. **(D)** The phrase "were lying" correctly uses the past progressive plural form of "to lie," indicating what the plural strikers were doing over an extended period in the past. The appropriate form of "lie" should be used since it means "being still," while "lay" means "put something down." The strikers were being still as they awaited the barges.

18. **(A)** This choice provides the most vivid details about the events while maintaining the more scholarly tone of the essay. The other options are too vague and informal.

19. **(C)** After considering the paragraph that immediately follows, you can see that it is logical to connect Frick's fears about the consequences of these events to the fact that he was correct in his prediction. Choices (A) and (B) connect to what happens in the next paragraph but are too vague to be solid explanations. Choice (D) contradicts Frick's goals.

20. **(D)** The mill is singular, and it possesses the grounds. Also, the two complete sentences need clear separation, which the semicolon, but not a comma, can provide. Choice (A) provides no possession, choice (B) is correct for plural mills, and choice (C) causes a comma splice.

21. **(A)** The paragraph should stay where it currently is. It concludes the essay, and generally refers to events that come later than the events discussed in the paragraphs beforehand. The other placements would change the chronology of the essay and interrupt the essay's narrative flow.

22. **(C)** The word "but" correctly indicates the logical contrast between the first and second halves of the sentence. The other options do not indicate contrast.

23. **(A)** This sentence begins the paragraph with a general introduction to the subject that is specifically elaborated upon in the next sentence. Choices (B) and (D) are too broad. Choice (C) is too specific.

24. **(D)** In this context, the word "claimed" should be followed by the word "that" in order to fit the common idiomatic phrasing, "claimed that." The other options do not use the proper idiomatic phrasing.

25. **(B)** This choice gives by far the most specific support for Dali's beliefs about his highly-developed abilities by mentioning the "dematerializing lighting technique." The other choices are too vague.

26. **(C)** "Completed" uses the correct singular past tense in reference to Dali's actions in the past. Choice (A) is present tense, choice (B) is present perfect, and choice (D) uses an improper form of the verb.

27. **(B)** It is most logical to state that there are "several symbols present in this painting," since this means that several symbols can be found in the painting.

28. **(D)** This choice maintains the original meaning while eliminating unnecessary wording. Choices (A) and (B) are too wordy. The meaning of choice (C) is unclear.

29. **(A)** "Reclaimed" is the only wording given that would be appropriately applied to a renewal of one's religion, which is what happened based on Dali's actions in the following sentences, making "rejected" incorrect. A person does not "reproduce" or "redomesticate" his or her religion.

30. **(C)** "For instance" provides a connection between the general statement made about the artwork in the previous sentence and the specific example given in the current sentence. Choices (A) and (B) do not provide this sort of transition. Choice (D) is too wordy.

31. **(B)** A boat is best described as passing "over" the sea since it travels along the sea's surface. A boat does not pass "to" or "sequence" over the sea, making choices (A) and (D) incorrect. Choice (C) is too wordy.

32. **(C)** The first part of the sentence mentions that Dali had a wide range of interests. This choice elaborates on what those specific interests were. In addition, the next several sentences describe Dali as creating sculptural pieces and writing a book.

33. **(B)** "Brought" is the correctly used tense of "to bring" in this context.

34. **(A)** The following sentence particularly clarifies which choice makes the most sense. The "former" would be referring to "knowledge and wisdom"—a sensible rationale for changing to robotic exploration since such exploration would increase our knowledge but wouldn't give humans bragging rights as the first to land on another planet. Choices (B) and (C) each present only one option instead of two. Choice (D) does not give an option that is the focus of the context that follows.

35. **(D)** This is consistent with the use of "we" elsewhere in the paragraph.

36. **(A)** Without this sentence, there would be no logical transition from the discussion of human exploration to the discussion of what the author considers to be a better, robotic alternative. Choice (B) is not correct because it does not provide any details.

37. **(C)** The commas correctly surround the clarification of what Io is. This grammatical construction is known as an "appositive," which is when an interchangeable name for what comes before is surrounded with commas. For example, "My oldest daughter, the Prime Minister, is well respected." The other options do not provide sufficient pauses.

38. **(D)** Each of the previous phrases in the sentence start with "that." Choice (D) is the only answer that continues this parallel structure.

39. **(A)** "Made-for-television" is an appropriate idiomatic expression that indicates that something was done with the intent of turning it into a television program. The other choices are nonsensical.

40. **(B)** This choice is the only one that focuses on the key argument of the passage, that it is time to move from human-centered to robot-centered exploration. The other choices present pairings that are not both discussed in the passage.

41. **(B)** The "it" refers to the act of involving humans in exploration, which is singular. "Does" is the correct form of the verb "to do" when coupled with a singular subject. Choice (D) could potentially work if instead of "that," the sentence used "the" immediately before the underlined phrase and if instead of "increase," it used "increased" immediately following the underlined phrase.

42. **(D)** The word "than" is used when comparing. While "to" is used in conjunction with a verb like "to run" and "too" in comparisons like "too much," neither of these is needed because (D) is the only choice that is parallel to the earlier phrasing in the sentence, "would rather hear."

43. **(C)** This is the only choice that does not have an unnecessary comma between the first and second contrasting parts of the sentence. This section of the sentence has only one subject—"volunteers." With only one subject, the two contrasting sections must be linked and therefore not be separated by a comma. Choice (A) is illogical, choice (B) includes an unnecessary pause, and choice (D) has two unnecessary commas.

44. **(A)** The paragraph discusses how strong public motivation to explore space will increase interest in it, citing the Mars One project as a good example. Choice (A) is the only option that correctly connects to the general theme of the paragraph to the specific example of Mars One.

Math Test (No Calculator)

1. **(C)** x and y could both be either negative or positive to make this true. Therefore, the only thing you can safely assume is that x and y are different. You can try this with sample values that make this expression true:

x	y	$x^2 > y^2$
−5	4	$25 > 16$
6	−1	$36 > 1$
3	0	$9 > 0$

2. **(B)** The easiest method is to substitute x into the first equation.

$$2x = 10 \rightarrow x = 5$$

Substitute 5 into the first equation:

$$5 = y^2 - 3y + 1 \rightarrow y^2 - 3y - 4 = 0 \rightarrow$$

Factor it: $(y + 1)(y - 4) = 0$

Therefore, the solutions are −1 and 4.

3. **(C)** Multiplying or dividing an inequality by a negative number requires that the direction of the inequality sign be reversed. The other operations mentioned do not do so. Here is how the inequality can be solved when dividing by −2:

$$-2x > 4 \rightarrow \frac{-2x}{-2} < \frac{4}{-2} \rightarrow x < -2$$

If you try some sample values that work for x, such as −3 or −5, you will see that the inequality is true.

4. **(D)** You could work backward from the choices if you are so inclined. Algebraically, divide the expression by 3 to simplify:

$$3a^2 - 27a - 108 = 0 \rightarrow a^2 - 9a - 36 = 0 \rightarrow$$

Factor it: $(a - 12)(a + 3) = 0$

If $a = 12$, the whole left-hand side equals 0. Similarly, if $a = -3$, the whole left-hand side equals 0.

Therefore, the solutions are 12, −3.

5. **(C)** Whenever Andrew starts a problem, he always takes the 10 minutes of time to set up. Then he completes 1 problem every 5 minutes of actual study. So the number of minutes he takes to do p problems is $10 + 5p$. If you set up the equation for this, it is $m = 10 + 5p$. Solving for p gives the correct answer:

$$m = 10 + 5p \rightarrow m - 10 = 5p \rightarrow \frac{(m - 10)}{5} = p \rightarrow p = \frac{1}{5}(m - 10)$$

6. **(A)** Take the slope of the line using relatively simple points from the table, like (1, 2) and (5, 18):

$$\text{Slope} = \frac{Rise}{Run} = \frac{y_2 - y_1}{x_2 - x_1} = \frac{18 - 2}{5 - 1} = \frac{16}{4} = 4$$

The only choice with a slope of 4 is (A).

7. **(D)** Since this is one equation with two variables, it has infinite solutions. If you knew another line with which this equation intersected, the two equations would have a single solution. To see how this equation has more than two solutions, substitute some sample values for x and y into the equation:

$$3x - 4y = 73$$

If x is 1, y is −17.5.

If x is 2, y is −16.75.

If x is 3, y is −16.

You can keep on going, and you will find endless possibilities for x and y.

8. **(B)** Solve for x and y by using substitution:

$$4 + y = 32x \text{ and } y = 2x + 2 \rightarrow$$

$$4 + (2x + 2) = 32x \rightarrow 6 = 30x \rightarrow x = \frac{1}{5} \rightarrow$$

Substitute $\frac{1}{5}$ for x to solve for y: $y = \left(2 \times \frac{1}{5}\right) + 2 = \frac{12}{5}$

Then multiply x and y to solve for their product: $\frac{1}{5} \times \frac{12}{5} = \frac{12}{25}$

9. **(C)** For each year she has the portfolio, its value increases 10%. Therefore, the amount after one year of growth over the original amount at the beginning of that year will be 1.1 times the original amount. This process will repeat for each year Maria has the portfolio growing at this rate, making $f(n) = 10,000 \times 1.1^n$.

You can also see this using concrete numbers. If Maria starts with $10,000, after 1 year, she will have 10% interest added to the original amount:

$$10\% \text{ of } 10,000 = 0.1 \times 10,000 = 1,000$$

Then you can add 1,000 to the original 10,000 to have $11,000 after the first year. To see how much money Maria will have after two years, find 10% of this new total:

$$10\% \text{ of } 11,000 = 0.1 \times 11,000 = 1,100$$

Then add this to the original 11,000 to find how much she will have in her account at the end of year 2:

$$11,000 + 1,100 = 12,100$$

The only option that fits these concrete numbers is choice (C).

10. **(D)** Minimizing all of the variables will decrease the amount of money in the account after a given period of time. You could plug in a variety of sample values and test the impact of changing each variable on the overall amount of money in the account. However, determining the answer is easier simply by using common sense. If you start off with less money, have a lower interest rate, and have less frequent compounding of interest, less money will be in the account.

11. **(B)** Begin by determining the slope of the line in the given equation by putting it in slope-intercept form ($y = mx + b$):

$$4x = 2y - 6 \rightarrow 2y = 4x + 6 \rightarrow y = 2x + 3$$

The line portrayed in choice (B), $y = 2x + 10$, is the only option that has the same slope as the line in the problem. This means that the two lines will never intersect and will have no common solutions since they are parallel to one another. Be mindful that this will be true only as long as the y-intercepts of the lines are different. If the y-intercepts are the same, the lines will overlap, resulting in an infinite number of solutions.

12. **(A)** No matter how many shirts or pants are cleaned, the cleaner charges a $5 fee. The only logical explanation out of the given choices is that this is some kind of set fee. The cost to clean a shirt is $10 since the shirt variable is multiplied by 10. The cost to clean a pair of pants is $6 since the pants variable is multiplied by 6. The total minimum cost to clean either one shirt or one pair of pants is $11:

$$C = 10S + 6P + 5 \rightarrow C = (10 \times 0) + (6 \times 1) + 5 = 11$$

13. **(B)** When you add a positive number to the y-value of a function, the function shifts up. When you subtract a number from the x-value of a function, the function shifts to the right. This function has had 2 subtracted from its x-value, so the function shifts to the right 2 units. This function has had 3 added to its y-value, so the function shifts up 3 units.

Grid-in Questions

14.

12 Triple the given equation $2x + 3 = 4$ to give you the equation $6x + 9 = 12$:

$$2x + 3 = 4 \rightarrow 3 \cdot 2x + 3 \cdot 3 = 3 \cdot 4 \rightarrow 6x + 9 = 12$$

15.

6 Look for a way to seamlessly make the original expression a variation of $x + 5$. Add 25 to both sides of the equation $x^2 + 10x = 11$ to form $x^2 + 10x + 25 = 36$. The result can be expressed as $(x + 5)^2 = 36$. Therefore, $x + 5 = 6$.

Alternatively, you could determine the value of x using the quadratic formula, $\dfrac{-b \pm \sqrt{b^2 - 4ac}}{2a}$. However, this will be more labor intensive than if you use the shortcut.

16.

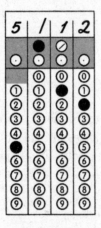

3 There are 3 values of the function where it will intersect the *x*-axis. You can see this by looking at the graph of the equation below:

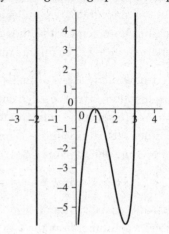

The values of 3, −2, and 1 are all zeros of the function.

You can perhaps more easily determine the zeros of the function if you recognize that the function is already factored:

$$f(x) = (x - 3)(x + 2)((x - 1)^2)$$

All you need to do is look at the values of *x* that would make the entire expression equal to zero. If $(x - 3) = 0$, if $(x + 2) = 0$, or if $(x - 1) = 0$, the entire expression is equal to zero. Since $(x - 1)$ is squared, the $(x - 1)$ term repeats. So you will have only three zeros even though this equation is actually to the 4th power.

17.

$\dfrac{5}{12}$ The triangle as described looks like this:

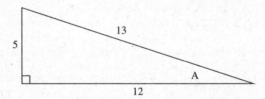

Given this sine and cosine, the triangle will be a multiple of the special right triangle 5-12-13. The smallest side is 5, and the median side is 12. So the ratio of the smallest side of the triangle to the median side of the triangle is $\dfrac{5}{12}$.

Another way to think about the answer is to realize that the question is asking for the tangent of angle *A*. The tangent is the opposite side over the adjacent side, which is $\dfrac{5}{12}$.

Math Test (With Calculator)

1. **(C)** The "difference" between two terms is the result when you subtract one term from another. Subtract one term from another. This is easiest to do if you place one term over the other so you can easily match up common terms and carefully apply the negative sign:

$$\begin{array}{r} (7a^2 + 3ab - 8b) \\ -(-2a^2 + ab - 2b) \\ \hline 9a^2 + 2ab - 6b \end{array}$$

2. **(A)**

$$\left(2x^2 + 4xy + 2y^2\right) \times \frac{1}{2x+2y} = \frac{2x^2 + 4xy + 2y^2}{2x+2y} \rightarrow$$

$$\frac{x^2 + 2xy + y^2}{x+y} = \frac{(x+y)(x+y)}{(x+y)} = x + y = y + x$$

3. **(B)** The professor will cancel if there are 10 or fewer students in the class. So more than 10 students must be present for the professor to conduct the class. Therefore, the answer is $S > 10$.

4. **(C)** What is a possible value for x in the expression below?

   Take the original expression: $-6 < \frac{8}{3}x < -\frac{1}{4}$

   Multiply everything by $\frac{3}{8}$ in order to get x by itself:

   $$-\frac{9}{4} < x < -\frac{3}{32}$$

   Make solving the inequality easier by converting each fraction to a decimal. Then determine what numbers fall within this range. The fractions would convert to the following range when expressed as decimals:

   $$-2.25 < x < -0.09375$$

   -2 is the only choice within this range.

5. **(B)** As the age groups gradually increase in value (from 12 through 61+), the number of group members using video sharing steadily decreases (from 40 to 2). A negative correlation is defined as the relationship between two variables such that when one variable increases, the other variable decreases. So the relationship between age groups and percentage of group members using video sharing can best be described as a negative correlation. A positive correlation is when the variables increase with one another. Equivalence simply means the variables are equal. An exponentially inverse relationship means that as one variable increases, the other decreases at an exponential rate. The decrease in video sharing is relatively steady, so the terms cannot be described as having an exponentially inverse relationship.

6. **(D)** Take the fractions of the portion of each group who uses that type of social media and divide by the total of each group; then multiply:

$$\frac{12-18\text{-year-olds who photo share}}{\text{Total number of } 12-18\text{-year-olds}} \times \frac{31-45\text{-year-olds who text share}}{\text{Total number of } 31-45\text{-year-olds}} = \frac{32}{94} \times \frac{40}{104} \approx 0.13$$

7. **(D)** Calling people from as large a group as possible from as many phone types and age groups as possible will ensure that the results are highly accurate. The other choices limit the samples to groups who do particular types of activities. The other choices would give results accurate for that sample but not for the population as a whole.

8. **(C)** Take how much money from the $62,000 total falls in each tax bracket, and calculate the amount of tax applied to it:

$$\text{First, } \$9,000 \text{ at } 15\% = \$9,000 \times 0.15 = \$1,350$$

$$\text{Next, } \$41,000 \text{ at } 20\% = \$41,000 \times 0.20 = \$8,200$$

$$\text{Next, } \$12,000 \text{ at } 30\% = \$12,000 \times 0.30 = \$3,600$$

$$\text{Finally, } \$1,350 + \$8,200 + \$3,600 = \$13,150 \text{ total}$$

As an alternative solution or as a way of checking your math, you could estimate. The answer must fall somewhere within the range of 15% to 30% of $62,000 since all of the tax brackets are within this range. Most of the money is taxed at 20%, so the answer should be close to 20%. Since more money is taxed at 30% and since 30% is twice as far away from 20% as is 15%, the amount of tax should be a bit more than 20% of the total. 20% of $62,000 is $12,400, and the answer is a bit greater than this.

9. **(A)** Multiply both the slope and the y-intercept of the given line by -1 to get the reflection of the line. For $y = 4x + 7$, this is the equation $y = -4x - 7$.

The general rule to find the reflection of a function $f(x)$ across the x-axis is that the reflection is $-f(x)$.

10. **(D)** Solve for x as follows:

$$\frac{12}{\sqrt[3]{x}} = 4 \to 12 = 4\sqrt[3]{x} \to 3 = \sqrt[3]{x} \to \text{Cube both sides} \to 27 = x$$

11. **(C)** The slope of the function is steady and linear until around week 6, at which point it starts curving upward exponentially. An exponential function is one that goes up at a rapidly increasing rate or goes down at a rapidly decreasing rate, as opposed to a steady, linear rate.

12. **(A)** "Geometric" is synonymous with "exponential." Estimate the approximate increase given the rate of exponential growth and starting point at week 12. Fortunately, the answers are far enough apart that 450 is the only reasonable option. The other options all represent far too large an increase.

13. **(A)** $m + 2n = 1$ and $6n + 3m = 9$ are parallel lines that will not intersect since they have the same slopes and different y-intercepts. Since they never intersect, they have no common solutions.

14. **(D)** Each penny is worth 1 cent, and each nickel is worth 5 cents. So the total number of cents given by the total coins in the change bowl is $P + 5N$. This needs to be less than 1 dollar total, i.e., 100 cents. So the inequality $P + 5N < 100$ is the solution.

15. **(B)** Since the data set would be far larger than either of the data sets portrayed and since the values are selected at random, it is most reasonable to conclude that the average (mean) of the set of 1,000 randomly selected values would be 50. Generally speaking, the larger your data sample, the more likely your actual mean will approach your estimated mean.

16. **(B)** Since the values are selected at random, such a high proportion of values greater than 50 in the selection of 50 random numbers is most surprising. With a larger data set, the values would be expected to average closer to the mean than those in the set of 20 random numbers. Since values are taken between 1 and 100, both sets of data should have a range between 1–100, which explains why choice (A) is incorrect. Choice (C) is incorrect because the ranges of the data sets are similar even though the means of the sets are different. Choice (D) is not correct because portraying these random values in a scatter plot is logical. You can impose a best-fit line on top of the scattered data if you would like to determine a trend.

17. **(A)** The range is the difference between the maximum and minimum values in the set. With such large data sets, it is highly likely that both sets would have a wide range of large and small values, with both almost certainly having a value close to or at 1 and a value close to or at 100. So the range for both sets would be about 100. The difference between the ranges is calculated by subtracting one range from the other: $100 - 100 = 0$.

18. **(B)** A best-fit line is a line on the graph that shows the overall direction the points seem to be going. The best-fit lines of both of these sets would most likely be a horizontal line with a y-intercept of approximately 50. Horizontal lines have a slope of 0, so the average of the slopes of both of these lines would most likely be 0 as well.

19. **(C)** A value of 4 for n will ensure that the expression has exponential growth since any power of 2 or greater will ensure exponential growth in the function. Anything raised to the 0 power simply equals 1. Anything raised to an exponent of 1 is simply itself. So choices (A) and (B) result in lines, not exponential functions.

20. **(C)** The best way to increase a confidence level is to increase the amount of relevant sample data. A more accurate scale could be of minor help but not as much as increasing the overall data samples. Choices (A) and (B) would provide irrelevant and less accurate data, respectively.

21. **(D)** The weight of the balloon itself is irrelevant since the balloon is identical in both situations.

    $1.2 - 0.179 = 1.021$ is the difference in density between the two balloons. Since you have a 2 cubic meter balloon, simply multiply 1.021×2 to give approximately 2.04.

22. **(B)** The smaller the range of values in a data set, the lower the standard deviation will be. If the smallest and largest values are removed, the range of values will decrease, thereby decreasing the standard deviation.

    To be more precise, you can calculate standard deviation using this formula:

$$\text{Standard deviation} = \sqrt{\text{Average of the squared distances of the data points from their mean}}$$

    For example, the standard deviation of the set $\{1, 5, 6, 7, 10\}$ is approximately 3.3. The standard deviation of the same set with the highest and lowest values removed $\{5, 6, 7\}$ is 1. By using this example, you can see that removing the smallest and largest values from the set decreases the standard deviation of the set.

23. **(B)** After purchasing gifts for his other friends, Jay has $50 left. Since 200 quarters equals $50, the range of what Jay can give his friend is between 1 and 200 quarters, inclusive. This is expressed as $1 \leq Q \leq 200$.

24. **(C)** The fixed costs for the pretzel stand are $500, and the variable costs are $2 per pretzel. So the cost function $c(x)$ given x pretzels is $c(x) = 2x + 500$. The graph of this function has a y-intercept of 500 and a slope of 2:

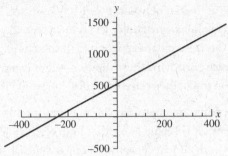

25. **(C)** Since this is a 2nd-degree equation, it should have two solutions.

$$8x^2 = -16x - 2$$
$$8x^2 + 16x = -2$$
$$x^2 + 2x = -\frac{1}{4}$$

Complete the square:

$$(x+1)^2 = \frac{3}{4} \rightarrow x^2 + 2x + 1 = \frac{3}{4} \rightarrow x^2 + 2x + \frac{1}{4} = 0$$

Use the quadratic equation to find the answers:

$$\frac{-b \pm \sqrt{b^2 - 4ac}}{2a} \rightarrow \frac{-2 \pm \sqrt{2^2 - 4 \cdot 1 \cdot \frac{1}{4}}}{2 \cdot 1} = \frac{-2 \pm \sqrt{3}}{2 \cdot 1} = -1 \pm \frac{\sqrt{3}}{2}$$

Then simplify the two solutions to see what they equal:

$$-1 + \frac{\sqrt{3}}{2} = \frac{-2}{2} + \frac{\sqrt{3}}{2} = \frac{1}{2}(\sqrt{3} - 2)$$

and

$$-1 - \frac{\sqrt{3}}{2} = \frac{-2}{2} - \frac{\sqrt{3}}{2} = -1 - \frac{\sqrt{3}}{2}$$

26. **(A)** In order to maximize the area of flooring while minimizing the floor's perimeter, a square floor would be the best choice. A square always has at least as much and typically more area for a particular perimeter than a rectangle of the same perimeter. Therefore, the length and width should be equivalent.

To see this, try using concrete numbers. If you have a square and a rectangle, each with a perimeter of 20 units, the length of each side for the square must be 5 and the lengths of the sides of the rectangle could be a wide range of possibilities, such as 2, 8, 2, 8. The area of the square with a side of 5 is $5^2 = 25$. The area of the rectangle is $2 \times 8 = 16$, which is much less than the area of the square. You can try this with other sample values for the rectangle's sides. However, you will consistently find that having the sides equivalent will lead to the greatest possible area.

27. **(D)** $i^4 + i^{12} = 1 + 1 = 2$. Know that the powers of i repeat in a cycle of four:

$$i^1 = i, \ i^2 = -1, \ i^3 = -i, \ i^4 = 1, \ i^5 = i, \ldots$$

That way, you can look at the value of the exponent and know what the value of i^x will be without having to do any long calculations.

Grid-in Questions

28.

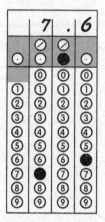

21 In a typical week, Eloise should get $9 \times 7 = 63$ hours of sleep. To see how many hours she has actually slept, subtract the total hours she has been awake from the total hours in a week:

$$(24 \times 7) - 126 = 42$$

Then calculate the additional hours of sleep she should get by subtracting how many hours she *actually* got (42) from the amount of sleep she *should have* gotten (63):

Eloise should get an additional $63 - 42 = 21$ hours of sleep.

29.

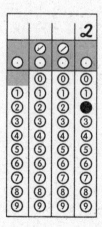

7.6 Plug in the given values for m and n to determine what the value of the constant k is:

$$m = kn$$
$$10 = k \times 2$$
$$5 = k$$

Now plug in 38 for m and 5 for k to get the value of n:

$$38 = 5n$$
$$7.6 = n$$

30.

2 The plant increases 3 inches in height every 2 months. Simply backtrack 2 months from the time when it is 5 inches tall in order to see how tall it was when it was planted:

$$5 - 3 = 2 \text{ inches}$$

31.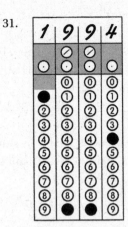

1994 1994 is the year during which the college had the largest spike in applications. Moreover, the number of admissions began to decrease at that time. This decrease most likely occurred because the college knew that, since it could secure a large number of students from early decision (since students admitted early were committed to going), it could fill all of its student spots without having to offer as many admissions. Having more applications and fewer admissions results in greater selectivity because being accepted to the college is more difficult for the majority of students applying.

Reading

Reading

1

FREQUENTLY ASKED QUESTIONS
How Is the Reading Section Structured?

- First section of the test
- 60 minutes long
- Five total passages, each with 9–10 questions, for 47 questions all together

  - One fiction passage (a short story or excerpt from a novel)
  - One social science passage (e.g., sociology, economics, psychology)
  - One "great global conversation" passage (typically a historical document related to the ideas of democracy)
  - Two science passages (could be an article or a book excerpt about biology, geology, astronomy, or another science field)
  - One of the non-fiction passages will be split into two smaller selections to compare

- Questions appear in a random order of difficulty
- Questions generally go in order of where the answers will be found in the passage

What Is Tested on the Reading Section?

- Approximately 9 questions on defining words in context
- Approximately 4 questions on data interpretation
- Approximately 9–10 questions related to finding evidence in the passage
- Remaining 24 questions a mixture of sentence-level, paragraph-level, and whole-passage comprehension

How Should I Use this Chapter?

- Carefully read the "Reading Passage Strategies" and "Reading Questions Strategies" sections, and think about what best applies to your personal situation.
- Review the section "Tactics for Specific Reading Question Types" for certain types of questions.
- See how the various strategies and tactics come together on a full-length passage with questions.
- Target your preparation with drills for particular question types:

  - Big picture and inference questions
  - Evidence-based questions
  - Words-in-context questions
  - Graph analysis questions

- Practice with samples from each type of passage:
    - Fiction
    - Social Science
    - Historical document
    - Science
    - Passage 1 and passage 2

- Fine-tune your approach to the PSAT Reading Test by consulting the "Troubleshooting" section at the end of the chapter and adjusting your test-taking behavior or tactics accordingly.

READING PASSAGE STRATEGIES

1. Read a Passage Before Reading the Questions.

TIP

When in doubt on how you should attack the reading, simply ask yourself, "how would I want to read something to truly understand it?" Your answer to that fundamental question will guide you to your best approach.

Most students find it helpful to read the passage first. Why? Because the PSAT Reading Test primarily has questions that require you to make inferences about the text. So having a general understanding of the passage is essential. For questions that ask about the purpose of the passage, the tone of the passage, the function of a paragraph, and what a phrase suggests, you will not be able to figure out the answer if you do not understand the overall meaning of the passage. Some students like to take a quick look at what the questions ask before they start. If you do this, *be sure you don't focus too much on specifics when you go back and read the passage—be sure you focus on the big picture.* Look at the questions with the mindset that you are trying to get a quick preview of what the passage will likely be about. Students run into trouble when they use the question preview as a "mental checklist" as they read because they focus too heavily on the details and not on the larger connections.

2. Focus on the Most Important Parts of the Passage.

You should be able to summarize the passage in one or two sentences. This summary should contain the "gist" of what you have read—don't worry about memorizing details from the passage. You can change your focus depending on the passage type in order to maximize your comprehension.

FICTION AND LITERATURE: Read the first paragraph or two a bit more slowly and carefully (at around 100 words a minute), and read the remainder of the passage at a more typical speed (at around 150 words a minute). This can help you fully grasp the beginning of the plot, the setting, and the characters before you move to the rest of the story.

NONFICTION (SOCIAL SCIENCE AND SCIENCE): Read the first paragraph, first sentence of each paragraph, and last paragraph a bit more slowly and carefully (at around 100 words a minute) and the rest at a more typical speed (at around 150 words a minute). Nonfiction is typically more structured than fiction. So the first and last paragraphs as well as the first sentence of each paragraph will typically give you critical information, such as the thesis of the essay and the general topic of each paragraph. Focusing on these parts also gives you a "mental map" of where information can most likely be located in the passage.

PASSAGE 1 AND PASSAGE 2: Read these with a focus on the overall meaning, but pay close attention to the *overall relationship* between the two passages. Why? Because there will be several questions that involve comparing the similarities and differences between the two reading selections. Be aware that the questions about just passage 1 come first, the questions about just passage 2 come second, and the questions about both passages come last. If you have trouble understanding the big picture of the passage, you may want read passage 1 and do the passage 1 questions first, followed by reading passage 2 and the passage 2 questions. If you choose to break it up like this, be sure you think about the overall relationship between the passages as you are reading the second passage, since 2–3 questions will typically ask about this relationship.

If you have extraordinary reading comprehension and speed (i.e., if you can read over 300 words per minute with excellent comprehension), do not worry about the above recommendations for how to focus your energy differently on different passages. Just read the passages the way you normally would. After all, the PSAT Reading Test is fundamentally a test of your general reading skill, so if that skill is solid, keep doing what you're doing.

3. Use the Full Amount of Time on the Passages—Don't Rush.

There is no need to speed-read on the PSAT. If you can read about as quickly as you can talk— for most people around 120–150 words per minute—you will be fine finishing the test. Since the passages all have 9–10 questions, you can pace yourself by taking about **12 minutes per passage**. This would involve taking about **5 minutes to read the passage** and about **7 minutes to answer the accompanying questions**. Table 1.1 shows how you might want to allocate your time for a typical Reading Test as a whole. (You can adjust this general outline if you need more or less time on the passages or if you think you may need to skip a passage. This timing break-down will work for most students, ensuring they can complete the reading test on time without rushing. Also, keep in mind that while the fiction passage always comes first, the order of the four non-fiction passages can vary.)

Table 1.1. Reading Timing

A Total of 5 Passages, 47 Questions, 60 Minutes		
Passage 1, fiction, 9 questions	5 minutes reading	7 minutes answering questions
Passage 2, social science, 9–10 questions	5 minutes reading	7 minutes answering questions
Passage 3, science, 9–10 questions	5 minutes reading	7 minutes answering questions
Passage 4, social science (great global conversation), 9–10 questions	5 minutes reading	7 minutes answering questions
Passage 5, science, 9–10 questions	5 minutes reading	7 minutes answering questions

Remember that Table 1 contains only guidelines. You can *take more time on the passage(s) that is/ are tough for you and less time on the passage(s) that is/are easier for you*. After you practice with the passages in this book, you will have a good sense of which passages demand more time and which demand less time. Some students even find it helpful to adopt the extreme tactic of rereading an entire passage. If you have the time to do so, this can absolutely be justified, especially if it helps you have a firm grasp of a passage before doing the questions.

TIP

Remember that you are in control— allocate your time as works best for you.

4. Read the "Introductory Text" Before the Passage.

Before each passage is a very brief summary that will give you some information about what you are about to read. This summary typically provides a passage title, information about when and where the passage was written, and occasionally some other helpful details. Here is an example of what a background blurb may look like:

This passage is adapted from Gerry Thompson, *Social Media: Connector of People or Waster of Time?* ©2016 by Gerry Thompson.

Be sure to read the background blurb before reading the actual passage as it will help you preview the general meaning of what follows. If any of the topics are unfamiliar or a passage's language seems too lofty, don't be alarmed. If you carefully read the passages, you will have the information necessary to answer the questions well—the PSAT makers do not expect you to be a master of all potential topics and potential writing styles.

5. Underline and Annotate the Passage If It Helps You Stay Focused.

You are absolutely permitted to write all over the test if it is paper-based (the most common situation). So if making notes and underlining key words helps you stay focused while you read, go for it. You do not need to underline and annotate as you would when reading a school textbook—for a textbook, you need to take notes in such a way that you will be able to look over your notebook or highlights prior to the big exam. On the PSAT, you will immediately go from reading the passage to answering the questions, so you do not need to underline and annotate as thoroughly as you would if you were reading material for school and then being tested on it several weeks later. You do not need to commit the passage to your long-term memory. If you are taking a digitally-based version of the PSAT or the PSAT 10, you will have some scrap paper available that you can use to take notes as you read.

6. Read *Actively*, Not *Passively*.

Simply moving your eyes over the page is not enough to be sure that you understand what you are reading. What makes active reading and passive reading different? Table 1.2 answers that question.

Table 1.2. Active Versus Passive Reading

Active Reading	Passive Reading
Paraphrase—You put the ideas of the passage into your own words. You are able to state the main idea of what you read.	No paraphrasing—You get lost in the details and are unable to summarize what is happening.
Ask questions—You ask yourself questions about the passage, such as, "Who is this character?" "What is going to happen next?" "What is the point of the passage?"	Don't ask questions—Although you may be reading, you are not interacting with the passage.
Focus on the task at hand—You think about the passage, and if your mind wanders, you quickly refocus.	Your mind is elsewhere—You may look like you're reading but don't actually refocus when you become bored or distracted.

If you have trouble reading actively, what can you do to improve?

FIND *SOMETHING* ABOUT THE PASSAGE THAT CAN INTEREST YOU: Reading actively is easy when the passage is something you would read for pleasure. If the passage is not on a topic you find particularly interesting, try to think of some connection you can make to the passage from your schoolwork or life experiences. Suppose you had a passage about human anatomy. Even if you haven't specifically studied the subject in school, you might be able to understand the concepts based on experiences you had going to the doctor or studying the biology of different animals.

PRACTICE WITH TEXTS YOU FIND MORE CHALLENGING: The PSAT Reading Test consistently has (1) a fiction passage, (2) a historical document, (3) a social science passage, and (4) two science passages. If you consistently have difficulty focusing on a certain type of passage, make an effort to read more of that type of material on your own or take coursework that assigns that type of reading.

CONSIDER LOOKING AT THE QUESTIONS BEFORE READING THE PASSAGE: If you are having a hard time staying focused while you read, scanning the questions before you start reading can help you. This could give you a preview of what you will need to comprehend from your reading. Just be sure you are able to keep the big picture in mind as you read.

MAKE SURE YOU ARE WELL RESTED: It is definitely more difficult to focus on reading when you are fatigued. Try your best to get about 8–9 hours of sleep on the nights leading up to the PSAT.

RECOGNIZE WHICH PASSAGE TYPES ARE MORE CHALLENGING FOR YOU AND ALLOW MORE TIME ON THEM: Often, students find the fiction and historical document passages to require more time to fully comprehend. The fiction passage may have flashbacks and metaphors that require a closer reading; the historical document may be over 200 years old, making some of the language antiquated. Experiment with reading the different passage types so that you have a sense of which passages you can complete in less than 12 minutes and which may need more than 12.

7. Most Students Find Doing the Passages *in Order* Is Better.

Most students prefer to do the passages in order, since they will not have to spend extra time and energy jumping around in the test. However, it can be helpful to do the passages out of order if either of these applies to you.

YOU LIKE TO BUILD MOMENTUM: The Reading Test comes first on the PSAT, so you may benefit from a little warm-up before you tackle the most challenging passages. Perhaps you know that a certain type of passage—say, Social Science—is always easiest for you. If so, locate this passage and start with it. Perhaps you can start with the passages that happen to have topics that are naturally much more interesting to you. If so, check out the introductory blurbs of the different passages. Start with the passage that intrigues you the most, and save the most difficult one for the end.

YOU LIKE TO GET THE TOUGHEST PASSAGE OUT OF THE WAY: If you are likely to be fresh and energized at the beginning of the test, you may want to start with the passage that is typically most difficult for you. Why? Because you will be able to give it your maximum focus and energy before you feel depleted after completing other passages. You can decide which passage to start with either ahead of time if you know that a certain type of passage is consistently most challenging or on the morning of the test after you briefly survey the passage topics.

READING QUESTIONS STRATEGIES

1. Focus on the *Front* of a Question, Not the *Back* of a Question.

Spend the majority of your time on a question by carefully reading the question and formulating your own answer. Doing this will allow you to be much more decisive when you evaluate the choices, just as you are more decisive when you go to a store if you have a list of what you want to purchase ahead of time. Strive to minimize or eliminate time that you spend after you have made a decision on your answer—double-checking and redoing questions is usually a recipe for trouble on reading questions because you will allow the wrong answers to get inside your head.

2. Underline and Circle Key Words as You Read the Questions.

A careless mistake in reading a question can cause you to pick the incorrect answer. Instead of quickly reading through the question and then having to reread it, *read it well one time* and underline and/or circle the most important words as you do so. This will ensure that you do not miss wording critical to understanding what the question is asking, such as "not," "primary," "infer," "suggest," etc. If your PSAT is paper-based (the most common situation), you are able to write on the PSAT booklet—take advantage of it! If you are taking a digital version of the PSAT, you won't be able to write on the screen. Just be sure to read the questions extremely thoroughly, perhaps using your finger to carefully follow along with the question text on the screen.

3. Go Back to the Passage as Often as Needed.

Do not hesitate to go back to the passage—this is an open-book test, and you will likely have plenty of time to review enough context. You will probably want to go back to the passage on about 75–80 percent of the questions. The ones that do not necessitate going back to review the passage are more general questions about the purpose or tone of the passage—you likely will be fine with these from your initial reading. The PSAT makes it easy for you to go back and review context, *generally putting the questions in the order of where they are in the passage*, and giving you plenty of line references. Go back and check out as much context as you need to answer the questions successfully.

4. Create an Answer in Your Own Words.

Once you fully understand the question and have considered the context in the passage related to the question, create your own idea for an answer. Sometimes you will be able to be pretty specific in your idea, like if the question asks for a synonym or for you to paraphrase a couple of sentences from the passage. At other times, you may need to have a more general idea, like if the question asks you to determine the purpose or tone of the passage as a whole. Ultimately, having some idea of what you are looking for is better than having no idea at all.

5. A Single Flaw Makes an Answer 100 Percent Wrong.

A single word can contaminate an answer, making it completely wrong. When you narrow the choices down to two options, don't just look for the "best" answer—look for the "flawless" answer. Try to deliberate quickly the correctness or incorrectness of each answer, knowing that there is one that is definitely correct and three that are definitely wrong. The College Board has put a great deal of effort into creating the questions you will see on the PSAT, so you can safely assume they will be of the very highest quality. Do not waste time looking for flaws in the test, and instead give the PSAT the benefit of the doubt.

6. Focus on *Meaning*, Not Matching.

On ordinary school tests, students are often used to matching the choices with facts they recall from the assigned reading or from the in-class lecture. On the PSAT, though, the fact that an answer has wording that matches parts of the passage text is no guarantee that it is correct. There is nothing wrong with picking an answer because it *does* have wording that is in the passage; just don't pick an answer *only because* it has matching wording. Be certain the overall meaning correctly answers the question.

7. Come Back to a Question If You Are Stuck.

If you are stuck, simply circle the question and move on to the next one. Doing so does not mean that you have given up on the question. On the contrary—you are allowing yourself more time to read other parts of the passage that will help you arrive at the answer. You are also allowing more time for your subconscious mind to process the question further. When you come back to the question with fresh eyes, you will likely find that it is far easier than it appeared at first glance.

8. If the Passage Is Unclear, Start with Specific Questions and Finish with Big-Picture Questions.

The first question on a reading passage is frequently a big-picture question, asking about the main idea, function, or tone of the whole passage. If you didn't quite understand the passage, wait on questions like these. Instead, answer the questions that ask about the meanings of words or about what can be inferred from small parts of the passage. After answering these more specific questions, revisit the big-picture questions, and the answers will come much more easily.

TIP

Sometimes it helps to start with the "trees" and gradually move toward the "forest." In other words, you might want to begin with questions that are straightforward and include line references and then move to those that are big picture.

9. Trust Your Intuition.

If you understand the passage, understand the question, and feel confident in your choice, pick that choice and don't look back. Your job while taking the PSAT is not to come up with an elaborate justification for your answer—you simply must answer the questions correctly. If you have approached the question with patience and care, you have done all you can do. It is now time to trust yourself.

TACTICS FOR SPECIFIC READING QUESTION TYPES

Evidence-Based Questions

TACTIC 1: USE THE LINE SELECTIONS IN EVIDENCE-BASED QUESTIONS TO HELP YOU ANSWER THE QUESTIONS THAT COME RIGHT BEFORE.

There will be several evidence-based questions on the PSAT Reading Test. They will ask you to find textual evidence that best supports the answer to a previous question. They typically look like this.

8. Which choice provides the best evidence for the answer to the previous question?

    (A) Lines 1–4 ("When . . . ends")
    (B) Lines 16–18 ("Sophistication . . . truth")
    (C) Lines 37–40 ("However . . . suggestion")
    (D) Lines 45–46 ("Beliefs . . . refusal")

If you are stuck on a question that *comes before* an evidence-based question, check out the lines mentioned in the choices of the evidence-based question to help you formulate an answer. The necessary supporting information will be found in the lines cited by one of those choices. The supporting evidence will allow you to make an inference as to the best answer to the previous question.

Word-Meaning Questions

There will be several "word meaning" questions that typically look like the following question.

13. As used in line 47, "compromise" most nearly means

    (A) endanger.
    (B) settle.
    (C) weaken.
    (D) accommodate.

TACTIC 2: USE CONTEXT CLUES FROM THE PASSAGE TO DETERMINE THE WORD'S MEANING.

Go back to the passage, and come up with a synonym for the word based on how the word is used in the sentence. Although memorizing vocabulary can help you prepare for word-meaning questions, you should especially sharpen your skills in picking up on the meanings of words based on context. Even if you know the definitions of words, you will need to determine which definition is most applicable in the particular situation. Just as in the example above, the given choices will all often work as a potential definition—the correct answer depends on the intended meaning of the author.

TACTIC 3: JUST BECAUSE YOU DO NOT KNOW A WORD'S MEANING DOES NOT MEAN A CHOICE IS WRONG.

One of the most frequent mistakes students make on words-in-context questions is going with a word that "sort of works" simply because they know the meaning of the word. If you narrow down the question to two words, one of which you know and doesn't quite fit and the other of which you do not know, go with the word you *do not know* since it has the *potential* to be 100 percent correct.

PUTTING IT ALL TOGETHER

What follows is a nonfiction passage. When reading the passage, focus on paraphrasing the general meaning of the passage. Do not worry about memorizing details because you can go back to the passage as often as you would like. Since it is nonfiction, pay particular attention to the first paragraph, the topic sentences, and the last paragraph to maximize your overall understanding while still reading everything else in the passage well. Try to take about 5 minutes to read the passage, feeling free to annotate and underline as you read.

Questions 1–9 are based on the following passage.

This passage is from "Arcology," taken from a journal article written in 2013.

As "low-impact" or "green" architecture grows steadily *en vogue* into the 21st century, it will become rapidly apparent that reclaimed building materials and energy-efficient designs alone cannot offset the backlash of the deleterious customs modern cities have endorsed at
Line least since the start of the Industrial Revolution. Only a profound and comprehensive rein-
(5) vention of our homes and communities will carry our societies onward into the coming ages.

Fortunately, a handful of premonitory architects and civil engineers have already been grappling with this predicament for nearly 100 years. Frank Lloyd Wright—the esteemed leader of the Prairie School—proposed his solution to chaotic suburban development and impractical land use in the form of Broadacre City: a preplanned community in which each
(10) resident would possess one acre of land arranged in such a way as to provide easy access to an extensive and efficient network of roads and public transportation. Broadacre—which never

evolved beyond the design phase—could hardly be described as "green" by today's standards, but it constitutes one of the first endeavors of the modern era to integrate fully the residential and the commercial, the consumer and the consumed, on an efficacious, city-wide scale.

(15) "Arcology", a portmanteau of "architecture" and "ecology", is the term coined by architect Paolo Soleri to describe the largely theoretical self-contained cities he's been designing since the late 1950's. Like Broadacre, one goal of an arcological structure is to maximize the efficiency of land use in a community. For Soleri, this means combating "suburban sprawl" by balancing urban expansion in three dimensions. But by incorporating significant agricul-
(20) tural and industrial components alongside commercial facilities and residences, arcology takes civic efficiency a step further than Broadacre. According to Soleri, a true arcological city would be both economically and ecologically self-sufficient. It would contain all the resources necessary for power and food production, for climate control, and for air and water treatment. But perhaps even more radically, it would eliminate the need for private transpor-
(25) tation through a combination of high-population density housing and carefully calculated infrastructural design.

Although Soleri has designed hundreds of buildings, to date his only large-scale arcological project to be realized—Arcosanti in central Arizona, a town intended to sustain up to 5,000 residents—today houses just 150 individuals. But while the American public's response to
(30) Soleri's bold innovations is, by and large, resistant, certain facets of arcology have already permeated more conventional cities. Comprehensive pedestrian skyways like those in downtown Calgary, Minneapolis, and the Las Vegas strip are derived from arcological notions of multi-dimensional public transit, and Co-op City in the Bronx, New York, reflects arcological influences in its high-density residential construction and self-contained resources which
(35) include public schools, shopping centers, religious centers, medical facilities, a fire station and a power plant.

Community projects that embrace the revolutionary precepts of arcology have always struggled for funding, and all too often are abandoned by their investors prior to completion. But over the past ten years the world has seen a steady groundswell of interest in "green,"
(40) arcological structures, with ambitious and novel projects cropping up from Tokyo to Moscow. In 2006, the United Arab Emirates initiated the construction of Masdar City, which will incorporate a fully sustainable "zero-waste and zero-carbon" ecology with a projected metropolitan community of 50,000 inhabitants—all on just six square kilometers of land.

What should be your overall understanding of the passage? It should be something like the following.

- Arcology is a movement to try to make cities more sustainable and self-sufficient.
- Architects like Wright and Soleri have designed many arcological developments, but few have actually been implemented in real life.
- Even though not many arcological cities have been created, the movement has inspired the construction of arcological components, like skyways. Also, there may be more actual arcological cities in the future.

Now, let's go through the questions from the passage one by one. With each question, be sure to take these steps.

- Cover the answer choices.
- Underline/circle key words as you carefully read the question.
- Create an answer in your own words based on the context in the passage.
- Critically analyze the choices, focusing on the overall meaning needed and eliminating choices with even a single flaw.

1. The author's overall point of view on the need for arcology is best described as

   (A) tepid appreciation.
   (B) mild skepticism.
   (C) strong advocacy.
   (D) outright rejection.

Solution: **(C)** Try to formulate your own answer before looking at the choices. Also, notice that the question that follows gives you the possible line selections that can help you answer this question. The author states his/her thesis at the end of the first paragraph, saying in lines 4–5 that "only a profound and comprehensive reinvention of our homes and communities will carry our societies onward into the coming ages." Put another way, the author believes that society will be in serious trouble unless significant changes are made to how cities are structured. So the answer needs to express that the author has a firm stance that arcology, which would support such changes, is needed—this is most like "strong advocacy" in choice (C). It is not choice (A) because "tepid" means "mild or lukewarm," and the author has a very strong belief in favor of arcology. The answer is not choice (B) because the author is not skeptical, or questioning, about the need for arcology—he/she believes that it must happen. The correct answer is certainly not choice (D) because the author accepts, not rejects, the need for arcology.

2. Which choice provides the best evidence for the answer to the previous question?

   (A) Lines 4–5 ("Only . . . ages")
   (B) Lines 15–17 ("Arcology . . . 1950's")
   (C) Lines 21–24 ("According . . . treatment")
   (D) Lines 37–38 ("Community . . . completion")

Solution: **(A)** The PSAT has several questions like this one that expect you to demonstrate your command of evidence. That way, the test can ascertain whether you actually understand what you have read or whether you were just lucky in answering the previous question correctly. The correct answer is choice (A) because this selection gives the thesis of the essay, expressing that the author believes that it is vital for society to change how it constructs cities in order to prevent a decline in society. The answer is not choice (B) because this selection simply defines arcology. It is not choice (C) because this selection simply explains what an arcological city would be like. The correct answer is not choice (D) because this selection states that arcology has had difficulty earning widespread public support.

3. The example of Broadacre City primarily serves as an example of

   (A) the first successfully implemented arcological urban development.
   (B) an early proposed solution to suburban sprawl.
   (C) the architectural masterpiece of world-renowned designer Frank Lloyd Wright.
   (D) a significant instance of cutting-edge environmental technology.

Solution: **(B)** Be sure you focus on what the question is asking—you need to determine the primary function of the example of Broadacre City. Lines 8–9 best provide this information, stating that Frank Lloyd Wright "proposed his solution to chaotic suburban development and impractical land use in the form of Broadacre City." So Broadacre City is given as an example of how a famous architect proposed a solution to suburban sprawl, which is the overexpansion of urban development. The correct answer is not choice (A) or choice (C) because the city was not actually made. It is also not choice (D) because line 12 states that Broadacre "could hardly be described as 'green' by today's standards."

4. As used in line 15, "portmanteau" most nearly means

(A) innovation.
(B) transition.
(C) environment.
(D) combination.

Solution: **(D)** Line 15 define arcology as "a portmanteau of 'architecture' and 'ecology.'" You can reasonably infer that this comes from the prefix "arc-" in "architecture" and the suffix "-ology" in "ecology," which combine to give the word "arcology." Given how the word "arcology" is used elsewhere, it makes sense that it would be a combination of architectural elements and ecological elements, since it is focused on designing cities in an environmentally sustainable way. Although "innovation," "transition," and "environment" are related to architectural and ecological ideas, they do not capture the overall meaning of the term.

5. The passage suggests that Paolo Soleri would have what view about the economic activity of major cities?

(A) Both imports and exports should be maximized.
(B) Both imports and exports should be minimized.
(C) Imports should be maximized while exports minimized.
(D) Imports should be minimized while exports maximized.

Solution: **(B)** Try looking ahead to the line selections in question 6 to help you find the information you need to answer this question. Imports are goods that are brought into a city, and exports are goods sold from a city. According to lines 21–24, Soleri believes that "a true arcological city would be both economically and ecologically self-sufficient. It would contain all the resources necessary for power and food production, for climate control, and for air and water treatment." If a city is to contain all its necessities within its borders, it will not need to import or export anything. So choice (B) is the correct option.

6. Which choice provides the best evidence for the answer to the previous question?

(A) Lines 18–19 ("For Soleri . . . dimensions")
(B) Lines 19–21 ("But by . . . Broadacre")
(C) Lines 21–24 ("According . . . treatment")
(D) Lines 24–26 ("But perhaps . . . design")

Solution: **(C)** These lines focus on the economic nature of the arcological cities, stating that they would be self-sufficient, which would remove any need for the import or exports of goods. The answer is not choice (A) because this focuses on the spatial aspects of cities. It is not choice (B) because this highlights issues of civic efficiency. The answer is not choice (D) because this focuses on transportation.

7. It can be reasonably inferred from the passage that the overall attitude of the American public toward arcology is

    (A) generally skeptical.
    (B) positively enthusiastic
    (C) bitterly cynical.
    (D) largely neutral.

Solution: **(A)** This is best seen in lines 29–31, which state that "the American public's response to Soleri's bold innovations is, by and large, resistant, certain facets of arcology have already permeated more conventional cities." In other words, Americans are generally skeptical of arcology because although they have been open to its implementation in some situations, they have not embraced it completely. The answer is not choice (B) because if the American public was positively enthusiastic about arcology, we would expect to see much more implementation of it than has happened. It is not choice (C) because being "cynical" means to have extremely negative views toward something, which is not the case here. The correct answer is not choice (D) because there is "resistance" in general to arcology, which is negative, preventing the public's attitude from being labeled as "neutral."

8. As used in line 37, "precepts" most nearly means

    (A) warrants.
    (B) buildings.
    (C) politics.
    (D) principles.

Solution: **(D)** Lines 37–38 state, "Community projects that embrace the revolutionary precepts of arcology have always struggled for funding, and all too often are abandoned by their investors prior to completion." "Principles" makes the most sense as the meaning of "precepts" here because arcology is described in the passage as a general philosophy of design that has certain key ideas, or principles, about methods of sustainable development. The correct is not choice (A) because arcology was not inspired by government documents. It is not choice (B) because arcology is an entire philosophy of design, not just a type of structure. The answer is not choice (C) because arcology is more of a design philosophy than a political one.

**Metropolitan Area Population
Changes (in millions of people)***

*Source: United Nations, World Urbanization Prospects: The 2007 Revision.
http://www.prb.org/Publications/Lesson-Plans/HumanPopulation/Urbanization.aspx.*

9. Assume that the urban areas in the chart have achieved the maximum of their geographic expansion. The passage author would think that which of the following cities (assuming that they continue on their current trajectories of growth) will be most likely in the year 2125 to have the greatest need to implement arcological principles?

(A) London

(B) New York

(C) Bombay

(D) Tokyo

Solution: **(C)** Be prepared to have a few graph analysis questions on the PSAT. If you are familiar with the ACT test, you may recognize that these questions test similar skills to those tested on the ACT Science Section. You will be asked to use graphical information to come to a conclusion that often incorporates information from the reading passage. To attack this question, focus on what it is asking—you need to determine which city would most need arcology. Arcology is focused on sustainable development in response to the growth of urban areas. So the author would most likely believe that a city that was experiencing the most significant growth in population would probably be in most need of more sustainable design principles. London is barely growing at all, and New York and Tokyo are growing at relatively slow rates. Bombay, however, is on a steep growth curve. If Bombay's growth continues at its current rate, it will be the largest of these cities by 2125, making it the one the author would most likely believe to be in need of arcological principles.

READING QUESTIONS DRILLS

Now that you have tried the different types of questions you will encounter on the PSAT, target your practice with the following drills:

- Big Picture and Inference Questions
- Evidence-Based Questions
- Words-in-Context Questions
- Graph Analysis Questions

Big Picture and Inference Questions Drill

The PSAT has quite a few questions that test your ability to understand the primary point of a passage and to make inferences. To perform well on questions like these, make sure you understand the overall narrative of the passage. Skimming the passage will not put you in a position to do well. Thorough reading—taking about 5 minutes to actually read the passage and reading actively, not passively—will help you do much better. When you think about the questions, be certain to paraphrase an answer before examining the choices.

Questions 1–8 are based on the following passage.

"The Boardwalk at Rehoboth Beach," written in 2012.

When I was younger, much younger—almost in another life—I spent every other summer at Rehoboth Beach. The day of departure had something of the quiet, methodical frenzy that I suspect surrounds the evacuation en masse of infantry. All morning we marched in and out of *Line* the house, hauling tin coolers and huge, blue Samsonite suitcases, piling them like bulwarks (5) in the driveway; while my Father—his body half-buried in the back of a County Squire station wagon—hollered out his orders for what should be loaded next. Being second to youngest, my place was invariably in the last row of the wagon, walled in on all three sides by the inevitable impediment of annual beachgoers—rope sandals, snorkels, the bright, polychrome canopies of sun umbrellas—all of it still somehow shedding fine, gray streams of sand with (10) every nudge. While pressing my nose to the glass for a farewell glimpse of our vacated home, my Mother put the car in gear, and I smacked my forehead on the window as it lurched forward. Between the bobbing heads of five siblings I could see my Father's blue Chevy Bel Air, bearing my three older brothers and whatever luggage refused to fit into the meticulously overloaded wagon, leading us, like a harbinger, six hundred miles east to the Atlantic Ocean.

(15) The beach itself at Rehoboth was neither exceptional nor squalid. It was entirely ordinary, of middling breadth, and middling color, made up of more sand than mud, and of more jagged shells and bottle caps than one typically prefers. In early and late summer the water was really too cold to stay in longer than half an hour or so, and in hue it remained a murky green all year. But Rehoboth Beach was special, perhaps even magical because it was, in its entire (20) length, rimmed by a magnificent boardwalk. At Rehoboth Beach, save for breakfast and supper, my siblings and I were autonomous, and from the age of about eight onward I spent hours wandering alone among the lush, interminable spectacles and seminude crowds of the boardwalk.

Being both pale and somewhat plain, the people were, I suppose, predominately rust belt (25) Midwesterners like myself, there at the shore to terminate their brief annual vacations. But they seemed so different, so transformed in manner and appearance by the proximity of the sea, that I often imagined the beach populated by denizens of an exotic, epicurean culture, and when I stepped upon the boardwalk, I saw myself entering one the strange and majestic bazaars so tantalizingly pervasive of my serial adventure novels. I snaked between vendors of (30) blown glass, odd, multifarious souvenirs constructed of driftwood and jetsam, and heaps of beachwear proclaimed by the hand-painted signs that accompanied them as the latest fashion on the French Riviera. Running my palm along a rack of wooden popguns, I imagined myself a soldier of the Foreign Legion, on leave in Lisbon, Yalta or Algiers. In the distance I could see the pier; indomitable, bisecting the boardwalk at a right angle and jutting far out (35) over the water.

The vendor appraised my interest, "We have some very nice beads here as well—genuine sea glass."

"No, thank you," I answered, and pressed onward. Overhead, between the fluttering, variegated canopies, I saw no fewer than two dozen kites hanging in the sky, and everywhere the (40) smells of the ocean comingled with those of chilidogs, cola, and Dolle's saltwater taffy.

Around sunset, with the breeze still sweeping in from the Atlantic, it turned a little chilly; women pulled lace and cotton dresses over their bikinis, and the men strode back from the shore wearing blue and white blazers above their sandy, dampened swimming trunks. I shivered and crossed my arms. The children on the boardwalk were becoming scarce, and I more (45) conspicuously unattended. But this was by far my favorite time at Rehoboth. As more orange rays of sunlight fell behind the houses to the west and were extinguished, the boardwalk grew more vibrant, more fantastic. All around bulbs of blue, red, orange and green incandescent light flashed to life. Voices became more boisterous as people sought to speak over the sprightly marching tunes that blasted from the horns of carnival rides, which always seemed (50) much louder in the evening air. I had walked quite far, I realized—the ferris wheel was far behind me; I could see it writing huge, luminous O's in the darkening distance. Childless couples were leaving the restaurants, some of them staggering a little as they opened the door onto the boardwalk. In the dim alcoves there grew a vague but thrilling sense of danger.

I wanted to walk out to the very edge of the pier; it was only another several hundred yards, (55) I thought. I wanted to stand there, and look for far off lights on the ocean where ships were traversing the deep, dark water. I felt a large hand grasp my bare shoulder.

"Lost, missy? Need someone to call your folks?"

"No. I know my way around," I shuddered. Slowly, begrudgingly, I turned away from the place where the pier issued from the shore, and started back along the boardwalk. One day (60) my body would learn contentment, steeling it against the ill-defined threats of wanderlust. But my mind would remain an endless boardwalk, from which I might ascend any one of the infinite ocean piers, and go anywhere, anywhere at all.

1. The narrator can best be described as a/an

   (A) anxious explorer.
   (B) adventurous misanthrope.
   (C) imaginative observer.
   (D) rebellious pedestrian.

2. The passage is primarily organized

   (A) by cause and effect.
   (B) chronologically.
   (C) in gradually increasing order of importance.
   (D) from microcosm to macrocosm.

3. The narrator's father's manner of speaking to his children as they prepare to leave for vacation is best characterized as

(A) patient.
(B) imperious.
(C) relaxed.
(D) insulting.

4. The boardwalk is most appealing to the narrator as a result of

(A) the widespread practice of kite-flying by users of it.
(B) the happy memories she has of time she spent there with family.
(C) the opportunities it gives for independent scholarly research.
(D) the freedom it gives her to explore independently.

5. The point of view from which the story is told is that of a/an

(A) adult looking back at a childhood experience.
(B) child contemplating her future opportunities.
(C) adolescent fixating on her past obstacles.
(D) third-person omniscient narrator.

6. It can be inferred that which of the narrator's four siblings is most likely to be in the same row that the narrator occupies in the car?

(A) The youngest one
(B) The middle child
(C) The next to the oldest
(D) The oldest

7. In the eyes of the narrator, the relationship of the beach to the boardwalk is most analogous to

(A) a forest floor in the mountains occasionally populated by wildlife.
(B) a clear, blue sky that is polluted with the smoke from human activity.
(C) an amusement park that incorporates the latest computer technology.
(D) a commonplace platter that is topped with a spectacular dessert.

8. The passage suggests that the person who grasps her "bare shoulder" (line 56) is likely motivated by

(A) avarice.
(B) power.
(C) vigilance.
(D) fear.

Answer Explanations

1. **(C)** The narrator is recounting her experiences as a young child, enjoying the unusual freedom of exploring a boardwalk. As she observes various things on the boardwalk, she imagines herself to be a soldier or like someone from an adventure novel. So she can best be described as an imaginative observer. The correct answer is not choice (A) because she does not demonstrate a consistent level of anxiety; rather, she finds the looming danger thrilling. It is not choice (B) because a misanthrope is someone who does not like people while she is enjoying the interactions with and observations of people. The answer is not choice (D) because she is far more than a mere pedestrian, i.e., someone who is walking along.

2. **(B)** The passage starts with a recounting of the narrator's car trip, followed by a step-by-step retelling of her adventures exploring the boardwalk. Therefore, the structure is best described as "chronological." Although certain factors have surely caused the narrator's behavior, the passage does not focus on connecting the causes of her behavior to its effects. Instead, it focuses on her general impressions, making choice (A) incorrect. One event does not seem to have more significance than another as the passage progresses—instead, a number of interesting personal impressions are provided throughout, making choice (C) incorrect. The answer is not choice (D) because such an organization would go from a small-picture to a big-picture perspective, but the first-person perspective remains fairly consistent throughout.

3. **(B)** Line 6 state that the narrator's father "hollered out his orders for what should be loaded next" to describe the setting when the family is packing to leave on the trip. It can most reasonably be inferred that the father's manner of speaking to his children as they prepare to leave for vacation would be best characterized as "imperious," or *commanding*, given how he orders his family around. The answer is not choice (A) or choice (C) because the father is not acting patiently or relaxed—he is suggesting that everyone move with urgency. It is not choice (D) because the father is not insulting his children; he is simply ordering them around.

4. **(D)** Immediately after introducing the boardwalk in line 20, the narrator states that she was able to spend "hours wandering alone" on the boardwalk (lines 22–23). Additionally, the narrator discusses in lines 43–45 that she enjoyed being unattended. So the narrator clearly enjoys how the boardwalk gives her the freedom to explore independently. Choice (A) mentions something too specific and irrelevant to her overall opinion of the boardwalk. She doesn't seem to spend much time with her family on the boardwalk, wandering alone along it instead, making choice (B) incorrect. She is a young child having fun, not a researcher, making choice (C) incorrect.

5. **(A)** The passage begins by stating, "When I was younger, much younger . . . I spent every other summer at Rehoboth Beach." The narrator goes on to tell a story about the boardwalk at the beach. Establishing the setting in this way most strongly suggests that the point of view from which the passage is told is that of an adult looking back at a childhood experience. It is not choice (B) because the story is told in the past tense. The answer is not choice (C) because it would not make sense for an adolescent to describe childhood experiences as "much younger"; moreover, the narrator is not "fixating" on past obstacles. Instead, she is able to learn from them and move on as indicated in line 60, where she says she "would learn contentment." Finally, the correct answer is not choice (D) because the story is told from a first-person perspective.

6. **(A)** Lines 6–8 explain that because she was the second-to-youngest child, the narrator had to sit in the last row of the station wagon. Since her birth order is cited as the only reason for this and since the narrator also mentions that she was surrounded by so much clutter making it easier for a smaller person to make do with the seating arrangement, her youngest sibling would most likely join her in the back.

7. **(D)** The answer is best seen in the second paragraph, where the beach itself is described as "ordinary," while the boardwalk rimming it is described as "special" and "magical." This is like an ordinary plate (like the beach) that would have a spectacular dessert (like the boardwalk) on top of it. Choice (A) is too focused on the natural aspects of the relationship. Choice (B) portrays human activity in a negative light, while the narrator very much enjoys partaking in and observing a variety of human activities. Choice (C) narrowly focuses on enjoyment that the boardwalk provides while neglecting the relationship of the boardwalk to the beach.

8. **(C)** When the person places his hand on the narrator's shoulders, she is walking about all alone on a pier, which could be very dangerous were she to fall off into the water. The person offers to help by asking the narrator whether she needs someone to reconnect her with her parents. So the motivation is one of "vigilance," or watchfulness. The person is not greedy, not showing avarice as in choice (A), and is not interested in maintaining power over the narrator as in choice (B). Although he might be fearful that she could fall into the water as in choice (D), "vigilance" is a better way to describe the person's calm, helpful interactions with the narrator.

Evidence-Based Questions

There are about nine evidence-based questions on the PSAT. These questions often take a bit longer to answer than other questions because you need to consider carefully four possible excerpts from the passage. Recall the tactic that it is often helpful to use the line selections in evidence-based questions to help you answer the questions that come right beforehand. For example in the following passage, you could read question 1, and then use the line selections in question 2 to help you answer question 1. Also, keep in mind that the evidence will require some inference and interpretation to answer the question that precedes it—you will almost certainly not find a word-for-word excerpt that matches up with an answer to the previous question.

Questions 1–8 are based on the following passages.

A political economist and a political philosopher present their views on the state of interest rates as of the beginning of the year 2016.

Passage 1

The economy is a delicate creature. In its fragility, it must be coddled and swaddled; prune and trim it, water and bathe it in sunlight as needed and it shall bear forth all the fruits of a healthy capitalist market. Contrarily, abandon the economy and she shall grow wild with
Line thorns jutting out at the flanks—the rebellion of the shrubbery overshadowing the beauty of
(5) the roses within.

The economy now is that rose bush; she has been left alone too long. Graciously, amazingly, she has not collapsed in her solitude. In fact, modest growth has occurred, and, for this, we must be ecstatic at our good fortune. But, that growth has soured of late, and we have fallen into a state of inertia.

(10) Yes, I will readily admit that a recession most likely is not imminent, but the time is not now to count our blessings and bask in the complacent contentment of a tragedy averted. No, we must act with haste. Money has been too cheap for far too long now, and such low interest rates are not the remedy for economic stagnation. Currently rates are next to nothing, which was a fine solution during the crisis of 2008 and 2009. But, the stock market no longer is in a
(15) state of crisis; in fact, both equities and bonds are criminally overpriced.

As a value investor, with the exception of a handful of companies, there simply is not a stock that I can pinpoint as a wise investment at this juncture. Historically, the price to earnings ratio of the S&P 500 stock index has hovered around 15 to 1. Now, however, that ratio has ballooned to nearly 21, and opportunities for investment are scarce. Simply put, everything is
(20) overpriced, and our rose bush must be reined back in.

These minuscule interest rates just are not sustainable. Economic growth is no longer occurring, but investors continue driving up prices as if it were. Overall, I fear we are reaching a bubble, and bubbles, as you might well know, are prone to not being bubbles for long.

Passage 2

(25) The tragedy of asking the wrong question is that, no matter how poignant or precise the diction, one cannot possibly attain the right answer. For instance, if my goal were to locate a wrench, I could go to my local improvement store using my most ornate of vocabulary and ask, "Where doth thou maintain thy hammers?" Alas, the store clerk might find me educated and mysterious, but he would direct me toward the wrong tool.

(30)   When I sit at the diner for lunch, I hear voices at the table next to me debating whether the Federal Reserve should raise interest rates. "Of course they should," one voice will opine. "Inflation sows the seeds of collapse." And, when I wait in line at the Bureau of Motor Vehicles to renew my license, I hear the same debate. "Why in the world should we raise interest rates?" asks another. "Do we really believe the economy is strong enough to withstand the
(35)   crunch that will follow?"

See, the crisis is not to do with interest rates, but in our questioning. It is not a matter of raising or maintaining rates, but whether the federal government should be so heavily involved in fiscal policy in the first place. We must look to Thomas Jefferson for our guidance on this matter. "That government is best which governs least because its people discipline themselves."

(40)   We must return to our Laissez Faire roots, for the economy will take care of itself if given the opportunity. Interest rates are not the issue. And, like my example at the home improvement store, the situation calls for a wrench, but all we ever ask ourselves is which hammer to swing.

1. The narrator of Passage 1 most strongly suggests the economy in 2008 and 2009 could be described as

   (A) deeply troubled.
   (B) growing exponentially.
   (C) steadily improving.
   (D) moderately declining.

2. Which option gives the best evidence for the answer to the previous question?

   (A) Lines 3–4 ("Contrarily . . . flanks")
   (B) Line 6 ("The economy . . . long")
   (C) Lines 13–15 ("Currently . . . crisis")
   (D) Lines 19–20 ("Simply . . . back in")

3. The narrator of Passage 1 would most likely want to see the government have what approach towards interest rates and the economy in 2016?

   (A) Detached
   (B) Patient
   (C) Complacent
   (D) Interventionist

4. Which option gives the best evidence for the answer to the previous question?

   (A) Lines 1–3 ("In its . . . market")
   (B) Line 10 ("Yes, . . . imminent")
   (C) Lines 11–13 ("No, . . . stagnation")
   (D) Lines 16–17 ("As a . . . juncture")

5. It is reasonable to infer that the narrator of Passage 2 believes the primary issue with the approach to economics at the time the passage was written is that we

   (A) are unwilling to consider alternative viewpoints.
   (B) fail to make relevant inquiries.
   (C) do not engage in interpersonal debate.
   (D) do not know biographical details of historical figures.

6. Which option gives the best evidence for the answer to the previous question?

    (A) Lines 30–32 ("When . . . collapse'")

    (B) Lines 32–35 ("And, . . . follow'")

    (C) Lines 36–38 ("See, . . . place")

    (D) Lines 38–39 ("We . . . themselves'")

7. The attitude of the narrator of Passage 2 toward governmental involvement in the economy could be best described as

    (A) skeptical.

    (B) supportive.

    (C) underhanded.

    (D) exultant.

8. Which option gives the best evidence for the answer to the previous question?

    (A) Lines 25–26 ("The tragedy . . . answer")

    (B) Lines 31–32 ("'Of course . . . collapse'")

    (C) Lines 33–35 ("'Why . . . follow'")

    (D) Lines 40–41 ("We must . . . opportunity")

Answer Explanations

1. **(A)** Lines 13–15 state that there was a crisis in 2008–2009, most strongly suggesting that the economy was deeply troubled at the time. Choices (B) and (C) are associated with a good and growing economy, while choice (D) does not go far enough to describe the status of the economy at the time.

2. **(C)** Choice (C) directly states that the economy was in crisis, which is most closely related to the economy being deeply troubled. Choice (A) suggests a course of action instead of describing the economy in 2008–2009, choice (B) refers to the economy in 2016, and choice (D) assesses a problem with the economy in 2016.

3. **(D)** Lines 11–13 suggest that the solution to the economic problems of 2016 are to act with "haste" and not allow interest rates to remain as low as they are—this is best described as "interventionist." Since the narrator wants to take action, sitting back and being detached, being complacent, or being patient would be unsatisfactory.

4. **(C)** These lines give the best insight into the approach the narrator would like to see to solve the problems he sees in the economy in 2016. Choice (A) uses metaphorical language that introduces the passage but does not give clarity as to what policies would be advisable. Choice (B) acknowledges the potential objection that a recession is not imminent but does not help explain what actions should be taken. Choice (D) speaks to what an individual should do given current economic conditions instead of focusing on what the government as a whole should do.

5. **(B)** When we look at lines 36–38, it becomes clear that the primary issue the author believes we have with our current approach to economics is that we fail to ask the right questions—in other words, we fail to make relevant inquiries, making choice (B) correct. The answer is not choice (A) or choice (C) because the narrator uses examples of people having disagreements and discussions over economic policy to show that people are definitely open to considering alternative viewpoints and having interpersonal debate. It is not choice (D) because at no point does the narrator suggest that if people knew more about the biographical details of historical figures, they would be better able to understand economic issues. Although the narrator does cite Jefferson, he does so in order to quote Jefferson's political theory, not to share his biography.

6. **(C)** By looking at the excerpts in choices (A), (B), and (D), we see that none give a clear indication as to the author's sense of what is currently "the primary issue with the approach to economics." Choice (A) and choice (B) focus on recounting an interpersonal discussion. Choice (D) quotes Jefferson and does not tie into why failing to make relevant inquiries would be a problem.

7. **(A)** Lines 40–41 state that the economy will "take care of itself if given the opportunity." Therefore, the narrator would like to see the government avoid intervention in the economy and would be "skeptical" of efforts to do so. The narrator of Passage 1 would be "supportive," but not the narrator of Passage 2. At no point does the narrator of Passage 2 suggest that being deceptive and underhanded would be wise. Finally, the narrator has skeptical views toward government intervention; being "exultant" would be far a more positive attitude, which is not supported by the text.

8. **(D)** These lines clearly state that the narrator believes the economy will be better off if the government gets out of the way. Choice (A) simply introduces the passage topic using general language. Choices (B) and (C) recount the opinions of different people.

Questions 1–8 are based on the following passage.

"A Quiet Revolutionary," written in 2014

Though today the familiar names of French Impressionism—Degas, Pissarro, Cézanne, Renoir, and Monet—are nearly synonymous with what we may inscrutably refer to as "great art", in its own time the impressionist movement was often identified with artistic dissidence, Line the avant-garde, and painterly provocateurs. In its development, the impressionist style (5) boldly challenged the entrenched principles of French painting, and ultimately transformed art for most of the Western world.

There is one linchpin name, however, too frequently omitted from surveys of early impressionism. Eugène Boudin—a friend and contemporary of the Paris Impressionists—never described himself as an innovator or revolutionary, and yet his work tremendously influ-(10) enced the transmigration of impressionism from the walls of radical art galleries to those of homes and businesses throughout Europe.

Primarily, Boudin painted beach scenes on the shores of Brittany and Normandy. Alongside Monet, he was among the first of the impressionists to embrace painting *en plein air*, and he was also one of very few artists to show canvases in all eight of the Paris Impressionist (15) Exhibitions. But despite his proximity to the avant-garde, Boudin's work remained, for the most part, conspicuously marketable throughout his career.

Employing slightly subtler brushstrokes than most of his counterparts, Boudin focused his labors on capturing the tranquil, shore-side recreations of bourgeois vacationers. Around this time it was becoming fashionable among the middle-class to possess commemorative depic-(20) tions of the places one had traveled, and Boudin managed to fill this niche masterfully.

By painting the idle vacationers from behind, and obscuring any visible faces in the impressionist-landscape style, his patrons could purchase premade a work articulating the mood, activity, colors and locale of their holiday without the monetary and temporal obstacles of a traditional, commissioned painting. For comparison, Renoir's painting of models from the (25) rear—far from making the work more commercially viable—was executed as a stylistic affront to classical notions of portraiture. Suffice it to say that Boudin's mercantile techniques were, at least among the impressionists, rather unique.

Boudin's beachscapes made French impressionism not only familiar to the masses, but pleasing and even preferable. But that is not to say that his talents were inferior to those of (30) the other preeminent impressionists. During his lifetime Boudin's work was well respected among the artistic elite; fellow landscape painter Jean-Baptiste Corot described him as "the master of the sky", and the poet Baudelaire was a lifelong admirer of his paintings. Monet himself cited Boudin as a profound influence on his early work.

More recently Boudin has garnered attention for his less common—and far less popular—(35) paintings depicting the seaside labors of working-class men and women. Though these works brought him very little financial profit, it is known that he was exceptionally fond of them. Having worked as a bay fisherman in his youth, it has been claimed that Boudin was perhaps somewhat ashamed of his reputation as painter of "les gens de la mode." In any case, these works provide us with a compelling contrast to those of the languorous, well-to-do beach-(40) goers; and together they provide a rare, panoptical insight into the full social spectrum of French life by the sea in the mid-to-late 19th century.

1. It can reasonably be inferred that the narrator's general attitude toward impressionism can best be characterized as

   (A) warm appreciation.
   (B) awestruck reverence.
   (C) dispassionate objectivity.
   (D) mild contempt.

2. Which choice provides the best evidence for the answer to the previous question?

   (A) Lines 4–6 ("In its . . . world")
   (B) Lines 18–20 ("Around . . . masterfully")
   (C) Lines 25–26 ("Was . . . portraiture")
   (D) Lines 34–35 ("More . . . women")

3. Based on the information in the passage, relative to painters like Renoir and Monet, Boudin is today considered to be

   (A) less artistic.
   (B) more emotionally troubled.
   (C) more intellectually curious.
   (D) less well-known.

4. Which choice provides the best evidence for the answer to the previous question?

   (A) Lines 7–8 ("There . . . Boudin")
   (B) Lines 21–24 ("By painting... painting")
   (C) Lines 30–33 ("During . . . work")
   (D) Lines 37–38 ("Having . . . mode'")

5. The passage suggests that a major factor that distinguished Boudin from his contemporaries was his

   (A) business innovation.
   (B) impressionist style.
   (C) focus on urban landscapes.
   (D) affront to common sensibilities.

6. Which choice provides the best evidence for the answer to the previous question?

   (A) Lines 3–6 ("In its...world")
   (B) Lines 26–27 ("Suffice . . . unique")
   (C) Lines 30–33 ("During . . . work")
   (D) Lines 35–36 ("Though . . . them")

7. Which choice provides the best supporting information that Boudin popularized a style of painting?

    (A) Lines 17–18 ("Employing . . . vacationers")

    (B) Lines 28–29 ("Boudin's . . . preferable")

    (C) Lines 30–31 ("During . . . elite")

    (D) Lines 34–35 ("More . . . women")

8. Which choice best supports the claim that Boudin's paintings had subjects from a variety of socioeconomic classes?

    (A) Lines 1–4 ("Though . . . provocateurs")

    (B) Lines 12–15 ("Primarily, . . . Exhibitions")

    (C) Lines 24–27 ("For comparison, . . . unique")

    (D) Lines 38–41 ("In any case, . . . century")

Answer Explanations

1. **(A)** The narrator has an attitude of warm appreciation as evidenced especially by the first paragraph of the essay, in which the narrator describes impressionist art as "boldly" challenging the older principles of art, "transforming" it into something new. Choice (B) is too positive, choice (C) too neutral, and choice (D) too negative.

2. **(A)** Lines 4–6 most clearly support the author's warm appreciation toward impressionist art because they cite its boldness and transformative power. Choice (B) is too vague with respect to the narrator's attitude, choice (C) focuses on the specific approach of Renoir, and choice (D) mentions increasing interest by others in Boudin without mentioning the narrator's attitude.

3. **(D)** The passage as a whole attempts to persuade the reader that Boudin was an artist worthy of the recognition given to other famous impressionists. This is explicitly seen in lines 7–8 when the narrator states that Boudin has been too frequently omitted from surveys of early impressionism and is therefore less well-known. The answer is not choice (A) because Boudin's artwork is praised throughout the passage. It is not choice (B) because the passage does not focus on the emotional states of these artists.

4. **(A)** Lines 7–8 strongly suggest that Boudin was not as famous as some other major impressionists since his name is omitted from surveys of the topic. Choice (B) focuses on Boudin's innovative techniques. Choice (C) focuses on how Boudin was considered by his contemporaries instead of focusing on a current-day standpoint. Choice (D) focuses on Boudin's early life experiences.

5. **(A)** Lines 26–27 state that his "mercantile techniques" were rather unique—in other words, making beautiful paintings that vacationers could purchase to memorialize their vacations was quite innovative. The correct response is not choice (B) since other artists shared an impressionist style. It is not choice (C) since Boudin focused on beachscapes, not urban landscapes. It is not choice (D) since Boudin's artwork was not offensive.

6. **(B)** Lines 26–27 say that Boudin's mercantile techniques were unique when compared to those of other impressionists. Choice (A) generally introduces impressionism. Choice (C) highlights the respect that Boudin's colleagues had for him but does not discuss differences. Choice (D) focuses on Boudin's personal opinions of his own creations.

7. **(B)** By stating that Boudin's beachscapes increased the familiarity and esteem of French impressionism, he would have helped popularize the painting style of French impressionism. Choice (A) discusses Boudin's artistic techniques, choice (C) focuses on what certain other artists thought of him instead of speaking about his popularity at large, and choice (D) emphasizes Boudin's less popular works.

8. **(D)** "A variety of socioeconomic classes" would include both well-off and poor people. Lines 38–41 say that Boudin was able to provide insight into the "full social spectrum of French life" because he painted both working-class people and "well-to-do beach-goers." The other choices do not examine the social and economic backgrounds of Boudin's artistic subjects.

Words-in-Context Questions

There will be approximately nine words-in-context questions on the PSAT. Knowing the definition of a word is not sufficient to answer these correctly, since the appropriate meaning can change based on how the word is used. So be certain that you look at enough context—at least the sentence the word is in and sometimes more—to determine the correct synonym.

Questions 1–8 are based on the following passage.

"Profanity," written in 2013

Profanity is a curious phenomenon in human speech—it exists in most every language, and consists of a small subset of words that carry inside them some incredible social power. Distinct from pejoratives and slurs—which are derived from traditions of racism, jingoism,
Line homophobia, and gross, general ignorance—true profanity only encompasses those precious
(5) few lexemes that might be applied to and by any individual within a given linguistic culture. They are, in a sense, universals, and by and large they derive from elemental human experiences; none more so than those concerning sexuality, and egesta.*

In the sense of Ferdinand Saussure's theory of Semiotics, one might suggest that the use of literal profanity—as opposed to figurative, which only possesses social sway based on its
(10) proximity to the literal—garners part of its power by being the closest available union of signifier and signified in subjects that, as a culture, we tend to avoid in polite and formal conversations. That is, the word is rude because the thing itself—in a general context—is also considered rude. In English, we tend to use either circumlocution or euphemisms to avoid the literal forms of our profanity in informal settings where swearing would be inappropriate,
(15) while in formal conversations, we turn to the Latin derivatives—words like "intercourse" and "excrement", which are tolerated socially, albeit with some reluctance because they represent the mother language of both medical science, and the Christian church. Our infamous "four letter words," meanwhile, are almost exclusively descended from the Germanic components of English. Even without an expertise in linguistics, one might sense this simply by the way
(20) they sound—phonically, most profanity in English is composed of short, terse syllables, and rounds off abruptly with a hard consonant.

Many accounts from people immersed in a language that is not their own have, throughout several centuries, pointed to profanity as by far the most difficult aspect of a novel language to master. There is, in our profanity, a high cultural learning curve that demands intimate
(25) knowledge and sensitivity to the subtleties of social interactions. Swearing is, in its own way, a kind of national art—one shared and apprehended almost exclusively by the members of a particular language community. Ernest Hemingway speaks of the artistry of another culture's profanity with admiration in his celebrated novel, *For Whom the Bell Tolls*, wherein the narrator bears witness as obscenities and insults build to a high formalism, and eventually collapse
(30) upon themselves, leaving the profanities implied rather than stated.

At least for the Western languages, it is impossible to ignore an additional—albeit wholly separate—source of profanity; and that is the Christian church. The word "profane" itself is a classical Latin derivative meaning "outside the temple". In early use, it referred to anything belonging to the secular world, but by the Middle Ages it had come to represent anything
(35) that demonstrated an active or passive indifference to the "religious" and the "sacred"—no

longer was a thing profane if it did not belong *to* the Church, but also if it did not belong *in* the Church. This included, as we have noted, the age-old obscenities of sex and excrement—whose profane statuses predate the church by several thousand years—as well as a kind of profanity that, while certainly not invented by the church, is preserved more or less intact (40) within our languages to this day.

*"Egesta" refers to matter excreted from the body.

1. As used in line 3, "distinct" most nearly means

   (A) individualized.
   (B) honored.
   (C) different.
   (D) repetitive.

2. As used in line 6, "elemental" most nearly means

   (A) molecular.
   (B) essential.
   (C) environmental.
   (D) experiential.

3. As used in line 9, "sway" most nearly means

   (A) governance.
   (B) oscillation.
   (C) rocking.
   (D) influence.

4. As used in line 21, "hard" most nearly refers to a word's

   (A) challenges.
   (B) pronunciation.
   (C) density.
   (D) difficulty.

5. As used in line 23, "novel" most nearly means

   (A) new.
   (B) literary.
   (C) wordy.
   (D) challenging.

6. As used in line 28, "celebrated" most nearly means

   (A) observed.
   (B) admired.
   (C) performed.
   (D) solemnized.

7. As used in line 33, "meaning" most nearly means

   (A) resulting in.
   (B) inspired by.
   (C) destined to.
   (D) defined as.

8. As used in line 38, "predate" most nearly means

   (A) obscure.
   (B) vilify.
   (C) precede.
   (D) span.

Answer Explanations

1. **(C)** "Distinct" is used to indicate that true profanity is "different" from pejoratives and slurs. Something that is "individualized" could perhaps be different from other things but is not necessarily so. Profanity is in no way considered "honored," and there is nothing to indicate that it is used in a "repetitive" way based on this sentence.

2. **(B)** "Essential" is the most logical definition, since without human reproduction, or sexuality, we would not exist; without producing bodily waste products, we would not survive. Therefore, these processes are essential to humans. Although there would be "molecular," "environmental," and "experiential" aspects to reproduction, these do not capture the intended meaning in this context.

3. **(D)** In the context of being "social," "sway" most logically means "influence" over opinions. "Oscillation" and "rocking" both signify physical motion, which could work in other contexts but not in this one. "Governance" suggests an overly rigid and hierarchical control over people's opinions, which would be illogical here.

4. **(B)** In line 20, the author mentions the way a word sounds and goes on to elaborate about what makes profanity have a distinct pronunciation, namely a "hard" ending. The other definitions would correctly define "hard" in different contexts but would not work in this situation.

5. **(A)** "New" makes the most sense because the author refers to people who have been immersed in a different language, i.e., a new language. The other options are not strongly associated with this newness.

6. **(B)** "Celebrated" as it is used in line 28 describes a book in a way that indicates it is widely admired. A book cannot very well be "observed" or "performed." Also "solemnizes" means performed a formal ceremony of some kind, which would be illogical as a definition here.

7. **(D)** Immediately after "meaning" is used, a definition in quotation marks is provided: "outside the temple." There is not a cause-and-effect relationship, making "resulting in" and "inspired by" incorrect. Since the word "profane" is immediately defined, it would not make sense to associate it with destiny.

8. **(C)** The surrounding context makes clear that the author is referring to "age-old" ideas that have been around for "several thousand years," making "precede" correct. The correct response is not "obscure," since "predate" refers to time, not to confusion. It is not "vilify" because there is no indication of belittling or insulting something. Although "span" is associated with time, it signifies a duration of time rather than a specific time in the past.

Questions 1–8 are based on the following passages.

Both passages are excerpts from The World is a Museum, *written in 2014.*

Passage 1

Where does art live? Where do we encounter it? Most of us would tend to answer that art belongs in galleries and museums—perhaps even that the limited environmental context of art is part of what defines it. However, many of the most recognizable, impactful, and dynamic
Line pieces of artwork the world over are not contained within the walls of museums, but out in
(5) public, where citizens encounter and engage them every day of their lives. Public art has a rich and storied history, dating at least from the classical era right up into the Renaissance. Consider the iconic *Trevi Fountain* in Rome, or Ghiberti's magnificent *Gates of Paradise*. Both the city of Paris itself and the critical heights of European industrial era ingenuity are epitomized in the unmistakable form of the Eiffel Tower. Even today, public art continues to evolve.
(10) In 2005, Christo and Jeanne-Claude conceived and executed a massive installation artwork entitled *The Gates*, consisting of 7,503 saffron-colored panels arching over 23 miles of public walkways in New York's Central Park.

Aesthetically, the success of *The Gates* lies in its harmonious interplay of color and composition. The vibrant saffron-orange fabric conveys energy, which is amplified by the natural
(15) movement of the material in the wind. Further, the orange against the ashen grey background of Manhattan in the winter is especially fresh and invigorating. In contrast, *The Gates* also elicit a serene, calming effect through repetition, with over 7,000 individual banners blustering in graceful arches. Together, the dynamism of its energy and steadiness of flow work to keep the viewer engaged and moving—both of which are elemental to a successful
(20) work of art.

Beyond the success of its composition, the installation of *The Gates* in a public park intrinsically influences how we encounter and react to it. Regardless of one's interest in the work, to any New Yorker passing by Central Park during its display, it could not be avoided or ignored. It compels the viewer to react, and ponder its purpose and meaning. As public art, it acts as
(25) an ephemeral social equalizer, briefly dissolving the distance between the homeless man and the business man. Both have free access to *The Gates*; both are equally entitled to encounter and to interpret it.

Passage 2

Few critics will deny that the transgressive idea for the sake of transgression has often been the operative principle in the modern evolution of art. And it is not nearly so much the writ-
(30) erly platitudes and sober dialectics of past eras that embody the trend of visual art in the 20th and 21st centuries as it is the anarchist battle-cry of Mikhail Bakunin that "the passion for destruction is also a creative passion".

To speak generally, crossing boundaries in order to expand the fields of our consciousness has been accepted in our contemporary culture as a vital component (and indeed, perhaps
(35) the only remaining component) demarcating a line between art and object, between ideation and decoration. However, there is an implied value to this perspective that few—artists and critics alike—will care to acknowledge. Boundaries matter.

It is well known that this nuance essentially eluded the likes of Marcel Duchamp and his Dadaist zealots. If we were to accept, as they did, that indeed there is no intrinsic quality—

(40) no ineluctable aspect of creation, or innovation, or craft—that defines "art" outside its being described as exactly that, the very notion of aesthetics collapses upon itself; for such a world is necessarily predicated on the principle that either everything is art, or else it is not. And I fear that it must be the latter.

The pluralistic ignorance of our "art-is-whatever-the-artist-says-it-is" society has reached

(45) a new and too infrequently criticized summit in the latest charade of self-described artists Christo and Jeanne-Claude, *The Gates* of Central Park. The distinctive fabric used in the *The Gates* was not sewn or dyed by the artists; the posts holding them aloft were not welded or painted by the artists. In this sense alone, Christo and Jeanne-Claude may be considered artists to the same extent that one is an artist in selecting new drapes for a sitting room.

(50) But more important (and more brazen) is the setting chosen by Christo and Jeanne-Claude for their pseudo-aesthetic stunt. Most every person who has walked the paths and bridges of Central Park—chiefly conceived by Frederick Law Olmstead and Calvert Vaux—and appreciated both the thoughtfulness and elegance of its design will readily agree that it is, already, a work of public art. To dress it, even for a day, in the costume of Christo's and Jeanne-Claude's

(55) creatively bankrupt brand of expressionist pretension is tantamount to drawing a mustache on the Mona Lisa—a ploy, in fact, already executed by Duchamp in his insipid 1919 "objet trouvé", *L.H.O.O.Q.*

It would perhaps make for an apt cautionary tale to Christo and Jeanne-Claude to realize that less than one hundred years later, the sophomoric antics of Duchamp are all but forgot-

(60) ten, whereas after half a millennium, da Vinci's painting remains one of the most iconic works of art in the Western world.

1. As used in line 1, "tend" most nearly means

   (A) wait on.
   (B) look over.
   (C) move toward.
   (D) be inclined.

2. As used in line 5, "engage" most nearly means

   (A) pledge.
   (B) fight with.
   (C) interact with.
   (D) create.

3. As used in line 9, "form" most nearly means

   (A) design.
   (B) variety.
   (C) dream.
   (D) classification.

4. As used in in line 10, "massive" most nearly means

   (A) dense.
   (B) large.
   (C) heavy.
   (D) severe.

5. As used in line 19, "elemental" most nearly means

   (A) environmental.
   (B) stable.
   (C) inorganic.
   (D) essential.

6. As used in line 35, "demarcating" most nearly means

   (A) destroying.
   (B) enabling.
   (C) separating.
   (D) crossing.

7. As used in line 53, "agree" most nearly means

   (A) negotiate.
   (B) acknowledge.
   (C) undertake.
   (D) contradict.

8. As used in line 56, "executed" most nearly means

   (A) done.
   (B) murdered.
   (C) surmised.
   (D) imagined.

Answer Explanations

1. **(D)** The sentence is referring to what people might think about how to properly respond to questions about the nature of art. Since it refers to their opinions on these questions, "be inclined" would be the best fit. People are not waiting on, looking over, or moving toward thoughts on the essence of art.

2. **(C)** The passage in which "engage" occurs describes citizens coming across public art on a daily basis, making it much more likely that they would "interact with" it in some way. They are not pledging to it or fighting with it, making choice (A) and choice (B) incorrect. They are also not creating it, unless they themselves are the artists, making choice (D) incorrect.

3. **(A)** The sentence mentions the ingenuity of the industrial era in creating the Eiffel Tower, something that has an unmistakable form, or "design." There is no "variety" of Eiffel Tower, just one. There is no "dream" of the tower since it actually exists. The "classification" of the tower is not unmistakable but, rather, the way it looks.

4. **(B)** In lines 10–12, the author describes the large size of the artwork, highlighting how it spanned over 23 miles of walkways. Something that is "massive" could be "dense," like a black hole, or "heavy," like a blue whale. In this context, the large size is emphasized. There is not a negative association with "massive" at it is used here, so "severe" would not work.

5. **(D)** The author states that dynamic energy and steady flow are "elemental," or "essential," to an artwork—they make it what it is. "Environmental," "stable," and "inorganic" would all describe elements one might find in a periodic table but not the essential features of a work of art.

6. **(C)** "Demarcating" signifies the separation between what makes something art vs. object and ideation vs. decoration. The sentence does not indicate that anything is destroyed, enabled, or crossed; instead, clear boundaries between the definitions of these artistic categories are laid out.

7. **(B)** The author is suggesting that anyone who walks through Central Park would "acknowledge" that it is already a work of public art. This signifies a mental realization, not a negotiation, an undertaking of a task, or a contradiction of some kind.

8. **(A)** The narrator is citing an artwork actually created by Duchamp that he finds mindless and offensive, so "executed" most nearly means "done." Choice (B) gives a common definition of "executed" that is not applicable here. Choice (C) and choice (D) provide incorrect definitions of "executed."

Graph Analysis Questions

A few graph analysis questions will appear on the PSAT Reading Test. They will be on two of the passages—the social science and two science passages are the potential candidates. On graph analysis questions, remember the following tactic.

TACTIC 4: LIMIT YOUR ANALYSIS TO THE *EVIDENCE* THAT IS PROVIDED IN THE GRAPHS—DO NOT JUMP TO CONCLUSIONS THAT ARE UNSUPPORTED BY THE INFORMATION PRESENTED.

Graph analysis questions test your understanding of the information in the graphs, not your background knowledge.

Questions 1–2 are based on the following graph.

Types of Transportation Companies from 1990–2015

	1990	1995	2000	2005	2010	2015
Air Carriers	70	96	91	85	77	63
Railroads	530	541	560	560	565	562
Interstate Motor Carriers	216,000	346,000	560,393	679,744	739,421	746,142
Marine Vessel Operators	1,420	1,381	1,114	733	603	1,189

Source: Adapted from the United States Department of Transportation Statistics, 2018.

1. According to the table, between the years 1995 and 2015, which type of transportation underwent the largest percentage decline in number of companies?

   (A) Air carriers
   (B) Railroads
   (C) Interstate motor carriers
   (D) Marine vessel operators

2. Which of the following is an accurate statement based on the data in the table?

   (A) The number of marine vessel operators has consistently increased from 1990–2015.
   (B) The number of air carriers has consistently decreased from 1990–2015.
   (C) The number of interstate motor carriers has consistently increased from 1990–2015.
   (D) The number of marine vessel operators has consistently decreased from 1990–2015.

Questions 3–4 are based on the following graph.

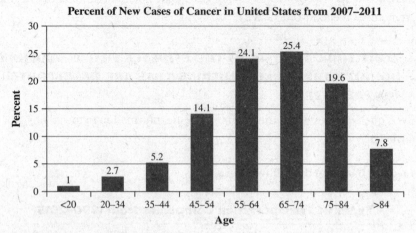

Percent of New Cases of Cancer in United States from 2007–2011

Source: Adapted from the National Cancer Institute.
https://www.cancer.gov/about-cancer/causes-prevention/risk/age.

3. Based on the information in the table, approximately half of all new cases of cancer in the United States were from people in which age ranges?

(A) 20–44
(B) 35–54
(C) 55–74
(D) 75–90

4. What additional piece of information would be most helpful in determining the number of people in the U.S. over age 84 who had a new case of cancer in the years 2007–2011?

(A) The total number of new cancer cases between 2007 and 2011 in the United States
(B) The total number of male cancer patients between 2007 and 2011
(C) The total number of lung cancer cases in the elderly between 2007 and 2011
(D) The total number of emergency room visits by the elderly between 2007 and 2011

Questions 5–6 are based on the following graph.

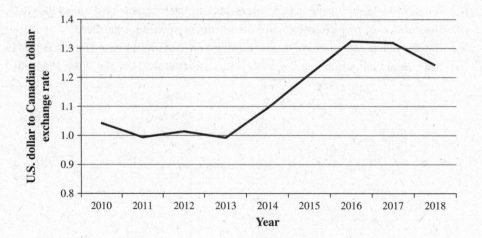

5. Based on the graph, during which of the following years was the Canadian dollar strongest relative to the United States dollar?

   (A) 2010
   (B) 2013
   (C) 2016
   (D) 2018

6. Considering the data in the graph, during which period did the strength of the U.S. dollar increase the most relative to the Canadian dollar?

   (A) 2010–2012
   (B) 2012–2014
   (C) 2014–2016
   (D) 2014–2018

Answer Explanations

1. **(A)** Between 1990–1995, the number of air carriers steadily decreased from 96 to 63, giving this a reduction of about 34 percent. The number of railroads and interstate motor carriers both declined. Although the number of marine vessel operators also declined, it did not come close to the same level of percentage decline as the number of air carriers. The number of marine vessel operators decreased by approximately 14 percent. You will not need a calculator to solve this problem since estimation will be sufficient.

2. **(C)** Between 1990 and 2015, the number of interstate motor carriers increased from 346,000 to 746,142; at each five-year interval, the number of interstate motor carriers was greater than it was at the previous time. The correct answer is not choice (A) because the number of marine vessel operators varied during this period. It is not choice (B) because between 1990 and 1995, the number of air carriers increased. It is not choice (D) because between 2010 and 2015, the number of marine vessel operators increased.

3. **(C)** If you add the percentages between 55 and 74, they come close to 50 percent:

$$24.1 + 25.4 = 49.5$$

The other combinations are significantly less than 50 percent, or half.

4. **(A)** If we knew the total number of new cancer cases between 2007 and 2011, we could multiply it by the percentage of new cases of cancer in the age group over 84 provided in the figure, giving us the total number of people in the U.S. over age 84 who had a new case of cancer in 2007–2011. The other options, although providing some interesting data, would not allow for a specific calculation of what we are asked to find.

5. **(B)** The graph portrays the exchange rate of the U.S. dollar relative to the Canadian dollar. As this ratio *increases*, the U.S. dollar can be exchanged for *more* Canadian dollars, making the U.S. dollar relatively stronger and the Canadian dollar relatively weaker. As this ratio *decreases*, the Canadian dollar is stronger relative to the U.S. dollar. So 2013 is correct since it shows the *lowest* ratio out of the four options.

6. **(C)** Between 2014 and 2016, the U.S dollar goes from being able to be exchanged for only about 1.05 Canadian dollars to over 1.3 Canadian dollars. This is by far the biggest increase in U.S. dollar strength relative to the Canadian dollar out of the given choices.

READING PASSAGES DRILLS

Now that you have completed the question drills, try some full-length passages that are just like those you will encounter on the PSAT Reading Test.

- Fiction
- Social Science
- Historical Document
- Science
- Passage 1 and Passage 2

Take about 12 minutes total per passage—devote about 5 minutes to read and about 7 minutes to answer the questions.

Fiction Passage Practice

The PSAT Reading Test will begin with a fiction passage, and it may be from an earlier time—possibly the 18th or 19th century. If it is an older passage, the language may be a bit more challenging to understand. Take things slowly at the beginning so you develop a feel for the writer's style, then read at a normal pace as the story develops.

Questions 1–9 are based on the following passage.

The following passage is an excerpt from the 1877 novel The American. *Christopher Newman, a civil war hero and self-made millionaire, is visiting Europe for the first time. In Paris, he meets and dines with the wife of an old friend, Mrs. Lizzie Tristram.*

She had an especial wish to know whether he had ever been in love—seriously, passionately—and, failing to gather any satisfaction from his allusions, at last closely pressed him. He hesitated a while, but finally said, "Hang it then, no!" She declared that she was delighted to
Line hear it, as it confirmed her private conviction that he was a man of no real feeling.
(5)   "Is that so?" he asked, very gravely. "But how do you recognize a man of real feeling?"

"I can't make out," said Mrs. Tristram, "whether you're very simple or very deep."

"I'm very deep. That's a fact."

"I believe that if I were to tell you with a certain air that you're as cold as a fish, you would implicitly believe me."

(10)   "A certain air?" said Newman. "Well try your air and see."

"You would believe me, but you would not care," said Mrs. Tristram.

"You've got it all wrong. I should care immensely, but I shouldn't believe you. The fact is I have never had time to 'feel' things. I have had to *do* them, had to make myself felt."

"Oh, I can imagine indeed that you may have sometimes done that tremendously."

(15)   "Yes, there's no mistake about that."

"When you're in one of your furies it can't be pleasant."

"I am never in a fury."

"I don't, nevertheless, see you always as you are now. You've *something* or other behind, beneath. You get harder or you get softer. You're more pleased—or you're more displeased."

(20)   "Well, a man of any sense doesn't lay his plans to be angry," said Newman, "and it's in fact so long since I have been displeased that I've quite forgotten it."

"I don't believe," she returned, "that you're never angry. A man ought to be angry sometimes, and you are neither good enough nor bad enough always to keep your temper."

"I lose it perhaps every five years."

(25)   "The time is coming round, then," said his hostess. "Before I've known you six months I shall see you in a magnificent rage."

"Do you mean to put me into one?"

"I should not be sorry. You take things too coolly. It quite exasperates me. And then you're too happy. You have what must be the most agreeable thing in the world: the consciousness
(30) of having bought your pleasure beforehand, having paid for it in advance. You have not a day of reckoning staring you in the face. Your reckonings are over."

"Well, I suppose I am happy," said Newman, almost pensively.

"You've been odiously successful."

"Successful in copper," said Newman, "but very mixed in other ventures. And I've had to
(35) take quite a back seat on oil."

"It's very disagreeable to know how Americans have come by their money," his companion sighed. "Now, at all events, you've the world before you. You've only to enjoy."

"Oh, I suppose I'm all right," said Newman. "Only I'm tired of having it thrown up at me. Besides, there are several drawbacks. I don't come up to my own standard of culture."

(40) "One doesn't expect it of you," Mrs. Tristram answered. Then in a moment: "Besides, you do come up. You *are* up!"

"Well, I mean to have a good time, wherever I am," said Newman. "I am not cultivated, I am not even educated; I know nothing about history, or art, or foreign tongues, or any other learned matters. But I am not a fool, either, and I shall undertake to know something about

(45) Europe by the time I have done with it. I feel something under my ribs here," he added in a moment, "that I can't explain—a sort of a mighty hankering, a desire to stretch out and haul in."

"Bravo!" Mrs. Tristram cried; "that's what I want to hear you say. You're the great Western Barbarian, stepping forth in his innocence and might, to gaze a while at this poor corrupt old world before swooping down on it."

(50) "Oh come," Newman protested; "I'm not an honest barbarian either, by a good deal. I've seen honest barbarians; I know what they are."

"There are different shades."

"I have instincts—have them deeply—if I haven't the forms of a high old civilization," Newman went on. "I stick to that. If you don't believe me, I should like to prove it to you."

(55) Mrs. Tristram was silent a while. "I should like to make you prove it," she said at last. "I should like to put you in a difficult place."

"Well, put me!" said Newman.

"Vous ne doutez de rien!" his companion rejoined.

"Oh," he insisted, "I've a very good opinion of myself."

(60) "I wish I could put it to the test. Give me time and I will."

1. Based on the passage as a whole, Newman is best characterized as

   (A) easily flustered and emotionally vulnerable.
   (B) even-tempered and business savvy.
   (C) odiously successful and frighteningly barbaric
   (D) innocently optimistic and personally intimidating.

2. The conversation between Mrs. Tristram and Newman is essentially a/an

   (A) philosophical dialogue.
   (B) insulting accusation.
   (C) complimentary platitude.
   (D) playful exchange.

3. As used in line 6, "deep" most nearly means

   (A) profound.
   (B) engrossed.
   (C) extended.
   (D) saturated.

4. It can be inferred from the passage that Mrs. Tristram most strongly believes that she can bear witness to a greater emotional range from Newman if she has sufficient

   (A) money.
   (B) culture.
   (C) time.
   (D) empathy.

5. Which choice provides the best evidence for the answer to the previous question?

   (A) Lines 8–9 ("'I believe . . . me'")
   (B) Lines 12–13 ("'You've . . . felt'")
   (C) Lines 25–26 ("'The time . . . rage'")
   (D) Lines 29–31 ("'You have . . . over'")

6. When Newman says "I'm tired of having it thrown up at me" (line 38), he most likely means that he is

   (A) sorry that he continues to fall ill.
   (B) annoyed with European culture.
   (C) wishful that he could be more successful.
   (D) weary of being reminded of his wealth.

7. As used in line 46, "hankering" most nearly means

   (A) confusion.
   (B) cultivation.
   (C) appreciation.
   (D) desire.

8. Newman's opinion of his capacity to understand higher culture is

   (A) drearily pessimistic
   (B) unquestionably recognized.
   (C) intuitively confident.
   (D) jealously guarded.

9. Which choice provides the best evidence for the answer to the previous question?

   (A) Lines 40–41 ("'One . . . up")
   (B) Line 42 ("'Well . . . Newman")
   (C) Line 50 ("'Oh . . . deal")
   (D) Line 53 ("'I have . . . civilization'")

Answer Explanations

1. **(B)** Tristram describes Newman as someone without "real feeling" in line 5. Tristram continues to try to press Newman's emotional buttons to demonstrate that her assumptions about his even-tempered nature are correct. Also, Newman has been "successful in copper" (line 34), which allows him to live a more free and luxurious life, so he must have business savvy (know-how or smarts). Choice (A) is incorrect because Newman does not demonstrate much emotion. Choice (C) and choice (D) are incorrect because Newman is in no way a frightening or an intimidating person.

2. **(D)** Throughout the conversation, Tristram playfully attempts to touch on the emotions of Newman, while Newman eagerly engages her with thoughtful responses. This is best described as a "playful exchange." Choice (A) is incorrect because the conversation is more superficial, preventing it from being considered philosophical. Choice (B) is wrong because they are getting along well with one another. Choice (C) is not the answer because Tristram is trying to find Newman's emotional vulnerability. A complimentary platitude would involve her saying nice yet meaningless things to him.

3. **(A)** In this context, they are referring to feelings. So "deep" refers to Newman's capacity for feeling. It would be synonymous in this context to call his feelings "profound." Choice (B) is incorrect because "engrossed" would be more applicable in describing one's intellectual focus. Choice (C) is incorrect because "extended" would refer more to breadth than to depth. Choice (D) is wrong because "saturated" would refer to having a great deal of some quality but not necessarily having it in depth.

4. **(C)** Lines 28–29 state that Tristram believes that surely by the time she has known Newman for at least six months, she will have seen him demonstrate great emotional passion. There is no indication that her lack of money or her European culture contributes to this. She seems to have plenty of empathy already, given how she is able to read his emotions quite well.

5. **(C)** Lines 25–26 provide the most direct support for the idea that if Mrs. Tristram has more time to get to know Newman, she will see him demonstrate passion. Choice (A) is wrong because these lines refer to Mrs. Tristram's belief in her own capacities. Choice (B) is wrong because it gives Newman's reasoning as to why he does not demonstrate much feeling. Choice (D) is incorrect because it states that Newman is financially prosperous.

6. **(D)** Considering the context before answering this is critical. Prior to line 38, Tristram and Newman are discussing Newman's success in business. So following this discussion, it makes the most sense to infer that the meaning of "I'm tired of having it thrown up at me" is referring to Newman's weariness at hearing that he is quite wealthy. Choice (A) is incorrect because it has nothing to do with physical illness. Choice (B) is wrong because Newman cannot get enough of European culture. Choice (C) is not correct because Newman is satisfied with the business success he has had.

7. **(D)** Immediately after mentioning the word "hankering," Newman clarifies that he has a "desire to stretch out and haul in." Therefore, "desire" is the correct answer. Although he cannot precisely explain his feelings, he is certain that he does have them, making "confusion," choice (A), incorrect. Choices (B) and (C) are incorrect because Newman is working on cultivating his cultural awareness and appreciation—he does not yet have such awareness and appreciation.

8. **(C)** Newman states that he has deep instincts for high civilization even though he does not have the forms of it quite yet. So he is intuitive (instinctive) in his confidence that he will someday be able to master European culture. Choice (A) is wrong because Newman is optimistic. Choice (B) is not correct because his capacity is not recognized by others or even explicitly and fully by himself. Choice (D) is not right because Newman is very forthcoming about his opinions.

9. **(D)** These lines provide the best evidence that Newman is intuitively confident about his ability to understand the higher cultures he is studying. Choice (A) focuses on Tristram's opinion of Newman. Choice (B) gives only an introduction to Newman's self-assessment. Choice (C) responds to Tristram's playfully insulting comments immediately beforehand.

Social Science Practice

The passage that follows is a historical analysis. You will not need to use outside knowledge to answer the accompanying questions—all of the answers will be provided in the text. Since it is non-fiction, read the first paragraph, topic sentences, and last paragraph a bit more carefully so that you fully grasp the overall point of the passage.

Questions 1–10 are based on the following passage.

The following excerpt is from a 2013 history article titled "The Great Seal."

In the wake of the wild and lucrative conspiracy theories that swept through our nation's popular culture in the last decade, widely disseminated misinformation seems still to haunt an alarming portion of our national symbols. Yet in many cases the reality behind
Line these symbols is far richer in meaning and profundity than any farfetched tale spun by a
(5) Hollywood screenwriter; and while the truth may not ensnare our sense of fantasy, it can still capture our imaginations with an illuminating insight into our nation's history, and the minds of early American patriots.

Take for instance the Great Seal of the United States, which was first commissioned by the Continental Congress on the very day that they declared independence from Great
(10) Britain (though it was not fully completed for another six years). For the most part, the symbolism of the obverse side is readily discernible to those versed in the story of the American Revolution; the bald eagle—our ubiquitous symbol for natural power and majesty—is displayed with a striped escutcheon and splayed wings in a formation that echoes (but is distinct from) English heraldry. The eagle was selected over the traditional heraldic animal of
(15) power—the lion—both because it is native to North America, and to avoid the overtones of kingship historically associated with the lion. The thirteen red and white stripes (or Pieces) and single blue cap (or Chief) of the escutcheon are described by Charles Thomson—who presented the final design of the Seal before Congress in 1782—as representing "the several states all joined in one solid compact entire, supporting a Chief, which unites the whole
(20) and represents Congress".

The constellation of thirteen stars in a blue field above the eagle also signify the colonies, and their capacity to shine independently while remaining integral components of a larger structure. The number appears again in the thirteen arrows and thirteen leaves of the olive branch clutched, respectively, in the left and right talons of the eagle. Together,
(25) the branch (which is said to derive from the Judeo-Christian symbol of peace in the story of Noah) and arrows represent a dichotomy—a national preparedness in both times of war and peace. Surrounding the stars above the eagle is a design described in heraldry as "clouds and glory," another symbol of religious origin (meant to invoke the Saint's Halo of Judeo-Christian iconography) that alludes to a belief held by many American revolutionar-
(30) ies that the victory of their new nation was the result of "divine providence". The arrangement of the stars themselves mimics the geometry of the Star of David.

The reverse side of the Great Seal is slightly more esoteric in its significance, and as such has been more vulnerable to exploitation at the hands of those who would popularize baseless myth at the expense of obscuring our national symbols. The "Eye of Providence"—
(35) which floats near the top of the Seal—is admittedly a derivative of the ancient Egyptian symbol for the Eye of Horus (which stood for royal power and good health), but it is also a symbol of tremendous distribution that has meant many different things to many different

cultures. The incarnation of the Eye that appears on the Great Seal emerges from the far more recent Christian tradition of the European Renaissance, in which the eye symbolized
(40) the universal presence of the Judeo-Christian God, and the triangle surrounding it the Holy Trinity. If one takes into account the motto above the Eye—"Annuit Cœptis", or "[He] has approved our undertakings"—as well as the prevalent belief among those American revolutionaries of the Christian persuasion that the founding of the United States was a literal act of Providence, there is little room for doubt that the Eye of Providence itself is meant
(45) to symbolize the "grace of God" as it were, and not, by any means, the nobility of ancient Egyptian monarchy.

The absurd suggestion that the Eye is meant to invoke Horus would likely never have been uttered but for the inclusion of an unfinished pyramid—consisting of thirteen steps— at the Seal's base. However, Charles Thomson describes the pyramid explicitly as signifying,
(50) "Strength and Duration", while, "the Eye over it & the Motto allude to the many signal interpositions of providence in favour of the American cause". In light of these words, one can surmise that the pyramid was selected because it is a worldwide symbol for a remarkable and enduring civilization—a thing manmade that stands the test of unfathomable time. In contrast to the pyramid's (in this case) wholly secular implications, the Eye of Providence
(55) hovers above it near the heavens; together they constitute another symbolic duality: the secular and spiritual foundations of our nation as envisioned by many of the Founding Fathers. The true symbolic beauty of the Seal's pyramid lies rather in its unfinished aspect; it demonstrates that—for all their accomplishments—the American Revolutionaries recognized that their work was but a beginning. To achieve its full splendor, the pyramid would
(60) require the equally impactful contributions of countless generations, building a still greater nation onward throughout time.

1. The author's overall purpose in writing the essay is to

   (A) analyze public opinion.
   (B) dispel misconceptions.
   (C) postulate a hypothesis.
   (D) confirm widespread views.

2. The passage primarily uses which of the following to make its argument?

   (A) Primary source quotation
   (B) Religious dogma
   (C) Symbolic analysis
   (D) Archaeological findings

3. As used in line 6, "illuminating" most nearly means

   (A) enlightening.
   (B) bright.
   (C) shiny.
   (D) creative.

4. Lines 10–14 suggest that a viewer of the Great Seal could generally understand it with some

   (A) in-depth scholarly investigation.
   (B) basic historical knowledge.
   (C) background information about bird anatomy.
   (D) familiarity with English heraldry.

5. Which symbol in the Great Seal of the United States does the author suggest was chosen in an effort to differentiate the U.S. from more aristocratic countries?

   (A) The eagle
   (B) The olive branch
   (C) The "Eye of Providence"
   (D) The unfinished pyramid

6. Which choice provides the best evidence for the answer to the previous question?

   (A) Lines 14–16 ("The eagle . . . lion")
   (B) Lines 24–27 ("Together, . . . peace")
   (C) Lines 34–38 ("The . . . cultures")
   (D) Lines 47–49 ("The absurd . . . base")

7. As used in line 19, "compact" most nearly means

   (A) small.
   (B) firm.
   (C) grouping.
   (D) union.

8. It can reasonably be inferred that the author believes the "Eye of Providence" is widely misinterpreted on account of the presence of what other symbol on the Great Seal?

   (A) The eagle
   (B) The triangle of the Holy Trinity
   (C) The unfinished pyramid
   (D) The Star of David

9. The author suggests that many early Americans believed that divine power had what role in the formation of the United States?

   (A) A negative and revolutionary role
   (B) A neutral and removed role
   (C) A positive and instrumental role
   (D) A helpful yet tangential role

10. Which choice provides the best evidence for the answer to the previous question?

   (A) Lines 1–7 ("In the . . . patriots")
   (B) Lines 21–27 ("The constellation . . . peace")
   (C) Lines 41–46 ("If one . . . monarchy")
   (D) Lines 57–61 ("The true . . . time")

Answer Explanations

1. **(B)** The first sentence of the passage refers to the widespread presence of "misinformation" about the national symbols of the United States. The essay goes on to dispel a number of misconceptions readers may have about the Great Seal of the United States. Choice (A) is incorrect because the passage does not focus on what the public as a whole thinks. Choice (C) is wrong because the excerpt is sharing information, not making a hypothesis. Choice (D) is not right because the information refutes commonly held views.

2. **(C)** The passage makes its argument by thoroughly analyzing the symbols in the Great Seal of the United States, from its eagle to its constellation. Choice (A) is wrong because the visual images of the Seal are primarily analyzed. Choice (B) is not correct because religion is mentioned only as an aside, not as the primary focus of the argument. Choice (D) is not correct. Although this is a historical symbol, it is one still in use today, so it does not involve archaeology.

3. **(A)** In this context, "illuminating" is describing the type of insight that people may gain from learning the true history of American symbols. Since this has to do with learning, it can best be described as "enlightening." The word in this context does not mean "bright" or "shiny" because it does not refer to the physical aspects of the symbol. The word does not mean "creative" because the insight we have is more informational and factual.

4. **(B)** Lines 10–12 state that "the symbolism of the obverse side is readily discernible to those versed in the story of the American Revolution." This means that if someone has basic historical knowledge about U.S. history, he or she will be able to make sense of the symbolism. Choice (A) is wrong because such in-depth knowledge is not necessary. Choice (C) is wrong because it is too narrowly focused on the eagle. Choice (D) is not correct because the Great Seal of the United States is "distinct from" English heraldry according to line 14.

5. **(A)** Lines 14–16 indicate that the eagle was chosen because it would avoid the "overtones of kingship" that the more common lion symbol would have. Although the other symbols are on the Great Seal, they are not as clearly present in order to differentiate the U.S. from more aristocratic countries.

6. **(A)** This choice refers to the lines that discuss the eagle in the Great Seal of the United States. The other choices refer to the symbols in each of the incorrect answers to the previous question.

7. **(D)** "Compact" in this context refers to the "union" of the different states joined into one country. It is not referring to size as in choice (A) or to texture as in choice (B). Also, a "grouping," found in choice (C), is too weak a word to describe the joining of states together into a country.

8. **(C)** Lines 45–48 explain that the suggestion that the Eye on the Great Seal refers to an Egyptian deity is based on the unfinished pyramid underneath the Great Seal. The other symbols, although present on the Great Seal, do not contribute to the misinterpretation of the Eye.

9. **(C)** Lines 39-45 report the belief of many American revolutionaries that "the grace of God" contributed to the founding of the United States. This can best be described as positive and instrumental since they believed divine power was vital to the formation of the country. This belief would not then be described as negative or neutral as in choices (A) and (B). The word "helpful" in choice (D) could be applicable. However, "tangential" is not correct since the definition of tangential is "diverging from the main topic."

10. **(C)** These lines address the role that many American revolutionaries believed divine providence played in the founding of the country. Choice (A) gives an introduction to the essay. Choice (B) touches on only religion. Choice (D) focuses on the contributions of future generations of Americans.

Historical Document Practice

One of the reading selections on the PSAT will be a great global conversation document from the 1700s to the present day. Common themes of these documents are the foundations of democracy, the abolition of slavery, and women's rights. The document is sometimes a speech, a letter, or a government publication. Be prepared to read this type of a passage a bit more slowly if the language in it is unfamiliar to you. Here is an example of such a passage.

Questions 1–9 are based on the following excerpt.

Excerpt from George Washington's "Farewell Address to the United States of America," 1796.

Against the insidious wiles of foreign influence (I conjure you to believe me, fellow-citizens) the jealousy of a free people ought to be constantly awake, since history and experience prove that foreign influence is one of the most baneful foes of republican government.

Line But that jealousy to be useful must be impartial; else it becomes the instrument of the very
(5) influence to be avoided, instead of a defense against it. Excessive partiality for one foreign nation and excessive dislike of another cause those whom they actuate to see danger only on one side, and serve to veil and even second the arts of influence on the other. Real patriots who may resist the intrigues of the favorite are liable to become suspected and odious, while its tools and dupes usurp the applause and confidence of the people, to surrender
(10) their interests.

The great rule of conduct for us in regard to foreign nations is in extending our commercial relations, to have with them as little political connection as possible. So far as we have already formed engagements, let them be fulfilled with perfect good faith. Here let us stop. Europe has a set of primary interests which to us have none; or a very remote relation. Hence she
(15) must be engaged in frequent controversies, the causes of which are essentially foreign to our concerns. Hence, therefore, it must be unwise in us to implicate ourselves by artificial ties in the ordinary vicissitudes of her politics, or the ordinary combinations and collisions of her friendships or enmities.

Our detached and distant situation invites and enables us to pursue a different course.
(20) If we remain one people under an efficient government, the period is not far off when we may defy material injury from external annoyance; when we may take such an attitude as will cause the neutrality we may at any time resolve upon to be scrupulously respected; when belligerent nations, under the impossibility of making acquisitions upon us, will not lightly hazard the giving us provocation; when we may choose peace or war, as our interest, guided
(25) by justice, shall counsel.

Why forego the advantages of so peculiar a situation? Why quit our own to stand upon foreign ground? Why, by interweaving our destiny with that of any part of Europe, entangle our peace and prosperity in the toils of European ambition, rivalship, interest, humor or caprice?

It is our true policy to steer clear of permanent alliances with any portion of the foreign
(30) world; so far, I mean, as we are now at liberty to do it; for let me not be understood as capable of patronizing infidelity to existing engagements. I hold the maxim no less applicable to public than to private affairs, that honesty is always the best policy. I repeat it, therefore, let those engagements be observed in their genuine sense. But, in my opinion, it is unnecessary and would be unwise to extend them.
(35) Taking care always to keep ourselves by suitable establishments on a respectable defensive posture, we may safely trust to temporary alliances for extraordinary emergencies.

1. The principle thesis of the passage is best summarized in

   (A) lines 2–3 ("Since . . . government").
   (B) lines 12–13 ("So far . . . stop").
   (C) lines 23–24 ("Belligerent . . . provocation").
   (D) line 36 ("We may . . . emergencies").

2. The passage suggests that Washington's primary concern is which of the following sorts of foreign interactions?

   (A) The U.S. is invaded by land from European aggressors, who quickly dismantle the fragile early republic.
   (B) The U.S. is drawn into a foreign war based not on our inherent interests but on treaty obligations.
   (C) The U.S. is taken over by foreign saboteurs who infiltrate the federal government and assume positions of power.
   (D) The U.S. is enmeshed in a long-lasting trade war over tariffs and fees on exports and imports.

3. Lines 7–10 ("Real . . . interests") most directly warn against what potential outcome?

   (A) Devoted, capable Americans are impugned while gullible Americans become pawns.
   (B) Patriotic, reputable Americans are praised while less capable Americans are impoverished.
   (C) Traitorous, clever Americans rise to power while lower-class Americans are disregarded.
   (D) Meddling, crafty Europeans successfully invade the U.S. while Americans surrender easily.

4. Paragraph 2 (lines 11–18) suggests that the principle aim of American's foreign relations should be

   (A) to encourage the development of new allies.
   (B) to isolate the U.S. from European interactions.
   (C) to promote commerce without alliance.
   (D) to seize new territories unchecked.

5. Washington postulates that the major domestic threat to American independence and prosperity is

   (A) patriotism.
   (B) disunity.
   (C) political isolationism.
   (D) impartiality.

6. Which choice provides the best evidence for the answer to the previous question?

   (A) Lines 11–12 ("The great . . . possible")
   (B) Lines 14–16 ("Hence . . . concerns")
   (C) Lines 20–21 ("If we . . . annoyance")
   (D) Lines 32–34 ("I repeat . . . them")

7. As used in line 24, "hazard" most nearly means

    (A) endanger.
    (B) confuse.
    (C) chance.
    (D) stop.

8. As used in line 26, "peculiar" most nearly means

    (A) distinct.
    (B) strange.
    (C) undesirable.
    (D) eccentric.

9. Suppose that at the time of the passage's writing the United States had a trade pact with a European country that had been in place for some time. We can reasonably infer that Washington would suggest what should be done to this pact?

    (A) It should be maintained.
    (B) It should be renegotiated.
    (C) It should be abandoned.
    (D) It should be built upon with political agreements.

Answer Explanations

1. **(A)** The overall argument of the passage is that the young United States should avoid alliances with foreign powers and focus instead on its own affairs. This is best summarized by lines 2–3, which state that "history and experience prove that foreign influence is one of the most baneful foes of republican government." This means that being influenced by other countries will hurt governments elected by the people. Choice (B) is incorrect because it is addressing a potential objection. Choice (C) is not right because it is making a related point but not the primary point of the passage's argument by advocating a stronger military posture to thwart potential invaders. Choice (D) is incorrect because it is noting an exception.

2. **(B)** Lines 13–18 state that European powers are likely to engage in frequent conflicts and that the U.S. should not entangle itself with "artificial ties," i.e., treaties that would oblige it to fight in wars in which the U.S. has no interest. So choice (B) is the best option. Choice (A) is incorrect. Although it is a concern, the primary argument of the excerpt is focused on avoiding foreign obligations, not on preparing for foreign invasion. Choice (C) is not correct because internal treason is not a focus of the passage. Choice (D) is wrong because Washington advocates foreign economic interaction in lines 11–12.

3. **(A)** In these lines, Washington expresses concern that "real patriots" will be considered suspicious simply because they side with a different foreign power, while "tools and dupes" will receive unwarranted praise. So Washington is expressing his concern that highly capable Americans truly devoted to the U.S. will be condemned, while easily manipulated Americans will become pawns for European powers. Choices (B) and (C) are incorrect because there is no discussion of economic status. Choice (D) is not right because Washington is not concerned with whether or not Americans can fight but with whether or not Americans will unnecessarily turn against one another.

4. **(C)** Washington uses this paragraph to argue that the U.S. should extend "commercial relations" but should not implicate itself "by artificial ties" to foreign powers that would require the U.S. to fight foreign wars. Choice (A) is wrong because Washington wants to avoid alliances. Choice (B) is not correct because trade is an interaction with Europe that Washington does want. Choice (D) is incorrect because Washington does not discuss American territorial expansion in this paragraph.

5. **(B)** Lines 19–20 state that if Americans remain "one people," they will be able to fend off foreign threats. So by implication, if Americans are disunited, they will encounter major threats to their independence and prosperity. Choice (A) is not correct because these statements about unity would serve to encourage patriotism as a helpful virtue to American independence. Choices (C) and (D) are not right because Washington advocates avoiding "artificial ties" (line 16) with other countries by being more neutral and isolated.

6. **(C)** These lines provide the most direct evidence that Washington thought of disunity as a major threat to American independence and prosperity since they mention the need to be "one people." Choice (A) is incorrect because these lines do not focus on threats. Choice (B) is wrong because these lines focus more on Europe. Choice (D) is wrong because these lines discuss how the U.S. can balance treaty obligations.

7. **(C)** Washington argues that the U.S. should get to a point where other countries will not take war with the U.S. lightly, thereby not wishing to "hazard" (risk or chance) war. Choices (A), (B), and (D) are all incorrect. Stating that other countries do not want to "endanger," "confuse," or "stop" giving the U.S. provocation does not make sense. These words do not have the secondary definition of "risk" that "chance" does.

8. **(A)** In ordinary usage, "peculiar" is something strange, eccentric, or even undesirable. In this context of antiquated English, though, Washington is arguing that the United States should not give up the advantages of its unique, or distinct, situation by making alliances with other countries.

9. **(A)** Washington states in lines 32–33 that when it comes to existing treaty obligations, he wishes for "those engagements" to be observed since doing otherwise would be dishonest. So Washington would want to maintain an existing trade treaty (pact). Choice (A) is also supported by Washington's advocacy of economic interactions with other nations.

Science Practice

The PSAT will include two scientific reading selections. Some of the terminology and concepts may be beyond what you have studied, but there will always be enough information given to you in the passage to answer the questions. The writers of the PSAT will not assume that you have outside knowledge on the topics.

Questions 1–10 are based on the following passage and supplementary material.

This is a passage from a 2013 science blog on the search for the Higgs boson particle, entitled "The God Particle." This particle is considered fundamental to the modern understanding of subatomic physics because it is assumed to give rise to all mass.

"The God Particle"—from a 2013 science blog.

In the early 1960's, theoretical physicists were racing to design a consistent and verifiable explanation to the question of how matter becomes massive at the subatomic level. Before the winter of 1964, three similar solutions emerged independently of one another—all of
Line which posited mechanisms that would resolve the issue—but only one of which predicted
(5) a theoretical, undiscovered particle that would mediate such a mechanism. Searching experimentally for this particle—dubbed the Higgs boson in the physics community, and known as the "God Particle" in the media—has been the task of hundreds of physicists since Fermilab's four-mile long Tevatron particle accelerator first came online in 1983.

A satisfying verbal definition for the Higgs boson is difficult to articulate, even for the
(10) theory's founder Dr. Peter Higgs. It is somewhat simpler to first describe how the universe would behave—according to the Standard Model of particle physics—without the activity of the Higgs boson. To begin with, matter would be essentially without mass. Gauge particles,* like photons,** would travel about at the speed of light, colliding occasionally, and sometimes even forming proton-like complexes. However, these complexes would decay
(15) almost instantaneously; the stable, atomic matter that constitutes our material world would be unsustainable.

In rough terms, the Higgs boson's role in imparting mass to the universe involves the propagation of a pervasive "Higgs field", which mediates the collision of subatomic gauge bosons, allowing them to acquire and maintain a mass. It is thought that this occurs because
(20) the Higgs field's non-zero amplitude in a vacuum spontaneously splits the electroweak gauge invariance of W, Z and Higgs bosons and gluons, resulting in a gauge transformation called "the Higgs mechanism". Metaphorically, the Higgs field might be thought of as a pool of molasses, slowing the bosons and gluons, allowing them to become massive, and ultimately reducing the elasticity of their collisions such that they may form larger, stable
(25) subatomic complexes like protons.

The Higgs boson is the only component of the Standard model—a set of physical theories that explain all interactions in the universe apart from gravity—that has yet to be observed experimentally. Because its discovery would mean a tremendous step toward validating the Standard model experimentally, it has often been referred to
(30) as a "holy grail" of particle physics. However, attempts to find the Higgs have proven

exceptionally troublesome for scientists. Together, the world's two largest and most powerful particle accelerators—Tevatron in Illinois, and the Large Hadron Collider in France and Switzerland—have sifted through roughly 70% of the particle's estimated vectors without returning any evidence for its existence. On one hand this suggests that—if

(35) the Higgs exists—its discovery is imminent, as the remaining "places" to look for it are becoming fewer and fewer. However, the cost of infrastructure and operation at these facilities is becoming, some believe, prohibitively expensive. Reduced federal funding at Fermilab has necessitated the cancellation of many projects involved with the search for the Higgs boson.

(40)   The protracted and arduous search for this singular particle has led some physicists to suspect that, in fact, it does not exist. Several theories competing with the Standard model—including Technicolor, and several extra-dimensional models—have postulated ways to break the electroweak gauge symmetry while maintaining unitarity without the presence of the Higgs boson. Of course, mathematical consistency is only half the battle in particle phys-

(45) ics; without evidence, these models cannot be considered more credible than the Standard. What's more, most physicists remain a far cry from abandoning Higgs boson-reliant models. M-theory, a cutting-edge, theoretical branch of string theory that may someday resolve the mathematical inconsistencies of modern physics, has successfully integrated the Standard and Supersymmetric gauge models—both of which currently rely on the presence of the

(50) Higgs boson.

    In any event, the answer looms near on the horizon. Though Tevatron continues to encounter financial setbacks, since coming online in 2009, CERN's seventeen-mile long Large Hadron Collider continues to advance and expand the search for the Higgs boson. At the LHC's current pace of operation, many predict that—if indeed the particle exists—a Higgs

(55) event will be observed and recorded in the very near future. And while it will necessarily require several years of analysis and experimental replication to fully verify such a discovery, the world hasn't much longer to wait for the first firm, material evidence for or against the existence of the elusive "God particle."

*A gauge particle is an elementary particle that carries a fundamental interaction of nature.
**A photon is a gauge particle responsible for electromagnetic radiation and is also known as the particle of light.

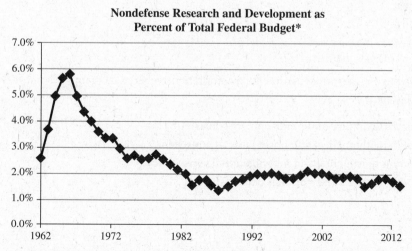

Nondefense Research and Development as Percent of Total Federal Budget*

*Source: AAAS estimates based on Budget of the U.S. Government Historical Tables.
http://www.aaas.org/page/historical-trends-federal-rd

1. It can reasonably be inferred that the author's overall stance on the existence of the Higgs boson particle is

   (A) studied neutrality.
   (B) a strong belief in its existence.
   (C) ignorant confusion.
   (D) a strong skepticism about its existence.

2. The passage suggests that at the time the passage was written, the scientific consensus about the existence of the Higgs boson was

   (A) indubitably conclusive.
   (B) generally unsettled.
   (C) worryingly confused.
   (D) unwaveringly skeptical.

3. As used in line 17, "imparting" most nearly means

   (A) breaking.
   (B) defining.
   (C) reproducing.
   (D) bestowing.

4. The primary function of lines 22–25 ("Metaphorically, . . . protons") in the paragraph as a whole is to

   (A) introduce poetic rhetorical devices to provide aesthetic language.
   (B) summarize the principle argument of the passage.
   (C) explain the mechanism whereby the Higgs particle can be detected.
   (D) clarify an esoteric concept for laypeople.

5. The passage indicates that at the time of the author's writing there remained about what percent of potential particle vectors of the Higgs for physicists to investigate?

   (A) 30%
   (B) 60%
   (C) 70%
   (D) 95%

6. The passage suggests that in order for a comprehensive physical theory to achieve widespread acceptance, it must have

   (A) both theoretical and philosophical consistency.
   (B) both mathematical and observational consistency.
   (C) both experimental and investigational consistency.
   (D) both standard and symmetrical consistency.

7. Which choice provides the best evidence for the answer to the previous question?

    (A) Lines 34–36 ("On the . . . fewer")
    (B) Lines 41–44 ("Several . . . Higgs boson")
    (C) Lines 44–45 ("Of course, . . . Standard")
    (D) Lines 55–58 ("And while . . . particle'")

8. As used in line 57, "material" most nearly means

    (A) stuff.
    (B) physical.
    (C) bodily.
    (D) theoretical.

9. Scientists eager to confirm or deny the existence of the Higgs boson would most likely want to see the percentage portrayed in the *y*-axis of the graph at

    (A) 6.5%.
    (B) 5.3%.
    (C) 4.8%.
    (D) 1.7%.

10. Based on the graph, would it be possible for overall U.S. governmental spending on research and development to have increased between 2004 and 2006?

    (A) No, because research and development decreased as a percent of the overall federal budget
    (B) No, because overall governmental spending decreased between 2004 and 2006
    (C) Yes, if the growth in overall governmental spending was sufficiently large
    (D) Yes, since the percentage of federal spending on research and development increased during this period

Answer Explanations

1. **(A)** The author presents a wide range of viewpoints on the plausibility of the existence of the Higgs boson particle and concludes the essay by stating that the world will find out relatively soon whether the Higgs boson exists. So this could best be described as "studied neutrality." The author clearly understands the subject matter well and has adopted a wait-and-see attitude rather than jumping to a conclusion. Choices (B) and (D) are too extreme. Given the author's in-depth analysis of the current status of particle physics, his stance could hardly be described as one of ignorant confusion as stated in choice (C).

2. **(B)** Line 51 states, "In any event, the answer looms near on the horizon," meaning that scientists do not yet definitively know whether or not the Higgs boson exists. If its existence is confirmed, then choice (A) could work. However, that is not the status at the time of the writing of this passage. Although the passage contains some confusion and some skepticism about the Higgs boson, choices (C) and (D) are too extreme in their descriptions.

3. **(D)** Based on the context of the paragraph, the Higgs boson is giving or "bestowing" mass to particles that would otherwise be massless. It is not breaking down particles but, instead, slowing them down, making choice (A) incorrect. The Higgs boson is not defining the particles, as in choice (B), since it is helping the particles come into a masslike form rather than giving them their essence. It is not causing more particles to be created from each other, making choice (C) incorrect.

4. **(D)** Immediately before this metaphor is a rather complicated discussion of how the Higgs boson field is thought to operate to give particles mass. The function of these lines is to help clarify this difficult (esoteric) concept for laypeople (nonphysicists) so they can understand a challenging idea in terms they can relate to. Choice (A) is wrong because the objective is to help the reader understand a difficult idea, not to insert a poetic aside. Choice (B) is not correct because this is a minor point of the passage. Choice (C) is incorrect because it focuses on how the Higgs boson provides mass, not on how it can be detected.

5. **(A)** Line 33 reports that scientists have sifted through 70% of the particle's estimated vectors, meaning 100% – 70% = 30% of the particle vectors are left for physicists to investigate.

6. **(B)** Lines 44–45 speak of an answer to this. They state that half of the battle in creating a physical theory is mathematical consistency and the other half is experimental evidence. So there will be both mathematical and observational (from experimental observations) consistency. Choice (A) is wrong because the passage does not mention philosophical consistency. Choice (C) is incorrect because investigational and experimental are synonymous. Choice (D) is not right because these terms focus on minor specific names and aspects of theories rather than on their general characteristics.

7. **(C)** These lines most directly support the notion that one needs both mathematical and observational consistency to have a sound theory. Choice (A) focuses on the difficulty of finding the Higgs boson. Choice (B) focuses on different theories about the Higgs. Choice (D) focuses on the hope that the Higgs boson will be discovered in the near future.

8. **(B)** The scientists are seeking experimental, observational, physical evidence that the Higgs boson exists because they already have a mathematically consistent model for it. Referring to the evidence as "stuff," as in choice (A), would not be appropriate. "Bodily," choice (C), is incorrect because the evidence would come from physical observations of nonliving things, not from humans and other animals. Choice (D) is not right because the theory is already mathematically consistent—the actual observation is lacking.

9. **(A)** In order for scientists to confirm or deny the existence of the Higgs boson particle, they would want to invest as much money as possible into scientific research and development so they could create more experimental opportunities to observe the particle. Choice (A) has the highest percent of the options, so it is correct.

10. **(C)** This question involves thinking critically and creatively about the numbers and statistics presented in the graph. In the graph, the percentage of the budget devoted to research and development remained fairly level, even dropping slightly. Despite this, if the amount from which these percentages are taken goes up enough, then the overall amount can increase even though the percentage remains about the same. If you take 10 percent of 100 dollars and then take 10 percent of 300 dollars, the value will increase from 10 dollars to 30 dollars even though the percentage remains the same. So if the overall growth in government spending was sufficiently large, it would allow for an increase in research spending even though the percentage remained level. Choices (A) and (B) are incorrect because it is possible that research and development spending increased. Choice (D) is not right because it contradicts the fact that spending on research decreased.

Passage 1 and Passage 2 Practice

One of the nonfiction passages you will come across will contain two shorter selections. The last few questions for this passage will relate to the relationship between the two selections. Consider the following tactics.

TACTIC 5: CONSIDER READING PASSAGE 1 AND DOING ITS QUESTIONS FIRST, AND THEN READING PASSAGE 2 AND DOING ITS QUESTIONS AFTERWARD.

This is a good approach if you have trouble focusing on two different passages simultaneously. Since the questions go in order of where they are found in the passage, the first few questions will be just about Passage 1 and the next few will be just about Passage 2. Then you can try the questions about both passages at the end.

TACTIC 6: BE MINDFUL OF HOW THE PASSAGES RELATE TO ONE ANOTHER SINCE AT LEAST A COUPLE QUESTIONS WILL ASK YOU ABOUT THE PASSAGE RELATIONSHIP.

Actively ask questions about what the main thesis of each passage is while you are reading, and you will be in great shape when it comes time to do the last few questions for a Passage 1 and Passage 2 combination.

Questions 1–10 are based on the following passages.

Two scientists analyze the impact of advances in genetic research.

Passage 1

The completion of the Human Genome Project in February 2001 marked a new era for individualized patient medicine. With a complete genetic map of humans available to scientists and researchers all over the world, new diagnostic tools, prevention methods, and treatments for diseases are created on a daily basis. While many new genetic technologies are decades away from being introduced to the general public, there are still many other genetic technologies in use today that are changing previously negative outcomes to positive ones for many patients.

The move from broad-spectrum interventions to individualized treatments based on a patient's genetic map is a sign that the future of medicine is here. For example, 20 years ago, if a patient were diagnosed with breast cancer, she would be offered the routine treatment of surgery, chemotherapy, and radiation. While this treatment plan was successful for many, there was still a very high percentage of disease relapse in patients. Treatment options for breast cancer patients today have radically changed with the discovery of genetic variation in cancers. While the previous medical professional theory was that breast cancer was the same in all patients, the finding of *BRCA1* and *BRCA2* genes revolutionized the way physicians prevent and treat breast cancer in women. With a focused treatment plan such as dietary changes, targeted chemotherapy, and general lifestyle changes, patients are experiencing better outcomes. Testing for *BRCA1* and *BRCA2* genes in family lines has also given women the opportunity to know if they are susceptible to the disease, which can significantly decrease the rate of occurrence.

Individualized patient medicine is not limited to the prevention and treatment of cancer. As genetic technologies continue to improve, parents can determine if they are a carrier of a recessive gene that may be passed to their child or adults can prepare to tackle a degenerative disease, such as Huntington's disease. For some, it is extremely helpful to know what medical trials they may face in the future so that they can make informed decisions about early intervention options. While many treatment options are still in the trial phase, patients receiving the treatment have not only seen an increase in life expectancy, but an increase in quality of life during those years. This is a triumphant achievement in medicine, as just a few years ago some patients, upon receiving a diagnosis, would be told that there were no treatment options even available. However, now physicians are able to provide targeted treatment options based on a patient's genetic make-up. As genetic technologies continue to develop, additional treatments will become available that will hopefully eradicate many prominent diseases.

Passage 2

Where do we draw the line with the advancement of genetic research? This is an important question to answer as new genetic research is performed on a daily basis and only some regulations are in place to monitor the research on an international level. While many argue that genetic research, thus far, has been positive, others have expressed concern that the continued development of genetic research could lead to severe consequences for society.

The completion of the human genome sequence has helped researchers identify key components of what makes a human. While the identification of certain genes in the genome has led to the advancement of treatment for prominent diseases, like cancer, other identified genes have started the discussion of "designer babies." Since we now know what genes

The *Line* marker appears at line 5, and line numbers (5), (10), (15), (20), (25), (30), (35), (40) appear in the left margin.

contribute to our hair, eye, and skin color, it is possible to create a baby that displays many desired physical attributes. To some, this genetic alteration is harmless, but others believe

(45) it could cause irrevocable harm to nature. Medical professionals have expressed additional concern with the unknown, long-term effects of deleting and inserting gene sequences as this technology is only in the beginning stages. Due to many unknowns of this technology, the United States government has placed a ban on germline manipulation until research can confirm that the benefits outweigh the risks.

(50) Others worry about the possibility of genetic discrimination. As the genetic research community continues to explore the human genome, there will be an increase in the identification of different genes that contribute to diseases such as diabetes and mental illness. Some fear that identification of such genes could lead to discrimination against individuals seeking health insurance coverage or even a job. Finding a balance with genetic research will be

(55) vitally important as researchers navigate new discoveries, so that advancements will help society, not harm it.

1. The author of Passage 1 suggests that a current advantage of genetically based medical treatments over more conventional treatments is their

   (A) greater future potential.
   (B) greater precision.
   (C) ethical objectivity.
   (D) increased popularity.

2. Which option gives the best evidence for the answer to the previous question?

   (A) Lines 1–2 ("The completion . . . medicine")
   (B) Lines 4–5 ("While many . . . public")
   (C) Lines 16–18 ("With a . . . outcomes")
   (D) Lines 22–24 ("As genetic . . . disease")

3. The sentence in lines 4–7 ("While many . . . patients") primarily serves to

   (A) consider objections to the author's views.
   (B) describe details of newfound medical processes.
   (C) suggest that science is slow to advance.
   (D) state the thesis of the passage.

4. As used in line 10, "routine" most closely means

   (A) typical.
   (B) repetitive.
   (C) personalized.
   (D) simple.

5. What is the point of Passage 2?

   (A) To consider the possible implications of an issue
   (B) To forecast the results of a scientific advance
   (C) To survey scholarly opinion on the foundations of genetics
   (D) To argue against scientific progress

6. As used in line 50, "discrimination" most closely means

(A) racism.
(B) bias.
(C) hatred.
(D) prosecution.

7. The author of Passage 2 would most likely categorize the author of Passage 1 under which of the following labels?

(A) "Many," line 36
(B) "Others," line 37
(C) "Researchers," line 39
(D) "Professionals," line 45

8. The author of Passage 2 would most likely raise which of the following concerns about the situation mentioned in lines 22–24 of Passage 1 ("As genetic . . . disease")?

(A) That the child who has a chance of receiving the gene may be discriminated against by insurance companies
(B) That the parents would not be able to predict the likelihood of their child developing the disease
(C) That the child would have his or her facial features artificially manipulated in his or her childhood
(D) That the resources spent on the child's care could be better spent on other scientific research

9. Which option gives the best evidence for the answer to the previous question?

(A) Lines 34–36 ("This is . . . level")
(B) Lines 42–44 ("Since we . . . attributes")
(C) Lines 45–47 ("Medical . . . stages")
(D) Lines 52–54 ("Some . . . job")

10. The authors of Passage 1 and Passage 2 have respective attitudes toward genetic research that are best described as

(A) positive, negative.
(B) scientific, historical.
(C) optimistic, cautious.
(D) hopeful, apocalyptic.

Answer Explanations

1. **(B)** The author states in line 16 that individualized (genetically based) treatments are more focused than broad-spectrum (traditional) treatments. Therefore, individualized treatments are more precise, as in choice (B). Furthermore, the author also states in lines 9–12 that although traditional methods do work for many patients, many patients also relapse. This shows that precision is lacking in the traditional methods. Choice (A) is incorrect because the question asks for a current advantage rather than a future one. Choice (C) is incorrect because the ethics of treatment are not discussed in the passage. Choice (D) is wrong because the author states in lines 4–6 that many of these new methods are far from being available to the general public.

2. **(C)** The correct answer is choice (C) because these lines champion individualized medicine as more "focused" than traditional methods; in other words, they are more precise. Even without knowing the correct answer to the previous question, you could have used the process of elimination to realize that only choice (C) discusses a current advantage of utilizing genetic advances in medicine. Choice (A) is incorrect because it merely says that the Human Genome Project revolutionized individualized medicine but doesn't give any advantages. Choice (B) is wrong because it states that much of individualized medicine is not yet readily available to the public, which clearly is not a current advantage. Choice (D) discusses the potential future directions of individualized medicine but not the current advantages.

3. **(D)** It's best to approach this question by summing up the lines in your own words. The gist of these lines is that the field of genetic medicine still has a long way to go but is already making a positive difference in the lives of patients. Because this also sums up the passage, it's a good thesis statement, choice (D). It supports the author's view rather than considering objections, making choice (A) incorrect. Choice (B) is incorrect because it certainly doesn't describe any medical processes in detail. Choice (C) may be tempting because these lines say that much of this technology isn't readily available to the public. However, the author is simply stating this rather than passing judgment about the pace of development.

4. **(A)** For this question, you can come up with your own synonym for the word given the context and then match it to an answer choice. In this case, "routine treatment" may be replaced with something like standard treatment. The closest choice to standard is choice (A), "typical." This makes sense given the context because the author is referring to this treatment in contrast with the cutting-edge genetic treatment. Choice (B) doesn't make sense because we don't know how repetitive the standard treatment is. Choice (C) would be correct in referring to the genetic treatment but not to the broad-spectrum treatment referenced here. Choice (D) is wrong because it's unlikely that the combination of surgery, chemotherapy, and radiation is simple.

5. **(A)** Passage 2 raises the question of how far people are willing to go with genetic research and then considers possible implications, such as negative effects from altering genes and discrimination against those with certain genes. Therefore, this could be described as considering the implications of an issue, as in answer choice (A). Choice (B) doesn't work because the author is just considering what might happen, not predicting or forecasting, it. Choice (C) is wrong because no scholarly opinions are considered. Choice (D) is incorrect because the author admits that genetic research can be very helpful in treating certain diseases.

6. **(B)** This line is about the discrimination of people with certain genes; another way to say this is that these people may experience a "bias," choice (B). "Racism," in choice (A), is another type of discrimination. However in this case, the discrimination is against people with certain genes rather than of certain races. Choice (C) is too extreme. Choice (D) is wrong because legal action isn't going to be taken against these people.

7. **(A)** Choice (A) refers to "many" people who argue that genetic research has been positive. The author of Passage 1 could certainly fall into this group of people, because Passage 1 is about how genetic research is leading to more effective, individualized medical treatment. Choice (B) is wrong because Passage 1 does not consider any severe consequences of genetic research. Choices (C) and (D) don't work because we have no reason to believe that the author of Passage 1 is either a researcher or a medical professional.

8. **(A)** The author of Passage 2 would most likely be concerned that this sort of information could actually be harmful because of the potential for genetic discrimination. The excerpt from lines 52-54 supports this notion. Passage 2 does not indicate that any of the other instances would present major concerns.

9. **(D)** These lines provide direct support to the notion that parents may have trouble finding health insurance for a child who had a condition that was expensive to cover. The other options do not provide direct support for this claim.

10. **(C)** Passage 1's author primarily considers the benefits of genetic research, so his viewpoint could be expressed as positive, optimistic, or hopeful. Passage 2's author concedes that genetic research can be very helpful in treating some diseases but is not without risks. Therefore, this author can best be described as cautious or balanced. Choice (C) has correct adjectives for both authors. Choice (A) is incorrect because Passage 2's author is more balanced than negative. Choice (B) is incorrect because neither passage is overly scientific or historical. Choice (D) is incorrect because "apocalyptic" is far too negative for Passage 2.

TROUBLESHOOTING

Here are some further pointers for common issues.

"I can't stay focused when I read."

- Be certain you get a good night's sleep before the PSAT. You will start the PSAT with the Reading Section. So if you are tired and groggy, it will go poorly. Staying focused is extremely difficult when you are exhausted. Don't stay up late the night before the test doing last-minute cramming; it is not worth it.

- Don't try to remember too much when you read. You only need to remember the general meaning of the passage—you should go back when you need to find details. This is not a school-based test for which you need to memorize many details.

- Try doing the passages in an order you choose. The simple act of choosing what passages to try first empowers you to take more ownership of what you read, instead of feeling that you're stuck reading a boring passage out of necessity. Build momentum by starting with the passages that come easiest to you.

"I finish too early."

- Consider what would be the best use of your extra time—surely it is not to just sit there and stare off into space for several minutes at the end of the test. Perhaps you can spend more time reading the passages, formulating your own answers to questions, or carefully dissecting the answer choices. Experiment with some practice passages to see where the extra time will be most helpful for you.

- Have a watch when you take the test so you can be mindful of how quickly you are working. Try to maintain about a 5 minute pace in reading the passages, and about a 7 minute pace for completing the set of accompanying questions for each passage.

"I go too slowly."

- Diagnose what is taking you the most time. Typically, students spend too much time either reading the passages or evaluating each answer choice. If you are spending too much time reading the passage, remind yourself that this is an open-book test and that you only need to paraphrase the general idea of the passage. If you are spending too much time breaking down the choices, shift your energy to reading the questions more carefully and formulating your own answer; that way, you will be much more decisive when you go to the answer choices.

- Let go of perfectionist tendencies. You will not have time to double-check every answer, and you may not have time to do every question. The PSAT is heavily curved, and you can still achieve National Merit recognition even if you miss some questions.

"I get it down to two choices, and I can't decide."

- Even though this isn't the Math section know that there will be one answer that is definitely correct. If you are not seeing it, make sure you understand the context of the passage and make sure you have a firm grasp of what the question is asking. Do not allow yourself to become frantic and panicked because you feel you have come across a "trick" question.

- Look for "contamination" in the choices. Even one incorrect word can ruin an entire answer choice. Instead of looking for the "best" answer, look for the "flawless" answer—this mindset will help you more rigorously analyze the answer choices without being seduced by the incorrect options.

 TIP
Do not underestimate how important it is to be well-rested for test day.

TIP
Practice under timed conditions so that proper pacing becomes second nature.

FURTHER PREPARATION

What else can I do beyond this book to prepare for the PSAT Reading Test?

TIP

Don't forget to try reading passages in the next chapter, "Advanced Reading Drills," for more challenging practice.

- Practice with Barron's books for the SAT: *Barron's SAT* has plenty of practice tests you can try.
- Use the online vocabulary resource that accompanies this book if you have trouble with the words-in-context questions. See the card at the front of this book for online access.
- Use the free reading practice tests and resources provided by College Board on *KhanAcademy.org*.
- Focus on your most difficult passage types—fiction, global documents, science, etc.—and turn them into strengths. To challenge yourself even further, you may want to try reading passages for the GRE, GMAT, and MCAT; the passages you find on graduate school admissions tests will surely be more challenging than what you will face on test day.
- Read, read, read. At a minimum, read high-quality books for pleasure, such as ones that have won the Pulitzer Prize or Booker Prize. At a maximum, seek out articles and books that you find most challenging, and read those in your spare time. The more widely you read, the greater the likelihood that you will have some baseline familiarity with the topics you encounter on the PSAT.

Advanced Reading Drills 2

To earn National Merit recognition, you will need to score at an elite level on the PSAT. The following 12 drills represent the most challenging types of reading passages and questions you will encounter on the PSAT. You can practice all of these or focus on the passages that give you the most difficulty:

- Fiction: *Almayer's Folly*
- Fiction: "The Fall of the House of Usher"
- Fiction: "Adventure"
- Great Global Conversation: Jefferson
- Great Global Conversation: Frederick Douglass
- Great Global Conversation: Emerson and Arnold
- Social Science: Russian Depopulation
- Social Science: The Emu War
- Science: Caffeine
- Science: Fungi
- Science: Methanogenesis
- Science: Wound Healing

To practice these passages under timed conditions, take about 12 minutes per drill. Answer explanations for each drill are at the end of the chapter.

FICTION

Fiction: *Almayer's Folly*

Almayer's Folly is Joseph Conrad's first novel, published in 1895. Almayer, a poor businessman, dreams of acquiring wealth.

"Kaspar! Makan!"

The well-known shrill voice startled Almayer from his dream of splendid future into the unpleasant realities of the present hour. An unpleasant voice too. He had heard it for many years, and with every year he liked it less. No matter; there would be an end to all this soon.

Line

(5)   He shuffled uneasily, but took no further notice of the call. Leaning with both his elbows on the balustrade of the verandah, he went on looking fixedly at the great river that flowed—indifferent and hurried—before his eyes. He liked to look at it about the time of sunset; perhaps because at that time the sinking sun would spread a glowing gold tinge on the waters of the Pantai, and Almayer's thoughts were often busy with gold; gold he had failed to secure;

(10) gold the others had secured—dishonestly, of course—or gold he meant to secure yet, through his own honest exertions, for himself and Nina. He absorbed himself in his dream of wealth and power away from this coast where he had dwelt for so many years, forgetting the bitterness of toil and strife in the vision of a great and splendid reward. They would live in Europe, he and his daughter. They would be rich and respected. Nobody would think of her mixed

(15) blood in the presence of her great beauty and of his immense wealth. Witnessing her triumphs he would grow young again, he would forget the twenty-five years of heart-breaking struggle on this coast where he felt like a prisoner. All this was nearly within his reach. Let only Dain return! And return soon he must—in his own interest, for his own share. He was now more than a week late! Perhaps he would return to-night. Such were Almayer's thoughts

(20) as, standing on the verandah of his new but already decaying house—that last failure of his life—he looked on the broad river. There was no tinge of gold on it this evening, for it had been swollen by the rains, and rolled an angry and muddy flood under his inattentive eyes, carrying small driftwood and big dead logs, and whole uprooted trees with branches and foliage, amongst which the water swirled and roared angrily.

(25)   One of those drifting trees grounded on the shelving shore, just by the house, and Almayer, neglecting his dream, watched it with languid interest. The tree swung slowly round, amid the hiss and foam of the water, and soon getting free of the obstruction began to move down stream again, rolling slowly over, raising upwards a long, denuded branch, like a hand lifted in mute appeal to heaven against the river's brutal and unnecessary violence. Almayer's interest

(30) in the fate of that tree increased rapidly. He leaned over to see if it would clear the low point below. It did; then he drew back, thinking that now its course was free down to the sea, and he envied the lot of that inanimate thing now growing small and indistinct in the deepening darkness. As he lost sight of it altogether he began to wonder how far out to sea it would drift. Would the current carry it north or south? South, probably, till it drifted in sight of Celebes, as

(35) far as Macassar, perhaps!

Macassar! Almayer's quickened fancy distanced the tree on its imaginary voyage, but his memory lagging behind some twenty years or more in point of time saw a young and slim Almayer, clad all in white and modest-looking, landing from the Dutch mail-boat on the dusty jetty of Macassar, coming to woo fortune in the godowns of old Hudig. It was an important

(40) epoch in his life, the beginning of a new existence for him. His father, a subordinate official employed in the Botanical Gardens of Buitenzorg, was no doubt delighted to place his son

in such a firm. The young man himself too was nothing loth to leave the poisonous shores of Java, and the meagre comforts of the parental bungalow, where the father grumbled all day at the stupidity of native gardeners, and the mother from the depths of her long easy-chair
(45) bewailed the lost glories of Amsterdam, where she had been brought up, and of her position as the daughter of a cigar dealer there.

Almayer had left his home with a light heart and a lighter pocket, speaking English well, and strong in arithmetic; ready to conquer the world, never doubting that he would.

1. How do the opening lines of the essay, lines 1–4 ("Kaspar . . . this soon"), serve to illustrate the overall internal conflict throughout the passage?

   (A) Almayer's dreams of wealth are interrupted by mundane reality.
   (B) Almayer's lack of cultural proficiency prevents him from achieving internal peace.
   (C) Almayer's relatively low personal assertiveness keeps him from having fulfilling relationships.
   (D) Almayer's struggles with hallucinations haunt his quest for rational thought.

2. How does Almayer contrast himself with those who have been more financially successful?

   (A) He argues that he is more intelligent.
   (B) He acknowledges that they are more motivated.
   (C) He asserts that he is more virtuous.
   (D) He grants that they are more clever.

3. Which option gives the best evidence for the answer to the previous question?

   (A) Lines 5–7 ("He shuffled . . . his eyes")
   (B) Lines 9–11 ("Almayer's . . . Nina")
   (C) Lines 14–17 ("They would . . . prisoner")
   (D) Lines 18–21 ("He was . . . river")

4. As used in line 18, "share" most closely means

   (A) part.
   (B) communication.
   (C) gift.
   (D) disclosure.

5. Almayer's attitude as expressed in lines 31–33 ("It did . . . darkness") compares in what way to his attitude when he first set out on his journey?

   (A) More optimistic
   (B) Less troubled
   (C) More hopeless
   (D) Less honest

6. Which option gives the best evidence for the answer to the previous question?

   (A) Lines 15–17 ("Witnessing . . . prisoner")
   (B) Lines 25–26 ("One of . . . interest")
   (C) Lines 44–46 ("the mother . . . there")
   (D) Lines 47–48 ("Almayer . . . would")

7. It is most reasonable to infer that Dain is someone who Almayer believes

   (A) is a skilled seafarer.
   (B) will help him become rich.
   (C) is a close relative.
   (D) will take him and his daughter to Europe.

8. As used in line 31, "free" most closely means

   (A) willful.
   (B) unhindered.
   (C) empowered.
   (D) inexpensive.

9. What personality characteristic does the author most strongly suggest that Almayer has taken from his parents?

   (A) A disappointment that he is continually unable to find adequate nourishment.
   (B) A cosmopolitan open-mindedness to new cultures and experiences.
   (C) A fear of venturing too far from one's native land.
   (D) A disregard for what he believes his station in life should be and what it actually is.

Fiction: "The Fall of the House of Usher"

Below is the opening excerpt from Edgar Allan Poe's 1839 short story, "The Fall of the House of Usher," in which an unnamed narrator approaches the home of his childhood friend Roderick Usher after not having seen him for many years.

During the whole of a dull, dark, and soundless day in the autumn of the year, when the clouds hung oppressively low in the heavens, I had been passing alone, on horseback, through a singularly dreary tract of country, and at length found myself, as the shades of the evening

Line drew on, within view of the melancholy House of Usher. I know not how it was—but, with the

(5) first glimpse of the building, a sense of insufferable gloom pervaded my spirit. I say insufferable; for the feeling was unrelieved by any of that half-pleasurable, because poetic, sentiment, with which the mind usually receives even the sternest natural images of the desolate or terrible. I looked upon the scene before me—upon the mere house, and the simple landscape features of the domain—upon the bleak walls—upon the vacant eye-like windows—upon a

(10) few rank sedges—and upon a few white trunks of decayed trees—with an utter depression of soul which I can compare to no earthly sensation more properly than to the after-dream of the reveller upon opium—the bitter lapse into every-day life—the hideous dropping off of the veil. There was an iciness, a sinking, a sickening of the heart—an unredeemed dreariness of thought which no goading of the imagination could torture into aught of the sublime. What

(15) was it—I paused to think—what was it that so unnerved me in the contemplation of the House of Usher? It was a mystery all insoluble; nor could I grapple with the shadowy fancies that crowded upon me as I pondered. I was forced to fall back upon the unsatisfactory conclusion, that while, beyond doubt, there *are* combinations of very simple natural objects which have the power of thus affecting us, still the analysis of this power lies among considerations

(20) beyond our depth. It was possible, I reflected, that a mere different arrangement of the particulars of the scene, of the details of the picture, would be sufficient to modify, or perhaps to annihilate its capacity for sorrowful impression; and, acting upon this idea, I reined my horse to the precipitous brink of a black and lurid tarn that lay in unruffled lustre by the dwelling, and gazed down—but with a shudder even more thrilling than before—upon the remodelled

(25) and inverted images of the gray sedge, and the ghastly tree-stems, and the vacant and eye-like windows.

Nevertheless, in this mansion of gloom I now proposed to myself a sojourn of some weeks. Its proprietor, Roderick Usher, had been one of my boon companions in boyhood; but many years had elapsed since our last meeting. A letter, however, had lately reached me in a distant

(30) part of the country—a letter from him—which, in its wildly importunate nature, had admitted of no other than a personal reply. The MS. gave evidence of nervous agitation. The writer spoke of acute bodily illness—of a mental disorder which oppressed him—and of an earnest desire to see me, as his best and indeed his only personal friend, with a view of attempting, by the cheerfulness of my society, some alleviation of his malady. It was the manner in which all

(35) this, and much more, was said—it was the apparent *heart* that went with his request—which allowed me no room for hesitation; and I accordingly obeyed forthwith what I still considered a very singular summons.

Although, as boys, we had been even intimate associates, yet I really knew little of my friend. His reserve had been always excessive and habitual. I was aware, however, that his

(40) very ancient family had been noted, time out of mind, for a peculiar sensibility of temperament, displaying itself, through long ages, in many works of exalted art, and manifested, of

late, in repeated deeds of munificent yet unobtrusive charity, as well as in a passionate devotion to the intricacies, perhaps even more than to the orthodox and easily recognizable beauties, of musical science. I had learned, too, the very remarkable fact, that the stem of the Usher *(45)* race, all time-honored as it was, had put forth, at no period, any enduring branch; in other words, that the entire family lay in the direct line of descent, and had always, with very trifling and very temporary variation, so lain.

1. Which option best describes what happens in the passage?

   (A) A traveler contemplates the best solution to a problem.
   (B) A man attempts to reconnect with his childhood best friend.
   (C) A character recounts his impressions and analysis of a situation.
   (D) A narrator tells the story of a famous and idiosyncratic family.

2. The tone of the first paragraph is one of

   (A) destruction.
   (B) sorrow.
   (C) foreboding.
   (D) mindfulness.

3. What best captures the narrator's sentiments about his capacity to understand the mystery of the House of Usher?

   (A) He feels intellectually capable.
   (B) He feels professionally untrained.
   (C) He feels largely optimistic.
   (D) He feels generally inadequate.

4. Which option gives the best evidence for the answer to the previous question?

   (A) Lines 5–8 ("I say . . . terrible")
   (B) Lines 13–14 ("There was . . . sublime")
   (C) Lines 16–17 ("It was . . . pondered")
   (D) Lines 22–24 ("I reined . . . before")

5. As used in line 34, "society" most closely means

   (A) civilization.
   (B) culture.
   (C) association.
   (D) order.

6. It can most reasonably be inferred from the passage that the narrator responds as he did to the letter out of a sense of

   (A) obligation.
   (B) sorrow.
   (C) longing.
   (D) terror.

7. Which option gives the best evidence for the answer to the previous question?

    (A) Lines 4–5 ("I know . . . spirit")

    (B) Lines 13–16 ("There was . . . Usher")

    (C) Lines 34–37 ("It was . . . summons")

    (D) Lines 39–41 ("I was . . . exalted art")

8. As used in line 39, "reserve" most closely means

    (A) greed.

    (B) openhandedness.

    (C) preparedness.

    (D) detachment.

9. Lines 44–47 ("I had . . . so lain") suggest that at any point in its history, the Usher family would have had how many heirs at a given time?

    (A) None

    (B) One

    (C) Two or more

    (D) The family had no heirs.

Fiction: "Adventure"

The passage below is adapted from "Adventure," in Sherwood Anderson's 1919 short-story collection Winesburg, Ohio.

Alice Hindman, a woman of twenty-seven when George Willard was a mere boy, had lived in Winesburg all her life. She clerked in Winney's Dry Goods Store and lived with her mother, who had married a second husband.

Line
(5) At twenty-seven Alice was tall and somewhat slight. Her head was large and overshadowed her body. Her shoulders were a little stooped and her hair and eyes brown. She was very quiet but beneath a placid exterior a continual ferment went on.

When she was a girl of sixteen and before she began to work in the store, Alice had an affair with a young man. The young man, named Ned Currie, was older than Alice. He, like George Willard, was employed on the *Winesburg Eagle* and for a long time he went to see Alice almost
(10) every evening. Together the two walked under the trees through the streets of the town and talked of what they would do with their lives. Alice was then a very pretty girl and Ned Currie took her into his arms and kissed her. He became excited and said things he did not intend to say and Alice, betrayed by her desire to have something beautiful come into her rather narrow life, also grew excited. She also talked. The outer crust of her life, all of her natural diffidence
(15) and reserve, was torn away and she gave herself over to the emotions of love. When, late in the fall of her sixteenth year, Ned Currie went away to Cleveland where he hoped to get a place on a city newspaper and rise in the world, she wanted to go with him. With a trembling voice she told him what was in her mind. "I will work and you can work," she said. "I do not want to harness you to a needless expense that will prevent your making progress. Don't marry me
(20) now. We will get along without that and we can be together. Even though we live in the same house no one will say anything. In the city we will be unknown and people will pay no attention to us."

Ned Currie was puzzled by the determination and abandon of his sweetheart and was also deeply touched. He had wanted the girl to become his mistress but changed his mind.
(25) He wanted to protect and care for her. "You don't know what you're talking about," he said sharply; "you may be sure I'll let you do no such thing. As soon as I get a good job I'll come back. For the present you'll have to stay here. It's the only thing we can do."

On the evening before he left Winesburg to take up his new life in the city, Ned Currie went to call on Alice. They walked about through the streets for an hour and then got a rig from
(30) Wesley Moyer's livery and went for a drive in the country. The moon came up and they found themselves unable to talk. In his sadness the young man forgot the resolutions he had made regarding his conduct with the girl.

They got out of the buggy at a place where a long meadow ran down to the bank of Wine Creek and there in the dim light became lovers. When at midnight they returned to town they
(35) were both glad. It did not seem to them that anything that could happen in the future could blot out the wonder and beauty of the thing that had happened. "Now we will have to stick to each other, whatever happens we will have to do that," Ned Currie said as he left the girl at her father's door.

The young newspaper man did not succeed in getting a place on a Cleveland paper and
(40) went west to Chicago. For a time he was lonely and wrote to Alice almost every day. Then he was caught up by the life of the city; he began to make friends and found new interests in life. In Chicago he boarded at a house where there were several women. One of them attracted his

attention and he forgot Alice in Winesburg. At the end of a year he had stopped writing letters, and only once in a long time, when he was lonely or when he went into one of the city parks (45) and saw the moon shining on the grass as it had shone that night on the meadow by Wine Creek, did he think of her at all.

1. The major thematic focus of the passage is on what characteristic of love?

   (A) Its impermanence
   (B) Its beauty
   (C) Its wholesomeness
   (D) Its potential for abuse

2. It is reasonable to infer that George Willard was approximately what age at the time that Alice initiated her affair with Ned Currie?

   (A) Unborn
   (B) Seven
   (C) Sixteen
   (D) Twenty-three

3. As an adult, the attitude that Alice has toward her past is best described as

   (A) fond.
   (B) forgetful.
   (C) unsettled.
   (D) sedate.

4. Which option gives the best evidence for the answer to the previous question?

   (A) Lines 4–5 ("At twenty-seven . . . brown")
   (B) Lines 5–6 ("She was . . . went on")
   (C) Lines 39–40 ("The young . . . every day")
   (D) Lines 43–46 ("At the end . . . her at all")

5. As used in line 24, "touched" most closely means

   (A) assaulted.
   (B) dashed.
   (C) matched.
   (D) moved.

6. Compared to Ned, Alice is much more

   (A) willing to make sacrifices for the benefit of their relationship.
   (B) determined to advanced her professional status.
   (C) motivated by physical attractiveness.
   (D) interested in moving away from their provincial small-town life.

7. Which option gives the best evidence for the answer to the previous question?

    (A) Lines 7–8 ("When she . . . man")

    (B) Lines 14–15 ("She also . . . love")

    (C) Lines 23–24 ("Ned . . . touched")

    (D) Lines 28–29 ("On the . . . Alice")

8. As used in line 31, "resolutions" most closely means

    (A) promises.

    (B) purposes.

    (C) solutions.

    (D) entreaties.

9. The surrounding context around Ned's statement in lines 36–37, "Now we . . . do that," suggests that this quote was

    (A) an outright deception.

    (B) somewhat disingenuous.

    (C) given under duress.

    (D) motivated by true love.

Great Global Conversation: Jefferson

Below are two letters sent by Thomas Jefferson of the United States of America, the first to Benjamin Franklin in 1777 and the second to George Washington in 1781.

Passage 1

Honorable Sir,

I forbear to write you news, as the time of Mr. Shore's departure being uncertain, it might be old before you receive it, and he can, in person, possess you of all we have. With respect to the
Line State of Virginia in particular, the people seem to have laid aside the monarchical, and taken
(5) up the republican government, with as much ease as would have attended their throwing off an old and putting on a new suit of clothes. Not a single throe has attended this important transformation. A half dozen aristocratical gentlemen, agonizing under the loss of pre-eminence, have sometimes ventured their sarcasms on our political metamorphosis. They have been thought fitter objects of pity than of punishment. We are at present in the complete and
(10) quiet exercise of well organized government, save only that our courts of justice do not open till the fall. I think nothing can bring the security of our continent and its cause into danger, if we can support the credit of our paper. To do that, I apprehend one of two steps must be taken. Either to procure free trade by alliance with some naval power able to protect it; or, if we find there is no prospect of that, to shut our ports totally to all the world, and turn our colonies
(15) into manufactories. The former would be most eligible, because most conformable to the habits and wishes of our people. Were the British Court to return to their senses in time to seize the little advantage which still remains within their reach from this quarter, I judge that, on acknowledging our absolute independence and sovereignty, a commercial treaty beneficial to them, and perhaps even a league of mutual offence and defence, might, not seeing the expense
(20) or consequences of such a measure, be approved by our people, if nothing in the mean time, done on your part, should prevent it. But they will continue to grasp at their desperate sovereignty, till every benefit short of that is for ever out of their reach. I wish my domestic situation had rendered it possible for me to join you in the very honorable charge confided to you. Residence in a polite Court, society of literati of the first order, a just cause and an approving
(25) God, will add length to a life for which all men pray, and none more than

Your most obedient
and humble servant,
Th: Jefferson.

Passage 2

Sir,

(30)   I have just received intelligence, which, though from a private hand, I believe is to be relied on, that a fleet of the enemy's ships have entered Cape Fear river, that eight of them had got over the bar, and many others were lying off; and that it was supposed to be a reinforcement to Lord Cornwallis, under the command of General Prevost. This account, which had come

through another channel, is confirmed by a letter from General Parsons at Halifax, to the
(35) gentleman who forwards it to me. I thought it of sufficient importance to be communicated
to your Excellency by the stationed expresses. The fatal want of arms puts it out of our power
to bring a greater force into the field, than will barely suffice to restrain the adventures of the
pitiful body of men they have at Portsmouth. Should any more be added to them, this country
will be perfectly open to them, by land as well as water.

(40) I have the honor to be, with all possible respect,
Your Excellency's most obedient
and most humble servant,
Th: Jefferson.

1. In Passage 1, Jefferson describes the Virginia governmental transition as

   (A) peaceful and orderly.
   (B) challenging and violent.
   (C) vengeful and political.
   (D) easy and trivial.

2. In Passage 1, Jefferson suggests that the American people would be open to which of the following with the British?

   (A) Political dependence
   (B) Economic reconciliation
   (C) Religious integration
   (D) Intellectual exchange

3. Which option gives the best evidence for the answer to the previous question?

   (A) Lines 9–12 ("We are . . . our paper")
   (B) Lines 13–15 ("Either to . . . manufactories")
   (C) Lines 18–21 ("a commercial . . . prevent it")
   (D) Lines 22–25 ("I wish . . . more than")

4. As used in line 12, "apprehend" most closely means

   (A) believe.
   (B) capture.
   (C) cease.
   (D) invent.

5. Jefferson uses lines 15–16 ("The former . . . people") to imply most directly that

   (A) Americans would prefer to continue to be able to purchase manufactured goods from abroad.
   (B) Americans are eager to achieve economic independence by creating domestic factories.
   (C) Americans are unwilling to engage in an entangling alliance with another country that would require the United States to enter foreign conflicts.
   (D) Americans are weary of the revolutionary conflict and would like to see its swift end.

6. The implied meaning of Jefferson's message in Passage 2 is that at the time of the letter, the American defense against the invading British force was

   (A) incapable of resistance.
   (B) likely to collapse if there were British reinforcements.
   (C) likely to defeat the insignificant force at Portsmouth.
   (D) capable of meeting and defeating the British on an open battlefield.

7. As used in line 36, "want" most closely means

   (A) desire.
   (B) abundance.
   (C) lack.
   (D) danger.

8. Both Passage 1 and Passage 2 have a tone of

   (A) obedience and inferiority.
   (B) aggression and anxiety.
   (C) practicality and avarice.
   (D) formality and deference.

9. Which of Jefferson's statements from Passage 1 demonstrated the greatest foresight given the issues mentioned in Passage 2?

   (A) Lines 7–8 ("A half dozen . . . metamorphosis")
   (B) Lines 9–11 ("We are . . . the fall")
   (C) Line 13 ("Either to . . . protect it")
   (D) Lines 22–23 ("I wish . . . to you")

10. The respective general themes of Passage 1 and Passage 2 are

    (A) militaristic and economic.
    (B) personal and reflective.
    (C) strategic and tactical.
    (D) pedestrian and urgent.

Great Global Conversation: Frederick Douglass

Below is the beginning of the autobiography Narrative of the Life of Frederick Douglass, *which was published in 1845 and became significant to the abolitionist movement.*

I was born in Tuckahoe, near Hillsborough, and about twelve miles from Easton, in Talbot County, Maryland. I have no accurate knowledge of my age, never having seen any authentic record containing it. By far the larger part of the slaves know as little of their ages as horses
Line know of theirs, and it is the wish of most masters within my knowledge to keep their slaves
(5) thus ignorant. I do not remember to have ever met a slave who could tell of his birthday. They seldom come nearer to it than planting-time, harvest-time, cherry-time, spring-time, or fall-time. A want of information concerning my own was a source of unhappiness to me even during childhood. The white children could tell their ages. I could not tell why I ought to be deprived of the same privilege. I was not allowed to make any inquiries of my master con-
(10) cerning it. He deemed all such inquiries on the part of a slave improper and impertinent, and evidence of a restless spirit. The nearest estimate I can give makes me now between twenty-seven and twenty-eight years of age. I come to this, from hearing my master say, some time during 1835, I was about seventeen years old.

My mother was named Harriet Bailey. She was the daughter of Isaac and Betsey Bailey,
(15) both colored, and quite dark. My mother was of a darker complexion than either my grand-mother or grandfather.

My father was a white man. He was admitted to be such by all I ever heard speak of my par-entage. The opinion was also whispered that my master was my father; but of the correctness of this opinion, I know nothing; the means of knowing was withheld from me. My mother and
(20) I were separated when I was but an infant—before I knew her as my mother. It is a common custom, in the part of Maryland from which I ran away, to part children from their mothers at a very early age. Frequently, before the child has reached its twelfth month, its mother is taken from it, and hired out on some farm a considerable distance off, and the child is placed under the care of an old woman, too old for field labor. For what this separation is done, I do not
(25) know, unless it be to hinder the development of the child's affection toward its mother, and to blunt and destroy the natural affection of the mother for the child. This is the inevitable result.

I never saw my mother, to know her as such, more than four or five times in my life; and each of these times was very short in duration, and at night. She was hired by a Mr. Stewart, who lived about twelve miles from my home. She made her journeys to see me in the night,
(30) travelling the whole distance on foot, after the performance of her day's work. She was a field hand, and a whipping is the penalty of not being in the field at sunrise, unless a slave has spe-cial permission from his or her master to the contrary—a permission which they seldom get, and one that gives to him that gives it the proud name of being a kind master. I do not recollect of ever seeing my mother by the light of day. She was with me in the night. She would lie down
(35) with me, and get me to sleep, but long before I waked she was gone. Very little communica-tion ever took place between us. Death soon ended what little we could have while she lived, and with it her hardships and suffering. She died when I was about seven years old, on one of my master's farms, near Lee's Mill. I was not allowed to be present during her illness, at her death, or burial.
(40) She was gone long before I knew any thing about it. Never having enjoyed, to any consid-erable extent, her soothing presence, her tender and watchful care, I received the tidings of her death with much the same emotions I should have probably felt at the death of a stranger.

1. The general point Douglass conveys in the first paragraph (lines 1–13) about knowing one's age is that

    (A) slaves managed to celebrate birthdays through careful estimations of their actual ages.
    (B) slaves were not granted basic personal identifying characteristics taken for granted by others.
    (C) there were some kind masters who overcame societal prejudice to see slaves as people, not property.
    (D) slaves did not know the fundamentals of arithmetic, having been denied math education by their masters.

2. As used in line 7, "want" most closely means

    (A) desire.
    (B) obstacle.
    (C) lack.
    (D) command.

3. Douglass expresses that his primary vehicle for learning about his origins was

    (A) his mother's private conversations.
    (B) the anecdotes of others.
    (C) documentary evidence.
    (D) spiritual revelation.

4. Which option gives the best evidence for the answer to the previous question?

    (A) Lines 10–11 ("He deemed . . . spirit")
    (B) Lines 17–18 ("My father . . . my father")
    (C) Lines 31–33 ("unless . . . master")
    (D) Lines 34–35 ("She was . . . gone")

5. It can reasonably be inferred from lines 24–26 that Frederick Douglass

    (A) was disappointed in his mother's lack of affection toward him.
    (B) was conditioned to feel little emotion toward his mother.
    (C) understands the true reason for the separation from his mother.
    (D) feels that the lack of his mother in his life hindered his intellectual development.

6. Douglass suggests that he met his father at what point in time?

    (A) As an infant
    (B) As a young child
    (C) As an adult
    (D) At no point

7. Douglass implies that his mother visited him only during the night because

    (A) she would face a harsh reprisal if she visited during the day.

    (B) she had other economic priorities besides child rearing.

    (C) she lived at an insurmountable distance from her son.

    (D) she had an unusual biological clock that made daytime activity a challenge.

8. Which option gives the best evidence for the answer to the previous question?

    (A) Lines 27–29 ("I never . . . home")

    (B) Lines 30–33 ("She was . . . master")

    (C) Lines 34–35 ("She was . . . gone")

    (D) Lines 35–37 ("Very little . . . suffering")

9. As used in line 41, "tidings" most closely means

    (A) news.

    (B) offerings.

    (C) remnants.

    (D) causes.

Great Global Conversation: Emerson and Arnold

The first passage is adapted from Ralph Waldo Emerson's essay "Nature," a foundational text of transcendentalism. Matthew Arnold, inspired by Emerson, wrote Literature and Science, *which is adapted for the second passage.*

Passage 1

Our age is retrospective. It builds the sepulchres of the fathers. It writes biographies, histo-
ries, and criticism. The foregoing generations beheld God and nature face to face; we, through
their eyes. Why should not we also enjoy an original relation to the universe? Why should not
Line we have a poetry and philosophy of insight and not of tradition, and a religion by revelation
(5) to us, and not the history of theirs? Embosomed for a season in nature, whose floods of life
stream around and through us, and invite us by the powers they supply, to action propor-
tioned to nature, why should we grope among the dry bones of the past, or put the living
generation into masquerade out of its faded wardrobe? The sun shines to-day also. There are
new lands, new men, new thoughts. Let us demand our own works and laws and worship.
(10) Undoubtedly we have no questions to ask which are unanswerable. We must trust the
perfection of the creation so far, as to believe that whatever curiosity the order of things has
awakened in our minds, the order of things can satisfy. Every man's condition is a solution
in hieroglyphic to those inquiries he would put. He acts it as life, before he apprehends it as
truth. In like manner, nature is already, in its forms and tendencies, describing its own design.
(15) Let us interrogate the great apparition, that shines so peacefully around us. Let us inquire, to
what end is nature?

All science has one aim, namely, to find a theory of nature. We have theories of races and
of functions, but scarcely yet a remote approach to an idea of creation. We are now so far from
the road to truth, that religious teachers dispute and hate each other, and speculative men
(20) are esteemed unsound and frivolous. But to a sound judgment, the most abstract truth is the
most practical. Whenever a true theory appears, it will be its own evidence.

Passage 2

Practical people talk with a smile of Plato and of his absolute ideas; and it is impossible
to deny that Plato's ideas do often seem unpractical and impracticable, and especially when
one views them in connexion with the life of a great work-a-day world like the United States.
(25) The necessary staple of the life of such a world Plato regards with disdain; handicraft and
trade and the working professions he regards with disdain; but what becomes of the life of an
industrial modern community if you take handicraft and trade and the working professions
out of it? The base mechanic arts and handicrafts, says Plato, bring about a natural weakness
in the principle of excellence in a man, so that he cannot govern the ignoble growths in him,
(30) but nurses them, and cannot understand fostering any other. Those who exercise such arts
and trades, as they have their bodies, he says, marred by their vulgar businesses, so they have
their souls, too, bowed and broken by them.

Nor do the working professions fare any better than trade at the hands of Plato. He draws
for us an inimitable picture of the working lawyer, and of his life of bondage; he shows how this
(35) bondage from his youth up has stunted and warped him, and made him small and crooked
of soul, encompassing him with difficulties which he is not man enough to rely on justice and
truth as means to encounter, but has recourse, for help out of them, to falsehood and wrong.

And so, says Plato, this poor creature is bent and broken, and grows up from boy to man without a particle of soundness in him, although exceedingly smart and clever in his own esteem.

(40)   One cannot refuse to admire the artist who draws these pictures. But we say to ourselves that his ideas show the influence of a primitive and obsolete order of things, when the warrior caste and the priestly caste were alone in honour, and the humble work of the world was done by slaves. We have now changed all that; the modern majority consists in work, as Emerson declares; and in work, we may add, principally of such plain and dusty kind as the work of

(45) cultivators of the ground, handicraftsmen, men of trade and business, men of the working professions.

1. The fundamental question raised by the first paragraph of Passage 1 is

   (A) why is it that scientific inquiry is dismissed in favor of political dogma?
   (B) why are philosophers considered superior to more practical professionals?
   (C) why shouldn't archaeology take precedence over historical research?
   (D) why can't modern society directly have transcendental experiences?

2. As used in line 3, "original" most closely means

   (A) special.
   (B) creative.
   (C) inventive.
   (D) formal.

3. According to Passage 1, Emerson has what attitude toward the human capacity for understanding?

   (A) Optimism
   (B) Skepticism
   (C) Abstraction
   (D) Historicism

4. Which option gives the best evidence for the answer to the previous question?

   (A) Lines 3–5 ("Why should . . . theirs")
   (B) Lines 10–12 ("Undoubtedly . . . satisfy")
   (C) Lines 15–16 ("Let us . . . nature")
   (D) Line 17 ("All science . . . nature")

5. According to Passage 2, Matthew Arnold has what overall feelings about Plato's ideas?

   (A) That they are interesting yet overly practical
   (B) That they are comprehensive yet indecipherable
   (C) That they are admirable yet outdated
   (D) That they are melancholy yet applicable

6. Which option gives the best evidence for the answer to the previous question?

   (A) Lines 30–32 ("Those who . . . by them")
   (B) Lines 38–39 ("And so . . . his own esteem")
   (C) Lines 40–43 ("But we say . . . by slaves")
   (D) Lines 44–46 ("and in work . . . professions")

7. As used in line 39, "soundness" most closely means

   (A) safety.
   (B) strength.
   (C) intelligence.
   (D) eloquence.

8. In Passage 2, Arnold's description of Plato's philosophy toward work can be summarized as

   (A) true strength is evident only in those who put the needs of others before themselves.
   (B) those who cannot make themselves useful to society are little more than parasites.
   (C) the demands of one's profession will limit the loftiness of one's being.
   (D) true nobility of soul is more likely to be found among those who work by hand than in those who use machines.

9. According to Passage 1 and Passage 2, Emerson and Plato, respectively, place great value on what in their pursuits of wisdom?

   (A) Religious revelation and scientific inquiry
   (B) Practical observation and abstract ideas
   (C) Legal theory and mathematical reasoning
   (D) Professional experience and industrial engineering

10. Which statement from Passage 1 is it reasonable to infer that Plato would have found most offensive?

   (A) Line 3 ("Why should . . universe")
   (B) Lines 8–9 ("There are . . . thoughts")
   (C) Line 15 ("Let us . . . around us")
   (D) Lines 19–20 ("speculative . . . frivolous")

SOCIAL SCIENCE

Social Science: Russian Depopulation

Russia, the geographically largest country in the world, is facing the biggest long-term problem any country can: depopulation. This problem is difficult to solve, however, as no one factor caused it. Rather, the roots of the issue lie in low life expectancy, low birth rates, and the gradual disintegration of the traditional Russian family.

(5) The beginning of the demographic problem is in Russia's low life expectancy. The life expectancy at birth for Russian males is only 64.7 years, and while the life expectancy for women is much longer, having the male half of the population die so early, before many men in the United States even retire, causes great concern.[1] This low male life expectancy has been attributed to both an increase in alcoholism and to the breakup of the Soviet Union, which

(10) have led to high labor turnover and increased crime rates.[2] Compared to many less developed countries in the world, a life expectancy of 64.7 is fairly high. These less developed countries, however, are not experiencing the drastic drop in population with which Russia is currently struggling. This is due to the high birth rates that counteract the low life expectancy. Russia, unfortunately, has no such advantage.

(15) Low birth rates are the most critical factor in the Russian population crisis. The average fertility rate for Russian women is at 1.61 children per women; this results in a population growth rate of –0.04 each year. Russian women have practically ceased having children altogether, putting extreme pressure on the population.

These demographic numbers show a society that desires family and children very little.

(20) Generally, in richer countries, the birth rate drops as the quality of life increases. Yet in Russia, the high quality of life that would justify the present low rates does not exist. The low birth rates must then point to some societal lack of value of family and children. Interestingly, this contention is not supported by a survey conducted in 2007 that found that sixty-seven percent of Russian people thought that the love of the parents was the most important aspect in rais-

(25) ing any child, and around sixty percent of all age groups found family, home, and comfort to be "very important" in their lives.[3]

Despite Russian people espousing these values of family life, reality says something different. Studies of the artwork of children who draw family life, as well as the children's game of "house" show that the average Russian father is often absent in daily life.[4] Thus, while

(30) Russians see parental love and care as being vital to the wellbeing of their children, in general, men in Russia do not act to give this love and care to their children. As rational humans, it can be concluded that the women of Russia, wanting their children to have good lives, are less likely to have kids since they know that it is very possible that their children will have absentee fathers. This may be a conscious or unconscious decision but it seems to have been

(35) imprinted upon the people of Russia, giving the entire society an attitude whereby they value children but they don't have any themselves. With each generation that passes, this mindset grows, the men drift further, and the birth rate drops. This low birth rate is the main factor in the population decline in Russia.

All of these problems—the low life expectancy, low birth rate, and dissolution of the tradi-
(40) tional family—are contributing to population declines in Russia. Vladimir Putin, in his 2006
State of the Nation Address, showed that he fails to see the underlying causes of the problem:
the lack of family support and the deep societal lack of desire for children. He focused on
the economic problems instead, encouraging social programs to help pay for children.[5] He
understands there is a problem but doesn't know how to fix it, which lies in the mindset, not
(45) necessarily the pocketbooks, of the Russian people. Without a change in mindset, the population of Russia is destined to grow ever smaller.

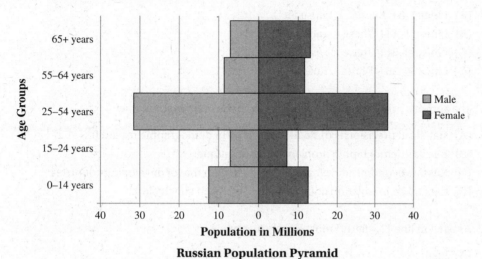

Russian Population Pyramid

Information Source: CIA World Factbook

[1] All demographic information sourced from the CIA World Factbook. https://www.cia.gov/library/
publications/the-world-factbook/
[2] Julie DaVanzo and Clifford Grammich, *Dire Demographics: Population Trends in the Russian Federation*
(Santa Monica: Rand, 2001), 40.
[3] E.I. Pakhomova, "Is it Reasonable to Speak of a Crisis of the Family?" *Russian Social Science Review* 48, no.
5(2007): 70, 79.
[4] Pakomova, 70, 79.
[5] Vladimir Putin, "State of the Nation Address 2006," *Population and Development Review* 32, no. 2 (2006), 386.

1. It is most reasonable to infer that the author considers the problem of Russian depopulation to be

   (A) complex yet manageable.
   (B) dire yet common.
   (C) serious and multifaceted.
   (D) unfortunate and nebulous.

2. Which option gives the best evidence for the answer to the previous question?

   (A) Lines 1–3 ("Russia . . . caused it")
   (B) Lines 11–14 ("These . . . advantage")
   (C) Lines 19–21 ("These . . . exist")
   (D) Lines 36–38 ("With . . . Russia")

3. The author's primary purpose in lines 10–14 is to demonstrate how

   (A) statistical precision is difficult to come by in demographic research.
   (B) Russia's demographic problems are not unique.
   (C) Russia's economic development is worse than that of developing countries.
   (D) data taken in isolation could lead to a mistaken conclusion.

4. As used in line 11, "fairly" most closely means

   (A) justly.
   (B) relatively.
   (C) equally.
   (D) exclusively.

5. As used in line 34, "absentee" most closely means

   (A) dead.
   (B) uninvolved.
   (C) far away.
   (D) incarcerated.

6. It can be reasonably inferred that Vladimir Putin's approach to depopulation as presented in lines 42–43 ("He focused . . . children") focuses on

   (A) the shifting mindset in the Russian population over the past century.
   (B) what is within the power of government to do.
   (C) the root causes of the issue.
   (D) centralized family planning.

7. Which of the following would be the most effective solution (unmentioned by the author) to the major problem that the author argues Russia faces?

   (A) More precise statistical study of demographic trends
   (B) Changing the Russian attitude toward fatherhood
   (C) Allowing increased immigration to Russia
   (D) Convincing Russians of the value of childhood

8. If Russia were able to follow the advice of the author, how would a reformed population distribution chart compare to the figure provided in the passage?

(A) It would have a greater percentage of youth.
(B) It would have a greater percentage of elderly.
(C) It would have a greater percentage of people in their 40s and 50s.
(D) It would have relatively more males than females.

9. Based on the figure provided and the passage, how does the distribution of ages within the 65+ group of women most likely compare to the distribution of ages within the 65+ group of men?

(A) More divergent
(B) Less divergent
(C) Nearly identical
(D) Differing values for the youngest ages

10. Which option gives the best evidence for the answer to the previous question?

(A) Lines 5–8 ("The beginning . . . concern")
(B) Lines 8–11 ("This low . . . high")
(C) Lines 15–18 ("Low birth . . . population")
(D) Lines 21–26 ("The low . . . their lives")

Social Science: The Emu War

The best-laid plans often have unexpected consequences. Popular among chaos theorists, the butterfly effect refers to the interdependence of all events, and how even seemingly trivial changes in any of these can cause disproportional differences in the non-linear space-time continuum. Chances are that following World War I, when British veterans were encouraged by the government to farm wheat in Western Australia, they had no idea they would be setting into motion another deadly conflict: The Great Emu War of 1932.

The end of World War I had many positive effects on the world: the end of world violence, the beginning of talks of worldwide peace organizations and treaties. However, there were also negative impacts. The end of the war also meant the end of many war-related jobs. Additionally, thousands of soldiers were returning home to economies already unable to provide enough employment opportunities to citizens. While different countries had different solutions to the problem, in Australia the government encouraged British veterans to take up farming. Subsidies were guaranteed but either failed to be provided, or weren't enough. As a result, by October 1932, wheat prices fell dangerously low.

Justifiably outraged, the farmers and government entered a time of rising tensions. Matters were made appreciably worse when over 20,000 emus entered the scene. Emus follow predictable migration patterns and when the farmers settled the land, the emus were residing in the coastal regions. In October, they started their migration toward the warmer, inland areas of Australia. Due to the extensive farming that had taken place, the land had been cleared—allowing easier migration—and there was a plentiful water supply from irrigation systems. In essence, the emus had found a perfect habitat. They destroyed much of the underpriced crop the farmers had painstakingly grown. This was the final straw for the farmers and they demanded the government provide them military aid.

The government assigned the emu mission to Major G.P.W. Meredith along with two soldiers to assist him. Beginning in November, Major Meredith, the two soldiers, two Lewis guns, and 10,000 rounds of ammunition arrived to "take care of" the emu problem. Similar to a typical war involving humans on both sides, there were several "engagements" in this "war." A variety of borderline comical events took place from the soldiers underestimating the emus' military prowess (they broke into several guerilla like groups), to the Lewis guns jamming, to Major Meredith deciding to mount the guns on a military vehicle. In the end, the war was an overall failure and Major Meredith and his men returned home with only a fraction of the emu pelts they were supposed to have acquired.

The retreat of Major Meredith allowed the emus to return to the farmlands and once again ravage the crops. The farmers again called on the government for aid, and the Minister of Defense approved another military engagement with the emus. Despite his previous failure, Major Meredith was sent back to the field. Drawing on his previous experience, he was reportedly much more successful this time around.

Following the "war," word travelled and eventually reached Great Britain. Several newspapers had comical responses to the so-called "Great Emu War." While it undoubtedly had comedic threads, the emus did have a devastating effect on an already tenuous situation. A bounty system was reinstated to avoid government involvement and potential future embarrassment should they lose another "war" to these large, flightless birds. Despite this, the

farmers called again for government aid in 1934, 1943, and 1948. However, the bounty system
(45) ended up being much more effective as locals were more well equipped and knowledgeable
about hunting the emus than was the military.

Significant Events in Emu War

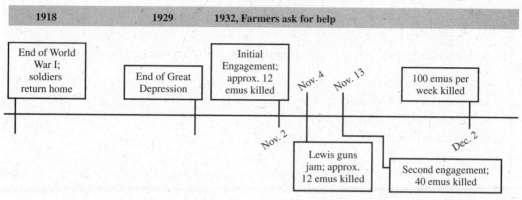

1. The author uses the introductory paragraph (lines 1–7) to

   (A) demonstrate how a military decision led to environmental catastrophe.
   (B) anticipate objections that the reader will have to the main argument.
   (C) provide a personal anecdote to draw the reader's attention.
   (D) place the topic of the passage in a greater context.

2. The author suggests that the military's initial mindset on their capacity to remove the emus
   was one of

   (A) overconfidence.
   (B) bravery.
   (C) humility.
   (D) fanaticism.

3. Which option gives the best evidence for the answer to the previous question?

   (A) Lines 4–7 ("Chances . . . 1932")
   (B) Lines 22–24 ("They . . . military aid")
   (C) Lines 28–30 ("A variety . . . groups")
   (D) Lines 34–36 ("The retreat . . . emus")

4. As used in line 13, the phrase "take up" most closely means

   (A) seize.
   (B) engage in.
   (C) study for.
   (D) invent.

5. Out of the following choices, which does the narrator suggest was of the greatest importance for people to fight the emus effectively?

(A) Military training from elite academies
(B) First-hand experience with the emus
(C) A scholarly understanding of emu anatomy
(D) A sophisticated relationship with the media

6. Which option gives the best evidence for the answer to the previous question?

(A) Lines 23–24 ("This was . . . aid")
(B) Lines 39–40 ("Following . . . War")
(C) Lines 41–43 ("A bounty . . . birds")
(D) Lines 44–46 ("However . . . military")

7. What is the author's primary purpose in using quotation marks in the sentence in lines 27–28 ("Similar . . . 'war'")?

(A) To quote primary source information
(B) To highlight the global importance of this event
(C) To underscore the irony of these labels
(D) To dispute the veracity of certain claims

8. As used in line 41, "tenuous" most closely means

(A) precarious.
(B) fatalistic.
(C) biological.
(D) cosmopolitan.

9. The figure is most useful in elaborating on which of the following selections from the passage?

(A) Lines 25–26 ("The government . . . him")
(B) Lines 26–27 ("Beginning . . . problem")
(C) Lines 27–28 ("Similar . . . 'war'")
(D) Lines 28–31 ("A variety . . . vehicle")

10. Based on the figure, the military's effectiveness in fighting the emus can best be described as

(A) gradually increasing over time.
(B) steadily decreasing over time.
(C) relatively constant over time.
(D) generally inconsistent.

SCIENCE

Science: Caffeine

Passage 1

All told, there exist just over sixty species of plant known to produce caffeine, among the mostly widely cultivated of which are coffee from the berries of the *Coffea arabica* plant, tea from the leaves of *Camellia sinesis*, and chocolate from the seeds of the *Theobroma cacao* tree.

Line Caffeine, curiously enough, is in its structure quite closely related to adenine and guanine,
(5) the two purine nitrogenous bases that comprise about half of our DNA. Moreover, it is precisely this structural similarity between caffeine and nucleic acids that gives coffee, tea, and chocolate their uniquely stimulating properties. While amphetamine, ephedrine, nicotine, cocaine, and the vast majority of other common psychoactive stimulants work to modulate the dopaminergic circuits of the central nervous system, the stimulation we feel from ingest-
(10) ing caffeine arises from a completely distinct neural pathway.

Within every metabolically active cell of the human body, a molecule called adenosine triphosphate acts as a major reservoir of transferrable chemical energy. That is, in the thermodynamically favorable liberation of phosphate groups from adenosine, free energy is released that can be harnessed to drive forward a variety of the thermodynamically unfavorable chem-
(15) ical reactions required to sustain life. For our purposes, the main implications of this system are fairly intuitive: cells with significant energy reserves will be those with a large amount of adenosine triphosphate at their disposal, while those that have exhausted their reserves will contain merely adenosine, and inorganic phosphate.

Throughout our evolution, the neurons that make up our brain and spinal cord have
(20) adapted to detect the presence of adenosine, and to react to it by increasing the secretion of melatonin from the pineal gland, which in turn mediates feelings of "drowsiness" or somnolence. The purpose, one might reason, is simply to promote sleep; a state that is minimally taxing to the metabolism of the central nervous system, and will allow its cells an opportunity to replenish their energy stores.

(25) Adenosine itself is made up merely of an adenine nitrogenous base attached via a betaglycosidic bond to a pentose sugar. Thus, it is simply the approximate structural correspondence between caffeine and adenosine that enables caffeine to interact with and antagonize adenosine-sensing receptors without chemically activating them. The end result is a general blunting of the brain's ability to perceive how much energy it has expended; though the effect,
(30) it should be mentioned, is self-limited. As the concentration of adenosine increases to critical levels, adenosine displaces caffeine from its inhibitory position on the receptor in a phenomenon known colloquially to some consumers of coffee and cola beverages as "the crash."

Passage 2

Caffeine, admittedly, seldom kills. A toxic dose to an adult is roughly equivalent to the amount contained in somewhere between eighty and one-hundred mid-sized cups of coffee. This is
(35) not to say, however, that caffeine is completely innocuous. By some estimates, more than 90% of the American adult population uses caffeine on a daily basis, and it is far and away the most widely consumed psychostimulant worldwide. It is somewhat shocking, therefore, that its distribution remains wholly unregulated by the Food and Drug Administration.

While the recreational use of caffeine is infrequently fatal, abuse of caffeinated supple-
(40) ments, medications, and beverages can precipitate a wide range of detrimental effects on the
body, particularly among individuals with underlying vulnerabilities. For instance, in those
already at risk for osteoporosis—such as post-menopausal women, and those suffering from
hyperparathyroidism—caffeine has been shown to significantly accelerate the rate of bone
loss, chiefly by increasing basal metabolic rate. Similarly, multiple studies have demonstrated
(45) a positive correlation between the agitating, stimulant-effects of caffeine use on the limbic
system and acute exacerbations of panic disorder and anxiety disorders. Caffeine increases
blood pressure. It promotes electrical dysrhythmias of the heart. It is anything but harmless,
and yet contrary to popular belief, the most commonly heard health complaint concerning
caffeine is something of a fallacy. That is to say, while chemical dependence, tolerance, and
(50) withdrawal from the stimulant are familiar entities to those who consume large quantities,
genuine pathological addiction to caffeine has not been documented in humans, and as such
is omitted from both the DSM-5, and the ICD-10 as well.

1. The respective purposes of Passage 1 and Passage 2 are best described as

   (A) analytical and narrative.
   (B) persuasive and descriptive.
   (C) expository and argumentative.
   (D) medical and economic.

2. Which of these gives the correct sequence of processes as described in the paragraphs in
   lines 11–24?

   (A) Adenosine triphosphate is formed in the pineal gland from the reaction between natural
       melatonin and artificial adenosine.
   (B) Adenosine and adenosine triphosphate stimulate the production of melatonin in the
       pineal gland.
   (C) Adenosine and melatonin from the pineal gland cause energy to be released in the cre-
       ation of adenosine triphosphate.
   (D) Melatonin is released from the pineal gland as a result of detection of adenosine, which
       comes from the breakdown of adenosine triphosphate.

3. As used in lines 12–13, the phrase "thermodynamically favorable" most closely refers to a
   reaction in which

   (A) the reactants are exclusively biological.
   (B) a subject consciously chooses to undergo the process because of its positive effects.
   (C) the reactants have more energy than the products.
   (D) the products have more energy than the reactants.

4. The process whereby caffeine works, according to Passage 1, is best paraphrased as

   (A) caffeine tricks the body into thinking it has not used as much energy as it in fact has.
   (B) caffeine causes the release of adenosine, stimulating the central nervous system.
   (C) caffeine strongly hinders the body's ability to produce adenosine, resulting in greater
       alertness.
   (D) caffeine helps the body generate more adenosine triphosphate storage, creating greater
       stores of energy.

5. Which option gives the best evidence for the answer to the previous question?

   (A) Lines 11–15 ("Within . . . life")
   (B) Lines 22–24 ("The purpose . . . stores")
   (C) Lines 26–30 ("Thus . . . self-limited")
   (D) Lines 30–32 ("As the . . . 'the crash'")

6. As used in line 35, "innocuous" most closely means

   (A) harmless.
   (B) stimulating.
   (C) legal.
   (D) popular.

7. Which of the following does the author of Passage 2 suggest is a way that caffeine does NOT present a danger to humans?

   (A) Through exacerbation of panic disorders
   (B) Through pathological addiction
   (C) Through increasing blood pressure
   (D) By accelerating bone loss among at-risk populations

8. Which option gives the best evidence for the answer to the previous question?

   (A) Lines 41–44 ("For instance . . . rate")
   (B) Lines 44–46 ("Similarly . . . disorders")
   (C) Lines 46–47 ("Caffeine . . . heart")
   (D) Lines 49–52 ("That is . . . well")

9. When taken together, these two passages present a solid overview of caffeinated stimulation's

   (A) origins and history.
   (B) benefits and pitfalls.
   (C) causes and effects.
   (D) evolution and devolution.

Science: Fungi

With good reason, biologists have frequently described fungi as the "forgotten kingdom." Despite demonstrating a diversity and evolutionary resilience to rival plants and animals alike, for many of us, our day-to-day familiarity with fungi reaches little further than to a
Line handful of domesticated mushrooms, and perhaps the *Penicillium* molds that imbue blue
(5) cheese with their distinctive color and smell. In reality, fungi are all around us, and contribute biochemically to a remarkable variety of both natural and artificial processes: from the vital decomposition of organic matter commonly described as "rotting" to the yeast-mediated fermentation of polysaccharides into ethanol and gaseous carbon dioxide which allows a baker's bread to rise. Even so, perhaps due to their obscure, soil-dwelling lifestyles, the manifold
(10) functions that fungi execute in our lives are more often than not inconspicuous, and all too easily overlooked.

The health sciences especially are rife with novel applications for mycology (that is, the branch of biology emphasizing fungi). Famously, the first commercially available antibiotics capable of curing streptococcal and staphylococcal infections were discovered quite by
(15) accident when Scottish scientist Alexander Fleming noticed how the growth of a staphylococcus culture had been drastically inhibited following its contamination with a *Penicillium chrysogenum* mold. Notably, the unique mechanism by which this inhibitory effect is accomplished has since led to the development of not one but three distinct classes of antimicrobial medications—penicillins, cephalosporins, and beta-lactamase inhibitors—and accelerated
(20) a set of fascinating genetic mutations which confer antibiotic resistance among strains of bacteria.

In penicillins and cephalosporins, the so-called "beta-lactam ring" is known to be the principle structure responsible for their antimicrobial properties. This ring binds avidly to specialized cross-linking proteins found within the peptidoglycan layer of bacterial cell walls,
(25) subsequently blocking a bacterium's attempts at reproduction, as well as the replication of its intracellular organelles. As it is not found naturally within the cells of animals, plants, or fungi, peptidoglycan polymers are highly peculiar to bacteria, and antimicrobial agents targeting peptidoglycan possess a very low potential for toxic cross-reactivity with other types of cells.

(30) Even into the 21st century, beta-lactam compounds still comprise more than half of all antibiotics prescribed worldwide, and it is widely believed that their pervasive usage has helped to promote the novel synthesis of beta-lactamases among a wide array of common pathogenic bacterial species. To clarify, beta-lactamases are a class of enzymes capable of hydrolyzing the beta-lactam ring, and are often secreted in the presence of antibiotics. While
(35) these enzymes are nigh ubiquitous among bacteria today, prior to the commercial availability of penicillin, their endogenous synthesis was limited to a fairly small number of gram-negative organisms. The startling rapidity with which bacteria have developed resistance against beta-lactams may have far reaching implications for the health of human populations in the future.

(40) Although penicillin is perhaps the most memorable example, it is hardly the only contribution fungi have made to improving human health. In recent years, a number of medicinally significant fungal isolates have emerged to treat not just infection, but metabolic, immunologic, and neoplastic diseases as well. Of particular note, 3-hydroxy-3-methylglutaryl-CoA reductase inhibitors—more commonly called "statins"—are considered the first-line phar-
(45) macological therapy for hypercholesterolemia, and are the only cholesterol-lowering class of medications that have been proven in peer-reviewed longitudinal studies to lower an

individual's risk of major cardiovascular disease. Mechanistically, rather than blocking the absorption of dietary cholesterol or enhancing its excretion, statins work to reduce the *de novo* biosynthesis of cholesterol molecules in the body by inhibiting the rate-limiting enzyme
(50) in its anabolic pathway.

It would not be overstating the matter to say that statins have transformed the treatment of both acquired and congenital cholesterol-related diseases. But what's more, the first generation of statins was discovered, oddly enough, by Japanese scientist Akira Endo during his research into the antimicrobial properties of the mold *Penicillium citrinum*. Not unlike
(55) Alexander Fleming one-half century earlier, Endo serendipitously discovered yet another compound from this curious genus of fungi destined to do no less than revolutionize the medical maintenance of human health. One must wonder, therefore, what more we stand to learn from fungi, and what still-greater mysteries they may yet be concealing in the soil.

1. As described in the passage, the gradual process of changes in bacterial resistance to antibiotics is most similar to which of the following situations?

(A) An artificial intelligence program analyzes multiple instances of computer viruses, increasing its antiviral effectiveness as it gathers more applicable data.
(B) A television show is extremely popular in its first season but becomes less popular as its novelty wears off.
(C) A school initiates antiplagiarism software that is highly useful in stopping cheating at the outset but becomes less useful as more students catch on.
(D) A car's tires become worn thin after thousands of miles of wear and tear.

2. The author primarily uses the introductory paragraph, lines 1–11, to

(A) demonstrate the applications of fungi in cooking.
(B) refute widespread misinformation about fungi.
(C) establish the relevance of the essay's topic.
(D) point out the easy visibility of fungal influence.

3. As used in line 10, "execute" most closely means

(A) destroy.
(B) camouflage.
(C) entice.
(D) perform.

4. The author suggests that some of the most important fungi-related medical innovations came about primarily as a result of

(A) luck.
(B) evolution.
(C) economic investment.
(D) genetic engineering.

5. Which option gives the best evidence for the answer to the previous question?

   (A) Lines 17–21 ("Notably . . . bacteria")
   (B) Lines 30–33 ("Even into . . . species")
   (C) Lines 43–47 ("Of particular . . . disease")
   (D) Lines 54–57 ("Not unlike . . . health")

6. As used in line 27, "peculiar" most closely means

   (A) strange.
   (B) unique.
   (C) diseased.
   (D) helpful.

7. The author implies that a property of antibiotics that makes them particularly helpful to diseased animals is that they

   (A) are not widely recognized and can therefore be inconspicuous.
   (B) cause the diseased tissue to mutate into healthy tissue.
   (C) help the organism develop long-term immunity against infection.
   (D) attack the bacteria without attacking the host organism.

8. Which option gives the best evidence for the answer to the previous question?

   (A) Lines 9–11 ("Even so . . . overlooked")
   (B) Lines 17–21 ("Notably . . . bacteria")
   (C) Lines 26–29 ("As it is . . . cells")
   (D) Lines 37–39 ("The startling . . . future")

9. The author most likely uses the final sentence of the passage (lines 57–58, "One must . . . soil") to suggest

   (A) that geological exploration deserves funding.
   (B) that further study of fungi is warranted.
   (C) skepticism about the prospects for scientific research.
   (D) a more balanced approach to the analysis of fungi.

Science: Methanogenesis

Methanosphaera stadtmanae, the first single-celled (archaeal) commensal (i.e., two organisms have a relationship wherein one benefits, and the other has no harm nor benefit) organism to have its genome sequenced, is an anaerobic, non-moving, sphere-shaped
Line organism that inhabits the human gastrointestinal tract. Of all methanogenic (methane-pro-
(5) ducing) Archaea, *Methanosphaera stadtmanae* has been found to have the most restrictive energy metabolism as it can generate methane only by reduction of methanol with H_2 and is dependent on acetate as a carbon source. These unique energy conservation traits are what make *Methanosphaera stadtmanae* beneficial to its human host and not an opportunistic pathogen.

(10) *Methanosphaera stadtmanae*'s genome lacks 37 protein-coding sequences present in the genomes of all other methanogens. Among these are the protein coding sequences for synthesis of molybdopterin, which is required for the enzyme catalyzing the first step of methanogenesis from CO_2 and H_2, as well as for the synthesis of the CO dehydrogenase/acetyl-coenzyme A synthase complex. This explains why *Methanosphaera stadtmanae* cannot
(15) reduce CO_2 to methane nor oxidize methanol to CO_2. While this is the typical path of methanogenesis for many archaeal methanogens, it is not the path for *Methanosphaera stadtmanae*.

Methanogenic Archaea are naturally occurring components of the human gut microbiota. The two original methanogenic species belonging to the order Methanobacteriales, *Methanobrevibacter smithii* and *Methanosphaera stadtmanae,* were identified over 30 years
(20) ago by the detection of methane in the breath, and eventually isolated from fecal samples. *Methanosphaera stadtmanae*, one of the major archaeal inhabitants of the gut, is able to thrive in the human digestive system because methanol is a product of pectin degradation in the intestine by *Bacterioides* species and other anaerobic bacteria. *Methanosphaera stadtmanae* reduces methanol produced by the anaerobic bacteria with H_2 present to produce
(25) methane. Production of methane in this manner is beneficial to the human host because of energy conservation. Methanogens, like *Methanosphaera stadtmanae*, also play an important role in digestion by improving efficiency of polysaccharide fermentation by helping to prevent accumulation of acids, reaction end products, and gaseous hydrogen. It is thought that *Methanosphaera stadtmanae*'s energy conserving methanogenesis process is one of
(30) the ways it helps in maintaining homeostasis (biological equilibrium) within the human gut microbiota.

Homeostasis of the human gut microbiota is a delicate balance, and if disrupted can cause serious issues for humans. One of these issues is the growing number of cases of IBD (Inflammatory Bowel Disease). IBD is a term used in the medical field to describe conditions
(35) of the gastrointestinal tract that have chronic or recurring immune responses and inflammation. *Methanosphaera stadtmanae*'s commensal role with the human can be disrupted when other bacteria in the highly immunologically active intestinal tract stop performing their normal processes. While the details of all of the processes that bacteria perform are not completely known, it is understood that *Methanosphaera stadtmanae* reacts to the adverse effects
(40) by inducing the release of proinflammatory cytokine TNF in peripheral blood cells. By releasing this, *Methanosphaera stadtmanae* produces a four-times stronger response than any other methanogen of the gut microbiota. This response causes increased inflammation in the gastrointestinal tract, and can only stop when balance within the gut microbiota is restored.

One method physicians have found to help restore the homeostasis of the gut microbiota
(45) is the administration of archaebiotics. Archaebiotics colonize in the gastrointestinal tract to help restore balance by eliminating and controlling bacteria or archaea that disrupted the

balance in the first place. Archaebiotics also help by keeping commensal methanogens, like *Methanosphaera stadtmanae*, so that they can continue to perform their necessary role of methanogenesis. It is imperative to maintain methanogenesis so that proper digestion and

(50) energy conservation can happen for the human.

Understanding the role *Methanosphaera stadtmanae* plays in the human gastrointestinal tract has been extremely important in the advancement of understanding IBD, as well as the development of treatments. Identification of additional archaeal and bacterial species will continue to help develop the field so that scientists and physicians can better understand how

(55) different organisms work with each other or against each other.

Pathway	Complete/Incomplete/Absent	Intermediates
Glycolysis (Embden-Meyerhof)	Incomplete	Missing glucose and D-glucose 6-phosphate
Entner-Doudoroff (Semi-phosphorylative Form)	Both Absent	Missing all intermediates
Pentose Phosphate	Incomplete	Missing all intermediates except D-ribulose-5-phosphate and D-ribose-5-phosphate
Pyruvate Oxidation	Complete	All intermediates present
Citrate Cycle (Glyoxylate Cycle)	Both Incomplete	Missing citrate and isocitrate as intermediates. Pyruvate feeds into the Citrate Cycle via oxaloacetate. Glyoxylate Cycle only contains oxaloacetate and malate.
Reductive Citrate Cycle	Incomplete	Missing all intermediates except oxaloacetate and malate
Calvin Cycle	Incomplete	Missing Erythrose-4P, Sedoheptulose 1,7P, Sedoheptulose 7P, and Ribulose 1,5P
Methanogenesis	Complete	All intermediates present (can only use methanol and H_2 to produce methane)
Reductive Acetyl-CoA	Incomplete	Missing all intermediates except 5,10-Methylene-THF and THF (come in from a different pathway)

Figure 1. The above chart lists the known mechanisms that bacterial and archaeal organisms use for energy purposes. The chart lists if *M. stadtmanae* has the necessary intermediates present in the human digestive system to have a functional energy pathway given a particular mechanism.

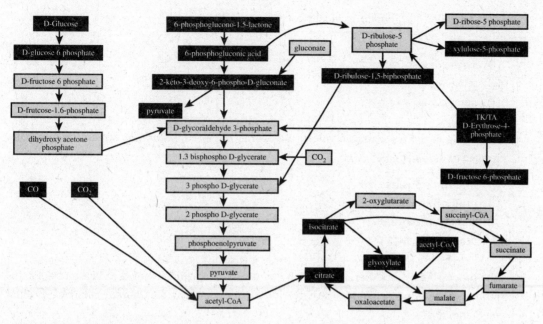

Figure 2. The intermediates in the black boxes are ones that *M. stadtmanae* cannot use or does not have. The intermediates in the gray boxes are ones that *M. stadtmanae* does use or has.

1. It is most reasonable to infer that the author of the passage believes that scientific understanding of how archaeal and bacterial species interact with the human digestive system is

   (A) largely settled.
   (B) making progress.
   (C) generally mystified.
   (D) static.

2. According to the third paragraph (lines 17–31), the presence of methanogenic species in the human digestive system was first detected from

   (A) observation of a product of a chemical reaction.
   (B) isolation from human bowel movements.
   (C) the decoding of the DNA of methanogens.
   (D) the discovery of its essential role in human homeostasis.

3. As used in line 24, "reduces" most closely means

   (A) subtracts.
   (B) diminishes.
   (C) transforms.
   (D) persecutes.

4. What is the primary purpose of lines 39–40 ("it is . . . cells")?

   (A) To address an objection
   (B) To provide speculation
   (C) To explain a process
   (D) To cite an authority

5. As used in line 40, "inducing" most closely means

    (A) causing.

    (B) suggesting.

    (C) releasing.

    (D) persuading.

6. According to the passage as a whole, the overall role of *Methanosphaera stadtmanae* with respect to human health is

    (A) uniformly positive.

    (B) primarily beneficial.

    (C) somewhat harmful.

    (D) mostly parasitic.

7. The processing or lack thereof of which chemical intermediate shown in Figure 2 does the author argue is particularly distinctive for *Methanosphaera stadtmanae* relative to other methanogens?

    (A) H_2

    (B) oxaloacetate

    (C) CO_2

    (D) succinate

8. Which option gives the best evidence for the answer to the previous question?

    (A) Lines 10–11 ("*Methanosphaera* . . . methanogens")

    (B) Lines 14–16 ("This explains . . . *stadtmanae*")

    (C) Lines 21–23 ("*Methanosphaera* . . . bacteria")

    (D) Lines 26–28 ("Methanogens . . . hydrogen")

9. How does the information in Figures 1 and 2 help make the author's case that *Methanosphaera stadtmanae* is helpful to humans, relative to many other similar bacteria and archaeal organisms?

    (A) The figures show that pentose phosphate does not have the needed intermediates to carry out the development of methanol.

    (B) The figures demonstrate that *M. stadtmanae* is genetically similar to the more common *Methanobrevibacter smithii*.

    (C) The figures detail the chemical process whereby inflammatory bowel disease can be avoided.

    (D) The figures show that *M. stadtmanae* lacks the necessary intermediates for most of the common energy pathways.

10. Which option gives the best evidence for the answer to the previous question?

    (A) Lines 4–9 ("Of all . . . pathogen")

    (B) Lines 18–20 ("The two . . . samples")

    (C) Lines 32–38 ("Homeostasis . . . processes")

    (D) Lines 44–49 ("One method . . . methanogenesis")

Science: Wound Healing

An Occupational Therapist Describes the Process of Wound Healing

Even when a laceration as small as a paper cut happens to a person, complex reactions begin within the body almost instantaneously. Were these processes to be disrupted for any number of reasons, even the most insignificant of scrapes could prove fatal for the victim.
Line Thus, it is of the utmost importance to know the typical progression for how a wound heals so
(5) that the afflicted can seek medical attention should the wound prove aggravated.

Immediately after the initial laceration transpires, the body responds and initiates action. Known as the "inflammatory phase" of wound healing, this is when the body first begins to repair the damage it encountered. In order to prevent excessive blood loss, the first step is vasoconstriction in which the blood vessels near the affected area are constricted. Nearly
(10) concurrently, phagocytosis begins as white blood cells are sent to the wound. Phagocytes are cells that consume the debris in the wound, which aids in the cleansing of damaged tissue as well as foreign matter.

Phagocytosis is completed quite quickly—a mere 30 minutes for culmination and inception of the next stage. Following the cleaning, mast cells arrive and release histamine which
(15) causes vasodilation; this opening of the blood vessels vastly increases the flow of fluid into the affected area and results in the inflammation for which this stage is named. This inflammation decreases the available capacity of the area and leads to increased amounts of pain and discoloration in and around the wound site. From vasoconstriction to dilation, the inflammatory phase may last between two days and two weeks (depending on the severity of the
(20) wound).

Following this somewhat preparatory stage, the proliferative phase marks the beginning of the actual healing process. Within this second stage, there are four mini steps that are crucial for the wound to close properly. Granulation is the first of these four steps. It is indicated by the body beginning to lay down different connective tissues like collagen; these
(25) tissues help fill the empty space or hole created by the affliction. The body, however, is not only constructed of connective tissue. Angiogenesis, the second of the four steps, is when the body embarks on the arduous process of growing new blood vessels. Intertwining networks of vessels are laid down, oft called capillary beds. These growing, weaving vessels give a new wound its distinctive pink coloration. The third stage, wound contraction, is the first stage in
(30) which the raw edges of the wound begin to adjoin to each other. The wound does not experience complete closure until the final stage of the four stages of proliferation—epithelization. Epithelial cells—or skin cells—move over the granulated tissue from the first step. The four stages of the proliferative phase can last anywhere from 3–21 days. The timeline is, once again, dependent on how poignant the wound is.

(35) It is critical to be protective of a newly healed wound at the beginning of the third stage: maturation. The new skin is quite fragile and can easily reopen if too much stress is placed on it. The maturation stage can last up to two years as the scar forms and hardens. In some cases the scar will disappear with time, but in others it's a permanent addendum to a person's body. Even once the scar has fully matured, scar tissue is only 80% as strong as skin, meaning it is
(40) prone to re-injury.

Several factors can influence the quality and timeliness of wound healing, many of which—circulation, chemical stress, temperature of the wound bed, amount of moisture in and around the wound, and age—are outside the control of the individual. The individual can

control other factors, like nutrition, medication, and infection. Maintaining a well-balanced
(45) diet, consulting a doctor about medications, and keeping the wound site clean can all have a
positive effect on wound closure and healing.

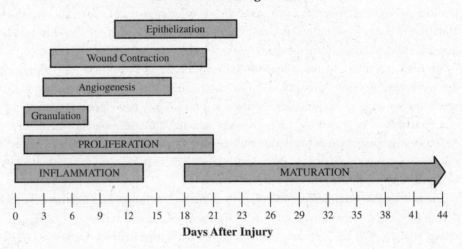

The Wound Healing Process

1. What is the overall structure of the passage?

    (A) Chronological
    (B) Pro and con
    (C) Spatial
    (D) Persuasive

2. What is the primary purpose of the passage?

    (A) To highlight medical abnormalities
    (B) To argue in favor of a theory
    (C) To detail helpful information
    (D) To confront conventional wisdom

3. Which option gives the best evidence for the answer to the previous question?

    (A) Lines 1–2 ("Even . . . instantaneously")
    (B) Lines 4–5 ("Thus . . . aggravated")
    (C) Lines 41–43 ("many . . . individual")
    (D) Lines 44–46 ("Maintaining . . . healing")

4. What is the primary function of the sentence in lines 10–12 ("Phagocytes . . . matter")?

    (A) To clarify a specialized term
    (B) To explain the derivation of a word
    (C) To highlight an irony
    (D) To offer a solution to a health care predicament

5. As used in line 30, "raw" most closely means

   (A) unprocessed.
   (B) primal.
   (C) uncooked.
   (D) inflamed.

6. As used in line 35, "critical" most closely means

   (A) important.
   (B) harsh.
   (C) negative.
   (D) analytical.

7. The passage and the figure, respectively, portray the steps of wound healing in which of the following different ways?

   (A) Concurrent and chronological
   (B) Gradual and sudden
   (C) Sequential and simultaneous
   (D) Internal and external

8. If the author wished to extend the *x*-axis of the figure to portray the point at which a wound would nearly certainly be healed without extending the graph unnecessarily, which of the following would serve as the most logical final value for days?

   (A) 10
   (B) 100
   (C) 1,000
   (D) 10,000

9. Which option gives the best evidence for the answer to the previous question?

   (A) Lines 13–15 ("Phagocytosis . . . vasodilation")
   (B) Lines 21–23 ("Following . . . steps")
   (C) Lines 32–34 ("Epithelial . . . wound is")
   (D) Lines 36–37 ("The new . . . hardens")

ANSWER EXPLANATIONS

Fiction: *Almayer's Folly*

1. **(A)** The passage begins with an "unpleasant voice" interrupting Almayer's dreams of a "splendid future." This pattern is characteristic of the passage as a whole. Almayer imagines a life of wealth but is constantly reminded of his dull, wretched reality, making choice (A) correct. Choices (B) and (C) are not evidenced by the passage; actually, Almayer demonstrates both cultural proficiency and assertiveness. Choice (D) wrongfully assumes that Almayer wishes to be grounded in the rational when actually he prefers his wishful fantasies.

2. **(C)** Almayer justifies his failure to secure gold by asserting that those successful few have secured it dishonestly. He, instead, hopes to gain wealth and power "through his own honest exertions." Therefore, his contrast is one of virtue and morality. Choice (A) is not evidenced, although he might, too, believe this. Choices (B) and (D) are not only without evidence but contrary to Almayer's character.

3. **(B)** Lines 8–11 tell us that Almayer contrasts himself to the dishonest procurers of gold, providing evidence for the previous question. Choice (A) provides detail of Almayer's response to the call but does not talk about financial circumstances. Choice (C) creates images of Almayer's fantasy of wealth and power but does not address his opinion toward those more financially successful. Choice (D) reports Almayer's thoughts about Dain and his belated return but, again, doesn't address the previous question.

4. **(A)** Here, Almayer reassures himself that his fantasies are within reach if only Dain returns. Likewise, Dain must return for "his own share." Since Dain is obviously connected to Almayer's desire for wealth, we can substitute "share" with "part of the money," making choice (A) the correct option. It is nonsensical to think that Dain must return for his own "communication" or "disclosure." Although choice (C) may be tempting, we cannot assume that Almayer is gifting something to Dain but, instead, that Dain has a stake in the gold per previous agreement.

5. **(C)** Throughout the passage, we can see that Almayer still wishes for wealth but is constantly in despair because of his grim, impoverished circumstances. In comparison to the hopeful Almayer who "left his home with a light heart . . . ready to conquer the world," we can infer that he is now more hopeless than earlier in life when he never doubted his success. Now, he hopes for wealth but certainly has doubts and dark thoughts, making choices (A) and (B) incorrect. We have no evidence for choice (D), particularly because Almayer still considers himself to be very honest.

6. **(D)** Lines 47–48 reference the beginning of Almayer's journey when he embarked optimistically and "ready to conquer the world." This is in stark contrast to his current internal turmoil that reveals his feelings of hopelessness and disempowerment. Choice (A) actually refers to how he imagines he will feel when he obtains wealth. Choice (B) might be tempting because it is close to the lines referenced in the above question and deals with Almayer's interest in the tree; however, it reveals nothing about his attitude earlier in life. Choice (C) does, in fact, deal with Almayer's early life but with the attitude of his mother rather than of himself.

7. **(B)** To approach this question, ask yourself what we know about Dain. We know that Almayer impatiently awaits Dain's return because his arrival is somehow tied to a prosperous future—a future "nearly within his reach." Therefore, we can reasonably conclude that Dain is somehow aiding Almayer in his financial goals. Although choices (A), (C), and (D) could all be true, they are not evidenced and so could equally be false.

8. **(B)** Here, the powerless and formerly stuck tree is now "free" to drift into the sea. So we could substitute *unimpeded* or *no longer restrained*, which makes choice (B) correct. Choice (A) conveys the idea that the tree has a feeling or an attitude of its own. Choice (C) is tempting but again evokes the idea that the tree has gained power rather than merely escaped to freedom. Choice (D) refers to free as a financial concept, as in *without cost*, which does not fit here.

9. **(D)** Look for evidence about what Almayer's parents believed. His father, a "subordinate," is delighted at his son's prospects for a better future. His mother is nostalgic for Amsterdam and her former "position." Thus, both parents are concerned with social mobility. Since this pattern coincides with Almayer's own refusal to accept a low social position, choice (D) is the correct choice. Choices (A) and (C) are not evidenced in the passage. Choice (B) can be ruled out by Almayer's father's intolerant reaction to the natives.

Fiction: "The Fall of the House of Usher"

1. **(C)** This is a big-picture question. First, the narrator tells us about a time when he approached a particularly gloomy-looking house, explains the events that led to his arrival, and then delivers a general sense of his relationship to the home's occupant. Choice (C) is the only option that fits this pattern, an impression of the house and then an analysis of how the narrator came to be there. The narrator does not suggest that he is solving a problem as in choice (A). Although he may attempt to reconnect with an old friend, the events of the passage take place before that. Choice (D) serves as a detail of the passage but not an overall description.

2. **(C)** Words like "dull," "dark," "dreary," "gloom," and "desolate" provide evidence to support choice (C). Although the narrator is certainly aware, as in choice (D), of how the home is in a destructive state, as mentioned in choice (A), and that he feels both despair and melancholy, found in choice (B), none of these describes the tone, or the general attitude of the paragraph. Since "foreboding" means a feeling that something bad will happen, it is the correct answer.

3. **(D)** Throughout the passage, the narrator is generally aware of the gloomy, ominous feeling the house gives off, but he cannot explain it. Even after trying to change his attitude and his view of the house, he cannot express why or how it has such power over him. So choice (D) is correct. Choices (A) and (C) describe feelings opposite of uncertainty. Since it doesn't have to do with professional training, you can rule out choice (B) as well.

4. **(C)** Lines 16–17 explicitly state the narrator's feeling that "[i]t was a mystery" and thus back up the answer for the previous question. Choices (A), (B), and (D) depict scenes in which the narrator feels unnerved but cannot shake his apprehension. As such, they evidence how the house makes the narrator feel but not how he understands his ability to assess that reaction.

5. **(C)** A good approach to this question is to replace "society" with a simple synonym like *company*, which is closest to choice (C). The other choices all refer to the alternate meaning of society that refers to an aggregate of people living together under a system of order.

6. **(A)** From the passage, we know the narrator and his friend haven't seen each other for a long time. However, they were friends "in boyhood" and Roderick is ill, hoping to feel better in the presence of "his only personal friend." Thus, we can infer the narrator feels obligated, as in choice (A), to submit to the request. His feelings of "sorrow" and "terror" are brought on by the house, not by his friend's letter. Choice (C) is too extreme since it implies that the narrator held a strong desire or yearning to visit his old friend.

7. **(C)** Here, the narrator states that "it was the apparent *heart*" of the letter, despite the odd request, that made him say yes. This provides sufficient evidence that the narrator feels a certain responsibility to his friend and yields the answer for the previous question. Choices (A) and (B) merely discuss his uneasiness upon approaching the house. Choice (D) highlights the narrator's limited knowledge concerning Roderick's family history.

8. **(D)** Use context clues. Despite their intimacy, the narrator doesn't know much about his friend. So "reserve" must mean something like shyness or reticence, making choice (D) the correct answer. Choice (B) is an antonym. On the other hand, neither greed nor preparedness means that Roderick is detached or unwilling to share much about himself.

9. **(B)** This is tough reading, but don't be intimidated; break it down. The family is peculiar, or odd; has a great interest in art, charity, and musical science; but is not enduring. In fact, the line of descent is direct and has always been so. Thus, there is only one descendant. We know that the family has a long history and that Roderick is the current heir, ruling out choices (A) and (D). The word "direct" implies that the inheritance has always been passed down from one to the next without any extra heirs, eliminating choice (C).

Fiction: "Adventure"

1. **(A)** The question asks for the thematic focus, which can be summarized as two lovers whose circumstances bring them together and then gradually apart. Thus, love is fleeting, transient, or temporary, making choice (A) the correct answer. Although love may be beautiful or wholesome more generally speaking, this passage focuses on its impermanence. Choice (D) is misleading because the two characters do not wish to abuse love but, instead, drift apart despite their good intentions.

2. **(A)** We know from lines 1–2 that George is only a boy when Alice is twenty-seven. Since her affair with Ned began when she was sixteen, eleven years have passed. If George is a small boy now, we can reasonably assume that eleven years ago, he was unborn. Choices (C) and (D) would make him much older than he is. Although choice (B) might be tempting, that would make George eighteen at the time of this passage, not a boy.

3. **(C)** The imagery in lines 4–6 reveals a lot about Alice as an adult. She is "stooped" and "quiet," despite the "ferment" brewing under her surface. Synonyms of *ferment* include tumult, turmoil, and disquiet, so "unsettled" is the correct answer. Although she may be fond of Ned, their unresolved love affair has taken its toll on her—she still lives with her mother and there is no evidence to suggest she has since moved on to another lover. Choice (B) is characteristic of Ned, not Alice. The word "sedate," which means calm and peaceful, describes Alice's exterior but remains in contrast to her restless interior.

4. **(B)** As stated above, the description of the adult Alice occurs in the first two paragraphs, eliminating choices (C) and (D), which describe instances of Alice's teenage years. When deciding between choices (A) and (B), you should focus on the words "beneath a placid exterior a continual ferment went on." Even if you don't know what "ferment" means, you can assume that it is in contrast to her placid, quiet exterior. Choice (A), in contrast, deals more with her physical appearance and not her attitude.

5. **(D)** Here, Ned is "puzzled" but "touched." He had desired Alice only physically, but here "changed his mind" and became more emotionally attached to her. So if you substitute a word or words for "touched," you might use *stirred emotionally* or "moved" as in choice (D). Choice (A) refers to touching someone physically in a violent manner. Choice (B) can be used as a verb meaning to hurry or as a feeling of disappointment as in *dashed hopes*; neither fits here. Choice (C) is irrelevant since it might mean to correspond or resemble another, or to be equal to something in quality or strength.

6. **(A)** The evidence for this question is scattered throughout the essay. Alice is both willing to move to a new city and to live unmarried with Ned. For her, their being together is most important. Ned is "puzzled," or confused, by her devotion. Despite his intention to "protect and care" for Alice, he is unwilling to take her with him, becomes interested in other women, and very nearly forgets her altogether. Choices (B), (C), and (D) better describe Ned than Alice.

7. **(C)** Lines 23–24 reveal much about both Alice's and Ned's feelings. He is confused but pleased by Alice's devotion. A good approach to this question is to eliminate the other answer choices. Choice (A) gives us only facts about Alice, not anything about their attitudes toward the affair itself. Choice (B) gives us information about Alice's infatuation but nothing about Ned's feelings. Choice (D), like choice (A), reports facts but reveals little about the couple's inward emotions. Choose choice (C) because it's the only choice that provides evidence of how both lovers feel toward one another.

8. **(A)** Ned, sad about leaving his home and his sweetheart, forgets his "resolutions" concerning Alice. Before this, he has refused to live with her unmarried and, instead, resolves to return to care for her in more traditionally appropriate ways. Instead, he forgets that plan. The couple, ignited by emotions, becomes lovers and makes further promises that are likewise disregarded. Thus, choice (A) is the correct option. It is not appropriate to say he forgot his "purposes" or "solutions." Choice (D) means requests rather than pledges.

9. **(B)** Lines 36–38 consist of Ned's promise to always be with Alice. Since he later glosses over this commitment to Alice, it is appropriate to infer that he was disingenuous, misleading, or insincere. Choice (A) is an extreme that is ultimately unfair to Ned, who attempts, somewhat halfheartedly, to keep the love alive through his letters. Choice (C) indicates that he committed himself to Alice under great pressure or force, which is untrue. Choice (D) is another extreme that lacks evidence; later, he casually neglects Alice for present, temporary amusements.

Great Global Conversation: Jefferson

1. **(A)** Jefferson explains the transition from monarchy to republic as one as natural and easy as "throwing off an old and putting on a new suit of clothes." Hence, choice (A) is correct. Choices (B) and (C) describe situations contradictory to the one Jefferson presents. Choice (D) is incorrect because of the word "trivial," which means "insignificant" or "inconsequential."

2. **(B)** Jefferson prefers the first of his two proposals, "Free trade by alliance with some naval power." He argues that if the British Court were willing, an alliance "might . . . be approved by our people." Hence, Jefferson suggests that the people would see the benefits of economic trade with the British, as in choice (B). Choices (A) and (D) don't express the idea of free trade. Choice (C) does not work because the passage does not focus on the desire of the American people as a whole for religious integration with the British.

3. **(C)** Lines 18–21 supply Jefferson's direct proposal that a free trade alliance with Britain will benefit both countries and be generally supported by the American people. Choice (A) discusses Virginia's smooth transition into a republic. Choice (B) is Jefferson's proposal but fails to address how the American people might react. Choice (D) expresses Jefferson's desire to be serving with Benjamin Franklin, for whom he obviously has great respect.

4. **(A)** Read the sentence before looking at the answer choices. You might substitute "apprehend" with *anticipate* or *think* since Jefferson is proposing his ideas. Thus, choice (A) is correct. Choices (B) and (C) refer to the other meaning of "apprehend," as in arresting someone for an offense or crime. Choice (D) implies creation rather than opinion.

5. **(A)** Check the sentence before this one. Jefferson says free trade with an alliance is preferable because it aligns with the American people's "habits and wishes." Here, he implies that Americans would like to have access to imports from abroad rather than making everything themselves. This coincides with choice (A) but contradicts choices (B) and (C). Choice (D) brings up the American Revolution. Although it seems plausible that Americans do not desire further conflict, that is not the subject of these lines.

6. **(B)** The meaning of his second letter concerns "a fleet of the enemy's ships" that will easily have access to America's shores "[s]hould any more be added to them." Hence, Jefferson worries that American defenses will fail if more British ships arrive, as in choice (B). Choice (C) says the opposite. Choice (D) is wrongly concerned with the "open battlefield." Although choice (A) is tempting, it is too extreme. Certainly, Jefferson believes American defenses can resist. However, he also believes that they will be quickly overcome if the situation gets any worse.

7. **(C)** Here, the "want of arms" inhibits America from bringing the amount of forces necessary to defeat the British fleet. So Jefferson means that there is a continual need or demand for limited military power. It is the "lack" of arms that prevents appropriate defense operations. If America had an abundance of military powers, as in choice (B), this would not be an issue. Since this is dealing with the availability of military forces, "danger" is not an appropriate choice. Choice (A) is appealing because Jefferson does desire more forces. However, read the sentence with "desire" in place before you choose it. It is not the desire for arms itself that prevents adequate defense but, instead, that the desire cannot be fulfilled.

8. **(D)** The tone, or overall feel/attitude, of the passages can be described as serious, official, and respectful. Choice (D) best describes these feelings since "formality" refers to a stateliness and "deference" implies a respectfulness. Jefferson offers ideas of his own, rather than submitting himself as subservient like in choice (A). Although Jefferson may be anxious because of the severity of his letters, he is far from aggressive. Practical could readily describe Jefferson's tone, but avarice, or greed, does not.

9. **(C)** First, think about what the question is asking. "Foresight" means that Jefferson was able to predict what might happen. So we are looking in the first passage for a prediction that comes true or could come true according to the second passage. Choice (C) is the only choice in which Jefferson anticipates America's vulnerability at its coasts, which is the topic of the second passage.

10. **(C)** Notice the word "respective" in the question, meaning that these answers have to go in order: the first word has to describe the first passage and the second should apply to Passage 2. In the first passage, Jefferson proposes ideas about how to move forward economically. In the second, he plans for military engagement. Choice (A) has these switched, so eliminate it. Jefferson never shows evidence of being overly concerned with his personal issues, as in choice (B). The first passage is far from "pedestrian," or dull and unconcerned.

Great Global Conversation: Frederick Douglass

1. **(B)** Notice the question asks for a general point, or main idea, from the first paragraph. In these lines, Douglass discusses his broad autobiographical information, his birthplace and age, emphasizing the obscurity about his age. The rest of the paragraph expresses that this ignorance is commonplace among slaves. Choice (A) wrongly assumes celebration, which is not mentioned here. Choice (C) is not evidenced; "kind" masters are referenced as those who give their slaves permission to visit another plantation—an allowance that is far from overcoming prejudice. Math education, although conceivable as a detail, is not the main point of the first paragraph, eliminating choice (D).

2. **(C)** In lines 6–8, Douglass validates his distress at not having access to his own basic personal information. If you replace "want" with *absence*, you can see that choice (C) is appropriate. Although choice (A) might be tempting, read the sentence with *obstacle* substituted for "want." You'll quickly see that the desire for information is not what produced unhappiness but that the need was denied. It isn't appropriate to say the "obstacle" or "command" of information produced unhappiness.

3. **(B)** What the author does know about himself comes from others' conversations or stories, making choice (B) correct. We know Douglass didn't speak much with his mother, and she died while he was very young. Choice (C) is incorrect because this evidence was purposefully denied him. Choice (D) is not discussed in the passage.

4. **(B)** To approach this question, look for lines in which Douglass receives information about his past through others, as in choice (B). Choice (A) evidences the master's tendency to refuse to answer questions concerning a slave's past. Choice (C) explains why it was especially tough for Douglass's mother to visit him. Choice (D) gives the only example of Douglass's history that he seems to remember for himself.

5. **(B)** In these lines, Douglass describes the effects of taking mothers from their children under institutionalized slavery. He concludes that this tendency impeded the child's affection and curtailed the mother's nurturing. Hence, choice (B) is correct. Although Douglass may have wished for a better relationship with his mother, he seems quite fond of, rather than disappointed by, her commitment to seeing him whenever possible. Choice (C) is appealing, but Douglass says himself that he can't be sure why. He doesn't discuss his intellectual development, eliminating choice (D).

6. **(D)** Douglass is unsure of who his father is, so choice (D) is correct. Although Douglass admits that a rumor spread that his master was his father, the rumor was never confirmed. So Douglass does not suggest that he actually met his father. Since this information is completely withheld from him, we cannot assume choices (A), (B), or (C).

7. **(A)** Douglass's mother sneaks out at night, walks 12 miles to visit him, and then has to make the journey again before morning so she can work in the fields all day. Her priorities are not economic as in choice (B). Although 12 miles is quite a bit to walk, her presence proves that it is not insurmountable, making choice (C) incorrect. Choice (D) is never mentioned.

8. **(B)** Beginning in line 30, we learn about the circumstances under which Douglass's mother visits him, risking "a whipping" if not back "in the field at sunrise." Hence, these lines provide direct evidence for the previous question. Choices (A), (C), and (D) tell us briefly about Douglass's relationship with his mother but not why she was forced to visit only at night.

9. **(A)** Here, Douglass describes his numbness at the news of his mother's death. "Tidings" means news or information, making choice (A) correct. Although choices (B) and (C) don't describe this same idea of hearing about her death, choice (D) might tempt you. Just remember that it's inaccurate to say Douglass would receive the "causes" of her death.

Great Global Conversation: Emerson and Arnold

1. **(D)** In the first passage, Emerson is concerned with why the current age is retrospective, or always looking back into the past. He advocates, instead, for "a poetry and philosophy of insight" rather than relying on traditional discourses. Similarly, he says we should "demand our own works" and interrogate what is natural. Hence, he raises the question of why we rely on what others have said instead of having our own experiences and creating our own theories, making choice (D) correct. He is not concerned with feuds or inconsistencies between separate fields as in choices (A), (B), and (C).

2. **(A)** Here, Emerson argues that past generations "beheld God and nature face to face" while the current generation experiences them only through the words and records of those who have come before. So "original" means "unique" or "special," making choice (A) correct. We can rule out choices (B) and (C) because they mean the same thing, both suggesting that the new ways be somehow groundbreaking. Choice (D) is wrong because Emerson does not suggest that the relationship be ceremonial in any way.

3. **(A)** Emerson believes in "the perfection of the creation so far," arguing that man can "satisfy" all "curiosity." So Emerson's attitude is optimistic that as long as we pose questions, we can intelligently and coherently discover answers. Choice (B) is the opposite. Although Emerson's argument is abstract, or existing through ideas and theoretical concepts, this doesn't describe his attitude toward human understanding. Similarly, historicism is the theory that culture is determined by history. This is what Emerson desires to change. Again, it is not accurate in describing his attitude toward human understanding.

4. **(B)** These lines summarize Emerson's belief that all questions can be answered, all curiosities can be satisfied, and thus provide evidence that he is optimistic that the current generation can come to their own understanding of the human experience. Choice (A) is merely where Emerson's question is posed. Choice (C) suggests that the current generation must look for its own answers but does not explicitly reveal his attitude toward the possibility of accomplishing this task. Choice (D) simply states what Emerson believes is the objective of science.

5. **(C)** Of Plato, Arnold says that "[o]ne cannot refuse to admire the artist," yet his notions are "primitive," making choice (C) correct. Plato, who held disdain for the man who worked rather than spent all his time thinking and speculating, is viewed as neither practical nor applicable, ruling out choices (A) and (D). Since Arnold summarizes Plato's beliefs, it is not accurate to call them "indecipherable" as in choice (B).

6. **(C)** Here, Plato's ideas are called "primitive," based on a time when society was categorized into warriors, priests, and slaves. Further, his ideas are "admirable" because the first sentence of the selection states that one "cannot refuse to admire the artist who draws these pictures." Choices (A) and (B) both explain Plato's argument. Choice (D) does not focus on what Arnold thinks of Plato's ideas.

7. **(B)** This word is used in Plato's description of the "working lawyer" who is bonded, "bent and broken . . . without a particle of soundness in him." A good approach to this question is to substitute a word like *health*. The example paints the picture of a man "smart and clever" who has not been able to meet his potential because of the strains of life, ruling out choice (C). It is inaccurate to say somebody doesn't have "safety" in them. The word "eloquence" means being articulate or expressive. Plato does not think the lawyer cannot be persuasive but, instead, that the lawyer doesn't have the time or strength to devote to his own refinement.

8. **(C)** Simply put, Plato is scornful of all working professions. So look for an answer that says something to the effect of labor detracting from one's self-worth. That is choice (C). Choices (A) and (D) favor those who work or service others and so contradict Plato's belief. Choice (B) is too extreme since Plato seems to pity the "bent and broken" victims of the labor force.

9. **(B)** To approach this question, think of what we know Emerson and Plato value. In the first passage, Emerson values independent thinking, observing, and asking questions. Emerson is briefly mentioned in the second passage as advocating for working professionals since they are "the modern majority." Plato, on the other hand, believes any kind of organized work or profession detracts from one's strength and intellectual potential. Hence, choice (B) is correct. Plato never advocates for mathematical reasoning or industrial engineering, eliminating choices (C) and (D). Although choice (A) is tempting, recall that religious revelation is only one detail of Emerson's argument and that Plato is not focused on the sciences but on the pursuit of knowledge apart from the burden of a job.

10. **(D)** Know what you are looking for by paraphrasing this question. We want to find what Emerson said that would explicitly offend Plato. Choice (D) is correct because here Emerson voices a common belief that "speculative men," or men like Plato who spend their time thinking, are "unsound and frivolous." Choices (A), (B), and (C) consist of Emerson's argument that the current generation should seek its own knowledge, an idea with which Plato would most likely agree.

Social Science: Russian Depopulation

1. **(C)** The author presents several contributing factors to the population problem and ends on a less than hopeful note that the population will continue to decline if great changes are not made. Thus choice (C) makes the most sense here. Choice (A) might tempt you, but "manageable" implies that the problem could be taken care of without difficulty, which is not the author's opinion. Since Russia seems to be an aberration rather than the norm, we can rule out choice (B). "Nebulous" means "unclear," but the author seems to believe he knows the factors behind the decline in population, which eliminates choice (D).

2. **(A)** In the very first paragraph, the author states that Russia faces "the biggest long-term problem" and lists the many factors influencing the problem. This provides direct evidence for the previous question, making choice (A) correct. Choice (B) supports the idea that Russia is an anomaly. Choices (C) and (D) discuss the author's opinions regarding Russian family values. Only choice (A) gives evidence of the author's overall attitude toward the issue.

3. **(D)** This is a purpose question. Ask yourself what the author is doing in these lines. These lines compare Russia to less-developed countries, illustrating how life expectancy alone cannot explain Russia's decline in population. Instead, Russia is combatting a more complex problem where life expectancy and birth rates are simultaneously low. These lines show how we need more than one number to evaluate Russia's situation effectively, making choice (D) correct. We are given precise data, so choice (A) doesn't work. These lines actually contradict choice (B). Be careful with choice (C); we are examining demographics, not economics.

4. **(B)** "Fairly" can be substituted with *comparably* here. So choice (B) is the correct choice. The idea is that the expectancy can be considered high in relation to less-developed countries. Choice (A) wrongly assumes we are using morals as judgment measures. Choice (C) inaccurately equates the expectancy rates. Choice (D) would mean that we are looking at a sole figure rather than comparing multiple figures.

5. **(B)** This line refers to fathers who are often absent, or "uninvolved," in the raising of their children. We cannot assume the fathers are in jail, deceased, or geographically distant.

6. **(B)** The author sees Putin's solution as limited because it "fails to see the underlying causes" and instead focuses on "economic programs." Choices (A) and (C) contradict this view. Choice (D) assumes too much; although the article references social programs, it does not include details.

7. **(C)** We are looking for two things here. First, we want a solution that would increase Russia's population. Second, we want something that was not considered in the passage. Hence, choice (C) is correct. Choices (B) and (D) were both mentioned by the author. Choice (A) wouldn't actually change the population at all.

8. **(A)** This question has two parts. First, decide what the author offered as advice. The author argues that the mindset of Russians has to change. She identifies the causes as lack of family support and lack of desire for children. So if those two things changed to increase the population, Russians would have more children. Hence, the new figure would show an increase in the youth population. Choice (A) accurately describes that change. Choice (B) wrongly implies that the author suggests a solution that extends life expectancy. Choices (C) and (D), by emphasizing other subsections of the population, both fail to account for the rise in births that the author ultimately advocates for.

9. **(A)** The question asks for the difference in Russia's male and female elderly populations. We know from the passage that women live much longer than men in Russia. Hence, their ages will diverge more. Choice (D) is nonsensical, claiming different values for the same numbers. Choices (B) and (C) don't account for the tendency for elderly women to live longer than elderly men.

10. **(A)** Look for the lines that indicate the gap in life expectancy between males and females in Russia. Since that occurs around lines 5–8, choice (A) is correct. Choice (B) explains some causes of the low male life expectancy. Choice (C) transitions into birth rates. Choice (D) examines the inconsistencies between demographic data and supposed family values.

Social Science: The Emu War

1. **(D)** The question is asking what the first paragraph *does*. That paragraph discusses the butterfly effect generally before closing in on a particular instance between British veterans and emus in Western Australia. So choice (D) is correct. This paragraph is concerned with introducing the topic in a creative way, not in demonstrating a decision (which comes much later in the passage) or countering objections. Choice (C) is incorrect because the first paragraph does not utilize a personal story.

2. **(A)** We know that the military initially thought they could easily handle the emus, but they failed miserably, making choice (A) correct. The author does not suggest that it requires extraordinary bravery to face flightless birds, ruling out choice (B). Choice (C) is actually the lesson learned from the military's overconfidence: because it was particularly presumptuous, the military learned a lesson in modesty. Choice (D) means excessively enthusiastic or extreme, which is not accurate here.

3. **(C)** These lines specifically state that the troops underestimated the emus and failed to accomplish their mission. Hence, they give direct support for the previous question. Choice (A) introduces the event but doesn't reveal the military mindset toward the emus. Choice (B) explains the damage inflicted by the emus. Choice (D) affirms the major's failure but, again, doesn't give evidence of his initial attitude.

4. **(B)** Here, the veterans are encouraged to participate in farming. Choice (B) sounds most like that. Choice (A) inaccurately implies that the veterans should *grab* farming. Choice (C) is wrong because no evidence is given that the veterans had to study farming first; instead, they are involved in actual farming. Of course, the veterans were not inventing or creating farming for the first time, making choice (D) incorrect.

5. **(B)** It might be helpful to paraphrase this question. *What changed between the ineffective and the effective raids on the emus?* The passage attributes Major Meredith's minimal success his second time around to "his previous experience." Later, the locals succeed because they are "well equipped and knowledgeable." So choice (B) is the correct answer. No evidence indicates that the major or the locals receive further training, academic or military. Choice (D) inappropriately implies that the media was somehow responsible for the more successful onslaughts.

6. **(D)** These lines state that the bounty system—a measure that prevented government involvement—worked well because the locals were better able to hunt the emus. Thus, we can infer that their first-hand experience gave them an advantage. Choice (A) states only that government aid was requested. Choice (B) references the media's involvement but, of course, does not connect the media with the successful fight against the emu population. Choice (C) includes the lines where the bounty system is explained, but fails to explain why it was successful. So choice (D) is the only answer that gives evidence as to what attributed to the effective attacks on the emus.

7. **(C)** Why might the author choose to use quotation marks here? You might be thinking for dramatic effect. The usage of "war" in this context is comical because a military force is being called in to fight birds, and the birds are ironically winning. So these terms usually mean something very different in warfare. Hence, choice (C) is correct. The author is not citing quotations or research. This event is actually quite trivial in the global context of war. Choice (D) is tempting but implies that the author is disputing facts, whereas he/she is actually calling attention to the absurdity of equating a fowl hunt to true warfare.

8. **(A)** To approach this question, use context clues and substitute your own synonym. The successful resistance of the emus, though humorous, was actually harmful to the veterans' already dangerously uncertain situation. Choice (A) sounds most like *uncertain* or *unpredictable*. Choice (B) is too extreme because it implies a submission to fate, but the veterans/ farmers are not merely resigned to fail. Choice (C) just means that the situation is related to living organisms. Choice (D) means cultivated in the sense of being well-traveled.

9. **(C)** This question focuses on what the figure can help explain. So first ask what the figure does. It gives a general timeline of the war very similar to the ones constructed to outline the battles of extended warfare. Then ask which of these choices discusses the varied events of the so-called war. Choice (C) specifically mentions the engagements of the war, and so it is correct. Choice (A) just tells who was assigned to the task. Choice (B) describes what the forces took for the first engagement. Choice (D) again describes one event but doesn't reference several like (C) does.

10. **(A)** From the figure, we can see that the forces were generally ineffective at first, improved with time, and then became particularly efficient by December. Choice (A) accurately accounts for this gradual increase in efficiency. Choices (B) and (C) do not reflect this improvement, and choice (D) inaccurately implies that we cannot find a general pattern.

Science: Caffeine

1. **(C)** Passage 1 examines how caffeine works in the body by inhibiting the body's ability to sense how much adenosine is in the body. It is neutral and informative. Passage 2 seems to serve as a warning to the reader that although caffeine isn't typically deadly, it does have many negative health consequences. Passage 2 is primarily persuasive. Therefore, choice (C) is correct. Choice (A) is wrong because although Passage 1 is analytical, Passage 2 is not narrative, or telling a story. Choice (B) is wrong because it flips the two passages. Choice (D) is incorrect because although Passage 1 is somewhat medical, Passage 2 doesn't focus on economics.

2. **(D)** The first of these two paragraphs says that in a thermodynamically favorable reaction, adenosine triphosphate releases its phosphates and free energy, leaving just adenosine and inorganic phosphate. The next paragraph talks about how we have neurons that have evolved to detect the presence of adenosine and then to direct the pineal gland to secrete melatonin. This sequence is described by answer choice (D). Choice (A) is wrong because the pineal gland secretes melatonin, rather than forms adenosine triphosphate. Choice (B) is wrong because the detection of just adenosine triggers the melatonin response; the presence of adenosine triphosphate does not have this effect. Choice (C) doesn't work because the energy is released when adenosine triphosphate decomposes to adenosine and inorganic phosphate.

3. **(C)** This paragraph describes the process by which adenosine triphosphate undergoes a thermodynamically favorable process to form adenosine and inorganic phosphate and to release free energy. If energy is released in the reaction, it means that energy was being stored in the reactants, so the reactants have more energy than the products, choice (C). Choices (A) and (B) are incorrect because this term refers to an energy differential. Choice (D) is backward.

4. **(A)** In paragraph 3, the author talks about how the body knows to sleep when a large amount of adenosine is sensed by receptors in the neurons. In the last paragraph, the author says that caffeine (because it has a very similar structure to adenine) can interact with these receptors, tricking the body into thinking less adenosine is present than really is. This corresponds to choice (A), because energy consumption in the body corresponds to conversion of adenosine triphosphate into adenosine. Choices (B), (C), and (D) aren't supported anywhere in the passage.

5. **(C)** The correct answer is choice (C) because this is the part of the passage that discusses how caffeine works. These lines talk about caffeine interacting with adenosine receptors that are intended to sense how much energy the body has expended. Choice (A) is wrong because it introduces the concept of adenosine triphosphate as a source of energy. Choice (B) merely suggests a purpose for sleep. Choice (D) is wrong because it talks about a time when caffeine doesn't work—when the body has simply expended too much energy and the body's adenosine levels have become too high.

6. **(A)** This line is used to contrast the beginning of the paragraph, which states that caffeine isn't typically deadly. The "however" in this line tips us off to the fact that the author wants to make a contrast. What he's saying is that although caffeine isn't deadly, it's also not ____. It makes sense to say that although caffeine isn't deadly, it's also not "harmless," which is choice (A). Choices (B), (C), and (D) are incorrect because caffeine is all of these things.

7. **(B)** The author states in the final paragraph that pathological addiction to caffeine has never been documented in humans, so the correct answer is choice (B). The rest of the answer choices are mentioned as detriments of caffeine (choice (A): lines 44–46; choice (C): lines 46–47; choice (D): lines 43–44).

8. **(D)** Choice (D) is correct because these lines state that pathological addiction to caffeine has never been documented. The other choices all mention negative effects of caffeine: bone loss, anxiety, and heart dysrhythmias.

9. **(C)** Passage 1 primarily examines how caffeine stimulation works in the body. Passage 2 argues that although caffeine isn't deadly, it can have many negative side effects in certain groups of people. Therefore, the correct answer is choice (C). Choice (A) is wrong because although Passage 1 does touch on the origins of caffeine, it doesn't discuss the history. Choice (B) is wrong because Passage 1 talks about how caffeine works rather than its benefits. Choice (D) is incorrect because neither passage discusses the evolution of caffeine stimulation.

Science: Fungi

1. **(C)** First summarize what happened with antibiotics and antibiotic resistance: certain classes of antibiotics were wildly effective in eradicating bacteria, but some were resistant. As these classes of antibiotics were used more rampantly, much larger numbers of the bacteria became resistant. Thus, the situation described is one in which initial efficiency decreases as something becomes better at beating the system. This matches choice (C): the software is initially effective. However, as more students learn to beat the system, the software loses its effectiveness. Choice (A) isn't the same, because its efficiency increases over time. Choices (B) and (D) are tempting, but nothing is learning to beat the system in either case.

2. **(C)** This paragraph gives a general introduction of fungi, emphasizing that many people don't realize how prevalent they are in our lives. The essay then goes on to discuss several examples of the applications of fungi. Therefore, the answer is choice (C): the author relates fungi to our lives. Choice (A) is wrong because the author mentions fungi only as food here, but the essay doesn't focus on it. Chocie (B) doesn't work because the author simply says that many people don't realize how important fungi are—not that they're wrong about fungi. Choice (D) is incorrect because the author says that the importance of fungi is easily overlooked rather than easily visible.

3. **(D)** This line says that fungi execute many functions in our lives. In other words, they *perform* many functions, which is choice (D). Choice (A) is another definition of "execute." However, the fungi aren't destroying functions, they're carrying out functions. They're also not hiding functions, as in choice (B), or enticing functions, as in choice (C).

4. **(A)** The author talks about Alexander Fleming somewhat accidentally discovering the antibiotic properties of penicillin (lines 12–17) and Akiro Endo discovering the benefits of statins while attempting to study *Penicillium citrinum*'s antimicrobial properties. What these major discoveries have in common is that they were somewhat accidental. Thus, the answer is choice (A). These discoveries weren't a product of evolution or genetic engineering as in choices (B) or (D). Although they may have required economic investment, as in choice (C), the author doesn't mention this.

5. **(D)** The correct answer is choice (D) because these lines state that both Alexander Fleming and Akira Endo made their discoveries serendipitously, meaning with a bit of chance or luck. Choice (A) talks about how Fleming's discovery contributed to science, but none of the answer choices from the previous question apply. Choice (B) talks about how widespread use of antibiotics contributed to antibiotic resistance—not exactly a medical innovation. Choice (C) simply defines statins.

6. **(B)** Consider the context. These lines state that peptidoglycan polymers are highly peculiar to bacteria and that the antimicrobial agents that target peptidoglycan don't harm other cells. In other words, only bacteria are affected by these agents because only bacteria have peptidoglycan polymers. Therefore, the polymers are *unique* to bacteria, choice (B). Choice (A) is another common use of the word "peculiar." In this case, though, it is somewhat opposite of what the author means since peptidoglycans are common to bacteria. Choice (C) is wrong because these polymers are normal, not diseased. Choice (D) is wrong because although peptidoglycans certainly are helpful, this doesn't fit the contrast in the latter part of the sentence.

7. **(D)** The answer can be found in the third paragraph, where the author details the mechanism by which antibiotics work. He says that antibiotics target peptidoglycan polymers, which are present only in bacteria. Therefore, antibiotics harm the bacteria without harming the host's cells, choice (D). Choice (A) is incorrect as evidenced by the fact that many bacteria have developed antibiotic resistance. Neither choice (B) nor choice (C) is supported anywhere in the passage.

8. **(C)** The correct answer is choice (C) These lines state that antibiotics work by targeting something present strictly in bacteria. Choice (A) doesn't discuss antibiotics. Choice (B) merely mentions that a fungus led to the development of three classes of antibiotics. Choice (D) references antibiotic resistance but not what makes antibiotics effective.

9. **(B)** This sentence beckons the reader to ask what is left to be discovered if some of our biggest findings in medicine have been the accidental results of studying fungi. The author is hinting that it's almost certain that fungi have more benefits to provide but that we must look for them. Thus, choice (B) is correct. Choice (A) is wrong because the author mentions neither geology nor funding. Choice (C) is wrong because the author thinks there's much research left to be done, and choice (D) is wrong because nowhere in the passage does the author criticize mycology.

Science: Methanogenesis

1. **(B)** The answer to this question can be found in the last paragraph. The author states that understanding *Methanosphaera stadtmanae* has been immensely helpful in understanding and treating IBD. He also acknowledges that further understanding of archaeal and bacterial species will lead to a better understanding of how all of these things interact. Therefore, progress is being made on the subject, choice (B). It isn't choice (A), "largely settled," because he admits that it can be better understood. It isn't choice (C) because he talks about how scientists have come to better understand the relationships. It isn't choice (D) because scientists are still working to understand how archaeal and bacterial species interact with the human anatomy.

2. **(A)** According to lines 17–20, methanogenic bacteria were first identified in the gut microbiota after methane was detected in the breath. Methanogens are defined throughout the passage as species that produce methane, so this presence of methane in the breath eventually led to the identification of methanogenic species in the human digestive system. Thus, the answer is choice (A). Choice (B) is incorrect because it says that the methanogens were eventually identified in fecal samples, but this wasn't how they were originally discovered. Choices (C) and (D) are details of the passage mentioned in other paragraphs but not in the third paragraph and not about how methanogens were discovered.

3. **(C)** In these lines, the author is referring to methanol being reduced to methane. Since these are two different chemical compounds, you can infer that methanol is being converted or *transformed* into methane, choice (C). The other choices are all different meanings of the word that don't apply here, as methanol cannot be subtracted, diminished, or persecuted into methane.

4. **(C)** Consider the context. Prior to these lines, the author stated that *Methanosphaera stadtmanae* is somehow connected to the occurrence of IBD. These lines serve to explain to the reader the role that *M. stadtmanae* plays in this process—it triggers the proinflammatory cytokines. Thus, he is explaining a process, choice (C). The answer isn't choice (A) because the author hasn't introduced any objections that he's trying to disprove. The answer isn't choice (B) because he's talking about a partially known scientific fact rather than a speculation. Choice (D) is incorrect because the author doesn't attribute this fact to anyone.

5. **(A)** This line says that *Methanosphaera stadtmanae* induces the release of proinflammatory cytokine TNF. This seems to be a cause-and-effect relationship: *M. stadtmanae* senses something and makes something else happen. Another way to describe this might be that *M. stadtmanae* triggers the release, or *causes* the release, choice (A). Choices (B) and (D) are too personified—it's more automated than something that is suggested or persuaded. Choice (C) doesn't work because the organisms can't release a release.

6. **(B)** The author states that *Methanosphaera stadtmanae* is helpful to humans because it conserves energy and aids in digestion (lines 44–50). He also says that it likely contributes to IBD in some individuals. Therefore, *M. stadtmanae* plays an important and helpful role in the body. However, if homeostasis is not maintained, it can also have negative effects in the body. Therefore, it is primarily beneficial, choice (B). It isn't uniformly positive, choice (A), because of its role in IBD. It isn't somewhat harmful, as in choice (D), because the author explicitly states in the first paragraph that *M. stadtmanae* is beneficial to humans. It's necessary for energy conservation and digestion.

7. **(C)** In the second paragraph, the author explains how *Methanosphaera stadtmanae* is different from other methanogens. These other methanogens can reduce CO_2 to methane, but *M. stadtmanae* lacks the enzyme to initiate this pathway. Thus, *M. stadtmanae* can reduce methanol only to methane. Therefore, the inability to process CO_2 sets the species apart from other methanogens. Choice (A) is incorrect because all of the methanogens the author references use H_2 in reduction. Choices (B) and (D) aren't mentioned in the passage.

8. **(B)** Choice (B) is the correct answer because these lines explicitly state that the inability of *Methanosphaera stadtmanae* to reduce carbon dioxide to methane is what sets it apart from other methanogens. Lines 10–11 and 21–23 also give examples of differences among *M. stadtmanae* and other methanogens, but these lines don't mention any of the answers to the previous question. Choice (D) provides a similarity between *M. stadtmanae* and the other methanogens.

9. **(D)** First, consider why the author says that *Methanosphaera stadtmanae* is beneficial to the host. In the first paragraph, he talks about how this species has a particularly restrictive energy metabolism, stating that "these unique energy conservation traits are what make *Methanosphaera stadtmanae* beneficial to its human host and not an opportunistic pathogen." Thus, we're looking for an answer choice from the figures that shows that this species conserves energy. Notice that for most of the pathways, Figure 1 says that at least some sort of intermediate is missing. In Figure 2, many of the boxes are black, meaning intermediates are missing. Thus, the answer is choice (D). Choices (A) and (B) aren't mentioned in the passage, and choice (C) isn't supported by the figures.

10. **(A)** The correct answer is choice (A). These lines suggest that this species is helpful to humans rather than harmful because it has a very restrictive metabolism, meaning it's limited in its pathways. This is what's being shown by the two figures. Choice (B) is about the history of the discovery of methanogens in the gut. Choice (C) is a negative side effect of what can happen if the balance of methanogens isn't maintained, so it's about how they can be harmful to humans, rather than helpful. Choice (D) is about how homeostasis of the gut microbiota may be restored when it's disturbed. However, choice (D) is unrelated to the figures, as well as to how *M. stadtmanae* is beneficial to humans.

Science: Wound Healing

1. **(A)** The passage starts with what happens immediately after a laceration occurs and continues through the stages of wound healing; thus, it is chronological as in choice (A). Choices (B) and (D) are incorrect because the passage is merely informative and does not consider pros and cons or attempt to be persuasive. Choice (C) is incorrect because these steps all occur in the same space.

2. **(C)** The main purpose of the passage is to inform the reader of what happens after a person sustains a wound so that he or she may know to seek medical attention if a wound isn't properly healing. This makes choice (C) the correct answer. Choice (A) is wrong because the author details the normal healing process rather than any abnormalities. Choices (B) and (D) are incorrect because the author is simply stating the current understanding of wound healing rather than arguing anything.

3. **(B)** Lines 4–5 give the author's purpose: to detail the typical wound progression so that a reader may know what to expect and when to be concerned. So choice (B) is correct. Furthermore, either the beginning or the end of the first paragraph is often where the author will clearly state his or her thesis, so it is unsurprising to find the answer in these lines. Choice (A) only introduces the reader to the topic of wound healing without stating why it is important that a reader understands the subject. Choice (C) lists aspects of wound healing that a reader can't control. Choice (D) gives the reader some advice. However, both choices (C) and (D) miss the big picture by merely providing details.

4. **(A)** Consider the context here. The previous sentence introduces the term *phagocytosis*. Because this is a scientific term that not all readers will know, the author then clarifies what phagocytes do in the process of phagocytosis. Therefore, the author is clarifying a specialized term, making choice (A) correct. Choice (B) is incorrect because the author doesn't tell where the word comes from. Choices (C) and (D) are incorrect because the sentence does neither of these things.

5. **(D)** In this case, "raw" is referring to the edges of the wound. The author means raw as in damaged or inflamed, as is expected after the inflammatory stage, choice (D). Choice (A) is incorrect because although it is a definition of the word "raw," it refers to materials rather than a wound. Choice (B) doesn't work because the skin isn't primitive. Choice (C) is a common definition of raw, but it refers more to uncooked food rather than to a wound.

6. **(A)** The author is emphasizing here that it is important to protect a wound in this stage, choice (A). Neither choice (B) nor choice (C) works because each has a negative connotation. The author is just emphasizing something, not passing judgment. Choice (D) is wrong because one wouldn't say that protecting something is analytical.

7. **(C)** The passage lists the steps in terms of one occurring then the body moving on to the next. Therefore, the passage lists the steps in a sequential or chronological order. However, the figure shows great overlap among the steps; for instance, angiogenesis and wound contraction occur almost entirely at the same time. Therefore, the figure shows them as being concurrent or simultaneous. Thus, the correct answer is choice (C) as it classifies the passage's description as sequential and the figure's description as simultaneous. Choice (A) has the passage and the figure backward. Choice (B) is incorrect because both show that the processes are gradual. Choice (D) is wrong because the figure simply shows a time depiction of when the steps occur but states nothing of where they occur.

8. **(C)** Line 37 states that the last step of healing, the maturation stage, may last up to two years. The inflammatory phase lasts between 2 and 14 days, and the proliferative phase lasts between 3 and 21 days. Therefore, the whole healing phase may last $14 + 21 + 365 + 365 = 765$ days. Thus, the closest answer is 1,000. In 1,000 days, the wound will almost certainly be healed, choice (C).

9. **(D)** Lines 35–38 give the timeline for the longest-lasting stage—up to two years. Therefore, we know that even the worst wounds should be healed in just over two years, making 1,000 days a reasonable estimate. Choices (A) and (C) give the timeline for much faster steps, but they don't give a reasonable estimate of the whole timeline. Choice (B) doesn't discuss time.

Writing and Language

Writing and Language

3

FREQUENTLY ASKED QUESTIONS

How Is the Writing and Language Section Structured?

- It is the second section of the PSAT, following Reading.
- There are 44 questions.
- There is a time limit of 35 minutes.
- There are 4 passages.
- Questions are in a random order of difficulty.

What Is Tested on the Writing and Language Section?

The Writing and Language section tests the fundamentals of English grammar and essential editing skills. More specifically, the following are overviews of the concepts assessed:

IDEA DEVELOPMENT: Is the writing well developed, clear, well supported, and focused? Can the student integrate information from quantitative graphs into the passage?

ORGANIZATION: Does the writing follow a logical sequence? Are the transitions, introductions, and conclusions effective?

LANGUAGE USE: Is the writing appropriately precise and concise? Is the style and tone consistent? Is proper syntax used?

SENTENCE STRUCTURE: Are sentences complete? Is parallel structure and proper word order used?

USAGE RULES: Is the verb tense and number use (singular and plural) consistent? Is the language consistent with conventional expressions?

PUNCTUATION: Does the student know how to use commas, semicolons, colons, and dashes properly?

What Are the Most Important Things I Can Do to Be Successful?

CAREFULLY REVIEW THIS CHAPTER. It comprehensively covers the major grammar and editing concepts you will need to know for the PSAT.

WORK THROUGH THE WRITING AND LANGUAGE PRACTICE TESTS IN THIS BOOK. They are carefully designed to align with what you will face on test day and are based on careful analysis of the released PSATs from College Board.

READ WIDELY! The more familiar you are with what good writing should look like, the easier it will be for you to spot the best options on this section.

PRACTICE WITH OTHER MATERIALS IF NEEDED. The PSAT Writing and Language section is virtually identical to the SAT Writing and Language section. So, if you run out of practice materials in this book, check out *Barron's SAT* or any of the other Barron's books for the SAT. You can find further practice at *KhanAcademy.org*, the official College Board practice website. Also, since the PSAT Writing and Language section closely mirrors the content covered by the ACT English section, you can improve your PSAT Writing and Language performance by practicing ACT English passages.

WRITING AND LANGUAGE STRATEGIES

1. Use the Full Amount of Time

The PSAT Writing and Language section is typically easy to finish for most students. With 35 minutes and 4 passages, you should take about *9 minutes per passage* to finish. You are much more likely to make careless errors if you rush through the questions. Instead, do the questions one time well so that you do not miss the subtle issues that many questions test. Even though with many tests it makes sense to finish early so that you have time to check your work, it is advisable with the PSAT Writing and Language test to pace yourself to finish right on time. You are more likely to avoid careless errors if you catch them the first time, rather than if you go through the test quickly and then quickly scan over your answers to check. If you find that you are able to comfortably finish the PSAT Writing and Language text with time to spare, you may consider reading through the passages before doing the questions so that you have a better understanding of the meaning and flow of the essay. Although this is not necessary to perform well, it can sometimes be advisable for those students who would otherwise simply waste this time just sitting there during the last few minutes of the test.

2. Write on the Test Booklet

With many school tests, teachers require students to avoid marking on the test booklets—this makes sense, as they want to reuse the booklets for other classes. No one is going to use your PSAT booklet but you. So, write on it whenever and wherever you find it helpful. If you are taking a digital version of the test, make notations on the provided scrap paper if needed. Here are a couple of common cases where writing can make a difference:

You can carefully underline and circle key words in the questions. If a question asks you about "specific" information and you miss this word, you will miss the question. If you underline the key words as you read, you are much less likely to make careless reading mistakes.

You can write down possible placements for reordering sentences and paragraphs. It is not necessary to keep all of the possible placements of a sentence straight in your head. Write down where choice (A) should go in the paragraph, where choice (B) should go, and so on. The less you have to keep track of in your head, the more mental power you will free up to think through the questions.

3. Mouth It Out as You Read

"Hear" the passage in your head and test out the sound of the different options. You don't have to know the exact rules for misplaced modifiers and proper sentence construction to recognize that this sounds wrong: "Excited was I the brand new science fiction movie to see." When you are doing the PSAT Writing and Language test, you must answer the questions correctly—you do not need to write out a justification for each answer. This chapter comprehensively covers the grammar rules you will need to know—study them, and you will be much more confident and decisive. Coupled with this knowledge, you will put yourself in the best position to succeed if you filter the questions not just through your eyes but through your ears as well.

4. Make Sure That Everything Makes Sense Given the Context

To determine if a sentence provides an effective introduction, you must understand the paragraph as a whole. To see if a verb has the correct tense, you must see how the verbs in nearby sentences are used. Some questions will require that you look only at the sentence that the underlined portion is in, whereas other questions will require a couple of paragraphs of context. When you have any doubt about how much of the surrounding context to consider, err on the side of reading *too much* rather than *too little*. Since the Writing and Language section is relatively easy to finish, you should take the necessary time to be certain everything is consistent and logical.

5. Understand That There Will Not Be Grammar Gimmicks—Just Grammar Rules

The PSAT will only test you on topics where there are clearly defined grammar rules. Topics on which there is disagreement on proper English usage (using the Oxford comma, using "but" or "because" to start a sentence, and whether it is OK to use the first person "I" or second person "you" in formal papers) will not be tested. In addition, you do not need to worry about if there will be two right answers—the PSAT is an extremely well-crafted test, and it is a virtual certainty that it will be free of errors. So, instead of wasting your time trying to determine the "tricks" of the test, boost your grammar knowledge and go in with confidence.

6. Guess Smart, Not Just Randomly

Remember—there is no penalty for guessing on the PSAT. Thus, be certain that you answer every single test question. If you do feel unsure about a question, here are some tips that can help you make an educated guess.

If two or three of the answers are extremely similar, it is highly unlikely that one of those will be the correct choice. For example, if a question has these choices—(A) but, (B) however, (C) nevertheless, and (D) consequently—the answer is most likely choice (D) because the other choices are all synonymous.

NO CHANGE has just as much of a chance of being correct as any other answer. Many students unfairly dismiss this as a possibility, believing that questions *must* have some kind of a change.

Come back to questions if you do not feel confident. Doing this will allow you to reexamine the question with fresh eyes after you've given your mind a chance to subconsciously process what the question was asking.

BIG PICTURE IDEA QUESTIONS

Big picture idea questions require you to consider how the writer's message and structure can be clarified. You may need to consider *thesis statements* (which express the primary argument of the passage), *topic sentences* (which are usually the first sentence of a paragraph and state its overall message), and *claims* and *counterclaims* (statements in favor of or against the author's argument).

Tactic 1: Put the General Meaning of the Passage or Paragraph into Your Own Words. Then Think About What Would Be the Most Logical Choice.

If you approach these types of questions by looking at a limited amount of context, you will likely choose an incorrect answer. Take the time necessary to paraphrase the meaning of as much of the passage as is relevant. Also, be certain that you carefully read the question to be clear on what is being asked.

Example

❶ Students will not be prepared for the real world if they cannot do simple mental math. This is true not just for those who are in science and math fields but for anyone who needs to approximate discounts for sales and calculate the appropriate tip at a restaurant. Schools should give students the tools they need to succeed by, ironically, taking away the tool of a calculator on occasion.

1. Which sentence, if inserted at the beginning of the paragraph, would provide the best introduction to what follows?

   (A) Scientific careers give students the best opportunity for high-paying jobs.

   (B) Many students are far too dependent on their calculators for basic computations.

   (C) I, for one, do not see the relevance of learning calculus if I am going to be a humanities major.

   (D) The funding for mathematical education across all age groups needs to be increased.

Start a question like this by carefully reading what is asked—we need a good introductory topic sentence. Before reading the choices, go ahead and read the paragraph that follows and put its general meaning into your own words. For example, this paragraph could be paraphrased as "No matter what profession students have later in life, they will need to be able to do basic math calculations." Now that we have an idea of what the paragraph is about, we can look at the choices one by one. Choice (B) is correct because it gives a clear statement of the argument that the remainder of the paragraph will support. The other choices all go on loosely related but ultimately irrelevant tangents.

BIG PICTURE IDEA DRILL

Write an introductory sentence to this paragraph. A sample good introduction follows.

_____

_____

First, without a good night's sleep, teens will be more likely to fall asleep in class, falling behind in their studies. Second, if teenagers who are of driving age are tired, they will be more susceptible to automotive accidents. Third, teens who do not have adequate rest are far more vulnerable to illness—both physical and mental. In conclusion, teens should make it a priority to get the recommended nine hours of nightly rest.

Sample Introductory Sentence: Teenagers need to make a good night's sleep a top priority for several key reasons.

SUPPORT QUESTIONS

In contrast to the previous question type, support questions are more focused on how to develop more specific ideas. You will need to consider how to use details and examples to give support to the author's argument.

Tactic 2: Think *Specific*, Not *Vague*, When It Comes to Supporting Main Ideas.

If someone is making a convincing argument, he or she will use specific and relevant facts and figures instead of vague generalities. Suppose you are trying to convince your parent to extend your curfew from 10 p.m. to midnight. Which of these statements would be more convincing to your parent?

- I would really like to stay out later because I think I'll act really well and not get into trouble. You don't have anything to worry about after all. You really should let me for the reasons I just discussed.
- I have demonstrated increased responsibility these past few months by making sure my room is kept tidy, keeping my GPA at its highest level ever, and becoming the president of two clubs at school. With my improved maturity, it is time for an extended curfew.

Clearly, the second one is more persuasive—it gives three specific and relevant reasons as to why you have earned the right to an extended curfew.

Example

I felt quite comfortable with the physician's assessment of my illness. ❸

3. Which choice, if inserted here, would give the most specific support for the statement in the preceding sentence?

(A) After all, she is a world-renowned expert in her field.
(B) I was worried about how I would manage having to take time off from work.
(C) My husband, on the other hand, was not so sure.
(D) She gave me reason to be hopeful about my outcome.

To support the previous sentence, we need something that would demonstrate why the narrator feels comfortable in the physician's ability to accurately diagnose the illness. Choices (B) and (C) are irrelevant, and choice (D) is far too vague. Choice (A) gives a concrete reason why the narrator would be confident in the doctor's assessment—if someone is a world-renowned expert, she is likely the best at what she does.

SUPPORT DRILL

Create a sentence at the underlined point in the paragraph that provides excellent support for the surrounding context.

The once-in-a-lifetime snowstorm was among the worst storms ever recorded in my city.

_____

_____

_____

With ice and snowfall like that, I hope that such a storm never occurs again as long as I live.

Sample Supporting Sentence: It left an inch of freezing rain coating all the roads and over a foot of snow on all surfaces, causing some roofs to collapse under the immense weight.

FOCUS QUESTIONS

When writing papers for school, you may be tempted to expand your word count by inserting unnecessary wording that *seems* relevant but actually is not. The PSAT will evaluate your skill in determining whether statements are closely tied to the purpose of the essay, or if they go off on tangents.

Tactic 3: Make Sure the Wording is Actually Relevant, Not Just Superficially Related.

The incorrect choices on questions like these will often look connected to the given context, but upon closer examination, you can see that they are off topic. Be sure to take your time in carefully thinking through these types of questions.

Example

When making pasta from scratch, start with fresh ingredients— **⓬** eating this type of food is delicious.

12. Which choice best maintains the focus of the sentence?

    (A) NO CHANGE

    (B) pasta-making can be a labor-intensive project.

    (C) trust your instincts, not hearsay.

    (D) the best flour and eggs you can find.

Do not worry about whether the choices are true—the only thing you need to consider is if the choice best accomplishes the author's goal. The first sentence tells the reader to "start with fresh ingredients." Choice (D) is the only one that does this, giving the specific examples of "flour and eggs." Choices (A) and (B) are somewhat related to the topic but are unfocused. If you were rushing through this question, these two choices would be quite tempting. Choice (C) is far too off topic.

FOCUS DRILL

Which numbered selections should be removed from the paragraph because they are irrelevant?

Apartment hunting in a large city is an involved process. **❶** Large cities can be found in many countries around the globe. While it would be nice if there were one comprehensive list of apartments that met your needs **❷** for location, price, and amenities, such a list doesn't exist. **❸** Lists can be found, however, for popular restaurants and coffee shops. Instead, you must do extensive searching yourself; you will become quite proficient at combing through online listings, tips on social media, and newspaper advertisements. **❹** The time you will devote to your apartment search will approach the time spent on a part-time job. When it comes to selecting a residence, this investment of time is well worth it. **❺** One day, you may have time to go on the vacation of a lifetime.

Answer

Keep sentences 2 and 4 because they maintain focus on the paragraph's topic of apartment hunting. Remove sentences 1, 3, and 5 because of irrelevance.

QUANTITATIVE INFORMATION QUESTIONS

The PSAT has questions that require you to analyze quantitative graphics and integrate statements about them into the passage. You will need to be sure that the statement is both supported by the graph and connected to the passage.

Tactic 4: Carefully Examine the Axes and Labels of the Graphs to Be Clear on the Data Presented.

The graphs can come in all sorts of forms: tables, charts, maps, diagrams, and more. You won't need to have any background knowledge on the data to understand it, but given the sheer variety of graphics you may find, it is easy to make careless errors. So, take time to fully grasp the information presented before you jump to the accompanying questions.

Example

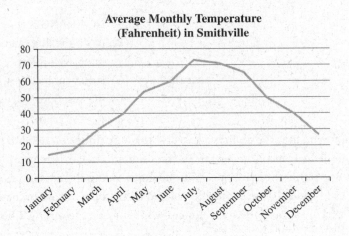

21. Which choice provides an accurate interpretation of the data in this chart?

(A) The warmest day of the year was found in July.

(B) A randomly selected day in June is going to be warmer than a randomly selected day in March.

(C) The average temperature in Smithville generally decreases between August and January.

(D) The months of December and January have the most inhospitable weather out of any of the months in Smithville.

It is critical that you come to conclusions based *only on the evidence given*. Choice (C) gives the only correct option, since the graph provides information about the average temperature during these months only. Choice (A) is incorrect because we do not have detailed information about the temperatures on each day. Choice (B) is incorrect because a randomly selected day could be quite hot or cool—we only have information about the *average* temperature for the entire month. Choice (D) is incorrect because temperature is not the sole factor determining how nice the weather is; air pressure, precipitation, wind, and pollution can all play major roles.

QUANTITATIVE INFORMATION DRILL

Consider the following graph. Which of the five statements that follow is/are justifiable based on the graph?

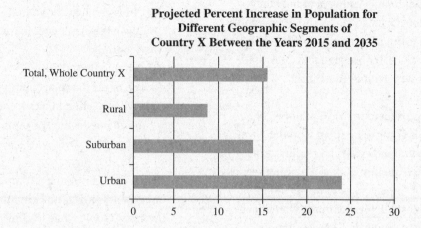

Projected Percent Increase in Population for Different Geographic Segments of Country X Between the Years 2015 and 2035

1. In 2035, there will be at least twice as many residents in urban areas of country X as in rural areas of country X.
2. The projected rate of increase in the urban population of country X is nearly three times the projected rate of increase in the rural population of country X over the twenty-year period starting in 2015.
3. The rate of increase in the suburban population of country X between the years 2020 and 2030 will be greater than the rate of increase in the rural population of country X during the same time period.
4. The majority of the residents of country X reside in urban and suburban areas.
5. The projected rate of growth in the rural population during the years 2015 through 2035 is less than the projected rate of growth for the population of country X as a whole.

Answers

1. Not justifiable
2. Justifiable
3. Not justifiable
4. Not justifiable
5. Justifiable

IDEA DEVELOPMENT PRACTICE

The eternal question about careers is ❶ "how do I decide which career I would like to do when I'm out of school?" This is a concern that haunts young people as they decide upon a college major and older people as they confront mid-life crises. ❷ While there is not a clear answer to this question, there are several things that merit consideration.

It is important to realize that not all of your time is going to be spent working. If you have a job that pays well and requires only a reasonable amount of time, you can treat the job as a "means to an end." ❸ Some of the wealthiest billionaires in the world have net worths in excess of the gross domestic products of small countries.

1. Which choice would most effectively introduce the major theme of the essay?

   (A) NO CHANGE
   (B) "how can I go about finding a job given the challenges in today's economy?"
   (C) "should I prioritize enjoyment of my job or my monetary compensation?"
   (D) "what is it that makes some careers more intellectually stimulating than others?"

2. Which option would best emphasize the uncertainty and complexity surrounding the essay's topic while leading into the rest of the sentence?

   (A) NO CHANGE
   (B) While many have successfully chosen their career paths,
   (C) Since competition for high-paying jobs is a fierce as ever,
   (D) Because advanced machines are rapidly replacing many jobs that have been done by humans,

3. Which option provides the most focused and relevant elaboration on the previous sentence?

   (A) NO CHANGE
   (B) Many people will never successfully sort out the intractable dilemma of how to prioritize the demands of their supervisors with the demands of their customers.
   (C) The social welfare programs in many Scandinavian countries enable both mothers and fathers to spend significant time at home with their kids.
   (D) In other words, if the job provides you the money and time that you need to enjoy hobbies and spend quality time with your family outside of work, it can be worth pursuing.

If it is possible to have a career that you truly enjoy, then it probably will not feel like work. The time you spend there will not feel like a drain on your other interests. ❹ Most people can determine the most appropriate careers based on which subjects they enjoy the most in school. If you are like most people, try to find a less dreamy niche at which you excel and that you enjoy.

You should excel at your chosen profession to the point where you are making enough money to live "comfortably" for your needs and lifestyle. If you are ❺ terrified due to financial concerns, it will be challenging to enjoy your work, no matter how fun it is. When you come home each day from a job that pays decently and that you find stimulating, you will feel fulfilled and rejuvenated instead of ❻ frustrated and drained.

4. Which option sets up the most relevant contrast with the sentence that follows?

   (A) NO CHANGE
   (B) Some careers involve long hours and great demands, with workers expected to be "on-call" 24 hours a day, and 7 days a week.
   (C) If you are so talented that you can pursue a fantasy job as a professional athlete or musician, go for it.
   (D) Instead, have your work be the equivalent of play, and you'll never "work" a day in your life.

5. Which phrasing would best express a degree of moderate concern?

   (A) NO CHANGE
   (B) preoccupied with
   (C) optimistic about
   (D) despondent over

6. Which choice of words would most consistently complete the contrast in the sentence?

   (A) NO CHANGE
   (B) saddened and unhappy.
   (C) exhausted and disloyal.
   (D) burdened and morose.

To summarize, **7** make sure you have a profession that commands the respect of your peers. Try to find a balance between work and non-work interests, and be sure the expected compensation will be sufficient to meet your needs. And be open to changing your mind about your priorities— **8** according to current research, people are mostly consistent throughout their lives as to their major career priorities.

**Primary Career Priority
for 40- to 60-Year-Olds**

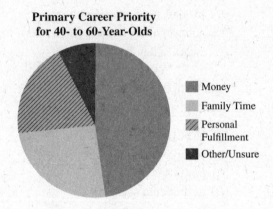

**Primary Career Priority
for 20- to 30-Year-Olds**

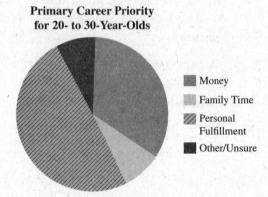

Surveys of 100 randomly selected 40- to 60-year-olds and 100 randomly selected 20- to 30-year-olds about their primary career priorities.

7. Which option most effectively introduces the concluding paragraph?

(A) NO CHANGE

(B) do not look at choosing a career as an "either-or" decision.

(C) realize that ultimately, family must come first.

(D) be certain your job will not be subject to lay-offs and unexpected shifts in the economy.

8. Which option uses the most relevant and justifiable conclusion based on the data in the graphs to build on the point made in the first part of the sentence?

(A) NO CHANGE

(B) Based on current surveys, monetary compensation is consistently the most important factor in making a career choice, regardless of age.

(C) According to recent surveys, as people age, they tend to prefer spending more time with family to having a satisfying profession.

(D) Based on the latest research, age is a more important factor in choosing a career than race or other demographics.

Answers

1. **(C)** Since this question asks about the major theme of the essay, it is helpful to quickly read through the essay, or at a minimum, read the topic sentences of each paragraph. Doing so will help you paraphrase the overall topic and message of the passage. Throughout the essay, the narrator focuses on how to prioritize money or enjoyment in a career. Accordingly, choice (C) makes the most sense because it addresses these two themes. It is not choice (A) or (D) because these themes are too narrow. It is not choice (B) because the author does not focus on job-finding prospects.

2. **(A)** Focus on the key words in the question: "emphasize the uncertainty and complexity." Choices (B), (C), and (D) all assert a great deal of certainty. Choice (A) stands out as being much less certain and emphatic.

3. **(D)** The question requires an elaboration on the previous sentence, which states that it is possible to consider a job to be tolerable if it gives you the financial means to enjoy non-work activities. Choice (D) is the only option that elaborates on this theme. The other options are all loosely related to the topic of the essay, but none directly elaborates on the sentence that comes before.

4. **(C)** The question requires that we set up a contrast with the sentence that comes immediately afterward. The sentence that follows states that people should have less lofty and more realistic expectations for what type of job they should pursue. Choice (C) sets up the most logical contrast with the sentence that follows because it acknowledges that if someone can actually obtain a position in a "dream job," it is a no-brainer to do so. Choices (A), (B), and (D) all are related to the essay's focus on the workplace but fail to offer a clear contrast with the sentence that follows.

5. **(B)** The question asks for "moderate concern," making it important to avoid an answer that uses emotionally extreme language. Choices (A) and (D) both convey extreme negativity, whereas choice (C) conveys a positive emotion. Choice (B) is correct because to be "preoccupied" is consistent with feeling moderately concerned about something.

6. **(A)** The words with which a contrast needs to be made are "fulfilled and rejuvenated." Choice (A) sets up the most logical contrast, since "frustrated and drained" express a negative attitude and a lack of energy. Choices (B), (C), and (D) all express negativity, but not in a way that provides a logical contrast with the preceding language.

7. **(B)** The paragraph goes on to state that balance and flexibility in choosing a career are critically important. Choice (B) provides a logical introduction to this theme, asserting that the choice of a career should not be an all-or-nothing proposition. All of the other options express extremes, making them inconsistent with the balanced attitude advocated in this paragraph.

8. **(C)** The first part of the sentence encourages readers to have an open mind. It is most logical to go with choice (C) because it gives statistical evidence that having an open mind is important because career priorities can change quite a bit as people age. Choices (A) and (B) do not logically build off the first part of the sentence, and choice (D) focuses on irrelevant information.

LOGICAL SEQUENCE QUESTIONS

These questions assess your ability to put sentences and ideas in the most logical sequence. The PSAT will generally prefer events to be in the order in which they happened, and for the ideas to be clear as the passage unfolds. The writer should not confuse the reader as to how things unfold.

Tactic 5: Try Labeling the Possible Placements of Sentences in the Passage, Making It Easier to Visualize the Potential Options.

You are able to write on the PSAT, so take advantage of this and physically write down where the different choices would be in the passage. If you are taking a digital version of the test, use the provided scrap paper to make organizational notes if needed. This will make you less likely to make careless errors than if you try to keep track of everything in your head.

Example

[1] Online discussion is both a blessing and a curse for politeness. [2] It is a blessing when participants feel comfortable openly sharing their views. [3] As a general rule, online discourse is best when there is transparency among those posting commentary. [4] It is a curse when participants can hide behind the shroud of anonymity to bully and intimidate. [5] That way, commenters will be more inclined to be fair and polite when they present their views. ⓫

11. What would be the most logical placement of sentence 3?

(A) Where it is now
(B) Before sentence 1
(C) After sentence 4
(D) After sentence 5

Sometimes the proper order of sentences becomes clear based on what *follows* the sentence, not just on what comes before. In this case, sentence 3 leads into the topic of sentence 5—mentioning that there should be "transparency" (i.e., openness) in online discourse would logically justify the message of sentence 5 that commenters will be more inclined to be fair and polite. After all, if everyone knew who was talking, the participants would not be able to say hurtful things without fear of reprisal. Therefore, the answer is choice (C). The other placements are illogical because they would not logically connect to statements about the need for openness with personal identity.

LOGICAL SEQUENCE DRILL

Put these sentences into a paragraph in the most logical order:

[1] On the one hand, there are teenagers who are inclined to use and trust what they find online.

[2] There need not be such a conflict if teachers are willing to see how far online resources have come in their quality, and students are willing to see the ease with which they can use printed materials.

[3] There is a fundamental conflict when it comes to high school research projects.

[4] Ultimately, good librarians are needed to help bridge the gap between teens and their teachers.

[5] On the other hand, there are teachers who encourage students to use time-tested printed material for their sources.

Answer

[3] There is a fundamental conflict when it comes to high school research projects. [1] On the one hand, there are teenagers who are inclined to use and trust what they find online. [5] On the other hand, there are teachers who encourage students to use time-tested printed material for their sources. [2] There need not be such a conflict if teachers are willing to see how far online resources have come in their quality, and students are willing to see the ease with which they can use printed materials. [4] Ultimately, good librarians are needed to help bridge the gap between teens and their teachers.

INTRODUCTIONS, CONCLUSIONS, AND TRANSITIONS QUESTIONS

Questions about the best connections between different parts of the passage *are among the most frequent question types on the PSAT*. These questions require you to consider what wording would make the flow of the passage most logical and meaningful. Be sure you know the "big three" transitional words—"but," "also," and "because"—and some of their common synonyms.

BUT: however, on the other hand, in contrast to, yet, still, nevertheless, conversely, in spite of, despite, unlike, besides, although, instead, rather, otherwise, regardless, notwithstanding

ALSO: additionally, moreover, further, as well, besides, likewise, what is more, furthermore, in addition, similarly

BECAUSE: consequently, so, therefore, as a result, thus, hence, in order to, if . . . then, since, so that, due to, whenever

Tactic 6: Treat the Transitional Wording as A Blank, and Then Consider What Type of Transition is Needed Given What Comes Before and After it.

What comes before and after the transitional wording could be in contrast to one another, be in support of one another, or have some other relationship. Look at as much of the passage as needed—sometimes just a couple of sentences, sometimes a couple of paragraphs—to determine what wording is needed.

Example

Those not accustomed to the effects of caffeine may experience jitteriness upon initial consumption. Despite this, many students try caffeine for the first time the morning of the PSAT in an effort to be alert. ❼ As a result, they should rely on a good night's sleep and natural adrenaline to maximize performance.

7. Which choice provides the most logical transition at this point in the paragraph?

(A) NO CHANGE
(B) Instead,
(C) Consequently,
(D) Moreover,

The sentence that precedes the question states that students try caffeine in order to improve their test performance. The sentence that follows states that students should rely on more natural solutions to improve performance. Choice (B) is the only option that shows the needed contrast between these two ideas. "As a result" and "consequently" both show cause and effect, and "moreover" is synonymous with "also."

TRANSITIONAL WORDING DRILL

Write appropriate transitional words in the underlined portions. Use the "word bank" of transitions—each word will be used only once.

Word Bank

while	and	in fact
but	since	perhaps

_____ it is unusual that I enjoy waiting in line for hours on the opening night of a big movie, _____ I am not alone. _____, dozens of other moviegoers wait along with me, _____ we enjoy passing the time speculating on the movie's potential plot twists. _____ it could be expected that tempers would be short as people stood patiently in line, the truth is that people are extremely polite. _____ we are all full of hopeful anticipation, everyone is in a fairly good mood.

Answer

Perhaps it is unusual that I enjoy waiting in line for hours on the opening night of a big movie, but I am not alone. In fact, dozens of other moviegoers wait along with me, and we enjoy passing the time speculating on the movie's potential plot twists. While it could be expected that tempers would be short as people stood patiently in line, the truth is that people are extremely polite. Since we are all full of hopeful anticipation, everyone is in a fairly good mood.

ORGANIZATION PRACTICE

❶ When I was young, I could not put down books. I read all the Harry Potter books several times over and was a big fan of other fantasy and science fiction texts. Once I entered middle school, I lost much of the joy of reading. ❷ Since I loved reading for fun, I had to read certain books for summer reading. Not only did I have to read them, I had to take careful notes on the texts ❸ from when school started again, there would inevitably be a major reading test. I suppose it is like going to see a

1. Which choice provides the best introduction to the paragraph?

   (A) NO CHANGE
   (B) Books have always fascinated me.
   (C) Some of the best books are ones you would not expect.
   (D) Some of my happiest memories come from my childhood travel.

2. (A) NO CHANGE
   (B) As a result of
   (C) In addition to
   (D) Instead of

3. (A) NO CHANGE
   (B) until
   (C) because
   (D) by

④ movie—if you had to take notes for a quiz while watching the film, you would probably just stay out in the lobby!

[1] Fortunately, my new English teacher helped reawaken my love of reading. [2] Not surprisingly, when you can read a book that actually interests you, you tend to do much better when it comes to recall. [3] **⑤** In contrast, I don't even mind taking a few notes or highlighting key phrases if it helps me understand a well-written story's plot. **⑥** Rather than forcing us to read certain books, she gave us considerable leeway in choosing which books most interested us.

My newfound attitude toward reading comes at just the right time. I am about to take some much more challenging AP courses, and **⑦** you surely cannot believe what happened, there will be some material in the classes that will be rather dry. If I still had my middle-school mentality toward reading, I would likely surf the web for book summaries instead of actually reading the texts.

4. Which choice best concludes the sentence with a logical explanation?

(A) NO CHANGE
(B) Who has the money to see a movie in a crowded theater when you can enjoy it much more comfortably at home?
(C) Both movies and books have plot lines, character development, and metaphorical imagery.
(D) Nobody enjoys a movie when it is interrupted by delinquents who talk and text through its entirety.

5. (A) NO CHANGE
(B) In fact,
(C) Without equivocation,
(D) Unfortunately,

6. What is the most logical placement of the underlined sentence in this paragraph?

(A) Where it is now
(B) Before sentence 1
(C) Before sentence 2
(D) Before sentence 3

7. Which choice provides the best transition at this point in the sentence?

(A) NO CHANGE
(B) the classes will take place in my school
(C) despite my misgivings about the teachers
(D) let's face it

8 On the other hand, I am able to find interesting articles and blogs to divert my attention from studying.

8. Which option would provide the best conclusion to the paragraph?

   (A) NO CHANGE
   (B) Instead, I am able to buckle down when I need to read an antiquated historical document or a chapter about balancing chemical equations.
   (C) Middle school was a tough time for me in general—it was difficult for me to figure out to which group I really belonged.
   (D) After all, online videos are far more interesting than the boring films our teachers force upon us in school.

Answers

1. **(A)** The paragraph shows a shift in the narrator's attitude toward reading—as a young child, she enjoyed reading, and as she progressed in school, she lost her joy in reading. Choice (A) best introduces this paragraph because it is the only option that previews this transition in attitude. Choices (B) and (D) are simply positive, and choice (C) is too loosely related to what follows.

2. **(D)** The previous sentence establishes that the narrator has lost joy in reading. The current sentence serves to explain how this shift in attitude came about—namely, rather than reading recreationally, the narrator was required to read certain texts. Choice (D) is the only option that shows this contrast. Choices (A) and (B) both show cause and effect, and choice (C) indicates a list.

3. **(C)** A cause-and-effect transition is needed here because the narrator is stating that she has to take notes so that she could be prepared for the test upon her return from vacation— choice (C) is the only option that provides a cause-and-effect transition.

4. **(A)** The paragraph as a whole states that the narrator became progressively less interested in reading as it became something she was required to do, instead of something she chose to do. Choice (A) makes sense in this context because it provides an analogy that shows how being forced to watch a movie for school makes the experience much less enjoyable. Choices (B), (C), and (D) are somewhat connected to the sentence but are not relevant to the paragraph.

5. **(B)** The sentence that comes before this makes the general point that it is easier to read books that are interesting to you. The remainder of the current sentence states that the narrator is fine with taking notes and highlighting words if doing so will help her better understand a story she finds interesting. Choice (B) is the best option because it provides a transition indicating a clarification. None of the other options indicates a clarification is taking place— choices (A) and (D) show contrast, and choice (C) shows certainty.

6. **(C)** This sentence should be placed before sentence 2 because it provides a logical transition after sentence 1, which states that the English teacher helped the narrator become interested once again in reading. Without having this sentence moved to this place, the paragraph would not have a clear elaboration on how the teacher accomplished this shift in the narrator's attitude. All of the other options would prevent this clear elaboration from taking place.

7. **(D)** "Let's face it" uses concise language that matches the relatively informal tone of the essay. Choice (A) is too wordy and extreme, choice (B) is illogical and irrelevant, and choice (C) changes the emphasis from the reading requirements to the teachers themselves.

8. **(B)** This paragraph states that the narrator now has a mindset that enables her to read material that is academic and dry. Choice (B) concludes this paragraph well because it concretely illustrates how being able to read less entertaining texts can be helpful. Choice (A) confuses the intended meaning, and choices (C) and (D) are too disconnected from the topic of the paragraph.

EFFECTIVE LANGUAGE USE

PRECISION QUESTIONS

Choosing the appropriate word for a given situation is extremely important to effective writing. Consider the following words:

dishonest   grumpy   careless
lazy   confrontational

All of the above words could reasonably be used to express a "bad" attitude. A writer should use the most *precise* word to express his or her intended idea—if the author's subject is "bad" because of constant fibbing, then "dishonest" would be correct; if the subject is "bad" because of violent disrespect, "confrontational" would be correct. The PSAT will have questions where you will need to choose the most precise wording to express the intended meaning.

Tactic 7: Go Beyond the Simple Dictionary Definitions of Words. Instead, Consider the Subtle Ways That Word Meaning Can Change Depending on Context.

Many of the incorrect options on precision questions will probably be loosely synonymous with the correct option. Be careful that your choice truly is the best way to express the author's message.

Example

An eagle can spot its prey from a great distance, since it has an extremely ❹ <u>acute</u> sense of sight.

4. (A) NO CHANGE
   (B) interesting
   (C) good
   (D) rigorous

All of the options are adjectives that generally mean positive characteristics. Choice (A) is correct because "acute" means "very perceptive," which is appropriate given that the eagle has an excellent sense of sight. "Good" could work, but it is too vague. "Interesting" and "rigorous" are illogical given the context.

Choose which of the two words is more appropriate, given the context of the sentence.

1. Down by 30 points near the end of the game, the team was clearly (finished or completed).
2. John was (emotional or passionate) about his career choice, believing he had finally found his calling.
3. I hope the servers are not too (conservative or conservationist) with the portion sizes—I am really hungry!
4. The e-mail demonstrated significant (disrespect or negativity) by addressing the professor so informally.
5. Your hotel room is quite (luxurious or expensive); the linens are really soft, the bathroom is capacious, and the view is magnificent.

Answers

1. finished
2. passionate
3. conservative
4. disrespect
5. luxurious

CONCISION QUESTIONS

When you write your college application essay, you will face what is likely an unusual situation—you will have a *word maximum* instead of a word minimum for your essay. Teachers often give students general guidance on the word count of a paper, and many students respond by being overly repetitive and wordy so that their papers meet the word count requirement. If you are accustomed to inflating your paper word count, be very careful when it comes to questions about concision. These questions require you to determine what phrasing expresses the author's meaning in the most concise way possible while preserving descriptive ideas. This concept is among the most commonly tested on the PSAT Writing and Language section.

Tactic 8: Shorter is Not Necessarily Sweeter—Consider Which Choice Expresses All the Intended Meaning While Not Being Repetitive.

Example

He has been the preeminent expert on the subject for ⑯ the duration of the past twenty years.

16. (A) NO CHANGE
    (B) the past.
    (C) the past two decades.
    (D) for the time that has passed in the previous two decades.

The original wording is unnecessarily repetitive—readers will understand that "years" are units that have duration. Choice (B) removes the descriptive language about the length of time that has passed. Choice (D) is far too wordy. Choice (C) correctly preserves the meaning about the twenty years that have passed, but it does so using far fewer words than choices (A) and (D).

CONCISION DRILL

Cross out any part of the sentence that is needlessly repetitive or irrelevant, but leave in descriptive wording.

1. Blue Dog Democrats—Democrats who side with Republicans on some issues—have become rarer in the increasingly polarized political climate.
2. My boss received my e-mail that I wrote to her late last night.
3. Trucks that drive on the roadway cause more wear on roads than do cars.
4. The winner of the Miss America Pageant was excited to use her newfound fame to advocate for underrepresented groups.
5. Choose the book you most want to read from the teacher's list—make sure you make a decision that aligns with what the teacher has selected.

Answers

1. Fine as is.
2. My boss received my e-mail ~~that I wrote to her~~ late last night.
3. Trucks ~~that drive on the roadways~~ cause more wear on roads than do cars.
4. Fine as is.
5. Choose the book you most want to read from the teacher's list.~~—make sure you make a decision that aligns with what the teacher has selected.~~

STYLE AND TONE QUESTIONS

There is nothing inherently wrong with more formal or informal language. As long as a writer has a consistent "voice," it is perfectly fine. Suppose you are hanging out with your friends. Which statement would be more appropriate?

> **"My, it was most serendipitous that my colleague shared the magnificent portraiture that was bequeathed to him by his associate."**
>
> **"It was cool that my friend shared the picture his buddy took."**

Obviously, the second choice would be preferable. Your job on questions about style and tone is to determine what choice expresses a given idea in a way that "fits" with the voice of the passage.

Tactic 9: Look at Enough Context to Determine How the Writer is Expressing Him- or Herself.

Do not assume that a writer will avoid using "you" or has to use technical language. Analyze enough of the passage so you can make a good judgment.

Example

When you enter the theme park, you will be too excited to think clearly, so be sure to have a plan ahead of time. First, know which rides you want to ride the most. Second, be aware of the height requirements. Finally, **⑫** determine a meeting place for your party.

12. Which option most closely matches the stylistic pattern used in the paragraph?

(A) NO CHANGE
(B) it would be great to know of a meeting place for you and your party beforehand.
(C) a place to meet with your party should be known.
(D) a meeting place for you and your party it is vital to determine.

If we look at the two sentences that precede the question, the stylistic pattern becomes clear: the author is giving a series of general recommendations. Choice (A) is the only option that follows the structure of the previous two sentences. The other options use convoluted wording that does not match the voice of what comes before.

STYLE AND TONE DRILL

Choose which of the two words or phrases is more stylistically appropriate, given the context of the sentence.

1. The Chief of Staff to the President strongly agreed with the President's (spin or stance).
2. It is incumbent upon the newly elected club officers to (build rapport with or be comfy with) their fellow club members.
3. The lethal parasitic infection was (invading or flocking to) the countryside.
4. Whenever you're feeling blue, be sure to (chronicle your contentment or count your blessings).
5. Upon hearing the tragic news of the building collapse, the building owner felt (despondent or unenthusiastic).

Answers

1. stance
2. build rapport with
3. invading
4. count your blessings
5. despondent

COMBINING SENTENCES QUESTIONS

The PSAT will assess your understanding of syntax by asking you sentence combination questions. You will need to pick the option that best joins two sentences in a way that improves the flow and organization of the words.

Tactic 10: Join the Sentences in the Clearest Way That Preserves the Original Meaning.

Example

32 Surprisingly, the man had a difficult time in making a decision. He had to make a choice between accepting a harsh sentence and a much milder one.

32. Which option most effectively joins the underlined sentences?

(A) Surprisingly, the man had a difficult time in making a decision between the options of first, a harsh sentence, and second, a much milder one.

(B) Surprisingly, a difficult time was had by the man between the acceptance of a harsh sentence and a much milder one.

(C) Surprisingly, the man had a difficult time deciding between accepting a harsh sentence and a much milder one.

(D) A choice between a much milder sentence and a harsh one presented difficulty for the man when he had to make a decision on the matter.

Choice (C) is correct because it preserves the original meaning of the two separate sentences, while joining them in a way that is concise and consistent. Choices (A) and (D) are unnecessarily wordy, and choice (B) uses the passive voice.

SENTENCE COMBINATION DRILL

Write a combined version of the following pairs of sentences or phrases. There are a variety of ways this can be done—sample answers follow.

1. My dog was interested in going for a walk. However, he was more interested in having his dinner.
2. It is critical that we spend frugally. It is also vitally important that we save for a rainy day.
3. My telescope needs batteries. Due to this fact, I am unable to use it.
4. While he should not be considered a good friend. In fact, he is one of my greatest enemies.
5. During those moments of time when you take out the trash, here is another thing you should do. Be sure to also take out the recycling.

Sample Answers

1. While my dog was interested in going for a walk, he was more interested in having his dinner.
2. It is critical that we both spend frugally and save for a rainy day.
3. Since my telescope needs batteries, I am unable to use it.
4. Far from being a good friend, he is one of my greatest enemies.
5. Whenever you take out the trash, also take out the recycling.

EFFECTIVE LANGUAGE USE PRACTICE

Test anxiety has become an increasingly ❶ <u>prevalent and widespread</u> problem among standardized test-takers. ❷ <u>While some measure of anxiety is to be expected. For it is in fact welcome in order to sharpen one's focus, so many students today find that their anxiety hinders their ability to perform on high-stakes tests.</u> What are some things that can be done to alleviate test anxiety?

1. (A) NO CHANGE
   (B) prevalent
   (C) spread from near to far
   (D) wide-ranging and quite impactful

2. How could the two sentences most effectively be combined?

   (A) While some measure of anxiety is to be expected, for the reason that it is in fact welcome in order to sharpen one's focus because many students today find that their anxiety hinders their ability to perform on high-stakes tests.

   (B) While some measure of anxiety is to be expected and is in fact welcome in order to sharpen one's focus; many students today find that their anxiety hinders their ability to perform on high-stakes tests.

   (C) While some measure of anxiety is to be expected and is, in fact, welcome in order to sharpen one's focus, many students today find that their anxiety hinders their ability to perform on high-stakes tests.

   (D) While some measure of anxiety is to be expected because it is in fact welcome in order to sharpen one's focus, the fact remains that many students today find that their anxiety hinders their ability to perform on high-stakes tests.

First, students should strive to have realistic expectations. It is becoming more and more competitive to earn admission to highly selective schools. ❸ Online applications and common essay prompts make it as easy to apply to ten schools as it once was to apply to only one. With the increased competition, students should set themselves up for success by striving to go to the school that is the best fit for them, ❹ rather than just chasing the most highly ranked school.

3. Which of the following statements, if inserted here, would provide the most specific and relevant support for the statement made in the previous sentence?

(A) College admission is a process that is carried out by teams of admissions representatives to ensure a thorough and reasonably objective process.

(B) In your application, be sure to state your grade point average, SAT and ACT test scores, and major extracurricular leadership positions.

(C) For example, at the University of Pennsylvania, an Ivy League institution, the admissions rate in 1991 was 47 percent—in 2015, it was less than 10 percent.

(D) Average salaries for those graduating in math and science programs can often be 30 percent higher than the salaries of those graduating from humanities programs.

4. Which statement provides the most precise and relevant contrast with what comes before in the sentence?

(A) NO CHANGE
(B) and doing what feels right.
(C) and struggling to achieve their childhood dreams of college acceptance.
(D) while bearing in mind the financial consequences of academic missteps.

Second, students can think through worst-case scenarios **⑤** to help calm their nerves and relieve internal tension. If the very worst outcome that could happen is not actually that bad, students' fears about mediocre test performance will decrease greatly. Suppose a major test doesn't go well. In all likelihood, there are many other times one can take the test to demonstrate one's knowledge and skills. Even with the all-important PSAT, which determines National Merit Scholarship eligibility, there are many more opportunities to take the SAT or ACT **⑥** , which play a major role in determining academic scholarships.

The bottom line is that if someone wants anything too badly, he or she will be **⑦** lesser in likelihood to obtain it. It is the same idea as when an overeager salesperson keeps pestering a customer in an attempt to make a deal—such desperation will turn him off, making him less likely to make a purchase. **⑧** To do the best on major tests, students should set reasonable expectations and think about worst case scenarios so that their minds are focused, not panicked.

5. (A) NO CHANGE
    (B) to calm their nerves.
    (C) to break free from the tension and anxiety that plagues them.
    (D) to achieve an internal equilibrium of peacefulness.

6. The author is considering deleting the underlined portion. Should it be kept or deleted?

    (A) Kept, because it provides a helpful elaboration.
    (B) Kept, because it details what the tests assess.
    (C) Deleted, because it contradicts information presented elsewhere in the paragraph.
    (D) Deleted, because it is irrelevant to the focus of the sentence.

7. (A) NO CHANGE
    (B) far, far less likely
    (C) for better or worse less expectedly
    (D) less likely

8. The author is considering inserting the following sentence at this point in the essay:

    "It is also similar to when somebody acts desperate in interpersonal relationships—no one wants to hang out with someone who is too intent on doing so."

    Should he do so?

    (A) Yes, because it continues the metaphorical discussion from the previous sentence.
    (B) Yes, because it introduces a new way of framing a topic critical to the argument of the essay.
    (C) No, because it repeats an idea already expressed in the previous sentence.
    (D) No, because it shifts the essay's focus away from the business practices of sales professionals.

Answers

1. **(B)** "Prevalent" is synonymous with "widespread," so it is repetitive to have both of these words. Choice (B) preserves the original meaning without adding extra words. Choices (A) and (D) are repetitive, and choice (C) uses excessive and awkward language to make the same point as choice (B).

2. **(C)** Choice (C) preserves the original meaning of the underlined sentences while joining them into a single complete sentence. Choice (A) has convoluted word order in the phrase "for the reason that it is in fact welcome," choice (B) does not have a complete sentence before the semicolon, and choice (D) is unnecessarily wordy.

3. **(C)** The statement in the previous sentence is that it is becoming increasingly difficult to earn admission to highly selective schools. Choice (C) provides the most specific support for this claim, since it gives relevant statistics that demonstrate just how much the selectivity of an elite school has increased over the years. Choice (A) is vague, and choices (B) and (D) provide specific information that does not relate to the previous sentence.

4. **(A)** The first part of the sentence encourages students to pick a school based on what is the best fit for them. Based on the context of the passage, choice (A) provides the most logical contrast because many students might instead focus unnecessarily on school rankings. Choice (B) is too vague, and choices (C) and (D) do not provide a clear contrast.

5. **(B)** Choice (B) preserves the original meaning while deleting repetitive wording. Choices (A), (C), and (D) are all wordy and repetitive.

6. **(A)** Without the underlined portion, it would not be entirely clear as to why the statement about taking the SAT or ACT would be relevant. Having this portion clarifies their connectedness to scholarship opportunities. Thus, it provides a helpful elaboration. It is not choice (B) because it mentions the tests very broadly and does not go into detail about what they assess. It is not choice (C) or (D) because these advocate removing the selection.

7. **(D)** "Less likely" expresses the intended meaning without adding in unnecessary words. Choice (A) uses an awkward construction, and choices (B) and (C) are clearly repetitive.

8. **(C)** The sentence that comes before this already makes this point using an analogy about a salesperson whose eagerness makes him seem desperate. It is not choice (D) because the focus of the essay is not on the business practices of sales professionals. It is not choice (A) or (B) because they advocate keeping a repetitive sentence.

SENTENCE STRUCTURE

SENTENCE FRAGMENTS AND RUN-ON QUESTIONS

A **sentence** expresses a complete thought with both a subject and predicate (i.e., a subject and a verb). A subject will be a noun—a person, place, or thing. The predicate will have a verb—a word that expresses an *action*, such as "is," "were," "ate," "choose," or "eat." Here are some examples of complete sentences:

What is this?
He won the match.
There is great trouble brewing in the town.

A *sentence fragment* expresses an incomplete thought with only a subject or a predicate. Here are some examples of sentence fragments:

From my place.
Homework for tomorrow's big test.
Your neighbor's house, which is next to the spooky mansion on the hill.

A *run-on sentence* consists of two or more complete sentences that are not joined together with appropriate punctuation or transitions. Here are some examples of run-on sentences.

Finish your meal it is really good for you to do so.
I was excited to see the new show I stayed up really late to see it.
The moon will be full tonight, let's stay up and enjoy its beauty.

Tactic 11: Evaluate Whether A Sentence is Complete by Determining If It Has a Subject and a Verb—Don't Make Assumptions Based Simply on the Length of the Sentence.

A sentence can be complete while being quite short. For example, "I am" is a complete sentence. A selection can be a fragment even though it is rather long. For example, "For the benefit of the United States of America, today, tomorrow, and in the years to come" is a fragment. Consider each sentence on a case-by-case basis to make a determination.

Example

We will need to get to the bottom of this news **8** story. Whether he is a winner in the hotly contested election.

8. (A) NO CHANGE
(B) story. If
(C) story. Whether or not
(D) story as to whether

Choices (A), (B), and (C) all have a sentence fragment after the period. Choice (D) is the only option that joins the wording together in a way that provides one complete sentence.

SENTENCE STRUCTURE DRILL

Determine if the sentence is complete, a run-on, or a fragment.

1. To whom this letter may concern.
2. She wept.
3. I am looking forward to the movie I plan on standing in line for a couple of hours.
4. Whenever they leave the doors unlocked of their brand new automobile.
5. My best friend, whom I have known since childhood, will be visiting from out of town this upcoming weekend.

Answers

1. Fragment
2. Complete
3. Run-on
4. Fragment
5. Complete

SUBORDINATION AND COORDINATION QUESTIONS

Coordinating conjunctions include words like "for," "and," and "but" to make compound sentences. Subordinating conjunctions include words like "if," "unless," and "whereas" to create sentence variety by making sentences more complex. For example, here is a sentence that does have an appropriate conjunction, "whereas," to illustrate a logical connection:

That politician is known for telling the truth, whereas his rival is known for deceit.

Tactic 12: When It Comes to Conjunctions, Be Careful That the Word Provides Both a Logical Connection and a Complete Sentence.

Example

I forgot to take my backpack ⑲ home, and I didn't have the materials I needed for my homework.

19. (A) NO CHANGE
    (B) home, also
    (C) home, so
    (D) home,

The part of the sentence before the comma and the part after the comma show a cause-and-effect relationship—it was because of not taking the backpack home that the narrator did not have the materials she needed. Choice (C) is the only option that uses a cause-and-effect conjunction, "so." Choices (A) and (B) use improper conjunctions, and choice (D) results in a run-on sentence.

SUBORDINATION AND COORDINATION DRILL

Make changes, if needed, to correct any subordination/coordination issues in the sentences. There are multiple ways these sentences can be fixed.

1. Whenever I go out with my friends, I am certain to tell my parents where I will be.
2. I love running distance races, and I am excited about my upcoming marathon.
3. It is either going to be sunny and be bad weather tomorrow.
4. No matter the outcome, and play your very best and you should be satisfied.
5. I am extremely disappointed in your lack of truthfulness; and I am willing to give you a second chance.

Answers with Possible Corrections

1. Fine as is.
2. I love running distance races, **so** I am excited about my upcoming marathon.
3. It is either going to be sunny **or** be bad weather tomorrow.
4. No matter the outcome, ~~and~~ play your very best and you should be satisfied.
5. I am extremely disappointed in your lack of truthfulness; **however,** I am willing to give you a second chance.

PARALLELISM QUESTIONS

It is not just what you say, it is how you say it. To make one's writing flow as well as possible, having parallel structure is key. For an example of excellent parallelism, consider the Oath of Office for the President of the United States:

> "I do solemnly swear that I will faithfully execute the office of President of the United States, and will to the best of my ability, preserve, protect, and defend the Constitution of the United States."

Imagine if instead the oath read like this:

> I do solemnly swear that I will execute with faith the office of President of the United States, and to the best of my ability will preserving, to protect, and defense of the Constitution for United States.

If you had to momentarily pause while reading the second version, you intuitively recognized the lack of parallel structure.

Tactic 13: Consider the Context Around the Underlined Portion, and Be Certain That Your Choice is Consistent with the Phrasing Surrounding it.

Example

Be sure to get a good night's sleep, **41** take your number 2 pencils, and arrive at the test site early.

41. (A) NO CHANGE
(B) taking your number 2 pencils
(C) your number 2 pencils take with you
(D) to take your number 2 pencils

The style of the phrasing in the other parts of the sentence is "Be sure . . . ," and "arrive . . . ," giving the reader direct advice. Choice (A) is the only option consistent with this style. The other options all use phrasing that does not match the other parts of the sentence.

PARALLEL STRUCTURE DRILL

Make corrections, if needed, to give the sentences parallel structure. There are multiple ways to fix these sentences.

1. Some of the best forms of exercise are running, swimming, and to go on a bike.
2. It is not whether you win or losing; it's how you play the game.
3. Her character garners the respect of colleagues and reporters alike.
4. Hard work and to persevere go hand in hand.
5. Lacking endorsements, donations, and media coverage, the candidate had little hope of winning.

Answers with Possible Corrections

1. Some of the best forms of exercise are running, swimming, and **biking.**
2. It is not whether you win or **lose**; it's how you play the game.
3. Fine as is.
4. Hard work and **perseverance** go hand in hand.
5. Fine as is.

MODIFIER PLACEMENT QUESTIONS

Consider these two improper sentences:

The fish loved its new aquarium, swimming quickly.

While reading the brand new book, many people were annoying.

These two sentences have confusing meaning. The first sentence literally expressed that the aquarium is swimming quickly. In the second sentence, it is unclear who is reading the new book. These sentences can be fixed by making sure the modifying words, like adjectives, and the words they modify, like nouns, are clearly stated and in a proper sequence. Here are proper versions of the two sentences:

The fish, swimming quickly, loved its new aquarium.

While I was reading the brand new book, many people annoyed me.

When it comes to modifier clarity and placement, remember this tip:

Tactic 14: Make Sure That the *Literal* Meaning and the *Intended* Meaning are the Same.

Example

My teacher asked me a question, but **32** too tired was I for giving a prompt response.

32. (A) NO CHANGE
    (B) giving was too tired for me
    (C) I was giving too tired
    (D) I was too tired to give

To clearly express what is doing the action, "I" should follow the "but." Choices (A) and (B) have convoluted word order. Choice (C) has the correct placement of "I," but jumbles the wording later in the selection. Choice (D) has clarity of wording and a logical sequence throughout.

MODIFIER PLACEMENT DRILL

Make corrections, if needed, to give the sentences proper modifier placement and word order. There are multiple ways to fix these sentences.

1. While reading the book, forgot to leave a bookmark I did.
2. My car was unavailable for the road trip, which was in the repair shop.
3. The player's last game was rather abysmal, not practice very well leading up to it.
4. Route 1 was a beautiful stretch of freeway on our way to vacation, a six-lane superhighway.
5. Read all the way to the end of the book, and confusion will be replaced with clarity.

Answers with Possible Corrections

1. While reading the book, **I forgot to leave a bookmark.**
2. My car, **which was in the repair shop,** was unavailable for the road trip.
3. The player's last game was rather abysmal **since he did** not practice very well leading up to it.
4. Route 1, **a six-lane superhighway,** was a beautiful stretch of freeway on our way to vacation.
5. Fine as is. The sentence implies that the reader is being directly addressed.

VERB USE QUESTIONS

The PSAT requires you to be comfortable with the essentials of verb conjugation. Most students become familiar with the terminology for proper verb conjugation when they take a foreign language in high school—here is an overview of the key verb conjugation information that you may already know intuitively.

Table 3.1 contains a summary of some of the basic conjugation patterns of verbs.

Table 3.1. Basic Verb Conjugations

Past	Present	Future
He ate They were She ran We walked	He eats They are She runs We walk	He will eat They will She will run We will walk
Past Perfect	**Present Perfect**	**Future Perfect**
I had eaten They had been She had run We had walked	I have eaten They have been She has run We have walked	I will have eaten They will have been She will have run They will have walked

Although many verbs follow a simple pattern, quite a few verbs have irregular conjugations, particularly for the past and past perfect forms. These irregular verbs are often called "strong" verbs since they form a past tense without the aid of the "ed" ending as with "weak" verbs. Table 3.2 shows a sampling of some irregular verbs you might encounter.

Table 3.2. Irregular Verb Conjugations

Present Tense (*I am.*)	Past Tense (*I was.*)	Past Participle (What comes after "have" in the Present Perfect— "*I have been.*")
Become	Became	Become
Begin	Began	Begun
Bring	Brought	Brought
Choose	Chose	Chosen
Do	Did	Done
Draw	Drew	Drawn
Drink	Drank	Drunk
Drive	Drove	Driven
Fly	Flew	Flown
Get	Got	Gotten
Go	Went	Gone
Grow	Grew	Grown
Have	Had	Had
Hear	Heard	Heard
Know	Knew	Known

Present Tense (*I am.*)	Past Tense (*I was.*)	Past Participle (What comes after "have" in the Present Perfect— "*I have been.*")
Lay (i.e., place)	Laid	Laid
Lead	Led	Led
Lie (i.e., recline)	Lay	Lain
Light	Lit	Lit
Ride	Rode	Ridden
Ring	Rang	Rung
Rise	Rose	Risen
Run	Ran	Run
See	Saw	Seen
Shine	Shone	Shone
Show	Showed	Shown
Sing	Sang	Sung
Sink	Sank	Sunk
Swim	Swam	Swum
Swing	Swung	Swung
Take	Took	Taken
Wake	Woke	Woken
Wear	Wore	Worn

Tactic 15: Look at the Context Surrounding the Verb to See What Verb Tense, Mood, or Voice is Appropriate.

Example

Three years ago on our trip to India, we visited Humayan's Tomb and **24** see the Siddhivinayak Temple.

24. (A) NO CHANGE
    (B) saw
    (C) seeing
    (D) shall see

The sentence refers to events that took place three years ago, making the entire sentence in the past tense. Choice (B) is the only option in the past tense. Choice (A) is in the present tense, choice (C) uses the gerund form of the verb, and choice (D) uses the future tense.

VERB USE DRILL

Make corrections, if needed, to give the sentences proper verb use. There are multiple ways to fix these sentences.

1. A decade ago, I decide to focus more intently on my studies.
2. The customer service message needs to be answered by you.
3. If you was able to find a job, you would not have the financial worries you currently did.
4. In 1992, Caitlin won the prize, but only after she practice for many months.
5. My teacher demands that I am quiet during the test.

Answers with Possible Corrections

1. A decade ago I **decided** to focus more intently on my studies. *Put it in the past tense since it was a decade ago.*

2. **You need to answer** the customer service message. *Avoid the passive voice—use the active voice instead.*

3. If you **were** able to find a job, you would not have the financial worries you currently **do**. *Use the subjunctive mood to express something contrary to fact, and use the present tense since the sentence says "currently."*

4. In 1992, Caitlin won the prize, but only after she **had practiced** for many months. *Use the past perfect tense to indicate that the practice was ongoing for a period in the past.*

5. My teacher demands that I **be** quiet during the test. *Since this is a demand, use "be" rather than "is."*

PRONOUN NUMBER QUESTIONS

Matching pronouns with the nouns they represent is easy when the words are close to each other. For example,

Darnell ate her entire lunch.

It becomes more challenging to match pronouns when the pronouns and the nouns are more separated. For example,

The man who left the calculator on top of the board games cabinet needs to pick up his property.

Tactic 16: Match Singular Pronouns with Singular Nouns and Plural Pronouns with Plural Nouns.

Even though the pronouns and nouns may be separated from one another, be sure they are numerically consistent. These types of questions take a bit more focus because simply "mouthing them out" won't necessarily alert you to a grammatical problem; the separation between the pronouns and nouns makes the sentences sound pretty good as they are.

Example

If only each respondent to the survey would have given ❸ their full name.

3. (A) NO CHANGE
   (B) they're
   (C) his or her
   (D) its

The full name is to be given by "each respondent," which is a singular person. Also, we do not know the gender of the respondents, so it is proper to refer to them individually as "his or her," making choice (C) correct. Choice (A) uses the plural "their," choice (B) means "they are," and choice (D) would not be used when referring to people.

PRONOUN NUMBER DRILL

Make corrections, if needed, to give the sentences proper pronoun number. There are multiple ways to fix these sentences.

1. No matter your feelings on the vote, be sure that you are true to oneself.
2. Whenever I see someone struggling with math, I can't help but wonder if they missed some of the fundamentals earlier in school.
3. A sperm whale will probably have scars from deep-sea battles with giant squids all over their skin.
4. Members of the orchestra have to submit practice records before you are allowed to attend rehearsal.
5. A skilled surgeon will likely be quite proud of his rigorous training.

ANSWERS WITH POSSIBLE CORRECTIONS

1. No matter your feelings on the vote, be sure that you are true to **yourself**. *Keep it consistent with "your" throughout.*
2. Whenever I see someone struggling with math, I can't help but wonder if **he or she** missed some of the fundamentals earlier in school. *This is referring to a singular person given the use of "someone."*
3. A sperm whale will probably have scars from deep-sea battles with giant squids all over **its** skin. *This refers to "a" sperm whale, so use the singular.*
4. Members of the orchestra have to submit practice records before **they** are allowed to attend rehearsal. *"They" will be consistent with "members of the orchestra."*
5. A skilled surgeon will likely be quite proud of **his or her** rigorous training. *It is unclear if this is a male or female, since it refers to skilled surgeons in general, so use "his or her."*

SENTENCE STRUCTURE PRACTICE

❶ The increased use of smartphones and Internet technology profoundly interaction with our friends and family. Class reunions and opening holiday

1. (A) NO CHANGE
   (B) The increased use of smartphones and Internet technology have profoundly influenced how we interact with our friends and family.
   (C) The increased using of smartphones and Internet technology had profoundly affected how we will interact with our friends and family.
   (D) The increased use of smartphones and Internet technology has profoundly affected how we interact with our friends and family.

greeting cards **②** <u>was once</u> highly anticipated events that would offer updates on the goings-on of distant acquaintances. Now, a quick scan of a social media feed gives a real-time update. On the other hand, look at any group of people out for dinner or just hanging out, and you will inevitably find many of the group members buried in their phones, **③** <u>immersed in their own stimulation instead of meaningful interactions to be had with the people right in front of them.</u> Is it possible to have both the blessings of instantaneous communication and the minimization of the effects of distraction and **④** <u>dehumanization</u>?

It is possible to do so if we put ourselves on an "information diet." Instead of having your phone set to notify you every time there is a message or a new post, give **⑤** <u>oneself</u> a reasonable schedule for updates. If you are working on a major project with other people, **⑥** <u>and</u> you should probably check your phone more frequently. If you are on vacation, take advantage of "away" messages and **⑦** <u>as your gatekeeper let the computer serve,</u> informing people that you will be available to respond upon your return. If you can take control of technology rather than letting it control you, you **⑧** <u>will be</u> empowered to have the benefits of new technology while minimizing its pitfalls.

2. (A) NO CHANGE
   (B) has been the
   (C) were once
   (D) is now

3. (A) NO CHANGE
   (B) immersed in stimulation of their own instead of with the people right in front of them having meaningful interactions.
   (C) immersed in their own stimulation instead of having meaningful interactions with the people right in front of them.
   (D) immersed with the people right in front of them with meaningful interactions instead in their own stimulation.

4. (A) NO CHANGE
   (B) dehumanizing
   (C) to dehumanize
   (D) for the dehumanizing

5. (A) NO CHANGE
   (B) yourself
   (C) themselves
   (D) us

6. (A) NO CHANGE
   (B) but
   (C) because
   (D) DELETE the underlined portion.

7. (A) NO CHANGE
   (B) the computer you should let as your gatekeeper serve,
   (C) let the computer serve as your gatekeeper,
   (D) the computer should be served by you as the gatekeeper,

8. (A) NO CHANGE
   (B) shall
   (C) had been
   (D) have

Answers

1. **(D)** Choice (D) uses parallel structure and proper tense to make a clear, flowing sentence. Choice (A) is a sentence fragment. Choice (B) uses the plural "have" instead of "has" to match up with the singular "use." Choice (C) improperly uses "using" instead of "use."

2. **(C)** Choice (C) uses a plural and past tense verb, "were," which is consistent with the fact that this refers to a past state of affairs, and that there is a compound subject of "reunions" and "cards." All of the other choices use singular verb forms.

3. **(C)** Choice (C) puts the words in the most logical and flowing order and clarifies the meaning of the sentence. Choice (A) does not have a parallel structure, choice (B) has jumbled word order with the phrase "instead of with the people right in front of them having," and choice (D) changes the intended meaning.

4. **(A)** Choice (A) is the only option to use wording that parallels the "communication" and "distraction" that come before in the sentence. Choices (B), (C), and (D) all convey the same idea, but they do not do so in a way consistent with the rest of the sentence.

5. **(B)** The author is directly addressing the reader using the informal second person in this sentence, earlier stating "your phone" and "notify you." To be consistent with this wording, "yourself" is correct. The other options are inconsistent with the use of "you" elsewhere in the sentence.

6. **(D)** The "If" at the beginning of the sentence already serves to create an implied transition. Because of this, no transitional word is needed at this point.

7. **(C)** Choice (C) maintains the parallel structure established earlier in the sentence in which the narrator directly addresses the reader, stating that he or she should "take advantage." The other options all lack this parallel structure.

8. **(A)** Choice (A) is the only option that properly uses the future tense. Choice (B) could work if it said "shall be," and choices (C) and (D) both would be used to refer to past actions.

CONVENTIONS OF USAGE

PRONOUN CLARITY QUESTIONS

Pronouns can improve the flow of one's writing. Consider this sentence:

> Bill went to Bill's house before Bill decided what Bill was going to have for Bill's dinner.

It would be far preferable to rewrite the sentence like this:

> Bill went to his house before deciding what he was going to have for dinner.

The second version is far less choppy because it doesn't continually reintroduce the subject. If what a pronoun refers to is unclear, clarification is needed. For example:

> Mark and Jason could not wait to see his new car.

There are two men mentioned—Mark and Jason—but we do not know whose car they cannot wait to see since the "his" could refer to either Mark or Jason. The sentence could be fixed by saying "Mark and Jason could not wait to see Mark's new car." If a PSAT question clarifies a vague pronoun with a noun, *do not worry about whether the replacement is true*—focus only on if the substitution is grammatically correct.

Tactic 17: Pronouns are Fine to Use, as Long as What They Stand for is 100 Percent Clear.

If what the pronoun stands for is not 100 percent clear, choose an option that provides a clarification.

Example

When I go to Susan and Marsha's hometown, I love to visit with **14** her family.

14. (A) NO CHANGE
    (B) this
    (C) Susan's
    (D) they're

Susan and Marsha both live in the same town, but the narrator has not made clear which of the two families she wishes to visit. Choice (C) is the only option that clarifies which family the narrator will see. Choice (A) could refer to either Susan or Marsha. Choice (B) is also vague. Choice (D) means "they are" and is not a possessive pronoun.

PRONOUN CLARITY DRILL

Make corrections, if needed, to clarify vague pronouns. There are multiple ways to fix these sentences.

1. At the business, they do a nice job of making customers happy.
2. Whenever Kristen decides to take on a project, she always manages to do an excellent job.
3. Eloise laughed with her mother as she told the funny story.
4. Soon after the school contracted with the company, they were disappointed.
5. My brother enjoyed reading the book by the famous author that opened his mind to the new possibilities of space travel.

Answers with Possible Corrections

When a pronoun is vague, there are many possible ways it can be clarified. On the PSAT, as long as the substitution for a vague pronoun is grammatically appropriate, it is a valid choice.

1. At the business, **the sales associates** do a nice job of making customers happy.
2. Fine as is.
3. Eloise laughed with her mother as **Eloise** told the funny story.
4. Soon after the school contracted with the company, **the school officials** were disappointed.
5. My brother enjoyed reading the book by the famous author—**it opened my brother's** mind to the new possibilities of space travel.

POSSESSION QUESTIONS

The PSAT will assess your understanding of possessive pronouns. Table 3.3 summarizes what you need to know.

Table 3.3. Possessive Pronouns

Pronoun	Meaning	Example
There vs. Their vs. They're	*there*: place *their*: possession *they're*: "they are"	They're excited to implement their new ideas when they travel over there.
Its vs. It's	*its*: possession *it's*: "it is" (*its'* is always incorrect)	It's a great day to take the car to be washed and vacuum all of its carpeting.
Your vs. You're	*your*: possession *you're*: "you are"	Your best friend tells you when you're not acting like yourself.
Whose vs. Who's	*whose*: possession *who's*: "who is"	Who's about to decide whose project wins the grand prize?

Tactic 18: Pronouns That Show Possession Do Not Have Apostrophes, Unlike Most Nouns.

Pronouns that use apostrophes are the contraction forms, like "they're" and "you're." Pronouns are different from most other words in that they show possession without apostrophes.

Example

When you try to turn on your computer, be sure that **③⑧** it's plugged into the wall outlet.

38. (A) NO CHANGE
    (B) its
    (C) its'
    (D) it is going to be

In the above sentence, the required meaning of the underlined portion is "it is," making choice (A) correct. Choice (B) is used to show possession, choice (C) is never correct, and choice (D) is too wordy.

POSSESSION DRILL

Make corrections, if needed, to clarify possession. There are multiple ways to fix these sentences.

1. The chair was nonfunctional—its' legs no longer worked.
2. You're patience is appreciated as you wait for the next customer service representative.
3. I am confident that they're going to be on time.
4. Whose calculator needs new batteries?
5. While it's a nice day, please be sure to wash your car—it's windows are filthy.

Answers with Possible Corrections

1. The chair was nonfunctional—**its** legs no longer worked.
2. **Your** patience is appreciated as you wait for the next customer service representative.
3. Fine as is.
4. Fine as is.
5. While it's a nice day, please be sure to wash your car—**its** windows are filthy.

SUBJECT-VERB AGREEMENT QUESTIONS

Subject-verb agreement would be easy to determine if all sentences had the subject and verb close to one another. For example,

> Birds fly in the air.

When the subject and verb are separated from each other, creating agreement can be more challenging. For example,

> The movie about the terrifying monsters and evil ghosts were most frightening.

The subject "movie" and the verb "were" do not match numerically. Here is the corrected version:

> The movie about the terrifying monsters and evil ghosts <u>was</u> most frightening.

When you encounter subject-verb agreement questions remember this next tactic.

Tactic 19: Cut Out the Words Between the Subject and Verb to See if the Subject and Verb are Both Singular or Both Plural.

Example

The general who led legions of soldiers
25 <u>were</u> triumphant in the battle.

25. (A) NO CHANGE
    (B) are
    (C) was
    (D) have been

The subject in the sentence is "general," which is singular. Choice (C) is the only option that has a singular verb. Choices (A), (B), and (D) are all plural, and thus incorrect. It would be easy to be confused about the subject and think that it was the plural "legions" or "soldiers."

NUMBER AGREEMENT DRILL

Make corrections, if needed, to a lack of number agreement. There are multiple ways to fix these sentences.

1. The company of actors do a wonderful production.
2. My teacher or his teaching assistant is in charge of grading the assignment.
3. Gender roles over the past century has evolved significantly.
4. My favorite summer diversion, reading and swimming, are quite enjoyable.
5. Each person on the train were glad to arrive at the destination.

Answers with Possible Corrections

1. The company of actors **does** a wonderful production.
2. Fine as is.
3. Gender roles over the past century **have** evolved significantly.
4. My favorite summer **diversions**, reading and swimming, are quite enjoyable.
5. Each person on the train **was** glad to arrive at the destination.

FREQUENTLY CONFUSED WORDS QUESTIONS

There are many words in the English language that sound similar, yet have different meanings. Take a look at Table 3.4, and memorize any rules about these commonly confused words that you do not already know.

Table 3.4. Frequently Confused Words

Confused Words	General Rules	Examples of Proper Use
Accept vs. Except	*accept*: receive *except*: excluding	The college is eager to <u>accept</u> his application, <u>except</u> for the fact that he did not pay the application fee.
Affect vs. Effect	*affect*: typically a verb *effect*: typically a noun	The <u>effect</u> of the speaker's inspirational message on me was profound: it <u>affected</u> how I conducted myself in the years that followed.
Allude vs. Elude	*allude:* indirectly refer to *elude*: escape from	The newspaper report <u>alluded</u> to some interesting information: the criminal continued to <u>elude</u> the police.
Amount vs. Number	*amount*: usually not countable *number*: usually countable	A <u>number</u> of my classmates told my teacher that the <u>amount</u> of homework was excessive.
Beside vs. Besides	*beside*: next to *besides*: in addition to	<u>Besides</u> being a beautiful building in and of itself, the skyscraper is made even more appealing since it stands <u>beside</u> another gorgeous building.
Between vs. Among	*between*: comparing one thing at a time, typically just two objects *among*: comparing non-distinct items, or three or more objects	<u>Among</u> all the people who applied for the prestigious scholarship, it came down to a choice <u>between</u> two incredible candidates.
Choose vs. Chose	*choose*: present tense *chose*: past tense	You do not have to <u>choose</u> the same thing off the menu as what you <u>chose</u> the last time you ate here.
Complement vs. Compliment	*complement*: complete something *compliment*: flattery	My friend <u>complimented</u> my fashion sense, noting how my choice of shoes <u>complemented</u> my outfit.
Elicit vs. Illicit	*elicit*: evoke or obtain *illicit*: illegal	It is difficult to <u>elicit</u> cooperation from those who engage in <u>illicit</u> activities.
Have vs. Of	*have*: verb (action word) *of*: preposition (connecting word)	I would <u>have</u> edited the paper. (Do not say "would of.")
I vs. Me	*I*: subject *me*: object	<u>I</u> love it when you give <u>me</u> a ride to school.

Confused Words	General Rules	Examples of Proper Use
Less/much vs. Fewer/many	*less/much*: usually not countable *fewer/many*: usually countable	Many people believe that the candidate ahead in the polls is actually less qualified than his closest rival.
Lie vs. Lay	*lie*: recline *lay*: place	Lay your pillow on the mattress before you lie down to take a nap.
Lose vs. Loose	*lose*: suffer a loss *loose*: not tight-fitting	The jacket is so loose that I am afraid I may lose it in the wind.
Principal vs. Principle	*principal*: high-ranking person, or primary *principle*: rule or belief	The high school principal is known for her outstanding academic and disciplinary principles.
Than vs. Then	*than*: for comparisons *then*: for time	It is a better time to find a job now than it was back then when I didn't have a high school diploma.
To vs. Too vs. Two	*to*: connecting preposition *two*: number *too*: comparisons	Too often students narrow their options to just two college choices, ignoring many schools that would potentially be excellent fits.
Which vs. That	*which*: nonrestrictive (extra information) *that*: restrictive (essential information)	The car that was driving quickly nearly ran over a pedestrian, which gave me major cause for concern.
Who vs. Whom	*who*: subject *whom*: object (Use "who" when you would use "he," and use "whom" when you would use "him.")	Who is going to finish the pizza? To whom will we give the leftover if no one eats the rest of it?

Tactic 20: Practice the Commonly Confused Words You Don't Know by Making an Effort to Use Them in Your Conversation and Writing.

If you only have a rough feel for the proper use of the words in the table above, you will want to practice using them until you know them extremely well. The PSAT will present you with very tempting incorrect answers, so it is important to be very comfortable with proper word usage.

Example

My mother had a profound **16** effect on me when I was young.

16. (A) NO CHANGE
    (B) affect
    (C) affectiveness
    (D) effective

In this case, a noun is required for the underlined portion, since there is the adjective "profound" modifying it. Choice (B) is typically used as a verb; choice (C) means "emotional character," which does not fit the context; and choice (D) is an adjective. Choice (A) correctly uses a noun that fits the context.

CONFUSED WORDS DRILL

Make corrections, if needed, to the wording. There are multiple ways to fix these sentences.

1. I have far more clocks then watches in my apartment.
2. My friend was delighted to receive his exceptance letter to his favorite university.
3. I am sure you wish you would of practiced more for the big game.
4. Be sure to lay down your pencils at the end of the exam.
5. The emergency personnel will treat the car which is on fire.

Answers with Possible Corrections

1. I have far more clocks **than** watches in my apartment.
2. My friend was delighted to receive his **acceptance** letter to his favorite university.
3. I am sure you wish you would **have** practiced more for the big game.
4. Fine as is.
5. The emergency personnel will treat the car **that** is on fire.

LOGICAL COMPARISON QUESTIONS

For these types of questions, it is important to be more formal in your approach. In a casual conversation, if someone made a statement like "The price of food in my cafeteria is far more than your cafeteria," you would reasonably conclude the person was comparing the price of food in one cafeteria to the price of food in the other. However, this is not what was literally said. The comparison as written was between "price" and "cafeteria," which would be illogical. When you encounter comparisons, keep this tip in mind:

Tactic 21: Compare a Part to a Part, and a Whole to a Whole.

Logical comparison problems usually come from a writer comparing the part of a group to another group. The following sample question has an issue like this,

Example

The principal of my high school is better than your **17** high school.

17. (A) NO CHANGE
    (B) high school's.
    (C) high schools one is.
    (D) high schools' one.

In this question, the "part" is "principal," while the larger "group" is the "high school." To make this comparison logical, clarify that the sentence is comparing a principal to another principal. Choice (B) is the only option that does this, since writing "high school's" implies that the writer is referring to the principal of the high school. Choice (A) makes an illogical comparison, choice (C) does not have an apostrophe in "schools" and is too wordy, and choice (D) makes "school" plural instead of singular because of the apostrophe placement.

LOGICAL COMPARISON DRILL

Make corrections, if needed, to the wording. There are multiple ways to fix these sentences.

1. Susan's house is much more expensive than Mary.
2. My supervisor is nicer than anyone at my company.
3. Gas prices downtown are far greater than the countryside.
4. Hannah's car was messier than Caitlin's.
5. Among broccoli, cauliflower, and asparagus, which one do you like better?

Answers with Possible Corrections

1. Susan's house is much more expensive than **Mary's**.
2. My supervisor is nicer than **anyone else** at my company.
3. Gas prices downtown are far greater than **those in** the countryside.
4. Fine as is.
5. Among broccoli, cauliflower, and asparagus, which one do you like **the best**?

CONVENTIONAL EXPRESSIONS

These questions are the "wild card" of the PSAT Writing and Language section. The other types of issues you will encounter mostly come down to clear rules; however, these questions involve the proper use of common English phrases. For example, in casual conversation, people sometimes improperly use the word "irregardless." This is actually not a word—"regardless" should be used instead.

Tactic 22: Trust Your Instincts When it Comes to Conventional Expressions.

The more widely you read, the easier these sorts of questions will become—you will have greater familiarity with conventional expressions and you will be more confident in your intuition.

Example

Many of the questions on the PSAT and the SAT are ㉚ <u>one in the same.</u>

30. (A) NO CHANGE
    (B) one of the same.
    (C) one and the same.
    (D) ones of the same.

The proper phrase based on common English practice is "one and the same," making choice (C) correct. Choices (A) and (B) use incorrect prepositions ("in" and "of"), and choice (D) uses the plural "ones," which does not conform to common English usage for this phrase.

CONVENTIONAL EXPRESSIONS DRILL

Make corrections, if needed, to the expressions. There are multiple ways to fix these sentences.

1. It is far less expensive to purchase the ingredients on bulk.
2. For lacking of a better idea, we opted for his suggestion.
3. The movie's duration was quite little—I was disappointed it was over so soon.
4. Will all those in favor for the motion raise their hands?
5. The criminal was not concerned about going to prison because the statue of limitations had passed.

Answers with Possible Corrections

1. It is far less expensive to purchase the ingredients **in** bulk.
2. For **lack** of a better idea, we opted for his suggestion.
3. The movie's duration was quite **short**—I was disappointed it was over so soon.
4. Will all those in favor **of** the motion raise their hands?
5. The criminal was not concerned about going to prison because the **statute** of limitations had passed.

CONVENTIONAL EXPRESSIONS PRACTICE

Picking a good birthday present for my friend Sarah is nearly impossible. ❶ Irregardless of what I buy her—be it new clothing, electronics, or even concert tickets—she never seems satisfied. Perhaps this is because Sarah is the girl ❷ whom has nearly everything already. She makes enough money from her job such that if ❸ there is an item she really wants, she will simply ❹ buy them for herself. Even a gift card causes a hostile reaction from her—"why did you get ❺ her something that I can only use at one store?"

In the gift exchange this year, I could get Sarah, Bethany, or my Mother, but I ❻ was worried I could have ❼ her. Purchasing a present for Bethany is far easier ❽ than Sarah.

1. (A) NO CHANGE
    (B) Giving regarding to
    (C) Regardless
    (D) Regarding

2. (A) NO CHANGE
    (B) who has
    (C) whom have
    (D) who have

3. (A) NO CHANGE
    (B) their's
    (C) their is
    (D) they'res

4. (A) NO CHANGE
    (B) purchase those
    (C) exchange
    (D) buy it

5. (A) NO CHANGE
    (B) them
    (C) me
    (D) it

6. (A) NO CHANGE
    (B) had been
    (C) will be
    (D) am

7. (A) NO CHANGE
    (B) Sarah.
    (C) a gift for her.
    (D) an excellent present for her.

8. (A) NO CHANGE
    (B) then her.
    (C) then Sarah.
    (D) than doing so for Sarah.

Answers

1. **(C)** Choice (C) uses "regardless," which means "in spite of." This makes sense given the context because the narrator is expressing that no matter what she tries to buy her friend, she is unsatisfied. Choice (A) is not a word, choice (B) is too wordy and improperly uses "regarding," and choice (D), "regarding," means "concerning."

2. **(B)** Choice (B) properly uses the subject form of "who" instead of the object form of "whom." Moreover, it uses the singular "has" instead of "have." The other options all either improperly use "whom," or use the plural "have."

3. **(A)** Choice (A) correctly uses "there is," which is used to make a statement about something. Choices (B) and (C) use "their," which is used for possession, and choice (D) is not a word. ("They're" means "they are.")

4. **(D)** This part of the sentence is referring to purchasing a singular "item," so the singular pronoun "it" is needed. Choices (A) and (B) use plural pronouns, and choice (C) lacks a needed pronoun while making a subtle change to the original meaning from "purchase" to "exchange."

5. **(C)** The sentence in quotation marks is from the first person point of view, making a reference to the speaker logical. So, "me" is appropriate in referring back to the speaker. The other options all do not refer to the speaker in the first person.

6. **(D)** Immediately after the underlined portion, it says "currently," indicating that this should be in the present tense. Choice (D), "am," is the only option in the present tense.

7. **(B)** In the previous sentence, there are three females mentioned: Sarah, Bethany, and the narrator's mother. So, a pronoun would not be appropriate at this point because it is unclear to whom the pronoun refers. On the PSAT, you never need to worry about whether the word substituted for a vague pronoun is true—if the pronoun needs to be clarified, whatever logical noun they use will be fine. Choice (A) keeps the vague pronoun, and choices (C) and (D) change the original meaning.

8. **(D)** Although it may seem a bit wordy, it is necessary to clarify this phrase by explicitly stating "doing so for Sarah" so that there can be a logical comparison. With the other options, the writer would be literally comparing the act of purchasing to a person, which does not make sense.

PUNCTUATION

Proper use of punctuation is a major area that is tested on the PSAT. Tables 3.5 through 3.9 show the rules for proper usage of commas, semicolons, colons, dashes, and apostrophes. These tables also include examples showing the correct usage of punctuation marks.

COMMAS

Table 3.5. Comma Rules and Examples

General Rule	Proper Use
Separate a phrase (dependent clause) from a complete sentence (independent clause).	When you open your birthday present, remember to whom you should send thank you notes.
Join two complete sentences when there is a transitional word, like the "FANBOYS": *for, and, nor, but, or, yet,* and *so.*	I am eager to receive my PSAT test scores online, but they will not come out for several weeks.
Separate extra information from the rest of the sentence.	The Hubble Telescope, which orbits our planet, has provided fantastic pictures of deep space.
Separate items in a list with commas.[1]	I will order a pizza topped with cheese, pepperoni, mushrooms, and green peppers.
Don't use commas to separate parts of a sentence if everything in the sentence is needed to make it clear and logical. (In this case, clarifying that the boat is sinking).	The boat that is sinking needs Coast Guard personnel to come rescue its passengers.
Just because a sentence is long doesn't mean that it needs a comma. Look more at the structure of the sentence than at its length.	The Great Barrier Reef off the coast of Australia offers some of the best snorkeling and scuba diving anywhere in the world.
A clarifying parenthetical phrase needs to be separated with commas. If the name is sufficient to know who the person is, commas are needed to separate the description. If the description is too vague to precisely narrow down the item, then no commas should separate descriptive phrases.	Eddie George, winner of the 1995 Heisman Trophy, had a successful professional football career after college.

[1]The PSAT has traditionally preferred the serial or "Oxford" comma (i.e., having a comma between the second-to-last and last items in a list), but since there is not a universally accepted rule about whether the serial comma should be used, it is extremely unlikely that the PSAT would include a test question about it.

COMMA DRILL

Make changes, if needed, to the comma usage.

1. Joe Montana winner of multiple Super Bowls, is undoubtedly one of the best to ever play football.
2. You are doing pretty well but you could be doing even better.
3. No I did not call the doctor.
4. *Gone With the Wind,* a nearly four-hour-long movie is so long that it has an intermission.
5. The horse currently winning the race will probably finish first.

Answers

1. Joe Montana, winner of multiple Super Bowls, is undoubtedly one of the best to ever play football.
2. You are doing pretty well, but you could be doing even better.
3. No, I did not call the doctor.
4. *Gone With the Wind*, a nearly four-hour-long movie, is so long that it has an intermission.
5. Fine as is.

SEMICOLONS

Table 3.6. Semicolon Rules and Examples

General Rule	Proper Use
You can use a semicolon to separate two complete, related sentences.	My friend did most of the driving on our trip; she has much better stamina than I do.
Use a semicolon to separate items in a list when each item has a comma or commas within it.	On my European trip during college, I went to Paris, France; London, England; and Rome, Italy.
Put a semicolon before a conjunctive adverb (e.g., however, consequently, and nevertheless) when it joins two independent clauses.	Be sure to wear a raincoat today; otherwise, you will be soaked.

SEMICOLON DRILL

Make changes, if needed, to the semicolon usage.

1. Please clean up after yourself I don't want to find any messes.
2. My dad was convinced she was lying, however, I was not so sure.
3. Although my husband's snoring is quite annoying, I try my best to ignore it.
4. Cyberbullying is a major problem, consequently, we need to do something to stop it.
5. On our "foundation of the nation" vacation we traveled to Boston, Massachusetts, Philadelphia, Pennsylvania, and Washington, D.C.

Answers

1. Please clean up after yourself; I don't want to find any messes.
2. My dad was convinced she was lying; however, I was not so sure.
3. Fine as is.
4. Cyberbullying is a major problem; consequently, we need to do something to stop it.
5. On our "foundation of the nation" vacation we traveled to Boston, Massachusetts; Philadelphia, Pennsylvania; and Washington, D.C.

COLONS

Table 3.7. Colon Rules and Examples

General Rule	Proper Use
Use a colon after a complete sentence to set off a list.	Whenever I go on a trip, I am certain to take the following items: my passport, a cell phone, and my wallet.
Use a colon after a complete sentence to set off a clarification. (A colon can work if it can be replaced by the word "namely.")	I was surprised at how my boyfriend proposed to me: he did so at the spot of our very first date.

COLON DRILL

Make changes, if needed, to the colon usage.

1. Be sure to do the following in the interview, make eye contact, listen carefully, and answer from the heart.
2. I whiffed something burning from downstairs it was the stove.
3. Lead paint should be avoided it can cause lower intelligence and delayed growth.
4. The player had a major announcement: he was retiring for good.
5. Both of the job candidates have major flaws, one candidate is inexperienced and the other is unprofessional.

Answers

1. Be sure to do the following in the interview: make eye contact, listen carefully, and answer from the heart.
2. I whiffed something burning from downstairs: it was the stove.
3. Lead paint should be avoided: it can cause lower intelligence and delayed growth.
4. Fine as is.
5. Both of the job candidates have major flaws: one candidate is inexperienced and the other is unprofessional.

DASHES

Table 3.8. Dashes Rules and Examples

General Rule	Proper Use
While other punctuation can often work (in this case, a colon or semicolon could work instead of the dash), the dash can provide variety in your writing when you need to indicate an interruption or change of thought.	Shut the door behind you—it is freezing outside.
A dash can be used to interrupt a sentence and provide a change of voice.	She won the prize—this came as no surprise to me—and shared her prize money with all her friends.
Dashes can set off a parenthetical phrase. If you start with a dash on one end of the phrase, you need to use a dash on the other end of it for consistency.	Summer vacation—considered by many educators to be outdated—is probably my favorite time of year.

DASH DRILL

Make changes, if needed, to the dash usage.

1. Hold on a second please wait for me to finish.
2. Sam took just three things with him to class a laptop, reading glasses, and a ballpoint pen.
3. New York City—home of the Statue of Liberty and the Empire State Building, is a major tourist attraction.
4. My brand new phone charger does not work nearly as well as my old one did.
5. My stomach was full I couldn't eat another bite.

Answers

1. Hold on a second—please wait for me to finish.
2. Sam took just three things with him to class—a laptop, reading glasses, and a ballpoint pen.
3. New York City—home of the Statue of Liberty and the Empire State Building—is a major tourist attraction.
4. Fine as is.
5. My stomach was full—I couldn't eat another bite.

APOSTROPHES

Table 3.9. Apostrophes Rules and Examples

General Rule	Proper Use
Use an apostrophe before the "s" to indicate that a singular entity possesses something.	The cat's claws needed to be trimmed.
Use an apostrophe after the "s" to indicate that a plural entity possesses something.	The class officers' retreat was extremely productive.
Use an apostrophe before the "s" to indicate possession after an already-plural noun.	Children's theater is often far more interesting than adults'.

APOSTROPHE DRILL

Make changes, if needed, to the apostrophe usage.

1. One dog's leash is sometimes just as expensive as two dog's leashes.
2. Womens restrooms frequently have longer lines than mens.
3. Your car's windows are so dirty I can write my name on them with my finger.
4. My one friends house is quite a bit more spacious than his.
5. Whale's skin is extremely thick in order to protect the animals from cold water.

Answers

1. One dog's leash is sometimes just as expensive as two **dogs'** leashes.
2. **Women's** restrooms frequently have longer lines than **men's**.
3. Fine as is.
4. My one **friend's** house is quite a bit more spacious than his.
5. **Whales'** skin is extremely thick in order to protect the animals from cold water.

END-OF-SENTENCE QUESTIONS

It is unlikely that you will find an end-of-sentence punctuation question that asks you to identify the basic usage of a period or a question mark, since these concepts are typically mastered in elementary school.

Tactic 23: End-of-Sentence Punctuation Questions Will Probably Be About Unusual Situations.

Example

My friend was wondering if it would be OK for me **6** to take him home?

6. (A) NO CHANGE
   (B) taking him home?
   (C) to take him home.
   (D) take him home!

Although the friend is asking a question, it is given indirectly. As a result, no question mark is needed, making choice (C) the correct choice. Choices (A) and (B) both improperly make this into a direct question, and choice (D) incorrectly makes this into an exclamation.

ITEMS-IN-A-SERIES QUESTIONS

As with end-of-sentence punctuation questions, items-in-a-series questions are unlikely to test basic concepts, such as knowing that a list of three or more items requires each item to be separated by punctuation of some kind. Be on the lookout for unusual situations with items in a series of questions, paying close attention to this next tactic.

Tactic 24: Make Sure the Punctuation Separates One Complete Item from Another.

Example

When traveling in the Western United States, be sure to visit **29** Yosemite National Park, Yellowstone National Park, and San Francisco.

29. (A) NO CHANGE
   (B) Yosemite National Park Yellowstone National Park, and San Francisco.
   (C) Yosemite, National Park, Yellowstone National Park, and San Francisco.
   (D) Yosemite National Park Yellowstone National Park and San Francisco.

Choice (A) is the only option that correctly separates each destination from one another. Choices (B) and (D) jumble the destination names together, and choice (C) breaks up "Yosemite National Park" unnecessarily.

PARENTHETICAL-PHRASE QUESTIONS

A parenthetical phrase provides extra, clarifying information that can be removed and the sentence will still be complete. For example,

> My good friend Jen—a champion horseback rider—is one of the most talented people I have ever met.

Commas, dashes, and parentheses can all set off parenthetical phrases. Be sure of one thing:

Tactic 25: Start a Parenthetical Phrase in the Same Way That You End it.

If the parenthetical phrase begins with a comma, end it with a comma; if it starts with a dash, end it with a dash. Do not mix and match punctuation types in these cases.

Example

The widely respected **8** engineer, winner of numerous industry awards—was able to develop a solution to the seemingly intractable problem.

8. (A) NO CHANGE
   (B) engineer—winner of numerous industry awards—was
   (C) engineer, winner of numerous industry awards was
   (D) engineer winner of numerous industry awards was

The phrase "winner of numerous industry awards" is not essential to making this sentence complete, although it does provide helpful clarifying information. The only option that sets this phrase out of the way using consistent punctuation is choice (B). Choice (A) mixes a comma with a dash, and choices (C) and (D) do not set the parenthetical phrase aside.

UNNECESSARY-PUNCTUATION QUESTIONS

Some students tend to over-punctuate, feeling that PSAT answer choices with more elaborate punctuation are more sophisticated. Other students tend to under-punctuate, picking options that read like a stream of consciousness.

Tactic 26: Find a Balance Between Too Much and Too Little Punctuation. Use Exactly What is Needed, No More and No Less.

Example

In the **22** summer months before, you start college, be sure to enjoy time with your family and high school friends.

22. (A) NO CHANGE
    (B) summer months, before you start college be
    (C) summer months before you start college, be
    (D) summer months before you start college be

The introductory phrase of the sentence, "In the summer months before you start college," needs to be kept unified because it gives a precise description of the time period under discussion. Choices (A) and (B) interrupt this phrase. Choice (D) has no punctuation to separate the introductory clause from the complete sentence that follows. Choice (C) is the only option that correctly places a comma just after the introductory phrase.

PUNCTUATION PRACTICE

The extent of one's extracurricular ❶ participation is a vital factor in college admissions decisions. There are innumerable ways to become involved in your school and ❷ community, running for class office, starting a new club, and volunteering as a tutor or mentor. Extracurricular participation should not be ❸ burdensome you should find activities that you find enjoyable and pursue them with passion. ❹ Despite what many people think, selective colleges are looking for a well-rounded class, not necessarily well-rounded students. What do we mean ❺ by this! An elite college would rather have a community of specialists than a group of generalists. ❻ So in choosing your extracurricular activity; go for in-depth involvement in one or two areas instead of superficial involvement in many areas.

1. (A) NO CHANGE
   (B) participation, is a vital factor in college admissions decisions.
   (C) participation is a vital factor, in college admissions decisions.
   (D) participation, is a vital factor in college, admissions decisions.

2. (A) NO CHANGE
   (B) community running, for class office starting
   (C) community running for class office; starting
   (D) community: running for class office, starting

3. (A) NO CHANGE
   (B) burdensome, you should
   (C) burdensome—you should
   (D) burdensome; you, should

4. (A) NO CHANGE
   (B) Despite what many people—think selective
   (C) Despite what many people think selective
   (D) Despite—what many people think— selective

5. (A) NO CHANGE
   (B) by this? An
   (C) by this. An
   (D) by this; an

6. (A) NO CHANGE
   (B) So, in choosing your extracurricular activity, go
   (C) So, in choosing your extracurricular activity; go
   (D) So, in choosing your extracurricular activity: go

Answers

1. **(A)** Even though this is a longer phrase, no commas are required. Choices (B) and (D) would separate the subject from the verb, and choice (C) interrupts the phrase "factor in college admissions."

2. **(D)** A colon is appropriate here as it sets off a list of three different ways that one can become involved. Choices (A) and (B) do not provide a sufficient pause, and choice (C) does not work because a semicolon must have a complete sentence both before and after.

3. **(C)** The dash provides an appropriately heavy pause to break up the two independent clauses. Choice (A) provides no break, choice (B) makes this a run-on sentence, and choice (D) has a comma inappropriately placed after "you."

4. **(A)** Choice (A) has a comma after the introductory dependent clause. Choice (B) places the pause too soon, choice (C) has no breaks at all, and choice (D) has too many breaks.

5. **(B)** This is the only option that correctly treats this as a question. Given the first part of the sentence, "What do we mean . . . ," it is clear that this should take the form of a question.

6. **(B)** This option correctly places commas around the parenthetical phrase. Choices (A), (C), and (D) are all incorrect because there must be a complete sentence before both a semicolon and a colon—"So, in choosing your extracurricular activity" is instead a fragment.

PRACTICE EXERCISES

Punctuation Exercise

Recovering History

The title of Erna ❶ Brodber's third novel, *Louisiana*, has a triple meaning: it refers to a state in the United States, a place of the same name in Jamaica, and the name taken by Ella ❷ Townsend the novel's protagonist. Ultimately, the word's fluidity emphasizes the connection between African Americans and African Caribbeans, as well as between the living and dead. The eponymous ❸ protagonist: a Colombian anthropology student ventures to St. Mary, Louisiana, to study Black folk life and, instead, finds herself taken over by the spirit of Mammy. Mammy, formally civil rights activist Sue Ann Grant King and more generally called Anna, is Ella's research target. A matriarch of

1. (A) NO CHANGE
   (B) Brodber's third novel *Louisiana*, has
   (C) Brodbers' third novel, *Louisiana* has
   (D) Brodber's third novel, *Louisiana*—has

2. (A) NO CHANGE
   (B) Townsend; the novel's protagonist.
   (C) Townsend, the novel's protagonist.
   (D) Townsend: the novels protagonist.

3. (A) NO CHANGE
   (B) protagonist, a Colombian anthropology student, ventures
   (C) protagonist, a Colombian anthropology student ventures
   (D) protagonist a Colombian anthropology student ventures

obscure but certain significance, Mammy gradually reveals her own history (as well as Ella's) via a psychic, spiritual **④** connection that changes the young academic's trajectory in unexpected ways.

Ella Townsend earned a fellowship in 1936 to collect and record the history of Blacks of Southwest Louisiana using one of the university's first tape recorders but never returned. The text opens with a confusing transcript of multiple voices that are all but nonsense to the **⑤** reader, Ella, later called Louisiana, endeavors for most of the novel to make sense of the data collected on the tape recorder, confronting her own preconceptions of voodoo and acknowledging her supernatural connection with two dead women, Anna (Mammy) and Louise. **⑥** Ella embraces this spiritual connection only after listening through the tape recorder's reel and witnessing her own out-of-body experiences. Although she has no recollection of her interactions on the tape, she hears her voice speaking unintelligibly, a phenomenon that she must either investigate or accept as proof of her insanity.

After Mammy's funeral, Ella begins to understand the recorded transcript as a tri-party **⑦** dialogue an interaction among her, Anna, and Anna's long-dead friend, Louise. Louisiana then gets her name by combining those of her spiritual sisters. When Caribbean sailors visit Ella and sing folk songs to her, Ella's past is revealed to her in a trance-like vision and formally initiates her into the art

4. (A) NO CHANGE
   (B) connection, that changes the young academic's trajectory in unexpected ways.
   (C) connection that changes, the young academic's trajectory, in unexpected ways.
   (D) connection that changes the young academics' trajectory, in unexpected ways.

5. (A) NO CHANGE
   (B) reader; Ella later called Louisiana, endeavors
   (C) reader: Ella—later called Louisiana, endeavors
   (D) reader; Ella, later called Louisiana, endeavors

6. (A) NO CHANGE
   (B) Ella embraces this spiritual connection, only after listening through, the tape recorder's reel and witnessing her own out-of-body experiences.
   (C) Ella embraces this spiritual connection only after listening through the tape recorder's reel; and witnessing her own out-of-body experiences.
   (D) Ella embraces this spiritual connection only after listening, through the tape recorder's reel and witnessing her own out-of-body experiences.

7. (A) NO CHANGE
   (B) dialogue—an interaction among her, Anna, and
   (C) dialogue, an interaction among her Anna and
   (D) dialogue; an interaction among her, Anna and

of prophecy. **8** From then on: her journey is one of guiding other diaspora in reliving their pasts and speaking with Louise and Anna to recover a communal history of resistance.

9 Louisianas supernatural powers however, are not universally commended. She faces isolation from academia, her parents, and the larger Western social sphere. When she finally completes her project and sketches out Mammy's family history, Louisiana nears death. The reader accompanies Louisiana on her revelation and expansion of the original transcription, engaging with oral folk traditions to rewrite history. Brodber's novel testifies to African **10** survivals; folk traditions that have made it through the Middle Passage.

8. (A) NO CHANGE
   (B) From then on, her journey is one of guiding
   (C) From then on; her journey is one of guiding
   (D) From then on her journey, is one of guiding

9. (A) NO CHANGE
   (B) Louisianas' supernatural powers, however are
   (C) Louisiana's supernatural powers, however are
   (D) Louisiana's supernatural powers, however, are

10. (A) NO CHANGE
    (B) survivals; folk traditions, that
    (C) survivals: folk traditions that
    (D) survivals: folk traditions, that

Answer Explanations

1. **(A)** "Erna Brodber" is a singular person. To show that she possesses the novel, the apostrophe must be placed like this: *Brodber's*. The name of the novel can also be set off/separated from the rest of the sentence by commas because the description that precedes it—Brodber's third novel—is sufficient to narrow down the information to exactly which novel it is. The answer is not choice (B) because there is not a comma after "novel." It is not choice (C) because of improper apostrophe and comma use. It is not choice (D) because the punctuation that starts and ends a parenthetical description must be consistent. Parenthetical information cannot start with a comma and end with a dash.

2. **(C)** This choice properly places a comma before the clarifying description; it also correctly uses the apostrophe and *s* after "novel" to indicate singular possession. Choice (A) is incorrect because there is no break before the clarifying phrase. The answer is not choice (B) because a semicolon must have a complete sentence both before and after it. Choice (D) is wrong because this option does not properly show possession.

3. **(B)** This is the only option that properly sets off the appositive phrase with commas. Choice (C) does so only at the beginning of the phrase. Choice (D) has no commas. Choice (A) does not correctly use the colon since a colon must have a complete sentence before it.

4. **(A)** There is no need to insert commas into this phrase since the phrase is describing an essential characteristic of the spiritual connection. All of the other options insert unnecessary punctuation.

5. **(D)** This choice separates the two independent clauses with a semicolon. Moreover, it surrounds the parenthetical phrase with commas. Choice (A) is wrong because this option results in a run-on sentence. Choice (B) is incorrect because there is not a comma at the beginning of the parenthetical phrase. The answer is not choice (C) because there is inconsistent punctuation around the parenthetical phrase.

6. **(A)** No additional punctuation is needed in this complete and logical sentence. Choices (B) and (D) insert unnecessary commas, which interrupt the sentence. Choice (C) does not have a complete sentence after the semicolon.

7. **(B)** A dash can provide the heavy pause needed to come before a clarification like this. The answer is not choice (A) because there is no pause between "dialogue" and the clarification that follows. It is not choice (C) because this option lacks needed commas to differentiate the items in the list. The answer is not choice (D) because there is not a complete sentence after the semicolon.

8. **(B)** This choice provides a break between the introductory phrase and the complete sentence that follows. The answer is not choice (A) because there is not a complete sentence before the colon. Choice (C) is incorrect because there is not a complete sentence before the semicolon. Choice (D) is wrong because the comma provides an interruption too late in the sentence.

9. **(D)** This is the only option that places needed commas around the word "however." In addition, this option properly uses the apostrophe to indicate singular ownership.

10. **(C)** This option provides a clear break before the clarification. The answer is not choice (A) or (B) because there is not a complete sentence after the semicolon. It is not choice (D) because there is an unnecessary comma after "traditions."

Transitions Exercise

The Benefits of Earthquakes

An earthquake results from tectonic plate activity, which starts from forces within the Earth that eventually break blocks of rock in the outer layers of the Earth. The rocks then move along a fault, or crack, ❶ and most of the energy that is released travels away from the fault in different types of seismic waves.

❷ Because earthquakes are often called natural disasters, in and of themselves, they

1. (A) NO CHANGE
   (B) but
   (C) since
   (D) while

2. (A) NO CHANGE
   (B) For
   (C) Although
   (D) Therefore

are part of the forces of nature that actually help to sustain life on Earth. **3** On the other hand, the carbon cycle is made possible by plate tectonics, which, together with the water cycle, keep nutrients, water, and land available for life. This process also regulates the global temperature. Tectonic activity builds mountains and forms lakes and waterfalls as well, providing an environment in which plant and animal life can flourish. **4** In addition to their contributions to Earth's habitability, earthquakes also help scientists to make discoveries. By using seismographs around the Earth to measure seismic waves, geophysicists can determine the structure of Earth's interior.

Despite these benefits, it is still common to think of the damage that earthquakes cause. **5** Unfortunately, most earthquakes have not been disastrous. There are as many as a million earthquakes per year, **6** because most occur below the oceans sometimes as deep as about 435 miles below the Earth's surface. There was also more tectonic plate activity earlier in Earth's history, which released trapped nutrients, methane, and hydrogen that provided sufficient energy for some life-forms. Providing for a greater diversity and amount of life **7** although prepared an environment that could support advanced life. Today, the amount of earthquakes is not so great as to prevent humans from living in cities.

8 Furthermore, some earthquakes are destructive. Such destruction, however, could be avoided. About ninety-five percent of earthquakes happen in the Pacific Belt and the Mediterranean Belt. Even though it is known where earthquakes are likely to happen with a strong degree of confidence, there are still

3. (A) NO CHANGE
   (B) For example,
   (C) As a result,
   (D) Nevertheless,

4. (A) NO CHANGE
   (B) Of
   (C) In consideration with
   (D) As a result of

5. (A) NO CHANGE
   (B) Also,
   (C) And,
   (D) However,

6. (A) NO CHANGE
   (B) but
   (C) with
   (D) moreover

7. (A) NO CHANGE
   (B) shall
   (C) in turn
   (D) as

8. (A) NO CHANGE
   (B) To illustrate,
   (C) Subsequently,
   (D) Nevertheless,

large cities in these areas that people have chosen to develop. Building cities **9** <u>to</u> soft ground in earthquake-prone areas leads to more damage and a greater loss of life. Structures can be built that are able to withstand even the most intense earthquakes, but this has often not been done. While tectonic plate activity provides a number of benefits, moving to locations **10** <u>when</u> earthquakes occur without the proper structures sometimes results in disasters.

9. (A) NO CHANGE
    (B) on
    (C) through
    (D) with

10. (A) NO CHANGE
    (B) which
    (C) where
    (D) that

Answer Explanations

1. **(A)** "And" correctly expresses that the author is simply continuing the line of thought from the first part of the sentence into the second part of the sentence.

2. **(C)** "Although" gives a contrast between the ideas that earthquakes are both natural disasters and life-sustaining events.

3. **(B)** "For example" connects the previous statement that earthquakes are life sustaining and the example of the carbon cycle that follows.

4. **(A)** "In addition to" connects the previous sentence, which focuses on some of the ways in which earthquakes make Earth more habitable, to the current sentence, which makes the additional statement that earthquakes help scientific research.

5. **(D)** The previous sentence acknowledges that there is a widespread belief that earthquakes are associated with damage. The current sentence states that this is not as widespread as is commonly thought, so the contrast that "however" provides is appropriate.

6. **(B)** "But" provides a contrast between the statement that there are so many earthquakes and the statement that many earthquakes happen deep within the planet.

7. **(C)** "In turn" is the only option that uses proper wording to express the cause-and-effect relationship within the sentence.

8. **(D)** The previous paragraph asserts that earthquakes are not all that harmful, while the current paragraph starts with the assertion that some earthquakes are destructive. Therefore, a contrasting word like "nevertheless" is appropriate.

9. **(B)** Although "building" can be paired with any of these options, in this context, "building on" is logical since one would build a city *on* the ground.

10. **(C)** Since the sentence is referring to physical locations, "where" is appropriate.

Sentence and Paragraph Ordering Exercise

Art Theft by Government—The Issues
with the British Museum

{1}

[1] The spoils of war have always gone to the winning side. [2] That has long been the general consensus among warring nations. [3] It seems quite obvious that those who win should take what they want. [4] However in recent years, this practice has become more and more common and not just within wars. [5] They took control of vast swaths of land and the people and items on them. [6] During this colonial time, the British government removed much artwork they deemed valuable and shipped it back to the British Museum. ❶

{2}

[1] Indeed, it isn't difficult to understand why the British people don't want to give up parts of one of the most amazing historical art collections in the world. [2] The British Museum has carefully cultivated the collection to reflect worldwide cultures. [3] However, many of these pieces were not purchased but were taken as spoils of war and colonization. [4] Egyptian, Iraqi, and Greek peoples, along with people from many other cultures, must travel around the world and pay an entry fee to see pieces of their own history. ❷

{3}

[1] For this reason, if you visit the British Museum today, you can see artifacts from everywhere from ancient Egypt to ancient Greece, from India to China. [2] For a long time the British government has justified the exhibits simply by pointing out that the artifacts have been safer in Great Britain than in their native countries. [3] However, this argument can no longer be generally accepted. [4] Governments like the one in Greece are very well equipped to keep their cultural

1. The author would like to insert the following sentence into paragraph {1}:

   "The British government at one point in time had colonies around the world."

   Where would it most logically be placed?

   (A) Before sentence 2
   (B) Before sentence 3
   (C) Before sentence 4
   (D) Before sentence 5

2. To make paragraph {2} most logical, sentence 4 should be placed

   (A) where it is now.
   (B) before sentence 1.
   (C) before sentence 2.
   (D) before sentence 3.

artifacts safe. [5] However, now that the time has come to return some of these artifacts to their rightful owners, the British government is dragging its feet. ❸

{4}

Although it is true that the British Museum has kept these pieces safe for decades, that doesn't mean the pieces belong to it. Even in cases where the pieces would be undiscovered if not for British archaeology, they should still belong to the people who created them, not to those who discovered them. The British Museum and museums around the world should accumulate foreign collections only through purchase, not by claiming "finders keepers." The time has come for people around the world to say a polite "thank you" to Britain for keeping their treasures safe and for Britain to send those treasures home. ❹

3. The author would like to insert the following sentence into paragraph {3}:

"Look at the recent ransacking of the National Museum of Iraq, for example."

Where would it most logically be placed?

(A) Before sentence 2
(B) Before sentence 3
(C) Before sentence 4
(D) Before sentence 5

4. Which ordering of the paragraphs is most logical?

(A) As they currently are
(B) 1, 4, 2, 3
(C) 1, 3, 2, 4
(D) 4, 1, 2, 3

Answer Explanations

1. **(D)** Placing this sentence before sentence 5 is the most logical choice. Unless this is done, the "they" that starts sentence 5 would be completely vague.

2. **(A)** If this sentence were moved from its current placement, it would interrupt the narrative flow of paragraph 2. In its current location, the sentence concludes the paragraph by demonstrating the modern-day impact of the British collection of artwork from other countries.

3. **(B)** This sentence provides evidence in support of the claim made in sentence 2 that artifacts may be safer if they are taken away from their native countries. Therefore, this sentence logically follows sentence 2.

4. **(C)** Paragraphs 1 and 4 are appropriate where they are as they provide a logical introduction and conclusion, respectively. Paragraph 3 should be moved to follow paragraph 1 since the last sentence of paragraph 1 provides the "reason" mentioned at the beginning of paragraph 3. Also, paragraph 2 should come after paragraph 3. Paragraph 2 elaborates on why moving the artifacts back to their native countries would be sensible.

TIP

Perhaps more than any other type of question on the Writing and Language section, questions about paragraph and sentence order demand patience.

Writing Concisely Exercise

A Name That Says It All

As a high school student, I always appreciated the frankness of the War of 1812—it declared **❶** its milieu in its very name, making it the subject of the most painless question on the semester exam. You guessed it: the war took place in 1812. This two-and a-half-year-conflict, however, was far more complex **❷** than this. At best, it can be said to have been a war of mixed results.

James Madison **❸** , known as the "Father of the Constitution," put the fledgling founding document to its earliest test as the first president to ask Congress to declare war. At the top of the commander in chief's list of reasons for going to war were Great Britain's restrictions on U.S. trade, disregard and violation of maritime rights, and encouragement of Native-American attacks on U.S. colonies. **❹** Ultimately, he was afraid of what might happen if there were a reconquest of the colonies by Great Britain's powerful naval forces.

According to the Federalists, particularly those of New England who depended on trade with Great Britain, the rationale for going to war wasn't as sincere as Madison would have liked everyone to believe. **❺** They argued, instead, that the justifications for war were barely camouflaged excuses to expand the

---

1. (A) NO CHANGE
   (B) the very naming of its
   (C) that its nomenclature of this
   (D) the precise background of

2. (A) NO CHANGE
   (B) than what people have called it for some time.
   (C) than its name.
   (D) OMIT the underlined portion.

3. The author is considering removing the underlined phrase from the sentence. Should it be kept or removed?

   (A) Kept, because it provides a relevant and helpful detail
   (B) Kept, because it explains the origins of the United States
   (C) Removed, because it distracts from the essay's theme
   (D) Removed, because it unnecessarily changes the subject

4. (A) NO CHANGE
   (B) Ultimately, he feared the reconquest
   (C) Ultimately, a reconquest
   (D) In conclusion, he was mostly afraid of the ultimate reconquest and dismantling

5. The author is considering inserting the following sentence at this point in the essay:

   "Trade with Great Britain was instrumental to the jobs and fortunes of some American citizens."

   Should this sentence be inserted?

   (A) Yes, because it underscores the importance of an international relationship.
   (B) Yes, because it explains how economic policy influenced political thinking.
   (C) No, because it essentially repeats ideas already expressed in the essay.
   (D) No, because it shifts the topic of the paragraph.

colonies without further ❻ meddling and intrusion by Great Britain. At the time, British support of Tecumseh and the Shawnee Indians impeded westward expansion. Regardless of its ambiguous roots, in June of 1812, a divided Congress voted in favor of war.

By the time the Treaty of Ghent was signed in February 1815, Americans felt victory ❼ but had achieved very little. Despite the War of 1812 being celebrated as a second war of independence, the original motivations for war were all but forgotten by its close. The U.S. had surrendered Detroit but found success in the Battle of Lake Erie, defended Baltimore and New Orleans just to have Washington, D.C. captured and burned. When Britain moved for an armistice, American patriotism soared, casually ignoring the ❽ severely serious losses on its own end.

The war proved particularly useful for the military and political careers of famous American men like Andrew Jackson, John Quincy Adams, James Monroe, and William Henry Harrison, who in most cases entered the war as relatively anonymous but came out as eminent patriots. ❾ Most of these men were recognized by few people before the war but afterward were widely known and respected by their countrymen. The real loss, on the other hand, befell the Native Americans. An armistice between the colonies and Great Britain not only marked a major failure in the Native-American end goal of self-government but also catalyzed a century of imperial expansion into Native-American territories ❿ , which were areas of land.

6. (A) NO CHANGE
   (B) prying and interloping
   (C) interference
   (D) and additional involvement

7. (A) NO CHANGE
   (B) yet did not feel that they had achieved many of their aims.
   (C) but less too.
   (D) OMIT the underlined portion and end the sentence with a period.

8. (A) NO CHANGE
   (B) momentously dispiriting
   (C) grave
   (D) vitally important due to their infamy

9. The author is considering removing the underlined sentence from the essay. Should it be kept or removed?

   (A) Kept, because it clarifies the previous sentence
   (B) Kept, because it elaborates on personal motivations
   (C) Removed, because it repeats assertions made earlier in the paragraph
   (D) Removed, because it contradicts information found elsewhere in the essay

10. (A) NO CHANGE
    (B) , which consisted of land areas found in parts of North America
    (C) , which are relevant to geographic concepts
    (D) OMIT the underlined portion.

Answer Explanations

1. **(A)** The last noun to which this could refer is "War of 1812." "Its" is sufficient because there is no other noun to which "its" could refer. The other choices are too wordy and repetitive.

2. **(C)** Choices (A) and (D) would leave this too vague. Choice (B) is far too wordy. Choice (C) provides the needed wording to make this a logical contrast.

3. **(A)** This phrase is relevant because it connects James Madison to the discussion of the "founding document" that immediately follows.

4. **(B)** This is the most concise option that will keep this as a complete sentence. Choice (C) would turn this into a fragment, and choices (A) and (D) are too wordy.

5. **(C)** The beginning of the paragraph already mentions "those of New England who depended on trade with Great Britain." So inserting this sentence is unnecessary since it repeats an idea that has already been expressed.

6. **(C)** "Interference" means the same as all of the other choices yet expresses in a single word what the other choices express in multiple words.

7. **(A)** This choice expresses the idea fully and concisely. Choice (B) is too wordy and somewhat contradictory to the beginning of the sentence. Choices (C) and (D) are too vague.

8. **(C)** "Grave" when used as an adjective means "very serious." So it concisely expresses the same idea that the other choices express using multiple words.

9. **(C)** Immediately before the underlined portion, the passage states that many famous men entered the war as little-known figures and emerged from the war as respected patriots. Therefore, the underlined sentence repeats an assertion made earlier in the paragraph. So the underlined sentence should be removed.

10. **(D)** A reader can reasonably conclude that a "territory" is an area of land, both from the context of the passage and from the common understanding of the definition of "territory." Therefore, the wording should simply be removed as it is unnecessarily repetitive. If a sophisticated word that few readers would understand were used, including a definition of that word would be sensible.

Questions 1–11 are based on the following passage and supplementary material.

The Boy Who Lived

The craze surrounding the *Harry Potter* series in the late 1990s and early 2000s was, in many ways, unprecedented. **❶** Developed into eight films and setting sales records that were nothing less than monumental. All of this established J. K. Rowling, a British author, as someone whose world of wizarding became a cornerstone of young adult fiction. Its achievements include the best-selling book series in history and the fastest-selling book ever; as of 2015, **❷** its film adaptations had grossed over $7 billion. So much was made of the young wizard Harry Potter and his friends, Ronald Weasley and Hermione Granger, as they endeavor to locate and destroy horcruxes **❸** for the purposes and reasons of the defeat the evil Lord Voldemort that the series gained a large adult audience and even had entire college-level courses devoted to it.

Certainly, fantasy is the genre that comes to mind when thinking of *Harry Potter*. **❹** Yet, adventure, romance, and coming-of-age all equally describe the series. In the first book, the

1. Which of the following provides the best combined version of the underlined sentences?

    (A) These eight films were developed into seven fantasy novels, making her world a cornerstone of young adult fiction.

    (B) The seven fantasy novels developed into eight films and set monumental records in sales, establishing British author J. K. Rowling's wizarding world as a cornerstone of young adult fiction.

    (C) With sales that were monumental, the development of J. K. Rowling's wizarding world became a young adult fiction cornerstone— additionally, she was a British author.

    (D) As the cornerstone of young adult fiction, J. K. Rowling, a British author, created a wizarding world that had eight films and set monumental sales records.

2. (A) NO CHANGE
    (B) it's
    (C) its'
    (D) much

3. (A) NO CHANGE
    (B) for
    (C) by
    (D) in order to

4. (A) NO CHANGE
    (B) Therefore
    (C) Coupled with these
    (D) So

Opening U.S. Domestic Weekend Box Office Totals

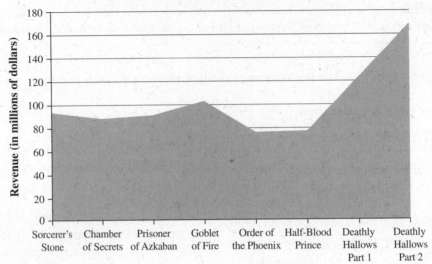

Source: *www.the-numbers.com*

young Harry, raised by his muggle (non-magical) aunt **5** and uncle learns his true identity, enrolls in Hogwarts School of Witchcraft and Wizardry, and manages to keep Lord Voldemort from procuring immortality. During his next three years of grade school, Harry defeats Voldemort's murderous basilisk, rescues his godfather who is wrongly accused of betraying Harry's parents, and witnesses Voldemort's return to power during a wizarding tournament. In the fifth and sixth books, an order of wizards **6** reemerge to defeat Voldemort and his followers, but suffers the deaths of Sirius Black (Harry's godfather) and Albus Dumbledore (headmaster of Hogwarts). And, in the **7** closing and last book of the series, Harry secures the Deathly Hallows and, with the help of his friends, finally defeats the Dark Lord. The intricate plot to the final Harry Potter installment demanded not one, but two movies to portray it. Interest in the stories increased with the final installment, as the corresponding pair of movies grossed **8** nearly 300 million dollars combined in the United States on their opening weekends.

5. (A) NO CHANGE
   (B) and uncle, learns his true identity, enrolls in Hogwarts School of Witchcraft and
   (C) and uncle, learns his true identity enrolls in Hogwarts School of Witchcraft and
   (D) and uncle learns his true identity enrolls in Hogwarts School of Witchcraft and

6. (A) NO CHANGE
   (B) reemerge for defeating
   (C) reemerges for defeat
   (D) reemerges to defeat

7. (A) NO CHANGE
   (B) ultimate ending finale text
   (C) final book
   (D) terminating wind-up tome

8. Which of the following provides a relevant, supporting detail consistent with the information in the graph?

   (A) NO CHANGE
   (B) an average of 100 million dollars per weekend during the first four installments.
   (C) 170 million dollars a piece.
   (D) slightly less than average for the *Order of the Phoenix* and the *Half-Blood Prince*.

(1) Though the series has been lauded for nearly two decades, controversy over its themes of witchcraft and politics **9** have nearly equaled its acclaim. (2) Subject of school-wide bans and book burnings, *Harry Potter* has failed to be categorized with harmless fairy tales or even the works of C. S. Lewis like many supporters believe it should be. (3) Furthermore, illegal pre-releasing of content has resulted in legal controversy over copyrights. (4) Despite opposition and dissension, J. K. Rowling made history with her fantastical imaginings of "the boy who lived." (5) And for those muggles who aren't satisfied with visiting Harry via computer screen, Universal Studios Orlando hosts *The Wizarding World of Harry Potter*. (6) **10** One thing is certain, there isn't a millennial out there who cannot recognize the lightning bolt scar etched into Harry's forehead. **11**

9. (A) NO CHANGE
    (B) has
    (C) is
    (D) are

10. (A) NO CHANGE
    (B) One thing is certain there
    (C) One thing is certain: there
    (D) One thing, is certain there

11. The author would like to insert the following sentence into the preceding paragraph.

    "Today, she continues the journey into the magical world on her interactive website, *Pottermore*."

    Where would this sentence most logically be placed?

    (A) Before sentence 2
    (B) Before sentence 3
    (C) Before sentence 5
    (D) Before sentence 6

Questions 12–22 are based on the following passage.

Up With the Rooster's Crow

(1) Depending on where you attend high school, your ⑫ teachers and peers might express confusion when you say you want to attend college to be a farmer. (2) Traditionally, we limit our conceptions of farming to the small family business portrayed in Hollywood movies. (3) A rooster crows long before the sunrise, and an exhausted adolescent clamors out of bed to join an already lively household. (4) Another misconception might involve the near extinction of farming. (5) Farming, largely a matter of the federal government or sizable corporations, simply doesn't exist for the public. (6) Despite these misconceptions and conspiratorial thinking, a college degree isn't the first thing you think about when imagining what it takes to be a successful farmer. (7) While these notions aren't completely artificial, they do limit our ⑬ sympathy of modern agriculture. ⑭

A rise in agricultural science degrees contradicts these widely held conceptions about farming. Students in agricultural science programs across the nation specialize in everything from forest to wildlife technologies, agricultural business to food science, and ⑮ biological engineering with veterinary medicine. The science behind planting, fertilizing, harvesting, and herding remains far from simple; often, it demands extensive education. However, if you enjoy working outdoors and using your hands, doing strenuous physical work, and have an

12. (A) NO CHANGE
     (B) teachers and peers, might express confusion when you say, you want to attend college to be a farmer.
     (C) teachers and peers might express confusion, when you say you want to attend, college to be a farmer.
     (D) teachers and peers might express, confusion when you say you want to attend college to be a farmer.

13. (A) NO CHANGE
     (B) wisdom
     (C) statistics
     (D) understanding

14. The author wishes to insert the following sentence into the previous paragraph.

     "An elusive and unnamed stronghold somewhere steadily reduces the land dedicated to farming but still manages to increase food production—*it's a conspiracy*."

     Where should it be placed?

     (A) Before sentence 2
     (B) Before sentence 3
     (C) Before sentence 6
     (D) Before sentence 7

15. (A) NO CHANGE
     (B) biological engineering to veterinary medicine.
     (C) engineering of the biological variety and medicine of the veterinary type.
     (D) veterinarians doing medicine and biologists engineering.

interest in the chemical and biological aspects of food and livestock, farming might be the path for you. **16** Moreover, it can be an excellent choice for those interested in working hard for a living.

Food science, one specific path of the agricultural science degree, undertakes the study and inspection of food production, storage, and distribution. A food scientist is a **17** special type of farmer, one charged with the role of improving the productivity and sustainability of farms. By finding better ways to grow, process, and deliver foods to consumers, the food scientist concerns **18** themselves with the health and nutrition of the entire planet. In a time of increased food processing, the food scientist's job necessitates the break down and analysis of basic food content to forge processed foods that are both safe and nutritional. Generally, the career calls for **19** extensive university education that could entail four or five years of schooling.

16. The author is considering deleting the underlined sentence. Should this sentence be removed?

(A) Yes, because it shifts the essay's focus to the expected lifestyle of a farmer.
(B) Yes, because it repeats information already previously implied in the paragraph.
(C) No, because it provides a fitting conclusion to the paragraph.
(D) No, because it clarifies a claim made previously in the paragraph.

17. (A) NO CHANGE
(B) special type, of farmer one
(C) special type of farmer; one
(D) special type of farmer one

18. (A) NO CHANGE
(B) theirselves
(C) yourself
(D) himself or herself

19. Which of the following provides the most specific and relevant information to complete this sentence?

(A) NO CHANGE
(B) a college diploma in an area that relates to agriculture.
(C) a Bachelor's degree and yields an annual income of $60,000–65,000.
(D) further education beyond high school, with earnings in the five figures.

A closely related career path, animal science, unites food science with research on domestic farm animals. **[20]** An animal scientist studies animal nutrition, breeding, genetics, etc., to improve the production and processing of meat, poultry, eggs, and milk. This career differs from **[21]** those of a food scientists because it has the specific goal of increasing the quality and efficiency of livestock. Many times, the animal scientist pursues a graduate or doctoral degree in order to treat and care for farm animals, opening up doors for higher salaries.

[22] Because of popular opinion, farms overflow with college degrees.

20. The author is considering removing the underlined sentence from the passage. Should it be kept or deleted?

(A) Kept, because it gives details to expand upon the general ideas of the previous sentence.

(B) Kept, because it explains the specific ways that the flavor of meat can be improved.

(C) Deleted, because it repeats information already expressed in the passage.

(D) Deleted, because it is only loosely related to the main focus of the passage.

21. (A) NO CHANGE
   (B) the food scientist's
   (C) the careers of food scientists'
   (D) food scientist

22. Which of the following provides an introductory phrase consistent with the overall message of the passage?

(A) NO CHANGE
   (B) Given
   (C) Despite
   (D) Coupled with

Questions 23–33 are based on the following passage.

Social Media: Good or Evil?

(1) I have 🟢23 sweared off all social media on my phone, computer, and tablet. (2) While I am computer literate and I enjoy my family and friends, I would rather have a conversation with a live person sitting across from me than engage in frivolous texting and chatting. (3) 🟢24 Yes, I do use e-mail in my work as an educator and will light up the search engines if I want to find something right away, but I have seen the harm that can be done by this new construct. (4) My pupils also hear my warning that an addicted social media adherent can never do any serious scholarship because there is just not enough time in the day. (5) I tell my classes about how I have seen students who had previously paid attention in class, only to have their participation plummet as soon as they had smartphones. 🟢25

When I was in the classroom, I would ask my honors students how 🟢26 much hours a day they spent with social media and video games, and these students always averaged between three and four hours a day. In my syllabus, I asked for one hour per day for outside work, and in my nine years working with these 🟢27 terrible students, not a single student admitted at the end of the course that he or she had given the course one hour per day.

I have a number of professional friends and family members who manage businesses, and 🟢28 they're number one challenge working

23. (A) NO CHANGE
    (B) swear
    (C) sworned
    (D) sworn

24. Which of the following options would provide the most logical introduction to this sentence?

    (A) NO CHANGE
    (B) Mildly,
    (C) Exceptionally,
    (D) Wrong,

25. What is the most logical placement of the sentence 5 in this paragraph?

    (A) Where it currently is
    (B) Before sentence 1
    (C) Before sentence 2
    (D) After sentence 3

26. (A) NO CHANGE
    (B) numbered
    (C) many
    (D) quantity

27. The author wishes to use wording at this point that will convey the narrator's mild sarcasm. Which of these choices would be most effective?

    (A) NO CHANGE
    (B) "advanced"
    (C) abysmal
    (D) "lazy"

28. (A) NO CHANGE
    (B) there
    (C) their
    (D) they are

with professional employees is dealing with social media in the workplace. **❷⁹** People will not have the action of staying away from this temptation, which is ever-present. The temptation is to experience some news, somewhere, in cyberspace. It is an ongoing issue in my brother's business with production employees and young engineers. He has actually fired several employees who could not **❸⁰** stay away from their phones.

I won't even go down the road of the connection of social media with **❸¹** problems and issues around the globe or cyberbullying in our schools. Essentially, I see this as one more example of playing to the addictive tendencies of humans, and I believe it is as capable of diverting time and energy from productive uses as mildly powerful drugs. When you combine this with interactive video games, chat rooms, and phone apps for every diversionary interest, **❸²** it is a minor miracle that anything productive really happens in our daily lives. When was the last time you sat down and read an interesting book, or took out a sketchpad to record your visual observations? **❸³** Who has time, for quiet contemplation and creativity with the siren of the cellphone drawing you near for another glimpse of "reality"?

29. Which of the following provides the most effective combination of the underlined sentences?

(A) People will give into the new temptation of cyberspace.

(B) People will not stay away from this ever-present temptation to experience some news from somewhere in cyberspace.

(C) While people are interested in the act of avoiding temptation, this temptation of cyberspace (to find news somewhere) is present ever-more.

(D) Ever-present, the temptation to find out the news from somewhere provides cyberspace with an experience.

30. (A) NO CHANGE
(B) stay off from
(C) stay a grand and immense distance away from
(D) stay

31. (A) NO CHANGE
(B) complications and difficulties
(C) worries, snags, and hitches
(D) troubles

32. Which of the following options conveys that the narrator is amazed that productive endeavors can occur despite the widespread use of modern communications technology?

(A) NO CHANGE
(B) it comes as no surprise
(C) it is a cause for concern
(D) it is welcome news

33. (A) NO CHANGE
(B) Who has time for quiet contemplation and creativity
(C) Who has time, for quiet contemplation, and creativity
(D) Who has time? For quiet contemplation and creativity

Questions 34–44 are based on the following information and supplementary material.

Killer Cells

My mother brags that her children have ㉞ especially resilient immune systems. As an adolescent, I understood this only as a vague, obscure advantage ㉟ of sorts my sister and I, paragons of robustness—defied infectious organisms. I recall being sick only twice during my childhood; the two to three days of rest, cool baths, pungent medicines, and bland broths seemed destined to go on forever, and I couldn't fathom the somber lives of other students in my class who were ill several times each year. As I ㊱ aging, my apparent durability only increased; occasionally, I suffered from a runny nose or a sore throat, ㊲ considering nothing more.

I never felt a need to investigate my favorable strength further ㊳ because my father was diagnosed with Lupus. Lupus is a chronic autoimmune disorder in which the immune system—the source of my vigor—mistakenly attacks healthy cells causing muscle and joint pain and inflammation. In essence, his microscopic armor had gone rogue. Imagine that—the cells that freed me from routine sicknesses like the common cold to life-threatening diseases like cancer were murderous in my father, unable to differentiate allies from ㊴ helpful cells.

In a healthy immune system, white blood cells, or leukocytes, work closely with the circular system and lymphatic system to locate and destroy threatening pathogens.

34. Which of the following provides the most logical introduction to the paragraph?

   (A) NO CHANGE
   (B) overcome a plethora of lethal maladies.
   (C) a tendency to be overly dramatic.
   (D) unmatched aerobic endurance.

35. (A) NO CHANGE
   (B) of sorts—my sister and I, paragons of robustness, defied infectious organisms.
   (C) of sorts, my sister and I: paragons of robustness, defied infectious organisms.
   (D) of sorts; my sister and I paragons of robustness defied infectious organisms.

36. (A) NO CHANGE
   (B) had aging
   (C) age
   (D) aged

37. (A) NO CHANGE
   (B) for
   (C) but
   (D) of

38. Which of the following provides the most logical transition at this point in the sentence?

   (A) NO CHANGE
   (B) until
   (C) for
   (D) when

39. Which phrase would create the most sensible contrast within the sentence?

   (A) NO CHANGE
   (B) neutral intermediaries.
   (C) foreign invaders.
   (D) wicked sorcery.

40 Unlike other systems of the body the immune system, is relatively invisible with soldiers housed throughout the body in the spleen, lymph nodes, thymus, and bone marrow. These leukocytes produce antibodies to destroy disease-causing invaders called antigens. Some cells are responsible for sending messages, generating specific antibodies, destroying infected cells, or **41** remembering previous invaders so that the body is ready for them the next time. While the body fights, you often experience fever, fatigue, **42** having swelling, or runny nose—hence, my rare ailments. Immunity looks different for everyone: we are born with some immunity, acquire more as we grow, and obtain others through vaccination. Even then, each body defends differently and with varying degrees of efficiency.

A confused immune system, like that of my father, doesn't operate so. Instead, the leukocytes cannot determine friend from foe and attack healthy tissues in the same way they might attack virus and bacteria. Lupus can affect almost any organ in the body and varies in symptoms making it tough to diagnose and even more difficult to treat. My father experiences pain on a daily basis; his joints and muscles ache constantly, and he is often too tired to perform routine daily activities. His form of Lupus, Systemic Lupus Erythematosus, infects millions of people and **43** produces symptoms similar to Crohn's disease and Lyme disease. It is as if his troops simply turned against him. **44**

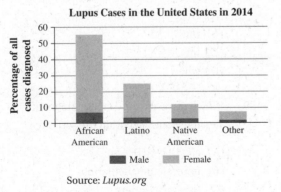

Lupus Cases in the United States in 2014

Source: *Lupus.org*

40. (A) NO CHANGE
    (B) Unlike other systems of the body, the immune system is relatively invisible with soldiers housed throughout the body in the spleen lymph nodes, thymus, and bone marrow.
    (C) Unlike, other systems of the body the immune system is, relatively, invisible with soldiers housed throughout the body in the spleen, lymph nodes, thymus, and bone marrow.
    (D) Unlike other systems of the body, the immune system is relatively invisible, with soldiers housed throughout the body in the spleen, lymph nodes, thymus, and bone marrow.

41. The author wishes to use a word that makes sense given the information that follows in the sentence. Which would best accomplish this goal?

    (A) NO CHANGE
    (B) trivializing
    (C) surrounding
    (D) approaching

42. (A) NO CHANGE
    (B) swelling
    (C) to swell
    (D) swellingness

43. (A) NO CHANGE
    (B) produced
    (C) producing
    (D) had produced

44. What new information about the narrator's father would make the statistics in the table most relevant in placing his illness in a greater societal context?

    (A) His age
    (B) His ethnicity
    (C) His gender
    (D) His salary

Answer Explanations

1. **(B)** Choice (A) is flawed in that it eliminates the name of J. K. Rowling, thus leading to ambiguity. Choice (D) incorrectly identifies J. K. Rowling as the "cornerstone of young adult fiction," rather than her literature. Choice (C), with its opening clause of, "With sales that were monumental," must refer to the Harry Potter series rather than the *development* of the series, as it does incorrectly. Choice (B), however, is perfect—it maintains all relevant information while avoiding awkward word ordering.

2. **(A)** This is a good moment to review the various forms of "it." The first, "it's," is a contraction of *it is*. The second, "its," is the possessive form of *it*. The third, "its'," is always grammatically incorrect. We are looking for the possessive form, so "its" is the correct answer.

3. **(D)** Notice the context of what we're attempting to connect: it is cause and effect. When we paraphrase, it is, "Harry and his friends must defeat horcruxes *so that* Lord Voldemort can be defeated." The best cause-and-effect transition here (to substitute for *so that*) is "in order to." Choice (A) expresses our intended sentiment, but it does so in a manner that is far too wordy. Choices (B) and (C) neglect cause and effect entirely.

4. **(A)** This requires a *contrasting* transition. Paraphrased, the sentences are, "Fantasy is Harry Potter's genre, *but* there are aspects of adventure and romance, as well." "Yet," choice (A), is our best substitute for "but."

5. **(B)** The phrase, "raised by his muggle aunt and uncle" is a parenthetical phrase; we can eliminate those words and still have the sentence function perfectly well. Accordingly, we can surround the phrase with two commas or two dashes to separate it from our main clause. Eliminate choices (A) and (D) as a result. Thereafter, we are listing actions. A comma is thus required between the actions of "learns his true identity" and "enrolls in Hogwarts . . . ." Choice (C) incorrectly omits that comma.

6. **(D)** The subject here was tricky: it was "order of wizards," with "order" being the operative word, not "wizards." "Order" is a singular noun, so we will need a singular verb to match. As "reemerge" is a plural verb, eliminate choices (A) and (B). Now, after "reemerges," the *infinitive* form of the verb is required: "to defeat." Choice (D), "reemerges to defeat," therefore, is the correct answer.

7. **(C)** All four choices express the same sentiment of *last book*. However, while choices (A), (B), and (D) achieve that in an overly verbose manner, choice (C) manages to do so while maintaining concision.

8. **(A)** Analyze the graph, specifically looking at "Deathly Hallows: Part 1" and "Deathly Hallows: Part 2." Choice (B) is incorrect in that it doesn't answer the question, but instead refers to the wrong movies. Choice (C) is incorrect, as "Part 1" grossed only 120 million dollars. Choice (D) is incorrect, as the two grossed significantly more than "Half-Blood Prince" and "Order of the Phoenix." The correct answer is choice (A): the sum of the two movies was 280 million dollars, which is "nearly 300 million."

9. **(B)** The subject is "controversy," which is a singular noun. Eliminate choices (A) and (D) as they are plural verbs, and thus can't be paired with a singular noun. Choice (C) is close to correct, but the passage would need to read as, "is nearly equaled *by* its acclaim." That requisite "by" is not there, however. Thus, "has equaled" is our best choice.

10. **(C)** Both "one thing is certain" and "there isn't a millennial out there who cannot recognize the lightning bolt scar etched into Harry's forehead" could be complete sentences independently. Therefore, proper punctuation is required to separate these two clauses. A colon is the best option here, as seen in choice (C). The colon serves as a sort of lead-in from clause 1 to clause 2. Choice (A) causes a run-on sentence while choices (B) and (D) neglect punctuation entirely.

11. **(C)** Sentence 5 references a "computer screen," which is a perfect follow-up to our proposed insertion about Rowling's website. Otherwise, the proposed insertion isn't logical in the context of the other choices.

12. **(A)** Be careful not to confuse *length* with a *run-on sentence.* There is nothing in this clause that requires a comma to delineate it from something else, so be aware of avoiding unnecessary punctuation. Choices (B), (C), and (D) all include unnecessary commas that break with the flow of the sentence.

13. **(D)** In essence, the sentence is stating that we have little *knowledge* of modern agriculture. "Understanding" is the most apt synonym for "knowledge." "Wisdom" is similar to "knowledge," but it typically implies good decision making. As the old saying goes, "*Knowledge* is knowing that a tomato is a fruit. *Wisdom* is knowing not to put a tomato in a fruit salad."

14. **(C)** It makes the most sense to have this sentence connect sentences 5 and 6 because sentence 5 focuses on the idea of a big business and governmental conspiracy, and sentence 6 transitions away from the discussion of misconceptions and conspiracies. Placing this sentence any earlier would interrupt the introduction of the paragraph's topic, and placing it later would revert to conspiratorial thinking when that line of analysis had already stopped.

15. **(B)** Notice the parallelism of the sentence, specifically in the recurring reference of the word "to." Choice (A) breaks with that pattern by swapping "to" for "with." Choice (D) also breaks with the pattern by omitting "to." Choice (C) is wordy. Choice (B), "biological engineering *to* veterinary medicine," maintains our desired parallelism.

16. **(B)** When deciding whether to delete the underlined sentence, ask two questions: *is it relevant, and is the information new?* If the answer is "no" to either of those questions, then the sentence should be deleted. In this case, "interested in working hard for a living" is simply a restatement of "if you enjoy . . . doing strenuous physical work." Thus, the information is not new, and the sentence should be deleted.

17. **(A)** The main clause in our sentence is, "A food scientist is a special type of farmer . . . ." We must separate this from any information that comes after. In this case, that is, "one charged with the role of improving the productivity and sustainability of farms." Choices (B) and (D) neglect a pause between "farmer" and "one," so they can be eliminated accordingly. The problem with choice (C) is that a semicolon requires the joining of two complete clauses. As the second clause is a fragment, the sentence therefore requires a comma as appropriately used in choice (A).

18. **(D)** We must choose the proper reflexive pronoun to match "the food scientist." "The food scientist" is a single person of indeterminate gender, so our reflexive pronoun should reflect that. "Theirselves" can be eliminated, as it is not a word. "Themselves" can be eliminated, as the food scientist is one person. "Yourself" can also be eliminated, as "the food scientist" is third person and "yourself" is second person. "Himself or herself" is the correct answer.

19. **(C)** The key to this question is the requirement for *specific* as all four choices are *relevant*. Choice (C) mentions a Bachelor's degree, which we can infer takes four or five years to complete. It also mentions a specific salary of $60,000–$65,000, which makes for three pieces of *specific* information—the degree, the required length of time, and the salary. Choice (A) gives us the length of the degree, choice (B) only tells us that a degree is needed, and choice (D) mentions that a degree is needed while mentioning that the salary could be between $10,000 and $99,999. It's clear to see the choice (C) is most *specific*.

20. **(A)** When deciding whether to delete the underlined sentence, ask two questions: *is it relevant, and is the information new?* If the answer is "no" to either of those questions, then the sentence should be deleted. In this case, the information about the animal scientist is both relevant and new. In fact, without this sentence, the reader would be left with an incomplete picture of what animal science actually is. Choice (B) correctly insists on keeping the sentence, but its logic is flawed, as it doesn't actually "explain the specific ways that the flavor of meat can be improved."

21. **(B)** Remember to compare apples to apples, so to speak, in order to preserve parallelism. We are comparing "this career" to *the food scientist's career*, or simply "the food scientist's," as choice (B) correctly states. Choice (A) is incorrect as "those" implies *multiple careers*, and choice (C) is wrong for the same reason. Choice (D) is incorrect as we are comparing careers, not the people actually working in those careers.

22. **(C)** The point that the author is making is that it is assumed that higher education has no place in agriculture. However, as she has demonstrated and proceeds to state in this sentence, "farms overflow with college degrees." Thus, a contrasting transition is required. "Despite" is our only option that fulfills that need for contrast.

23. **(D)** The "have" indicates to us that our verb tense will be *present perfect*. The present perfect tense of "swore" is irregular—"sworn" is the correct answer.

24. **(A)** This is a question where it is probably easier to eliminate incorrect choices rather than zeroing in our correct answer immediately. "Wrong, I do use e-mail . . ." implies that an incorrect assumption has been made, which is not the case. "Mildly, I do use e-mail . . ." is nonsensical. Similarly, "exceptionally, I use e-mail . . ." does not make sense, either. The correct choice was choice (A). Notice how the "yes" works in context: it is given as a concession that, even though the narrator is not terribly fond of technology, he still uses *some* technology.

25. **(D)** Sentence four references the pupils hearing the narrator's warning. Our proposed insertion is, in fact, that warning. Thus, the sentence must be placed before sentence 4, or "after sentence 3," as choice (D) states.

26. **(C)** Recall that "many" and "few" are words used to describe concrete things that can be quantified. "Much" or "little" refer to more abstract concepts that are not easily quantifiable. In this case, *hours* are something that can be counted. Accordingly, we would say, "too *many* hours," which is choice (C).

27. **(B)** Read the question carefully. We need a choice that will use "mild sarcasm" to describe honors students who do not spend enough time studying. "Lazy" is an apt description of these students, but it conveys nothing of sarcasm or of sarcasm's cousin: irony. "Terrible" and "abysmal" aren't so much sarcastic as insulting. "Advanced" is a perfect choice here; it is ironic and certainly fits the definition of sarcasm.

28. **(C)** We need a possessive word to use as a stand-in for the "professional friends" and "family members" mentioned earlier in the sentence. Recall that "their" is a possessive word for multiple people, whereas "there" refers to *something over there*, for instance. "They're" is the contraction of *they are*. Thus, choice (C) is the only adequate answer.

29. **(B)** The best way to combine the two sentences hinges on "temptation," as it was used once in each sentence. We can eliminate the need for two sentences by using "temptation" as the figurative fulcrum of the clause, as choice (B) effectively executes. Choice (A) eliminates key information from our initial two sentences. Choice (C) changes the meaning, particularly in its statement of how "people are interested in the act of avoiding temptation." Nothing in the initial two sentences suggests that. Choice (D)'s flaw is most apparent in its change of subject by omitting the word "people."

30. **(A)** Choice (B) is flawed in that it includes the extra preposition "from." Choice (D), "stay their phones," is incorrect. Choices (A) and (C) both express the same sentiment, but choice (C) is terribly wordy next to the concision of choice (A).

31. **(D)** We must strike the proper balance between the inclusion of relevant information and the exclusion of repetitive, unnecessary information. All four choices express the same sentiment, but choices (A), (B), and (C) all do so by including multiple words that mean the exact same thing. For instance, we can say "complications and difficulties," but these two words are practically identical. In the interest of concision, simply say, "troubles."

32. **(A)** The operative word in the question is "amazed," and we will accordingly need a choice that indicates something of amazement. "It comes as no surprise" does not indicate amazement, just as "it is welcome news" does not. "It is a cause for concern" expresses a negative sentiment, which is certainly not amazement. People are amazed by miracles, however. "It is a minor miracle"—"NO CHANGE"—is the correct answer.

33. **(B)** Recall that length alone does not necessarily indicate a run-on sentence or a need for punctuation. In this case, "Who has time for quiet contemplation and creativity . . ." is the core part of our main clause. Accordingly, it should not be dissected with commas but should instead be allowed to remain intact. Choices (A), (C), and (D) all insert unnecessary punctuation that breaks that main clause.

34. **(A)** In order to find the most logical introduction to the paragraph, we in fact need to *read* the entire paragraph. The theme is that the narrator and her siblings were rarely sick, whereas her peers were sick quite frequently. In this context, "especially resilient immune systems" would be most appropriate, as it was the immunity that prevented them from becoming sick in the first place. Choices (C) and (D) are off topic. Choice (B) is incorrect in that the kids never became sick in the first place.

35. **(B)** This was a difficult one. Notice the first principal clause: "I understood this only as a vague, obscure advantage of sorts . . . ." That alone could be a full sentence, so we need an appropriate break between it and what follows. Choice (A) has no break, and choice (C), with its comma, provides too little of a break; choice (C) is also flawed with its colon. With choice (D),

a semicolon would be acceptable, but "paragons of robustness" is a parenthetical phrase that can use commas or dashes to surround it.

36. **(D)** Notice the use of "increased" later in the sentence. That verb is in past tense, so the verb we choose must be in past tense to maintain parallelism. Choice (D) is the only past tense verb. "Had aging" could be confused for past tense, but the correct form would have been "had *aged*."

37. **(C)** A contrast is needed here. "I suffered from a runny nose or sore throat, *but* nothing more." Paraphrased so that the contrast requirement is more apparent, the sentence is, "*although* I was sick with little things, nothing big ever affected me." Choices (A), (B), and (D) are not effective contrasting transitions.

38. **(B)** Choices (A) and (C) provide a cause-and-effect relationship that is *opposite* of our intentions, as if her father having lupus was the reason she never investigated. In actuality, she never investigated "until" her father had lupus, which is an inversion of choices (A) and (C). Choice (D), similarly, provides an opposite meaning from our intended meaning.

39. **(C)** The sentence requires the most "sensible contrast," specifically with "allies." The opposite of an ally is an enemy. "Foreign invaders" would certainly be enemies.

40. **(D)** In a complex sentence such as this, it's probably easier to eliminate the three incorrect choices rather than initially diagnosing the correct one immediately. Choice (A) features an unnecessary comma separating the subject from the predicate. Choice (B) neglects a comma between "spleen" and "lymph nodes," and choice (C) is incorrect from the very beginning with an unnecessary comma after "unlike." Upon eliminating those three, analyze the remaining choice, choice (D), and notice that it is faultless.

41. **(A)** The operative part of the question is "given the information that follows in this sentence"; what follows is, "previous invaders so that the body is ready for them next time." "Approaching" and "surrounding" are logical choices scientifically, but these words fail to take into account that stipulation about connecting with the second part of the sentence. In this case, "remembering" is the best match for an action that could connect with previous information or, more specifically, "previous invaders." To trivialize something is to make light of it, which isn't logical.

42. **(B)** "Swelling" operates as a noun in this case, as gerunds can do under certain circumstances. Having the word in noun form makes it parallel to the rest of the sentence, unlike choices (A) and (C). Choice (D), "swellingness," is not a word.

43. **(A)** We want a verb that parallels "infects," which is a singular, present tense verb. "Produces" is also a singular, present tense verb. The other choices all sacrifice parallelism.

44. **(B)** Analyze the chart for this question. The only information listed in the chart pertains to gender and ethnicity. As we already know that it is his father, the only remaining piece of information unknown and potentially useful to us is his ethnicity.

TROUBLESHOOTING

Here are some further pointers for common issues.

"I never learned grammar rules."

- Review the concepts presented throughout this chapter—the rules are presented in an extremely concise, easy-to-grasp way.

- Realize that you don't need to know the precise grammatical terminology for a concept being tested. As long as you have a good sense of what is correct, you do not need to give an elaborate justification for your answer—simply get it right.

- Actually read the editing marks and comments teachers make on your papers. Instead of just looking at your grade, look at what grammar mistakes you made and be sure you understand *why* they were mistakes. That way, you will gradually remedy gaps in your grammar knowledge.

"I finish too quickly."

- Try reading the passage before you look at the questions. Having a sense of the broad flow of the passage can be useful to you in answering many of the big-picture questions. This will be a more effective use of your time than doing nothing for several minutes at the end of the Writing and Language section.

- Pace yourself to take the full amount of time per passage. If you do not check your time as you go, you will likely rush to the end. Try to take the full nine minutes for each passage.

"I finish too slowly."

- Do not spend time overanalyzing your choice after you have made it. If you have read enough context and fully understand the requirements of the question, you have done all you can do; it is time to pick an answer choice and move on.

- Practice with timing so that on test day you do not fall prey to "paralysis by analysis." Any tendencies you have to go too slowly will only be exacerbated by the stresses of the actual PSAT.

- Try to spend no more than 90 seconds on a difficult question. If you have spent this much time and are not getting anywhere, you should cut your losses and take a guess. After all, there is no guessing penalty on the PSAT. You will not need to answer every question correctly to achieve National Merit recognition.

FURTHER PREPARATION

What else can I do beyond the drills and practice tests in this book to prepare for the PSAT Writing and Language?

- Practice with the other Barron's books for the SAT: *Barron's SAT* has plenty of practice tests you can try.
- Use the free practice tests and resources provided by the College Board on *KhanAcademy.org*.
- Practice with ACT English tests—the grammar concepts and editing skills tested on the ACT are virtually identical to those tested on the PSAT Writing and Language section.
- Edit your friends' papers, and have them edit yours. Since the Writing and Language test is fundamentally an editing test, the more practice you have with editing, the better you will do.
- Read a variety of high-quality texts so that you develop a great feel for excellent writing.

Don't forget to try the drills in chapter 4, "Advanced Writing and Language Drills," for more challenging practice.

Advanced Writing and Language Drills

4

The following eight drills represent the most challenging types of writing and language passages and questions you will encounter on the PSAT. Completing these will help you prepare to score at the elite level required for National Merit recognition. The body of passages comprehensively covers the most difficult question types you might find. Here are the titles of the passages should you wish to mark them off as you complete them:

- *Abeng*
- Beauty and Peril
- Carbon
- Court Reporter
- Hatfields and McCoys
- Hornsby
- President
- Risk

To practice these passages under timed conditions, take about 9 minutes per drill. Answer explanations for each drill are at the end of the chapter.

ADVANCED WRITING AND LANGUAGE DRILLS

Abeng

[1] In contemporary critical work examining female subjectivities in **❶** womens' fiction, there is a tendency to privilege the overt insurgent over more **❷** direct instances of insubordination. [2] For most, it seems that the better story lies with psychically fragmented protagonists deviating from the world in which they live. [3] Michelle Cliff's 1984 *Abeng* tells the story of Clare Savage, a light-skinned Jamaican girl whose mixed racial heritage—in a world of strict oppositional binaries—incapacitates her chances for wholeness. [4] While Clare's complex subjectivity under the constraints of colonialist White supremacy certainly **❸** calls for examination as well as acclaim, other female characters' counter hegemonic personalities and actions, often less conspicuous, go predominantly **❹** unseen and unnoticed. [5] Thus, there is a presumption that these female characters are less courageous, less risky, less intellectual, less *something*. **❺**

The novel, in some ways, magnifies the difference between insurgent and pacifist women in its juxtaposition of Nanny and Sekesu—the former a legendary leader of the Windward Maroons, and **❻** the later her sister who remained a slave. Accordingly, the islanders descend from either one or the other—rebel or conformist—implying a congenital difference in the people of Jamaica. A closer reading of several of the characters, however, suggests an identity more complex than mere compliance with White

1. (A) NO CHANGE
   (B) women's
   (C) womans'
   (D) womens

2. Which of the following provides the most logical ending to this sentence?

   (A) NO CHANGE
   (B) conspicuous happenings of belligerence.
   (C) indirect depictions of inconsistency.
   (D) subtle representations of resistance.

3. (A) NO CHANGE
   (B) call for
   (C) calls of
   (D) call of

4. (A) NO CHANGE
   (B) without anyone actually seeing them.
   (C) mostly without being viewed.
   (D) unnoticed.

5. The author wishes to place the following sentence into the previous paragraph.

   "In Caribbean women's fiction specifically, this commonality likely coincides with the tradition's inclination to be inherently subversive."

   Where would it most logically be placed?

   (A) Before sentence 1
   (B) Before sentence 2
   (C) Before sentence 3
   (D) Before sentence 4

6. (A) NO CHANGE
   (B) the opposition
   (C) the latter
   (D) the other one

patriarchal ideologies, a subjectivity amid the mire of institutionalized oppression that resists and survives in more nuanced ways. **❼** Rather than relying on colonialist binaries, the female characters in *Abeng* demarcate a complex gradation of resistance from varying marginal spaces that ultimately works to dismantle the conceptual order of Western metaphysics. By interrogating the subjectivities of characters like Kitty, Mad Hannah, and Miss Winifred, readers can begin to understand various degrees of female resistance. **❽** Moreover, they will understand the roots of the motivations that empowered them to stand up for themselves.

Cliff's novel is within the tradition of Jamaica Kincaid's *Annie John* **❾** (1985) Merle Hodge's *Crick Crack Monkey* (1981), Oonya Kempadoo's *Buxton Spice* (1999), and Edwidge Danticat's *Clare of the Sea Light* (2013), in which young Caribbean girls' gender awakenings coincide with their political awakenings while they struggle to construct a Black female self without coherent mother-daughter relationships and without a clear sense of history. Clare typifies the **❿** double consciousness, her White external self attempts to reconcile internal feelings of Blackness. In essence, the quest for Black female subjectivity coexists with the struggle against patriarchy, concurring with the feminist perspective that loving Blackness is itself political resistance. **⓫** Hence, actions taken by women like Kitty, Mad Hannah, and Miss Winifred that may seem inconsequential actually serve socially and politically to challenge notions of patriarchal discourse by creating spaces of agency that refute, undermine, or opt out of systemic oppression.

7. Which of the following would provide the most effective and logical introduction to this sentence?

(A) NO CHANGE
(B) Instead of acting in a relativist fashion,
(C) In contrast with some documentary evidence,
(D) As opposed to seeing things along a spectrum,

8. The author is considering deleting the underlined sentence. Should it be kept or removed?

(A) Kept, because it provides a needed clarification
(B) Kept, because it justifies the author's line of thinking
(C) Removed, because it is unrelated to the previous sentence
(D) Removed, because it repeats an idea already expressed

9. (A) NO CHANGE
(B) (1985), Merle Hodge's *Crick Crack Monkey* (1981) Oonya
(C) (1985) Merle Hodge's, *Crick Crack Monkey* (1981) Oonya
(D) (1985), Merle Hodge's *Crick Crack Monkey* (1981), Oonya

10. (A) NO CHANGE
(B) double consciousness: her White external self attempts to reconcile internal feelings of Blackness.
(C) double consciousness her White external self, attempts to reconcile internal feelings of Blackness.
(D) double consciousness—her White external self—attempts to reconcile internal feelings of Blackness.

11. (A) NO CHANGE
(B) Additionally,
(C) Moreover,
(D) However,

Beauty and Peril

One would be hard-pressed to find more gorgeous scenery ❶ <u>than that in</u> California and the Pacific Northwest. From the Santa Monica Mountains to the Malibu lagoons, from the gorgeous Cascades and Mount Rainier to Puget Sound, the entirety of the coast from California to Washington is breathtaking. Tucked beneath that striking veneer, sinister and lurking, however, ❷ is secrets of a magnitude of which we are suspicious but uncertain. The reality, though, is as follows: ❸ <u>a conspiracy is afoot.</u>

For one, the region is threatened by the San Andreas fault line. Popularized by countless Hollywood films in the previous decades, San Andreas is perhaps the most recognizable (though, unfortunately, perhaps not even the most potentially destructive) of Pacific geological hazards. ❹ <u>Extending for 810 miles in length through</u> the bulk of California, the San Andreas fault line had its largest recorded earthquake in 1906, the infamous San Francisco earthquake with a magnitude of 7.8 on the Richter scale. The death count was 3,000, ❺ <u>and</u> that must be accompanied by the disclaimer that the population was significantly less than it is today.

❻ <u>In addition to the previously mentioned things, there is also the Juan de Fuca tectonic plate. This plate comprises part of the Cascadia subduction zone.</u> Cascadia stretches all the way from Northern California to Canada's

1. (A) NO CHANGE
   (B) than
   (C) then those in
   (D) then

2. (A) NO CHANGE
   (B) was
   (C) are
   (D) has

3. Which of the following would provide wording that focuses on the overall message of the essay?

   (A) NO CHANGE
   (B) people need to get their priorities straight.
   (C) leadership depends on deeds, not words.
   (D) something cataclysmic is coming this way.

4. (A) NO CHANGE
   (B) Extending through
   (C) Extending for 810 miles through
   (D) Passing by

5. (A) NO CHANGE
   (B) moreover
   (C) but
   (D) also

6. Which of the following provides the best combination of the underlined sentences?

   (A) Additionally to the Juan de Fuca plate is the following, a plate that comprises part of the Cascadia subduction zone.
   (B) What is more, the Juan de Fuca tectonic plate is comprised with the Cascadia subduction zone.
   (C) Furthermore, the Juan de Fuca tectonic plate is the major component which partially comprises the zone, known as the "Cascadia subduction" zone.
   (D) Then there is the Juan de Fuca tectonic plate, which comprises part of the Cascadia subduction zone.

British Columbia, and this is the place where seismologists predict is the most likely spot for the "Big One." ❼ For centuries North Americas continental shelf has ground against Juan de Fuca, and the shelf has been compressed upward all the while—every moment, every day, every century, a little bit more all the time. Predictions are that this sort of unrelenting stress ❽ is approaching its breaking point of both literal and figurative nature. When that finally occurs (and advanced computer models put the likelihood of that catastrophe at greater than one in three in the next fifty years), it's difficult to affix an accurate estimation of the impending damages. Tens of thousands of deaths, hundreds of thousands of casualties, and billions of dollars in damaged property are not outside the scope of possibility. ❾ Moreover, as both San Andreas and Juan de Fuca are coastal, subsequent tidal waves would accompany the earthquakes. And, at this point in our ❿ wild goose chase, perhaps it is best not to venture any further down our path of apocalyptic prediction.

⓫ Despite all of these frightening possibilities, by no means am I advocating avoiding the Pacific coastal states. We must refuse to allow fear to dictate the courses of our lives—refuse to be deterred in our pursuit of happiness by the fragile futility of, "Well, what if . . . ?"

7. (A) NO CHANGE
   (B) For centuries, North Americas' continental
   (C) For centuries, North America's continental
   (D) For centuries North Americas' continental

8. (A) NO CHANGE
   (B) is approaching their
   (C) are approaching its
   (D) are approaching their

9. (A) NO CHANGE
   (B) Moreover as both San Andreas, and Juan de Fuca are coastal subsequent
   (C) Moreover as both San Andreas and Juan de Fuca are coastal subsequent
   (D) Moreover—as both San Andreas and Juan de Fuca are coastal subsequent

10. Which of the following would be most consistent with the tone and meaning of the passage?

    (A) NO CHANGE
    (B) conjecture
    (C) guesstimate
    (D) wisdom

11. Which of these options provides the most effective introduction to this sentence and paragraph as a whole?

    (A) NO CHANGE
    (B) Given the imminent catastrophe,
    (C) With the utter pointlessness of rampant speculation,
    (D) Granted that this is all hypothetical,

Percent of Human Body

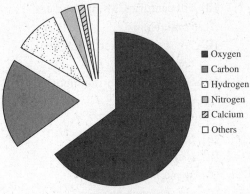

- ■ Oxygen
- ■ Carbon
- ☐ Hydrogen
- ■ Nitrogen
- ▨ Calcium
- ☐ Others

Source: OpenStax College

Carbon

You can burn me for energy or find me in plastics. When I am soft, pliable, and dark, I am used to write with. When I am diamond shaped and clear, I go on your left hand. I might be in your stocking or your gas tank, and I always show up to the family barbecues. I make up **❶** 2% of the human body, forming the basis of your very DNA. I am life when mixed with oxygen but death without enough of it. **❷** It takes a lot to melt me, my nature is quite unreactive. With an atomic number of 6 and a weight of 12.011, I am the fourth most common element in the entire universe. I'm all about the bonds, attaching to up to four atoms at one time. **❸** Chemists, casually refer to me as the basis of all plant and animal life, so you could say I have some big footprints to fill. **❹**

If you guessed iron, you're wrong. If you guessed nitrogen, you are equally incorrect. **❺** Sulfur, lacking in many of the characteristics of other atomic elements, is not suitable for this purpose. Carbon is the name; living organisms are the game.

1. Which of the following is supported by the information in the accompanying graph?

   (A) NO CHANGE
   (B) 10%
   (C) 19%
   (D) 65%

2. (A) NO CHANGE
   (B) It takes a lot to melt me my nature is quite unreactive.
   (C) It takes a lot to melt me: while my nature is quite unreactive.
   (D) It takes a lot to melt me; my nature is quite unreactive.

3. (A) NO CHANGE
   (B) Chemists casually refer to me, as the basis of all plant and animal life,
   (C) Chemists casually refer to me as the basis of all plant and animal life,
   (D) Chemists casually refer to me as the basis of all plant and animal life

4. Which option, if inserted here, would provide the most logical conclusion to the paragraph and the most effective transition to the next?

   (A) What am I?
   (B) Where am I?
   (C) What are these?
   (D) Who is this?

5. Which of the following is most consistent with the tone and style of the passage as a whole?

   (A) NO CHANGE
   (B) Nope, sulfur isn't cutting it either.
   (C) If you considered picking sulfur, that too would be a deleterious inclination.
   (D) Sulfur ain't right, too.

And it just so happens that I form more compounds than any other element, making me a building block of life on Earth. You might **6** have heard of my most common isotope, carbon-12, because it occurs naturally and makes up 99% of the carbon on your planet. If you happen to be more versed in the wonders of the chemical world, you might recognize me as the basis of graphene, a material stronger than steel but more flexible than rubber.

[1] My versatility is both gift and curse. [2] When I can find two oxygen atoms, I make carbon dioxide, which is found in Earth's atmosphere and used in photosynthesis. [3] Carbon footprint refers to the amount of greenhouse gas emissions generated by a particular country, organization, etc., and damages to Earth's ozone layer. [4] Hence, carbon dioxide—essential to life— can be detrimental in excess quantities. [5] **7** Accordingly, when I join with only one oxygen atom, I form a toxic gas known as carbon monoxide and **8** are responsible for fatal poisonings. **9**

For millions of years, I operated **10** between a balanced cycle. Plant life extracts me from the atmosphere in large quantities for food and energy, and I return to the atmosphere through respiration, **11** decomposing, and combustion. But humans disrupted my cycle by burning fossil fuels at rapid rates and destroying forests and plant life. Since I'm so critical to life, you may want to be more careful in the future.

6. (A) NO CHANGE
    (B) of heard of
    (C) have heard have
    (D) of heard have

7. (A) NO CHANGE
    (B) Furthermore,
    (C) Nevertheless,
    (D) Consequently,

8. (A) NO CHANGE
    (B) is
    (C) were
    (D) am

9. The author would like to insert the following sentence into the preceding paragraph.

    "However, too much of a good thing can be bad, really bad."

    Where would it most logically be placed?

    (A) After sentence 1
    (B) After sentence 2
    (C) After sentence 3
    (D) After sentence 4

10. (A) NO CHANGE
    (B) among
    (C) within
    (D) for

11. (A) NO CHANGE
    (B) decompose,
    (C) decomposed,
    (D) decomposition,

Court Reporter

In the court of law, a judge is the public official who presides over the hearing and is ultimately responsible for the administration of justice. An attorney or a lawyer advises and represents individuals, businesses, or agencies in legal disputes. Defense attorneys and prosecutors are the specific names given to lawyers ❶ whom represent the accused or whom represent local, state, or federal agencies as they accuse others of crimes, respectively. The jury consists of a body of people appointed to listen, consider evidence, and give a verdict on a ❷ specific trial—essentially, jurors represent a panel of judges. Responsible for maintaining order in the court is an officer, much like a police officer. And a court clerk maintains records of the court proceedings. Other than interested parties like the defendant and the witnesses, this list ❸ composes those occupants found in a normal legal proceeding. ❹ *Or will they?*

❺ Court reporting an often-overlooked occupation of legal services—is essential to trials, depositions, committee meetings, and basically any legal proceeding you can think of. A court reporter provides a verbatim record of court proceedings using recording equipment, stenographs, and stenomasks. ❻ For this reason, a court reporter transcribes any spoken dialogue, recorded speech, gestures, actions, etc. that occur in a legal environment where exact record of occurrences is mandatory. Hence, the oversight does not reflect the significance of the occupation itself. Court reporters are very important to the judicial system.

1. (A) NO CHANGE
   (B) who represent the accused or who
   (C) whom represent the accused or who
   (D) who represent the accused or whom

2. (A) NO CHANGE
   (B) specific trial, essentially jurors represent a panel of judges.
   (C) specific trial: essentially jurors represent, a panel of judges.
   (D) specific trial; essentially jurors, represent a panel of judges.

3. (A) NO CHANGE
   (B) compromises
   (C) comprises
   (D) comprising

4. Which of the following would provide the most logical and effective conclusion to this paragraph and transition to the next paragraph?

   (A) NO CHANGE
   (B) *Or does it?*
   (C) *Or can you?*
   (D) *Or did it?*

5. (A) NO CHANGE
   (B) Court reporting—an often-overlooked occupation of legal services, is essential to trials, depositions, committee
   (C) Court reporting, an often-overlooked occupation of legal services is essential to trials, depositions committee
   (D) Court reporting, an often-overlooked occupation of legal services, is essential to trials, depositions, committee

6. (A) NO CHANGE
   (B) In other words,
   (C) In contrast,
   (D) Because of this,

Stenographs are machines like keyboards that use key combinations rather than single characters **❼** for effective communication. A court reporter using a stenomask, on the other hand, actually speaks into a covered microphone recording dialogue and reporting actions that a computer then transcribes. Recording equipment might consist of anything from a traditional tape recorder to more advanced digital audio recording with voice recognition technology. Whatever a court reporter chooses to use, **❽** they are charged with generating exact records of what was said inside the courtroom and then providing accurate copies to courts, counsels, and other involved parties.

As you might guess, the occupational skills valued in a court reporter encompass clerical, listening, and writing skills; selective hearing; attention to detail; and knowledge of legal codes, jargon, and court procedures. That being said, it might surprise **❾** you to learn that most entry-level positions require only an associate's degree or certificate program, and completion of licensing exams. **❿** You are on your way to a six-figure salary and a front-row seat at local, state, or federal court proceedings in as little as two years. In addition, **⓫** a given court reporter's salary is more likely to be within a consistent range than the salaries of other major legal fields, making it a job you can count on to give you a solid paycheck.

Average Salaries for Legal Occupations, 2014

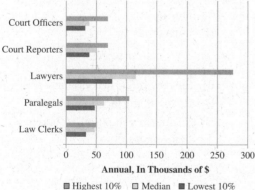

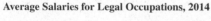

Source: Onetonline.org

7. Which of the following provides the most logical and effective ending to this sentence?

(A) NO CHANGE
(B) for technological advantage.
(C) for speedy typing.
(D) to discourage sickness.

8. (A) NO CHANGE
(B) you are
(C) one are
(D) he or she is

9. (A) NO CHANGE
(B) him or her
(C) one
(D) them

10. Which of the following is both the most logical introduction to the sentence and supported by the information in the accompanying graph?

(A) NO CHANGE
(B) You will earn more than the typical American worker
(C) You will pay off your student loans in no time
(D) You could be on your way to a $60,000 salary

11. Which of the following properly uses information from the graph to build upon the author's argument in this paragraph?

(A) NO CHANGE
(B) court reporters earn an average salary that exceeds the median legal professional salary,
(C) court reporters are more likely to be hired for entry-level positions,
(D) a given court reporter's compensation is likely to be as much as the salaries of the attorneys who appear before them,

Hatfields and McCoys

Like many of history's most legendary battles, the lawless family feud between the Hatfields and McCoys ❶ boiling down to the differences between two men. William Anderson Hatfield, known widely as "Devil Anse," was a mountain dweller and successful timber merchant. Randolph McCoy, or "Ole Ran'l," ❷ owned some land, and livestock in the same region; the borderlands dividing Kentucky and West Virginia. The clash between the two families brands the American memory—in the Midwest, the vendetta rivals that of the Capulets and Montagues but with a uniquely "hillbilly" twist.

Legend has it that the feud began somewhere near 1865 with the murder of Randolph's brother, Asa, who was accused of treason for fighting for the Union during the Civil War. ❸ As a result, the Hatfield family ran the Logan Wildcats, the local militia group responsible for Asa's murder. Years of deep dislike, bitter resentment, and minor confrontations passed before Randolph McCoy accused Floyd Hatfield of stealing a hog in 1878. Devil Anse's influence over the courts resulted in a quick clearing of Floyd's name but not before a McCoy relative testified on the Hatfield's behalf. ❹ The disloyalty sealed the witness's fate—he was violently killed by other McCoys.

It wasn't until the 1880s, though, that things spiraled out of control. Johnse Hatfield, son of Devil Anse, began dating Randolph's daughter, Roseanna. They devoted themselves to each other despite their ❺ family's disapproval. However, Johnse later left a pregnant Roseanna and married her cousin Nancy, stirring intra- and inter-familial conflicts. Things were unstable to say the least in August 1882, when three of Randolph's sons confronted two Hatfield brothers. ❻ The face-off turned to violence with quickness and rapidity, and Ellison Hatfield was stabbed and shot. To ❼ venge the family name, a group of Hatfields found the three

1. (A) NO CHANGE
   (B) boils
   (C) boil
   (D) OMIT the underlined portion.

2. (A) NO CHANGE
   (B) owned some land, and livestock in the same region, the borderlands dividing Kentucky and West Virginia.
   (C) owned some land and livestock in the same region, the borderlands dividing Kentucky and West Virginia.
   (D) owned some land and livestock in the same region the borderlands dividing Kentucky and West Virginia.

3. (A) NO CHANGE
   (B) Nonetheless, the
   (C) Contradictorily, the
   (D) The

4. Which of the following would provide the most logical and effective introduction to this sentence?

   (A) NO CHANGE
   (B) He managed to keep his word
   (C) The judge and jury were unimpressed
   (D) The historical record did him no favors

5. (A) NO CHANGE
   (B) families
   (C) familys
   (D) families'

6. (A) NO CHANGE
   (B) The face-off turned violent,
   (C) Violent to the face-off turned,
   (D) Turning to a situation of violent confrontation,

7. (A) NO CHANGE
   (B) revenging
   (C) vengeance
   (D) avenge

sons, bound them, and fired more than 50 bullets into them. Again, the prominent family ❽ eluded arrest.

[1] The media caught on, and the Hatfield/McCoy clash reached commercial popularity. [2] Suddenly newspapers produced article after article, painting the Hatfield family as particularly vicious and violent. [3] By 1887, the Hatfields spent most of their time dodging increasingly large bounties. [4] To put an end to the family rivalry, the Hatfields sought to end the McCoys once and for all. [5] In 1888, they ambushed the McCoy household, killing ❾ Old Ran'l's son and daughter, and brutally beating his wife. [6] Nine were arrested in connection to the atrocious crime. ❿

Eventually, the case made its way to the U.S. Supreme Court where eight of the nine received life in prison. ⓫ The ninth, a mentally handicapped Ellison Mounts, was hanged in February 1890. Today, both families hold celebrity status in the American consciousness.

8. (A) NO CHANGE
    (B) alluded
    (C) illuded
    (D) illuminated

9. The author is considering changing this phrase to "Mr. McCoy's." Is this change necessary?

    (A) Yes, because it provides a needed clarification.
    (B) Yes, because it uses more formal language.
    (C) No, because this logically refers to Mr. Hatfield.
    (D) No, because this nickname was already established in the essay.

10. The author would like to insert the following sentence into the previous paragraph:

    "With the journalistic sensationalism, the feud was revived."

    Where would it most logically be placed?

    (A) Before sentence 1
    (B) Before sentence 3
    (C) Before sentence 5
    (D) After sentence 6

11. Should the underlined sentence be kept or deleted?

    (A) Kept, because it provides a relevant clarification
    (B) Kept, because it gives a needed justification
    (C) Removed, because it is off topic
    (D) Removed, because it shifts the analysis too quickly

Hornsby

I struggle with the phenomenon of fame. ❶ Perhaps, as Andy Warhol once quipped, we are all destined to occupy the spotlight for fifteen minutes. But what, I ask, of those whose notoriety is longer sustained? How can a Hollywood family of dullards and never-do-wells mesmerize the whole of a nation with a smash-hit reality TV series, while someone of actual import and accomplishment—say, a heroic police officer or selfless organ donor— ❷ passes the entirety of his or her life in the thankless shadows? I don't wish to waste your time disputing the nature or purpose of celebrity, but pardon my tangential musing as I approach ❸ my true question, where is the love, for Bruce Hornsby?

❹ Powerfully, I now must tell you who Bruce Hornsby is, which further illustrates the criminality of his anonymity. A man so talented should require no introduction whatsoever. Alas, Hornsby is a singer, songwriter, and—in my esteemed opinion—as fine a piano player as Billy Joel (a man who requires no introduction, ❺ my point about the arbitrary nature of fame having been thus solidified). When Bruce plays the piano, the sound is so wonderfully rich that your brain can't help but be puzzled at the thought of human hands moving so deftly over the keys.

1. The author is considering deleting the underlined sentence. Should this sentence be kept or removed?

   (A) Kept, because it provides a relevant elaboration
   (B) Kept, because it introduces the main person to be analyzed
   (C) Deleted, because it is inconsistent with the essay's tone
   (D) Deleted, because it distracts from the essay's principal argument

2. (A) NO CHANGE
   (B) pass
   (C) passing
   (D) past

3. (A) NO CHANGE
   (B) my true, question; where is the love for Bruce Hornsby?
   (C) my true question—where is the love for Bruce Hornsby.
   (D) my true question: where is the love for Bruce Hornsby?

4. Which word provides the most logical transition at this point in the essay?

   (A) NO CHANGE
   (B) Imaginatively,
   (C) Inevitably,
   (D) Obliquely,

5. (A) NO CHANGE
   (B) giving the solidity of a case to my point about the arbitrary nature of fame.
   (C) further solidifying my point about fame's arbitrary nature
   (D) making my point about the solidifying of the arbitration of fame

And when he sings, there is a molasses-sweet timbre that communicates volumes about the human condition. ⑥

Even more puzzling about Hornsby's lack of name recognition is that he has had a moderate amount of success throughout his career. Hornsby has won three Grammy awards (most notably in 1987 for best new artist), and his album *The Way It Is* attained multiplatinum status by selling more than two million units. His songs continue to receive radio airplay on ⑦ <u>variety various</u> stations, and he has toured and collaborated with such dynamos as The Grateful Dead, Don Henley, Bob Dylan, Stevie Nicks, Bonnie Raitt, and Crosby Stills and Nash ⑧ <u>(all of whom have succeeded him greatly in notoriety and recognition)</u>. Moreover, Bruce Hornsby's music has transcended genre; it is a little-known fact that hip-hop legend Tupac Shakur's mega-hit "Changes" was actually an adaptation of Hornsby's "The Way It Is."

6. The author wishes to insert an aside to underscore his self-deprecating self-awareness that readers likely will not share his views about Hornsby. Which of the following would best be inserted at this point to accomplish the author's goal?

    (A) There are those who can appreciate Hornsby, and there are those who not only cannot appreciate his work, but have no artistic sensibility whatsoever.

    (B) Forgive my hyperbole, but so profound is my love for his music that I cannot help but get carried away with my adulation.

    (C) As someone with extensive musical training, I can assure you that if you miss out on Hornsby, you are truly missing out.

    (D) To listen to him play is like watching Michelangelo painting the Sistine Chapel—it is to see a master at work.

7. (A) NO CHANGE
    (B) various variety
    (C) variety, various
    (D) various, variety

8. The author is considering deleting the underlined portion of the sentence. Should this portion be removed?

    (A) Yes, because it does not focus on the essay's primary topic.

    (B) Yes, because it unfairly disparages the protagonist of the passage.

    (C) No, because it underscores the author's thoughts about Hornsby's lack of recognition.

    (D) No, because it provides specific details in support of the following sentence.

❾ Perhaps, like van Gogh's or F. Scott Fitzgerald's, Bruce Hornsby's legacy will grow with time. Perhaps society just isn't quite ready to award him his deserved credentials. **❿** Consequently, I fear the opposite: now more than ever, we are a Justin Bieber and Eminem crowd. Bruce's time is past, and his just deserts will forever elude him as we continue to turn our attention to increasingly **⓫** lessening worthy recipients.

9. (A) NO CHANGE
    (B) Perhaps like van Gogh or F. Scott Fitzgerald Bruce Hornsby's legacy
    (C) Perhaps, like van Gogh or F. Scott Fitzgerald Bruce Hornsby's, legacy
    (D) Perhaps, like van Gogh or F. Scott Fitzgerald Bruce Hornsby's legacy

10. (A) NO CHANGE
    (B) But,
    (C) Therefore,
    (D) Accordingly,

11. (A) NO CHANGE
    (B) less worthy
    (C) fewer worthy
    (D) fewer worth of the

President

{1}

The first three articles of a 1789 document—formally known as the United States Constitution—delineate the separation of powers ❶ in the core of American democracy. Divided into three branches, the federal government assigns law making to the legislative, law enforcing to the executive, and law interpreting to the judicial system. ❷ The separation of powers doctrine largely originated with the ideas of the French political philosopher, Baron de Montesquieu. The President of the United States is the nucleus of the Executive Branch, serving as both Head of State and Commander in Chief, and is the most prominent figure of American government. ❸ Thus, if one's career goals involve establishing oneself as one of the most important and well-known people in the world, then running for the national presidency makes a great deal of sense.

{2}

[1] The requirements are pretty straightforward: one must be a natural-born citizen who ❹ is at least the age of 35 years and for at least the duration of 14 years resided in the United States. [2] What it actually takes, however, is labyrinthine. [3] At the forefront of a successful campaign for presidency ❺ lie charisma. [4] One's public image must be maintained with a skeleton-free closet and consistent political views—nothing sabotages a presidential campaign like scandal or irregularity. [5] Even then, a likely candidate should endeavor to appeal to average Americans, appearing in churches and small businesses often and visiting frequently with

1. (A) NO CHANGE
   (B) with
   (C) at
   (D) on

2. The author is considering deleting the underlined sentence. Should it be removed?

   (A) Yes, because it interrupts the flow of the paragraph.
   (B) Yes, because it is unrelated to the facts of the paragraph.
   (C) No, because it defines a key term in the passage.
   (D) No, because it provides a relevant historical anecdote.

3. (A) NO CHANGE
   (B) Thus, if ones career goals involve establishing oneself
   (C) Thus if your career goals involve establishing yourself
   (D) Thus, if your career goals involve establishing oneself

4. (A) NO CHANGE
   (B) is at least 35 years old and has resided in the United States for 14 years or more.
   (C) is 35 and has lived in the U.S. for a long time.
   (D) meets the requirements as laid out in the Constitution.

5. (A) NO CHANGE
   (B) lay
   (C) lays
   (D) lies

veterans, blue-collar workers, and farmers.
[6] Personal military experience never hurt
anyone either. **6**

{3}

7 Past presidents' age ranges from 44 (John
F. Kennedy) to 76 (Ronald Reagan) but average
at about 55 years old. U.S. presidents tend to
be married with children and hold advanced
degrees in law or business from elite universities.
Most candidates possess resumes boasting of
years in public service and political positions; the
fast track to presidential candidacy comprises
elected posts like mayor, governor, and
senator. **8** Still allure, a spotless background,
and years in diplomatic service are a dime a
dozen in presidential races. One needs money,
and plenty of it, to run for the presidency.

{4}

Even after an exploratory committee
predicts success and a potential candidate
registers with the Federal Election Commission,
one has to win support in a caucus, triumph
in a primary, **9** following an earning
nationally in a convention, and raise millions
of dollars in funds before the general
election. **10** Surprisingly, the *Washington Post*
reported that both presidential candidates in
2012, Barack Obama and Mitt Romney, raised
over $1 billion each to run their campaigns.
Thinking of the White House as a future
residence? Work on that billion-dollar smile. **11**

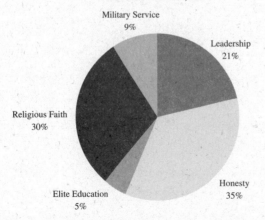

**Desirable Characteristics in the
next U.S. President, 2016**

Military Service 9%

Leadership 21%

Religious Faith 30%

Honesty 35%

Elite Education 5%

Survey of 1,000 randomly selected likely voters

6. The author would like to insert the
following sentence into the previous
paragraph:

"But mastering the charm, attractiveness,
and likability to please the cameras—
arguably one of the more mystifying
qualifications of presidency—by itself
falls short of an election."

Where would it most logically be inserted?

(A) After sentence 1
(B) After sentence 2
(C) After sentence 3
(D) After sentence 5

7. (A) NO CHANGE
(B) Past president's ages range
(C) Past president's age range
(D) Past presidents' ages range

8. (A) NO CHANGE
(B) Still, allure, a spotless background, and
(C) Still, allure a spotless background and
(D) Still, allure a spotless background, and

9. (A) NO CHANGE
(B) earn a following in a national
convention,
(C) follow an earning nationally in a
convention,
(D) follow a national earning in a
convention

10. (A) NO CHANGE
(B) As a result,
(C) For instance,
(D) However,

11. The author would like to use the data
from the accompanying chart to create a
relevant sentence to insert in the essay.
To which paragraph should such a
sentence be added?

(A) Paragraph 1
(B) Paragraph 2
(C) Paragraph 3
(D) Paragraph 4

Risk

I remember the class well. ❶ We seniors understood academic principles and knew the roles that we would play when we moved into management jobs after graduation ❷ since we felt well-prepared for the profession we were about to enter. Most programs had a capstone course that pulled all of our coursework together, and this was no different. Our guide for this course was an experienced executive and not the normal academic ❸ who walked these halls. "What is the basic job of a general manager?" he asked. Hands shot up. "Maximize shareholder equity!" "Maximize profit." "Develop a strategic vision!" "Increase market share." To these responses and others, he said a simple "no." Finally, he told us what we would be doing as managers ❹ for the field. "Your job is to take risk. When analysis will not provide an answer, you have to make a decision and move the ball forward. ❺ Your decision-making performance will determine your worth to the enterprise."

1. (A) NO CHANGE
   (B) Us
   (C) That
   (D) This

2. The author is considering deleting the underlined portion. Should this selection be removed?

   (A) Yes, because it digresses from the main idea of the sentence.
   (B) Yes, because it repeats ideas already implied in the sentence.
   (C) No, because it provides relevant details in support of a claim.
   (D) No, because it provides a needed contrast.

3. (A) NO CHANGE
   (B) whom walked
   (C) who walking
   (D) whom walking

4. (A) NO CHANGE
   (B) fielding.
   (C) out in the field.
   (D) with a field.

5. Which of the following provides the most logical and relevant conclusion to the paragraph?

   (A) NO CHANGE
   (B) Significant wealth will inevitably follow.
   (C) Be sure you incorporate thorough analysis before you decide on your course of action.
   (D) Remember these words of advice when you go back to school.

Taking risk involves the understanding that various outcomes can arise when you make a choice. ❻ Some outcomes may spell disaster for your company, others may create exceptional financial returns for the shareholders. But hiding behind every one of these possible futures is the uncertainty of which one or some hybrid of several will actually occur. An ❼ affective manager has the confidence to face these outcomes and the inherent unknowns.

[1] Let's take a simple example. [2] How much inventory of a certain item should you hold so that you can provide exceptional customer service and not run out of product? [3] What affects the success of a chosen number of items to put on the shelf? [4] The other is the lead time that it takes to replenish the inventory when it begins to run low. [5] The tricky part is that both the demand for the product and the lead time to replenish are typically not known with certainty. [6] ❽ Books are going the way of the record player—technology has made mobile electronics far more preferable. [7] The publisher may tell you that the standard lead time is 8 weeks, but this can change due to other business it may be running in the printing factory. [8] And if you are at Amazon. com, there are millions of these decisions that are made, and ❾ the success of the business will be driven by how well you manage these variations.

6. (A) NO CHANGE
    (B) Some outcomes, may spell disaster for your company: others may create exceptional financial returns for the shareholders.
    (C) Some outcomes—may spell disaster for your company—others may create exceptional financial returns for the shareholders.
    (D) Some outcomes may spell disaster for your company; others may create exceptional financial returns for the shareholders.

7. (A) NO CHANGE
    (B) affecting
    (C) effective
    (D) effecting

8. Which of the following would provide the most specific example in support of the claim made in the previous sentence?

    (A) NO CHANGE
    (B) If Oprah selects a given book for her monthly review, copies will run off of the shelves and backorders will occur.
    (C) The definition of "lead time" varies a great deal depending on the business professor to whom you speak.
    (D) Publishers try to increase demand for profitable books, using methods like online advertising and public relations firms.

9. (A) NO CHANGE
    (B) the success of the business, will be driven by how well you manage these variations.
    (C) the success, of the business will be driven, by how well you manage these variations.
    (D) the success of the business will be driven by how well, you manage these variations.

[9] If you don't have the item, the customer will simply click on a competitor's website and make the purchase. [10] If you put too much on the shelf, the investment cost of this **10** moving slowly inventory can consume the working capital of the business. **11**

10. (A) NO CHANGE
    (B) slow inventory with respect to moving
    (C) slowly moving inventory
    (D) inventory, which is slowly moving at times,

11. The author wishes to place the following sentence into the previous paragraph:

    "One factor is the demand that you expect over a given time period, such as a month or quarter."

    Where would it most logically be placed?

    (A) Before sentence 2
    (B) Before sentence 4
    (C) Before sentence 9
    (D) Before sentence 10

ANSWER EXPLANATIONS

Abeng

1. **(B)** A choice is needed that encompasses *fiction of women*. A possessive is required, and possession is demonstrated using *s*. Choice (D) can be eliminated, as it has no apostrophe. Choice (C) can be eliminated, as it reads as *fiction of womans*. Choice (A) can be eliminated as it reads as *fiction of womens*. Choice (B) is the only logical option.

2. **(D)** This question is largely about the vocabulary. A choice is needed that contrasts with "overt insurgent," which essentially means clear instance of rebellion. Choice (D), particularly with its usage of "subtle . . . resistance," forms a perfect contrast since *subtle* is an antonym for *overt*. Choices (A) and (B) are flawed in that they mean the same thing as "overt insurgent." Choice (C) is not logical in context. Instead, it is irrelevant to the topic.

3. **(A)** The subject is "subjectivity," which requires the singular verb form "calls." Eliminate choices (B) and (D) accordingly. One "calls for" rather than "calls of." Eliminate choice (C).

4. **(D)** All four choices represent the exact same sentiment. To be concise and avoid wordiness, choice (D) is the best option.

5. **(C)** The proposed insertion mentions "Caribbean women's fiction." Sentence 3 references a story in Jamaica, which would be an example of "Caribbean women's fiction." The new sentence should therefore be inserted before sentence 3. In that position, the new sentence can act as an introductory sentence to the discussion of *Abeng*.

6. **(C)** A common verbal pattern involves the usage of *former* and *latter* in conjunction. This sentence is a perfect example of that pattern, and "the latter" is the correct answer. Choice (A), "the later," is used as an adjective or adverb, not as a noun. Choices (B) and (D) break with the pattern completely.

7. **(A)** Immediately before this sentence, the author writes about resisting oppression in more "nuanced" ways. The author then states that the characters act along a more "complex gradation of resistance." In other words, the characters act in such a way that their behavior should be considered to be along a spectrum. Therefore, choice (A) is the most logical, because "relying on colonialist binaries" is a simplified way of interpreting their actions, as a "binary" provides only two extreme options. Choices (B) and (D) are incorrect because they express the opposite of what is intended. Choice (C) is incorrect because the author is suggesting how the interpretation of literature should be done—there is no question about the quality of the documentary sources themselves.

8. **(D)** In the sentence immediately before the underlined portion, the author states that "by interrogating the subjectivities of characters like Kitty, Mad Hannah, and Miss Winifred, readers can begin to understand various degrees of female resistance." Subjectivity refers to one's personal point of view, which gives insight into the person's motivations. The female resistance refers to actions one would take to stand up for oneself. Therefore, this sentence provides a subtle repetition of the idea expressed in the previous sentence. Choices (A) and (B) are incorrect because they would leave in an unneeded sentence. The answer is not choice (C) because the underlined sentence is, in fact, related to the previous sentence.

9. **(D)** Notice the pattern here: there is an author, a title, a year, and then a comma. Eliminate choices (A) and (C) for neglecting the comma after "(1985)." Eliminate choice (B) since it does not include a comma after "(1981)."

10. **(B)** This sentence first mentions "double consciousness" and then proceeds to define that phrase. There must be adequate punctuation to separate the term from the definition. With choice (A), a comma isn't a strong enough pause. A colon or dash would be ideal, and a semi-colon could arguably work. However, a comma is not appropriate since it leaves a comma splice. Choice (C) neglects punctuation altogether. Choice (D)'s initial dash is acceptable, but the second dash is unnecessary. This isn't a parenthetical phrase and should not be treated as such. After eliminating those three choices, analyze choice (B). Notice that it is properly punctuated, with the colon serving as a lead-in between the term and the definition.

11. **(A)** When working with transitions, analyze both the current sentence and the previous sentence to determine how they interrelate. In this case, there is a *cause-and-effect* relationship. "Hence" may not have been familiar to you, but it is a close approximation for *as a result, therefore,* or *accordingly.* Since "hence" can be used to transition between a cause and its effect, it is the best option. Notice that choices (B) and (C) mean the same thing. So they can be eliminated for that reason. The word "however," in choice (D) is a *contrasting* transition, but the sentences do not contrast.

Beauty and Peril

1. **(A)** Maintain a logical comparison in this sentence. "Then" is not used for comparisons, so eliminate choices (C) and (D). Keep in mind that this is comparing the *scenery* of California to the *scenery* of other places, as opposed to comparing *California* itself to other places. Choice (B) attempts to compare apples to oranges, so it must be eliminated. Choice (A) is the only option that logically compares one place's scenery to another place's scenery.

2. **(C)** The subject comes after the verb, which can be confusing. Nonetheless, the subject is "secrets," a plural noun that requires a plural verb for agreement. Choices (A), (B), and (D) are all *singular* verbs and therefore must be eliminated. "Are" is the only acceptable option.

3. **(D)** This is a question that perhaps requires reading a little bit further into the passage to diagnose the theme, which is the possibility of "cataclysmic" natural disasters on the Pacific Coast. The passage has nothing to do with a "conspiracy," with people who "need to get their priorities straight," or with the concept of "leadership." Choice (D), with its speculation on the possibility of impending, devastating natural disasters, is the only logical solution.

4. **(C)** Eliminate choice (D) immediately, as "passing by" California is incorrect; the San Andreas fault goes *through* California. From there, find the choice that has the perfect balance between concision and content. In choice (A), it is unnecessary to say "810 miles *in length.*" *Length* is already implied. Choice (B) eliminates too much, as "810 miles" is still relevant and provides new, productive information. Choice (C), then, is the perfect balance.

5. **(C)** This question illustrates the principle of coordination and subordination. Essentially, to paraphrase this sentence: *the death toll then was only 3,000,* **but** *keep in mind that the death toll from a similar earthquake would probably be much higher today.* Choice (C) is the only option that expresses that disclaimer effectively. Choices (A), (B), and (D) really all communicate the same message of *additionally,* which is not logical in this sentence; the clauses do not build on each other. Also keep in mind that there can be only one correct answer, so any choices that are essentially identical must be eliminated.

6. **(D)** Choices (A), (B), and (C) all have some major flaw, and sometimes they have multiple flaws. There are grammatical issues with choice (A), too, but its largest flaw is that it treats Juan de Fuca and Cascadia as two separate things, whereas the former is actually part of the latter. In choice (B), the proper phrase is *comprised of*, not "comprised with." Choice (C) uses "which" where it should use "that"; it also places an unnecessary comma after "zone." Choice (D) is without flaw, and its use of "which" rather than *that* is perfect.

7. **(C)** The idea that should be expressed as a possessive is *the continental shelf of North America*. Choice (A), by omitting an apostrophe, fails to illustrate possession. Choices (B) and (D) read as if the continent were *North Americas*, as opposed to the correct *North America*.

8. **(A)** It can be argued that the item "approaching its breaking point" is either "stress" or *the plate*. Nonetheless, both are singular nouns that require singular verbs for concordance. Eliminate choices (C) and (D) for using plural verbs. Next, the possessive pronoun form of one thing is "its." "Their" is used for multiple items, as in choice (B). Choice (A) is therefore the correct answer.

9. **(A)** The principal matter that separates the correct answer from all three incorrect choices is the issue of comma placement between "coastal" and "subsequent." The independent, main clause of the sentence is "subsequent tidal waves would accompany the earthquakes." The clause "as both San Andreas and Juan de Fuca are coastal," is separate and *dependent*. (It depends on the second clause to constitute a full sentence.) Since the two are separate clauses, the comma must be placed between them for separation.

10. **(B)** "Conjecture" most clearly means speculation, theory, or hypothesis. Since the author is speculating about the future throughout the passage, choice (B) is the correct answer. A "wild goose chase" is a hectic, often-futile undertaking. This doesn't fit in context. "Wisdom" doesn't fit in context since the author actually *knows* nothing of the future but is merely speculating. "Guesstimate" is a *portmanteau* (combination of two words) that is too casual for the purposes of this passage.

11. **(A)** Choice (B) can be quickly eliminated since the author has made clear that the catastrophe is not "imminent" but, rather, *probable given a long enough period of time*. The paragraph goes on to address fear and to warn that we must not allow it to dictate our lives. Choices (C) and (D) address the futility of speculation, which does capture part of the paragraph's theme. However, they ultimately fail to make any mention of "fear." Choice (A) is the only option that addresses the concept that fear based on speculation is unproductive.

Carbon

1. **(C)** Analyze the graph for this question. It's impossible to say *exactly* how much carbon is in the human body as there are no numbers provided. However, the carbon slice makes up just under one-fourth or one-fifth of the pie. The only answer that is even close to the 20% to 25% of the actual slice is 19%.

2. **(D)** The underlined section contains two *independent clauses:* they could be full sentences by themselves. Accordingly, we need to separate the two clauses. Choice (D) uses a semicolon to do this. Choice (A) is a comma splice. Choice (B) is a run-on sentence. Choice (C) would be acceptable if we had used a colon and maintained the two initial clauses. However, the use of "while" changes the second clause from independent to dependent, which doesn't function.

3. **(C)** There are two independent clauses here, with "so" used as a conjunction to unite them. Choice (A), by placing a comma after "chemists," breaks the first independent clause. Choice (B) incorrectly treats the phrase as an appositive. Choice (D) is a run-on sentence. Choice (C) is correct; it adds no unnecessary commas while still managing to insert the required one after "life."

4. **(A)** Analyze the first sentence of the next paragraph, "If you guessed iron, you're wrong." Iron is not a place, so eliminate choice (B). It is not plural, so eliminate choice (C). It is not a person, so eliminate choice (D). It is a singular thing, which makes choice (A) the correct answer.

5. **(B)** First, recognize tone: it is very casual, almost like an informal conversation. Choices (A) and (C) are far too formal. Choice (D) is incorrect, as one would say "sulfur ain't right, *either*" as opposed to "sulfur ain't right, *too*." Choice (B) is both informal and without enormous grammatical flaws.

6. **(A)** Eliminate choices (B) and (D) since the verb tense is "have heard." "Might of" is never a correct construction. Choice (C)'s error is in having an extra "have." One hears *of* something as opposed to hears *have* something.

7. **(B)** Analyze the relationship between this sentence and the previous sentence to diagnose the relationship between the two. In this case, each sentence independently builds on the statement in the first sentence of the paragraph that says that carbon can be a "curse." "Furthermore" is the best way to list an additional aspect to an argument. "Accordingly" and "consequently" express cause and effect, which is not what we want. "Nevertheless" is contrasting, which is equally incorrect.

8. **(D)** The subject is difficult to isolate, but it is "I." One would say, "I am," not *I are/is/were*.

9. **(B)** This sentence is most logically placed after sentence 2. A good thing, life-giving photosynthesis, is mentioned at the end of sentence 2. Then sentence 3 transitions to a contrasting bad thing, namely, the carbon footprint. Any of the other placements would make this logical transition unclear.

10. **(C)** When paraphrased, the clause becomes "I operated *inside* a balanced cycle," or "I operated *as part of* a balanced cycle." Choice (A), "between," requires operating *between two things*. Choice (B), "among," requires operating *among three or more things*. However, carbon is part of only *one thing*: as the cycle. Choice (D) implies a causal relationship that is not logical.

11. **(D)** Pay attention to context in order to maintain parallelism. The other words in the list are "respiration" and "combustion"—both nouns that end in *-tion*. "Decomposition" is one of two noun options, but it is the *-tion* ending that maintains parallelism better than the gerund "decomposing." Choices (B) and (C) are not nouns. Rather, they are verbs that do not maintain parallelism in the list.

Court Reporter

1. **(B)** When deciding on *who* versus *whom*, remember to rewrite the sentence using *he* or *him*. In this case, one would say *he represents* rather than *him represents*. Recall that he = who and him = whom, so one must use *who* here. Choices (A), (C), and (D) all have at least one instance of misusing *whom*, so choice (B) is the only possible answer.

2. **(A)** The clause up to the word "trial" is independent, as is the clause after "trial." Accordingly, sufficient punctuation is needed to separate the two. Eliminate choice (B) because it is a comma splice. In the second clause, "jurors represent a panel of judges," we want no punctuation separating the subject and predicate. Choices (C) and (D) both add unnecessary commas.

3. **(C)** This question is more a matter of vocabulary than anything else. After eliminating choice (D)—a gerund that leaves a fragment in its wake—one must simply select the most apt vocabulary. *To comprise* means "to consist of," so this is the most logical option. *To compromise* is to come to an agreement, which isn't logical. *To compose* is to create, which is equally illogical.

4. **(B)** First, maintain verb parallelism. The rest of the passage is in present tense, so eliminate choice (D) for being past tense. Our proposed question refers to the previous sentence that refers to a list that "comprises those occupants found in a normal legal proceeding." The most logical follow-up is "Or does it?" This phrase means *does this list really comprise the occupants in the legal proceeding*? Choices (A) and (C) use pronouns that aren't logical in context.

5. **(D)** The phrase "an often-overlooked occupation of legal services" is a parenthetical phrase. If you remove it from the sentence, the clause still functions perfectly well. The rule for parenthetical phrases is that they can be separated from the main clause using either two commas or two dashes. Choices (A) and (C) bungle the parenthetical phrase completely. Choice (B) is close, but it uses one dash and one comma, whereas one needs to use two of the same punctuation marks.

6. **(B)** Notice that choices (A) and (D) convey *the exact same meaning*. As there can be only one correct answer, eliminate those two (the relationship is not causal). Choice (C) declares a contrast, but this sentence does not contrast with the previous one. What actually happens is that the second sentence restates the first sentence in a more explanatory fashion. "In other words" is the correct answer.

7. **(C)** Consider what the sentence is implying: by using key combinations, it would be much quicker to type than if one had to punch each letter key individually. Choice (C) is most logical and effective. Choices (A) and (B) are logical, but they aren't terribly descriptive and thus not very effective. Choice (D) is completely irrelevant.

8. **(D)** The pronoun in the underlined portion must refer back to the singular "court reporter," which only choice (D) successfully does. Choice (A) uses the plural "they." Choice (B) changes this from third person to second person. Choice (C) uses an incorrect verb.

9. **(A)** Notice the context of this paragraph: it is written in second person, consistently referring to *you*. Maintain that parallelism by staying in second person instead of switching to third person as the other choices do.

10. **(D)** Analyze the graph for this question, particularly the data about court reporter salaries. Notice that the top 10% make roughly $60,000 dollars per year, thus making choice (D) the most logical and specific option. Choice (A) is incorrect, as this is a five-figure salary. Choice (B) is true but is not directly supported by the information in the graph since there are no statistics about the average American worker's salary, just statistics about those in legal professions. In this context, choice (C) and "student loans" are wholly irrelevant.

11. **(A)** Analyze the graph for this question. Choice (B) is simply not supported by the data. Choice (C) is equally unsupported as there is no data on entry-level hiring. Choice (D) is entirely false; attorneys earn much more. After eliminating the three illogical choices, all that remains is the correct answer. Analyze choice (A) just to make certain, and it is true.

Hatfields and McCoys

1. **(B)** The subject here is "feud," which is a singular noun that requires a singular verb. Eliminate choice (C) accordingly. Choice (A) would result in a sentence fragment. Delete choice (D) for producing a fragment. "Boils" is the correct answer.

2. **(C)** The first issue is not to include an unnecessary comma between "land and livestock." No comma is required in a list of just two items. Eliminate choices (A) and (B) for that reason. Choice (D) neglects necessary punctuation after "region," rendering it a run-on sentence.

3. **(D)** Choose the correct transitional word by analyzing the relationship between the current sentence and the previous sentence. There is no cause-and-effect relationship, so eliminate choice (A). There is no contrasting relationship, so eliminate choices (B) and (C). Ultimately, a transition wasn't necessary at all, and sometimes that is perfectly fine. Choice (D) is the correct answer.

4. **(A)** The concept here is that the McCoy witness's betrayal of his own family led to his death. The betrayal thus *sealed his fate*, and he was subsequently murdered by his family members. Choices (B), (C), and (D) provide no relevant, logical connection to the man being killed.

5. **(D)** In essence, we must select a possessive form of *disapproval of families*. Since there are plural *families,* eliminate choice (A). Choices (B) and (C) neglect the necessary apostrophe that demonstrates possession.

6. **(B)** This choice uses concise wording that is in a logical order. Choice (A) is too wordy. Choice (C) uses awkward word order along with an unneeded "to." Choice (D) is also too wordy.

7. **(D)** We must work with the "to" already provided at the beginning of the sentence. This demonstrates that we need an infinitive verb. "Venge" is an archaic verb that was abandoned centuries ago. "Vengeance" is a noun, not a verb. "Revenging" would not work with the preceding "to" to create an infinitive.

8. **(A)** To "illude" means to create an illusion, so this is not logical in context. To "allude" is to refer to something, which is equally illogical. To "illuminate" is to shine light upon, which still does not make sense. To "elude," however, means to escape or avoid, which is perfect in this sentence.

9. **(D)** In the first paragraph, Randolph McCoy is referred to as "Old Ran'l." Continuing to refer to him as "Old Ran'l" avoids the ambiguity that would be caused by referring to him as "Mr. McCoy." In effect, everyone in the passage is either a Hatfield or a McCoy. So writing *Mr. McCoy* leaves the reader uncertain as to which McCoy is intended. Eliminate choice (A), as this actually is *less* a clarification than a cause of confusion. Eliminate choice (B), as "old Ran'l" has already been established as acceptable and therefore formalities have already been abandoned. Choice (C)'s statement is simply incorrect.

10. **(B)** Sentence 2 refers to the publishing of inflammatory articles by newspapers, which matches the "journalistic sensationalism" mentioned in the proposed insertion. The insertion, then, must come either *before* or *after* sentence 2 in order to maintain coherence. As *before sentence 2* is not an option, "before sentence 3" (or *after sentence 2*) is the most logical selection.

11. **(A)** If the underlined sentence were deleted, most readers would wonder what was exceptional about the ninth person that permitted him to avoid life in prison. Thankfully, our underlined sentence answers this question for us: *the ninth wasn't so lucky; in fact, he was probably the least lucky of all.* Thus, the sentence must be kept as it "provides a relevant clarification" that removes confusion that might arise otherwise.

Hornsby

1. **(A)** If the author were to delete the sentence, it would then be unclear *why* he struggles with the phenomenon of fame. It "provides a relevant elaboration," as in choice (A). Choice (B) is incorrect as Bruce Hornsby, not Andy Warhol, is "the main person to be analyzed."

2. **(A)** The subject here is "someone of actual import," and *someone* is a singular noun that requires a singular verb. Eliminate choice (B) for being a plural verb, and eliminate choice (D) for not being a verb at all. Choice (C), *a gerund,* does not provide a complete sentence. "Passes," however, is a singular verb.

3. **(D)** Choice (A) places an unnecessary comma after "love." Choice (B) places an unnecessary comma after "true." Choice (C) neglects to end with a question mark. Choice (D) is correct; the colon acts as a nice lead-in to the question.

4. **(C)** "Obliquely" means *indirectly,* and there is nothing indirect about the statement, just as there is nothing *imaginative* or *powerful* about it, as described by choices (A) and (B). "Inevitably" means *unavoidably*. The author's point is that he *unavoidably* has to tell you who Hornsby is, and the fact that this is necessary is unfortunate.

5. **(C)** This question is difficult in that the choices are all fairly similar. Choice (A) transitions to passive voice, which is best to avoid if possible. In choice (B), saying both "case" and "point" is wordy and unnecessary. ("Case in point" is a common phrase, but using "case" and "point" separately in this instance does not use the common idiom.) In choice (D), "arbitration" is a process through which two parties resolve differences and is not connected with the adjective *arbitrary.*

6. **(B)** Choice (A) is not "self-deprecating" but, rather, deprecates *others.* Choice (C) is not self-deprecating in any way; rather it reads almost as more of a boast. Again, choice (D) features nothing of self-deprecation. Choice (B), however, fits the question. Its use of "forgive my hyperbole" is an acknowledgment that the author is aware that he is *going overboard* in his praise, so to speak.

7. **(B)** This sentence reads awkwardly at first, particularly with the use of both "various" and "variety." But if you look closer, you will see that a "variety station" is a genre of radio channel and the "various" refers to the prevalence of those stations. Eliminate choices (A) and (C) for not recognizing "variety stations." Just as one wouldn't say, "There are two, cars," one can't say, "various, variety stations." The quantifier must not be separate from what it is describing. Eliminate choice (D) because of that unnecessary comma.

8. **(C)** Without the underlined portion, many high school readers would not recognize the fame of the musicians mentioned; thus, it provides an important distinction that again "underscores the author's thoughts about Hornsby's lack of recognition." In effect, *why are Hornsby's peers so much more famous than he is?*

9. **(A)** "Like van Gogh's or F. Scott Fitzgerald's" is an *appositive*. If you remove this portion, the sentence still functions perfectly acceptably. A correctly used appositive must be set off from the surrounding sentence with two commas or two dashes. Choice (B) forgets the punctuation completely. Choice (C) incorrectly diagnoses what the appositive actually is by misplacing the second comma. Choice (D) neglects the second comma. In addition, choice (A) is the only option that makes a logical comparison, using the possessive "Gogh's" and "Fitzgerald's" to make these implicitly comparable to "Hornsby's legacy."

10. **(B)** The relationship between this sentence and the previous one is *contrasting*. When paraphrased, the sentences are *Maybe Hornsby will be famous later*. However, *I doubt it*. "But" is the only option that executes the contrast. Choices (A), (C), and (D) all are *cause-and-effect* transitions.

11. **(B)** To quantify adjectives, it is appropriate to use "less." For example, one would never say *he is fewer fast*. Rather, one would say *he is less fast*. Eliminate choices (C) and (D) accordingly. "Lessening" cannot be used as a determiner, which is what this sentence requires.

President

1. **(C)** Certain expressions are used frequently in the English language, and it is important to use the common preposition when using these expressions. The phrase "at the core" is an example of one of those expressions. Using "at" is far preferable to the other choices if only because that is the way this expression is typically written.

2. **(A)** The problem with this sentence is that it needed to be placed earlier if it was going to be used at all. The passage has drifted away from discussion of the separation of powers. To return to the topic would be flighty at this point, breaking with the flow of the passage. Choice (A) is the correct answer.

3. **(A)** Choice (B) is flawed because it omits an apostrophe on "one's." Choice (C) forgets a necessary comma after "thus." Choice (D) changes from second person to third person during the course of the sentence. Choice (A) is without blemish, and it is the correct answer.

4. **(B)** Choice (A) is very wordy. For instance, "for the duration of 14 years" can be much more effective if it is shortened to "for 14 years." Choice (C) reads as if the president must be exactly 35. Choice (D) is terribly general, providing us with no relevant, specific information. Choice (B) is the best combination of concision and specificity.

5. **(D)** "Charisma," a singular noun, is the subject. It requires a singular verb to maintain concordance. Eliminate choices (A) and (B) accordingly. At this point, the decision is about "lies" versus "lays," which are two commonly confused verbs. To *lay* is the act of physically taking something and placing it elsewhere. To *lie* is the act of an object remaining at rest. "Lies" is far more appropriate in this context.

6. **(C)** Sentence 3 mentions "charisma." The proposed insertion practically gives us the complete definition of charisma by using the words "charm, attractiveness, and likability." The insertion, then, is best placed after sentence 3, which is choice (C).

7. **(D)** The first part of the question regards proper use of the possessive for *the ages of presidents*. As there are multiple presidents, the apostrophe must go *after* the *s*. Eliminate choices (B) and (C) accordingly. Now, as there were multiple presidents, there were multiple ages. Choice (A) reads as if the presidents all had one age—the same age. Choice (D), then, is the correct answer.

8. **(B)** "Still" is separate from the main clause. (In effect, if we remove "still," the clause is still perfect.) So we must place a comma after "still" to denote that required separation. Eliminate choice (A) accordingly. From there is a list of three things: "allure, a spotless background, and years in diplomatic service." Eliminate choices (C) and (D) for neglecting the comma after "allure."

9. **(B)** Take note of parallelism in this sentence: "one has *to win*" (to win is an infinitive verb) and "triumph" (*one has to* is implied, which makes this an infinitive verb). Therefore, eliminate choice (A) since "following" is not an infinitive verb. We can eliminate choice (D) for omitting the listing comma after "convention." From there, we can analyze the context to see what is most *logical*. To "earn a following" means to gain supporters, while to "follow an earning" is nonsensical. Choice (B) is the best answer.

10. **(C)** For transitions, analyze both the current sentence and the previous sentence to determine how they interrelate. The second sentence here gives a supporting example to bolster the claim made in the first sentence. "For instance" is the best option to illustrate an example. The second sentence isn't surprising but, rather, is to be expected based on sentence 1. Eliminate choice (A) for that reason. Choice (B) implies a cause-and-effect relationship that is not apparent, while choice (D) implies a contrast that is equally absent.

11. **(B)** Analyze the chart for this question. Notice that the chart refers to personal characteristics that voters have stated would be important to them in a presidential candidate. Paragraph 2 refers to personal characteristics, which makes that paragraph the most suitable place to insert a relevant sentence based on the data in our chart. Paragraph 1 is introductory, and there isn't any mention of personal characteristics there. Paragraph 4 refers to financial matters. Paragraph 3 is close, but it refers to more *concrete* qualifications, like education, seniority, and political credentials. Choice (B) is the correct answer.

Risk

1. **(A)** For one, notice that "we" is used throughout the sentence. That's indicative of the need to remain in first person plural, so eliminate choices (C) and (D). Now ask, *Is it better to say "we understood" or "us understood"*? "We," of course, is the proper pronoun. Choice (A) is correct.

2. **(B)** When deciding to delete a portion, ask yourself, *Is this information relevant?* Then ask, *Does it repeat information or feature information that can be readily inferred?* Since the passage already states that the narrator knew the roles he or she would fulfill upon graduation, "we felt well-prepared for the profession we were about to enter" is a restatement of what is already known. Choice (B) is the correct answer. This portion must be deleted because it does not provide meaningful, new information.

3. **(A)** When deciding between *who* and *whom*, remember to rewrite the clause using *he* or *him*. We would say *he walked* rather than *him walked*, so we must use *who*. Eliminate choices (B) and (D) accordingly. "Who walking" would leave a fragment—and a rough one at that—so choice (A), "who walked," is the correct answer.

4. **(C)** There are certain phrases that the test writers assume are widely known. "Out in the field" is one of those. The meaning isn't that one is *literally* in a body of grass but, rather, that one is in a professional environment—i.e., the *field of business management* in this case. Choices (A), (B), and (D) simply do not suit the required purpose as choice (C) does.

5. **(A)** Choice (D) can be immediately deleted as the professor is referring to *after* leaving school rather than returning to it. Choice (B) is somewhat relevant but is not a logical, effective conclusion to the argument. Choice (C) is relevant, but it *isn't effective;* it lacks the attention-getting quality of choice (A), which essentially says, *You've taken all these courses to be a better manager. But the true value comes down to one simple question*: *can you take calculated risk?* Choice (A), then, is by far the best answer.

6. **(D)** There are two independent clauses, with the first ending at "company" and the second beginning at "others." Choice (A) is a comma splice. Choice (B) is flawed in multiple ways, but the first mistake is with the inclusion of an unnecessary comma after "outcomes." Choice (C) incorrectly attempts to employ a parenthetical phrase. Choice (D), however, correctly links the two independent clauses with a semicolon.

7. **(C)** "Affective" is a psychological term relating to moods and feelings, and it isn't logical here. Eliminate "affecting" for the same reason. "Effecting" is a word that isn't traditionally an adjective and isn't particularly logical in this case. This leaves only "effective," which is the correct answer.

8. **(B)** The question requires "the most specific example," with *specific* being the operative word. Choices (A) and (D) aren't relevant to the concept of trying to determine lead time. Choice (C) regards attempts to *define* lead time rather than calculate it for an actual business. Choice (B) provides a very *specific* example of how lead time can fluctuate in a *specific* industry after a *specific* event occurs.

9. **(A)** This is an example of an independent clause. The subject is "the success of the business," and the predicate is "will be driven by how well you manage these variations." There is no reason to insert any punctuation to separate the subject and predicate, so eliminate choices (B), (C), and (D) accordingly.

10. **(C)** Choices (B) and (D) lack concision; eliminate them because they are wordy. The adverb "slowly" functions much more effectively when placed before "moving" as opposed to after. Choice (C), then, is the correct answer.

11. **(B)** Notice how sentence 4 says "the other" but is ambiguous in context. *What is the other?* The proposed insertion clarifies this, beginning with "one factor." "The other," then, refers to *the other factor*, which is much more logical when the insertion is placed before sentence 4.

Math

Math Review

WHAT IS TESTED ON THE MATH SECTION?

The following is the typical breakdown of all the Math Test questions from both sections combined:

- Heart of Algebra (primarily linear equations and systems): 16 questions
- Problem Solving and Data Analysis (primarily demonstrating literacy with data and real-world applications): 16 questions
- Passport to Advanced Math (primarily more complicated equations): 14 questions
- Additional Topics in Math (geometry, trigonometry, and other advanced math): 2 questions

If you have studied Algebra 1, Geometry, and Algebra 2, then you most likely will have covered the concepts tested on the PSAT Math Sections.

HOW SHOULD I USE THIS CHAPTER?

Examine the following list. If there is anything you need to review or practice, check it out. After you complete the review, try the "Math Essentials Review Quiz" to be sure that you don't have any gaps in your knowledge.

Heart of Algebra

Problem Solving and Data Analysis

Passport to Advanced Math

Additional Topics in Math

ORDER OF OPERATIONS

Remember the proper sequence of mathematical operations by using the acronym **PEMDAS:** *Please Excuse My Dear Aunt Sally.*

Parentheses ( ) or other grouping symbols, like $\sqrt{}$ or { }
Exponents x^y
Multiplication $x \times y$
Division $x \div y$
Addition $x + y$
Subtraction $x - y$

 Example _____

$$(-2)(4+3)^2 = ?$$

Solution

Simplify what is in the parentheses first, square it, and then multiply it by –2.

$$(-2)(4+3)^2 =$$
$$(-2)(7)^2 =$$
$$(-2)49 = -98$$

FOIL

Remember how to multiply simple polynomials by "FOILing" the expression. This corresponds to the order in which you multiply parts of the factored expression:

First, **O**uter, **I**nner, **L**ast

In the expression $(a+b)(x+y)$, you can simplify by multiplying parts in the FOIL sequence and then simplifying like terms by combining them together:

First = ax Outer = ay Inner = bx Last = by
Add them all together: $ax + ay + bx + by$

Here are examples of FOIL in action:

$$(4+x)(2-x) = 4 \cdot 2 - 4x + 2x - x^2 = 8 - 2x - x^2$$

$$(x+2y)(x-3y) = x \cdot x - 3xy + 2xy - 6y^2 = x^2 - xy - 6y^2$$

ORDER OF OPERATIONS DRILL

1. $(x+4)+(x-2) = ?$
2. $3(m+n)-n = ?$
3. $x^2 + 2x^2 = ?$
4. $\dfrac{2x+3x}{x} = ?$
5. $\dfrac{3 \times (5n)^2}{n} = ?$

6. $(2+x)(5+x)=?$

7. $(3x-4)(2x+5)=?$

8. $5n(2n+1)^2=?$

9. Solve for x: $2x+5=7$

10. Solve for x: $\dfrac{-5}{x}=10$

Solutions

1. The parentheses can be ignored since there is nothing on the outside of the parentheses:

$$(x+4)+(x-2)=$$
$$x+4+x-2=2x+2$$

2. Distribute the 3 and multiply it by each term within the parentheses. Then combine like terms to simplify:

$$3(m+n)-n=$$
$$3m+3n-n=3m+2n$$

3. Add the like terms together:

$$x^2+2x^2=$$
$$1x^2+2x^2=3x^2$$

4. Combine the parts on the top, and then divide both the top and bottom by x:

$$\frac{2x+3x}{x}=$$
$$\frac{5x}{x}=$$
$$\frac{5\cancel{x}}{\cancel{x}}=5$$

5. First simplify what is in the parentheses by squaring it, and then multiply and divide:

$$\frac{3\times(5n)^2}{n}=$$
$$\frac{3\times(25n^2)}{n}=$$
$$\frac{75n^2}{n}=75n$$

6. FOIL the expression:

$$(2+x)(5+x)=$$
$$10+2x+5x+x^2=$$
$$10+7x+x^2 \rightarrow x^2+7x+10$$

7. FOIL the expression:

$$(3x-4)(2x+5)=$$
$$6x^2+15x-8x-20=6x^2+7x-20$$

8. First FOIL what is in the parentheses, and then distribute the $5n$ through the expression:

$$5n(2n+1)^2=$$
$$5n\big((2n+1)(2n+1)\big)=$$
$$5n\big(4n^2+4n+1\big)=20n^3+20n^2+5n$$

9. $2x + 5 = 7$

$\quad 2x = 7 - 5$

$\quad 2x = 2$

$\quad\; x = 1$

10. $\dfrac{-5}{x} = 10$

$\quad -5 = 10x$

$\quad -\dfrac{5}{10} = x$

$\quad -\dfrac{1}{2} = x$

SUBSTITUTION AND ELIMINATION TO SOLVE A SYSTEM OF EQUATIONS

Substitution

A common way to solve a system of equations with two variables is through *substitution* of one variable in terms of the other.

➡ **Example**_____

Solve for x and y in the equations below.

$$2x = y$$
$$y - 3x = -5$$

Solution

Substitute $2x$ for y in the second equation:

$$(2x) - 3x = -5$$
$$-x = -5$$
$$x = 5$$

Plug 5 in for x into the first equation to solve for y:

$$2x = y$$
$$2(5) = 10$$
$$y = 10$$

Elimination

When two equations are similar to one another, *elimination* of terms and variables may be the easiest way to solve for the variables. Multiply both sides of one of the equations by a number that allows you to add or subtract one equation easily from another, making it easy to eliminate one of the variables.

> Two equations have infinitely many solutions if the equations are identical. For example, $x + y = 2$ and $2x + 2y = 4$ together have infinitely many solutions since the equations are simply multiples of one another. Some equations, like $x + y = 2$ and $2x + 2y = 10$, have no solutions. They do not intersect at all because their graphs are parallel to each other.

➥ Example

Solve for both x and y in the system of equations below:

$$3x + 2y = 7$$
$$2x - y = 0$$

Solution

Multiply the second equation by 2:

$$3x + 2y = 7$$
$$4x - 2y = 0$$

Then add the second equation to the first equation to eliminate the y-variables:

$$3x + 2y = 7$$
$$+4x - 2y = 0$$
$$\overline{7x + 0\ = 7}$$

Divide both sides by 7 to get the answer: $x = 1$.

Then solve for y by plugging 1 in for x in the first equation:

$$3x + 2y = 7$$
$$3 \times 1 + 2y = 7$$
$$2y = 4$$
$$y = 2$$

The PSAT will generally have systems of equations with one or two variables. Be mindful that there should typically be as many *equations* as there are *variables* in order to solve a given system. For example, in order to solve for two variables, you should have two equations; to solve for three variables, you should have three equations.

Distance, Rate, and Time

When considering the relationship among distance, speed/rate, and time, use the following formula:

$$\text{Distance} = \text{Rate} \times \text{Time}$$

For example, if you were biking 80 miles at 10 miles per hour, it would take you 8 hours to do so. See how that situation fits into the equation:

$$80 \text{ miles} = 10 \ \frac{\text{miles}}{\text{hour}} \times 8 \text{ hours}$$

Variations on the distance, speed/rate, and time formula can also be used to solve for whichever variable is needed:

$$\text{Rate} = \frac{\text{Distance}}{\text{Time}} \text{ and } \text{Time} = \frac{\text{Distance}}{\text{Rate}}$$

➥ Example

If Fred has to drive 200 miles in 5 hours, at what average speed should he drive?

Solution

Insert the given information into the formula and solve for rate (speed):

$$\text{Distance} = \text{Rate} \times \text{Time}$$
$$200 \text{ miles} = \text{Rate} \times 5 \text{ hours}$$
$$\frac{200}{5} = 40 \text{ miles per hour}$$

With distance, rate, and time questions, be sure to check that the units in the solution (mph, miles, hours, etc.) match the units required by the question.

SUBSTITUTION AND ELIMINATION TO SOLVE A SYSTEM OF EQUATIONS DRILL

In questions 1–5, solve for x and y in these systems of equations:

1. $3x = 2y$
   $x = y + 1$

2. $y = x - 1$
   $7x = -3y + 2$

3. $x + 4y = 2$
   $-x + y = 8$

4. $x - \frac{1}{2}y = 3$
   $2x + y = 10$

5. $4x + 2y = 1$
   $8x + 4y = 2$

6. If Nischal is traveling at 40 miles per hour for 3 hours, how far will he have traveled?

7. What is the rate in feet per second a hockey puck travels if it goes 30 feet in 10 seconds?

Solutions

1. Use substitution to solve this system of equations:

   $$3x = 2y$$
   $$x = y + 1$$

   Plug in $y + 1$ for x into the first equation:

   $$3(y + 1) = 2y$$
   $$3y + 3 = 2y$$
   $$y + 3 = 0$$
   $$y = -3$$

   Then substitute -3 in for y into the second equation:

   $$x = y + 1$$
   $$x = -3 + 1$$
   $$x = -2$$

   So the solution is $x = -2$ and $y = -3$.

2. Use substitution to solve this system of equations:

   $$y = x - 1$$
   $$7x = -3y + 2$$

Plug in $x - 1$ for y into the second equation:

$$7x = -3(x-1)+2$$
$$7x = -3x+3+2$$
$$7x = -3x+5$$
$$10x = 5$$
$$x = \frac{1}{2}$$

Now, plug this value of x into the first equation:

$$y = x-1$$
$$y = \frac{1}{2}-1$$
$$y = -\frac{1}{2}$$

So the solution is $x = \frac{1}{2}$ and $y = -\frac{1}{2}$.

3. Use elimination to solve this system of equations:

$$x+4y = 2$$
$$-x+y = 8$$
$$\overline{0+5y = 10}$$

Then, solve for y:

$$5y = 10$$
$$y = \frac{10}{5}$$
$$y = 2$$

Then, plug 2 back in for y and solve for x:

$$x+4y = 2$$
$$x+4(2) = 2$$
$$x+8 = 2$$
$$x = -6$$

So the solution set is $x = -6$ and $y = 2$.

4. Solve using elimination by doubling the first equation and adding it to the second:

$$2\left(x-\frac{1}{2}y = 3\right) \rightarrow 2x-y = 6$$

$$2x-y = 6$$
$$2x+y = 10$$
$$\overline{4x+0 = 16}$$

Then solve for x and plug it into either original equation to solve for y:

$$4x = 16$$
$$x = 4$$

$$2x+y = 10$$
$$2(4)+y = 10$$
$$8+y = 10$$
$$y = 2$$

So the solution is $x = 4$ and $y = 2$.

5. Multiply the first equation by 2 to notice a pattern:

$$4x + 2y = 1$$
$$8x + 4y = 2$$

As you may recognize, this is identical to the second equation: $8x + 4y = 2$.

Since the two equations are identical and would therefore overlap if graphed in the *x-y* coordinate plane, there would be *infinitely* many solutions.

6. Multiply the rate by the time to find the total distance:

$$40 \times 3 = 120$$

So Nischal has traveled a total of 120 miles.

7. Divide the distance by the time to find the rate:

$$30 \div 10 = 3$$

So the puck is traveling 3 feet/second.

FRACTIONS

The *numerator* is the number on top of a fraction, while the *denominator* is the number on the bottom of the fraction. For example, in the fraction $\frac{1}{2}$, "1" is the numerator and "2" is the denominator. To simplify fractions, put them in their *lowest terms*. Do so by canceling out the same number as a factor of both the numerator and the denominator. For example:

$$\frac{6}{10} = \frac{3 \cdot 2}{5 \cdot 2} = \frac{3 \cdot \cancel{2}}{5 \cdot \cancel{2}} = \frac{3}{5}$$

The number 2 can be taken out of both the numerator and denominator, leaving just $\frac{3}{5}$. We know that the fraction is now in lowest terms because no factors are shared by 3 and 5 besides 1.

Adding and Subtracting Fractions

To add two fractions, follow these two simple steps.

STEP 1 Find the least common denominator of each fraction (i.e., the lowest common multiple of the denominators) so that the fractions have the same number on the bottom.

Consider the problem $\frac{3}{7} + \frac{5}{14}$. The least common multiple of the denominators is 14, so $\frac{3}{7}$ can be rewritten like this:

$$\frac{3}{7} \times \frac{2}{2} = \frac{6}{14}$$

Now both fractions have 14 as the denominator. The addition problem looks like this:

$$\frac{6}{14} + \frac{5}{14} =$$

Let's do our second step to solve the problem.

STEP 2 Once you have the same denominator for the fractions, add their numerators.

With $\frac{6}{14} + \frac{5}{14}$, just add the 6 and 5 together:

$$\frac{6}{14} + \frac{5}{14} = \frac{6+5}{14} = \frac{11}{14}$$

To subtract a fraction from another, find the least common denominator and subtract the numerators. For example:

$$\frac{8}{9}-\frac{1}{6}=$$

$$\frac{2}{2}\left(\frac{8}{9}\right)-\frac{3}{3}\left(\frac{1}{6}\right)=\frac{16}{18}-\frac{3}{18}$$

The least common denominator is 18. Now subtract one numerator from the other:

$$\frac{16-3}{18}=\frac{13}{18}$$

Multiplying and Dividing Fractions

Multiply fractions using this rule:

$$\frac{a}{b}\cdot\frac{c}{d}=\frac{ac}{bd}\quad\text{(Neither b nor d can equal zero, or it will be undefined.)}$$

Visualize fraction multiplication with actual numbers:

$$\frac{3}{4}\cdot\frac{2}{5}=\frac{3\cdot2}{4\cdot5}=\frac{6}{20}\to\text{reduce the fraction}\to\frac{3}{10}$$

Divide fractions using the following rule:

$$\frac{a}{b}\div\frac{c}{d}=\frac{a}{b}\cdot\frac{d}{c}\quad\text{(b, c, and d cannot equal zero, or it will be undefined.)}$$

Visualize fraction division with actual numbers:

$$\frac{2}{5}\div\frac{3}{4}=\frac{2}{5}\cdot\frac{4}{3}=\frac{8}{15}$$

FRACTIONS DRILL

1. Reduce $\frac{12}{18}$ to its lowest terms.

2. Reduce $\frac{2}{7}$ to its lowest terms.

3. $\frac{1}{4}+\frac{3}{4}=?$

4. $\frac{2}{3}+\frac{1}{9}=?$

5. $\frac{7}{8}-\frac{1}{2}=?$

6. $\frac{15}{16}-\frac{3}{4}=?$

7. $\frac{2}{9}\times\frac{4}{5}=?$

8. $\frac{2}{3}\times\frac{3}{8}=?$

9. $\frac{4}{3}\div\frac{1}{3}=?$

10. $\frac{5}{8}\div\frac{2}{3}=?$

Solutions

1. $\frac{12}{18}=$

   $\frac{2\cdot6}{3\cdot6}=$

   $\frac{2\cdot\cancel{6}}{3\cdot\cancel{6}}=\frac{2}{3}$

2. $\frac{2}{7}$ cannot be reduced further.

3. $\frac{1}{4}+\frac{3}{4}=$

   $\frac{1+3}{4}=$

   $\frac{4}{4}=1$

4. $\frac{2}{3}+\frac{1}{9}=$

   $\frac{6}{9}+\frac{1}{9}=\frac{7}{9}$

5. $\dfrac{7}{8} - \dfrac{1}{2} =$

$\dfrac{7}{8} - \dfrac{4}{8} = \dfrac{3}{8}$

6. $\dfrac{15}{16} - \dfrac{3}{4} =$

$\dfrac{15}{16} - \dfrac{12}{16} =$

$\dfrac{15-12}{16} = \dfrac{3}{16}$

7. $\dfrac{2}{9} \times \dfrac{4}{5} =$

$\dfrac{2 \times 4}{9 \times 5} = \dfrac{8}{45}$

8. $\dfrac{2}{3} \times \dfrac{3}{8} =$

$\dfrac{2}{\cancel{3}} \times \dfrac{\cancel{3}}{8} =$

$\dfrac{2}{8} = \dfrac{1}{4}$

9. $\dfrac{4}{3} \div \dfrac{1}{3} =$

$\dfrac{4}{3} \times \dfrac{3}{1} =$

$\dfrac{4}{\cancel{3}} \times \dfrac{\cancel{3}}{1} =$

$\dfrac{4}{1} = 4$

10. $\dfrac{5}{8} \div \dfrac{2}{3} =$

$\dfrac{5}{8} \times \dfrac{3}{2} =$

$\dfrac{5 \times 3}{8 \times 2} = \dfrac{15}{16}$

INEQUALITIES

An inequality is an expression that indicates that something is less than or greater than something else. The open end of the ">" goes toward the larger number. For example:

$$4 < 8 \text{ and } 7 > 2$$

When an inequality has a line underneath the "greater than" sign or the "less than" sign, it indicates that the terms on either side can also equal one another. For example:

$$x \leq 5 \text{ means that } x \text{ is less than or equal to 5}$$

When working with inequalities, solve them just as you would typical equations EXCEPT in two situations:

1. When you multiply or divide both sides of the inequality by a *negative* number, change the direction of the inequality sign.

➡ Example _____

Solve for x: $-5x > 2$

Solution

Divide both sides by –5 and turn the > around to <.

$$-5x > 2$$

$$\dfrac{-5x}{-5} < \dfrac{2}{-5}$$

$$\dfrac{\cancel{-5}x}{\cancel{-5}} < \dfrac{2}{-5}$$

$$x < -\dfrac{2}{5}$$

2. If you take the reciprocal with an inequality, and the variables have the same sign (positive or negative), you must change the direction of the inequality sign. If the variables have opposite signs, do not change the direction of the inequality sign.

➡ Example _____

Simplify this expression, in which x and y are both positive: $\frac{1}{x} > \frac{1}{y}$

Solution

Cross multiply, and then flip the sign to put the variables in the numerator:

$$\frac{1}{x} > \frac{1}{y}$$
$$x < y$$

When graphing inequalities on a number line, a hollow circle indicates < or > and a solid circle indicates ≤ or ≥. Figure 1 shows the graph of two different inequalities.

$n > 2$ is graphed as:

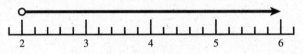

$n \leq 5$ is graphed as:

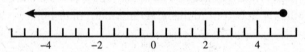

Figure 1

INEQUALITIES DRILL

1. Solve for x: $4x + 2 \leq 6$
2. How would you graph the inequality $x > 2$ on a number line?
3. Solve for x: $-3x \geq 9$

Solutions

1. $4x + 2 \leq 6$
   $4x \leq 4$
   $x \leq 1$

2. Since the inequality includes a > sign with no "equal" underneath, make the circle where it intersects 2 *hollow*:

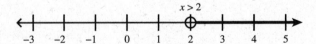

3. When you multiply or divide an inequality by a negative number, the direction of the inequality sign changes:

$$-3x \geq 9 \rightarrow x \leq -3$$

ABSOLUTE VALUE

Absolute value is the distance that a number is from zero along the number line. It doesn't matter if you are considering –3 or +3. Since both are the same distance from zero on the number line, both have an absolute value of 3.

If you want the absolute value of 9, express it like this: $|9|$.

When computing the value of an absolute value expression, simply determine the value of what is inside the two bars and then make that number positive, no matter if it was originally positive or negative. Here are some examples:

$$|25| = 25$$
$$|-12| = 12$$
$$|-3+8| = 5$$
$$|-2 \times 9| = 18$$

When solving absolute value equations, set them up as equal to both a positive and a negative value. If, for example, you are going to solve $|x+2| = 4$, you should write it as two different equations since what occurs inside the absolute value signs can have either a positive or a negative value and can make the expression true.

$$|x+2| = 4$$

$$x+2 = 4 \qquad \text{and} \qquad x+2 = -4$$
$$x = 2 \qquad\qquad\qquad x = -6$$

So x could be either 2 or –6.

ABSOLUTE VALUE DRILL

1. What is the value of $|8|$?
2. What is the value of $|-25+4|$?
3. What are the possible solutions for x: $|x+5| = 7$?
4. How many solutions are there for x in this equation? $|x-5| = -2$

Solutions

1. 8

2. $|-25+4| \rightarrow |-21| \rightarrow 21$

3. Turn $|x+5| = 7$ into two equations and solve:

$$x+5 = 7 \qquad \text{and} \qquad x+5 = -7$$
$$x = 2 \qquad\qquad\qquad x = -12$$

So the solutions for x are 2 and –12.

4. Since an absolute value must give a value that is greater than or equal to zero, there are *no* solutions to this equation.

LINEAR RELATIONSHIPS

Slope-Intercept Form

TIP

Since the PSAT has quite a few problems that don't allow you to use a calculator, be sure you don't have to rely on your calculator to graph a line.

Determine the graph of a line by putting it in *slope-intercept form*:

$$y = mx + b$$

m = slope of the line, the "rise" over the "run," calculated with $\dfrac{(y_2 - y_1)}{(x_2 - x_1)}$

b = y-intercept of the line, i.e., where the line intersects the y-axis

➡ Example

Graph the following equation:

$$y = 3x + 2$$

Solution

Based on the slope-intercept formula, the line has a slope of 3 and a y-intercept of 2.

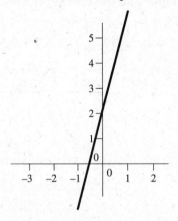

Parallel and Perpendicular Lines

Lines that are *parallel* to one another have *identical slopes*—they will never cross one another. (Parallel lines should have different y-intercepts, or they will simply be overlapping lines.) Figure 2 is a graph of two parallel lines in the x-y coordinate plane, $y = 3x$ and $y = 3x + 2$:

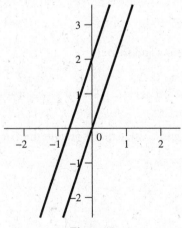

Figure 2

Perpendicular lines intersect at a 90° angle and have slopes that are *negative reciprocals* of one another. For example, if one line has a slope of 4, a line perpendicular to it has a slope of $-\frac{1}{4}$. Figure 3 is an example of two perpendicular lines and their graph, $y=-\frac{1}{5}x-1$ and $y=5x-3$:

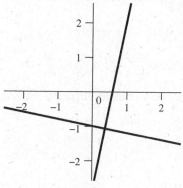

Figure 3

Slope Formula, Positive and Negative Correlations

To find the slope between two points, (x_1, y_1) and (x_2, y_2), plug the coordinates of the points into this formula:

$$\text{Slope} = \frac{\text{Change in } y}{\text{Change in } x} = \frac{(y_2 - y_1)}{(x_2 - x_1)}$$

(It is not important which point you consider the first or second set of coordinates, so long as your calculation is consistent.)

➥ Example

If a line includes the points (6, 4) and (2, 9), what is the slope of the line?

Solution

You can determine the slope as follows:

$$\frac{(y_2 - y_1)}{(x_2 - x_1)} = \frac{(9-4)}{(2-6)} = -\frac{5}{4}$$

You can examine the slope of a line to see whether the variables have a positive or a negative correlation. If the x-values and y-values increase together or decrease together, the variables have a *positive correlation*. The line has a *positive slope*. If the x-values increase while the y-values decrease, or vice versa, the variables have a *negative correlation*. The line has a *negative slope*.

LINEAR RELATIONSHIPS DRILL

1. What is the y-intercept of the line given by $y=-4x+13$?

2. What is the slope of a line with points $(1, -2)$ and $(-4, 6)$?

3. What is the slope of the line given by $-8x+2y=10$?

4. If $(3, 5)$ is a point on a line that goes through the origin, what is the slope of this line?

5. If a line has a slope of $-\frac{2}{3}$, what is the slope of a line perpendicular to it?

6. If two lines have the same slope but different y-intercepts, how often will the lines intersect?

7. In the equation $y=5x$, are x and y positively or negatively correlated?

Solutions

1. The line is in slope-intercept form, $y = mx + b$, so the y-intercept corresponds to the b: 13.

2. Use the slope formula, $\dfrac{(y_2 - y_1)}{(x_2 - x_1)}$, to solve for the slope of the line with these points:

$$\frac{(y_2 - y_1)}{(x_2 - x_1)}$$

$$\frac{(6 - -2)}{(-4 - 1)} = \frac{8}{-5} = -\frac{8}{5}$$

3. Rearrange the parts of the equation so that it is in slope-intercept form:

$$-8x + 2y = 10$$
$$2y = 8x + 10$$
$$y = 4x + 5$$

The slope is 4.

4. The origin has the coordinates $(0, 0)$. So take the slope of the two points using the slope formula:

$$\frac{(y_2 - y_1)}{(x_2 - x_1)}$$

$$\frac{(5 - 0)}{(3 - 0)} = \frac{5}{3}$$

5. Take the negative reciprocal of $-\dfrac{2}{3}$ to find the slope of a perpendicular line. Multiply $-\dfrac{2}{3}$ by -1 and flip the fraction.

$$-\frac{2}{3} \times -1 = \frac{2}{3}$$

$$\frac{3}{2}$$

6. Lines with the same slope but different y-intercepts are parallel to each other. Therefore, they never intersect. For example, the lines $y = 2x$ and $y = 2x + 2$ have identical slopes but different y-intercepts, making them parallel:

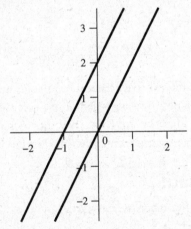

7. The variables are *positively* correlated with one another because the line of this equation has a positive slope. As x increases, y also increases.

INTERPRETING FUNCTIONS

Linear, Quadratic, and Exponential Models

A linear *relationship* between two variables is represented by a graph with a *constant slope*. For example, the equation $y = x$ represents a linear relationship between x and y, as you can see in the graph in Figure 4.

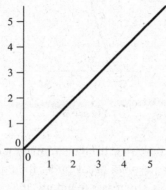

Figure 4

TIP

If you have a question that says some quantity is increasing at a "constant" rate, realize that this is code for a linear relationship.

A *quadratic relationship* between two variables, x and y, is generally represented by an equation of the form $y = kx^2$ or $y = ax^2 + bx + c$, in which k, a, b, and c are constants. It is called a quadratic relationship because "quad" means *square*. Figure 5 shows a portion of the graph of $y = x^2$, in which x and y have a quadratic relationship.

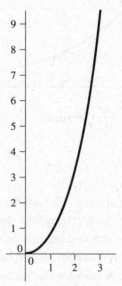

Figure 5

TIP

Generally the most rapid growth or decay is found with an exponential function, and the least rapid growth or decay is found with a linear function.

An *exponential relationship* between two variables, x and y, is generally expressed in the form $y = cb^x$ or $y = ab^x + c$, in which a, b, and c are constants. Figure 6 shows a portion of the graph of $y = 3^x - 1$, which is an exponential function. (Notice that the exponential relationship puts the x in the exponent part of the equation)

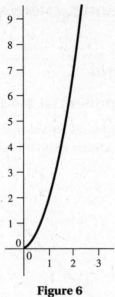

Figure 6

Keep in mind that functions can have negative linear, quadratic, and exponential relationships. In other words, these functions can express decay rather than growth. For example, the function $y = 20 \times 0.5^x$ shows decay because as x increases to infinity, the y-value decreases. The graph of the function is shown in Figure 7.

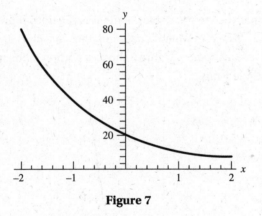

Figure 7

Scatter Plots

The PSAT will test your understanding of scatter plot graphs. Scatter plots provide a graph of different points that together show a relationship among data. To see the relationship among the data, draw a "line of best fit" that shows a line that bests approximate the data points. A line of best fit typically has roughly the same number of points above it and beneath it, unless there are significantly outlying points. Figure 8 is an example of a scatter plot with a line of best fit.

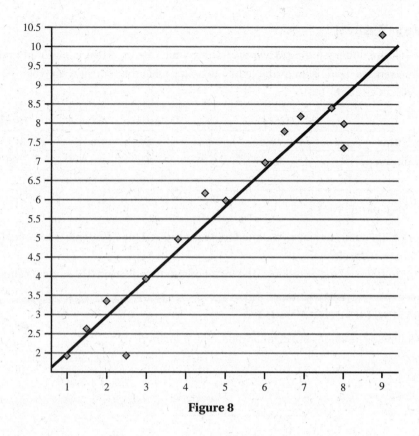

Figure 8

Histograms

Another type of graph on the PSAT is the histogram—it shows the frequency of different values in a data set. For example, consider the histogram in Figure 9.

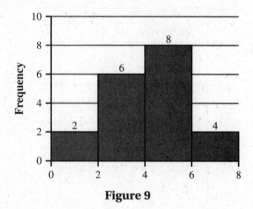

Figure 9

What does this histogram portray?

- 2 values in the set between 0 and 2
- 6 values between 2 and 4
- 8 values between 4 and 6
- 4 values between 6 and 8

Two-Way Tables

The PSAT tests your understanding of two-way tables, which are used to organize multiple variables and their frequencies. Here is an example of a two-way table that portrays the votes in a student council president election:

	Male	**Female**	**Total**
Voted for Liam	48	59	107
Voted for Emma	61	45	106
Total	109	104	213

What does this table tell you?

- There are 107 total students who voted for Liam and 106 total students who voted for Emma. So Liam won the election.
- There are 109 total male students, 104 total female students, and 213 students altogether.

INTERPRETING FUNCTIONS DRILL

1. Are the following functions linear, quadratic, or exponential?
   a. $y = 2x^2 - 5$
   b. $y = 4x + 2$
   c. $y = 6^x + 5$

2.

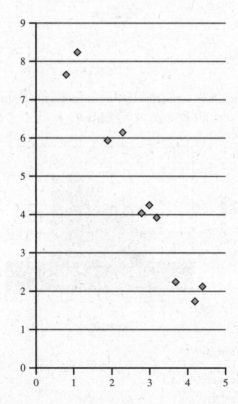

Consider the scatter plot above. When rounded to the nearest whole number, what is the slope of the line of best fit for this scatter plot?

3.

	Seniors Graduating With Honors	Seniors Graduating Without Honors	Total
Lincoln High School	50	240	290
Jefferson High School	80	170	250
Total	130	410	540

Consider the table above.

   a. How many seniors are graduating from Jefferson High School without honors?

   b. How many seniors are at both schools?

   c. How many seniors are at just Lincoln High School?

Solutions

1. a. $y = 2x^2 - 5$ is a quadratic function since the x is raised to the second power.

   b. $y = 4x + 2$ is a linear function since it has a constant slope of 4.

   c. $y = 6^x + 5$ is an exponential function since the 6 is raised to the x power.

2. To estimate the slope, sketch a best-fit line:

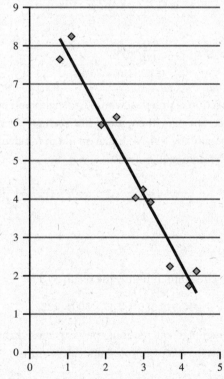

The line roughly has points at (1, 8) and (3, 4). So the slope would approximately be:

$$\frac{(y_2 - y_1)}{(x_2 - x_1)}$$

$$\frac{8 - 4}{1 - 3} =$$

$$\frac{4}{-2} = -2$$

3. a. 170

   b. 540. Include seniors from both schools, both those who are graduating with honors and those who are graduating without honors.

   c. 290. Include only seniors from Lincoln, both those who are graduating with honors and those who are graduating without honors.

PERCENTAGES

The general formula for percentages is:

$$\frac{\text{Part}}{\text{Whole}} \times 100 = \text{Percent}$$

➥ Example

You took a test with 80 questions, and you answered 60 of them correctly. What percentage of the questions did you answer correctly?

Solution

$$\frac{\text{Part}}{\text{Whole}} \times 100 = \text{Percent}$$

$$\frac{60}{80} \times 100 =$$

$$0.75 \times 100 = 75\%$$

On the calculator-permitted section, a practical way to work with percentages is to convert them to decimals. First, remove the percent sign. Then, move the decimal point 2 spots to the left. Finally, multiply the last decimal expression by 100. Note that on the non-calculator section, you may want to convert the percentages to a fraction, like $\frac{1}{2} = 50\%$.

➥ Example

What is 45 percent of 300?

Solution

Convert the percentage to a decimal and multiply the result by 300:

$$45\% \text{ of } 300 = 0.45 \times 300 = 135$$

When doing multistep percentage calculations, be very careful that you are considering the increases or decreases from previous steps in your later calculations.

➥ Example

A book regularly costs $20, but it is on sale for 10% off. A customer also has a coupon for 30% off the price of the book in addition to any sale discounts. What will be the price of the book the customer pays using only the sale? What will then be the price also using the coupon? Ignore any sales tax.

Solution

First determine the sale price of the book by subtracting the 10% discount from the original price:

$$\$20 - (0.1 \times \$20) = \$20 - \$2 = \$18$$

Then subtract 30% of the new price from the new price to find the fully discounted price:

$$\$18 - (0.3 \times \$18) = \$18 - \$5.40 = \$12.60$$

Alternatively, you could calculate 90% of the original amount and then calculate 70% of that new amount. This method takes away the need to do subtraction:

$$\$20 \times 0.9 = \$18 \rightarrow \$18 \times 0.7 = \$12.60$$

Another useful approach to percentage calculations is to use 100 as a sample starting value.

➥ Example

If Michal's blood pressure increased by 20% from 6 P.M. to 7 P.M. and then decreased by 10% from 7 P.M. to 8 P.M., what was the overall percentage change in her blood pressure from 6 P.M. to 8 P.M.?

Solution

Although you can calculate this percentage change using variables, it is far easier if you use 100 as the original number. If you assume Michal's initial blood pressure at 6 P.M. is 100, then a 20% increase will result in a new blood pressure of 120 at 7 P.M. Why? Because 20% of 100 is 20, and you add it to 100, giving 120. Then to calculate the change from 7 P.M. to 8 P.M., simply take 10% of 120, which is $120 \times 0.10 = 12$, and subtract it from 120, $120 - 12 = 108$. So 108 represents an 8% increase over 100. The overall percentage change in her blood pressure is 8%.

Sometimes you can save time on percentage problems by substituting fractions for the percentage. Certain percentages are easily converted to fractions, like $25\% \rightarrow \frac{1}{4}$ or $50\% \rightarrow \frac{1}{2}$.

➥ Example

If a shirt that costs $60 is on sale for 50% off, what is the discounted price of the shirt?

Solution

To solve this without the use of a calculator, use the fraction $\frac{1}{2}$ instead of 50% to easily find the discounted price:

$$\$60 \times \frac{1}{2} = \$30$$

$30 taken away from $60 gives you a discounted price of $30.

PERCENTAGES DRILL

1. What is 25% of 200?

2. What is 110% of 50?

3. If there are 50 questions on a test and you answered 36 questions correctly, what is your percent score on the test?

4. If a book regularly costs $20 but you have a coupon for 15% off the book, what would you pay altogether for the book after 7% sales tax is added?

5. Lydia has $1,000 in her savings account on January 1 of this year. If she earns 2% interest, compounded annually, how much money will she have on January 1 two years from now (assuming she makes no additional deposits or withdrawals)?

Solutions

1. $0.25 \times 200 = 50$

2. $1.10 \times 50 = 55$

3. $\dfrac{36}{50} \times 100 = 72\%$

4. First determine the discounted price for the book:

$$\$20 - (0.15 \times \$20) = \$17$$

Then, add the 7% sales tax to the price to get the total price paid:

$$\$17 + (0.07 \times \$17) = \$18.19$$

Alternatively, combine the addition and subtraction steps to save time in your calculations:

$$\$20 \times (0.85) = \$17$$
$$\$17 \times (1.07) = \$18.19$$

5. A 2% increase on an original amount of x is calculated like this:

$$x + 0.02x = 1.02x$$

To compound the 2% interest on the original sum of $1,000 over two years, multiply the original amount by 1.02 *twice* to get the total amount of money:

$$1.02 \times 1.02 \times \$1,000 = \$1,040.40$$

RATIOS, PROPORTIONS, AND DIRECT AND INVERSE VARIATION

Ratios and Proportions

Recognize when numbers and expressions involve the application of ratios and proportions. This will most frequently occur with word problems.

➥ Example

A cookie recipe calls for 6 cups of sugar and 4 cups of milk. Brendan has 18 cups of sugar. If Brendan wants to use all of that sugar, how many cups of milk will he need?

Solution

Set up a ratio that has the same units in the numerator and the same units in the denominator:

$$\frac{4 \text{ cups milk}}{6 \text{ cups sugar}} = \frac{x \text{ cups milk}}{18 \text{ cups sugar}}$$

$$\frac{2}{3} = \frac{x}{18}$$

Cross multiply:

$$2 \times 18 = 3x$$

Divide both sides by 3:

$$\frac{2 \times 18}{3} = x$$

$$\frac{36}{3} = 12 = x$$

Brendan will need 12 cups of milk.

Direct and Inverse Variation

The variables a and b vary *directly* with one another (also called "directly proportional") if as a increases, then b increases, and if as a decreases, then b also decreases. The general form for an equation in which a and b are directly proportional is:

$$b = ka \quad (k = \text{constant})$$

As a real-world example, the greater quantity of a certain food, the more calories there are in that food. You could say the food quantity and caloric quantity are directly proportional.

The variables a and b vary *indirectly* with one another (also called "inversely proportional") if as a increases, then b decreases, and if as a decreases, then b increases. The general form for an equation in which a and b are inversely related is:

$$b = \frac{k}{a} \quad (k = \text{constant})$$

As a real-world example, the more people who split a pizza, the smaller the size is of each person's piece of pizza. The number of people and the size of each piece are inversely related.

➥ Example

Consider the variable n in this equation:

$$n = \frac{x}{y}$$

To which variable is n directly proportional, and to which variable is n inversely proportional?

Solution

Since n and x are both on top in the equation, if x becomes greater, so does n. (You can consider n to be a fraction with n as the numerator and 1 as the denominator.) The variable y is in the denominator, so as y increases, n decreases. As a result, n is directly proportional to x and is inversely proportional to y.

RATIOS, PROPORTIONS, AND DIRECT AND INVERSE VARIATION DRILL

1. If 3 teaspoons are in 1 tablespoon, how many teaspoons are in 4 tablespoons?

2. If the U.S. dollar exchanges for 71 Indian rupees, how many dollars will be needed to purchase a toy that costs 426 rupees?

3. A town requires that in every new development, there are 2 acres of park for every 3 acres that are zoned for residential and/or commercial purposes. How many acres of park would be required in a new development that is 50 acres total?

4. When a car is traveling 40 kilometers per hour, how fast will it be going in meters per second (to the nearest tenth)? Note: There are 1,000 meters in a kilometer.

5. The physics equation that describes the relationship among pressure (p), force (F), and surface area (A) is $p = \frac{F}{A}$. Based on this equation, pressure is directly proportional and is inversely related to which variables?

6. Variables a and b are related by the equation $b = ka$, in which k is the constant of proportionality. If b is 5 when a is 10, what is the value of k?

Solutions

1. Set up a proportion to solve the problem:

$$\frac{3 \text{ teaspoons}}{1 \text{ tablespoon}} = \frac{x \text{ teaspoons}}{4 \text{ tablespoons}}$$

   Cross multiply:

$$3 \times 4 = 12 \text{ teaspoons}$$

2. Solve using a proportion:

$$\frac{1 \text{ dollar}}{71 \text{ rupees}} = \frac{x \text{ dollars}}{426 \text{ rupees}}$$

   Cross multiply:

$$426 = 71x$$
$$\frac{426}{71} = 6 \text{ dollars}$$

3. For a given development, there will be 2 park acres for every 5 total acres since 2 park acres + 3 non-park acres = 5 total acres. Solve this question using a proportion:

$$\frac{2 \text{ park acres}}{5 \text{ total acres}} = \frac{x \text{ park acres}}{50 \text{ total acres}}$$

   Cross multiply:

$$50 \times 2 = 5x$$
$$\frac{100}{5} = 20 \text{ park acres}$$

4. There are 1,000 meters in 1 kilometer and 3,600 seconds in an hour (60 minutes × 60 seconds = 3,600). Solve by converting the units:

$$40 \frac{\text{kilometers}}{\text{hour}} \times 1{,}000 \frac{\text{meters}}{\text{kilometer}} \times \frac{\text{hour}}{3{,}600 \text{ seconds}} \rightarrow$$

$$40 \frac{\cancel{\text{kilometers}}}{\cancel{\text{hour}}} \times 1{,}000 \frac{\text{meters}}{\cancel{\text{kilometer}}} \times \frac{\cancel{\text{hour}}}{3{,}600 \text{ seconds}} = \frac{40 \times 1{,}000}{3{,}600} = 11.1 \frac{\text{meters}}{\text{second}}$$

5. In this equation, $p = \frac{F}{A}$, p and F are both in the numerator. So pressure (p) and force (F) are directly proportional to one another—as p increases, F also increases. Surface area (A) is in the denominator while p is in the numerator. So A and p are inversely related to one another—as A increases, p decreases.

6. Plug the values for a and b into the equation to solve for k:

$$b = ka$$
$$5 = k(10)$$
$$\frac{5}{10} = k$$
$$\frac{1}{2} = k$$

MEAN, MEDIAN, AND MODE

Table 5.1 gives the definition of mean, median, and mode.

Table 5.1. Mean, Median, and Mode

	Definition
Mean	$$\frac{\text{Sum of Items}}{\text{Number of Items}} = \text{Mean}$$ What you usually think of when you calculate the average.
Median	The middle term of a set of numbers when those numbers are lined up from smallest to largest. When the number of terms is even and the two terms in the middle are not the same, take the mean of the two middle terms to find the median.
Mode	The most frequent term in a set of numbers. In a set of numbers, if each number appears only once, there is no mode. However, if 2 or more numbers are tied for appearing the most times, that set has multiple modes.

➡ Example

Compute the mean, median, and mode for the following set of numbers:

$$\{1, 4, 4, 5, 8, 13, 22\}$$

Solution

The mean:

$$\frac{1 + 4 + 4 + 5 + 8 + 13 + 22}{7} = \frac{57}{7} \approx 8.14$$

The mean is 8.14.

The median:

The numbers are already in order from smallest to largest. There are 7 numbers in the set. The median is 5 since it is in the middle of the set.

The mode:

The most frequent term is 4, so it is the mode.

A common application of the mean is when you calculate the missing term in a set when you already know the mean. Here is an example.

➡ Example

Sam has taken three exams, each worth a maximum of 50 points, over the course of her semester. She scored 40, 35, and 27 on her three exams. What must she score on a fourth exam, also out of 50 points, in order to average 35 points on her four exams?

Solution

Set up the problem using the formula for finding the mean:

$$\frac{\text{Sum of Items}}{\text{Number of Items}} = \text{Mean}$$

Plug in the terms that you know:

$$\frac{40+35+27+x}{4}=35$$

Cross multiply by 4:

$$(4)\frac{40+35+27+x}{4}=35(4)$$
$$40+35+27+x=140$$

Solve for x:

$$40+35+27+x=140$$
$$102+x=140$$
$$x=38$$

Sam would need to score a 38 on her fourth exam.

MEAN, MEDIAN, AND MODE DRILL

1. Consider this set of numbers: {1, 3, 4, 5, 5, 7, 10}
   a. What is the mean of this set?
   b. What is the median of this set?
   c. What is the mode of this set?

2. If the set of numbers {4, 6, 7, 7, 9} had the number 10 added to it, what would change?
   I. The set's mean
   II. The set's mode
   III. The set's median

3. A restaurant wants the average calories for each item in a meal to be 300. If a meal is to consist of a serving of pasta (500 calories), a salad (200 calories), and a side dish, what must the calories in the side dish be to meet the restaurant's requirement?

Solutions

1. a. The formula for the mean is $\frac{\text{Sum of Items}}{\text{Number of Items}}=\text{Mean}$. Add the numbers in the set together, and divide by how many numbers there are in the set:

$$\frac{1+3+4+5+5+7+10}{7}=\frac{35}{7}=5$$

   b. The numbers are already organized in order from least to greatest, so find the fourth value of the set since it is in the middle:

$$(1,\ 3,\ 4,\ 5,\ 5,\ 7,\ 10)$$

   The median is therefore 5.

   c. The mode is the most frequent member of the set. Since 5 appears twice while the other numbers appear only once, 5 is the mode of the set.

2. The current set is {4, 6, 7, 7, 9}, and the new set is {4, 6, 7, 7, 9, 10}.

   The mean of the set would change. The original mean is $\frac{4+6+7+7+9}{5}=\frac{33}{5}=6.6$, while the new mean would be $\frac{4+6+7+7+9+10}{6}=\frac{43}{6}\approx7.2$. You could also estimate that the mean would change because if you add only a number that is greater than the mean to a set, it will make the mean larger as a result.

The mode of the set would NOT change because 7 is still the most frequent number in each set.

The median of the set would NOT change. In the original set, 7 is the middle number. In the new set, 7 is the value we get when we take the average of the two middle values of the new set (since there is an even number of members of the set): $\frac{7+7}{2} = 7$. If the two middle values in a set that has an even number of elements are the same, then the median will simply be one of these middle values.

3. Set up an equation for the mean, where x represents the calories in the side dish:

$$\frac{500 + 200 + x}{3} = 300$$

$$\frac{700 + x}{3} = 300$$

Cross multiply:

$$700 + x = 3 \times 300$$
$$700 + x = 900$$
$$x = 200$$

There must be 200 calories in the side dish.

PROBABILITY AND STATISTICS

Probability Basics

Probability is the *likelihood that a given event will happen*, expressed as a fraction, decimal, or percentage. If there is no chance an event will occur, it has a probability of 0. If there is a 100 percent chance something will happen, it has a probability of 1.

To calculate probability, take the number of cases of a success and divide it by the total number of possible outcomes:

$$\text{Probability} = \frac{\text{Number of Successes}}{\text{Number of Possible Outcomes}}$$

➡ Example

If Janice has 3 red marbles out of the 200 total marbles in her collection, what is the probability that she will randomly pick a red marble?

Solution

The number of successes is 3, and the number of possible outcomes is 200:

$$\frac{\text{Number of red marbles}}{\text{Number of total marbles}} = \frac{3}{200} = 0.015 = 1.5\%$$

Independent/Dependent Counting Problems

Counting problems are either independent or dependent.

INDEPENDENT COUNTING PROBLEMS (DRAWING WITH REPLACEMENT)

Independent counting problems involve drawing an object and then replacing it before drawing again. In these types of problems, each choice is computed *independently*. In other words, what you pick the first time has *no impact* on what you pick the second time, which has no impact on what you pick the third time, and so on. Such problems include flipping a coin several times because the flip of one coin has no impact on the later coin flips.

 **Example** _____

Hazel is choosing a 3-letter combination for her safe. Whether or not the letters are repeated does not matter. How many unique combinations can Hazel make?

Solution

What Hazel picks for one letter does not impact what she picks for another letter. Since there are 26 letters in the alphabet, calculate the total number of possible combinations as follows:

$$26 \times 26 \times 26 = 17{,}576 \text{ possible combinations}$$

DEPENDENT COUNTING PROBLEMS (DRAWING WITHOUT REPLACEMENT)

Dependent counting problems involve drawing an object and not replacing it before drawing again. In these types of problems, each choice _depends_ on what was previously chosen. In other words, what you pick the first time _has an impact_ on what you pick the second time, which has an impact on what you pick the third time, and so on. Such problems include drawing names out of a hat because you do not want to pick the same name more than once.

Example _____

John is choosing a 3-letter combination for his locker. The letters _cannot_ be repeated. How many unique combinations can John make?

Solution

What John picks for the first letter does impact what he picks for the second, which impacts what he picks for the third. So he will have one fewer possible letters for each subsequent choice. He can compute the total number of unique 3-letter combinations with no repeating letters as follows:

$$26 \times 25 \times 24 = 15{,}600 \text{ possible combinations}$$

Range and Standard Deviation

The PSAT will emphasize analyzing data sets. So be comfortable with the important concepts of range and standard deviation.

RANGE

Range is defined as the difference between the smallest and the largest values in a set of data.

STANDARD DEVIATION

Standard deviation measures how spread out or how varied the data points are in a set. It can be calculated using the following equation:

$$\text{Standard deviation} = \sqrt{\text{Average of the squared distances of the data points from their mean}}$$

Rather than having you conduct elaborate calculations to find the standard deviation of a set of data, you will need to have a feel for what the standard deviation represents. If the standard deviation is small, the data points have little variation. If the standard deviation is large, the data points have great variation.

Compare the ranges and standard deviations of Set *A* and Set *B*.

Set *A*: {1, 3, 4, 6, 8}

Set *B*: {1, 8, 50, 200, 380}

Solution

The range and standard deviation of Set *B* are greater than the range and standard deviation of Set *A*. Why? The values in Set *A* range from only 1 to 8 and do not vary much from the average of Set *A* (4.4). The values in Set *B* range from 1 to 380 and vary quite a bit from the average of Set *B* (127.8). The sets are simple enough that you can likely determine the general trends with standard deviation and range without doing detailed calculations.

The most common graph involving standard deviation is the *normal distribution*—the typical distribution of a large sampling of values in a bell curve shape. Figure 10 shows a normal distribution. About 68% of the values are within 1 standard deviation of the mean. About 95% of the values are within 2 standard deviations of the mean. About 99.7% of the values are within 3 standard deviations of the mean.

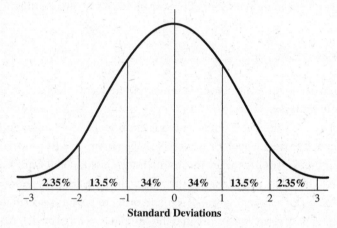

Figure 10

Confidence Interval and Margin of Error

When collecting a sample of data from a population, you need to be sure that the results give a true snapshot of the population as a whole. Two important terms are associated with the quality of data sampling: confidence interval and margin of error.

> Use common sense when thinking about data. To get an accurate snapshot of public opinion, you want to ask as MANY RANDOM people your questions as you can!

CONFIDENCE INTERVAL

The confidence interval is a range of values defined so that there is a predetermined probability that the value of an unknown parameter under investigation will fall within the range. The higher the confidence level is, the more likely the parameter will fall within that interval.

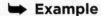 _____

Suppose a stockbroker has research indicating a 95% confidence interval that a company's stock will have a return between −7.8% and +9.5% during the next year. What does this mean?

Solution

In this case, the unknown parameter is the average stock return for the year. This means that if all economic conditions remain the same, there is a 95% chance that the stock will have an average return in this interval of −7.8% to +9.5%.

MARGIN OF ERROR

The margin of error is the maximum expected difference between the actual (unknown) parameter and the estimate for that parameter obtained through a sample. The smaller the margin of error is, the more accurate the survey results are.

➡ **Example** _____

Suppose that a survey has a margin of error of plus or minus 5% at 96% confidence. What does this mean?

Solution

This means that 96% of the time the survey is repeated, the results are within 5% of the amount reported in the original survey.

You do not need to know the details of calculating confidence level and margin of error for the PSAT. Instead, you need to have a feel for what will make survey results more reliable. The confidence level and margin of error for survey results are interrelated. If you want a smaller margin of error, you may have to have less confidence in the results. If you want to be more confident in your results, you should allow for a larger margin of error. In order to maximize confidence in the results and minimize the margin of error, make sure that the sample is as *large and as random* as possible.

PROBABILITY AND STATISTICS DRILL

1. If a particular pet store has five dogs, four cats, and 12 guinea pigs available for purchase (and no other pets for sale), what is the probability that a randomly purchased pet will be a cat?

2.

	Write Using Cursive	**Write Using Print**	**Total**
Teachers	12	4	16
Students	40	280	320
Total	52	284	336

Consider the table above that portrays the teachers and students at a particular high school and their preferred writing styles.

a. What is the probability that a randomly selected teacher prefers to write using print?

b. What is the probability that a randomly selected person at the school prefers to write using cursive?

3. At the school cafeteria, there are three main courses and four desserts from which to choose. What is the total number of possible meals that a student can choose, assuming he or she wants both a main course and a dessert?

4. In Kim's closet, she has eight different dresses. She is packing for a three-day trip; she wants to wear a different dress on each day of the trip. What is the total number of combinations of dresses Kim could pack?

5. Consider the set of numbers {3, 4, 7, 11}. What positive number could be added to the set to double the set's range?

6. If someone added the number 20 to the set of numbers {1, 2, 4, 5, 12}, would that increase or decrease the standard deviation of the set?

7. Which of these approaches would give the best indication of how a particular town is planning on voting on an issue in an election?
   a. Interviewing 100 political activists in the town as to their predictions
   b. Taking a phone survey of 500 randomly selected likely voters
   c. Having 500 pedestrians in the main city park complete a survey

Solutions

1. Total the number of pets:

$$5 + 4 + 12 = 21$$

Then divide the number of cats (4) by the number of total pets (21) to get the probability that a randomly purchased pet will be a cat:

$$\frac{4}{21}$$

2. a. There are 16 total teachers, and 4 of them prefer to write using print. So divide 4 by 16 to get the probability:

$$\frac{4}{16} = \frac{1}{4}$$

This is the same as 0.25 if you want to express the answer as a decimal.

   b. There are 336 total people in the school, and 52 of them prefer to write using cursive. So divide 52 by 336. Your answer can be expressed as a reduced fraction or as a decimal:

$$\frac{52}{336} = \frac{13}{84} \text{ or } 0.155$$

3. Multiply the number of main courses by the number of desserts to find the total number of possible meals:

$$3 \times 4 = 12$$

4. After Kim wears one dress, she does not want to wear it again. Therefore, the number of dress options each day decreases by 1. Calculate the total number of combinations as follows:

$$8 \times 7 \times 6 = 336 \text{ total possible combinations}$$

5. The range of the set {3, 4, 7, 11} is currently $11 - 3 = 8$.
   Double the current range to find the new range:

$$8 \times 2 = 16$$

Since the smallest number in the set is 3, add 16 to 3 to find the number that would need to be added to make the range of the set 16:

$$3 + 16 = 19$$

So the new set would be {3, 4, 7, 11, 19} with 19 as the added number. It would have a range of 16, twice the original range of 8.

6. If 20 was added to this set, the new set would be {1, 2, 4, 5, 12, 20}. The average deviation from the mean would increase since the spread of the numbers would increase. Therefore, the standard deviation would increase.

7. Interviewing the political activists and the park pedestrians would not be ideal since the sample set would not be randomized. Performing a phone survey of the randomly selected voters would ensure that the sample was randomized, giving much better results.

FACTORING

Factoring to Simplify Expressions

When simplifying an equation, take out any common factors.

➡ **Example** _____

Factor $nx + ny$.

Solution

$nx + ny$ can be expressed as $n(x + y)$ by factoring out the n.

➡ **Example** _____

Factor $\dfrac{2x^3 + 6x}{3x}$.

Solution

$\dfrac{2x^3 + 6x}{3x}$ can be expressed as $\dfrac{2x(x^2 + 3)}{3x}$ since you can factor $2x$ out of the numerator. Then you can cancel out an x from the numerator and denominator:

$$\frac{2x(x^2 + 3)}{3x} = \frac{2\cancel{x}(x^2 + 3)}{3\cancel{x}} = \frac{2}{3}(x^2 + 3)$$

You also should know how to factor equations like $x^2 - x - 12 = 0$. Try to express it as two binomials that are multiplied by each other. The factored form looks like:

$$(x + \text{something})(x - \text{something}) = 0$$

In the case of $x^2 - x - 12 = 0$, you can rewrite it as $(x + 3)(x - 4) = 0$. If you use FOIL to multiply the left-hand side (i.e., multiply the **F**irst terms together, then the **O**uter terms, then the **I**nner terms, and finally the **L**ast terms), you will get the original equation:

$$(x + 3)(x - 4) = 0$$
$$x^2 - 4x + 3x - 12 = 0$$
$$x^2 - x - 12 = 0$$

Common Factoring Patterns

Memorize these patterns so you can recognize them on the PSAT Math Test and save time.

- ■ Multiplying Binomials

$$(a+b)(a+b) = a^2 + 2ab + b^2$$

Example:

$$(x+3)(x+3) = x^2 + 6x + 9$$

$$(a+b)(a-b) = a^2 - b^2$$

Example:

$$(m+2)(m-2) = m^2 - 4$$

$$(a-b)(a-b) = a^2 - 2ab + b^2$$

Example:

$$(3-y)(3-y) = 9 - 6y + y^2$$

- ■ Sum of Cubes

$$(a+b)(a^2 - ab + b^2) = a^3 + b^3$$

Example:

$$(2+x)(4-2x+x^2) = 2^3 + x^3 = 8 + x^3$$

- ■ Difference of Cubes

$$(a-b)(a^2 + ab + b^2) = a^3 - b^3$$

Example:

$$(y-4)(y^2 + 4y + 16) = y^3 - 4^3 = y^3 - 64$$

FACTORING DRILL

1. Factor this expression: $4x + 8y$

2. Simplify this expression: $\dfrac{3x - 6y}{3}$

3. Simplify this expression: $\dfrac{12x^4}{3x^2}$

4. Factor this expression: $25x^2 - 9y^2$

5. Factor this expression: $27 - 8x^3$

Solutions

1. $4x + 8y \rightarrow 4(x + 2y)$

2. $\dfrac{3x - 6y}{3} =$

$\dfrac{3(x - 2y)}{3} =$

$\dfrac{\cancel{3}(x - 2y)}{\cancel{3}} = x - 2y$

3.
$$\frac{12x^4}{3x^2}=$$

$$\frac{3 \cdot 4 \cdot x^2 \cdot x^2}{3x^2}=$$

$$\frac{\cancel{3} \cdot 4 \cdot \cancel{x^2} \cdot x^2}{\cancel{3}\cancel{x^2}}=4x^2$$

4. $25x^2 - 9y^2 = (5x - 3y)(5x + 3y)$

5. This is a difference of cubes, where $a^3 - b^3 = (a-b)(a^2 + ab + b^2)$. In this case, a is equal to 3, and b is equal to $2x$. So the solution is:

$$27 - 8x^3 =$$
$$3^3 - \left((2x)^3\right) =$$
$$(3-2x)\left(3^2 + 3(2x) + (2x)^2\right) = (3-2x)\left(9 + 6x + 4x^2\right)$$

ADVANCED EQUATION CONCEPTS

Quadratic Formula

A second-degree equation containing the variable x, the constants a, b, and c, and written in the form $ax^2 + bx + c = 0$ can be solved using the quadratic formula:

$$x = \frac{-b \pm \sqrt{b^2 - 4ac}}{2a}$$

➥ Example _____

What are the values of x in the equation $2x^2 - 2x - 12 = 0$?

Solution

The values of the constants are $a = 2$, $b = -2$, and $c = -12$. Solve for x by plugging a, b, and c into the quadratic formula:

$$x = \frac{-b \pm \sqrt{b^2 - 4ac}}{2a}$$
$$x = \frac{-(-2) \pm \sqrt{(-2)^2 - 4(2)(-12)}}{2(2)}$$
$$x = \frac{2 \pm \sqrt{4 + 96}}{4}$$
$$x = \frac{2 \pm \sqrt{100}}{4}$$
$$x = \frac{2 \pm 10}{4}$$
$$x = \frac{1}{2} \pm \frac{5}{2}$$
$$x = 3 \text{ or } -2$$

Completing the Square

Another way to solve quadratic equations is by completing the square—turning each side of the equation into parts that can be squared. Here is how you can solve for x using this method. Consider the following equation:

$$x^2 - 6x - 16 = 0$$

Start by adding 16 to both sides so the x-terms are all on the left.

$$x^2 - 6x = 16$$

Then take half of –6, which is –3, square it, and add it to both sides of the equation.

$$x^2 - 6x + 9 = 16 + 9$$

You can now rewrite the left-hand side in simplified, squared form:

$$(x-3)^2 = 25$$

Take the square root of both sides:

$$x - 3 = \pm 5$$

Solve for x:

$$x - 3 = -5 \quad \text{and} \quad x - 3 = 5$$
$$x = -2 \qquad\qquad x = 8$$

Therefore, $x = 8$ and $x = -2$.

Undefined Functions

A function can be undefined when *it is divided by zero*. The value at which a function is undefined indicates that the function has *no solution* for that value. This makes sense because it would be impossible to divide something into *zero* parts.

➡ Example _____

When is this function undefined?

$$f(x) = \frac{x^2 + 5}{x - 7}$$

Solution

Find the value of x that would make this function have zero in the denominator. The denominator is $x - 7$, so set this equal to zero and solve for x:

$$x - 7 = 0$$
$$x = 7$$

So the function is undefined when $x = 7$.

Extraneous Solutions

Sometimes you should test solutions to see if they work in the original expression.

➡ Example _____

What are the solution(s) for x in this equation?

$$x = \sqrt{24 - 2x}$$

Solution

The logical first step to solve this equation is to square both sides:

$$x^2 = 24 - 2x$$

This can then be arranged and factored:

$$x^2 + 2x - 24 = 0$$
$$(x-4)(x+6) = 0$$
$$x - 4 = 0 \quad x + 6 = 0$$
$$x = 4 \qquad x = -6$$

So 4 and −6 both appear to be solutions. However, only 4 works in the original expression since the square root of a real number cannot be negative. Therefore, just 4 is the answer. Check for extraneous solutions when you start multiplying and dividing expressions containing square root symbols.

ADVANCED EQUATION CONCEPTS DRILL

1. Solve for x: $2x^2 - 5x + 1 = 0$

2. For what value of x is the following function undefined?

$$y = \frac{14x - 5}{2x + 3}$$

3. If x is going to have only imaginary solutions, what are the possible values of c in this equation? (If needed, see "Imaginary Numbers" on page 361.)

$$x^2 + 2x + c = 0$$

4. What is the solution (or solutions) to this equation?

$$x = \sqrt{12 - x}$$

5. Solve for x by completing the square: $x^2 - 8x - 20 = 0$.

Solutions

1. Use the quadratic equation to solve:

$$x = \frac{-b \pm \sqrt{b^2 - 4ac}}{2a}$$

$$x = \frac{-(-5) \pm \sqrt{(-5)^2 - 4(2)(1)}}{2 \cdot 2}$$

$$x = \frac{5 \pm \sqrt{25 - 8}}{4}$$

$$x = \frac{5 \pm \sqrt{17}}{4}$$

2. In order for the function $y = \frac{14x - 5}{2x + 3}$ to be undefined, the denominator, $2x + 3$, should equal zero. Set up an equation to solve:

$$2x + 3 = 0 \rightarrow 2x = -3 \rightarrow x = -\frac{3}{2}$$

3. Consider the quadratic equation: $x = \dfrac{-b \pm \sqrt{b^2 - 4ac}}{2a}$. If x is going to have only imaginary solutions, the *discriminant* ($b^2 - 4ac$) in the quadratic formula must be *negative*. Why? If the discriminant was negative, you would be taking the square root of a negative number, which will result in imaginary solutions. For the equation $x^2 + 2x + c = 0$, the value of a is 1, the value of b is 2, and c is a variable. Set up an inequality to solve:

$$b^2 - 4ac < 0$$
$$2^2 - 4 \cdot 1 \cdot c < 0$$
$$4 - 4c < 0$$
$$4 < 4c$$
$$1 < c$$

As long as c is greater than 1, there will be an imaginary solution to the equation.

4. Start by squaring both sides of the equation:

$$x = \sqrt{12 - x}$$
$$x^2 = 12 - x$$
$$x^2 + x - 12 = 0$$

Then factor the equation:

$$x^2 + x - 12 = 0$$
$$(x + 4)(x - 3) = 0$$

It looks like -4 and 3 will work as solutions. However, you need to check for extraneous solutions by plugging these possible solutions back into the original equation.

Plug in 3 for x:

$$x = \sqrt{12 - x}$$
$$3 = \sqrt{12 - 3}$$
$$3 = \sqrt{9}$$
$$3 = 3$$

So 3 works.

Now plug in -4 for x:

$$-4 = \sqrt{12 - (-4)}$$
$$-4 = \sqrt{12 - (-4)}$$
$$-4 = \sqrt{16}$$
$$-4 \neq 4$$

So -4 is extraneous, and the only solution is 3.

5. Start by adding 20 to each side of the equation:

$$x^2 - 8x - 20 = 0$$
$$x^2 - 8x = 20$$

Now take half of -8, which is -4, square it, and add it to both sides:

$$x^2 - 8x + 16 = 20 + 16$$
$$x^2 - 8x + 16 = 36$$
$$(x - 4)^2 = 6^2$$
$$\sqrt{(x - 4)^2} = \sqrt{6^2}$$
$$x - 4 = \pm 6$$

The two solutions for x can be found as follows:

$$x-4=6 \quad \text{and} \quad x-4=-6$$
$$x=10 \qquad\qquad x=-2$$

So x can be either 10 or –2.

SYNTHETIC DIVISION

Synthetic division is the way students typically learn how to divide polynomials. Here is a brief review of how $2x^2-5x+7$ would be divided by $x+1$ using synthetic division.

Set up the synthetic division by taking the coefficients of the terms of the polynomial (2, –5, 7) and placing the numerical term of the divisor $x+1$ (multiplied by –1) to the left of them as follows:

$$-1 \enclose{verticalstrike}{} \quad 2 \quad -5 \quad 7$$

Then, bring down each of the coefficients, multiplying the columns one by one by the –1. Create sums to determine the divided polynomial and remainder:

$$
\begin{array}{r|rrr}
-1 & 2 & -5 & 7 \\
   &   & -2 & 7 \\
\hline
   & 2 & -7 & 14
\end{array}
$$

So the answer is $2x-7$ with a remainder of $\dfrac{14}{x+1}$.

Important fact: $x+1$ is NOT a factor of $2x^2-5x+7$ since the remainder is not zero.

SYNTHETIC DIVISION DRILL

1. Is $(x-2)$ a factor of $x^2+3x-10$?

2. What is the remainder when $5x^2-3x+2$ is divided by $x-2$?

Solutions

1. To determine if $(x-2)$ is a factor of $x^2+3x-10$, divide $x^2+3x-10$ by $(x-2)$ to see if there is a remainder. If the remainder is zero, then $(x-2)$ is a factor. Use synthetic division to divide:

$$
\begin{array}{r|rrr}
2 & 1 & 3 & -10 \\
  &   & 2 & 10 \\
\hline
  & 1 & 5 & 0
\end{array}
$$

The remainder is zero, so $(x-2)$ is a factor.

2. Use synthetic division to divide:

$$
\begin{array}{r|rrr}
2 & 5 & -3 & 2 \\
  &   & 10 & 14 \\
\hline
  & 5 & 7 & 16
\end{array}
$$

The remainder is 16 divided by $x-2$:

$$\frac{16}{x-2}$$

FUNCTION NOTATION AND MANIPULATION

In school, you are probably comfortable with equations written in one of the following two ways:

A function written like this:

$$y = 4x - 2$$

is the same as a function written like this:

$$f(x) = 4x - 2$$

If you are told that $x = 3$, you can just plug 3 in for x into each equation:

$$y = 4(3) - 2$$
$$f(3) = 4 \cdot 3 - 2$$

The PSAT will also assess your understanding of *composite functions*, which involve functions that depend on one another. For example, consider these two functions:

$$f(x) = x + 5$$
$$g(x) = 3x - 1$$

If you are asked to solve $f(g(2))$, you need to work from the *inside out*. Start with the $g(x)$ function, plugging in 2 for x:

$$g(x) = 3x - 1$$
$$g(2) = 3 \cdot 2 - 1$$
$$g(2) = 5$$

Then, plug 5 into $f(x)$:

$$f(x) = x + 5$$
$$f(5) = 5 + 5$$
$$f(5) = 10$$

So $f(g(2)) = 10$.

FUNCTION NOTATION AND MANIPULATION DRILL

1. If $f(x) = -3x + 5$, what is the value of $f(4)$?

2. If $f(x) = 3x$ and $g(x) = x - 4$, what is the value of $f(g(5))$?

3. What is the value of $f(x + 2) = 5x - 6$ when $x = 4$?

Solutions

1. Plug in 4 for x:

$$f(x) = -3x + 5$$
$$f(4) = -3(4) + 5$$
$$f(4) = -12 + 5$$
$$f(4) = -7$$

2. Start by calculating the value of $g(5)$:

$$g(x) = x - 4$$
$$g(5) = 5 - 4$$
$$g(5) = 1$$

Now, plug 1 into $f(x)$:

$$f(x) = 3x$$
$$f(1) = 3(1)$$
$$f(1) = 3$$

3. Plug in 4 for x on the left-hand side to determine what value should be plugged in for x on the right-hand side:

$$f(x+2) = 5x - 6$$
$$f(4+2) = 5(4+2) - 6$$
$$f(6) = 5(6) - 6$$
$$f(6) = 24$$

EXPONENTS

Table 5.2 shows the most important exponent rules along with some concrete examples. It also includes ways to remember these rules.

Table 5.2. Exponent Rules

Exponent Rule	Concrete Example	Way to Remember
$x^a x^b = x^{(a+b)}$	$x^3 x^4 = x^{(3+4)} = x^7$	Remember the acronym **MADSPM**. **M**ultiply exponents, **A**dd them.
$\dfrac{x^a}{x^b} = x^{a-b}$	$\dfrac{x^7}{x^2} = x^{7-2} = x^5$	**D**ivide exponents, **S**ubtract them.
$(x^a)^b = x^{ab}$	$(x^3)^5 = x^{15}$	**P**arentheses with exponents, **M**ultiply them.
$x^{-a} = \dfrac{1}{x^a}$	$x^{-5} = \dfrac{1}{x^5}$	If you are "bad" (negative), you are sent down below!
$x^{\frac{a}{b}} = \sqrt[b]{x^a}$	$x^{\frac{2}{7}} = \sqrt[7]{x^2}$	The root of a tree is on the bottom. Similarly, the root is on the bottom and on the left-hand side!

Exponential Growth and Decay

One of the most common ways that the PSAT will assess your understanding of exponents is by asking you to calculate the future value of a quantity after interest is applied to it. Here is a formula you can use to determine *exponential growth*:

$$(\text{Future Value}) = (\text{Present Value})(1 + (\text{Interest Rate as a Decimal}))^{\text{Number of Periods}}$$

The number of periods indicates the number of times the interest is compounded.

➥ Example _____

If Sara starts a savings account with $500 and the money in the account earns 3% interest compounded once a year, how much money will she have in the account after 2 years?

Solution

The present value of the money is $500. The interest rate, expressed as a decimal, is 0.03. The number of periods for which the money is compounded is 2 since there are 2 years. By plugging this all into the formula, you get the following:

$$\text{(Future Value)} = (500)(1 + (0.03))^2$$
$$500 \times 1.03^2 = \$530.45$$

If a function decreases exponentially over time, slightly modify the formula by subtracting the interest rate to determine *exponential decay*:

$$\text{(Future Value)} = \text{(Present Value)}(1 - \text{(Interest Rate as a Decimal)})^{\text{Number of Periods}}$$

➥ Example _____

Suppose the cost of a television is currently $600, but the price of the television will decrease by 5% each year. What will be price of the television exactly three years from now?

Solution

The present value of the price is $600. The interest rate, expressed as a decimal, is 0.05. The number of periods for which the price is compounded is 3 since there are 3 years. By plugging this all into the formula, you get the following:

$$\text{(Future Value)} = (600)(1 - (0.05))^3$$
$$600 \times 0.95^3 \approx \$514.43$$

EXPONENTS DRILL

1. Simplify: $3x^2 + 7x^2$

2. Simplify: $4(x^3)^2$

3. Simplify: $\dfrac{5x^3 + 10x}{5x}$

4. Simplify without the negative exponent: $2x^{-4}$

5. Simplify without the exponent form: $x^{\left(-\frac{2}{5}\right)}$

6. Simplify this expression: $\dfrac{x^{\left(\frac{3}{4}\right)}}{x^{-\left(\frac{1}{4}\right)}}$

7. Simplify this expression: $\left(\sqrt[3]{x^2}\right)\left(\sqrt[6]{x^8}\right)$

8. If Neha is 50 inches tall and she grows 5% in height each year, what is her height after two years have passed?

Solutions

1. $3x^2 + 7x^2 = 10x^2$

2. $4\left(x^3\right)^2 = 4x^{(3\times 2)} = 4x^6$

3. $\dfrac{5x^3 + 10x}{5x} =$

    $\dfrac{5x(x^2 + 2)}{5x} =$

    $\dfrac{\cancel{5x}(x^2 + 2)}{\cancel{5x}} = x^2 + 2$

4. $2x^{-4} = \dfrac{2}{x^4}$

5. $x^{\left(-\frac{2}{5}\right)} = \dfrac{1}{x^{\left(\frac{2}{5}\right)}} = \dfrac{1}{\sqrt[5]{x^2}}$

6. $\dfrac{x^{\left(\frac{3}{4}\right)}}{x^{-\left(\frac{1}{4}\right)}} =$

    $x^{\left(\frac{3}{4}\right)} x^{\left(\frac{1}{4}\right)} =$

    $x^{\left(\frac{3}{4} + \frac{1}{4}\right)} = x^1 = x$

7. $\left(\sqrt[3]{x^2}\right)\left(\sqrt[6]{x^8}\right) =$

    $\left(x^{\frac{2}{3}}\right)\left(x^{\frac{8}{6}}\right) =$

    $\left(x^{\frac{2}{3}}\right)\left(x^{\frac{4}{3}}\right) =$

    $x^{\left(\frac{2}{3} + \frac{4}{3}\right)} = x^{\left(\frac{6}{3}\right)} = x^2$

8. You can use this equation to solve:

$$(\text{Future Value}) = (\text{Present Value})\left(1 + (\text{Interest Rate as a Decimal})\right)^{\text{Number of Periods}}$$

The present value is 50 inches, the interest rate expressed as a decimal is 0.05, and the number of periods is 2 since you need the height after 2 years. By plugging this all into the formula, you get the following:

$$(\text{Future Value}) = (50)(1 + 0.05)^2 = 55.125 \text{ inches}$$

ZEROS AND PARABOLAS

Roots or Zeros

The root or zero of a function is the value for which the function has a value of zero. A function can have more than one root/zero. To find the root(s) of a function, either examine the equation of the function or look at the function's graph.

➠ **Example** _____

What are the zeros of $y = x^2 - 10x + 21$?

Solution

The equation is graphed below:

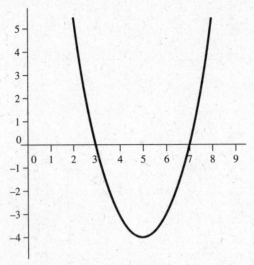

The function has roots/zeros at 3 and 7 since that is where the function intersects the *x*-axis. Since the function intersects the *x*-axis twice, the function has 2 solutions.

You can also determine the roots/zeros of the function by factoring it and setting the function equal to zero. Then solve for *x*. Let's do that with the above function:

$$y = x^2 - 10x + 21$$
$$0 = (x - 3)(x - 7)$$
$$(x - 3) = 0 \text{ and } (x - 7) = 0$$
$$x = 3 \text{ and } 7$$

The values of *x* that give a *y*-value of 0 are 3 and 7. Depending on the situation, use the graph or a simplified equation to determine roots/zeros.

Alternatively, you can use the quadratic formula to determine the roots:

$$y = x^2 - 10x + 21$$
$$x = \frac{-b \pm \sqrt{b^2 - 4ac}}{2a}$$
$$x = \frac{-(-10) \pm \sqrt{(-10)^2 - 4(1)(21)}}{2(1)}$$
$$x = \frac{10 \pm \sqrt{100 - 84}}{2}$$
$$x = \frac{10 \pm \sqrt{16}}{2}$$
$$x = \frac{10 \pm 4}{2}$$
$$x = 5 \pm 2$$
$$x = 3 \text{ or } 7$$

Parabolas

Sometimes you will need to look at the equation of a U-shaped curve, known as a parabola, and determine certain properties of it.

- The vertex form of a parabola is $y = a(x - h)^2 + k$.

- The vertex has the coordinates (h, k). If the parabola is facing up, the vertex is the bottom point of the U-shape. If the parabola is facing down, the vertex is the top point of the U-shape.
- The x-coordinate of the vertex provides the *axis of symmetry* for the parabola.

A parabola with the equation $y = (x - 1)^2 + 2$ has a vertex of $(1, 2)$. The equation for the axis of symmetry for the parabola is $x = 1$. The parabola is graphed in Figure 11:

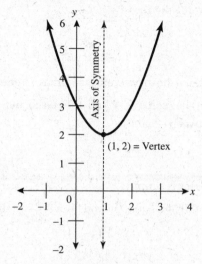

Figure 11

When a parabola is written in the form $y = ax^2 + bx + c$, you can determine the x-coordinate of the parabola's vertex using this formula:

$$x = -\frac{b}{2a}$$

➡ Example

Given a parabola with the equation $y = 5x^2 - 4x + 7$, what is the x-coordinate of the parabola's vertex?

Solution

Use the formula $x = -\dfrac{b}{2a}$, and plug in the correct values: $a = 5$ and $b = -4$. Therefore:

$$x = -\frac{b}{2a}$$
$$x = -\frac{(-4)}{2 \cdot 5}$$
$$x = \frac{4}{10}$$
$$x = 0.4$$

ZEROS AND PARABOLAS DRILL

1. What are the zeros of the function $y = (x-9)(x+1)$?

2. Where does the function $y = (x+4)(x-7)$ intersect the x-axis?

3. What are the zeros of the parabola $y = x^2 + x - 12$?

4. What is the x-coordinate of the vertex of a parabola with the equation $y = (x+2)(x-4)$?

5. A parabola with the equation $y + 4 = 3(x-5)^2$ has what coordinates for its vertex?

6. What are the x- and y-coordinates for the vertex of a parabola with the equation $y = 3x^2 - 6x + 5$?

Solutions

1. Consider where y will equal zero. If $x-9=0$ or $x+1=0$, the function will equal zero. Therefore, x can equal 9 or -1.

2. The function intersects the x-axis where the value of y is zero. Find the zeros of $y=(x+4)(x-7)$ to solve. If $(x+4)=0$ or $(x-7)=0$, y will be zero. So x could be -4 or 7.

3. Factor the equation to determine the zeros:

$$y=x^2+x-12$$
$$y=(x+4)(x-3)$$

So the zeros are at -4 and 3 since those two values of x make y equal zero.

4. The parabola $y=(x+2)(x-4)$ has zeros at -2 and 4. To easily determine the x-coordinate of the vertex, find the midpoint between -2 and 4:

$$\frac{-2+4}{2}=\frac{2}{2}=1$$

So the x-coordinate of the vertex is simply 1.

Alternatively, you could FOIL the equation and find $-\dfrac{b}{2a}$ in the new expression:

$$y=(x+2)(x-4)$$
$$y=x^2-4x+2x-8$$
$$y=x^2-2x-8$$

For this equation, $a=1$ and $b=-2$. So:

$$-\frac{b}{2a}\rightarrow-\frac{-2}{2(1)}=\frac{2}{2}=1$$

Therefore, this approach also results in 1 as the x-coordinate of the vertex.

5. Put the parabola with the equation $y+4=3(x-5)^2$ into vertex form, $y=a(x-h)^2+k$. Easily do so by subtracting 4 from both sides:

$$y+4=3(x-5)^2$$
$$y=3(x-5)^2-4$$

In parabolas of the form $y=a(x-h)^2+k$, (h,k) is the vertex. Therefore, in the equation $y=3(x-5)^2-4$, the vertex is $(5,-4)$.

6. For parabolas in the form $y=ax^2+bx+c$, the x-coordinate of the vertex is found using this formula: $x=-\dfrac{b}{2a}$. For the equation $y=3x^2-6x+5$, find the x-coordinate of the vertex:

$$x=-\frac{(-6)}{2(3)}=\frac{6}{6}=1$$

Then, solve for the y-coordinate of the vertex by plugging 1 into the equation for the parabola:

$$y=3x^2-6x+5$$
$$y=3(1)^2-6(1)+5$$
$$y=3-6+5$$
$$y=2$$

The coordinates of the vertex are $(1,2)$.

IMAGINARY NUMBERS

A complex number includes the square root of a negative number and is expressed using i, which is $\sqrt{-1}$. Some examples of imaginary numbers include:

$$\sqrt{-64} = 8i$$
$$\sqrt{-4} = 2i$$
$$7i + 4i = 11i$$
$$i \times i = -1$$
$$\frac{7i^3}{3i} = \frac{7}{3}i^2 = -\frac{7}{3}$$
$$3i^4 = 3 \times (i \times i) \times (i \times i)$$
$$= 3 \times (-1) \times (-1)$$
$$= 3$$

> Imaginary numbers have a recurring pattern when they are in exponential form:
> $$i^1 = i$$
> $$i^2 = -1$$
> $$i^3 = -i$$
> $$i^4 = 1$$
> $$i^5 = i$$
> $$i^6 = -1$$
> **and so on**

IMAGINARY NUMBERS DRILL

1. $3i + 8i = ?$

2. $(4i) \times (3i) = ?$

3. $\dfrac{-12i^2}{4i^4} = ?$

4. The *conjugate* of $a + bi$ is $a - bi$. Using the concept of conjugate, simplify the following expression so there are no imaginary numbers in the denominator: $\dfrac{12}{x+i}$.

Solutions

1. $3i + 8i = 11i$

2. $(4i) \times (3i) = 12i^2$
$$= 12(-1)$$
$$= -12$$

3. $\dfrac{-12i^2}{4i^4} = \dfrac{-12}{4} \times \dfrac{i^2}{i^4}$
$$= -3 \times i^{-2}$$
$$= \frac{-3}{i^2}$$
$$= \frac{-3}{-1}$$
$$= 3$$

4. To simplify this expression, multiply both the numerator and the denominator by the *conjugate* of the denominator, $x - i$. This will cause the imaginary numbers in the denominator to be canceled:

$$\frac{12}{x+i} \times \frac{x-i}{x-i} = \frac{12(x-i)}{x^2 - ix + ix - i^2}$$

$$= \frac{12x - 12i}{x^2 - i^2}$$

$$= \frac{12x - 12i}{x^2 + 1}$$

TRIGONOMETRY

The three sides in a right triangle (a triangle with a 90° angle) each have special names that are based on the angles.

- **Hypotenuse:** This side is always the longest and is across from the 90° angle.
- **Opposite:** This side depends on the location of the angle you are using. It is always *directly opposite* the angle.
- **Adjacent:** This side also changes depending on the location of the angle you are using. It is always *adjacent* (next) to the angle you are using.

People often confuse the adjacent with the hypotenuse. Just remember that the hypotenuse is always the longest side in a right triangle. All three sides in a right triangle are shown in Figure 12.

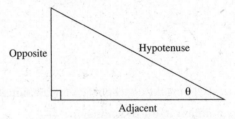

Figure 12

Use the acronym **SOH-CAH-TOA** to remember the key trigonometric ratios, as shown in Table 5.3.

Table 5.3. A Mnemonic to Remember Trigonometric Ratios

SOH	CAH	TOA
$\sin \theta = \dfrac{\text{Opposite}}{\text{Hypotenuse}}$	$\cos \theta = \dfrac{\text{Adjacent}}{\text{Hypotenuse}}$	$\tan \theta = \dfrac{\text{Opposite}}{\text{Adjacent}}$

Let's take a look at an example to see what the different trigonometric values are in the same right triangle.

➡ Example

A right triangle has side lengths of 3, 4, and 5. The angle θ is opposite from the side with length 3. What are the different trigonometric values for angle θ?

Solution

Draw the triangle to determine the different trigonometric values.

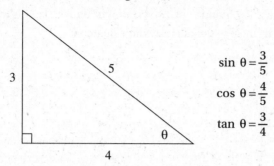

$$\sin\theta = \frac{3}{5}$$

$$\cos\theta = \frac{4}{5}$$

$$\tan\theta = \frac{3}{4}$$

To solve for an unknown angle in a right triangle, use an *inverse* of one of the trigonometry functions. In the triangle above, use an inverse function to solve for θ:

$$\sin\theta = \frac{3}{5}$$

$$\sin^{-1}(\sin\theta) = \sin^{-1}\left(\frac{3}{5}\right)$$

$$\theta \approx 36.87°$$

This could have been calculated using an inverse of the tangent or the cosine functions as well.

You can save time in your calculations if you recognize common special right triangles and Pythagorean triples:

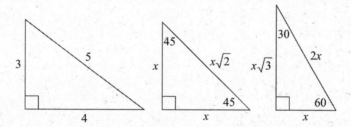

Some other common triples are **5-12-13** and **7-24-25**—you can plug these in to the Pythagorean theorem, and they will work as sides in a right triangle:

$$5^2 + 12^2 = 13^2 \text{ and } 7^2 + 24^2 = 25^2$$

TRIGONOMETRY DRILL

1.

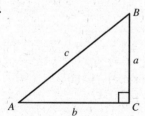

In this right triangle, what are the values of the following?

a. sin A

b. cos B

c. tan A

2. What is the length of the hypotenuse of a right triangle with two legs that each have a length of 4?

3. If $\sin X = \dfrac{1}{2}$ and angle X is between 0° and 90°, what is the degree measure of angle X?

4. If a right triangle has a hypotenuse of 13 and one of its legs is 5, what is the measure of the smallest angle in the triangle to the nearest whole degree?

Solutions

1.

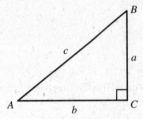

(a) $\sin A = \dfrac{\text{side opposite of angle A}}{\text{hypotenuse of the triangle}} = \dfrac{a}{c}$

(b) $\cos B = \dfrac{\text{side adjacent to angle B}}{\text{hypotenuse of the triangle}} = \dfrac{a}{c}$

(c) $\tan A = \dfrac{\text{side opposite of angle A}}{\text{side adjacent to angle A}} = \dfrac{a}{b}$

2. Use the Pythagorean theorem to solve, plugging in 4 for both a and b since the length of each leg is 4:

$$a^2 + b^2 = c^2$$
$$4^2 + 4^2 = c^2$$
$$16 + 16 = 32$$
$$c^2 = 32$$
$$c = \sqrt{32}$$
$$c = \sqrt{2 \times 16}$$
$$c = 4\sqrt{2}$$

Alternatively, you could recognize this is a multiple of a special right triangle: $x, x, \sqrt{2}x$. You could then just multiply 4 by $\sqrt{2}$ and get the same result.

3.
$$\sin X = \dfrac{1}{2}$$
$$\sin^{-1}(\sin X) = \sin^{-1}\left(\dfrac{1}{2}\right)$$
$$X = \sin^{-1}\left(\dfrac{1}{2}\right)$$

With the calculator set in degree mode (not radian mode), find that $\sin^{-1}\left(\dfrac{1}{2}\right) = 30°$.

4. If a right triangle has a hypotenuse of 13 and one of its legs as 5, the length of the other leg will be 12. You can find this by either realizing this is a 5-12-13 special right triangle or by calculating the unknown side by using the Pythagorean theorem:

$$a^2 + b^2 = c^2$$

$$5^2 + x^2 = 13^2$$
$$25 + x^2 = 169$$
$$x^2 = 169 - 25$$
$$x^2 = 144$$
$$\sqrt{x^2} = \sqrt{144}$$
$$x = 12$$

The triangle will look like this:

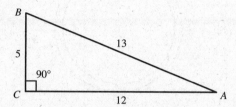

The smallest angle will be the one across from the side of length 5, angle A. So find the measure of angle A using trigonometry:

$$\sin A = \frac{5}{13}$$
$$\sin^{-1}(\sin A) = \sin^{-1}\left(\frac{5}{13}\right)$$
$$A \approx 22.62°$$

The answer is 23° since the question asks for the nearest whole degree. You could have calculated the value of this angle using tangent or cosine as well.

CIRCLES

Circumference and Area

You should know some important circle definitions.

- The *radius* goes from the center of the circle to the circle itself, as shown in Figure 13.

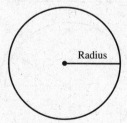

Figure 13

- The *diameter* goes from one point on a circle, through the center, to another point on the circle, as shown in Figure 14.

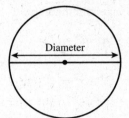

Diameter

Figure 14

- A circle has 360°, as shown in Figure 15.

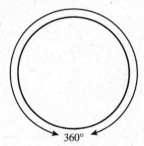

360°

Figure 15

The *area* of a circle is computed with the following formula, where *r* is the radius:

$$\text{Area} = \pi r^2$$

For example, the area of a circle that has a radius of 6 is $\pi 6^2 = 36\pi$.

The *circumference* of a circle is computed with the following formula, where *r* is the radius:

$$\text{Circumference} = 2\pi r$$

For example, the circumference of a circle that has a radius of 6 is $2\pi 6 = 12\pi$.

A common application of circle concepts on the PSAT is calculating the length of an arc or the area of a sector. The formula for *arc length* is the following:

$$\frac{\text{Part}}{\text{Whole}} = \frac{\text{Angle}}{360°} = \frac{\text{Length of Arc}}{\text{Circumference}}$$

➥ **Example** _____

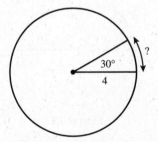

30°

4

?

If a circle has a radius of 4 with an arc of 30° as shown above, what is the length of the arc?

Solution

Use the part-whole ratio to solve this problem:

$$\frac{\text{Part}}{\text{Whole}} = \frac{30°}{360°} = \frac{1}{12} = \frac{\text{Length of Arc}}{\text{Circumference}} = \frac{x}{2\pi 4} = \frac{x}{8\pi}$$

Set up a proportion to solve for the arc length:

$$\frac{1}{12} = \frac{x}{8\pi}$$
$$8\pi = 12x$$
$$\frac{8\pi}{12} = x$$
$$\frac{2}{3}\pi = x$$

The formula for *sector area* is the following:

$$\frac{\text{Part}}{\text{Whole}} = \frac{\text{Angle}}{360°} = \frac{\text{Area of Sector}}{\text{Area of Circle}}$$

➡ Example

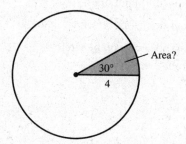

If a circle has a radius of 4 with a sector of 30° as shown above, what is the area of the sector?

Solution

Use the part-whole ratio to solve this problem:

$$\frac{\text{Part}}{\text{Whole}} = \frac{30°}{360°} = \frac{1}{12} = \frac{\text{Area of Sector}}{\text{Area of Circle}} = \frac{x}{\pi 4^2} = \frac{x}{16\pi}$$

Set up a proportion to solve for the sector area:

$$\frac{1}{12} = \frac{x}{16\pi} \rightarrow \frac{16\pi}{12} = x \rightarrow \frac{4}{3}\pi = x$$

Circle Formula

The following formula provides the graph of a circle in the *xy*-plane:

$$(x - h)^2 + (y - k)^2 = r^2$$
$$h = x\text{-coordinate of center}$$
$$k = y\text{-coordinate of center}$$
$$r = \text{radius}$$

➡ Example

What are the center and radius of the following equation? What is its graph?

$$(x - 3)^2 + (y - 2)^2 = 9$$

Solution

$(x-3)^2 + (y-2)^2 = 9$ has a center at $(3, 2)$ and a radius of 3. Its graph is shown:

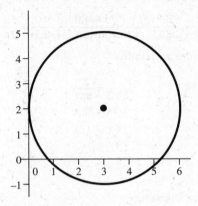

CIRCLES DRILL

1. What is the circumference of a circle with radius 5?

2. What is the area of a circle with a diameter of 6?

3. Consider a circle with the equation $(x-1)^2 + (y+4)^2 = 36$.

   a. What are the coordinates of the center of the circle?

   b. What is the radius of the circle?

4.

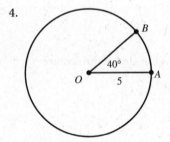

Consider a circle with a radius of 5 as shown above. Arc $\overarc{AB}$ in this circle has a measure of 40°.

a. What is the length of arc $\overarc{AB}$?

b. What is the area of the sector formed by arc $\overarc{AB}$?

Solutions

1. Use the formula for circumference, $2\pi r$, and plug in 5 for the radius:

$$C = 2\pi r$$
$$C = 2\pi 5$$
$$C = 10\pi$$

2. Use the area formula for a circle, πr^2, and plug in half the diameter, 3, for the radius:

$$A = \pi r^2$$
$$A = \pi(3)^2$$
$$A = 9\pi$$

3. a. From the formula for a circle, $(x-h)^2 + (y-k)^2 = r^2$, the center of the circle is point (h, k). So in the circle with the equation $(x-1)^2 + (y+4)^2 = 36$, the center is $(1, -4)$.

b. The radius of a circle of the form $(x-h)^2 + (y-k)^2 = r^2$ is r. So in the circle with the equation $(x-1)^2 + (y+4)^2 = 36$, take the square root of 36 to find the radius:

$$\sqrt{36} = 6$$

4. a. $\dfrac{\text{Part}}{\text{Whole}} = \dfrac{40°}{360°} = \dfrac{1}{9} = \dfrac{\text{Length of Arc}}{\text{Circumference}} = \dfrac{x}{2\pi5} = \dfrac{x}{10\pi}$

Set up a proportion to solve for the arc length:

$$\frac{1}{9} = \frac{x}{10\pi}$$
$$10\pi = 9x$$
$$\frac{10\pi}{9} = x$$

If you simplify without the π, the solution is approximately 3.49.

b. $\dfrac{\text{Part}}{\text{Whole}} = \dfrac{40°}{360°} = \dfrac{1}{9} = \dfrac{\text{Area of Sector}}{\text{Area of Circle}} = \dfrac{x}{\pi5^2} = \dfrac{x}{25\pi}$

Set up a proportion to solve for the sector area:

$$\frac{1}{9} = \frac{x}{25\pi}$$
$$25\pi = 9x$$
$$\frac{25\pi}{9} = x$$

If you simplify without the π, the solution is approximately 8.73.

The PSAT will provide you with the following facts and formulas. Memorizing these facts will save you time and help you think about what formula may be needed for a particular problem. However, if you do forget a formula, you can always go to the beginning of the Math section to see it.

Radius of a circle $= r$
Area of a circle $= \pi r^2$
Circumference of a circle $= 2\pi r$

Area of a rectangle $=$ **length** $\times$ **width** $= lw$

Area of a triangle $= \frac{1}{2} \times$ **base** $\times$ **height** $= \frac{1}{2} bh$

Pythagorean theorem: $a^2 + b^2 = c^2$

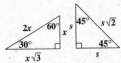

Special right triangles: 30-60-90 and 45-45-90

Volume of a box $=$ **length** $\times$ **width** $\times$ **height** $= lwh$

Volume of a cylinder $= \pi r^2 h$

Volume of a sphere $= \frac{4}{3} \pi r^3$

Volume of a cone $= \frac{1}{3} \pi r^2 h$

Volume of a pyramid $=$
$\frac{1}{3} \times$ **length** $\times$ **width** $\times$ **height** $= \frac{1}{3} lwh$

KEY FACTS:

- A circle has 360 degrees.
- There are 2π radians in a circle.
- There are 180 degrees in a triangle.

Even though the PSAT provides you with some formulas, it doesn't provide all the ones you will need. Complete this quiz to determine which concepts you may still need to memorize.

1. To find the perimeter P of a rectangle with length L and width W, what is the correct formula?

    (A) $P = L \times W$ OR   (B) $P = 2L + 2W$

2. Which of these statements is true?

    (A) An isosceles triangle is always equilateral.   OR   (B) An equilateral triangle is always isosceles.

3.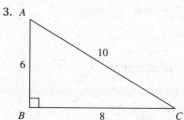

    What is the value of the sine of angle C in the triangle above?

    (A) $\dfrac{3}{5}$ OR   (B) $\dfrac{4}{5}$

4. What is the y-intercept and slope of the line with the equation $y = 4x + 3$?

    (A) y-intercept: 4 and slope: 3   OR   (B) y-intercept: 3 and slope: 4

5. What is an expression to calculate the slope between the points (A, B) and (C, D)?

    (A) $\dfrac{B-D}{A-C}$ OR   (B) $\dfrac{A-C}{B-D}$

6. A line that is parallel to the line $y = 5x - 3$ would have what slope?

    (A) 5   OR   (B) –3

7. What is the slope of a line perpendicular to the line with the equation $y = -\dfrac{1}{5}x - 7$?

    (A) –5   OR   (B) 5

8. What is another way of writing $(a + b)(a - b)$?

    (A) $a^2 - b^2$ OR   (B) $a^2 + b^2$

9. What does $(4x - 3)^2$ equal?

    (A) $16x^2 - 24x + 9$ OR   (B) $16x^2 + 9$

10. Which of these expresses an equivalent relationship?

    (A) $|-3| = -|3|$ OR   (B) $|3| = |-3|$

11. Which of these expresses that x is 40% of y?

    (A) $x = 0.4y$ OR   (B) $y = 0.4x$

12.

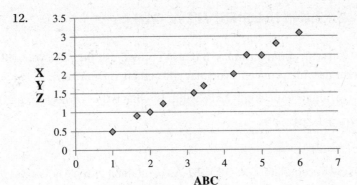

ABC

What is the best approximation of the slope of a best-fit line for the graph above?

(A) $\frac{1}{2}$ OR   (B) 2

13. How should you calculate the arithmetic mean of this set of numbers?

$$\{2, 3, 5, 7, 11\}$$

(A) Simply choose the middle value, 5   OR   (B) $\frac{2+3+5+7+11}{5}$

14. Which is larger for this set of numbers, the mode or the range?
$$\{1, 1, 4, 5, 12, 71\}$$

(A) Mode   OR   (B) Range

15. What is the probability that a two-sided coin will turn up heads when flipped?

(A) 0.5   OR   (B) 2

16. Which of these expressions states that x is less than or equal to 3?

(A) $x < 3$ OR   (B) $x \leq 3$

17. If $f(x) = 2x$ and $g(x) = x + 3$, what is the value of $f(g(2))$?

(A) 10   OR   (B) 13

18. Which of these is the correct quadratic formula for equations in the form $ax^2 + bx + c = 0$?

(A) $x = \dfrac{-b \pm \sqrt{b^2 - 4ac}}{2a}$ OR   (B) $x = \dfrac{b \pm \sqrt{b^2 + 4ac}}{a}$

19. Which of these systems of equations has infinitely many solutions?

(A) $y = 2x$ OR   (B) $y = 2x + 1$
    $y = x + 5$ $3y = 6x + 3$

20. The function $f(x) = \dfrac{x^2 + 5}{x - 3}$ is undefined when x equals what number?

(A) $x = 3$ OR   (B) $x = \sqrt{5}$

21. $\dfrac{2}{3} + \dfrac{1}{4} = ?$

(A) $\dfrac{11}{12}$ OR   (B) $\dfrac{3}{7}$

22. $\dfrac{x+3}{3} = ?$

(A) x OR   (B) $\dfrac{x}{3} + 1$

23. $x^3 x^4 = ?$

(A) x^7　OR　(B) x^{12}

24. $\left(x^2\right)^5 = ?$

(A) x^7　OR　(B) x^{10}

25. If $x > 0$, $\dfrac{\sqrt[3]{x^2}}{\sqrt[6]{x}} = ?$

(A) $\sqrt[3]{x}$　OR　(B) $\sqrt{x}$

26. What is 40% of 80?

(A) 32　OR　(B) 48

27. If someone travels 200 miles in 4 hours, what is the person's speed in miles per hour?

(A) 40 mph　OR　(B) 50 mph

28. What are the zeros of the function $y = (x+2)(x-4)$?

(A) −2 and 4　OR　(B) 2 and −4

29. What is the vertex of a parabola with the equation $y = 2(x-4)^2 - 5$?

(A) (4, −5)　OR　(B) (2, 4)

30. What is the x-coordinate of the vertex of a parabola with the equation $y = 2x^2 + 3x - 6$?

(A) $\dfrac{1}{3}$　OR　(B) $-\dfrac{3}{4}$

Answer Explanations

Solutions	Concept Review
1. **(B)** $P = 2L + 2W$ Perimeter is the sum of the lengths of the sides in the figure. As you can see in the figure below, the rectangle has two sides of width W and two sides of length L. The sum of all these sides is $L + L + W + W = 2L + 2W$. 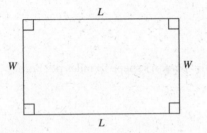	**Rectangle Area = Length × Width** and **Rectangle Perimeter =** **(2 × Length) + (2 × Width)**
2. **(B)** An equilateral triangle is always isosceles. An isosceles triangle needs to have only *two* sides and angles equivalent. In contrast, an equilateral triangle must have *all three sides and angles equivalent*. (An isosceles triangle can also have three angles and sides equivalent, but it is not a necessary condition to be isosceles.) So if a triangle is equilateral, it will definitely be isosceles as well. (This is similar to stating that a square is always a rectangle.)	**Isosceles Triangle:** At least 2 equal sides; at least 2 equal angles. 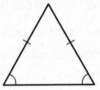 **Equilateral Triangle:** 3 equal sides; 3 equal angles (all 60°). 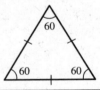
3. **(A)** $\dfrac{3}{5}$ Here is a drawing of the sides of the triangle relative to angle C: 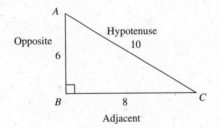	$\sin \theta = \dfrac{\text{Opposite}}{\text{Hypotenuse}}$ $\cos \theta = \dfrac{\text{Adjacent}}{\text{Hypotenuse}}$ $\tan \theta = \dfrac{\text{Opposite}}{\text{Adjacent}}$ **Pythagorean Theorem:** $$a^2 + b^2 = c^2$$

Calculate the sine of angle C by taking the length of the opposite side (length 6) and dividing it by the length of the hypotenuse (length 10):

$$\frac{6}{10} = \frac{3}{5}$$

Special Right Triangles and Pythagorean Triples:

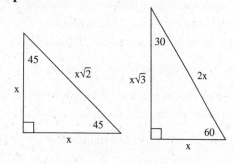

3-4-5   5-12-13   7-24-25

4. **(B)** y-intercept: 3 and slope: 4

The equation is in slope-intercept form. So the slope of the line is 4 and its y-intercept is 3. Here is a drawing of the line:

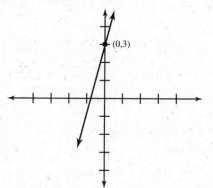

Slope-Intercept Form of a Line:

$y = mx + b$

$m = $ slope $b = y$-intercept

5. **(A)** $\dfrac{B-D}{A-C}$

Slope is the rise over the run. For the given two points, take the difference between the y-coordinates and divide it by the difference between the x-coordinates. Be careful to maintain the same order. If you subtract the y-coordinate of point 1 from the y-coordinate of point 2, you must subtract the x-coordinate of point 1 from the x-coordinate of point 2.

For a line with the points (x_1, y_1) and (x_2, y_2):

Slope $= \dfrac{y_2 - y_1}{x_2 - x_1}$

6. **(A)** 5

Parallel lines never intersect since they run parallel to one another. They therefore have identical slopes. Since this line is in slope-intercept form, we can tell that the slope is 5. So any line parallel to it will also have a slope of 5.

Parallel Lines: Slopes are the same.

7. (B) 5

Perpendicular lines intersect at a 90-degree angle and have slopes that are negative reciprocals of each other. The slope of the line in the equation is $-\frac{1}{5}$. To find the negative reciprocal, first find the reciprocal and then multiply that result by -1. To find the reciprocal of $-\frac{1}{5}$, determine what number you would multiply $-\frac{1}{5}$ by to get 1.

$$-\frac{1}{5} \times (-5) = 1$$

So the reciprocal is -5. To get the negative reciprocal, multiply this by -1, giving $(-1)(-5) = 5$. Thus, the slope of the line perpendicular to the given line is 5.

A shortcut to finding the slope of a line perpendicular to another is simply to invert the fraction and flip the sign.

Perpendicular Lines: Slopes are *negative reciprocals of each other* (e.g., 3 and $-\frac{1}{3}$).

---

8. (A) $a^2 - b^2$

If you don't remember this pattern, you can use FOIL (first, outer, inner, last) with this expression:

$(a+b)(a-b) \rightarrow$
$a^2 - ab + ab - b^2 \rightarrow$
$a^2 - b^2$

Common Factoring Patterns:

$(a+b)(a+b) = a^2 + 2ab + b^2$
Example:
$(x+4)(x+4) = x^2 + 8x + 16$

$(a+b)(a-b) = a^2 - b^2$
Example:
$(m+2)(m-2) = m^2 - 4$

---

9. (A) $16x^2 - 24x + 9$

FOIL the expression:

$(4x-3)^2 \rightarrow$
$(4x-3)(4x-3) \rightarrow$
$16x^2 - 12x - 12x + 9 \rightarrow$
$16x^2 - 24x + 9$

$(a-b)(a-b) = a^2 - 2ab + b^2$
Example:
$(5-y)(5-y) = 25 - 10y + y^2$

Sum of Cubes
$(a+b)(a^2 - ab + b^2) = a^3 + b^3$
Example:
$(2+x)(4 - 2x + x^2) = 8 + x^3$

Difference of Cubes
$(a-b)(a^2 + ab + b^2) = a^3 - b^3$
Example:
$(y-4)(y^2 + 4y + 16) = y^3 - 4^3 = y^3 - 64$

10. **(B)** $\lvert 3\rvert = \lvert -3\rvert$ Treat the absolute value sign like parentheses with the order of operations. Just like parentheses come first in the order of operations, you should calculate the absolute value expressions first before dealing with the negatives outside the absolute values. In choice (A), the left-hand side equals 3 since –3 is 3 units away from 0. However, on the right-hand side, the negative sign on the outside of the absolute value makes the expression negative: $$-\lvert 3\rvert = -3$$	**Absolute Value:** Distance along the number line from zero. Examples: $\lvert 8\rvert = 8$ and $\lvert -8\rvert = 8$ Remark: Taking the absolute value of something should always give a nonnegative result since absolute value represents a distance.
11. **(A)** $x = 0.4y$ To find the percent, turn 40% into a fraction by dividing 40 by 100: $$\frac{40}{100} = 0.4$$ Write an equation to show that x equals 40% of y: $$x = 0.4y$$	**General Percent Formula:** $$\frac{\text{Part}}{\text{Whole}} \times 100 = \text{Percent}$$
12. **(A)** $\frac{1}{2}$ Estimate the coordinates of a couple of points in the graph. Then calculate the slope. We can use (0, 0) and (6, 3). Plug these into the slope formula to solve: $$\frac{y_2 - y_1}{x_2 - x_1} = \frac{3-0}{6-0} = \frac{3}{6} = \frac{1}{2}$$	**Best-Fit Lines:** Look for a general trend in the data (if it exists), and draw a line to model the trend.
13. **(B)** $\dfrac{2+3+5+7+11}{5}$ The mean is the simple average. Add the individual values (2 + 3 + 5 + 7 + 11), and divide by the total number of values (5).	$$\text{Mean} = \frac{\text{Sum of Items}}{\text{Number of Items}}$$ **Median:** The middle term of a set of numbers when lined up small to large. Note that when the number of terms is even and the two terms in the middle are not equal, take the mean of the two middle terms to find the median. **Mode:** The most frequent term in a set of numbers. Note that if in a set of numbers, each number appears only once, there is no mode. If a set of numbers has 2 or more numbers tied for appearing the most times, the set has multiple modes.

14. **(B)** Range The mode is 1 for this set of numbers since 1 appears more frequently than any other number. The range is $71 - 1 = 70$ since that is the difference between the smallest and largest terms in the set. Therefore, the range is greater than the mode.	**Range:** The difference between the smallest and largest values in a set of data.
15. **(A)** 0.5 When the coin is flipped, it can land on either heads or tails. So there is a 1 out of 2 chance it will land on heads. In other words, 1 outcome results in success (heads) out of 2 possible outcomes (heads or tails). So the probability is $\frac{1}{2} = 0.5$.	**Probability:** The likelihood that a given event will happen, expressed as a fraction or decimal between 0 and 1 inclusive. Note that a probability of 0 means an event has no chance of occurring. A probability of 0.5 means there is a 50% chance it will occur. A probability of 1 means the event is certain to occur. In general, we can find the probability by taking the number of successes divided by the number of possible outcomes.
16. **(B)** $x \le 3$ The line underneath the $>$ or $<$ sign signifies equivalence.	$<$ means less than. $>$ means greater than. $\le$ means less than or equal to. $\ge$ means greater than or equal to.
17. **(A)** 10 First, calculate the value of $g(2)$: $$g(x) = x + 3$$ $$g(2) = 2 + 3 = 5$$ Then plug 5 into $f(x)$: $$f(x) = 2x$$ $$f(5) = 2 \times 5 = 10$$	**Composite Functions:** Calculate the value of the *inside* function first. Then calculate the value of the *outside* function, just as in the example problem.
18. **(A)** $x = \dfrac{-b \pm \sqrt{b^2 - 4ac}}{2a}$ This is a formula you absolutely must memorize.	**Quadratic Formula:** $x = \dfrac{-b \pm \sqrt{b^2 - 4ac}}{2a}$ An equation with the variable x and constants a, b, and c written in the form $ax^2 + bx + c = 0$ can be solved with the quadratic formula.

19. (B) $y = 2x + 1$
$\qquad 3y = 6x + 3$

These two equations have infinitely many solutions because the second equation is 3 times the first equation, making them different expressions of the same equation. Thus, any solution to one equation is a solution to the other as well. Since there are infinitely many solutions to the equations (both equations are linear and a line has infinitely many points), the system itself must have infinitely many solutions.

A system of equations will have **infinite solutions** if the equations are simple multiples of each other. The graphs of the equations are exactly the same.

A system of equations will have **no solutions** if no points are solutions to all equations in the system. Graphically, the graphs of the equations never intersect. In other words, the graphs are parallel.

20. (A) $x = 3$

If $x = 3$, the denominator (bottom) of the equation equals zero since $3 - 3 = 0$. If you divide a number by zero, the result is undefined. You cannot divide a number into zero parts.

A function is **undefined** at a point if inputting that value into the function produces an undefined number, such as $\dfrac{5}{0}$.

21. (A) $\dfrac{11}{12}$

$$\frac{2}{3} + \frac{1}{4} \rightarrow \frac{8}{12} + \frac{3}{12} \rightarrow \frac{11}{12}$$

Add fractions by (1) finding the least common denominator, (2) changing each fraction to have the same denominator, and (3) adding the numerators together.

22. (B) $\dfrac{x}{3} + 1$

$$\frac{x+3}{3} = \frac{x}{3} + \frac{3}{3} = \frac{x}{3} + 1$$

In general,

$$\frac{xy}{x} = \frac{\cancel{x}y}{\cancel{x}} = y \text{ and}$$

$$\frac{x+y}{y} = \frac{x}{y} + \frac{y}{y} = \frac{x}{y} + 1$$

23. (A) x^7

$$x^3 x^4 = x^{3+4} = x^7$$

24. (B) x^{10}

$$(x^2)^5 = x^{2 \times 5} = x^{10}$$

25. (B) $\sqrt{x}$

For $x > 0$,

$$\frac{\sqrt[3]{x^2}}{\sqrt[6]{x}} = \frac{x^{\frac{2}{3}}}{x^{\frac{1}{6}}} = x^{\frac{2}{3} - \frac{1}{6}} = x^{\frac{4}{6} - \frac{1}{6}} = x^{\frac{3}{6}} = x^{\frac{1}{2}} = \sqrt{x}$$

Exponent Rules:

$$a^x a^y = a^{x+y}$$

$$\frac{a^x}{a^y} = a^{x-y}$$

$$(a^x)^y = a^{xy}$$

$$a^{-x} = \frac{1}{a^x}$$

$$a^{\frac{x}{y}} = \sqrt[y]{a^x}$$

26. **(A)** 32 $$0.40 \times 80 = 32$$	$$\frac{\text{Part}}{\text{Whole}} \times 100 = \text{Percent}$$ Move the decimal point over two spots to calculate a percentage. $$40\% = 0.40$$
27. **(B)** 50 mph $$\frac{200 \text{ miles}}{4 \text{ hours}} = 50 \text{ mph}$$	Distance = Rate × Time
28. **(A)** −2 and 4 For $y = (x+2)(x-4)$, y will be zero when x equals −2 and 4.	**Zeros:** The root or zero of a function is the value for which the function has a value of zero. In other words, it is where the function intersects the x-axis.
29. **(A)** $(4, -5)$ In the function $y = 2(x-4)^2 - 5$, 4 is the h and −5 is the k.	The vertex form of a parabola is $y = a(x-h)^2 + k$ and the vertex (the bottom point of the U-shape) has the coordinates (h, k).
30. **(B)** $-\dfrac{3}{4}$ For $y = 2x^2 + 3x - 6$, the a is 2 and the b is 3: $$-\frac{b}{2a} = -\frac{3}{2 \cdot 2} = -\frac{3}{4}$$	When a parabola is written in the form $y = ax^2 + bx + c$, the x-coordinate of the parabola's vertex is $x = -\dfrac{b}{2a}$.

FURTHER PREPARATION

- Practice with other materials if needed. The PSAT Math Sections are very similar to the SAT Math Sections. You can use *Barron's SAT* for additional practice. Also, you can find further practice at *Khanacademy.org*, the official College Board practice website.
- Take the most rigorous math courses offered by your school.
- Practice all of the word problems and algebra problems you can find—these are the most prevalent types of problems you will find on the test.

Math Strategies, Tactics, and Problem Solving

6

HOW IS THE PSAT MATH TEST DESIGNED?

- Third and fourth sections of the test; first part no calculator, second part with calculator
- No-calculator Section:

  - 25 minutes
  - 17 questions: 13 multiple choice, 4 grid-in

- Calculator Section:

  - 45 minutes
  - 31 questions: 27 multiple choice, 4 grid-in

- Typical breakdown of all the test questions from both sections combined:

  - Heart of Algebra (primarily linear equations and systems): 16 questions
  - Problem Solving and Data Analysis (primarily demonstrating literacy with data and real-world applications): 16 questions
  - Passport to Advanced Math (primarily more complicated equations): 14 questions
  - Additional Topics in Math (geometry, trigonometry, and other advanced math): 2 questions

- The questions generally become more difficult as you go. The typical organization of difficulty is as follows:

  - No-calculator Section—Multiple-choice questions 1–13 progress from easy to hard. Grid-in questions 14–17 progress from easy to hard.
  - Calculator Section—Multiple-choice questions 1–27 progress from easy to hard. Grid-in questions 28–31 progress from easy to hard.

HOW CAN I PREPARE FOR AND BE SUCCESSFUL ON THE PSAT MATH TEST?

- Brush up on your content knowledge with the "Math Review" chapter.
- Review the timing strategies, question strategies, and math tactics in this chapter.
- Practice PSAT-style math questions in this chapter, targeting the question types that are most challenging to you. They are organized as follows:

  - Heart of Algebra
  - Problem Solving and Data Analysis
  - Passport to Advanced Math
  - Additional Topics in Math

- Use the "Troubleshooting" guide at the end of this chapter to help you work through strategic issues you have encountered in the past or are finding as you work through problems.

PSAT MATH TIMING STRATEGIES

1. Take About 1.5 Minutes per Question, Adjusting Based on Where You Are in the Test.

The questions follow the progression shown in the table below in difficulty on both the calculator and non-calculator Math sections.

Multiple-Choice Questions	Progress from **easy** to **difficult**
Grid-In Questions	Progress from **easy** to **difficult**

On the earlier multiple-choice and grid-in questions, take a little *less* than 1.5 minutes per question. On the later multiple-choice and grid-in questions, take a little *more* than 1.5 minutes per question.

If you are having trouble finishing the Math Test, on which questions would it make sense to guess? In general, if you are having difficulty finishing the Math Test, guess on the last couple of multiple-choice and the last couple of grid-in questions—these are usually the toughest ones. Every question is worth the same point value, and there is no penalty for guessing; so be sure to try the easy and medium questions.

2. Don't Rush Through the PSAT Math.

Compared to other major standardized tests, like the ACT, the PSAT will be easier to finish in the given time. Practice your pacing on the practice Math Tests in this book, and go into the test ready to be thorough rather than hasty. On school math tests if you finish early, you can typically take the remainder of the class period to do something else. On the PSAT, however, you won't be able to do anything but the test if you finish early—you might as well use all the time available. Rushing to the end may feel good and make you look smart to your fellow test takers, who may glance at you resting on your desk and assume you are a math genius. However, there is no prize for finishing early. There is a prize—thousands of dollars in scholarship money—if you answer the questions correctly. Also, even if you are a fast reader, realize that the dense, technical prose of PSAT math questions will require more time and focus than other sorts of reading material.

3. Don't Overthink Early Questions, and Don't Underthink Later Questions.

Solutions to earlier questions in the PSAT Math Test will be more straightforward, while solutions to later multiple-choice and grid-in questions will involve more critical thinking.

4. Do the Questions One Time Well, Instead of Double-checking.

The PSAT Math generally has far more lengthy word problems than you may be accustomed to seeing on typical school math tests, making it more difficult to correct careless reading errors. Instead of rushing through the questions and spending time second-guessing and double-checking your work, focus on doing the questions *one time well*. If you misread a PSAT Math question because you are going too quickly and then come back and read it over again quickly to double-check, it is far less likely that you will answer the question correctly than if you had simply taken the time to get it right the first time. If you are very thorough and *still* finish with some time remaining, go ahead and double-check. Go back to problems that are particularly susceptible to careless errors, like ones with negative numbers, fractions, and long word problems. Also, as you go through the test the first time, you can circle any questions you would like to come back to and double-check if time permits.

5. Come Back to Questions You Don't Understand.

Don't underestimate the power of your subconscious mind to work through something while your conscious mind is focused on a different problem. If you have given a problem a decent attempt to no avail, circle the question and come back. While you are working on other problems, your subconscious mind will be unlocking possible approaches to the problem you left behind. By coming back to the problem later and with fresh eyes, it may seem much easier than it did before. Since the math problems are of gradually increasing difficulty, you will likely want to return to the earlier problems rather than the later ones in the test if you want to attempt them again. Whatever you do, don't allow yourself to become bogged down on a single problem—you can still earn a top score while missing questions.

6. Check Your Pace at Reasonable Intervals.

Each time you turn the page on the PSAT Math is typically a good time to see if you are on track with your pacing. If you are going significantly faster than the 1.5 minutes per question, you may want to slow down. If you are going slower than 1.5 minutes per question, speed things up or consider guessing on the harder questions. If you never check your pacing, you may finish way ahead or way behind. If you check the pace too frequently, you will spend too much time looking at your watch instead of solving problems.

7. Since the PSAT Is Curved, Do Your Best to Stay Levelheaded.

As much as we can try to predict the precise difficulty of the test, even the College Board doesn't always know ahead of time exactly how difficult the test is—that is why the College Board will curve the exam. So no matter if the PSAT seems more challenging or less challenging than you anticipated, do your best to keep a level head and not to get too confident or too worried. Everyone taking the PSAT will be in the same situation, and the curve will reflect the relative difficulty of the test that particular day. As a point of reference, in 2018, a math score of 650 out of 760 would still be in the 95th percentile for a nationally representative sample; a math score of 480 out of 760 was approximately average for all test takers nationwide.*

PSAT MATH QUESTION STRATEGIES

1. Focus on What the Question Is Asking.

Try to underline and circle key words in the question as you go to ensure you don't miss anything important. (If you are taking a computer version of the test, while you cannot write on the screen, you can make notations on your scrap paper to paraphrase the question.) Rather than going on autopilot and quickly jumping into solving the question, really pay attention to what the question is asking you to do. Unless you are mindful about focusing on what the questions are asking, you will get tunnel vision and tune out vital information in the questions.

2. Stay in the Moment—Don't Skip Ahead to the Next Step.

When solving a problem, a desire to finish quickly will make you jump ahead to the next step instead of working through the step you are on. Fortunately, the PSAT Math problems generally *do not require many steps to solve them.* Many of the wrong answers, however, will be what many students would calculate if they skipped or rushed through a step. Channel all of your intellectual energy into rigorously solving the problem, one step at a time.

* *https://collegereadiness.collegeboard.org/pdf/psat-nmsqt-understanding-scores.pdf*

3. Don't Overthink the Questions.

Don't allow yourself to over-complicate the questions at the beginning of the test, as they will be more straightforward and simple to solve than the later questions. The PSAT questions may all be solved in fairly straightforward ways once you get past the surface.

- Drawings and figures are always drawn to scale.
- If a question involves factoring, it will typically use a common factoring pattern, e.g., $(x+1)(x-1) = x^2 - 1$.
- If a question involves right triangles, it will often use a special right triangle, e.g., $45° - 45° - 90°$ or 3-4-5.
- If a question asks you to calculate the value of an expression, like x^3 or $x-9$, look for ways that the expression can be simplified. For example, if you are asked to solve for x^4 in the equation $x^8 = 49$, simply take the square root of both sides to reach your answer: $x^8 = 49 \rightarrow \sqrt{x^8} = \sqrt{49} \rightarrow x^4 = 7$. This is much easier than solving for just the variable x and having to plug that value back in to x^4.
- Since the PSAT mainly tests algebra, many advanced students who are taking calculus or precalculus may overthink relatively easy questions. You will not need higher-order math to solve the questions on the PSAT—you will just need a firm grounding in the basics. If you have not studied algebra and geometry for a while, be sure to read the "Math Review" chapter in this book thoroughly —it should not take you very long to get back up to speed.

4. Don't Overuse Your Calculator.

The PSAT Math Test has a whole section in which you are not able to use your calculator. Even on the section that does allow calculator use, though, don't let your calculator be a crutch. PSAT Math problems will not require elaborate calculations, and having a bunch of sophisticated programs on your calculator won't make a difference. In fact, many of the answers to the problems keep radicals and fractions in their non-decimal form, so calculating too far ahead could set you behind. Use the calculator when necessary, but rely on your critical thinking first and your calculator second.

5. Mistakes Can Lead to Success.

If the PSAT problems involved 20–30 steps of calculations, a simple mistake would jeopardize your entire problem-solving process and would waste valuable time. In actuality, the PSAT Math problems do not require great numbers of steps, so a small mistake will not be catastrophic. As long as you find your mistakes quickly and are able to restart your thought process on a problem quickly, you will be fine.

6. Give the Questions the Benefit of the Doubt.

The College Board has spent a couple of years developing the materials you will see on the PSAT, and it has extensively field-tested possible questions on students to ensure the fairness and accuracy of those questions. As a result, when you encounter a tough problem on the PSAT Math, do not immediately assume that it is an unfair or a stupid question. Instead, know that quite a bit of work and care went into crafting the questions, and try to reexamine your understanding of the question.

7. It's Fine If You Cannot Precisely Justify Your Answers.

You simply need to answer the question correctly—you do not need to explain yourself. There are many ways to solve the PSAT Math problems; as long as you have a method that arrives at the correct answer, you are doing things perfectly. Let go of the little voice in your head that tells you that if you can't explain yourself, you must not truly understand it. Trust your intuition.

MATH TACTICS WITH EXAMPLES

Tactic 1: Translate Word Problems into Algebraic Expressions.

A major difference between the PSAT and school tests is the widespread use of word problems on the PSAT. Many PSAT problems will require you to translate several sentences into an algebraic expression. Table 6.1 lists some of the key phrases that may be used in place of mathematical notations.

Table 6.1. Key Phrases and Mathematical Operators

Wording Examples	Translation
Is, are, was, were, will be, results in, gives, yields, equals	$=$
Sum, increased by, more than, together, combined, total(s), added to, older than, farther than	$+$
Difference, decreased by, less than, fewer than, minus, younger than, shorter than	$-$
Multiplied by, times, of, product of, twice	$\times$
Divided by, per, out of, ratio of, half of, one third of, split	$\div$ or $\dfrac{x}{y}$

Here is an example of a typical PSAT word problem that is much easier to solve by translating the wording into algebra.

➡ Example_____

Katie rents an apartment in the spring and will rent it for the rest of the calendar year. To rent it, she must pay a $500 security deposit and a monthly rent of $750. In addition, she must pay monthly utilities of $40 for water and $50 for electricity. What expression gives the total amount of money Katie will spend if she rents the apartment for x months that year?

(A) $840 + 500x$

(B) $500 + 840x$

(C) $500x$

(D) $750x + 500$

Solution

As you read this problem, you can underline key words and write out important information. You should use abbreviations for the sake of time. For instructional purposes, though, everything is written out here using complete words. For example:

$$\$500 = \text{security deposit}$$
$$\$750 = \text{monthly rent}$$
$$\$40 + \$50 = \$90 \text{ for total monthly utilities}$$

To rent the apartment for x months, Katie will need to pay the $500 security deposit one time. Then, she will need to pay $750 in rent each month plus $90 in utilities each month for a total of $840 each month.

So the correct answer is choice (B) because there is a flat fee of $500 plus the $840 per month, varying with how many months she rents. Writing this out, rather than doing it in your head, makes this a much easier problem to solve. If you happen to be taking a digital version of the test, you will have scrap paper provided that you can use.

Tactic 2: Minimize Careless Errors by Writing Out Your Work.

Students often dismiss careless errors as ones that should not concern them in their preparation. However, if you make careless mistakes in your practice, you will likely make them on the real PSAT. Although it may be nice to focus your preparation on learning to solve the most challenging questions elegantly, realize that a couple of careless errors on easier problems may be more detrimental than having conceptual difficulties on a challenging question.

Here is a problem where careless errors can be avoided with careful writing.

➡ **Example**

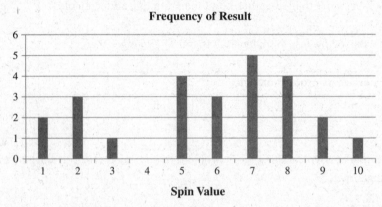

Frequency of Result

Spin Value

A board game has a circular wheel evenly divided into ten segments, each with a numerical value between 1 and 10. For the spins recorded in the above graph, what is the mean value of a spin, rounded to the nearest hundredth?

*Grid-In Question: Write Your Answer*_____

Solution

If you try to do this in your head, you will likely make a careless mistake. You need to use this formula:

$$\text{Mean} = \frac{\text{Sum of Values}}{\text{Total Number of Values}}$$

The sum of all of the responses is:

$$2(1) + 3(2) + 1(3) + 0(4) + 4(5) + 3(6) + 5(7) + 4(8) + 2(9) + 1(10) = 144$$

The total number of responses is:

$$2 + 3 + 1 + 0 + 4 + 3 + 5 + 4 + 2 + 1 = 25$$

Calculate the mean:

$$144 \div 25 = 5.76$$

Tactic 3: Patiently Visualize What the Parts of an Algebraic Expression Signify.

The PSAT will have questions that require you to interpret algebraic expressions. For many questions, it is helpful to look at the answer choices before solving to see where the question is headed. On questions like these, it is advisable to "look before you leap." The incorrect answers here will likely be very persuasive. So use writing to visualize what the parts of the algebraic expression signify before you evaluate the answer choices. Although this takes more time up front, it will probably save you time in the long run. Here is an example of the kind of problem that applies to this approach.

➡ **Example** _____

A book warehouse has an inventory of books, I, that is modeled by the equation $I = 42{,}500 - 600w$, where w represents the number of weeks that have gone by after the beginning of the year. What do the numbers 42,500 and 600 represent in the equation?

- (A) The average book inventory throughout the year is 42,500. The number of books at the end of the year is 600.
- (B) The book inventory in the warehouse at the end of the year is 42,500. The number of weeks that it takes for the book inventory to be gone is 600.
- (C) The initial monetary investment in the book warehouse is 42,500. The weekly revenue from outside book sales is 600.
- (D) The warehouse book inventory at the beginning of the year is 42,500. The number of books removed from the warehouse each week is 600.

Solution

Start by rewriting the provided equation:

$$I = 42{,}500 - 600w$$

Next, try plugging in different values for w to see how these impact the inventory, I.

When 0 weeks have gone by, w is 0. So the inventory is 42,500. This means that at the beginning of the year, the inventory is 42,500.

At the beginning of week 1, the initial inventory is still 42,500. At the end of week 1, though, 600 books have been subtracted from the inventory. After 2 weeks go by, the original inventory goes down by 1,200. So a pattern emerges—the 600 in the equation represents the amount by which the book inventory decreases each week. The correct answer is choice (D).

If you just jumped into the answer choices without thinking this question through and making some notes, it would have been quite easy to become trapped by a persuasive answer and overthink the question.

Tactic 4: Plug in the Answer Choices.

One of the most tried-and-true PSAT Math strategies is to plug the answers into an equation, starting with a middle value, like choice (B) or choice (C). Why? That way you will need to try only a maximum of two or three choices instead of potentially all four. The choices are almost certainly going to be in numerical order. So if the first value you choose is too large, you will know which choices to try next. Here is an example of where this technique can save you time.

What is a possible value of x that satisfies the equation below?

$$-(x-3)^2 = -25$$

(A) 6
(B) 8
(C) 10
(D) 12

Solution

If you write all of this, it will make for a relatively long, messy calculation. If you work backward from the choices, you will arrive at the answer with ease. Start with choice (C), where $x = 10$, because it is a middle value among your choices:

$$-(10-3)^2 = -25$$
$$-49 \neq -25$$

So choice (C) doesn't work. If you try a larger value, like 12, the difference between the answers will be even larger. So try choice (B) next, where $x = 8$:

$$-(8-3)^2 = -25$$
$$-(5)^2 = -25$$

Since $x = 8$ is true, the correct answer is choice (B). It is unlikely that some of the later, more challenging questions will permit this sort of backsolving. However, this method can save you time on earlier questions, giving you more time to work through the difficult questions.

Tactic 5: Plug in Numbers to Solve Certain Types of Problems More Easily.

A common situation where plugging in numbers can be helpful is when the problem provides a variable within a possible range. In this case, you can pick a number within the given range and plug it in to see the value of the expression. Here is an example.

➥ **Example**_____

Assuming that x is not equal to zero, what is the value of the following expression?

$$\frac{1}{4}\left(\frac{(2x)^3}{(3x)^3}\right)$$

Grid-In Question: Write Your Answer_____

Solution

Perhaps you see that you can cancel out the x^3 from the top and bottom. If you don't make that intellectual leap, plugging in a value can make things much easier and more concrete. Based on the question, any number that is not equal to zero would work for x. This provides you with infinite options to try for x. Instead of trying a really large number or a fraction, how about plugging in 1 for x? It is not equal to zero, so it is a valid input. It is easy to work with since it will remain 1 when cubed:

$$\frac{1}{4}\left(\frac{(2x)^3}{(3x)^3}\right)=$$

$$\frac{1}{4}\left(\frac{(2\cdot1)^3}{(3\cdot1)^3}\right)=$$

$$\frac{1}{4}\left(\frac{8}{27}\right)=$$

$$\frac{8}{108}=\frac{2}{27}$$

The answer is $\frac{2}{27}$.

Tactic 6: Isolate a Constant in Order to Find Its Value.

If a question asks you to find the value of a constant, simplify the expression so you can isolate the constant and determine its value.

➡ **Example** _____

In the equation that follows, a is a constant:

$$(2-3x)\left(x^2+4x-5\right)=-3x^3-10x^2+ax-10$$

Given that this equation is true for all values of x, what is the value of the constant a?

(A) −3
(B) 15
(C) 23
(D) 30

Solution

Solve this by first expanding the left-hand side of the equation:

$$(2-3x)\left(x^2+4x-5\right)$$

Multiply and distribute:

$$2x^2+8x-10-3x^3-12x^2+15x$$

Combine like terms:

$$-3x^3-10x^2+23x-10$$

Now that the left-hand side has been simplified, rewrite the original problem to see what matches up to the constant a:

$$-3x^3-10x^2+23x-10=-3x^3-10x^2+ax-10$$

After looking at this, it becomes clear that 23 corresponds to the constant a. Therefore, choice (C) is the correct answer. Whenever you encounter a problem involving constants, don't worry about solving for multiple variables—just isolate the constant.

Tactic 7: Use the Provided Formulas on Geometry and Trigonometry Problems.

Not many problems use geometry and trigonometry on the PSAT. Those that do are often toward the end of the test section. Because of this, it is easy to forget that the PSAT provides you with several extremely helpful formulas at the beginning of the test section. Although it would be best if you didn't have to look because you have the formulas memorized, here are the provided formulas in case you need them.

Radius of a circle = *r*
Area of a circle = πr^2
Circumference of a circle = $2\pi r$

Volume of a box = length × width × height = *lwh*

Area of a rectangle = length × width = *lw*

Volume of a cylinder = $\pi r^2 h$

Area of a triangle = $\frac{1}{2}$ × base × height = $\frac{1}{2} bh$

Volume of a sphere = $\frac{4}{3} \pi r^3$

Pythagorean theorem: $a^2 + b^2 = c^2$

Volume of a cone = $\frac{1}{3}\pi r^2 h$

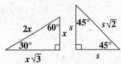

Special right triangles: 30-60-90 and 45-45-90

Volume of a pyramid =
$\frac{1}{3}$ × length × width × height = $\frac{1}{3} lwh$

KEY FACTS:

- A circle has 360 degrees.
- There are 2π radians in a circle.
- There are 180 degrees in a triangle.

The following example is the sort of problem where referring to the formulas can make a big difference.

➡ Example

The area of a sector of a circle represents 20% of the area of the entire circle. What is the central angle that corresponds to this sector in degrees?

(A) 72°

(B) 90°

(C) 120°

(D) 180°

Solution

A provided fact is key to solving this:

"A circle has 360 degrees."

If a sector is taking up 20% of the circle, it is also taking up 20% of the degrees in the center of that circle. Since a circle has 360 degrees, the sector is taking up:

$$(0.20)(360°) = 72°$$

The answer is choice (A).

Tactic 8: Use Proportions and Canceling to Solve Unit Conversion Problems.

TIP

Many students learn the process for unit conversions in chemistry or other science classes.

Converting among different types of units—such as mass measurements, currency conversion rates, and length measurements—is a major component of the PSAT. You can do unit conversions in several ways.

If you are doing a relatively straightforward conversion between just two units, you can set up a proportion or do simple multiplication. Here is an example.

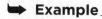 **Example** _____

A cook needs to measure $3\frac{1}{2}$ cups of flour for a recipe, but he has only a tablespoon available to measure the flour. Given that there are 16 tablespoons in 1 cup, how many tablespoons of flour will the cook need for the recipe?

(A) 32 tablespoons
(B) 56 tablespoons
(C) 64 tablespoons
(D) 73 tablespoons

Solution

Option 1: Set up a proportion. There are 16 tablespoons in 1 cup, and the cook needs 3.5 cups. So set up a proportion that has the tablespoons to cup ratio on either side:

$$\frac{16 \text{ tablespoons}}{1 \text{ cup}} = \frac{x \text{ tablespoons}}{3.5 \text{ cups}}$$

Cross multiply to solve for x:

$$3.5 \times 16 \text{ tablespoons} = 56 \text{ tablespoons}$$

The correct answer is choice (B), 56 tablespoons.

Option 2: If you are comfortable enough with conversions, you could simply jump to the last step of the above calculations and multiply 3.5 cups by 16 tablespoons to get the same result.

If you are doing a more intricate conversion that involves three or more units, you can set it up in the same way you probably learned to do unit conversions in your science classes. This method may have been called *dimensional analysis* or the *unit-factor method*. Here is an example.

If John traveled 20 miles in a straight line from his original destination, approximately how many meters is he from his original destination given that there are 1.609 kilometers in a mile and 1,000 meters in a kilometer?

(A) 32.18

(B) 12,430

(C) 24,154

(D) 32,180

Solution

Write this out in an organized way where you can see which units should be canceled:

$$20 \text{ miles} \times \frac{1.609 \text{ kilometers}}{1 \text{ mile}} \times \frac{1,000 \text{ meters}}{1 \text{ kilometer}} =$$

$$20 \text{ miles} \times \frac{1.609 \text{ kilometers}}{1 \text{ mile}} \times \frac{1,000 \text{ meters}}{1 \text{ kilometer}} =$$

$$20 \times 1.609 \times 1,000 \text{ meters} \approx 32,180 \text{ meters}$$

The miles and kilometers cancel, so 20 miles approximately equals 32,180 meters, choice (D).

Tactic 9: Use Estimation When Applicable to Save Time.

Don't be overly reliant on estimation, but use it when it can help avoid a longer calculation. Here is an example.

➡ **Example** _____

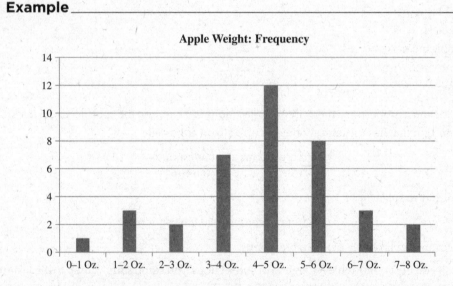

The chart above shows the distribution of individual apple weights that a customer at an apple-picking orchard placed into his bag. Which of the following could be the median weight of the 38 apples in his bag?

(A) 4.6 oz.

(B) 5.1 oz.

(C) 5.4 oz.

(D) 5.7 oz.

Solution

The median of a set of numbers is the middle value when the values are arranged from least to greatest. Although you could come up with sample values and do a laborious calculation, there is no need. The choices have only one possibility that is in the range between 4 and 5 ounces. Since the 4–5 oz. column clearly contains the median value based on a simple eyeball estimation, you can pick choice (A) and move on to the next question.

Another time when estimation is useful is when the numbers in the problem can be rounded to numbers that are easier to manipulate.

➡ **Example**_____

Annie initially has $1,997 in her checking account. After shopping for her friend's birthday, the amount of money in her checking account decreases by $603. To the nearest whole number, by what percentage has the amount in her checking account decreased?

(A) 25 percent
(B) 30 percent
(C) 35 percent
(D) 40 percent

Solution

Instead of using the numbers 1,997 and 603, estimate and use numbers that are easier to manipulate: 2,000 for 1,997 and 600 for 603. Use these numbers to estimate the percentage change in the amount of money in her checking account:

$$\frac{\text{Part}}{\text{Whole}} \times 100 = \text{Percentage}$$

$$\frac{600}{2,000} \times 100 =$$

$$\frac{6}{20} \times 100 =$$

$$\frac{3}{10} \times 100 = 30\%$$

This corresponds to choice (B)

Tactic 10: Don't Let Unusual Concepts Intimidate You.

You will be presented with concepts and situations on the PSAT Math that may intimidate you due to their unfamiliarity. Don't respond by quickly giving up because you were never officially taught the concept. Instead, use your intuition and reasoning to think through the problems. Your job is to get the right answer, not to explain your thought process to someone else. If you can devise a clever way to work through the problem, go with it. Remember that the PSAT is designed to assess your general mathematical thinking skills, not your memorization of formulas.

TIP

Keep in mind that the PSAT/ NMSQT is for students starting their junior year. If you have taken Algebra 1, Geometry, and some Algebra 2, you should have covered all the concepts you will see on test day. Use the "Math Review" chapter to go over anything you do not remember.

➡ Example

When measuring temperature, the equation to convert degrees Celsius, C, to degrees Fahrenheit, F, is $\frac{9}{5}C + 32 = F$. For the same actual temperature, what is the range of degrees Fahrenheit for which the given number is greater than the given number of degrees Celsius?

(A) $F < -78$

(B) $F > -40$

(C) $F < 26$

(D) $F > 30$

Solution

Although this problem seems as though you may need to incorporate outside knowledge from chemistry, everything you need to figure it out is right in front of you. First paraphrase what the question is asking, "For what temperatures will F be bigger than C?" To determine this, find a value for C and F that is identical. Why? Because if you know the point at which the values are equal to one another, you can then test values greater than or less than that value to determine the direction of the inequality sign.

Let x equal the value for which C and F are the same. Plug it into the equation and solve:

$$\frac{9}{5}C + 32 = F$$

$$\frac{9}{5}x + 32 = x$$

$$32 = -\frac{4}{5}x$$

$$x = -40$$

Since C and F are equivalent at -40 degrees, plug in a simple number for F to see if the expression should be $F > -40$ or $F < -40$. Try 0 for F since it is easy to plug in:

$$\frac{9}{5}C + 32 = F$$

$$\frac{9}{5}C + 32 = 0$$

$$\frac{9}{5}C = -32$$

$$C \approx -17.8$$

From this, you can see that when the F value is 0, it is greater than the value of C, which is a negative number. So the values for which F are greater than the values of C when both numbers represent the actual temperatures are $F > -40$, making the answer choice (B).

Alternatively, you can use an algebraic approach. Since the answers are in terms of F, first solve for C in terms of F:

$$\frac{9}{5}C + 32 = F$$

$$\frac{9}{5}C = F - 32$$

$$C = \frac{5}{9}(F - 32)$$

Then you can make $F > C$ and solve the inequality:

$$F > \frac{5}{9}(F - 32)$$

$$F > \frac{5}{9}F - \left(\frac{5}{9}\right)32$$

$$\frac{4}{9}F > -\left(\frac{5}{9}\right)32$$

$$F > -\left(\frac{9}{4}\right) \times \left(\frac{5}{9}\right) \times 32$$

$$F > -\frac{5}{4} \times 32$$

$$F > -40$$

If you did not realize the algebraic approaches to solving the problem, an alternative would be to take the time to test out the different answers by trying sample values from their ranges to see what would make them true. This approach can work, but it may take you more time than if you can recognize an algebraic solution.

Tactic 11: Approach the Questions Like a Puzzle, Not Like a Typical School Math Problem.

Challenging school math questions often require long calculations and cover tough concepts. The PSAT Math Test questions will not be difficult in these ways. In contrast, the tough questions will involve the patient and creative mindset needed to solve puzzles. Many of the PSAT Math problems can be solved using intuition, trying out sample values, and using the given diagrams. These approaches are not what you would find in a math textbook, yet they often work. Why? Because the PSAT Math Test has generally more *elegant* problems involving pattern recognition than the cut-and-dried problems found on typical school math tests. When you try to do a Sudoku puzzle, a jigsaw puzzle, or a challenging video game, you succeed by setting up the puzzle well instead of going full-speed ahead and doing unnecessary steps. The same applies to answering tough PSAT Math questions.

➡ Example _____

Consider a set of 25 different numbers. If two numbers are added to the set, one that is larger than the current median of the set and one that is smaller than the current median of the set, which of the following quantities about the set MUST NOT change?

(A) Range
(B) Mean
(C) Mode
(D) Median

Solution

On a problem like this, try visualizing what will happen by making up some sample values. Suppose you have a simple set of numbers something like this:

$$\{1, 1, 2, 3, 4, 5, 6, 7, 8, 9, 10, 11, 12, 13, 14, 15, 16, 17, 18, 19, 20, 21, 22, 23, 24\}$$

The range of the set is 23, which is the difference between the smallest value (1) and the largest value (24).

The mean for this set is all of the above numbers added together and then divided by 25.

The mode is 1 since it appears the most frequently.

The median is 12 since it is the middle value when the numbers are placed in order from smallest to largest.

If you can come up with even one set of values that will make one of these quantities change, that answer is out as a possibility.

If you add −5 and 100 to the set, the range of the set will become much larger—it will be 105. So choice (A) is not correct.

If you add 2 and 1,000 to the set, the mean will change because the average will shift significantly upward. So choice (B) is not correct.

If you add 7 and 17 to the set, it will have 3 different modes instead of just having 1 as the only mode. So choice (C) is not correct.

Choice (D) is correct. As long as you add any number less than 12 and any number greater than 12, the median will remain the same because 12 will still be in the middle of the set of numbers when they are all placed in order from smallest to largest.

You could also solve this more intuitively if you have a solid understanding of the concept of the median of a set. When given a particular median, if you add one number greater than and one number less than the median, the median will not change since it will remain in the very middle of the set.

Tactic 12: Don't Jump to an Answer Too Quickly.

Unlike in traditional math tests where the incorrect answers are often just random numbers, the answers on the PSAT are designed to reflect the errors students can make when solving the problems. Simply because an answer is on your calculator is no guarantee that it is correct. For example, in math class you typically solve for x and the answer is a given solution. On the PSAT, however, the question may be asking for the value of an expression, like $-2x^2 - x$.

> If you have absolutely no idea what the correct answer is to a question, then guess. There is no penalty for guessing. The PSAT does not consistently favor one answer choice letter over another. So before you take the test, choose a letter at random. When you have to guess an answer, just use that letter. Choosing a particular letter ahead of time and always using it when you are blindly guessing will help you avoid wasting time during the test deciding which letter to pick.

➡ **Example** _____

What is/are the real number value(s) of x in this equation?

$$x = \sqrt{2x + 15}$$

(A) −3 only

(B) 5 only

(C) −3 and 5

(D) Cannot determine based on the given information.

Solution

Although this looks fairly easy to solve, more is here than meets the eye. You have to be careful that what seems to be a solution actually is a solution. Start by squaring both sides and determining the potential values for x:

$$x = \sqrt{2x + 15}$$
$$x^2 = 2x + 15$$
$$0 = x^2 - 2x - 15$$
$$0 = (x + 3)(x - 5)$$

So if $(x + 3) = 0$ or if $(x - 5) = 0$, the entire expression equals 0. That means -3 can be a solution since you can set $(x + 3)$ equal to 0 and solve for x:

$$(x + 3) = 0$$

Subtract 3 from both sides:

$$x = -3$$

You can do the same procedure for $(x - 5)$:

$$(x - 5) = 0$$

Add 5 to both sides:

$$x = 5$$

So it appears that both -3 and 5 work as solutions since they both cause $(x + 3)(x - 5)$ to equal 0. When you try these in the original equation, however, only 5 works. Why? Because -3 cannot be the principal square root of 9 since -3 cannot equal the positive square root of a number. So -3 is an "extraneous solution," making choice (B) the answer.

Tactic 13: Know the Grid-In Question Rules.

On the PSAT Math Test, you will have a total of 8 grid-in questions: 4 on the calculator subsection and 4 on the non-calculator subsection. Here are some key things to know about these types of problems.

- It is possible that a question could have more than one correct answer. Enter just one correct answer.
- There are no negative answers.
- Long decimal answers that continue past the four spots allowed for gridding can be rounded up or shortened as long as you use all of the spaces on the grid. You can also express a decimal answer as a fraction. For example, you can write $\frac{7}{9}$ as 7/9, .777, or .778.
- You don't need to reduce fractions. For example, since $\frac{2}{3}$, $\frac{4}{6}$, and $\frac{6}{9}$ are equivalent, any of them will work as an answer.

➡ Example

What is the value of x if $(3x + 2) - (5x - 6) = -4$?

*Grid-In Question: Write Your Answer*_____

Solution

On a problem like this, the math is not too difficult. The challenge is to avoid making a careless error because of confusing a negative sign or incorrectly adding numbers. This is especially important on a grid-in question since you will not have four multiple choices to help you detect a major miscalculation. Avoid making careless mistakes by writing out all of your steps. Start by writing the original equation:

$$(3x + 2) - (5x - 6) = -4$$

Remove the parentheses around $(3x + 2)$ and distribute the -1 through the $(5x - 6)$:

$$3x + 2 - 5x + 6 = -4$$

Check that you distributed the negative sign correctly. Then combine like terms:

$$-2x + 8 = -4$$

Subtract the 8 from both sides:

$$-2x = -12$$

Divide both sides by -2 to solve for x:

$$x = 6$$

You can check your work by plugging in 6 for x into the original equation:

$$(3x + 2) - (5x - 6) = -4$$
$$(3(6) + 2) - (5(6) - 6) = -4$$
$$18 + 2 - 30 + 6 = -4$$
$$-4 = -4$$

It checks out. So the final answer is 6, which you need to put onto the grid-in sheet.

HEART OF ALGEBRA PRACTICE

1. Which ordered pair (x, y) satisfies the pair of equations below?

$$3x + y = -3$$
$$x - 2y = -8$$

(A) $(2, 4)$

(B) $(-2, 3)$

(C) $(-3, 2)$

(D) $(1, -4)$

2. The United States primarily uses a 12-hour clock with 12-hour periods for the morning (A.M.) and for the afternoon/evening (P.M.). Much of the rest of the world uses a 24-hour clock. Which of the following inequalities expresses the digits for hours, H, on a 24-hour clock that correspond to the business hours for a restaurant that is open from 7 P.M. until 11 P.M.?

(A) $7 \le H \le 11$

(B) $12 \le H \le 24$

(C) $19 \le H \le 23$

(D) $24 \le H \le 27$

3. A video arcade charges a set \$5 charge to purchase a game card and then charges \$0.50 for each video game played. What expression gives the relationship between the number of games played, G, and the total amount of dollars spent using the game card, T?

(A) $T = 5G - 0.50$

(B) $T = 4.50G + 5$

(C) $T = 0.50G - 2.5$

(D) $T = 0.50G + 5$

4.

Age	Maximum Recommended Heart Rate
50	165
55	160
60	155
65	150

A cardiologist uses the guidelines for maximum recommended heart rate (measured in beats per minute) shown in the table above, which vary based on a patient's age. One of the cardiologist's patients, age 55, wants to start an exercise program. The cardiologist recommends that the patient maintain a heart rate greater than 50% and less than 85% of the maximum recommended heart rate while exercising. Which of the following expressions gives the range in which the patient's heart rate, H, should be during exercise?

(A) $50 < H < 85$

(B) $80 < H < 136$

(C) $85 < H < 160$

(D) $150 < H < 160$

5. Hannah has only nickels and dimes in her wallet. She has a total of $2.50 and a total of 30 coins. How many nickels does she have?

(A) 10
(B) 12
(C) 15
(D) 16

6. A two-digit number has a tens place, t, and a units place, u. The digits have the following relationships:

$$t + u = 8$$
$$t = 2 + u$$

What is the value of the two-digit number given by these two digits?

(A) 41
(B) 53
(C) 63
(D) 79

7. 18-karat gold has 18 parts gold for 24 total parts metal (the difference comes from the 6 parts that are metals other than gold). 24-karat gold is pure gold. In order to make a piece of jewelry that is 2.4 ounces in weight and is 20-karat gold, how many ounces of 18-karat gold, X, and of 24-karat gold, Y, are needed to make this piece of jewelry?

(A) $X = 0.4$, $Y = 0.6$
(B) $X = 0.9$, $Y = 1.7$
(C) $X = 1.2$, $Y = 1.1$
(D) $X = 1.6$, $Y = 0.8$

8. For the equation $3 + 4x - 2 = k + 6x - 2x$, what does the constant k need to equal in order for there to be multiple solutions for x?

(A) 1
(B) 2
(C) 3
(D) 4

9. What is the value of y in the system of equations below?

$$16x - 4y = 12$$
$$8x + 2y = 4$$

(A) 2
(B) $\dfrac{3}{2}$
(C) $-\dfrac{1}{2}$
(D) -4

10. What are the solutions for x and y in the equations below?

$$-\frac{3}{4}x+2\left(y-\frac{1}{2}\right)=3$$

$$\frac{2}{3}x=6-2y$$

(A) $x=\frac{24}{17}$, $y=\frac{43}{17}$

(B) $x=\frac{2}{13}$, $y=\frac{14}{19}$

(C) $x=-3$, $y=\frac{7}{19}$

(D) $x=-\frac{4}{11}$, $y=\frac{18}{23}$

11. Electrical engineers use Ohm's law, $V = IR$, to give the relationship among voltage (V), current (I), and resistance (R). Which of the following statements is always true about the relationship among voltage, current, and resistance based on Ohm's law?

  I. If the current increases and the resistance remains the same, the voltage increases.

  II. If the voltage increases, the resistance must increase.

  III. If the resistance increases and the voltage remains the same, the current must decrease.

(A) I only

(B) II only

(C) I and III only

(D) II and III only

12. What is the graph of the following function?

$$3 + y = 2 + 3x$$

(A)

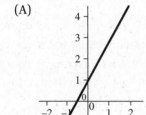

(C)

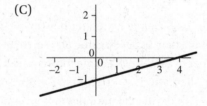

(B)

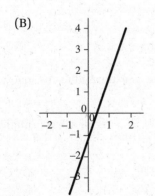

(D)

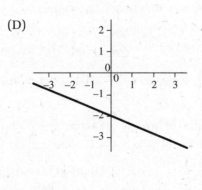

Answer Explanations

1. **(B)** You can use substitution to solve, although elimination could also work.

$$3x + y = -3$$
$$x - 2y = -8$$

Rearrange the second equation to be in terms of y:

$$x - 2y = -8$$
$$x = 2y - 8$$

Substitute into the first equation and solve for y:

$$3x + y = -3$$
$$3(2y - 8) + y = -3$$
$$6y - 24 + y = -3$$
$$7y - 24 = -3$$
$$7y = 21$$
$$y = 3$$

Then plug in 3 for y into the first equation to solve for x:

$$3x + y = -3$$
$$3x + 3 = -3$$
$$3x = -6$$
$$x = -2$$

2. **(C)** Simply add 12 to both 7 and 11 to find the correct range since all of the P.M. times are 12 hours less than the time on a 24-hour clock:

$$12 + 7 = 19 \text{ and } 12 + 11 = 23$$

This makes the range between 19 and 23 hours inclusive, which is expressed as the inequality $19 \leq H \leq 23$.

3. **(D)** There will be a $5 charge no matter how many games are played. So the $5 should be represented as a constant. For each game played, there is an additional $0.50 fee. Since G represents the number of games played, the total cost is $0.50G + 5$ dollars. This can be expressed as $T = 0.50G + 5$. Alternatively, you could make up a number of games played and the total dollars spent. Then find which of the equations gives an identical result.

4. **(B)** Use the table to find the maximum recommended heart rate for a 55-year-old person—160 beats per minute. Then take 50% and 85% of 160 to determine the lower and upper bounds of the recommended heart rate:

$$50\% \text{ of } 160 = 0.50 \times 160 = 80$$
$$85\% \text{ of } 160 = 0.85 \times 160 = 136$$

So the range is between 80 and 136 beats per minute, which is expressed as the inequality $80 < H < 136$.

5. **(A)** Set up a series of two equations. Put everything in terms of cents for sake of simplicity. Use N as the number of nickels and D as the number of dimes:

$$\text{The total number of coins: } N + D = 30$$
$$\text{The total number of cents: } 5N + 10D = 250$$

Express D in terms of N based on the first equation:

$$N + D = 30$$
$$D = 30 - N$$

Then, substitute this for D in the second equation:

$$5N + 10D = 250$$
$$5N + 10(30 - N) = 250$$
$$5N + 300 - 10N = 250$$
$$-5N = -50$$
$$N = 10$$

Alternatively, you can solve this by working backward from the answers. Since the total number of cents must be 250, try the different possible values of nickels from the choices to see which one works. You can try choice (B) or choice (C) since they are in the middle. Once you get to choice (A), you will find that if you have 10 nickels, you have 50 cents from nickels. That means there must be 200 cents from dimes, which also means there are 20 dimes. Since 20 dimes and 10 nickels add together to give you 30 coins total, choice (A) is correct.

6. **(B)** Use substitution to solve for t and u:

$$t + u = 8$$
$$t = 2 + u$$

Plug in $2 + u$ for t into the first equation:

$$(2 + u) + u = 8$$
$$2 + 2u = 8$$
$$2u = 6$$
$$u = 3$$

Plug in 3 for u into one of the original equations, and solve for t. This gives 5 in the tens place and 3 in the ones place, making 53 your answer.

Alternatively, you can solve this using elimination.

$$t + u = 8$$
$$t = 2 + u$$

Rearrange the second equation:

$$t = 2 + u$$
$$t - u = 2$$

Then you have this as the set of equations:

$$t + u = 8$$
$$t - u = 2$$

Add the two together to get:

$$2t = 10$$
$$t = 5$$

Then substitute $t = 5$ into the first equation to solve for u:

$$t + u = 8$$
$$5 + u = 8$$
$$u = 3$$

The answer is still 53.

7. **(D)** Set up a system of two equations. One equation models the number of actual gold karats:

$$\frac{18}{24}X + \frac{24}{24}Y = \frac{20}{24} \times 2.4 \rightarrow \frac{3}{4}X + Y = \frac{5}{6} \times 2.4$$

One equation models the weight of the jewelry:

$$X + Y = 2.4$$

You can use either substitution or elimination to solve this system. However, using elimination is better since a Y-term in each equation will be easily canceled. Start by simplifying the first equation:

$$\frac{3}{4}X + Y = \frac{5}{6} \times 2.4$$
$$\frac{3}{4}X + Y = 2$$

Now subtract it from $X + Y = 2.4$:

$$\begin{array}{r} X + Y = 2.4 \\ -\left(\frac{3}{4}X + Y = 2\right) \\ \hline \frac{1}{4}X \quad\quad = 0.4 \end{array}$$

Then solve for X:

$$\frac{1}{4}X = 0.4$$
$$X = 4 \times 0.4$$
$$X = 1.6$$

Now plug in 1.6 for X into one of the equations to solve for Y. Use $X + Y = 2.4$ since it is simpler:

$$X + Y = 2.4$$
$$1.6 + Y = 2.4$$
$$Y = 0.8$$

So the final answer is $X = 1.6$, $Y = 0.8$.

8. **(A)** Before proceeding too far, simplify the equation by grouping like terms:

$$3 + 4x - 2 = k + 6x - 2x$$
$$1 + 4x = k + 4x$$

So if $k = 1$, both sides of the equations are equivalent to one another. The equation reduces to $x = x$, which has an infinite number of solutions.

9. **(C)** Solve this using elimination by taking the first equation and multiplying it by $\frac{1}{2}$:

$$16x - 4y = 12$$
$$8x + 2y = 4$$

$$8x - 2y = 6$$
$$8x + 2y = 4$$

Subtract the two so we can easily find y:

$$8x - 2y = 6$$
$$-(8x + 2y = 4)$$
$$-4y = 2$$
$$y = -\frac{1}{2}$$

10. **(A)** Start by simplifying both equations:

$$-\frac{3}{4}x + 2\left(y - \frac{1}{2}\right) = 3$$
$$-\frac{3}{4}x + 2y - 1 = 3 \qquad \text{and} \qquad \frac{2}{3}x = 6 - 2y$$
$$-\frac{3}{4}x + 2y = 4 \qquad\qquad\qquad \frac{2}{3}x + 2y = 6$$

Then use elimination to solve:

$$-\frac{3}{4}x + 2y = 4$$
$$-\left(\frac{2}{3}x + 2y = 6\right)$$
$$-\frac{3}{4}x - \frac{2}{3}x = -2$$

$$-\frac{9}{12}x - \frac{8}{12}x = -2$$
$$\frac{-17}{12}x = -2$$
$$x = \frac{24}{17}$$

Since only choice (A) has x equal to $\frac{24}{17}$, you can save time by just picking it as the correct answer.

11. **(C)** Choice I is correct. Increasing current while keeping resistance constant increases the right side of the equation. This means the left side—the voltage—increases as well. Choice III is correct. If the voltage—the left side of the equation—remains the same while the resistance increases, the current must decrease in order for the value on the right side of the equation to remain the same. Choice II is NOT correct. The current could increase without the resistance increasing if the voltage increases.

12. **(B)** Put the equation into slope-intercept form:

$$3 + y = 2 + 3x$$
$$y = 3x - 1$$

This line has a slope of 3 and a y-intercept of -1, which has the following graph:

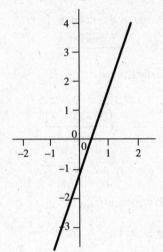

PROBLEM SOLVING AND DATA ANALYSIS PRACTICE

1. A subway map is drawn to scale so that 1 inch on the map corresponds to 2 miles of actual distance on the track. The subway train travels at a constant average rate of 30 miles per hour. How many minutes will a journey on the subway take if the track distance as portrayed on the map is 3 inches?

   (A) 6
   (B) 9
   (C) 12
   (D) 18

2. An electronic reader typically costs $100. However, the price is heavily discounted due to both a coupon and a sale that have the same percent off the regular price. If the price using both the coupon discount and the sale discount is $49, what is the percent off the regular price that the coupon and the sale each provide independently?

   (A) 25%
   (B) 30%
   (C) 35%
   (D) 40%

3. If n percent of 80 is 20, what is n percent of 220?

   (A) 42
   (B) 48
   (C) 55
   (D) 76

4. If 132 men and 168 women are living in a dormitory, what percent of the total dormitory residents are men?

   (A) 28%
   (B) 34%
   (C) 40%
   (D) 44%

5. If 1 Canadian dollar can be exchanged for 0.80 U.S. dollars and vice versa, how many Canadian dollars can a traveler receive in exchange for 120 U.S. dollars?

   (A) 60
   (B) 90
   (C) 150
   (D) 220

6. David is developing a fitness plan and wants to get his weight to a level that will be considered healthy in terms of the body mass index (BMI) calculation. The currently recommended BMI is between 18.6 and 24.9. To calculate BMI using inches and pounds, David takes his weight in pounds and divides it by the square of his height in inches. Then he multiplies the entire result by 703. David is 6 feet, 3 inches tall and currently weighs 260 pounds. To the nearest whole pound, what is the least number of whole pounds he needs to lose in order for his BMI to be within the healthy range?

(A) 61
(B) 68
(C) 75
(D) 83

Questions 7–9 refer to the following information.

A marine biologist has conducted research into the population of blue whales over the past few decades. The estimated global blue whale population is plotted against the given year in the graph below:

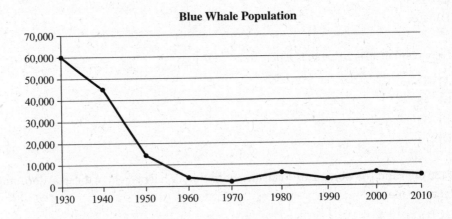

7. From 1940 until 1970, the best-fit equation for the values of the blue whale population has which general characteristic?

(A) Linear decay
(B) Linear growth
(C) Exponential decay
(D) Exponential growth

8. A worldwide treaty prohibiting commercial whaling (i.e., the hunting of whales) was passed at some point between 1930 and 2010. Based on the data, what is the year when this treaty most likely went into effect?

(A) 1930
(B) 1950
(C) 1970
(D) 2000

9. Another scientist is reviewing the results of the marine biologist's observations and assessing the impact of measurement error on such an ambitious project. The scientist is considering two possible sources of measurement error: (1) random error from any factor that would affect the scientist's measurements and (2) systematic error from a problem in the overall setup of the data-gathering project. Which of the following would be the best way that the marine biologist's measurement error could have been minimized?

(A) Collecting whale population data from as many possible points from an even distribution throughout all the world's oceans

(B) Comparing the blue whale data to data of other whales, such as the sperm whale, fin whale, and killer whale

(C) Gathering data from a consistent single point in the Atlantic Ocean, doing so at the same day/time each year

(D) Consistently taking a sample from a 100-square-mile range of the Pacific Ocean and electronically tagging each whale that is observed to ensure no whale is counted twice

Questions 10–11 refer to the following information.

The graph below gives the current GPA of every one of the 389 students at County High School.

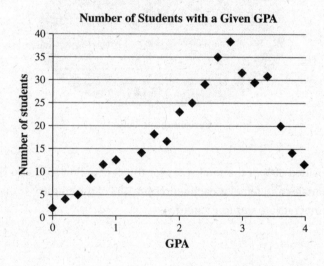

Number of Students with a Given GPA

10. Which of these values of the GPA for the students portrayed in the graph is between 2 and 3?

I. Mean

II. Median

III. Mode

(A) I only

(B) II only

(C) I and II only

(D) I, II, and III

11. The school administrators have decided that too much grade inflation occurs at the school. They believe the average GPA is skewed too high by teachers giving too many A's and B's and by not enough students receiving C's, D's, and F's. If the administrators want to ensure that grade inflation is minimized, which of these quantities would be important to bring close to 2.0?

(A) Median only
(B) Mean only
(C) Both mean and median
(D) Neither mean nor median

Questions 12–13 refer to the following information.

In a recent election in a European country, the political parties divided the vote among the Social Democrats, the Christian Democrats, the Socialists, and the Green Party.

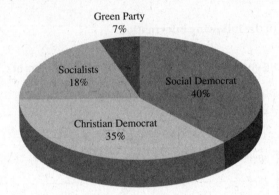

Percentage of Votes

12. If women provided 60% of the total votes for the Green, Socialist, and Christian Democrat parties and if males and females each represent 50% of the country's voters, what percent of the Social Democrat vote was from men?

(A) 45%
(B) 49%
(C) 56%
(D) 65%

13. The country's constitution states that in order for a party to come to power, it must have a majority of the votes. The constitution also states that the seats in the parliament are allocated proportionally to each party based on the percentage of votes each party received. So if no one political party receives a majority of the vote, a coalition party will have to be formed from 2 or more parties to give a governing majority. Which of the following combinations of political parties from this election would NOT result in a governing coalition?

(A) Christian Democrat and Social Democrat
(B) Green Party and Christian Democrat
(C) Socialist and Social Democrat
(D) Socialist and Christian Democrat

Questions 14–15 refer to the following information.

300 patients at a hospital were categorized based on whether they had high or low cholesterol and on whether they had high or low blood pressure. The results are tabulated in the table below.

	High Cholesterol	**Low Cholesterol**	**Total**
High Blood Pressure	40	30	70
Low Blood Pressure	50	180	230
Total	90	210	300

14. What is the probability that one of the 230 low blood pressure patients has high cholesterol?

    (A) $\dfrac{30}{230}$

    (B) $\dfrac{50}{230}$

    (C) $\dfrac{65}{230}$

    (D) $\dfrac{80}{230}$

15. What is the percent chance that one of the 300 patients will have at least one of the conditions—high cholesterol or high blood pressure?

    (A) 36%

    (B) 40%

    (C) 48%

    (D) 52%

Questions 16–17 refer to the following information.

A researcher surveyed several residents in a town about the types of vehicles the residents own. The results are shown in the table below.

	Car	**Van**	**Truck/SUV**	**Total**
Gas	104	31	43	178
Hybrid	10	1	m	n
Electric	6	3	0	9
Total	120	35	45	200

16. Jennifer and Bill were members of the group surveyed. They have a car and a van in their garage. What is the probability that both of the vehicles in their garage are hybrids?

    (A) $\dfrac{1}{420}$

    (B) $\dfrac{1}{380}$

    (C) $\dfrac{1}{360}$

    (D) $\dfrac{1}{240}$

17. What are the values of m and n in the table above?

    (A) $m = 4$ and $n = 8$

    (B) $m = 8$ and $n = 26$

    (C) $m = 2$ and $n = 13$

    (D) Cannot determine based on the given information.

Answer Explanations

1. **(C)** Since 1 inch on the map corresponds to 2 miles of actual distance, double the 3 inches shown on the map to determine that the subway has traveled 6 actual miles. Since the subway is traveling at 30 miles per hour, solve for the number of hours the subway has traveled:

$$\text{Distance} = \text{Rate} \times \text{Time}$$
$$6 = 30 \times \text{Time}$$
$$\text{Time} = \frac{1}{5} \text{ hours}$$

Then multiply $\frac{1}{5}$ by 60 minutes to determine how many minutes the train takes to travel 6 miles:

$$\frac{1}{5} \times 60 = 12 \text{ minutes}$$

2. **(B)** Since both the coupon and the sale provide the same percent discount, you can set up an equation to determine what you must multiply \$100 by in order to end up with a price of \$49. Alternatively, you can simply multiply \$100 by the same variable twice, which will let you determine the correct percentage:

$$(x)(x)(100) = 49$$
$$100x^2 = 49$$
$$x^2 = \frac{49}{100}$$
$$x^2 = 0.49$$
$$x = \sqrt{0.49}$$
$$x = 0.7$$

If x equals 0.7, subtract 0.7 from 1 to find the percent discount:

$$1 - 0.7 = 0.3 = 30\%$$

This means that a 30 percent discount has been applied to the original amount two times.

3. **(C)** Set this up as an equation to determine what n equals. Use the first bit of information in the question:

$$\frac{\text{Part}}{\text{Whole}} \times 100 = \text{Percent}$$
$$\frac{20}{80} \times 100 = n$$
$$\frac{1}{4} \times 100 = n$$
$$n = 25\%$$

Then take 25% of 220:

$$0.25 \times 220 = 55$$

4. **(D)** Since $\frac{\text{Part}}{\text{Whole}} \times 100 = \text{Percent}$, take the number of men and divide it by the total number of residents to determine the percentage of just men:

$$\frac{132}{132 + 168} \times 100 = 44\%$$

5. **(C)** This is easiest to solve using a simple proportion:

$$\frac{1 \text{ Canadian dollar}}{0.80 \text{ U.S. dollars}} = \frac{x}{120}$$

Cross multiply to find the solution:

$$(1 \text{ Canadian dollar})(120) = (0.80 \text{ U.S. dollars})(x)$$

$$x = \frac{120}{0.80} = 150 \text{ Canadian dollars}$$

6. **(A)** First solve for the weight that David must be in order to have a BMI of 24.9 given his height since this would put the BMI within the appropriate range. Use the wording in the question to set up an equation, "To calculate BMI using inches and pounds, David takes his weight in pounds and divides it by the square of his height in inches. Then he multiplies the entire result by 703." This gives the following BMI equation:

$$\frac{\text{Weight}}{\text{Height}^2} \times 703 = \text{BMI}$$

Since David is 6 feet, 3 inches tall, his height is $(12 \times 6) + 3 = 75$ inches. Plug in 24.9 for the BMI and 75 for the height into the equation, and solve for the weight:

$$\frac{\text{Weight}}{75^2} \times 703 = 24.9$$

$$\text{Weight} \times 703 = 24.9 \times 75^2$$

$$\text{Weight} = \frac{24.9 \times 75^2}{703}$$

$$\text{Weight} \approx 199$$

Then subtract the desired weight from David's current weight to determine how many whole pounds he should lose:

$$260 - 199 = 61$$

7. **(C)** Between 1940 and 1970, the blue whale population is decreasing and the function has a substantial curve. So the graph shows exponential decay. Note that if the decay were linear, the graph would have gone down in a straight line.

8. **(C)** After the passage of a treaty banning whaling, it is most reasonable to expect that the population of blue whales would gradually increase. 1970 is the only choice after which there is an increase in the global blue whale population.

9. **(A)** The arrangement described in choice (A) would ensure the most random gathering of data from as large a sample as possible, thereby minimizing both random and systematic error. The other options focus on irrelevant or extremely narrow samples. Choice (B) has a major systematic error since it does not focus on gathering blue whale data. Instead, this choice focuses on comparing data. Choice (C) minimizes random error for this particular data point due to its consistent measurement. However, this choice has the systematic issue of not gathering a wide enough sample of data. Although choice (D) is superior to choices (B) and (C), it falls short of choice (A). Choice (D) limits the sample to a relatively small part of one ocean instead of considering blue whales all over the world.

10. **(D)** Since there is a large cluster of students with GPAs between 2 and 3, it is possible to estimate that the mean and median will fall in that range. The most frequent value, the mode, will also be in that range since the greatest number of students with a particular GPA is between 2 and 3.

11. **(C)** The median is the middle value of all the GPAs. If the middle value was much above 2.0, it would be a strong indication that there was grade inflation. The mean is the arithmetic average of the GPAs, so if it was much above 2.0, it would also indicate grade inflation. So both the median and mean should be close to 2.0 in order to minimize grade inflation.

12. **(D)** Women provided 60% of the vote for the 60% of the total votes for the Green, Socialist, and Christian Democrat parties. That means that women provided $0.6 \times 0.6 \times$ Total votes = 36% of the Total votes, not including the Social Democrat votes. Since women make up 50% of the country's voters, 14% of the country's total voters are women who voted for the Social Democrats since $50 - 36 = 14$. That means that 26% of the total population of the country are males who voted for the Social Democrats. To determine the percentage of Social Democrat votes from males, take 26 and divide it by the total percentage of 40 and then convert that value to a percent:

$$\frac{26}{40} \times 100 = 65\%$$

13. **(B)** The Green Party and Christian Democrat Party together would represent $7\% + 35\% = 42\%$ of the entire vote. Since 42% is less than the 50% majority needed for a governing coalition, these two parties would not be able to form a governing coalition on their own. All of the other options would give combinations that would add up to at least 50% and could therefore form a majority governing coalition.

14. **(B)** There are 50 low blood pressure patients who have high cholesterol. So simply divide 50 by the 230 total patients:

$$\frac{50}{230}$$

15. **(B)** There are 40 patients with both conditions, 50 who have only high cholesterol, and 30 who have only high blood pressure:

$$40 + 50 + 30 = 120$$

Divide 120 by the 300 total to find the percent:

$$\frac{120}{300} \times 100 = 40\%$$

16. **(A)** Multiply the probability that the car is a hybrid, $\frac{10}{120}$, by the probability that the van is a hybrid, $\frac{1}{35}$:

$$\frac{10}{120} \times \frac{1}{35} = \frac{1}{12} \times \frac{1}{35} = \frac{1}{420}$$

17. **(C)** The value of m must be 2. All of the trucks and SUVs must add up to a total of 45, and there are 43 of the other truck/SUV types: $43 + 2 = 45$. The value of n must be 13. The total of all the different types of vehicles must add up to 200. The numbers in the last column show a total of $178 + 9 = 187$ and $187 + 13 = 200$.

PASSPORT TO ADVANCED MATH PRACTICE

1. Michele wants to design a floor that will have a length and width that add up to 30 feet. She also wants the area of the floor to be 216 square feet. What will the dimensions of the floor need to be?

   (A) 10 feet by 20 feet
   (B) 12 feet by 18 feet
   (C) 14 feet by 16 feet
   (D) 17 feet by 17 feet

2. $\left(\dfrac{n^2 - n^3}{n^4}\right)^{-2}$ is equivalent to which of the following?

   (A) $\dfrac{n^4}{1 - 2n + n^2}$

   (B) $\dfrac{n}{n^8}$

   (C) $\dfrac{1 - 2n + n^2}{n^2}$

   (D) $\dfrac{n^2}{1 + 4n - n^2}$

3. For the real integers x and y, what must $\dfrac{2x + 2y}{4}$ equal?

   (A) The mode of x and y
   (B) $x^2 + y^2$
   (C) The arithmetic mean of x and y
   (D) The median of $2x$ and $2y$

4. Factor: $16a^2 - 9b^2$

   (A) $(2a + b)(a - b)$
   (B) $(3a + 2b)(6a - 3b)$
   (C) $(4a + 3b)(4a - 3b)$
   (D) $(8a + 3b)(2a - 3b)$

5. What are the two solutions for x in the equation $4x^2 + 8x - 4 = 0$?

   (A) $x = 3\sqrt{2}$ and $x = -4$
   (B) $x = 2\sqrt{3}$ and $x = \sqrt{11} + 13$
   (C) $x = -\sqrt{7}$ and $x = -5$
   (D) $x = -1 - \sqrt{2}$ and $x = \sqrt{2} - 1$

6. Simplify: $x^4 y^2 + x^3 y^5 + x y^6 + 2x^3 y^5$

   (A) $xy(x^4 + 3x^2 y^3 + y^6)$
   (B) $y^2(x^4 + 4x^3 y^4 + y^3)$
   (C) $xy^2(x^3 + 3x^2 y^3 + y^4)$
   (D) $x(x^3 y^2 + x^2 y^5 + y^6 + 2x^4 y^4)$

7. $\dfrac{x}{2} = \dfrac{2(n^0)}{2} - \dfrac{1}{2x}$

What is the value of x?

(A) 0
(B) 1
(C) 2
(D) 3

8. What is the sum of $3x^3 + 5x - 3$ and $2x^2 - 4x + 6$?

(A) $x^2 - 9x + 9$
(B) $2x^3 + 4x^2 - x$
(C) $3x^3 - x^2 + 2x + 3$
(D) $3x^3 + 2x^2 + x + 3$

9. $(25a^4 + 40a^2b^4 + 16b^8) \div (5a^2 + 4b^4) = ?$

(A) $5b^4 + 40a^2b^4 + 5a^2$
(B) $4b^4 + 5a^2$
(C) $25a^4 + 8a^2b^4 + 4a^2$
(D) 1

10. The formula used by the National Weather Service to calculate wind chill in degrees Fahrenheit is:

$$35.74 + 0.6215 \times T - 35.75 \times \left(V^{(0.16)}\right) + 0.4275 \times T \times \left(V^{(0.16)}\right)$$

T represents the air temperature in degrees Fahrenheit, and V represents the wind velocity in miles per hour.

Which of these is an accurate statement about the relationship between wind chill and temperature?

I. The relative impact on wind chill of a particular increase in wind speed is more significant at lower wind speeds than at higher wind speeds.
II. Wind chill has an impact on the relative temperature feeling only at temperatures greater than or equal to 35.75 degrees Fahrenheit.
III. Wind chill and temperature are inversely related to one another.

(A) I only
(B) II only
(C) I and II only
(D) II and IIII only

11. Consider the function below.

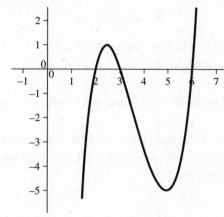

If the function is written as $f(x) = (x-2) \times A \times (x-3)$, what is the value of A?

(A) x

(B) $(x+2)$

(C) $(x-6)$

(D) $(x-14)$

12. The function $y = 6x^3 + 19x^2 - 24x + c$ has zeros at the values of $-\frac{1}{2}, \frac{4}{3}$, and -4. What is the value of the constant c in this function?

(A) -16

(B) -9

(C) 2

(D) 14

13. The graph of the function below is given by which equation?

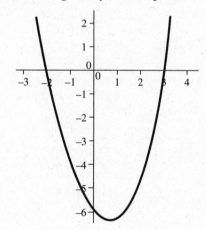

(A) $f(x) = 2x^2 - 2x - 4$

(B) $f(x) = 3x^2 - 6x - 7$

(C) $f(x) = x^2 + x - 3$

(D) $f(x) = x^2 - x - 6$

14. What will happen to the graph of $y = x^2$ in the xy-plane if it is changed to

$$y = (x+8)^2 + 4?$$

(A) It will shift to the left 8 units and shift up 4 units.

(B) It will shift to the right 8 units and shift up 4 units.

(C) It will shift to the left 8 units and shift down 4 units.

(D) It will shift to the right 8 units and shift down 4 units.

15. Calculating the total cost C, including the sales tax (and no other fees), of a good with an untaxed price of P is given by the expression $C = 1.07P$. How could you calculate the cost of only the sales tax on the good?

(A) P

(B) $0.07P$

(C) $0.13P$

(D) $0.17P$

Answer Explanations

1. **(B)** This is easiest to solve if you work your way backward from the answer choices. The only answer that multiplies to give an area of 216 is choice (B):

$$12 \times 18 = 216$$

If you wanted to solve this algebraically, finding the solution would be much more complicated. This question demonstrates that you should be open to plugging in answers when you anticipate a lengthy calculation. Set up two equations, one equation for the sum of the length and width and one equation for the area:

$$L + W = 30$$
$$L \times W = 216$$

Use substitution to solve:

$$L + W = 30$$
$$L = 30 - W$$

Substitute this in for L in the other equation:

$$L \times W = 216$$
$$(30 - W) \times W = 216$$
$$-W^2 + 30W - 216 = 0$$

This looks rather challenging to solve by factoring, so use the quadratic formula:

$$x = \frac{-b \pm \sqrt{b^2 - 4ac}}{2a}$$
$$x = \frac{-30 \pm \sqrt{30^2 - 4(-1)(-216)}}{2(-1)}$$
$$x = \frac{-30 \pm \sqrt{900 - 864}}{-2}$$
$$x = \frac{-30 \pm \sqrt{36}}{-2}$$
$$x = \frac{-30 \pm 6}{-2}$$
$$x = 15 \pm 3$$
$$x = 12, 18$$

If you plug in 12 as the width, you get 18 as the length. If you plug in 18 as the width, you get 12 as the length:

$$L \times W = 216$$
$$L \times 12 = 216$$
$$L = 18$$

$$L \times W = 216$$
$$L \times 18 = 216$$
$$L = 12$$

So the dimensions are 12 feet by 18 feet, regardless of what you call the length and width.

2. **(A)** Simplify the expression:

$$\left(\frac{n^2-n^3}{n^4}\right)^{-2} = \left(\frac{n^2}{n^2}\left(\frac{1-n}{n^2}\right)\right)^{-2}$$

Cancel the n^2 terms on the outside:

$$\left(\frac{\cancel{n^2}}{\cancel{n^2}}\left(\frac{1-n}{n^2}\right)\right)^{-2} = \left(\frac{1-n}{n^2}\right)^{-2}$$

Flip the fraction so it has a positive exponent:

$$\left(\frac{1-n}{n^2}\right)^{-2} = \left(\frac{n^2}{1-n}\right)^{2}$$

Square both the numerator and the denominator and simplify:

$$\left(\frac{(n^2)^2}{(1-n)^2}\right) = \left(\frac{n^4}{(1-n)(1-n)}\right) = \frac{n^4}{1-2n+n^2}$$

3. **(C)** $\frac{2x+2y}{4} = \frac{x+y}{2}$, which is the arithmetic mean (simple average) of x and y.

4. **(C)** Both the first term and the second term of the expression are squared terms. So the expression can be restated as the difference of squares, the general form of which is $x^2 - y^2 = (x+y)(x-y)$:

$$16a^2 - 9b^2 =$$
$$(4a)^2 - (3b)^2 = (4a+3b)(4a-3b)$$

5. **(D)** Solve by simplifying and completing the square:

$$4x^2 + 8x - 4 = 0$$
$$x^2 + 2x - 1 = 0$$
$$x^2 + 2x = 1$$

Then complete the square by adding 1 to both sides:

$$x^2 + 2x + 1 = 2$$

Then factor the left-hand side:

$$(x+1)^2 = 2$$

Then take the square root of both sides, remembering to include both the positive and the negative values on the right:

$$x+1 = \sqrt{2} \text{ and } x+1 = -\sqrt{2}$$

Solve for x to find the solutions:

$$x = \sqrt{2} - 1 \text{ and } x = -\sqrt{2} - 1$$

Alternatively, you could solve this using the quadratic equation. Start by dividing by 4 to simplify:

$$4x^2 + 8x - 4 = 0$$
$$x^2 + 2x - 1 = 0$$

$$x = \frac{-b \pm \sqrt{b^2 - 4ac}}{2a}$$

$$x = \frac{-2 \pm \sqrt{2^2 - 4(1)(-1)}}{2(1)}$$

$$x = \frac{-2 \pm \sqrt{8}}{2}$$

$$x = \frac{-2 \pm 2\sqrt{2}}{2}$$

$$x = \frac{-1 \pm \sqrt{2}}{1}$$

$$x = -1 \pm \sqrt{2}$$

This is equivalent to the answers $x = \sqrt{2} - 1$ and $x = -\sqrt{2} - 1$.

6. **(C)** Combine like terms, and then factor out what is common to all of the terms:

$$x^4 y^2 + x^3 y^5 + xy^6 + 2x^3 y^5 =$$
$$x^4 y^2 + 3x^3 y^5 + xy^6 =$$
$$xy^2(x^3 + 3x^2 y^3 + y^4)$$

7. **(B)** This is probably easiest to solve by plugging in the answers. Start with choice (B) or choice (C) as your first attempt since the answers are in order from smallest to largest. (Note that $n^0 = 1$ since anything to the zero power is 1.) If you plug in 1 for x, it works:

$$\frac{x}{2} = \frac{2\left(n^0\right)}{2} - \frac{1}{2x}$$

$$\frac{1}{2} = \frac{2(1)}{2} - \frac{1}{2(1)}$$

$$\frac{1}{2} = 1 - \frac{1}{2}$$

You can also solve the problem algebraically, but doing so may take more time:

$$\frac{x}{2} = \frac{2\left(n^0\right)}{2} - \frac{1}{2x}$$

$$x = 2\left(n^0\right) - \frac{1}{x}$$

$$x = 2 - \frac{1}{x}$$

Multiply by x:

$$x^2 = 2x - 1$$
$$x^2 - 2x + 1 = 0$$
$$(x-1)(x-1) = 0$$
$$(x-1)^2 = 0$$
$$x = 1$$

8. **(D)** Combine the like terms together to find the sum:

$$3x^3 + 5x - 3$$
$$+ 2x^2 - 4x + 6$$
$$\overline{3x^3 + 2x^2 + x + 3}$$

9. **(B)**

$$(25a^4 + 40a^2b^4 + 16b^8) \div (5a^2 + 4b^4) =$$
$$\frac{25a^4 + 40a^2b^4 + 16b^8}{5a^2 + 4b^4} =$$
$$\frac{(5a^2 + 4b^4)(5a^2 + 4b^4)}{5a^2 + 4b^4} =$$
$$5a^2 + 4b^4 = 4b^4 + 5a^2$$

10. **(A)** Choice I is correct. Since the velocity is raised to a fractional exponent, the impact of a certain amount of wind speed increase is more significant at lower wind speeds than at higher wind speeds. Choice II is not correct. Wind chill still has an impact when the temperature is less than 35.75 degrees Fahrenheit since this number is a constant, not a minimal temperature. Choice III is not correct. As temperature increases, the perceived temperature due to wind chill also increases.

11. **(C)** The function intersects the x-axis at $x = 6$, making 6 a zero of the function. Therefore, A can be expressed as $(x - 6)$.

12. **(A)** Plug in one of the zeros for x and plug in the number 0 for y since a zero intersects the x-axis. Remember that the y-value must be 0 for an x-intercept since that indicates where the function intersects the x-axis. Use this to solve for the constant c. Use -4 as that x-value so that you do not have to calculate with fractions:

$$y = 6x^3 + 19x^2 - 24x + c$$
$$0 = 6(-4)^3 + 19(-4)^2 - 24(-4) + c$$
$$0 = 6(-64) + 19(16) + 96 + c$$
$$0 = -384 + 304 + 96 + c$$
$$0 = 16 + c$$
$$-16 = c$$

13. **(D)** Since the parabola has zeros at 3 and -2, it can be written in this way:

$$f(x) = (x - 3)(x + 2)$$

Use FOIL:

$$f(x) = x^2 - x - 6$$

Alternatively, you can set $x = 0$. Then see which of the choices results in a y-value of -6 since this is the y-intercept of the parabola based on the graph. Only choice (D) works:

$$f(x) = x^2 - x - 6$$
$$f(0) = 0^2 - 0 - 6 = -6$$
$$f(0) = -6$$

14. **(A)** When you add a number to the x-value itself, the function shifts to the left by that number of places. When you add a number to the function as a whole, the function shifts upward by that number of places. Since 8 is added to the x-value itself and 4 is added to the function as a whole, the function shifts to the left 8 units and shifts up 4 units.

15. **(B)** The cost of the sales tax on the good is found by subtracting the untaxed price from the total cost:

$$1.07P - P = 0.07P$$

You can also visualize this by plugging in a sample value for the price of the good. A helpful sample value to use with percentages is 100 since it gives easily understood results. If, for example, you suppose that the price of the good is $100, the cost with the sales tax included is $1.07 \times \$100 = \$107$. So the sales tax on the good is $\$107 - \$100 = \$7$. This is equivalent to $0.07 \times \$100 = \$7$.

ADDITIONAL TOPICS IN MATH PRACTICE

1. If Alaina wishes to paint all six faces of a rectangular box that has dimensions in feet of $8 \times 4 \times 6$, how many square feet of paint does she need?

   (A) 124
   (B) 168
   (C) 208
   (D) 256

2. If a circle has a radius of 3 units, what is the length in units of the arc on the circle that measures $\frac{\pi}{2}$ radians?

   (A) π
   (B) $\frac{3}{2}\pi$
   (C) $\frac{5}{2}\pi$
   (D) 7π

3. If x represents the diameter of a circle, what is the area of a 60-degree sector of the circle?

   (A) πx^2
   (B) $\frac{\pi x^2}{24}$
   (C) $\frac{\pi x^2}{6}$
   (D) $\frac{\pi x^2}{36}$

4.

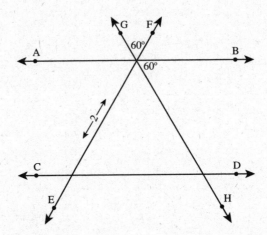

In the above drawing, lines *AB* and *CD* are parallel. Lines *EF* and *GH* intersect line *AB* at the same point and with the angle measures as indicated. What is the perimeter of the triangle formed by lines *CD, EF,* and *GH* between lines *AB* and *CD*?

   (A) 2
   (B) 4
   (C) 6
   (D) 8

5. A cube with edge length x has all of its edges doubled. Suppose the volume of the original cube is V cubic inches. What is the volume of the new cube in terms of the original cube?

(A) $2V$

(B) $4V$

(C) $8V$

(D) $16V$

6. The sides of a right triangle are 6, $6\sqrt{3}$, and 12. In a triangle similar to this triangle, what is the measure of the triangle's smallest interior angle?

(A) $10°$

(B) $30°$

(C) $40°$

(D) $45°$

7. What is an equivalent form of the following expression?

$$\frac{2i}{5-i}$$

(A) $\frac{2i-1}{17}$

(B) $\frac{4+2i}{5}$

(C) $\frac{1+i}{3}$

(D) $\frac{5i-1}{13}$

Answer Explanations

1. **(C)** The box is drawn below:

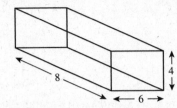

   Add up all of the surface areas of the six faces of the box. Since there are 2 of each face dimension, you can set up your equation as follows:

   $$2((8 \times 4) + (4 \times 6) + (8 \times 6)) = 208$$

2. **(B)** A measure of $\frac{\pi}{2}$ radians corresponds to $\frac{1}{4}$ of the distance around the circle since 2π radians is the entire distance around the circle. First find the circumference of a circle with radius of 3:

   $$2\pi r = 2\pi 3 = 6\pi$$

   Then calculate $\frac{1}{4}$ of the circumference:

   $$\frac{1}{4} \text{ of } 6\pi \text{ is } \frac{3}{2}\pi$$

3. **(B)** A 60-degree sector of the circle is $\frac{60}{360} = \frac{1}{6}$ of the total circle's area since there are 360 degrees in a circle. The area of a circle is calculated using πr^2. Since the diameter of the circle is x, the radius of the circle is half of x: $\frac{x}{2}$. So the area of this circle equals:

   $$\pi r^2 = \pi \left(\frac{x}{2}\right)^2 = \frac{\pi x^2}{4}$$

   Multiply the circle area by $\frac{1}{6}$ to find the area of the sector:

   $$\frac{1}{6} \times \frac{\pi x^2}{4} = \frac{\pi x^2}{24}$$

4. **(C)** Perimeter is the sum of the side measures of the triangle. The internal angles of the triangle formed are all 60 degrees. Since the angles are all congruent, the sides of the triangle are all congruent as well. Thus, the perimeter of the triangle is $2 + 2 + 2 = 6$ units. You can see this more clearly in the diagram below:

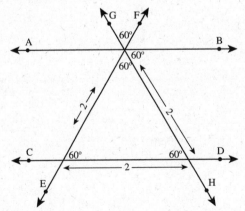

5. **(C)** Each edge of the cube is doubled. So instead of each edge having a length of x, each edge now has a length of $2x$. The volume formula for a cube is $V = x^3$. The original cube has a volume of x^3. The new cube has a volume of $(2x)^3 = 2^3 x^3 = 8x^3$. So the volume of the new cube is 8 times the volume of the original cube, which is $8V$.

6. **(B)** The sides given are a multiple of a special right triangle, the $30° - 60° - 90°$ triangle that has sides the length of x, $\sqrt{3}x$, and $2x$. In this problem, 6 corresponds to the x, $6\sqrt{3}$ corresponds to the $\sqrt{3}x$, and 12 corresponds to the $2x$. In this triangle, $30°$ is the smallest angle.

7. **(D)** A common way to simplify expressions with imaginary numbers is to multiply both the numerator and the denominator by the *conjugate* of the denominator. Doing so allows you to eliminate the imaginary components from the denominator. For $\dfrac{2i}{5-i}$, the conjugate is $5+i$. Simplify as follows:

$$\frac{2i}{5-i} \times \frac{5+i}{5+i} =$$
$$\frac{10i-2}{25+5i-5i-i^2} =$$
$$\frac{10i-2}{25+1} =$$
$$\frac{10i-2}{26} = \frac{5i-1}{13}$$

TROUBLESHOOTING

Here are some further pointers for common strategy issues.

"I haven't taken enough math yet."

- Most of the PSAT will be from Algebra 1 and Algebra 2. Don't worry about not having taken precalculus yet—just be comfortable using sine, cosine, and tangent.
- Review the key formulas at the beginning of the chapter. If you memorize these, you will feel much more confident.
- Keep in mind that the test primarily requires critical thinking. If you go into the PSAT Math Test ready to figure out things, you can often overcome a lack of advanced training.

"I take too long."

TIP

You only have so much energy to devote to thinking on test day. Focus on solving the problems and not on things like overanalyzing the questions, checking your pace too frequently, and excessively reviewing your work.

- Prioritize which problems you do. Don't worry about the last question or two on either PSAT Math section. They will likely be more difficult.
- If a question is taking you more than a couple of minutes to solve, consider circling it and coming back to it. You are not writing off the problem. You will continue to think about it. If you have time to revisit the problem, it will likely seem quite a bit easier the second time around. Skip very difficult problems here and there. Then go back to them if time is available. Do not initially spend too much time on very difficult problems, because you may not have enough time to finish the test. Because the test is graded on a curve, skipping a problem isn't a big deal. However, not finishing the Math Test because of poor time management could be detrimental to scholarship chances if you leave enough problems incomplete. All problems are worth the same number of points. So it is better to get to the later problems and earn a few more points than just get that one tricky question but not have time for other problems you could be capable of solving. At the very least, be certain that you guess on a very difficult problem because there is no guessing penalty on the test.
- Pace yourself—take about 1.5 minutes per question on average. The earlier questions should take less time than this. The later questions should take more time. Keep yourself moving along.

"I finish too quickly."

- Consider what would be the most effective use of your extra time. For most people, it will be taking more time the first time through the questions. For some, it may be helpful to start with the most challenging questions later in the test so that you will have a couple of chances to try them—both when you start the test and when you finish. **Note:** Be sure to try this approach first on a practice test before you try it on the actual test. It is not typically an effective strategy; most students end up rushing through easier questions because they become stuck on the more difficult questions.
- Pace yourself—be sure you are taking enough time on each question, on average about 1.5 minutes a question.

"I have math anxiety."

TIP

Don't forget to try the drills in the next chapter, "Advanced Math Drills," for more challenging practice.

- The confidence that comes with rigorous practice is the best way to overcome your anxiety. If you work through the problem sets throughout this book, you will be ready for the PSAT.
- Realize that some anxiety is welcome—it can help you stay focused and tune out distractions. It can also help push you to work through a challenging problem. Channel your nervous energy into action instead of letting it paralyze your thought process.
- Keep things in perspective. The Math Test represents half of the test; you can still miss several questions and achieve a top score. The PSAT, although vital for National Merit consideration, is primarily preparation for the SAT. You will have plenty of chances to take the SAT and/or ACT, the tests that colleges use for admissions decisions. All the practice you are doing for the PSAT will directly help you prepare for these later tests as well.

Advanced Math Drills 7

The following 14 drills represent the most challenging types of math questions you will encounter on the PSAT, helping prepare you to earn National Merit recognition. You can practice all of these or focus on your most challenging question types. The drills as a whole are designed to give you comprehensive coverage of the variety of questions you may face on test day. The passages are arranged by topic and type of question:

- Heart of Algebra Drill 1 (Calculator)
- Heart of Algebra Drill 2 (Calculator)
- Heart of Algebra Drill (No Calculator)
- Problem Solving and Data Analysis Drill 1 (Calculator)
- Problem Solving and Data Analysis Drill 2 (Calculator)
- Problem Solving and Data Analysis Drill (No Calculator)
- Passport to Advanced Math Drill 1 (Calculator)
- Passport to Advanced Math Drill 2 (Calculator)
- Passport to Advanced Math Drill (No Calculator)
- Additional Topics in Math Drill (Calculator)
- Calculator Problems Mixed Drill
- Free-Response Problems Drill (No Calculator)
- Free-Response Problems Drill (Calculator)
- No-Calculator Problems Mixed Drill

To practice these passages under timed conditions, take about 15 minutes per drill. Answer explanations for each drill appear at the end of the chapter.

HEART OF ALGEBRA

Heart of Algebra Drill 1 (Calculator)

1. What is the value of x in the following equation?

$$-\frac{3}{8}x + \frac{5}{16}x - \frac{1}{2}x = \frac{18}{32}$$

   (A) 1
   (B) −1
   (C) 3
   (D) $\frac{117}{8}$

2. What is the value of a in the following equation?

$$\frac{(3a-4)}{5} = \frac{(3a-4)}{8}$$

   (A) $\frac{4}{3}$
   (B) 0
   (C) $\frac{28}{9}$
   (D) $\frac{52}{9}$

3. What is the solution with the least possible y-value that satisfies both of the following inequalities?

$$y \geq 2x + 5$$
$$\text{and}$$
$$4 - y \leq x$$

   (A) $\left(\frac{1}{2}, \frac{5}{2}\right)$
   (B) $\left(\frac{1}{3}, \frac{11}{3}\right)$
   (C) $\left(-\frac{1}{2}, 4\right)$
   (D) $\left(-\frac{1}{3}, \frac{13}{3}\right)$

4. If $|3x - 1| = 4$, what are all of the possible value(s) of x?

   I. −1
   II. $\frac{5}{3}$
   III. 1

   (A) II only
   (B) III only
   (C) I and II only
   (D) All of the above

5. What is the value of x?

$$\frac{3}{2}x - \frac{2}{3} = \frac{x}{6} - \frac{10}{27}$$

   (A) $-\frac{7}{9}$
   (B) $\frac{2}{9}$
   (C) $\frac{17}{54}$
   (D) $\frac{9}{2}$

6. The graph of each equation in the system below is a line in the xy-plane.

$$y = 6x - 2$$
$$-6 = 12x - 2y$$

   What must be true about these two lines?

   (A) The lines are parallel.
   (B) The lines are perpendicular.
   (C) The lines intersect at $\left(\frac{3}{2}, 7\right)$.
   (D) The lines are the same.

7. Towns A and B are 200 miles apart. Caitlin starts driving from Town A to Town B at 3 P.M. at a rate of 30 miles per hour. Hannah starts driving from Town B to Town A at 4 P.M. on the same day at a rate of 40 miles per hour. At what time will they meet (to the nearest minute)?

   (A) 3:42 P.M.
   (B) 5:29 P.M.
   (C) 6:26 P.M.
   (D) 7:32 P.M.

8. A person can ride a roller coaster at an amusement park if he or she is between 36 and 72 inches tall. Which of the following inequalities models all possible values of permitted heights in inches for the ride?

(A) $|x - 36| < 72$
(B) $|x - 38| < 34$
(C) $|x - 30| < 42$
(D) $|x - 54| < 18$

9. A line in the xy-plane has a slope of $\frac{3}{5}$ and passes through the origin. Which of the following is a point on the line?

(A) $(15, 10)$
(B) $(3, 5)$
(C) $\left(0, \frac{3}{5}\right)$
(D) $(10, 6)$

10. A salesperson earns a commission (C) on the number of phone plans sold (x) if the value of C is positive. (There is no penalty or cost to the salesperson for a negative value of C; simply no commission is paid.) The amount of commission in dollars is modeled by this equation:

$$C = 50x + 25(x - 100) - 2{,}000$$

What is the least number of phone plans that the salesperson must sell in order to earn a commission?

(A) 60
(B) 61
(C) 75
(D) 100

Heart of Algebra Drill 2 (Calculator)

1. If the volume of a pyramid is given by the formula $V = \frac{1}{3} lwh$, where V is the volume, l is the length, w is the width, and h is the height, what is the width of the pyramid in terms of the other variables?

(A) $\dfrac{V}{3lh}$
(B) $\dfrac{3V}{lw}$
(C) $\dfrac{3V}{lh}$
(D) $\dfrac{lh}{3V}$

2. What is the negative solution to the following equation, rounded to one decimal place?

$$18x - \frac{21}{x} = \frac{2x}{3} + 12$$

(A) 1.5
(B) −0.8
(C) −0.6
(D) −1.5

3. An employee at a company has the following rules for days off from work:
   - Employees are granted 30 flex days paid time off in a year for non-weekend and holiday days.
   - Sick days with a doctor's note count as half a flex day.
   - Personal days count as a full flex day.

   If an employee wants to use at least half of the flex days but less than $\frac{5}{6}$ of them, what inequality would express the total number of sick days, S, and personal days, P, he or she could take in a year?

(A) $\dfrac{1}{2} \le \dfrac{1}{2}S + P < \dfrac{5}{6}$
(B) $15 \le \dfrac{1}{2}S + P < 25$
(C) $15 \le 2S + P < 25$
(D) $15 \le S + 2P < 30$

4. If $g(x) = 9x + 2$, what does $g(-4x)$ equal?

   (A) $-36x - 8$
   (B) $-36x + 2$
   (C) $5x + 2$
   (D) $-36x^2 + 2$

5. A carpenter charges a $40 initial fee for an in-home visit and $60 for each half hour worked. Which inequality models the total fee, F, for H hours worked where $H > 0$?

   (A) $F(H) = 40 + 30H$
   (B) $F(H) = 40 + 60H$
   (C) $F(H) = 40 + 120H$
   (D) $F(H) = 60 + 40H$

6. What are the values of x and y in the following equations?

   $$0.75x - 0.1y = 1.2$$
   $$2.6x + 3.4y = 15.4$$

   (A) $x = 1, y = -4.5$
   (B) $x = 2, y = 3$
   (C) $x = 3, y = 10.5$
   (D) $x = 4, y = 18$

7. If $\dfrac{m}{n} = -3$, what does $-2\dfrac{n}{m}$ equal?

   (A) -6
   (B) $\dfrac{2}{3}$
   (C) $\dfrac{3}{2}$
   (D) 6

8. If Equation A is defined by $y = \dfrac{2}{3}x - 4$ and if Equation B is defined by $3y = 2x + 3$, what must be done to Equation B so that the system of both Equation A and Equation B will have infinitely many solutions?

   (A) Add 9 to the right side
   (B) Subtract 5 from the right side
   (C) Subtract 7 from the right side
   (D) Subtract 15 from the right side

9. At 1:00 P.M., a blimp and a hot-air balloon are above the cities of Springfield and Washington, respectively. The two cities are 300 miles apart horizontally. The blimp is moving from Springfield to Washington at a horizontal speed of 10 miles per hour; the balloon is moving from Washington to Springfield at a horizontal speed of 200 miles per hour. The blimp starts at an altitude of 5,000 feet and is descending at a rate of 5 feet per minute; the balloon starts at an altitude of 500 feet and is ascending at a rate of 4 feet per minute. At what time will the blimp and balloon be at the same altitude, to the nearest minute?

   (A) 6:20 P.M.
   (B) 7:20 P.M.
   (C) 8:20 P.M.
   (D) 9:20 P.M.

10. Rosa's metabolism is 65 calories per hour when resting and 300 calories per hour when exercising. If Rosa wants to burn more than 2,000 calories per day, what is the range of hours, H, she should spend exercising, calculated to the nearest tenth, assuming that she is either resting or exercising at any time in a given day?

   (A) $24 > H > 1.9$
   (B) $24 > H > 2.4$
   (C) $24 > H > 6.7$
   (D) $24 > H > 22.1$

Heart of Algebra Drill (No Calculator)

1. If $\dfrac{-2x - 4}{5} > 2$, what is the range of x?

   (A) $x > -7$
   (B) $x < -\dfrac{11}{2}$
   (C) $x < -7$
   (D) $x > 7$

2. Susan is given a piggybank for her birthday that can hold a maximum of 500 quarters. The piggybank initially has 120 quarters. Each day after she receives the bank, 4 quarters are added. No coins or other objects are added to the piggybank. Which equation could be used to solve for the number of days (D) after Susan's birthday that it will take to fill the bank?

(A) $500 = 120 + 4D$
(B) $500 = 4D - 120$
(C) $120 = 4D$
(D) $500 = 4 + 120D$

3. In basketball, 1 point is awarded for a free throw, 2 points for a shot within the three-point line, and 3 points for shots outside the three-point line. If the number of points from x two-point shots is at least as great as the number of points from y three-point shots and z free throws, which expression would represent this relationship?

(A) $x \geq y + z$
(B) $x \geq 3y + z$
(C) $2x \geq 3y + z$
(D) $2x \geq y + 3z$

4. What is the value of x in this pair of equations?

$$5 - \frac{2}{3}y = x \text{ and } 4\left(10 - \frac{4}{3}y\right) = 2x + 5$$

(A) -20
(B) $\frac{5}{6}$
(C) $\frac{25}{4}$
(D) $\frac{75}{2}$

5. If $-2|-3| < -3|x + 5|$, what are all possible values of x?

(A) $-7 < x < -3$
(B) $-3 < x$ OR $-7 > x$
(C) $-3 < x$
(D) No solutions

6. Machine 1 can manufacture one box in A hours, and Machine 2 can manufacture an identical box in B hours. When working simultaneously, Machines A and B can produce 1 box in T hours. This relationship is given by the following formula:

$$\frac{1}{A} + \frac{1}{B} = \frac{1}{T}$$

What is the value of B in terms of the other two variables?

(A) $\dfrac{1}{\dfrac{1}{T} - \dfrac{1}{A}}$

(B) $\dfrac{1}{\dfrac{1}{A} - \dfrac{1}{T}}$

(C) $\dfrac{1}{T} - \dfrac{1}{A}$

(D) $\dfrac{AT}{T - A}$

7.

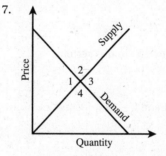

If the manufacturer of the XYZ machine develops new technology that makes creating the machine less expensive, in which zone(s) of the graph would the new supply curve most likely be?

(A) 1 and 2
(B) 2 and 3
(C) 3 and 4
(D) Unchanged

8. Line A has points $(1, -2)$ and $(-1, 0)$. Line B has point $(3, 4)$. What would the y-value of the y-intercept of line B need to be in order for line A and line B to intersect at a 90° angle?

(A) −7
(B) −1
(C) 1
(D) 4

9. A library fines a patron who fails to return a book on time the replacement cost of the book plus an additional 10 cents each day that the fine is not paid in full. On December 1, Jane borrowed a book with a replacement cost of $30. The book was due to be returned on December 14. Which function models the total amount of dollars (A) that Jane will need to pay x days after December 14?

(A) $A(x) = 30 + 10x$
(B) $A(x) = 30 + 0.1x$
(C) $A(x) = 30 + 1.4x$
(D) $A(x) = 30 - x$

10. What is the value of a in this system of equations?

$$a = \frac{2}{3}b + 1 \text{ and } 2 + 3a = -4(2b + 1)$$

(A) $-\frac{9}{10}$

(B) $\frac{2}{5}$

(C) $\frac{11}{15}$

(D) $\frac{16}{15}$

PROBLEM SOLVING AND DATA ANALYSIS

Problem Solving and Data Analysis Drill 1 (Calculator)

1. In an animal shelter consisting of only dogs and cats, the ratio of dogs to cats is 3 to 1. If there are 360 animals in the shelter, how many dogs must be present?

(A) 90
(B) 120
(C) 270
(D) 300

2. A reporter finds that on average, a particular politician receives 14 seconds of applause out of every minute of a speech. If the politician were to give a speech for exactly two hours, how many minutes of the speech would be devoted to applause?

(A) 14
(B) 28
(C) 37
(D) 1,680

3. Whole milk has 3.5% fat content. If you used equal amounts of 1% and 2% milk, how many total gallons of the combined milk would you use to equal the fat content in exactly 1 gallon of whole milk?

(A) $\frac{1}{200}$

(B) $\frac{1}{2}$

(C) $1\frac{1}{6}$

(D) $2\frac{1}{3}$

4. Katie is interested in running a marathon, which is 26.2 miles long. She just finished a 5-kilometer race, and she wants to see how many 5K races she would have to complete in order to equal a full marathon. Given that there are approximately 0.62 miles in 1 kilometer, how many complete 5K races would Katie have to finish to go at least the distance of a marathon?

(A) 6
(B) 8
(C) 9
(D) 10

5. At the beginning of the year, 1 U.S. dollar can be exchanged for 0.9 euros, and 1 Canadian dollar can be exchanged for 0.7 U.S. dollars. If someone wants to convert 100 Canadian dollars to euros at these exchange rates and assuming that there are no transaction fees, how many euros would the person have after the conversion?

(A) 63
(B) 78
(C) 129
(D) 158

6. **Spread of a Computer Virus**

Day	Number of Computers Infected
1	101
2	110
3	200
4	1,100
5	10,100

The table above gives the number of computers infected with a virus. Which of the following functions models the number of computers infected, $C(d)$, after d days?

(A) $C(d) = 10^{2d} + 10(d-1) + 1$
(B) $C(d) = 100 + 10^d$
(C) $C(d) = 100 + 10(d-1) + 1$
(D) $C(d) = 100 + 10^{(d-1)}$

7. Light travels at approximately 3.00×10^8 meters per second. When the planet Jupiter is at its closest point to Earth, it is 588 million kilometers away. When Earth and Jupiter are this close, approximately how many minutes does light reflected off of Jupiter take to reach Earth?

(A) 3 minutes
(B) 33 minutes
(C) 58 minutes
(D) 18 minutes

8.

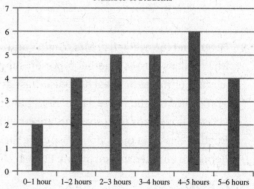

A group of 26 teenagers was asked about their daily smartphone usage. What was the median range of hours that this group used smartphones each day?

(A) Between 1 and 2
(B) Between 2 and 3
(C) Between 3 and 4
(D) Between 4 and 5

	Finished Summer Reading	Did Not Complete Summer Reading	
Mrs. Smith's Class	21	8	29
Mr. Walker's Class	14	17	31
	35	25	

9. Given that the average of Mrs. Smith's and Mr. Walker's classes together represents the average enrollment in each English class at the school and that there are a total of 14 English classes, how many total students are enrolled in English classes at the school, assuming that students are enrolled in exactly one English class?

    (A) 280
    (B) 420
    (C) 560
    (D) 840

10. The high school principal wants to evaluate the effectiveness of the teachers in getting their students to complete the summer reading assignments. The principal assigns 5 points to each student who completes the assignment and gives 0 points to each student who fails to complete the assignment. What is the difference between the mean and the median of the point values given to students in Mr. Walker's class?

    (A) 1.38
    (B) 1.60
    (C) 2.26
    (D) 2.74

Problem Solving and Data Analysis Drill 2 (Calculator)

1. A student writes a double-spaced typed paper using Times New Roman 12-point font. He finds that each page contains an average of 240 words. If the student changes to Comic Sans 12-point font, each page contains an average of only 170 words. If the student is required to write a 10-page double-spaced report, how many fewer words would he be required to write if the teacher accepts Comic Sans 12-point font instead of Times New Roman 12-point font?

    (A) 70
    (B) 170
    (C) 700
    (D) 1,700

2. On a map of a rectangular fenced-in area, the drawing of the enclosed area has a surface area of 20 square inches. If one side of the fenced-in area drawing is 4 inches long and the key of the map indicates that for every 1 inch drawn on the map there are 6 feet in actual distance, what is the perimeter of the actual fence, assuming there are no gaps or gates?

    (A) 18 ft
    (B) 108 ft
    (C) 120 ft
    (D) 720 ft

3. John's performance on his first test was only 60%. His performance increased by 20% on the next test, and it increased an additional 25% on the third test. What did John earn on the third test, to the nearest whole percent?

    (A) 72%
    (B) 75%
    (C) 90%
    (D) 105%

4. Linda's 15-gallon car tank has only 2 gallons left when she pulls into a gas station. She wants to purchase only the gas she will need to drive 240 miles and still have 1 gallon remaining. Her car gets 28 miles to the gallon. How many gallons should Linda purchase, to the nearest tenth of a gallon?

(A) 6.6 gallons
(B) 7.6 gallons
(C) 8.6 gallons
(D) 9.6 gallons

Questions 5–6 use the following graph.

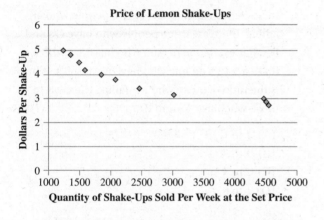

Price of Lemon Shake-Ups

5. If you were to graph dollars per shake-up along the *x*-axis and quantity of shake-ups sold per week at the set price on the *y*-axis, which of the following would be a property of the function between the values of 3 and 5 dollars?

(A) It would be a decreasing exponential function.
(B) It would be an increasing exponential function.
(C) It would be a decreasing linear function.
(D) It would be an increasing linear function.

6. At which of the following prices of a lemon shake-up would the total revenue be maximized?

(A) $2.50
(B) $3.00
(C) $3.50
(D) $5.00

Questions 7–8 use the following graph and information.

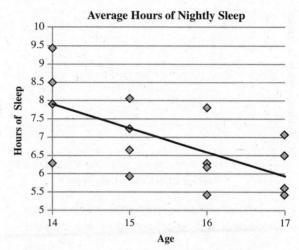

Average Hours of Nightly Sleep

A scientist surveys 16 randomly selected teenage students, recording their ages and their average number of hours of nightly sleep.

7. If *x* represents the age and *y* represents the average hours of sleep, which of the following gives the equation of the best-fit line for the survey results?

(A) $y = -0.6x + 7.8$
(B) $y = 0.8x + 7.8$
(C) $y = -0.6x + 16.2$
(D) $y = -1.9x + 16.2$

8. Which of the following would most likely cause the greatest obstacle to the accuracy of the sleep survey results?

(A) If the student survey responses are self-reported
(B) Whether the survey was conducted during the school year or during summer break
(C) If not all of the 16 teenagers respond
(D) If the scientist misreads the number of hours of one responder and records one more hour of sleep on average than what was reported

Questions 9–10 use the following graph.

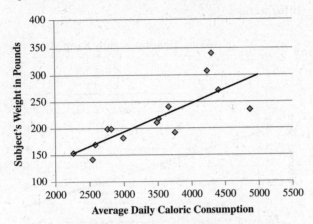

9. What choice most closely approximates the slope of the best-fit line of the graph above?

    (A) $-\dfrac{1}{10}$

    (B) $\dfrac{3}{50}$

    (C) $\dfrac{1}{5}$

    (D) $\dfrac{50}{3}$

10. What is the most logical explanation as to why the x- and y-axes begin as they do, as opposed to at zero values?

    (A) The researcher is not interested in the relationship between weight and caloric intake for a subject less than 100 pounds who eats under 2,000 calories per day.
    (B) No person weighs less than 100 pounds.
    (C) No person eats under 2,000 calories in a day.
    (D) A person cannot weigh zero pounds, and a person cannot consistently eat zero calories each day.

Problem Solving and Data Analysis Drill (No Calculator)

1. For every 8 units of x, there are consistently 12 units of y. If the relationship between x and y is given as an equation of the form $y = kx$, where k is a constant, what is the value of k?

    (A) $\dfrac{1}{4}$

    (B) $\dfrac{2}{3}$

    (C) $\dfrac{3}{2}$

    (D) 4

2. In a science class, for every two people who are failing, there are three people who have C's and D's. For every one person who has C's and D's, there are two people who have A's and B's. What is the ratio of those who are failing the class to those who have A's and B's?

    (A) 1 to 1
    (B) 1 to 3
    (C) 2 to 3
    (D) 1 to 6

3. A restaurant charges a $5 standard delivery fee plus a 15% tip on the amount of the bill before the delivery fee. Which of these expressions would model the total cost to have x dollars worth of food delivered?

    (A) $0.15x + 5$
    (B) $1.15x + 5$
    (C) $5x + 15$
    (D) $15x + 5$

Questions 4–5 use the following graph.

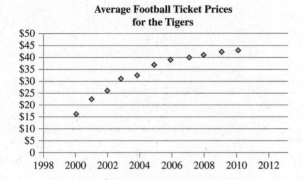

Average Football Ticket Prices
for the Tigers

4. Which of the following best describes the general relationship between years and average football ticket price?

   (A) As the years go by, the average football ticket price increases.
   (B) As the years go by, the average football ticket price decreases.
   (C) As the years go by, the average football ticket price stays the same.
   (D) There is no general relationship between years and average football ticket price.

5. Assuming that the trend represented in the graph continues over the next decade (which is not portrayed in the graph), the average price of a football ticket in the year 2014 would most likely be:

   (A) $41
   (B) $47
   (C) $56
   (D) $62

6.

Year	Exchange Rate of Currency X to Currency Y
2000	2.30
2001	15.35
2002	55.42
2003	121.56
2004	237.83

Which of these statements accurately represents the data in the table above?

   (A) As time goes by, Currency X is becoming relatively more valuable than Currency Y.
   (B) As time goes by, Currency Y is becoming relatively more valuable than Currency X.
   (C) As time goes by, Currency X is approaching the same value as Currency Y.
   (D) No relationship can be determined between Currency X and Currency Y.

7.

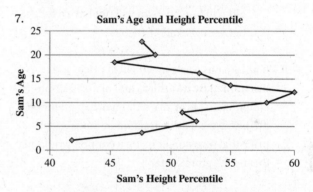

Sam's Age and Height Percentile

Which of the following is a logical conclusion about the data about Sam's age and height percentile?

   I. Sam's height grew exponentially quickly between ages 12 and 18.
   II. Sam's height relative to that of other men was lower when he was less than 5 years old than when he was between 10 and 15 years old.
   III. Sam continued to experience changes in his height between the ages of 18 and 22.

   (A) I only
   (B) II only
   (C) II and III only
   (D) I, II, and III

8. An amusement park researcher compiles data about the average height of ten-year-old children in a certain town to determine whether this age group will meet the minimum height requirements for a new attraction. The researcher selects 100 ten-year-old children at random from the town and finds that the average height has a 95% confidence interval between 42 and 48 inches. Which of the following conclusions could the researcher most reasonably make?

   (A) There is a 5% chance that the average ten-year-old child in the town will have a height between 42 and 48 inches.
   (B) It is very likely that the average ten-year-old child in the town will be less than 42 inches tall.
   (C) It is very likely that the average ten-year-old child in the town will have a height between 42 and 48 inches.
   (D) It is very likely that the average ten-year-old child in the town will not have a height between 42 and 48 inches.

9. If a store has a sale in which all prices are discounted by two-thirds and also distributes coupons that take an additional 20 percent off the price, what is the fraction of the original price that a customer using a coupon would pay during the store's sale?

   (A) $\dfrac{1}{15}$

   (B) $\dfrac{2}{15}$

   (C) $\dfrac{4}{15}$

   (D) $\dfrac{8}{15}$

10. A pollster wishes to project the winner for an upcoming election in her small city. Which of the following approaches to selecting a sample size would give the most accurate polling results?

    (A) Interviewing randomly selected shoppers at the grocery store
    (B) Contacting residents who live within half a mile of polling locations
    (C) Contacting a random selection of registered voters
    (D) Inviting voters to submit results to an online survey

PASSPORT TO ADVANCED MATH

Passport to Advanced Math Drill 1 (Calculator)

1. A cubic function would be most appropriate when modeling which of the following mathematical relationships?

   (A) A sphere's volume and its radius
   (B) A circle's circumference and its diameter
   (C) A triangle's area and its height
   (D) A cube's edge length and its total surface area

2. $\dfrac{a^3 - b^3 + 2a^2b - 2ab^2 + ab^2 - ba^2}{a^2 - b^2}$ equals which of the following, given that $a \neq \pm b$?

   (A) $a + b$
   (B) $a - b$
   (C) $a^2b - ab^2$
   (D) $a^2 + b^2$

3. If $-5m^5 + 3m^3 = 2m^7$, what is the sum of all possible values of m^2?

   (A) -2.5
   (B) 0
   (C) 0.5
   (D) 2.5

4. Solve for x: $\frac{1}{2}x^2 + \frac{1}{4}x - \frac{1}{8} = 0$

(A) $\frac{1}{2}\left(-1 \pm \sqrt{3}\right)$

(B) $\frac{1}{2}\left(-1 \pm \sqrt{5}\right)$

(C) $\frac{1}{4}\left(-1 \pm \sqrt{3}\right)$

(D) $\frac{1}{4}\left(-1 \pm \sqrt{5}\right)$

5. What is/are the solution(s) to the following equation?

$$a + 4 = \sqrt{a^2 - 2}$$

(A) $-\frac{9}{4}$

(B) $\frac{9}{4}$

(C) $\frac{-7}{4}$ and $\frac{9}{4}$

(D) No solutions

6. How many distinct zeros does the function $f(x) = (x-3)(x+7)(x-3)$ have?

(A) 0

(B) 1

(C) 2

(D) 3

7. Consider the function $f(x) = x^2 + 2$.
What operation could be performed on the right-hand side of the equation to expand the range to include negative values?

(A) Add 5

(B) Add −2

(C) Subtract 3

(D) Subtract 1

8. What is the vertex of the parabola $(y-4)^2 = 17(x+2)$?

(A) $(-2, 4)$

(B) $(2, -4)$

(C) $(-4, 2)$

(D) $(4, -2)$

9. The root mean squared speed of a molecule, v_{rms}, is calculated using the formula

$v_{rms} = \sqrt{\dfrac{3RT}{M}}$, where R is a gas constant, T is the temperature, and M is the molecular mass. The molecular mass of substance A is most likely to be less than the molecular mass of substance B if the temperature and v_{rms} of substance A compare in which ways to those of substance B?

(A) Greater v_{rms} and lower temperature

(B) Lower v_{rms} and greater temperature

(C) Lower v_{rms} and equal temperature

(D) Cannot be determined

10. Two different stock portfolios, A and B, have had no new deposits or withdrawals over a ten-year period and had the same initial amount in the account. If stock portfolio A has grown at an annual rate of $x\%$, if stock portfolio B has grown at an annual rate of $y\%$, and if $x > y$, what would represent the ratio of the value of portfolio A over that of portfolio B at the end of the ten-year period?

(A) $\left(\dfrac{1 + \dfrac{x}{100}}{1 + \dfrac{y}{100}}\right)^{10}$

(B) $\left(\dfrac{x}{y}\right)^{10}$

(C) $10\left(\dfrac{x}{y}\right)$

(D) $\left(\dfrac{1 - \dfrac{x}{100}}{1 - \dfrac{y}{100}}\right)^{10}$

Passport to Advanced Math Drill 2 (Calculator)

1. A car and a truck are initially 180 miles apart and are driving toward each other on a straight road when an observer measures their respective speeds. The car is driving at a constant speed of x miles per hour, and the truck is going twice this speed. If the car and the truck meet each other after three hours of driving, what is the speed of the truck?

   (A) 20 mph
   (B) 30 mph
   (C) 40 mph
   (D) 60 mph

2. The formula for the area of a trapezoid is $\frac{B_1 + B_2}{2} \times H$, where B_1 and B_2 are the bases of the trapezoid and H is its height. If the mean of the bases of the trapezoid is twice the height and if the area of the trapezoid is 72 square inches, what is the trapezoid's height in inches?

   (A) 6
   (B) $6\sqrt{2}$
   (C) 24
   (D) 36

3. $2m^{-2} - 4m^{-3}$ is equivalent to which of the following?

   (A) $\dfrac{2m-1}{4m^3}$

   (B) $\dfrac{-2}{m^5}$

   (C) $\dfrac{2m-4}{m^3}$

   (D) $-2m^2 + 4m^3$

4. $(2y^4 + 3x^6) + (5x^6 + 3y^4)$ is equivalent to which of the following?

   (A) $5y^4 + 8x^6$
   (B) $7y^4 + 6x^6$
   (C) $13y^4 x^6$
   (D) $5y^8 + 8x^{12}$

5. Which of the following is equivalent to the expression $\dfrac{2x^2 - 12x + 18}{3(x-3)^3}$?

   (A) $\dfrac{x^2 + 9}{x - 3}$

   (B) $\dfrac{2(x+3)}{3(x-3)^2}$

   (C) $\dfrac{2(x-6)}{(x-3)}$

   (D) $\dfrac{2}{3(x-3)}$

6. What are the solutions to $21x^2 = 15x + 18$?

   (A) $\dfrac{5 \pm \sqrt{193}}{14}$

   (B) $\dfrac{15 \pm \sqrt{1527}}{14}$

   (C) $\dfrac{5 \pm \sqrt{67}}{14}$

   (D) No real solutions

7. The supply for a given item at a varying price p (in dollars) is given by the equation $s(p) = 3p + 6p^2$. The demand for the same item at a varying price p is given by the equation $d(p) = 156 - 12p$. At what price are the supply and the demand for the item equivalent?

   (A) $3.50
   (B) $4
   (C) $6.50
   (D) $12

8. If x and y are variables and if c is a nonzero constant, which of the following choices would not necessarily have a y-intercept when graphed?

   I. $x = c$

   II. $y = -c$

   III. $y = cx$

(A) I only

(B) I and II only

(C) II and III only

(D) None of the above

9.

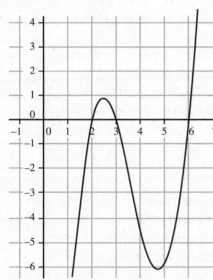

Which of the following equations represents the function graphed above?

(A) $x^3 + 11x^2 + 36x + 36$

(B) $x^3 - 11x^2 + 36x - 36$

(C) $x^3 + x^2 - 24x + 36$

(D) $x^2 - 5x + 6$

10. The formula for annual compounded interest is $A = P\left(1 + \dfrac{r}{n}\right)^{nt}$, where P is the initial amount invested, A is the future value of the initial amount, r is the annual interest rate expressed as a decimal, n is the number of times the investment is compounded each year, and t is the number of years the amount is invested. If an initial investment, P, is compounded once every 12 months, which expression is equivalent to the future value of the investment if its interest rate is 5% and if the money is invested for exactly 1 year?

(A) $0.05P$

(B) $0.5P$

(C) $1.05P$

(D) $1.50P$

Passport to Advanced Math Drill (No Calculator)

1. A square piece of paper is folded in half n times. If L is the length of an edge, what is the area of the piece of paper after it is folded in half n times?

(A) $\dfrac{L^2}{2^{n-1}}$

(B) $\dfrac{L^2}{2^n}$

(C) $\dfrac{L^2}{n}$

(D) $\dfrac{L^2}{2n}$

2. $\left(81^{-\frac{1}{4}}\right)\left(64^{\frac{1}{3}}\right)$ equals

(A) -12

(B) $-\dfrac{4}{3}$

(C) $\dfrac{1}{12}$

(D) $\dfrac{4}{3}$

3. Which of the following is equivalent to

$$\frac{3x^3 + 2x^2 - 5x + 6}{x + 2}$$ for x not equal to -2?

(A) $3x^2 - 4x + 3$

(B) $3x^2 + 8x + 11$

(C) $x^2 - 3x + 3$

(D) $3x^2 + 4x + 12$

4. What relationship must exist between the constants a, b, and c for the equation $ax^2 + bx + c = 0$ to have only real solutions?

(A) $b^2 \le 4ac$

(B) $b^2 \ge 4ac$

(C) $2a > -b$

(D) Cannot be determined

5. $(3x^3 - 2x^2 + 5x + 7) - (x^4 + x(x + 2)) = ?$

(A) $2x^3 - x^2 + 7x + 9$

(B) $-x^4 + 3x^3 - x^2 + 7x + 7$

(C) $2x^4 - 3x^2 + 5x + 5$

(D) $-x^4 + 3x^3 - 3x^2 + 3x + 7$

6. How many solutions does the following equation have?

$$a - \sqrt{a} = 6$$

(A) 0

(B) 1

(C) 2

(D) 4

7. Out of all possible solutions (x, y) to the pair of equations below, what is the greatest possible product xy that can be obtained?

$$x(y + 2) - 3x - 4(y + 2) = -12$$
and
$$3x - 6 = 3y$$

(A) 3

(B) 4

(C) 6

(D) 8

8.

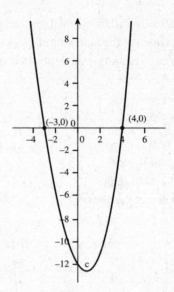

Based on the graph of $f(x)$ above, $f(x)$ is divisible by which of the following expressions?

I. $x - 4$

II. $x + 1$

III. $x + 3$

(A) I and II only

(B) I and III only

(C) All of the above

(D) None of the above

9. What happens to the vertex (h, k) of $y = x^2 + 3$ if the 3 is replaced by a 6 and if x is changed to $(x - 5)$?

(A) h decreases by 5, k increases by 6

(B) h increases by 5, k increases by 3

(C) h increases by 5, k increases by 6

(D) h remains the same, k increases by 31

10. If $f(x) = g(x) + 4$ and if $g(x) = x - \dfrac{5}{x}$, what is the value of $f(10)$?

(A) 9.5

(B) 10

(C) 13.5

(D) 14

ADDITIONAL TOPICS IN MATH

Additional Topics in Math Drill (Calculator)

1. A right circular cylinder has a volume of $30x$ cubic feet, and a cube has a volume of $21x$ cubic feet. What is the sum of the volumes of a cone with the same height and radius as the cylinder and of a pyramid with the same length, width, and height of the cube?

   (A) $7x$ cubic feet
   (B) $10x$ cubic feet
   (C) $17x$ cubic feet
   (D) $51x$ cubic feet

2. Andrew rides his bike 20 miles directly north and then 15 miles directly to the east. How many miles would he travel if he could fly directly from his starting point to his ending point?

   (A) 25
   (B) 31
   (C) 35
   (D) 625

3. In a right triangle with legs of length a and b, what is the value of the hypotenuse of the triangle?

   (A) $\sqrt{a+b}$
   (B) $\sqrt{a^2-b^2}$
   (C) $\sqrt{a^2+b^2}$
   (D) a^2+b^2

4. If $i = \sqrt{-1}$, $2i^2(3i)^4 = ?$

   (A) -162
   (B) -6
   (C) $162i$
   (D) 162

5. What would be the measure, in radians, of an arc on a circle if the measure of the arc in degrees was 270?

   (A) $\dfrac{2\pi}{3}$
   (B) $\dfrac{3\pi}{2}$
   (C) 270π
   (D) $\dfrac{48,600}{\pi}$

6.

A circular pizza has a radius of 8 inches. If the pizza is cut into 8 equal sectors as shown in the drawing above, what is the length of the crust on the edge of each piece, rounded to two decimal places?

   (A) 0.13 inches
   (B) 0.79 inches
   (C) 3.74 inches
   (D) 6.28 inches

7.

In the above drawing, lines AB and CD are parallel, and line EF is a transversal. How many angles made from the given lines measure 60 degrees?

   (A) 1
   (B) 2
   (C) 4
   (D) 6

8. $\dfrac{i^3 + 9i - 6}{3 + i} = ?$

   (A) $2i - 3$
   (B) $3i - 1$
   (C) $3 - i$
   (D) $2 + 3i$

9. In two similar isosceles triangles, triangle A has two sides each of length 5 and one side of length 7. Triangle B has exactly one side of length 28. What is the perimeter of triangle B?

   (A) 17
   (B) 20
   (C) 38
   (D) 68

10. Triangle XYZ has a right angle for angle Y and has side lengths of 24 for XY and 26 for XZ. For a triangle that is similar to XYZ, what would be the value of the tangent of its smallest angle?

   (A) $\dfrac{5}{12}$

   (B) $\dfrac{5}{13}$

   (C) $\dfrac{12}{13}$

   (D) $\dfrac{12}{5}$

CALCULATOR PROBLEMS

Calculator Problems Mixed Drill

1. Solve for x: $\dfrac{12\left(\dfrac{5x - 2x}{2}\right)}{6} = 18$

   (A) 24

   (B) $\dfrac{9}{4}$

   (C) $\dfrac{4}{3}$

   (D) 6

2. A rock is made up by volume of 32% coal, which has a specific gravity (expressed in grams per cubic centimeter) of 1.20. The rock contains 29% granite with a specific gravity of 2.60. The rock also contains 39% of an unknown mineral. If the specific gravity of the entire rock is 1.4, the unknown material has what approximate specific gravity?

   (A) 0.43
   (B) 0.54
   (C) 0.67
   (D) 0.81

3. A train is traveling for 5 hours at a constant rate of x miles per hour and then travels an additional $\dfrac{x}{10}$ hours at a speed of $\dfrac{x}{2}$ miles per hour. If the train travels a total of 300 miles during these two segments, which equation could be used to solve for x?

   (A) $x^2 + 100x - 6{,}000 = 0$
   (B) $x^2 + 100x - 300 = 0$
   (C) $x^2 + 5x - 300 = 0$
   (D) $3x^2 + 150x - 6{,}000 = 0$

4. $(6a^3)^3 - (2b)^4 + c^{-2} = ?$

   (A) $6a^9 - 2b^4 + \dfrac{1}{c^2}$

   (B) $18a^9 - 8b^4 + \dfrac{1}{c^2}$

   (C) $21a^6 - 16b^4 + \dfrac{1}{c^2}$

   (D) $216a^9 - 16b^4 + \dfrac{1}{c^2}$

Questions 5–7 use the following graph.

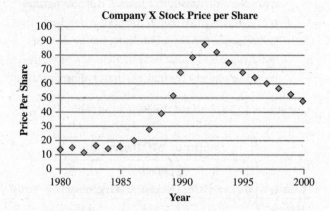

Company X Stock Price per Share

5. The relationship between year and stock price is most exponential during what range of years?

   (A) 1980–1983
   (B) 1984–1991
   (C) 1992–1996
   (D) 1997–2000

6. Between which two-year period does the Company X stock price undergo the greatest percentage increase?

   (A) Between 1983–1984
   (B) Between 1986–1987
   (C) Between 1988–1989
   (D) Between 1989–1990

7. A stockbroker sold $1,000 in shares of Company X stock. Approximately how many more shares would she have sold if the stock price is taken at the minimal value in the graph versus at the maximum value in the graph?

   (A) 8
   (B) 20
   (C) 40
   (D) 80

8. If $f(a) = a^2 - 12$, what is $f(b - a)$?

   (A) $a^2 + b^2 - 12$
   (B) $a^3 - b - 12$
   (C) $a^2 - 2ab - b^2 - 12$
   (D) $a^2 - 2ab + b^2 - 12$

9.

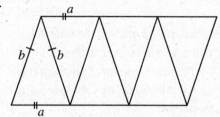

Six identical isosceles triangles are arranged as shown in the figure above. If one side of each triangle has length a and if the other two sides each have length b, what is the outside perimeter of the figure above in terms of a and b?

   (A) $4a + 4b$
   (B) $6a + 2b$
   (C) $6a + 7b$
   (D) $6a + 12b$

10.

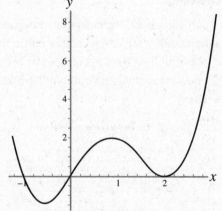

Which of the following could be an equation for the function graphed in the xy-plane above?

   (A) $x(x - 2)(x + 1)$
   (B) $x(x - 2)^2(x + 1)$
   (C) $x(x + 2)^2(x - 1)$
   (D) $x(x + 2)(x - 1)$

FREE-RESPONSE PROBLEMS

Free-Response Problems Drill (No Calculator)

1. A circle has the equation $x^2 + y^2 = 36$. What is the shortest distance in units from the origin to a point on the circle?

2. Jamie can run $\frac{3}{2}k$ miles in the time that Matt takes to run k miles. If Jamie and Matt run for the same amount of time and their combined mileage is 10 miles, how many miles did Jamie run?

3. What is the product of all solutions to $(x+2)^2 = (2x-3)^2$?

4. If $a^4 - 2a^3 + 2a^2 + ma + 2$ has $(a+1)$ as a factor, what is the value of the constant m?

5. What will be the new slope of the line $y = 2x + 3$ after it is translated 3 units to the right and 2 units down?

Free-Response Problems Drill (Calculator)

1. At a particular store, customers can purchase children's outfits for $20 and adults' outfits for $45. If a family purchased 22 outfits for a total of $765, how many children's outfits did the family purchase?

2.

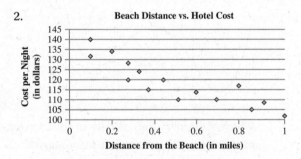

Beach Distance vs. Hotel Cost

The scatter plot above shows the price of a room per night at 15 different hotels versus the distance the hotels are from the beach. If Hotel M is the hotel at the median distance to the beach, how many hotel rooms must be booked for the hotel to make $2,280 in one night?

3. One face of a triangular building is portrayed in a photograph in which 1 inch in the photograph corresponds to 10 feet in the actual building. If the face of the actual building has an area of 960 square feet and a base of 48 feet, what is the building's height (in inches) in the photograph?

Questions 4–5 are about the following table.

	Major at ABC University			
Gender	**Humanities**	**Math/ Science**	**Engineering**	**Total**
Male	450	125	140	715
Female	520	100	155	775
Total	970	225	295	1490

4. What is the total percentage of STEM majors (math, science, engineering) out of all the students at ABC University, rounded to the nearest percent? (Ignore the percent symbol when entering your answer. For example, if your answer is 10%, enter 10 as your answer.)

5. What is the probability that a randomly selected student at ABC University will be both a male and a humanities major (calculated to the nearest hundredth)?

NO-CALCULATOR PROBLEMS

No-Calculator Problems Mixed Drill

1. What is the value of x in the following equation?

$$15x + \frac{1}{2} = -5\left(x - \frac{5}{2}\right)$$

(A) $-\dfrac{3}{20}$

(B) $-\dfrac{13}{20}$

(C) $\dfrac{3}{5}$

(D) $\dfrac{3}{10}$

2. If $i = \sqrt{-1}$, what is the value of $(3 - i)(4 + i)$?

   (A) $11 - i$
   (B) $12 + 7i$
   (C) $13 - i$
   (D) $13 + i$

3. What is the value of the constant c in the equation below?

$$(x - 6)(x - 10) = (x - 8)^2 + c$$

   (A) -4
   (B) 0
   (C) 4
   (D) 16

4.

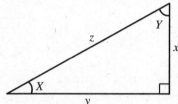

Which trigonometric expression would give the value of angle X?

   (A) $\sin^{-1}\left(\dfrac{x}{z}\right)$

   (B) $\cos^{-1}\left(\dfrac{x}{z}\right)$

   (C) $\sin\left(\dfrac{x}{z}\right)$

   (D) $\sin^{-1}\left(\dfrac{y}{z}\right)$

5. The ideal gas equation is $PV = nRT$, where P is the pressure, V is the volume, n is the number of moles, R is the gas constant, and T is the temperature. According to the equation, the volume of a gas is inversely related to

   (A) the number of moles.
   (B) gas constant.
   (C) temperature.
   (D) none of the above.

6. In physics, the mirror equation is

$$\frac{1}{f} = \frac{1}{d_o} + \frac{1}{d_i}, \text{ where } f \text{ represents the}$$

mirror's focal length, d_o is the distance of an object from the mirror, and d_i is the distance of the image from the mirror. Which expression gives d_o in terms of focal length and image distance?

   (A) $\dfrac{1}{\dfrac{1}{f} + \dfrac{1}{d_i}}$

   (B) $\dfrac{1}{f} - \dfrac{1}{d_i}$

   (C) $\dfrac{1}{\dfrac{1}{d_i} - \dfrac{1}{f}}$

   (D) $\dfrac{1}{\dfrac{1}{f} - \dfrac{1}{d_i}}$

7. If the following equation is true for every value of x and if a is a constant, what is the value of a?

$$(x + 4)(x^2 + ax + 2) = x^3 + x^2 - 10x + 8$$

   (A) -10
   (B) -3
   (C) -2
   (D) 1

8. $\left(6y^3 + \dfrac{1}{2}y - \dfrac{2}{3}\right) - \left(4y^3 - y^2 + \dfrac{1}{2}y + \dfrac{1}{6}\right) = ?$

   (A) $2y^3 + y^2 + y + \dfrac{5}{6}$

   (B) $2y^3 - y^2 + y - \dfrac{1}{2}$

   (C) $2y^3 - \dfrac{1}{2}y - \dfrac{1}{2}$

   (D) $2y^3 + y^2 - \dfrac{5}{6}$

9. If the slope of line A is $-\dfrac{x}{y}$, where x and y are positive numbers, what is the slope of a line that is perpendicular to A?

(A) $-\dfrac{x}{y}$

(B) $-\dfrac{y}{x}$

(C) $\dfrac{x}{y}$

(D) $\dfrac{y}{x}$

10. The formula for the surface area of a sphere is $A = 4\pi r^2$. If the volume of sphere A is 8 times the volume of sphere B, what is the ratio of the surface area of sphere A to that of sphere B?

(A) 1:2

(B) 2:1

(C) 4:1

(D) 8:1

ANSWER EXPLANATIONS

Heart of Algebra Drill 1 (Calculator)

1. **(B)** To add all of these fractions, you need a common denominator. The least common denominator for the three fractions is 16. However, because the other side has a denominator of 32, let's use 32 for ease. To convert $-\frac{3}{8}x$ to a fraction with a denominator of 32, multiply both the numerator and the denominator by 4. Thus, $-\frac{3}{8}x$ becomes $-\frac{12}{32}x$. Similarly, $\frac{5}{16}x$ becomes $\frac{10}{32}x$ after multiplying both the numerator and denominator by 2. Finally, $-\frac{1}{2}x$ becomes $-\frac{16}{32}x$ after multiplying both the numerator and denominator by 16. Therefore, we're left with:

$$-\frac{12}{32}x + \frac{10}{32}x - \frac{16}{32}x = \frac{18}{32}$$

Combining like terms gives:

$$-\frac{18}{32}x = \frac{18}{32}$$

To isolate x, divide both sides by $-\frac{18}{32}$. Dividing by a fraction is the same as multiplying by its reciprocal, so you're left with:

$$x = \left(\frac{18}{32}\right) \times \left(\frac{-32}{18}\right) = -1$$

So $x = -1$, or choice (B).

2. **(A)** Let's cross multiply here:

$$8(3a - 4) = 5(3a - 4)$$

Next we need to distribute both the 8 and the 5:

$$24a - 32 = 15a - 20$$

Combine both a terms by subtracting $15a$ from both sides:

$$9a - 32 = -20$$

Combine the constants by adding 32 to both sides:

$$9a = 12$$

Finally, solve for a by dividing both sides by 9. So $a = \frac{12}{9} = \frac{4}{3}$, choice (A).

Alternatively, realize that $3a - 4 = 0$ because if we plug in x for $3a - 4$, $\frac{x}{5} = \frac{x}{8}$, meaning $8x = 5x$. Therefore, x must be zero.

3. **(D)** First, get the second inequality in the same form as the first. To do this, subtract 4 from both sides of the second inequality:

$$-y \leq x - 4$$

Then divide by −1, remembering to flip the inequality since you're dividing by a negative:

$$y \geq -x + 4$$

If you graph these two inequalities, you'll see that the point where the lines intersect is the solution that they share that has the lowest y-value.

We can use this knowledge to set both inequalities equal to one another and solve:

$$2x + 5 = -x + 4$$

To solve for x, add an x to both sides to get all of the x-terms on the left. Subtract 5 from both sides to get all constants on the right:

$$3x = -1$$

Dividing by 3 tells us that $x = -\frac{1}{3}$. That's enough to narrow it down to choice (D).

However, if we wanted to know the y-value, we could plug the x-value into the equation for either of the two lines:

$$y = -x + 4 = -\left(-\frac{1}{3}\right) + 4 = \frac{1}{3} + \frac{12}{3} = \frac{13}{3}$$

This also agrees with choice (D).

Alternatively, you can plug in the values of the answers and see which set works for both equations.

4. **(C)** Recall that absolute value can be thought of as the distance of something from the origin. So if the absolute value of something is 4, it is 4 units away from the origin in either direction. This means that it can be either 4 or −4. Therefore, to solve for the values of x, we can set what's inside the absolute value equal to both 4 and −4 and solve. Setting it equal to 4 gives:

$$3x - 1 = 4$$

Adding 1 to both sides results in:

$$3x = 5$$

Dividing both sides by 3 gives us our first solution:

$$x = \frac{5}{3}$$

Next, set the inside of the absolute value sign equal to −4:

$$3x - 1 = -4$$

Adding 1 to both sides gives:

$$3x = -3$$

Dividing by 3 gives us our second solution:

$$x = -1$$

Therefore, there are two solutions, I and II, choice (C).

5. **(B)** To combine the x-terms, you need a common denominator, 6. To combine the constant terms, you also need a common denominator, 27:

$$\frac{9}{6}x - \frac{18}{27} = \frac{1}{6}x - \frac{10}{27}$$

To get all x-terms on the left, subtract $\frac{1}{6}x$ from both sides:

$$\frac{8}{6}x - \frac{18}{27} = -\frac{10}{27}$$

Next, add $\frac{18}{27}$ to both sides to get all constants on the right:

$$\frac{8}{6}x = \frac{8}{27}$$

Finally, divide both sides by $\frac{8}{6}$ (which is the same thing as multiplying both sides by $\frac{6}{8}$) to solve for x:

$$x = \frac{8(6)}{27(8)} = \frac{48}{216} = \frac{2}{9}$$

This matches choice (B).

6. **(A)** Let's get the second equation in $y = mx + b$ form. First, let's get the y-terms on the left by adding $2y$ to both sides:

$$2y - 6 = 12x$$

Next we need to bring the constant to the right side by adding 6 to both sides:

$$2y = 12x + 6$$

Finally, divide both sides by 2:

$$y = 6x + 3$$

Comparing the two lines shows they have the same slope but different y-intercepts. Therefore, they are parallel lines, choice (A).

If their slopes had been negative reciprocals of one another, they would have been perpendicular lines.

If the lines had had different slopes, they would have intersected at exactly one point.

If they had had the same slope and the same y-intercept, then they would have been the same line.

7. **(C)** The women will meet when their positions are equal, so we need to come up with equations to model each of their positions. First, notice that Caitlin leaves a full hour before Hannah. In that first hour, she'll travel 30 miles since she's traveling at 30 mph. Therefore, the women start out 170 miles apart at 4:00 P.M.

Let's say that Caitlin starts at position 0, while Hannah starts at position 170. Caitlin is moving toward 170, so she's moving in the positive direction at 30 mph. Keeping in mind that distance = rate × time, Caitlin's position, s, can then be described as:

$$s = 0 + 30t = 30t$$

On the other hand, Hannah is traveling from position 170 toward position 0, so she's traveling in the negative direction. Therefore, her position can be described as:

$$s = 170 - 40t$$

In order to solve for t, we must set the women's positions equal to one another:

$$30t = 170 - 40t$$

Adding $40t$ to both sides results in:

$$70t = 170$$

Dividing by 70 tells us:

$$t = 2.429$$

Because our rates were in miles per hour, this time is in hours. Therefore, it takes the women two full hours and a fraction of a third hour, so they meet sometime between 6 and 7. This is enough information to narrow down the solution to choice (C).

To find the exact time, we can figure out how many minutes 0.429 hours is by multiplying 0.429 hours by 60 minutes/hour. $0.429(60) = 25.74$ minutes. Therefore, Caitlin and Hannah meet 2 hours and 26 minutes after the time Hannah started traveling, 4:00 P.M. So the women arrive at the same place at 6:26 P.M.

8. **(D)** Recognize that those who are allowed to ride are the ones who aren't too far in either direction from the mean of the permitted heights. If you take the mean height of the constraints, you get:

$$\frac{36 + 72}{2} = 54$$

$72 - 54 = 18$ and $36 - 54 = -18$. Therefore, anyone who is less than 18 units away from 54 is allowed to ride, which is what choice (D) says.

If you didn't recognize this, you could use the process of elimination. You could pick heights that aren't allowed to ride. If you plug in a height that isn't allowed to ride but the inequality is still true, then you'd know that you could eliminate the choice. For instance:

Choice (A): $|35 - 36| = 1$. Since 1 is less than 72, we can rule out this answer choice.

Choice (B): $|35 - 38| = 3$. Since 3 is less than 34, we can rule out this answer choice as well.

Choice (C): $|35 - 30| = 5$. Since 5 is less than 42, we're left with choice (D).

9. **(D)** The answer choices are all positive, so let's come up with some of the positive points on the line. The line has a slope of $\frac{3}{5}$ and passes through the origin (thus has a y-intercept of 0). So the equation for the line is:

$$y = \frac{3}{5}x$$

The line starts at the origin and goes up 3 units and to the right 5 units. So (5, 3) is a point. From there, the line goes up 3 more units and to the right 5 more units, so (10, 6) is also a point, which is choice (D).

Alternatively, you could have used the process of elimination by plugging in the x-coordinates of the answer choices to get the y-coordinate at that value of x.

10. **(B)** In order for the commission to be positive, change the expression to an inequality where the commission will be positive and solve for x:

$$C = 50x + 25(x - 100) - 2{,}000 \boxed{?}$$
$$0 < 50x + 25(x - 100) - 2{,}000 \boxed{?}$$
$$0 < 50x + 25x - 2{,}500 - 2{,}000 \boxed{?}$$
$$0 < 75x - 4{,}500 \boxed{?}$$
$$4{,}500 < 75x \boxed{?}$$
$$60 < x$$

Since the salesperson cannot sell a partial phone plan, the least number of phone plans must be the first integer greater than 60, which is 61.

Heart of Algebra Drill 2 (Calculator)

1. **(C)** This problem is simply asking you to isolate the w variable. To begin, let's move the constant to the left side of the equation by dividing both sides by $\frac{1}{3}$.

Dividing by $\frac{1}{3}$ is the same as multiplying by 3. (Remember that dividing by a fraction is the same as multiplying by its reciprocal.) So we're left with:

$$3V = lwh$$

Next, let's divide both sides by l:

$$\frac{3V}{l} = wh$$

The final step is to divide both sides by h, giving us our final answer:

$$\frac{3V}{lh} = w$$

This is choice (C).

2. **(B)** First, we need to get the x out of the denominator by multiplying both sides of the equation by x:

$$18x^2 - 21 = \frac{2x^2}{3} + 12x$$

We have two x^2-terms to combine. So we need a common denominator, which is 3:

$$\frac{54x^2}{3} - 21 = \frac{2x^2}{3} + 12x$$

This is a quadratic equation since the highest degree of the terms is 2. We bring all terms to the same side so that we can eventually use the quadratic formula:

$$\frac{52x^2}{3} - 12x - 21 = 0$$

Recall the quadratic formula for a quadratic equation of the form $ax^2 + bx + c$:

$$x = \frac{-b \pm \sqrt{b^2 - 4ac}}{2a}$$

Filling in our values for a, b, and c gives:

$$x = \frac{12 \pm \sqrt{(-12)^2 - 4\left(\frac{52}{3}\right)(-21)}}{2\left(\frac{52}{3}\right)}$$

$$x = \frac{12 \pm \sqrt{1600}}{\left(\frac{104}{3}\right)} = \frac{12 \pm 40}{\left(\frac{104}{3}\right)}$$

So $x = \frac{3}{2}$ or $x = -\frac{21}{26}$.

We're looking only for the negative value of x, so we only care about the second value. This second value can also be expressed as −0.8077. Rounded to one decimal place, we get choice (B).

3. **(B)** First, figure out what $\frac{1}{2}$ and $\frac{5}{6}$ of 30 are so that you know what range of flex days an employee wants to take:

$$\frac{1}{2}(30)=15 \text{ and } \frac{5}{6}(30)=25$$

So the employee wants to take at least 15 days but fewer than 25 days. If we consider F to be the number of flex days taken, this can be expressed as:

$$15 \leq F < 25$$

Now we need an expression for flex days using sick days, S, and personal days, P. A sick day counts as half of a flex day, and a personal day counts as a total flex day. So the number of flex days used will be represented by:

$$\frac{1}{2}S+P=F$$

We can plug in this expression for F in our previous inequality:

$$15 \leq \frac{1}{2}S+P < 25$$

This is choice (B).

4. **(B)** For this question, we simply plug in $-4x$ for every x in the original function:

$$g(-4x)=9(-4x)+2=-36x+2$$

This answer matches choice (B).

5. **(C)** The carpenter charges a flat fee of \$40, so our equation will have a constant of 40. The carpenter also charges \$60 for each half hour worked. Therefore, the carpenter charges \$120 for each hour, H, worked. Therefore, the carpenter's total fee for working H hours is:

$$F(H)=40+120H$$

This is answer (C).

6. **(B)** Let's use elimination to get rid of the y-terms. Start by multiplying the first equation by 34: $34(0.75x-0.1y=1.2)$. This results in:

$$25.5x-3.4y=40.8$$

Now we can add this new equation to the second equation to eliminate the y-terms:

$$
\begin{aligned}
25.5x-3.4y&=40.8\\
+\ 2.6x+3.4y&=15.4\\
\hline
28.1x&=56.2
\end{aligned}
$$

Dividing by 28.1 tells us that $x = 2$. This is enough to narrow the answer down to choice (B). However, let's solve for y just for practice:

$$2.6(2)+3.4y=15.4$$
$$5.2+3.4y=15.4$$

Subtract 5.2 from both sides and then divide by 3.4 to learn that $y = 3$.

7. **(B)** If $\dfrac{m}{n} = -\dfrac{3}{1}$, then $\dfrac{n}{m} = -\dfrac{1}{3}$. Therefore, $-2\left(\dfrac{n}{m}\right) = -2\left(-\dfrac{1}{3}\right) = \dfrac{2}{3}$, which is choice (B).

8. **(D)** First, you must consider how two lines could have infinitely many solutions. The answer is that they need to have the same slope and the same y-intercept. In other words, they are the same line when graphed.

Let's start by rewriting Equation B in slope-intercept form by dividing both sides by 3:

$$y = \dfrac{2}{3}x + 1$$

The equations already have the same slope. However, they also need to have the same y-intercept: -4.

Let's subtract 5 from the right side of Equation B so that it matches Equation A:

$$y = \dfrac{2}{3}x - 4$$

However, we want to know what we need to change about the *original* Equation B. Therefore, we want to get Equation B back in its original form to see what changed. We can do this by multiplying both sides by 3:

$$3\left(y = \dfrac{2}{3}x - 4\right) \text{ becomes } 3y = 2x - 12.$$

Now we can see that from Equation B to this final equation, we subtracted 15 from the right side to change the y-intercept from $+3$ to -12. This matches choice (D).

9. **(D)** Don't get confused by all of the unnecessary information here! We want to know when the hot-air balloon and the blimp will be at the same altitude. Since altitude deals with only vertical movement, we only care about their vertical movements. The balloon and blimp will be at the same altitude when their vertical positions are equal.

Start with some notation. Let's say that traveling up is in the positive direction. So the balloon is traveling in the positive direction. Let's also say that traveling down is in the negative direction. So the blimp is traveling in the negative direction.

Remember that distance $=$ rate $\times$ time.

The blimp's position can be defined as $s = 5{,}000 - 5t$.

The balloon's position can be described as $s = 500 + 4t$.

The blimp and balloon will be at the same altitude when their positions are equal. So we can set the two expressions equal to one another:

$$5{,}000 - 5t = 500 + 4t$$

Add $5t$ to both sides while subtracting 500 from both sides:

$$4{,}500 = 9t$$

Dividing by 9 tells us that $t = 500$.

Because our rates were in feet/minute, our time is in minutes. Let's divide by 60 to convert this to hours:

$$\dfrac{500}{60} = 8.333$$

So it takes 8 hours and $\dfrac{1}{3}$ of the 9th hour. One-third of an hour is 20 minutes since $\dfrac{1}{3}(60) = 20$. So it takes 8 hours and 20 minutes. Since the balloon and blimp started moving toward one another at 1:00 P.M., they'll meet at 9:20 P.M., which is choice (D).

10. **(A)** Let's first set up an inequality that models this situation. Rosa wants to burn more than 2,000 calories, so we can represent this as 2,000 < calories.

Next we need to come up with an expression that represents the number of calories Rosa burns. Rosa is either burning 65 calories per hour by resting or burning 300 calories per hour while exercising. Let's call H the number of hours she spends exercising. Since there are 24 hours in a day and she's not exercising for the rest of the hours outside of H, the hours spent resting will be $24 - H$.

Therefore, the number of calories Rosa burns can be expressed as:

$$2,000 < 300H + 65(24 - H)$$

Now we solve for H. First, distribute the 65:

$$2,000 < 300H + 1560 - 65H$$

Combine like terms:

$$2,000 < 235H + 1560$$

Subtract 1,560 from both sides:

$$440 < 235H$$

Divide both sides by 235:

$$1.87 < H$$

This means that Rosa has to work out for at least 1.9 hours. She can't work out more than 24 hours per day since there are only 24 hours in a day. So the correct answer is (A).

Heart of Algebra Drill (No Calculator)

1. **(C)** Inequalities can be solved just like equations. The only difference is you must remember to flip the inequality sign if you multiply or divide by a negative number.

   The first step is to get rid of the denominator by multiplying both sides by 5:

   $$-2x - 4 > 10$$

   Add 4 to both sides:

   $$-2x > 14$$

   Divide both sides by -2 to solve for x. Since we are dividing by a negative number, we need to flip the inequality as follows:

   $$x < -7$$

   The answer is choice **(C)**.

2. **(A)** When the piggybank is full, it will have 500 quarters in it. Let's write an expression for how many quarters the piggybank contains on any given day, D, after Susan's birthday.

   Susan starts with 120 quarters on day 0 (her birthday), so 120 is a constant. Every day, 4 quarters are added to the bank. Thus, on day 1, 4 quarters have been added. On day 2, Susan adds an additional 4 quarters to the bank so that $4(2) = 8$ quarters total have been added since her birthday. On day 3, $4(3) = 12$ quarters total have been added, and so on. This part of the expression can be written as $4D$.

Adding in the original 120 quarters she started with gives an expression for the total number of quarters in the bank D days after Susan's birthday:

$$120 + 4D$$

We know the bank is full when it contains 500 quarters. So we can set our expression equal to 500 and solve for D to determine how many days after Susan's birthday the piggybank will be filled. Thus choice (A), $500 = 120 + 4D$, is correct.

3. **(C)** The number of points from x two-point shots will be $2x$. Similarly, making y three-point shots and z free throws corresponds to $3y$ points and z points, respectively. So the number of points earned from y three-point shots combined with z free throws will be $3y + z$. If the number of points from the two-point shots has to be at least as much (implying at least as much if not more) than the combined points from three-pointers and free throws, it follows that:

$$2x \geq 3y + z$$

This is choice (C).

Choice (A) doesn't work because it doesn't take into account the different values of each shot.

Choice (B) doesn't account for each two-point shot giving 2 points.

Choice (D) implies that three-point shots score only 1 point and that free throws score 3 points.

4. **(B)** First, let's distribute the 4 in the second equation:

$$40 - \frac{16}{3}y = 2x + 5$$

Next, notice that if you multiplied the first equation by 8, the y-terms (and in fact the entire left-hand side of both equations) would be the same:

$$8\left(5 - \frac{2}{3}y = x\right) = 40 - \frac{16}{3}y = 8x$$

You could subtract the second equation from the first to cancel the y-terms:

$$
\begin{array}{r}
40 - \dfrac{16}{3}y = 8x \\
-\left(40 - \dfrac{16}{3}y = 2x + 5\right) \\
\hline
0 = 6x - 5
\end{array}
$$

Add 5 to both sides:

$$5 = 6x$$

Now divide by 6 to solve for x:

$$\frac{5}{6} = x$$

This is choice (B).

5. **(A)** Let's start with the left side of the inequality. The absolute value of -3 is 3, so:

$$-2|-3| = -2(3) = -6$$

$$-6 < -3|x + 5|$$

We want to isolate our absolute value. So let's divide by −3, flipping the inequality since we are dividing by a negative number:

$$2 > |x + 5|$$

Because 2 has to be greater than the absolute value, the expression inside of the absolute value symbol can be anything between (−2, 2). In other words, $x − 5$ needs to be greater than −2 but less than 2. To find the x-values such that $x − 5$ is less than 2, simply take away the absolute value signs and solve for x:

$$2 > x + 5$$

Subtracting 5 from both sides gives:

$$-3 > x$$

Next, we want to find the values of x such that $x − 5$ is greater than −2. In other words, we want to solve for x in the inequality $−2 < x + 5$. Subtracting 5 tells us:

$$-7 < x$$

We have found that $−3 > x$ and that $−7 < x$. In other words, $−7 < x < −3$, which is choice (A).

6. **(A)** First, we'll solve for $\frac{1}{B}$. To do this, subtract $\frac{1}{A}$ from both sides:

$$\frac{1}{B} = \frac{1}{T} - \frac{1}{A}$$

Don't be tempted to pick choice (C)! We've solved for $\frac{1}{B}$, not for B as asked in the question. To solve for B, we must take the reciprocal of what we have:

$$B = \frac{1}{\dfrac{1}{T} - \dfrac{1}{A}}$$

This matches answer (A).

7. **(C)** If creating the machine is now less expensive, the manufacturer can afford to make more machines for a given price. Therefore for each price, the quantity will be higher. Thus, the supply curve should shift to the right, shifting it into zones 3 and 4, which is choice (C).

8. **(C)** Let's first find the slope of line A. The formula for slope is Change in y/Change in x:

$$\frac{0 - (-2)}{-1 - 1} = \frac{2}{-2} = -1$$

If the lines are to intersect at a 90° angle, they must be perpendicular. Any line perpendicular to this one would have a slope of 1, since 1 is the negative reciprocal of −1.

We can now use the one given point of line B and the slope in the point-slope formula in order to get the equation of line B.

The point-slope formula is given by the equation $y − y_1 = m(x − x_1)$:

$$y - 4 = 1(x - 3)$$

Distributing the 1 gives:

$$y - 4 = x - 3$$

To get the line into slope-intercept form, add 4 to both sides:

$$y = x + 1$$

Therefore, line B has a y-intercept of 1, which is answer (C).

Alternatively, once it is known that the slope of the new line is 1, the equation must be $y = x + b$. Plug in the point $(3, 4)$ to the line to solve for b:

$$4 = 3 + b \rightarrow b = 1$$

9. **(B)** The book will have a fixed replacement cost of $30, so +30 will be a constant term in the function. For each day that the book goes unreturned past December 14, Jane owes another 10 cents. Thus on day 1 after the return date, she owes a $30 replacement fee and 10 more cents, for a total of $30.10. On the second day, she owes the $30 replacement fee and 2 days' worth of late fees, $(2)(10) = 20$ cents, for a total of $30.20. By continuing in this manner, on day x, Jane will owe the $30 replacement fee and x days' worth of late fees, which is $(x)(10) = 10x$ cents or $0.1x$ dollars. The total cost is shown by $A(x) = 30 + 0.1x$.

This relationship is best described in choice (B).

Choice (A) is tempting, but you must remember that 10 cents is expressed in dollars as $0.10. Choice (A) instead indicates that Jane pays an additional $10 of fees every day plus the $30 replacement fee.

10. **(B)** Since a is already solved for in the first equation, let's plug the right side of that equation into the second equation wherever there is an a:

$$2 + 3\left(\frac{2}{3}b + 1\right) = -4(2b + 1)$$

Next, distribute the 3 and the -4:

$$2 + 2b + 3 = -8b - 4$$

You can combine the constants on the left side of the equation.

$$2b + 5 = -8b - 4$$

Now add $8b$ to both sides and subtract 5 from both sides:

$$10b = -9$$

Dividing by 10 gives you

$$b = -\frac{9}{10}$$

However, the question asks us for the value of a. So let's plug the b-value into the first equation:

$$a = \frac{2}{3}b + 1 = \frac{2}{3}\left(-\frac{9}{10}\right) + 1 = -\frac{18}{30} + 1 = -\frac{3}{5} + \frac{5}{5} = \frac{2}{5}$$

This is choice (B).

This can be solved in other ways, such as by trying elimination instead of substitution.

Problem Solving and Data Analysis Drill 1 (Calculator)

1. **(C)** Let's use the variable d to represent the number of dogs in the shelter and the variable c to represent the number of cats. If the ratio of dogs to cats is 3:1, then there are 3 times as many dogs as cats:

$$d = 3c$$

If there are 360 animals in the shelter:

$$d + c = 360$$

We want to know the number of dogs present. So let's solve the first equation for c in terms of d and plug this into the second equation. Dividing by 3 tells us:

$$\frac{1}{3}d = c$$

Plugging this into the second equation results in:

$$d + \frac{1}{3}d = 360$$

Combining like terms gives:

$$\frac{4}{3}d = 360$$

We can divide both sides by $\frac{4}{3}$ (in other words, multiply both sides by $\frac{3}{4}$) to learn that $d = 270$, which is answer choice (C).

Alternatively, you can solve this as a ratio problem:

$$\frac{d}{c} = \frac{3}{1}$$

As a fraction of the whole, the number of dogs can be expressed as $d = \frac{3}{(3+1)} = \frac{3}{4}$ of the total. Then take $\frac{3}{4}$ of the total number of animals to find the number of dogs:

$$\frac{3}{4} \times 360 = 270$$

2. **(B)** Let's set up a proportion for this problem. The politician receives 14 seconds of applause for every minute of a speech. We want our units to be the same, so let's call that minute 60 seconds. We can model this part of our proportion as $\frac{14}{60}$.

We want to know how many minutes of applause he'll get for 2 hours of speech. Since we want our answer in minutes, let's call 2 hours 120 minutes. We want applause on top again. Therefore, this side of the proportion can be modeled by $\frac{x}{120}$, where x represents the number of minutes of applause the politician will receive in 120 minutes.

You can then set both sides of the proportion equal to one another:

$$\frac{14}{60} = \frac{x}{120}$$

Next, cross multiply:

$$14(120) = 60x$$

$$1{,}680 = 60x$$

Dividing by 60 gives us $x = 28$, choice (B).

3. **(D)** A gallon of whole milk would have 3.5% of a gallon of fat, or 0.035 gallons. If we mix 1% milk and 2% milk in equal parts, we will essentially have 1.5% milk since the fat content will be the average of the two fat contents.

Therefore, the whole milk has $\frac{0.035}{0.015} = 2.333$ times the amount of fat of the 1% and 2% mixture. You would need 2.333 times the amount of milk of the mixture to have the same quantity of fat as in 1 gallon of whole milk. Because 0.333 can be represented as $\frac{1}{3}$, the answer is choice (D).

Alternatively, take the combined average of the lower-fat milks:

$$\frac{1+2}{2} = 1.5$$

Then using x as the number of gallons needed of the combined milks, you can set up this equation:

$$1.5x = 3.5$$

Then solve for x to get $2\frac{1}{3}$.

4. **(C)** Let's first convert the marathon distance to kilometers:

$$26.2 \text{ miles} \times \frac{1 \text{ kilometer}}{0.62 \text{ miles}} = 42.26 \text{ kilometers}$$

If Katie has to run 42.26 km and if she's doing it 5 km at a time, she would need to run:

$$\frac{42.26}{5} = 8.45 \text{ races}$$

Therefore, she would need to run a minimum of 9 whole races to run the distance of a marathon.

Alternatively, you could have done dimensional analysis for the last step, canceling out units that you don't want and leaving only the units that you do want. Katie wants to go 42.26 km, and she's running 5 km/race. Cancel out kilometers, so that we're left with number of races:

$$42.26 \text{ kilometers} \times \frac{1 \text{ race}}{5 \text{ kilometers}} = 8.45 \text{ races}$$

We again need to round up to 9 so that Katie runs the full marathon distance.

5. **(A)** Let's use dimensional analysis, canceling out the units that we don't want and leaving the units that we do want (euros). In the dimensional analysis, let CAD mean Canadian dollars, let USD mean U.S. dollars, and let EUR mean euros:

$$100 \text{ CAD} \times \frac{0.7 \text{ USD}}{1 \text{ CAD}} \times \frac{0.9 \text{ EUR}}{1 \text{ USD}} = 63 \text{ EUR}$$

The correct answer is choice (A).

6. **(D)** The easiest way to approach a problem like this is to test some points with each equation to see which equation works.

Choice (A):

$$C(1) = 10^{2(1)} + 10(1-1) + 1 = 100 + 1 = 101$$

So the equation works for day 1. Let's see if it works with day 2:

$$C(2) = 10^{2(2)} + 10(2-1) + 1 = 10{,}000 + 10 + 1 = 10{,}011$$

This doesn't match the number for day 2, so we can rule out choice (A).

Choice (B):

$$C(1) = 100 + 10^1 = 100 + 10 = 110$$

This isn't the right number for day 1, so we can rule out choice (B).

Choice (C):

$$C(1) = 100 + 10(1-1) + 1 = 100 + 1 = 101$$

This works, so let's try $C(2)$:

$$C(2) = 100 + 10(2 - 1) + 1 = 100 + 10 + 1 = 111$$

This doesn't work, so we can rule out choice (C).

Choice (D):

$$C(1) = 100 + 10^{1-1} = 100 + 1 = 101$$
$$C(2) = 100 + 10^{2-1} = 100 + 10 = 110$$
$$C(3) = 100 + 10^{3-1} = 100 + 100 = 200$$
$$C(4) = 100 + 10^{4-1} = 100 + 1,000 = 1,100$$
$$C(5) = 100 + 10^{5-1} = 100 + 10,000 = 10,100$$

Obviously, choice (D) is the correct answer.

7. **(B)** Let's first convert 588 million kilometers to meters:

$$588,000,000 \text{ kilometers} \times \frac{1,000 \text{ meters}}{\text{kilometer}} = 588,000,000,000 \text{ meters}$$

Because distance = rate × time, it follows that $t = \dfrac{d}{r}$. Therefore, the t in seconds is given by the following expression:

$$t = \frac{588,000,000,000}{3.00 \times 10^8} = 1,960 \text{ seconds}$$

Because there are 60 seconds in every minute,

$$1,960 \text{ sec} \times \frac{1 \text{ min}}{60 \text{ sec}} = 32.67 \text{ min}$$

This answer rounds to 33 minutes, which is choice (B).

8. **(C)** Since the total number of responses was 26, the median response will be the mean of the 13th and 14th terms.

Terms 1–2 were 0–1 hours.

Terms 3–6 were 1–2 hours.

Terms 7–11 were 2–3 hours.

Terms 12–16 were 3–4 hours.

Therefore, the 13th and 14th terms were both 3–4 hours, which is choice (C).

9. **(B)** Every student in each class either did or did not complete summer reading. So the total number of students enrolled in Mrs. Smith's class is 29, and the total number enrolled in Mr. Walker's class is 31. The average number of students enrolled in the two classes is:

$$\frac{29 + 31}{2} = 30$$

We can assume that each of the 14 English classes has, on average, 30 people. Therefore, the total number enrolled in English classes would be:

$$14(30) = 420$$

The correct answer is choice (B).

10. **(C)** In Mr. Walker's class, 14 students completed summer reading and earned 5 points, accounting for $14(5) = 70$ points. The remaining 17 students received 0 points. So the total points for the class were 70. There are 31 students in the class, so the mean is:

$$70 \div 31 = 2.26$$

To find the median, list the students' point values from smallest to largest. There are 17 students who earned 0 followed by 14 students who each earned 5. The median term in a 31-term series is the 16th term. (There are 15 terms on the left of the 16th term and 15 terms on the right of the 16th term.) The 16th value is 0, so the median is 0. The difference between the mean and the median, therefore, is:

$$2.26 - 0 = 2.26$$

Choice (C) is correct.

Problem Solving and Data Analysis Drill 2 (Calculator)

1. **(C)** First, figure out the number of words that each report would have. We know the number of words per page. So if we multiply this by the number of pages, the pages unit will cancel from the top and bottom. This will leave us with the number of words. If the student uses Times New Roman, he will write:

$$240(10) = 2,400 \text{ words}$$

However, if he uses Comic Sans, he will write only:

$$170(10) = 1,700 \text{ words}$$

We want to know how many fewer words he will write in the second situation.

$$2,400 - 1,700 = 700 \text{ words}$$

So choice (C) is correct.

2. **(B)** The area of a rectangle is given by the formula $A = lw$, where l is length and w is width. If the length of the drawing is 4 inches, we know from dividing both sides of our area equation by the length that:

$$w = \frac{A}{l} = \frac{20}{4} = 5 \text{ inches}$$

The key tells us that each inch on the map represents 6 feet. We can multiply 4 inches by 6 feet/inch to tell us that the length is 24 feet. Similarly, we can multiply the 5-inch width by 6 feet/inch to tell us that the width is 30 feet.

Alternatively, you could have solved for actual distance by setting up a proportion. For the length, the proportion might look something like:

$$\frac{1''}{6'} = \frac{4''}{x'}$$

Cross multiplying gives you:

$$1x = (4)(6)$$

So $x = 24$.

The question wants to know the perimeter of the fence. Perimeter of a rectangle is given by the formula $P = 2l + 2w$. Plugging our dimensions into the formula tells us:

$$P = 2(24) + 2(30) = 48 + 60 = 108$$

The correct answer is choice (B).

3. **(C)** If John's performance increased by 20%, then he performed at 120% of his original performance. 120% can be expressed in decimal form as 1.2, and we can find 120% of his original score of 60 by multiplying the two:

$$1.2(60) = 72$$

So John got a 72% on his second test. His performance then increased another 25%, so his third test performance was 125%, or 1.25, of test 2. Therefore, John's third score was:

$$1.25(72) = 90\%$$

The answer is choice (C).

Alternatively, you could have found John's second score by finding 20% of 60 and adding that to 60:

$$\text{Test } 2 = 60 + (0.2)(60) = 60 + 12 = 72$$

Then you could have found the third score by finding 25% of 72 and adding that to 72:

$$\text{Test } 3 = 72 + (0.25)(72) = 72 + 18 = 90$$

4. **(B)** If you were told that you had to travel 50 miles and that your car got 10 miles/gallon, you may intuitively see that you need 5 gallons of gas. You get that by dividing 50/10. Following this logic, we can get the number of gallons of gas Linda needs to travel 240 miles by dividing 240 by 28:

$$240 \div 28 = 8.57 \text{ gallons}$$

If this doesn't quite make sense, you could also do dimensional analysis to cancel out the units you don't want. You want to cancel out miles and end up with gallons:

$$240 \text{ miles} \times \frac{1 \text{ gallon}}{28 \text{ miles}} = 8.57 \text{ gallons}$$

Linda also wants to have 1 gallon left, so she'll want to have 9.57 gallons in her tank when she starts out. Linda already has 2 gallons in her tank, so she needs to buy $9.57 - 2 = 7.57$ gallons, or 7.6 rounded to the nearest tenth. This matches choice (B).

5. **(A)** We can see from the negative slope that as the quantity of shake-ups increases, price decreases. Therefore, we know that the function will be decreasing, eliminating choices (B) and (D). We can also see that the slope isn't constant. Therefore, it can't be linear, as in choice (C). The graph starts off fairly steep and then it becomes less steep, consistent with exponential decay, as in choice (A).

6. **(B)** Revenue means money made. The amount of money made at any price will be that price times the number of shake-ups sold. Find the approximate revenue at all of the given prices:

$$\text{Choice (A): } \$2.50(4,700) = \$11,750$$

$$\text{Choice (B): } \$3.00(4,600) = \$13,800$$

$$\text{Choice (C): } \$3.50(2,600) = \$9,100$$

$$\text{Choice (D): } \$5.00(1,300) = \$6,500$$

Therefore, the largest revenue occurs with choice (B).

7. **(C)** An equation of a line is given by $y = mx + b$, where m is the slope and b is the y-intercept. The formula for slope is calculated by finding the rise over the run, which is illustrated by this formula:

$$m = \frac{\Delta y}{\Delta x} = \frac{y_2 - y_1}{x_2 - x_1}$$

Plug in values for the endpoints:

$$m = \frac{5.9 - 7.8}{17 - 14} = \frac{-1.9}{3} = -0.633$$

Thus, the slope is approximately -0.6, so we can rule out choices (B) and (D).

Next, we need to determine the y-intercept b. To do this, we can plug a particular point on the line into the equation and solve for b. For instance, $(14, 7.8)$ appears to be a point on the line. Plugging these values into the equation gives:

$$7.8 = -0.6(14) + b$$

So $7.8 = -8.4 + b$.

Adding 8.4 to both sides gives $16.2 = b$. Therefore, choice (C) must be correct.

With this graph, you cannot find the y-intercept, b, just by looking at the where the line crosses the y-axis. On this graph, the y-axis crosses the x-axis at 14, not at 0. However, the y-intercept is, by definition, the value of y when the value of x equals 0.

8. **(A)** Students may be entirely unaware of how many hours they're sleeping. Alternatively, they may modify their answers for a variety of reasons, possibly to give the answers they suspect the researchers want to hear. This makes self-reporting a fairly inaccurate technique, as in choice (A).

Choice (B) isn't correct because although students may get a different number of hours of sleep during the school year versus the summer, the study asks for the average number of hours. This should take into account variations due to time of year.

Choice (C) isn't correct because the researchers could simply ask more teenagers.

Choice (D) isn't correct because changing one response by a small margin shouldn't have a large result on the accuracy of the entire study.

9. **(B)** We can rule out choice (A) because the slope is clearly positive. Use the slope formula:

$$m = \frac{\Delta y}{\Delta x} = \frac{y_2 - y_1}{x_2 - x_1}$$

Plug in the values for the approximate endpoints of the line of best fit to get:

$$m = \frac{300 - 150}{5,000 - 2,500} = \frac{150}{2,500} = \frac{3}{50}$$

The answer is choice (B).

10. **(D)** There's no need to start the y-axis at 0 pounds, because it's impossible to weigh 0 pounds. There's no reason to start the x-axis at 0 calories, because it's not possible to average 0 calories daily. This situation matches choice (D).

Problem Solving and Data Analysis Drill (No Calculator)

1. **(C)** When $x = 8$, $y = 12$. We want to know the proportionality constant. We can do this by plugging the values of x and y into the equation and solving for k:

$$12 = 8k$$

Dividing by 8 tells us that $k = \dfrac{12}{8}$. Reducing this fraction gives choice (C) as the answer, $k = \dfrac{3}{2}$.

2. **(B)** Let's imagine the simplest version of this and say that there are two people failing. Since for every two failing, three have C's and D's, that means that three in this class do have C's and D's. We also know that for every one person who has a C or a D, two people have A's and B's. Since three have C's and D's, $3(2) = 6$ have A's and B's.

   Therefore, the ratio of those failing to those with A's and B's is 2 to 6, or 1 to 3, which is choice (B).

3. **(B)** Think of this as 3 separate charges. Let's call x the cost of the food. That's the first charge. Then there's a tip charge that is 15% of the cost of food. The 15% tip charge can be expressed as $0.15x$ since x is the cost of food. Finally, there's a $5 flat fee delivery charge that doesn't depend on the cost of the food. Therefore, the cost can be represented by:

$$C = x + 0.15x + 5$$

Combining like terms gives:

$$C = 1.15x + 5$$

Choice (B) is the correct answer.

4. **(A)** The graph has a positive slope everywhere, so the variables are positively correlated. You can tell that as the year increases from 2000 to 2010, the price increases from about $16 to about $43. Choice (A) is the correct answer.

5. **(B)** As you can see from the graph, the trend is a slight decrease in slope each year (while remaining positive). Thus, we would expect ticket prices to rise again but only slightly. You can use the slope from the previous year to get an idea of an approximate increase in the next few years. It looks like from 2009 to 2010, the price increased from $42 to $43, so the price increased by $1. If it continues to increase about $1 for the next 4 years until 2014, the price will go up a total of $4, from $43 to $47, which is choice (B).

6. **(B)** As time goes by, the exchange rate increases drastically. In 2000, every unit of Currency Y was equal to 2.3 units of Currency X. However in 2004, 1 unit of Currency Y was equal to 237.83 units of Currency X. That means that Currency Y is becoming more valuable with respect to Currency X because Currency Y is becoming worth more than Currency X. This matches choice (B).

7. **(B)** Go through each possibility.

   Option I: Sam's height percentile actually decreased between ages 12 and 18, so it's extremely unlikely that he experienced exponential growth. By ruling this out, we can eliminate choices (A) and (D).

   Option II: When Sam was less than 5 years old, his height percentile ranged between about the 42nd percentile and the 50th percentile. Between the ages of 10 and 15, he ranged between the 54th and 60th percentile. Therefore, he was taller than more men during these later years, making this statement true.

Option III: We can't say for sure that Sam's height changed between these years, although it's probable. Percentiles measure only your status compared to others. We know only that Sam's height compared to others changed, not that his absolute height changed.

Therefore, the answer is choice (B).

8. **(C)** A 95% confidence interval means that if the study is done at random many times, the average height statistically should fall between these two heights 95% of the time. In other words, choice (C) is correct. It is very likely that an average child will fall between these two heights.

9. **(C)** If prices are discounted by $\frac{2}{3}$, that means you're still paying $\frac{1}{3}$ of the original price. If you also have a coupon that discounts 20%, you're still paying 80% of that price. Since the sale price is $\frac{1}{3}$ of the original price, the price with the coupon is 80% of $\frac{1}{3}$ of the original price. The fraction $\frac{4}{5}$ (or $\frac{8}{10}$ if that makes more sense to you) can represent 80%. So we can find 80% of $\frac{1}{3}$:

$$\left(\frac{4}{5}\right)\left(\frac{1}{3}\right) = \frac{4}{15}$$

Choice (C) is the answer.

10. **(C)** A random sample is useful if it is truly random and if it is truly representative of the people being studied.

Choice (C) is correct because it polls a randomly selected group and takes into account only registered voters, which is what you would want to sample if you wanted to predict the results of an election.

Choice (A) is incorrect because it polls only people who go to that grocery store and likely excludes voters who shop elsewhere, are too elderly to shop, or don't have money to spend. It also likely samples a significant number of nonregistered voters who won't be counted in the election.

Choice (B) is incorrect because it polls only people in certain geographical locations and therefore likely people of only certain socioeconomic statuses as well.

Choice (D) is incorrect because it polls only those who have access to the Internet and actually take the time to complete the survey.

Passport to Advanced Math Drill 1 (Calculator)

1. **(A)** A cubic function has a variable raised to the third degree or, in terms of geometry, has 3 dimensions. Therefore, we need a shape that is 3-dimensional. This rules out choices (B) and (C).

Choice (D) may be tempting because a cube is 3-dimensional. However, surface area is actually only 2 dimensions, so this wouldn't be a cubic function.

Choice (A) is correct because volume of a sphere varies proportionally to the cube of its radius. Volume is always in 3 dimensions, hence, the reason its units are always in cubic units.

Alternatively, you could have written out all of the relationships depicted in the answer choices.

The volume of a sphere is given by the formula $V = \frac{4}{3}\pi r^3$, which is a cubic function since the radius variable has degree 3. So choice (A) is correct.

The formula for a circle's circumference is $C = 2\pi r = \pi d$, where d represents diameter. This is a linear relationship between d and C, making choice (B) incorrect.

A triangle's area is $A = \frac{1}{2}bh$. This isn't a cubic function, so choice (C) can't be correct.

A cube's surface area is given by the formula $SA = 6x^2$, where x represents the length of each side of the cube. Again, this isn't a cubic function since the degree of x is only 2, so choice (D) is incorrect.

2. **(A)** From all of the answer choices, we can see that the whole denominator cancels out somehow. Let's use polynomial long division to figure out an equivalent expression for our original fraction. Before we use long division, let's first combine like terms in the numerator so that the long division isn't as complicated:

$$a^3 - b^3 + 2a^2b - 2ab^2 + ab^2 - ba^2 = a^3 - b^3 + a^2b - ab^2$$

Now do polynomial long division:

$$
\begin{array}{r}
a+b \\
a^2-b^2 \,\overline{\smash{\big)}\, a^3 - b^3 + a^2b - ab^2} \\
\underline{-\left(a^3 \qquad\quad -ab^2\right)} \\
-b^3 + a^2b \\
\underline{-\left(-b^3 + a^2b\right)} \\
0
\end{array}
$$

Thus, our original fraction is equal to $a + b$, which is choice (A).

Alternatively, you could have simplified directly by factoring. Since $a^3 - b^3 = (a - b)(a^2 + ab + b^2)$, we can rewrite the numerator:

$$a^3 - b^3 + 2a^2b - 2ab^2 + ab^2 - ba^2 = a^3 - b^3 + a^2b - ab^2 = (a - b)(a^2 + ab + b^2) + a^2b - ab^2$$

Notice that $a^2b - ab^2 = ab(a - b)$, so our numerator becomes:

$$(a - b)(a^2 + ab + b^2) + a^2b - ab^2 = (a - b)(a^2 + ab + b^2) + ab(a - b) =$$
$$(a - b)(a^2 + ab + b^2 + ab) = (a - b)(a^2 + 2ab + b^2) = (a - b)(a + b)^2$$

Thus, our original fraction can be rewritten as $\dfrac{(a-b)(a+b)^2}{a^2 - b^2}$. Since our denominator is a difference of squares, it can be rewritten as $a^2 - b^2 = (a + b)(a - b)$. Our entire expression becomes:

$$\frac{(a-b)(a+b)^2}{a^2 - b^2} = \frac{(a-b)(a+b)^2}{(a-b)(a+b)} = a + b$$

Choice (A) is correct.

3. **(C)** We can solve for all possible values of m^2 by subtracting $2m^7$ from both sides, factoring the left side, and setting the left side equal to 0:

$$-5m^5 + 3m^3 - 2m^7 = 0$$

First, factor out $-m^3$:

$$-m^3(5m^2 - 3 + 2m^4) = 0$$

Rearrange the polynomial inside the parentheses so that the terms are decreasing in degree for easier factoring:

$$-m^3(2m^4 + 5m^2 - 3) = 0.$$

Next factor the inside:

$$-m^3(2m^4 + 5m^2 - 3) = -m^3(m^2 + 3)(2m^2 - 1) = 0$$

Now set each factor equal to 0 to solve for possible values of m^2:

$$-m^3 = 0$$

Dividing both sides by $-m$ tells you that $m^2 = 0$, so this is one possible value.

$$m^2 + 3 = 0$$

Subtracting 3 from both sides gives $m^2 = -3$. However, you can't square a number and get a negative, so this solution is extraneous.

$$2m^2 - 1 = 0$$

Add 1 to both sides and divide by 2:

$$m^2 = \frac{1}{2}$$

This is another possible value. Therefore, the two possible values of m^2 are 0 and 0.5. Thus, their sum is 0.5, which is choice (C).

4. **(D)** First, multiply by 8 to avoid dealing with fractions:

$$4x^2 + 2x - 1 = 0$$

Next, use the quadratic formula:

$$x = \frac{-b \pm \sqrt{b^2 - 4ac}}{2a} = \frac{-2 \pm \sqrt{2^2 - 4(4)(-1)}}{2(4)} = \frac{-2 \pm \sqrt{4 + 16}}{8} = \frac{-2 \pm \sqrt{20}}{8} = -\frac{2}{8} \pm \frac{2\sqrt{5}}{8} = -\frac{1}{4} \pm \frac{\sqrt{5}}{4}$$

This still doesn't match any of the answer choices. All of the answer choices have a fraction factored out of them. We can factor $\frac{1}{4}$ out of our expression to get the answer:

$$\frac{1}{4}\left(-1 \pm \sqrt{5}\right)$$

Choice (D) is correct.

5. **(A)** Get rid of the square root by squaring both sides. Squaring the right side simply gets rid of the square root, but be careful to FOIL the left side:

$$a^2 + 8a + 16 = a^2 - 2$$

Subtract a^2 from both sides:

$$8a + 16 = -2$$

Next, subtract 16 from both sides:

$$8a = -18$$

Solve for a by dividing by 8:

$$a = -\frac{18}{8} = -\frac{9}{4}$$

This is choice (A).

Note that squaring equations can lead to extraneous answers. In this case, we don't get any extraneous solutions. However, you should get in the habit of checking your solutions by plugging them back into the original equation to ensure that your solution is truly a solution to the original.

6. **(C)** The zeros of a factored polynomial can be found by setting each distinct factor equal to 0 and solving for x. Here there are only 2 distinct factors, $(x-3)$ and $(x+7)$. So there will only be 2, choice (C).

$$x-3=0$$
$$x=3$$
$$x+7=0$$
$$x=-7$$

Note: Although $x-3$ occurs twice as a factor, this still corresponds to only one zero. We say that 3 is a zero of multiplicity 2 since its corresponding factor occurs twice.

7. **(C)** This function is a parabola. It opens upward because the coefficient in front of x^2 is positive. (In this case, the coefficient of x^2 is 1.) The function has a y-intercept of 2. Therefore, the range is $[2, \infty)$. In order for the range to include negative numbers, the new function either needs to open downward or have a negative y-intercept. In order for it to open downward, you would multiply the right side by a negative number, but this isn't a choice.

The only choice that works is subtracting 3, which would make the y-intercept negative. The y-intercept of the new function would be -1 because $2-3=-1$. The range of the new function would be expanded to $[-1, \infty)$.

8. **(A)** This equation is probably a bit different from the equations of the parabolas that you're used to seeing. To get it into standard form, we need to solve for x instead of the y as we usually do:

$$\frac{1}{17}(y-4)^2 - 2 = x$$

This is a parabola rotated 90 degrees clockwise. The standard form can be represented by the equation:

$$x = a(y-k)^2 + h$$

Therefore, in this problem, $k = 4$ and $h = -2$. So (h, k) is $(-2, 4)$, as shown in choice (A). Parabola problems like this may not be on the PSAT, but it is included here so that you will be as prepared as possible.

9. **(A)** The relationship is easiest to see if you solve for M first. First, square both sides:

$$\left(v_{rms}\right)^2 = \frac{3RT}{M}$$

Multiply both sides by M to get M out of the denominator:

$$M(v_{rms})^2 = 3RT$$

Now isolate M:

$$M = \frac{3RT}{\left(v_{rms}\right)^2}$$

We can now consider how we can lower M. First, M is directly proportional to T. So decreasing T will decrease M. Further, M is inversely proportional to the square of v_{rms}. So increasing v_{rms} will decrease M because you will be dividing by a larger number. Therefore, choice (A) is correct.

10. **(A)** None of the answer choices has a percentage in it, so convert the percentage to a decimal by dividing by 100:

$$x\% = \frac{x}{100} \quad \text{and} \quad y\% = \frac{y}{100}$$

Suppose P is the initial amount deposited into each portfolio. If portfolio A grows at a rate of $x\%$ yearly, the value after 1 year will be given by the expression:

$$P + \frac{x}{100}P = \left(1 + \frac{x}{100}\right)P.$$

The following year, the amount of money in portfolio A again increases by $x\%$. Therefore, the value after the second year will be given by the following expression:

$$\left(1 + \frac{x}{100}\right)\left[\left(1 + \frac{x}{100}\right)P\right] = \left(1 + \frac{x}{100}\right)\left(1 + \frac{x}{100}\right)P \quad \text{or} \quad \left(1 + \frac{x}{100}\right)^2 P$$

The third year, the interest will be compounded on the previous value. Therefore, the value will be:

$$\left(1 + \frac{x}{100}\right)^2\left(1 + \frac{x}{100}\right)P \quad \text{or} \quad \left(1 + \frac{x}{100}\right)^3 P$$

The value after n years is given by:

$$\left(1 + \frac{x}{100}\right)^n P$$

So after 10 years, the value of portfolio A will be $\left(1 + \frac{x}{100}\right)^{10} P$.

Repeat the thought process for portfolio B to arrive at the conclusion that the value of portfolio B after 10 years will be

$$\left(1 + \frac{y}{100}\right)^{10} P$$

since both portfolio A and B start out with the same amount initially, P. Therefore, the ratio of the value of portfolio A to the value of portfolio B is:

$$\frac{\left(1 + \frac{x}{100}\right)^{10} P}{\left(1 + \frac{y}{100}\right)^{10} P} \quad \text{or} \quad \left(\frac{1 + \frac{x}{100}}{1 + \frac{y}{100}}\right)^{10}$$

This matches choice (A).

Passport to Advanced Math Drill 2 (Calculator)

1. **(C)** We will use the formula $d = rt$, where d is distance, r is rate, and t is time. Let's define the car's initial position, s, as $s = 0$ and the truck's initial position as $s = 180$.

The car's position at time t will be its initial position (0) plus the distance it has traveled in that time. We are told that the car's rate r is x, so the distance the car travels in time t is xt. Since the car starts at an initial position of 0, its position at time t will be expressed as $s = xt + 0 = xt$.

The truck starts at position $s = 180$ and travels toward the 0 position. So the truck's position at time t will be expressed as 180 minus the distance it has traveled in time t. Its speed is twice the speed of the car, or $2x$. So the truck's position at time t will be expressed as $s = 180 - 2xt$.

They meet where their positions are equal. So set the two equations equal to one another to solve for x:

$$xt = 180 - 2xt$$

We know that the vehicles meet after 3 hours, so we can plug in 3 for t:

$$3x = 180 - 6x$$

Adding $6x$ to both sides gives:

$$9x = 180$$

Dividing both sides by 9 tells results in $x = 20$.

However, before selecting choice (A), make sure to finish the problem.

The question asks you what speed the truck is going. The truck has a speed of $2x$. So its speed is $2(20) = 40$, which is choice (C).

2. **(A)** This problem mentions the "mean of the bases." Notice that $\frac{B_1 + B_2}{2}$, the first part of the area formula, is another way of saying the mean of the bases. Since the mean of the bases is twice the height, we can replace this part of the formula with $2H$:

$$A = \frac{B_1 + B_2}{2} H = 2H \times H = 2H^2$$

The area is 72, so plug this in for A and solve for H:

$$72 = 2H^2$$

Divide by 2:

$$36 = H^2$$

Take the square root of both sides to arrive at the answer $6 = H$, which is choice (A).

3. **(C)** If the negative exponent is in the numerator, it can send whatever is being raised to that exponent to the denominator, but be careful here. In both terms, only the m is being raised to the negative exponents, so the constants stay in the numerator:

$$2m^{-2} - 4m^{-3} = \frac{2}{m^2} - \frac{4}{m^3}$$

However, this doesn't match an answer choice. Based on the answer choices, it looks like we may need to add the two fractions together to get just one fraction overall. To add the two fractions, we need a common denominator. If you multiplied the first fraction by $\frac{m}{m}$, both terms would have a denominator of m^3:

$$\frac{2}{m^2} - \frac{4}{m^3} = \frac{2m}{m^3} - \frac{4}{m^3}$$

Now that they have a common denominator, you can add the two fractions together:

$$\frac{2m}{m^3} - \frac{4}{m^3} = \frac{2m - 4}{m^3}$$

Choice (C) is correct.

4. **(A)** Since there's nothing to distribute, you can just drop the parentheses and combine like terms:

$$2y^4 + 3x^6 + 5x^6 + 3y^4 = 5y^4 + 8x^6$$

The correct answer is choice (A).

5. **(D)** Look at the answer choices. All of the choices indicate that at least one $(x-3)$ factor cancels out, so divide the numerator by $(x-3)$:

$$
\begin{array}{r}
2x-6 \\
x-3\overline{\smash{\big)}\,2x^2-12x+18} \\
-\left(2x^2-6x\right) \\
\hline
-6x+18 \\
-(-6x+18) \\
\hline
0
\end{array}
$$

So the expression can be rewritten as:

$$\frac{(x-3)(2x-6)}{3(x-3)^3}$$

You can cancel an $(x-3)$ term from the top and bottom:

$$\frac{(2x-6)}{3(x-3)^2}$$

The number 2 can be factored out of the numerator:

$$\frac{2(x-3)}{3(x-3)^2}$$

Another $(x-3)$ term cancels:

$$\frac{2}{3(x-3)}$$

This is choice (D).

Alternatively, you could have factored the numerator directly:

$$2x^2 - 12x + 18 = 2(x^2 - 6x + 9) = 2(x-3)^2$$

Then you could have canceled out the $(x-3)^2$ term from the denominator.

6. **(A)** To find the solutions, subtract $15x$ and 18 from both sides to get everything on the left side:

$$21x^2 - 15x - 18 = 0$$

Next, factor out a 3 to make the quadratic equation a bit simpler:

$$3(7x^2 - 5x - 6) = 0$$

Divide both sides by 3:

$$7x^2 - 5x - 6 = 0$$

Notice that the answer choices look similar in structure to the quadratic formula $x = \dfrac{-b \pm \sqrt{b^2 - 4ac}}{2a}$. This suggests that we try to factor our quadratic equation using the quadratic formula. Letting $a = 7$, $b = -5$, and $c = -6$ in the quadratic formula above, we get choice (A).

7. **(B)** Find where the supply and demand are equivalent by setting the two equations equal to one another and solving for p:

$$3p + 6p^2 = 156 - 12p$$

Subtract 156 and add $12p$ to both sides:

$$15p + 6p^2 - 156 = 0$$

Rearrange the equation to get it in $ax^2 + bx + c$ form while simultaneously factoring out a 3:

$$3(2p^2 + 5p - 52) = 0$$

Divide both sides by 3:

$$2p^2 + 5p - 52 = 0$$

Factor to get:

$$(2p + 13)(p - 4) = 0$$

Set each factor equal to 0 and solve for p to get the two possible values of p:

$$2p + 13 = 0 \text{ so } p = -\frac{13}{2}$$

$$p - 4 = 0 \text{ so } p = 4$$

In this situation, p must be positive since it represents the price of the item, which can't be negative. Therefore, p equals only 4, choice (B).

Alternatively, if you didn't recognize that the quadratic equation could be factored, you could have used the quadratic formula:

$$x = \frac{-5 \pm \sqrt{5^2 - 4(2)(-52)}}{2(2)} = \frac{-5 \pm \sqrt{441}}{4} = \frac{-5 \pm 21}{4}$$

$$x = 4 \text{ or } x = -\frac{13}{2}$$

8. **(A)** Look at each option to see whether it is an answer.

Option I: $x = c$ is a vertical line at c. The line will cross the y-axis only if $c = 0$. Since we are told that c is a nonzero constant, this equation does not have a y-intercept.

Option II: $y = -c$ is a horizontal line at the $-c$ value. The line will cross the y-axis at $-c$. This option, therefore, must have a y-intercept.

Option III: $y = cx$ is a line with slope c. Note that when $x = 0$, $y = c(0) = 0$. So the line has a y-intercept at 0.

Thus, only option I is true, which is choice (A).

9. **(B)** The function has zeros at 2, 3, and 6. We can use this to find the factors of the function.

If $x = 2$, $x - 2 = 0$. So $(x - 2)$ is a factor.

If $x = 3$, $x - 3 = 0$. So $(x - 3)$ is a factor.

If $x = 6$, $x - 6 = 0$. So $(x - 6)$ is a factor.

Therefore, the function can be rewritten as $y = (x - 2)(x - 3)(x - 6)$. All of the answer choices are in their unfactored forms, so use FOIL. Start by using FOIL with the first two-factors:

$$y = (x^2 - 5x + 6)(x - 6)$$

Then multiply the remaining factors:

$$y = x^3 - 11x^2 + 36x - 36$$

This matches choice (B).

10. **(C)** First, let's identify all of the givens.

Since we're not provided a value for P, we will leave it as is in the formula.

We're also given that the interest is compounded once every 12 months. In other words, it's compounded once every year. Since n is the number of times the investment is compounded yearly, $n = 1$.

We're also told that the investment rate is 5%. Because r is the interest rate expressed as a decimal, $r = \frac{5}{100} = 0.05$.

We want to know A after 1 year, so $t = 1$.

Now plug everything into the equation:

$$A = P\left(1 + \frac{0.05}{1}\right)^{(1)(1)} = P(1.05) = 1.05P$$

Choice (C) is the answer.

Passport to Advanced Math Drill (No Calculator)

1. **(B)**

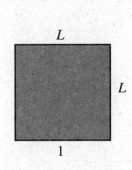 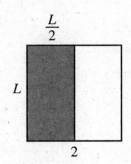

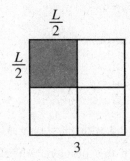 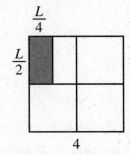

From the drawings, we can see that if the paper is folded in half once, the area is:

$$A = L\left(\frac{L}{2}\right) = \frac{L^2}{2}$$

After the second fold:

$$A = \left(\frac{L}{2}\right)\left(\frac{L}{2}\right) = \frac{L^2}{4}$$

After the third fold:

$$A = \left(\frac{L}{4}\right)\left(\frac{L}{2}\right) = \frac{L^2}{8}$$

We can see that each time, the numerator stays the same while the denominator is multiplied by 2. Therefore, the numerator will always be L^2 while the denominator will be 2^n. Therefore, area can be represented by:

$$A = \frac{L^2}{2^n}$$

Choice (B) is the correct answer.

Alternatively, you could have plugged the values for the areas for each fold into the answer choices to see that only choice (B) works.

2. **(D)** Numbers with negative exponents in the numerator can be rewritten with a positive exponent by moving that number to the denominator (i.e., $a^{-k} = \frac{1}{a^k}$). Fractional exponents are the same as roots. So the entire expression can be rewritten as:

$$\frac{\sqrt[3]{64}}{\sqrt[4]{81}} = \frac{4}{3}$$

The answer is choice (D).

3. **(A)** Let's use polynomial long division to divide the numerator by the denominator:

$$
\require{enclose}
\begin{array}{r}
3x^2 - 4x + 3 \\
x+2 \enclose{longdiv}{3x^3 + 2x^2 - 5x + 6} \\
-\left(3x^3 + 6x^2\right) \\
\hline
-4x^2 - 5x + 6 \\
-\left(-4x^2 - 8x\right) \\
\hline
3x + 6 \\
-(3x + 6) \\
\hline
0
\end{array}
$$

Therefore, $(3x^3 + 2x^2 - 5x + 6) \div (x + 2) = 3x^2 - 4x + 3$, which is choice (A).

You could also use synthetic division to solve this problem. Alternatively, if you were unsure of how to divide polynomials, you could have multiplied the answer choices by $x + 2$ to see which choice equaled the numerator.

4. **(B)** Recall that the quadratic formula tells us that solutions to the quadratic equation $ax^2 + bx + c = 0$ are $x = \frac{-b \pm \sqrt{b^2 - 4ac}}{2a}$. Thus, for a quadratic function to only have real solutions, we need $\frac{-b \pm \sqrt{b^2 - 4ac}}{2a}$ to be real numbers. This means that the expression under the square root, $b^2 - 4ac$, must be positive or 0. (If the value underneath the square root sign is negative, the solutions will be imaginary since the square roots of negative numbers are imaginary.)

In other words:

$$b^2 - 4ac \geq 0$$

If we add $4ac$ to both sides:

$$b^2 \geq 4ac$$

The answer is choice (B).

5. **(D)** First, distribute the x in the second part of the expression:

$$x^4 + x(x+2) = x^4 + x^2 + 2x$$

Next, distribute the negative sign:

$$(3x^3 - 2x^2 + 5x + 7) - (x^4 + x^2 + 2x) = 3x^3 - 2x^2 + 5x + 7 - x^4 - x^2 - 2x$$

Next, combine like terms:

$$3x^3 - 2x^2 + 5x + 7 - x^4 - x^2 - 2x = 3x^3 - 3x^2 + 3x + 7 - x^4$$

Rearrange the terms in descending order:

$$-x^4 + 3x^3 - 3x^2 + 3x + 7$$

So choice (D) is correct.

6. **(B)** Add $\sqrt{a}$ to both sides while subtracting 6 from both sides:

$$a - 6 = \sqrt{a}$$

If we square both sides, we can get rid of the square root:

$$a^2 - 12a + 36 = a$$

Subtract a from both sides to set the expression equal to 0:

$$a^2 - 13a + 36 = 0$$

Factoring tells us:

$$(a - 9)(a - 4) = 0$$

So a should equal 9 or 4. However, we have to be careful when square roots are involved. Although squaring both sides was useful when solving for a, this method can produce extraneous solutions. So we have to go back and check our answers to make sure that they are actually solutions to our original equation. Plug both numbers back in to the original equation to make sure that they work:

$$9 - \sqrt{9} = 6$$
$$9 - 3 = 6$$

So 9 does work and is a solution to the original equation.

$$4 - \sqrt{4} = 6$$
$$4 - 2 \neq 6$$

So 4 is an extraneous solution. Therefore, there is only one solution, choice (B).

7. **(D)** The second equation is simpler, so solve for y and then plug your expression for y back into the first equation:

$$3x - 6 = 3y$$

Divide by 3 to solve for y:

$$y = \frac{3x-6}{3} = \frac{3x}{3} - \frac{6}{3} = x - 2$$

Now you can plug $x - 2$ in for y in the first equality:

$$x[(x-2)+2] - 3x - 4[(x-2)+2] = -12$$

Combine like terms within the parentheses:

$$x(x) - 3x - 4(x) = -12$$

Combine like terms and bring the 12 to the left side:

$$x^2 - 7x + 12 = 0$$

Factor this, or use the quadratic equation if you're not great at factoring:

$$(x-3)(x-4) = 0$$

Set each factor equal to 0 to solve for the possible values of x:

$$x - 3 = 0$$

$$x = 3$$

$$x - 4 = 0$$

$$x = 4$$

Next, plug these values into either of the two equations to solve for y. It'll be easiest to plug them into the equation that you already solved for y:

$$y = x - 2 = 3 - 2 = 1$$

$$y = x - 2 = 4 - 2 = 2$$

So x can equal 3 or 4, and y can equal 1 or 2. Therefore, the greatest product xy will be:

$$4 \times 2 = 8$$

Choice (D) is the answer.

8. **(B)** From the graph, the function has zeros at $x = -3$ and at $x = 4$.

Starting with the $x = -3$, add 3 to both sides:

$$x + 3 = 0$$

Therefore, $x + 3$ is a factor. This means that the function must be divisible by $x + 3$.

Similarly, $x = 4$, so:

$$x - 4 = 0$$

Therefore, $x - 4$ is a factor of the function, meaning the function is divisible by $x - 4$. These are the only two zeros. So the function has only two distinct factors, which we have already found. Therefore, Options I and III are correct, which is choice (B).

9. **(B)** The vertex form of a parabola is $y = (x - h)^2 + k$, where (h, k) are the coordinates of the vertex. Our original equation can be written in this form as $y = (x - 0)^2 + 3$. So $h = 0$ and $k = 3$.

The second parabola would be written as $y = (x - 5)^2 + 6$. So $h = 5$ and $k = 6$.

Therefore, h increases by 5 and k increases by 3, which is choice (B).

10. **(C)** First, you must plug the expression for $g(x)$ into $f(x)$ where it's indicated:

$$f(x) = g(x) + 4 = x - \frac{5}{x} + 4$$

Next, plug 10 in for x in $f(x)$:

$$f(10) = 10 - \frac{5}{10} + 4 = 14 - \frac{1}{2} = 13\frac{1}{2} = 13.5$$

Choice (C) is the correct answer.

Additional Topics in Math Drill (Calculator)

1. **(C)** Let's do this one in two parts. First, we have a right cylinder with a volume of $30x$. We form a cone with the same height and radius as that cylinder. The formula for the volume of a cylinder is $V = \pi r^2 h$, while the formula for the volume of a cone is $V = \frac{1}{3}\pi r^2 h$.

   Notice that the volume of a cone is just $\frac{1}{3}$ the volume of a cylinder with the same dimensions. Thus, if the volume of the cylinder is $30x$, the volume of a cone with the same dimensions is $\frac{1}{3}(30x)$ or $10x$.

   For the second part of this problem, there's a cube with a volume of $21x$. We have a pyramid with the same length, width, and height as the cube. The formula for the volume of a cube is $V = LWH = L^3$ because the length, width, and height are all the same. The formula for the volume of a pyramid is $V = \frac{1}{3}LWH$.

   In this case, the pyramid has the same length, width, and height as the cube, so the volume for the pyramid can be expressed as $V = \frac{1}{3}L^3$.

   Notice that in this case, the volume of the pyramid is just $\frac{1}{3}$ of the volume of the cube.

   The volume of the cube is $21x$, so the volume of the pyramid is $\frac{1}{3}(21x) = 7x$.

   The question asked us the sum of the volume of the cone and the pyramid, which can be expressed by:

   $$V = V_{cone} + V_{pyramid} = 10x + 7x = 17x$$

   Choice (C) is correct.

2. **(A)** The length Andrew would fly would simply be the hypotenuse of a right triangle with side lengths of 20 miles and 15 miles. So we can use the Pythagorean theorem, which states that $a^2 + b^2 = c^2$, where a and b represent the sides and c represents the hypotenuse:

   $$(20)^2 + (15)^2 = c^2$$
   $$400 + 225 = c^2$$
   $$c = \sqrt{625} = 25$$

   Choice (A) is correct.

   Alternatively, you could have saved a bit of time by noticing that this is just a variation of a 3-4-5 triangle:

   $$15 = 3(5) \text{ and } 20 = 4(5)$$

   Thus, the hypotenuse will be 5(5) or 25.

3. **(C)** In a right triangle, we can use the Pythagorean theorem to solve for an unknown hypotenuse. $a^2 + b^2 = c^2$ where a and b are the 2 shorter legs and c is the hypotenuse. To solve for c, you take the square root of both sides:

$$c = \sqrt{a^2 + b^2}$$

This matches choice (C).

4. **(A)** Remember the cycle of how i^n repeats as we increase the integer n by 1 each time:

$$i = \sqrt{-1}$$
$$i^2 = -1$$
$$i^3 = -i$$
$$i^4 = 1$$

Therefore, $2i^2 = 2(-1) = -2$.

For $(3i)^4$, we have to remember to raise both the 3 and the i to the fourth power:

$$3^4 = 81$$
$$i^4 = 1$$
$$(3i)^4 = (81)(1) = 81$$

Multiply the two terms together:

$$2i^2(3i)^4 = (-2)(81) = -162$$

The answer is choice (A).

5. **(B)** To convert degrees to radians, simply multiply the number of degrees by $\frac{\pi}{180}$:

$$270\left(\frac{\pi}{180}\right) = \frac{3\pi}{2}$$

Choice (B) is the answer.

Alternatively, you could have realized that 270 degrees is $\frac{3}{4}$ of a circle. A circle is 2π radians, so 270 degrees corresponds to:

$$\frac{3}{4}(2\pi) = \frac{6\pi}{4} = \frac{3\pi}{2} \text{ radians}$$

Note: Radians may or may not be a topic tested on the PSAT. It is definitely something that could be on the SAT. So this problem was included here to prepare you.

6. **(D)** To find the length of the crust, we want to find $\frac{1}{8}$ of the total crust measure. The total crust measure is the circumference of a circle with radius 8. So the crust of one piece is $\frac{1}{8}C$. Because $C = 2\pi r$, the measure we're looking for is:

$$\frac{1}{8}2\pi r = \frac{\pi r}{4} = \frac{8\pi}{4} = 2\pi$$

Note that $2(3.14) = 6.28$, or choice (D).

7. **(C)** The angle next to the 120-degree angle on line *AB* is 60 degrees because two angles on a given line (supplementary angles) must add up to 180 degrees.

The angle directly opposite that first 60 degree angle must also be 60 degrees, because angles opposite one another (called vertical angles) are equal. Furthermore, that vertical angle is along line *EF* with the 120-degree angle. So the sum of these supplementary angles must also be 180 degrees, making the vertical angle 60 degrees.

Because lines *AB* and *CD* are parallel and line *EF* is a transversal, opposite interior angles are also congruent. Therefore, the acute angle along line *CD* is also 60 degrees.

Because that angle is 60 degrees, the acute angle across from it (also along line *CD*) is also 60 degrees since angles opposite one another (vertical angles) must be congruent.

8. **(B)** For this problem, we can employ a little trick so that we have an i^2 term and can factor out an i in the numerator. We can use the knowledge that $i^2 = -1$ to change -6 to $6(-1)$ or $6i^2$. Thus, we can rewrite the original numerator as:

$$i^3 + 6i^2 + 9i$$

An i can be factored out, leaving us with the following in the numerator:

$$i(i^2 + 6i + 9)$$

The part inside the parentheses can be factored as:

$$(i + 3)^2$$

Therefore, our whole expression can be rewritten as:

$$\frac{i(i+3)^2}{3+i}$$

Since $i + 3$ is the same as $3 + i$, we can cancel one of the $i + 3$ terms from the numerator with the $3 + i$ term in the denominator. This leaves:

$$i(i+3) \text{ or } i^2 + 3i$$

Because we know that $i^2 = -1$, we can rewrite this as $-1 + 3i$, which is the same as choice (B).

Alternatively, we can first simplify the numerator since $i^3 = -i$:

$$i^3 + 9i - 6 = -i + 9i - 6 = 8i - 6$$

Now notice that none of the answer choices are fractions, so we want to get rid of the denominator. We can get rid of the i-term in the denominator by multiplying by its complex conjugate. This is found by changing the sign of all terms with an i in them and leaving the signs of all real numbers the same. So in our case, the complex conjugate of the denominator $3 + i$ is $3 - i$. We multiply both the numerator and denominator by this conjugate:

$$\frac{8i-6}{3+i} \cdot \frac{3-i}{3-i} = \frac{(8i-6)(3-i)}{(3+i)(3-i)}$$

By using FOIL and simplifying, we have:

$$\frac{(8i-6)(3-i)}{(3+i)(3-i)} = \frac{24i - 8i^2 - 18 + 6i}{9 - 3i + 3i - i^2} = \frac{30i - 8(-1) - 18}{9 - (-1)} = \frac{30i - 10}{10}$$

Factoring out a 10 from the numerator gives:

$$\frac{10(3i-1)}{10} = 3i - 1$$

Choice (B) is the answer.

9. **(D)** Similar triangles have similar side lengths, meaning that the side lengths vary in fixed proportions. We know that triangle B has exactly one side length of 28. Since exactly one side of triangle A has length 7, this is $28 \div 7 = 4$ times the side length of the unique side in triangle A. Thus, the two shorter sides in triangle B will also be 4 times the side length of the shorter sides in triangle A. Since the two other sides of triangle A have length 5, triangle B has two sides of length $4(5) = 20$ and one side of length of 28.

This could have also been determined using a proportion:

$$\frac{28}{7} = \frac{x}{5}$$

Cross multiplication yields:

$$(28)(5) = 7x$$

$$140 = 7x$$

Dividing both sides by 7 tells us that $20 = x$.

Here we need to be careful. Notice that choice (B) is 20, so you may be tempted to pick choice (B). However, the question is asking us for the perimeter of the triangle rather than for the unknown side length.

The perimeter is $20 + 20 + 28 = 68$, choice (D).

An alternative approach would have been to recognize that the perimeters of similar triangles will vary in the same proportion as the side lengths. We know that triangle B has sides 4 times longer than those of triangle A, so triangle B will also have a perimeter 4 times that of triangle A.

Triangle A has a perimeter of $5 + 5 + 7 = 17$.

Triangle B therefore has a perimeter of $4(17) = 68$.

10. **(A)** We can solve for the unknown side using the Pythagorean theorem:

$$a^2 + b^2 = c^2$$

It follows that

$$b = \sqrt{c^2 - a^2} = \sqrt{26^2 - 24^2} = \sqrt{676 - 576} = \sqrt{100} = 10$$

Similar triangles have the same trigonometric ratios because the similar sides simplify to their lowest multiples.

The smallest angle in this triangle is angle X, as it is across from the shortest side length.

Therefore, a similar triangle will have a tangent of $\frac{\text{opposite}}{\text{adjacent}} = \frac{10}{24}$, which simplifies to $\frac{5}{12}$, choice (A).

Alternatively, you could have saved yourself some time by noticing that this is just a multiple of a 5-12-13 Pythagorean triple. The two known sides are $2(12) = 24$ and $2(13) = 26$. The only side length we were missing was the 5 side, which has a measure of:

$$2(5) = 10.$$

Calculator Problems Mixed Drill

1. **(D)** We want to isolate what's inside the parentheses with the goal of eventually isolating x. Let's first get that 6 out of the denominator by multiplying both sides by 6:

$$12\left(\frac{5x-2x}{2}\right)=108$$

To isolate what's inside the parentheses, we have to divide both sides by 12:

$$\left(\frac{5x-2x}{2}\right)=9$$

Now we can get rid of the parentheses:

$$\frac{5x-2x}{2}=9$$

To isolate our x-terms, multiply both sides by 2:

$$5x-2x=18$$

Combine the like x-terms:

$$5x-2x=3x=18$$

Because $3x=18$, it follows that $x=6$.

2. **(C)** Let's imagine the total volume of this rock to be 1 cubic centimeter. Therefore, 0.32 cubic centimeters are coal, 0.29 cubic centimeters are granite, and $1-0.32-0.29=0.39$ cubic centimeters are an unknown mineral. Using the specific gravities, we can calculate the mass of each species.

For coal:

$$0.32\text{ cm}^3 \times \frac{1.20\text{ grams}}{\text{cm}^3} = 0.384\text{ grams}$$

For granite:

$$0.29\text{ cm}^3 \times \frac{2.60\text{ grams}}{\text{cm}^3} = 0.754\text{ grams}$$

For the unknown:

$$0.39\text{ cm}^3 \times \frac{x\text{ grams}}{\text{cm}^3} = 0.39x\text{ grams}$$

We know that the specific gravity of the whole thing is 1.4 grams/centimeter cubed, so its mass is:

$$1\text{ cm}^3 \times \frac{1.4\text{ grams}}{\text{cm}^3} = 1.4\text{ grams}$$

Because all of the masses together must equal 1.4, it follows that:

$$0.384+0.754+0.39x=1.4$$

Subtract the first 2 terms from both sides:

$$0.39x=0.262$$

Divide both sides by 0.39:

$$x=0.67$$

3. **(A)** Remember that $d=rt$, where d is distance, r is rate, and t is time. We have two different rates and two different times. We can multiply the coinciding rates and times together and then can add them to obtain the total distance traveled, 300 miles:

$$5x+\left(\frac{x}{10}\right)\left(\frac{x}{2}\right)=300$$

Multiplying the two fractions together leaves:

$$5x + \frac{x^2}{20} = 300$$

None of the answer choices has a denominator, so let's multiply both sides by 20 to get rid of the denominator:

$$100x + x^2 = 6,000$$

Subtracting 6,000 from both sides and rearranging the terms gives:

$$x^2 + 100x - 6,000 = 0$$

This matches choice (A).

4. **(D)** Take each term one at a time. When you cube $6a^3$, you're cubing both the 6 and the a^3. When you raise an exponent to another exponent, multiply the exponents. Therefore:

$$(6a^3)^3 - (2b)^4 + c^{-2} = 216a^9 - (2b)^4 + c^{-2}$$

Next, raise $2b$ to the fourth power by raising 2 to the fourth power and raising b to the fourth power:

$$216a^9 - (2b)^4 + c^{-2} = 216a^9 - 16b^4 + c^{-2}$$

Lastly, deal with the negative exponent. Something with a negative exponent can be rewritten by moving that something to the denominator and making the corresponding exponent positive:

$$216a^9 - 16b^4 + c^{-2} = 216a^9 - 16b^4 + \frac{1}{c^2}$$

Choice (D) is the correct answer.

An alternative to solving this problem to completion is to realize that once there is the $216a^9$, the answer must have this term in it. Choice (D) is the only option with this term, so you can pick it without having to do the last steps as discussed above.

5. **(B)** Exponential growth has initially slow growth that later becomes fast growth. In other words, it starts with a small slope that quickly turns into a steep slope. Only choice (B) shows this kind of growth.

6. **(B)** Percent change is given by the following equation:

$$\frac{\text{New} - \text{Original}}{\text{Original}} \times 100\%$$

We can rule out choice (A) since stock price decreased between 1983 and 1984. Calculate the approximate percent increase for the remaining answer choices.

Choice (B):

$$\frac{29 - 20}{20} \times 100\% = 45\%$$

Choice (C):

$$\frac{52 - 39}{39} \times 100\% = 33\%$$

Choice (D):

$$\frac{68 - 52}{52} \times 100\% = 31\%$$

Therefore, choice (B) has the greatest percent increase.

7. **(D)** The minimal stock price is about \$11/share. Since the stockbroker sold \$1,000 in shares, she must have sold:

$$1,000 \times \frac{1\,\text{share}}{\$11} = 90.91\,\text{shares}$$

The maximum price is about \$88/share:

$$1,000 \times \frac{1\,\text{share}}{\$88} = 11.36\,\text{shares}$$

She would have sold $90.91 - 11.36 = 79.55$ more shares at the lower price, or about 80 as in choice (D).

8. **(D)** Just plug in $(b - a)$ wherever there is an a in the expression for $f(a)$:

$$f(b - a) = (b - a)^2 - 12$$

Next, use FOIL for $(b - a)^2$:

$$(b - a)^2 = (b - a)(b - a) = b^2 - ab - ab + a^2 = b^2 - 2ab + a^2$$

Plug this back into $f(b - a)$:

$$f(b - a) = b^2 - 2ab + a^2 - 12$$

This can be arranged as $f(b - a) = a^2 - 2ab + b^2 - 12$, choice (D).

9. **(B)** Notice that the top and bottom sides each have a length of $3a$, while the left and right sides will each have a length of b. Therefore, $P = 3a + b + 3a + b$. Combine like terms:

$$P = 6a + 2b$$

The answer is choice (B).

10. **(B)** This function turns 3 times, so it's a quartic function, meaning it must have 4 factors. Right away, we can eliminate choices (A) and (D) because these functions each have only 3 factors; they're cubics. To conceptualize, a quadratic function—a parabola—turns once. A cubic function turns twice.

The function has zeros at -1, 0, and 2. We can use this to solve for the factors.

If $x = -1$, $x + 1 = 0$. So $(x + 1)$ is a factor. From this, you can eliminate choice (C), thus leaving choice (B) as the correct answer. However, if you want to see where the rest of the factors come from, read on.

If $x = 0$, x must be a factor. Why? Because if $x = 0$, the whole function equals zero; so x must be a factor.

If $x = 2$, $x - 2 = 0$. So $(x - 2)$ must be a factor. This factor must actually be squared. In general, if $(x - a)^m$ is a factor of a function, then the function crosses the x-axis at a if m is odd and does not cross the x-axis at a if m is even. In our case, if we look at the graph at $x = 2$, we can see that the graph never crosses the x-axis at 2; it stays above the x-axis right before and after 2. This means that $(x - 2)$ must be raised to an even power. We know that our graph is quartic. Since we already have 2 other distinct factors, the only option is for the exponent to be 2. In other words, $(x - 2)^2$ is a factor. Notice that the graph crosses the x-axis at the other two zeros: -1 and 0. At -1, the graph goes from the positive side to the negative side of the x-axis. The graph goes from the negative side to the positive side of the x-axis at 0. So their corresponding factors must occur an odd number of times (in this case, they each occur once). This matches choice (B).

Free-Response Problems Drill (No Calculator)

1. **(6)** A circle has the formula $(x-h)^2 + (y-k)^2 = r^2$, where (h, k) provides the coordinates for the center of the circle and r is the radius of the circle. This circle, therefore, has a center at $(0, 0)$, otherwise known as the origin. It has a radius of 6. Therefore, a line from the origin to any point on the circle has a distance of 6 units.

2. **(6)** Jamie runs $\frac{3}{2}k$ miles in the time that Matt runs k miles. Their combined distance is 10 miles, so create an equation to show this situation:

$$\frac{3}{2}k + k = 10$$

Get a common denominator so you can add like terms:

$$\frac{3}{2}k + \frac{2}{2}k = 10$$

$$\frac{5}{2}k = 10$$

To solve for k, divide both sides by $\frac{5}{2}$. This is the same as multiplying both sides by the reciprocal, $\frac{2}{5}$:

$$k = 10\left(\frac{2}{5}\right) = \frac{20}{5} = 4$$

However, the question asks how much Jamie runs, so you need to plug this value into $\frac{3}{2}k$:

$$\frac{3}{2}(4) = \frac{12}{2} = 6$$

So Jamie will run 6 miles.

3. $\left(\dfrac{5}{3}\right)$ Both sides of the equation are squared:

$$(x+2)(x+2) = (2x-3)(2x-3)$$

If you FOIL both sides:

$$x^2 + 4x + 4 = 4x^2 - 12x + 9$$

To find the solutions, you want to get everything on one side. Moving all terms on the left-hand side to the right side of the equation by subtracting gives:

$$0 = 3x^2 - 16x + 5$$

If you don't see that it can be factored as $(3x-1)(x-5)$, then use the quadratic formula:

$$x = \frac{-b \pm \sqrt{b^2 - 4ac}}{2a} = \frac{16 \pm \sqrt{(-16)^2 - 4(3)(5)}}{2(3)} = \frac{16 \pm \sqrt{196}}{6} = \frac{16 \pm 14}{6}$$

Therefore, $x = \frac{1}{3}$ or $x = 5$.

The question asks for the product of all of the solutions, so the answer is

$$5\left(\frac{1}{3}\right) = \frac{5}{3}$$

4. **(7)** If $a + 1$ is a factor, it will divide evenly into the polynomial without a remainder. You can do polynomial long division or synthetic division. We will show the steps for long division:

$$a+1 \overline{\smash{\big)}\, a^4 - 2a^3 + 2a^2 + ma + 2} \quad \dfrac{a^3 - 3a^2 + 5a + (m-5)}{}$$

$$\begin{array}{r}
a^3 - 3a^2 + 5a + (m-5) \\
a+1 \overline{\smash{\big)}\, a^4 - 2a^3 + 2a^2 + ma + 2} \\
-\underline{\left(a^4 + a^3\right)} \\
-3a^3 + 2a^2 + ma + 2 \\
-\underline{\left(-3a^3 - 3a^2\right)} \\
5a^2 + ma + 2 \\
-\underline{\left(5a^2 + 5a\right)} \\
(m-5)a + 2 \\
-\underline{\left((m-5)a + (m-5)\right)} \\
2 - (m-5)
\end{array}$$

In order for there to be no remainder, $2 - (m - 5)$ must be equal to 0. Set it equal to 0 and solve for m:

$$2 - (m - 5) = 0$$

Distribute the negative sign:

$$2 - m + 5 = 0$$

Combine like terms on the right:

$$7 - m = 0$$

Adding m to both sides solves for m:

$$7 = m$$

5. **(2)** Translating the line will merely shift it to the right and down. It will not affect the slope. Therefore, the slope will still be 2. Picture moving a line down and to the right on a graph. Does the slope change? No, so the slope remains the same.

Free-Response Problems Drill (Calculator)

1. **(9)** Let's call c the number of children's outfits purchased and a the number of adults' outfits purchased. We can write two equations: one for the number of outfits purchased and one for the amount of money spent.

We know that the sum of children's outfits and adults' outfits purchased must add up to $22:

$$c + a = 22$$

We also know that each children's outfit was $20, so the amount of money spent on children's outfits was $20c$. Similarly, each adults' outfit was $45. So the amount of money spent on adults' outfits was $45a$. We are also told that the family spent a total of $765. Therefore, our second equation is:

$$20c + 45a = 765$$

We want to know how many children's outfits were purchased. Let's solve for a in the first equation so that we can substitute a out of the second equation, leaving only c-terms.

$$a = 22 - c$$

Plug this into the second equation:

$$20c + 45(22 - c) = 765$$

Distributing the 45 gives us:

$$20c + 990 - 45c = 765$$

We can now combine both c-terms on the left:

$$-25c + 990 = 765$$

Subtracting 990 from both sides leaves:

$$-25c = -225$$

Finally, dividing both sides by −25 will tell us the number of children's outfits purchased:

$$c = 9$$

2. **(19)** The hotel at the median distance in a series of 15 terms will have 7 terms on both sides. Therefore, the hotel that we are looking for is the 8th term. Count 8 points from the left. Then follow that point along to the y-axis to find its cost per night. The cost per night at Hotel M is $120.

Let x be the number of rooms the hotel books. Since the hotel wants to make $2,280 and each room costs $120, we have the following equation: $2,280 = 120x$. Divide $2,280 by $120 to tell how many rooms must be booked:

$$\$2,280 \div \$120 = 19$$

So 19 rooms must be booked. Alternatively, we could have used dimensional analysis in the last step to eliminate units that we didn't want:

$$2,280 \times \frac{1\,\text{room}}{120} = 19\,\text{rooms}$$

3. **(4)** The formula for the area of a triangle is $A = \frac{1}{2}BH$. Plug the given numbers in to solve for the building's actual height:

$$960 = \frac{1}{2}(48)H$$

Divide both sides by $\frac{1}{2}$ (in other words, multiply both sides by the reciprocal, 2):

$$1,920 = 48H$$

Isolate H by dividing both sides by 48:

$$H = 40\,\text{feet}$$

This is the building's actual height, but we want to know its height in the picture. Let's set up a proportion to find the height in the photograph:

$$\frac{1''}{10'} = \frac{x''}{40'}$$

If we cross multiply:

$$(1)(40) = 10x$$

Dividing both sides by 10 gives:

$$x = 4$$

4. **(35)** The number of math/science majors is 225, and the number of engineering majors is 295. So the total number of STEM majors is 225 + 295 = 520. The total number of students at the university is 1,490. Therefore, the total percentage of STEM majors at the university is:

$$\frac{520}{1,490} \times 100\% = 34.9\%$$

When rounded to the nearest percent, we get 35%.

5. **(0.30)** The probability is given by (number of successes) ÷ number of chances. The number of successes is the number of female humanities majors, which is 450. The total number of chances is the total number of students in the school, which is 1,490. Therefore, the probability is:

$$\frac{450}{1,490} = 0.302$$

When rounded to the nearest hundredth, we get 0.30.

No-Calculator Problems Mixed Drill

1. **(C)** First, distribute the −5:

$$15x + \frac{1}{2} = -5x + \frac{25}{2}$$

Now we want to get all of the x-terms on one side and all of the constant terms on the other side. Let's start by adding $5x$ to both sides:

$$20x + \frac{1}{2} = \frac{25}{2}$$

Now all of the x-terms are on the left, so we want all constant terms on the right. Let's subtract $\frac{1}{2}$ from both sides:

$$20x = \frac{24}{2} = 12$$

Dividing both sides by 20 will isolate the x:

$$x = \frac{12}{20}$$

This simplifies to $x = \frac{3}{5}$, which is choice (C).

2. **(C)** Use FOIL for this like you would anything else. When you FOIL the expression, you get:

$$12 + 3i - 4i - i^2 = 12 - i - i^2$$

Because $i = \sqrt{-1}$, $i^2 = -1$. Thus, we can rewrite our equation as:

$$12 - i - (-1)$$

Therefore, the final answer is $13 - i$, which is choice (C).

3. **(A)** Use FOIL on both sides to get:

$$x^2 - 16x + 60 = x^2 - 16x + 64 + c$$

The coefficients of like terms of both sides of the equation must equal one another. The coefficients of the x^2-terms and of the x-terms are already equal on both sides. However, the constant terms must equal one another as well:

$$60 = 64 + c$$

Subtract 64 from both sides:

$$-4 = c$$

Choice (A) is correct.

4. **(A)** Here we're looking for an angle measure, so we need an inverse trigonometry function. Let's go through the answer choices.

Choice (A) works because sine is the value of the opposite side over the hypotenuse. Side x is opposite of angle X, and side z is the hypotenuse. Thus, $\sin^{-1}\left(\dfrac{x}{z}\right)$ would provide the measure of angle X.

Choice (B) doesn't work because side x is opposite of angle X rather than adjacent, so we don't want to use $\cos^{-1}$.

Choice (C) won't work because we want an inverse trigonometry function rather than a trigonometry function. The output of an inverse trigonometry function is an angle. In contrast, the output of a trigonometry function is the ratio of two sides of a right triangle.

Choice (D) doesn't work because side y is adjacent to angle X, so $\sin^{-1}$ is not the appropriate inverse trigonometry function to use.

5. **(D)** Solve for V:

$$V = \frac{nRT}{P}$$

Recall that, in general, y is directly proportional to x if $y = cx$ for some constant c, and y is inversely proportional if $y = \dfrac{c}{x}$. In our case, we are told that R is the gas constant, so we can think of this as our constant. So V is directly proportional to n and T. If you increased either of these variables, V would also increase. V is inversely proportional only to P, which isn't an answer choice. So choice (D) is the correct answer.

6. **(D)** First, isolate $\dfrac{1}{d_o}$ by subtracting $\dfrac{1}{d_i}$ from both sides of the equation:

$$\frac{1}{f} - \frac{1}{d_i} = \frac{1}{d_o}$$

We want to find d_o, so we need the reciprocal of $\dfrac{1}{d_o}$, which is d_o. To find the reciprocal, simply take 1 over both sides:

$$\frac{1}{\dfrac{1}{f} - \dfrac{1}{d_i}} = d_o$$

The answer is choice (D).

7. **(B)** First, use FOIL for the left side of the equation:

$$x^3 + ax^2 + 2x + 4x^2 + 4ax + 8$$

Next, combine like terms:

$$x^3 + (a+4)x^2 + (2+4a)x + 8$$

We know that this has to equal the right side of the original equation:

$$x^3 + (a+4)x^2 + (2+4a)x + 8 = x^3 + x^2 - 10x + 8$$

The coefficients of the like terms on both sides of the equation must equal one another. The coefficients on the x^3-terms are already equal and the constants are equal. So we need to worry about only the x^2-terms and the x-terms. Set the coefficients on the x^2-terms equal to one another:

$$a + 4 = 1$$

Subtracting 4 from both sides reveals that $a = -3$, which is choice (B).

We also could have set the coefficients of the x-terms equal to each other to solve for a:

$$2 + 4a = -10$$

Subtracting 2 from both sides and then dividing by 4 gives $a = -3$ as well.

8. **(D)** Distribute the negative sign:

$$\left(6y^3 + \frac{1}{2}y - \frac{2}{3}\right) - \left(4y^3 - y^2 + \frac{1}{2}y + \frac{1}{6}\right) = 6y^3 + \frac{1}{2}y - \frac{2}{3} - 4y^3 + y^2 - \frac{1}{2}y - \frac{1}{6}$$

Next combine like terms:

$$6y^3 + \frac{1}{2}y - \frac{2}{3} - 4y^3 + y^2 - \frac{1}{2}y - \frac{1}{6} = 2y^3 + y^2 - \frac{5}{6}$$

This matches choice (D).

9. **(D)** A line perpendicular to line A has a slope that is the negative reciprocal of $-\dfrac{x}{y}$.

The negative reciprocal is $-\left(-\dfrac{y}{x}\right)$, or $\dfrac{y}{x}$.

10. **(C)** We're given that $V_A = 8V_B$. From the formula for the volume of a sphere ($V = \frac{4}{3}\pi r^3$), it follows that $\frac{4}{3}\pi r_A^3 = 8\left(\frac{4}{3}\pi r_B^3\right)$. The $\frac{4}{3}\pi$ term cancels out on both sides, leaving us with $r_A^3 = 8r_B^3$. Taking the cube root of both sides gives $r_A = 2r_B$. Thus, the radius of sphere A is twice the radius of sphere B. We ultimately want to find the ratio of the surface areas, so consider the surface areas of the two spheres:

$$SA_A = 4\pi r_A^2 = 4\pi(2r_B)^2 = 4\pi(4r_B^2)$$

and

$$SA_B = 4\pi r_B^2$$

To find the ratio of the surface area of sphere A to the surface area of sphere B, we divide the surface area of sphere A by the surface area of sphere B:

$$\frac{SA_A}{SA_B} = \frac{4\pi\left(4r_B^2\right)}{4\pi r_B^2}$$

We can cancel a 4π and an r_B^2 out of both the numerator and the denominator, which leaves us with $\dfrac{SA_A}{SA_B} = 4$.

Thus, the ratio of the surface area of sphere A to sphere B is $\dfrac{4}{1}$ or 4:1, which is choice (C).

Practice Tests

ANSWER SHEET
Practice Test 1

Reading Test

1. Ⓐ Ⓑ Ⓒ Ⓓ	13. Ⓐ Ⓑ Ⓒ Ⓓ	25. Ⓐ Ⓑ Ⓒ Ⓓ	37. Ⓐ Ⓑ Ⓒ Ⓓ
2. Ⓐ Ⓑ Ⓒ Ⓓ	14. Ⓐ Ⓑ Ⓒ Ⓓ	26. Ⓐ Ⓑ Ⓒ Ⓓ	38. Ⓐ Ⓑ Ⓒ Ⓓ
3. Ⓐ Ⓑ Ⓒ Ⓓ	15. Ⓐ Ⓑ Ⓒ Ⓓ	27. Ⓐ Ⓑ Ⓒ Ⓓ	39. Ⓐ Ⓑ Ⓒ Ⓓ
4. Ⓐ Ⓑ Ⓒ Ⓓ	16. Ⓐ Ⓑ Ⓒ Ⓓ	28. Ⓐ Ⓑ Ⓒ Ⓓ	40. Ⓐ Ⓑ Ⓒ Ⓓ
5. Ⓐ Ⓑ Ⓒ Ⓓ	17. Ⓐ Ⓑ Ⓒ Ⓓ	29. Ⓐ Ⓑ Ⓒ Ⓓ	41. Ⓐ Ⓑ Ⓒ Ⓓ
6. Ⓐ Ⓑ Ⓒ Ⓓ	18. Ⓐ Ⓑ Ⓒ Ⓓ	30. Ⓐ Ⓑ Ⓒ Ⓓ	42. Ⓐ Ⓑ Ⓒ Ⓓ
7. Ⓐ Ⓑ Ⓒ Ⓓ	19. Ⓐ Ⓑ Ⓒ Ⓓ	31. Ⓐ Ⓑ Ⓒ Ⓓ	43. Ⓐ Ⓑ Ⓒ Ⓓ
8. Ⓐ Ⓑ Ⓒ Ⓓ	20. Ⓐ Ⓑ Ⓒ Ⓓ	32. Ⓐ Ⓑ Ⓒ Ⓓ	44. Ⓐ Ⓑ Ⓒ Ⓓ
9. Ⓐ Ⓑ Ⓒ Ⓓ	21. Ⓐ Ⓑ Ⓒ Ⓓ	33. Ⓐ Ⓑ Ⓒ Ⓓ	45. Ⓐ Ⓑ Ⓒ Ⓓ
10. Ⓐ Ⓑ Ⓒ Ⓓ	22. Ⓐ Ⓑ Ⓒ Ⓓ	34. Ⓐ Ⓑ Ⓒ Ⓓ	46. Ⓐ Ⓑ Ⓒ Ⓓ
11. Ⓐ Ⓑ Ⓒ Ⓓ	23. Ⓐ Ⓑ Ⓒ Ⓓ	35. Ⓐ Ⓑ Ⓒ Ⓓ	47. Ⓐ Ⓑ Ⓒ Ⓓ
12. Ⓐ Ⓑ Ⓒ Ⓓ	24. Ⓐ Ⓑ Ⓒ Ⓓ	36. Ⓐ Ⓑ Ⓒ Ⓓ	

Writing and Language Test

1. Ⓐ Ⓑ Ⓒ Ⓓ	12. Ⓐ Ⓑ Ⓒ Ⓓ	23. Ⓐ Ⓑ Ⓒ Ⓓ	34. Ⓐ Ⓑ Ⓒ Ⓓ
2. Ⓐ Ⓑ Ⓒ Ⓓ	13. Ⓐ Ⓑ Ⓒ Ⓓ	24. Ⓐ Ⓑ Ⓒ Ⓓ	35. Ⓐ Ⓑ Ⓒ Ⓓ
3. Ⓐ Ⓑ Ⓒ Ⓓ	14. Ⓐ Ⓑ Ⓒ Ⓓ	25. Ⓐ Ⓑ Ⓒ Ⓓ	36. Ⓐ Ⓑ Ⓒ Ⓓ
4. Ⓐ Ⓑ Ⓒ Ⓓ	15. Ⓐ Ⓑ Ⓒ Ⓓ	26. Ⓐ Ⓑ Ⓒ Ⓓ	37. Ⓐ Ⓑ Ⓒ Ⓓ
5. Ⓐ Ⓑ Ⓒ Ⓓ	16. Ⓐ Ⓑ Ⓒ Ⓓ	27. Ⓐ Ⓑ Ⓒ Ⓓ	38. Ⓐ Ⓑ Ⓒ Ⓓ
6. Ⓐ Ⓑ Ⓒ Ⓓ	17. Ⓐ Ⓑ Ⓒ Ⓓ	28. Ⓐ Ⓑ Ⓒ Ⓓ	39. Ⓐ Ⓑ Ⓒ Ⓓ
7. Ⓐ Ⓑ Ⓒ Ⓓ	18. Ⓐ Ⓑ Ⓒ Ⓓ	29. Ⓐ Ⓑ Ⓒ Ⓓ	40. Ⓐ Ⓑ Ⓒ Ⓓ
8. Ⓐ Ⓑ Ⓒ Ⓓ	19. Ⓐ Ⓑ Ⓒ Ⓓ	30. Ⓐ Ⓑ Ⓒ Ⓓ	41. Ⓐ Ⓑ Ⓒ Ⓓ
9. Ⓐ Ⓑ Ⓒ Ⓓ	20. Ⓐ Ⓑ Ⓒ Ⓓ	31. Ⓐ Ⓑ Ⓒ Ⓓ	42. Ⓐ Ⓑ Ⓒ Ⓓ
10. Ⓐ Ⓑ Ⓒ Ⓓ	21. Ⓐ Ⓑ Ⓒ Ⓓ	32. Ⓐ Ⓑ Ⓒ Ⓓ	43. Ⓐ Ⓑ Ⓒ Ⓓ
11. Ⓐ Ⓑ Ⓒ Ⓓ	22. Ⓐ Ⓑ Ⓒ Ⓓ	33. Ⓐ Ⓑ Ⓒ Ⓓ	44. Ⓐ Ⓑ Ⓒ Ⓓ

ANSWER SHEET
Practice Test 1

Math Test (No Calculator)

1. Ⓐ Ⓑ Ⓒ Ⓓ
2. Ⓐ Ⓑ Ⓒ Ⓓ
3. Ⓐ Ⓑ Ⓒ Ⓓ
4. Ⓐ Ⓑ Ⓒ Ⓓ

5. Ⓐ Ⓑ Ⓒ Ⓓ
6. Ⓐ Ⓑ Ⓒ Ⓓ
7. Ⓐ Ⓑ Ⓒ Ⓓ
8. Ⓐ Ⓑ Ⓒ Ⓓ

9. Ⓐ Ⓑ Ⓒ Ⓓ
10. Ⓐ Ⓑ Ⓒ Ⓓ
11. Ⓐ Ⓑ Ⓒ Ⓓ
12. Ⓐ Ⓑ Ⓒ Ⓓ

13. Ⓐ Ⓑ Ⓒ Ⓓ

14.
15.
16.
17.

Math Test (With Calculator)

1. Ⓐ Ⓑ Ⓒ Ⓓ
2. Ⓐ Ⓑ Ⓒ Ⓓ
3. Ⓐ Ⓑ Ⓒ Ⓓ
4. Ⓐ Ⓑ Ⓒ Ⓓ
5. Ⓐ Ⓑ Ⓒ Ⓓ
6. Ⓐ Ⓑ Ⓒ Ⓓ
7. Ⓐ Ⓑ Ⓒ Ⓓ

8. Ⓐ Ⓑ Ⓒ Ⓓ
9. Ⓐ Ⓑ Ⓒ Ⓓ
10. Ⓐ Ⓑ Ⓒ Ⓓ
11. Ⓐ Ⓑ Ⓒ Ⓓ
12. Ⓐ Ⓑ Ⓒ Ⓓ
13. Ⓐ Ⓑ Ⓒ Ⓓ
14. Ⓐ Ⓑ Ⓒ Ⓓ

15. Ⓐ Ⓑ Ⓒ Ⓓ
16. Ⓐ Ⓑ Ⓒ Ⓓ
17. Ⓐ Ⓑ Ⓒ Ⓓ
18. Ⓐ Ⓑ Ⓒ Ⓓ
19. Ⓐ Ⓑ Ⓒ Ⓓ
20. Ⓐ Ⓑ Ⓒ Ⓓ
21. Ⓐ Ⓑ Ⓒ Ⓓ

22. Ⓐ Ⓑ Ⓒ Ⓓ
23. Ⓐ Ⓑ Ⓒ Ⓓ
24. Ⓐ Ⓑ Ⓒ Ⓓ
25. Ⓐ Ⓑ Ⓒ Ⓓ
26. Ⓐ Ⓑ Ⓒ Ⓓ
27. Ⓐ Ⓑ Ⓒ Ⓓ

28.
29.
30.
31.

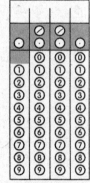

Practice Test 1

READING TEST

60 MINUTES, 47 QUESTIONS

Directions: Each passage or pair of passages is accompanied by several questions. After reading the passage(s), choose the best answer to each question based on what is indicated explicitly or implicitly in the passage(s) or in the associated graphics.

Questions 1–9 are based on the passage that follows.

Upton Sinclair's 1906 The Jungle *recounts the immigration of Jurgis Rudkus and Ona Lukoszaite from Lithuania to Chicago. The text raised social awareness of the unhealthy standards of industrial work at the turn of the century.*

Promptly at seven the next morning Jurgis
reported for work. He came to the door that
had been pointed out to him, and there he
line   waited for nearly two hours. The boss had
(5)   meant for him to enter, but had not said this,
and so it was only when on his way out to
hire another man that he came upon Jurgis.
He gave him a good cursing, but as Jurgis did
not understand a word of it he did not object.
(10)   He followed the boss, who showed him
where to put his street clothes, and waited
while he donned the working clothes he had
bought in a secondhand shop and brought
with him in a bundle; then he led him to the
(15)   "killing beds." The work which Jurgis was to
do here was very simple, and it took him but
a few minutes to learn it. He was provided
with a stiff besom, such as is used by street
sweepers, and it was his place to follow down
(20)   the line the man who drew out the smoking

entrails from the carcass of the steer; this
mass was to be swept into a trap, which was
then closed, so that no one might slip into
it. As Jurgis came in, the first cattle of the
(25)   morning were just making their appearance;
and so, with scarcely time to look about him,
and none to speak to any one, he fell to work.
It was a sweltering day in July, and the place
ran with steaming hot blood—one waded
(30)   in it on the floor. The stench was almost
overpowering, but to Jurgis it was nothing.
His whole soul was dancing with joy—he
was at work at last! He was at work and
earning money! All day long he was figuring
(35)   to himself. He was paid the fabulous sum
of seventeen and a half cents an hour; and
as it proved a rush day and he worked until
nearly seven o'clock in the evening, he went
home to the family with the tidings that he
(40)   had earned more than a dollar and a half in a
single day!
At home, also, there was more good news;
so much of it at once that there was quite a
celebration in Aniele's hall bedroom. Jonas
(45)   had been to have an interview with the
special policeman to whom Szedvilas had
introduced him, and had been taken to see
several of the bosses, with the result that
one had promised him a job the beginning

GO ON TO THE NEXT PAGE

(50) of the next week. And then there was Marija
Berczynskas, who, fired with jealousy by
the success of Jurgis, had set out upon her
own responsibility to get a place. Marija
had nothing to take with her save her two
(55) brawny arms and the word "job," laboriously
learned; but with these she had marched
about Packingtown all day, entering every
door where there were signs of activity. Out
of some she had been ordered with curses;
(60) but Marija was not afraid of man or devil,
and asked every one she saw—visitors and
strangers, or work-people like herself, and
once or twice even high and lofty office
personages, who stared at her as if they
(65) thought she was crazy. In the end, however,
she had reaped her reward. In one of the
smaller plants she had stumbled upon a
room where scores of women and girls were
sitting at long tables preparing smoked beef
(70) in cans; and wandering through room after
room, Marija came at last to the place where
the sealed cans were being painted and
labeled, and here she had the good fortune
to encounter the "forelady." Marija did not
(75) understand then, as she was destined to
understand later, what there was attractive
to a "forelady" about the combination of a
face full of boundless good nature and the
muscles of a dray horse; but the woman had
(80) told her to come the next day and she would
perhaps give her a chance to learn the trade
of painting cans. The painting of cans being
skilled piecework, and paying as much as two
dollars a day, Marija burst in upon the family
(85) with the yell of a Comanche Indian, and fell
to capering about the room so as to frighten
the baby almost into convulsions.

1. The major thematic contrast in the narrative is
   between
   (A) being motivated to find a job and deciding
       to take it easy.
   (B) strict vegetarianism and a willingness to eat
       meat.
   (C) becoming an immigrant and staying in one's
       native country.
   (D) the attitudes of the workers and the true
       nature of their work.

2. The two successful job seekers discussed in the
   passage have what general attitude upon being
   hired?

   (A) Optimism
   (B) Pessimism
   (C) Resignation
   (D) Peacefulness

3. It can be reasonably inferred from the passage
   that the supervisors in the meat-packing factories
   viewed employees as

   (A) skillful.
   (B) disposable.
   (C) valuable.
   (D) interesting.

4. Which option gives the best evidence for the
   answer to the previous question?

   (A) Lines 4–7 ("The boss . . . Jurgis")
   (B) Lines 15–17 ("The work . . . learn it")
   (C) Lines 32–35 ("His whole . . . himself")
   (D) Lines 42–44 ("At home . . . bedroom")

GO ON TO THE NEXT PAGE

5. What is the purpose of lines 15–24?

    (A) To analyze a character's motivations
    (B) To summarize the major point of the paragraph
    (C) To describe a character's professional tasks
    (D) To consider a likely objection by the reader

6. As used in line 34, "figuring" most closely means

    (A) believing.
    (B) calculating.
    (C) assuming.
    (D) doubting.

7. As used in line 67, "plants" most closely means

    (A) vegetation.
    (B) stations.
    (C) factories.
    (D) houses.

8. The passage suggests that Marija has what level of proficiency in the English language?

    (A) Totally fluent
    (B) Mostly fluent
    (C) Somewhat proficient
    (D) Very limited

9. Which option gives the best evidence for the answer to the previous question?

    (A) Lines 50–53 ("And then . . . place")
    (B) Lines 53–56 ("Marija . . . learned")
    (C) Lines 66–74 ("In one . . . 'forelady'")
    (D) Lines 82–87 ("The painting . . . convulsions")

Questions 10–19 are based on the passage and supplementary material that follow.

"Santa's Big Helpers"—An economist discusses American overnight-delivery logistics. Written in 2015.

Each year the holiday season rolls around and most people have difficulty doing all the things to get ready for family gatherings

Line and traditions. Black Friday is either an

(5) adrenaline-laced day of chaos when bargains can be garnered, or it is an experience to avoid by sitting at a keyboard and becoming part of the e-commerce movement. Some people love the thrill of the hunt and others

(10) enjoy the peace and quiet of working down a list with a company like Amazon.com.

Whatever your preference, the method by which a product finds its way to you, the consumer, is logistics. Originally a term

(15) that described the flow of materiel for the military in the conflicts around the globe, it has now found its way into every element of consumerism. Major retailers have emerged that specialize in online shopping; others

(20) have outlet stores and websites where the buyer can choose a channel for procurement. Other "big box" retailers have stores in malls and large distribution centers where product is delivered from the various manufacturers

(25) and moved through an integrated supply chain to the point-of-sale retail establishment. Making sure that your size and desired color of clothing is on the hanger is no small task and large teams of employees

(30) manage the information and product flows to provide a seamless experience for the customer.

GO ON TO THE NEXT PAGE

Companies like FedEx have grown to be an integral part of the American landscape.
(35) FedEx first specialized in overnight deliveries via aircraft and then grew into a full service provider using a truck network in conjunction with air transport. *"When it absolutely, positively has to be there*
(40) *overnight"* is its mantra, and it basically provides certainty of service for a premium price that consumers are willing to bear. Product is prepared for shipment and FedEx picks it up at the factory or distribution
(45) center. If it is traveling from New York City to Los Angeles, California, it is loaded on an aircraft in the early evening and flown to Memphis, TN, arriving after midnight or before. This massive influx of aircraft must
(50) be unloaded piece by piece, sorted to a new destination, loaded on an out-going aircraft and flown out in the early morning hours. In Los Angeles, the plane is unloaded, the items are taken by truck to a dispatching center and
(55) white delivery vans will navigate the perils of rush hour traffic to make the delivery to the person who wants the package.

FedEx and UPS now provide online tracking of packages for the consumer. It
(60) is interesting to log on and see the journey that a purchase has traveled to go from source to destination. Each time an arrival and a departure are scanned, that item has to be picked up by an employee, placed on
(65) a moving belt to take to a sortation system, and then placed on another vehicle for its next leg in the sojourn. Holiday seasons put these logistics systems to a severe test each year, and companies in the business of
(70) logistics are constantly investing in new ways to handle the information and the items as they flow through the pipelines. Billions of dollars have been invested in these types of

service industries, and the activity behind
(75) the scenes is something to behold. Santa does indeed have his helpers, but instead of a red sleigh and cute little reindeer, a 747 jet aircraft and a white or brown delivery truck are the real implements in keeping people
(80) happy in their gift giving. And if the recent past is any indication, consumer spending on e-commerce will only continue to increase.

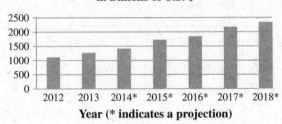

Worldwide Business to Consumer Sales in Billions of U.S. $

Year (* indicates a projection)

Figure 1

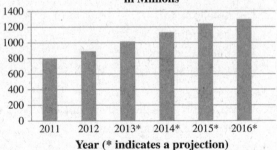

Number of Digital Buyers Worldwide in Millions

Year (* indicates a projection)

Figure 2

Source: Statista.com

GO ON TO THE NEXT PAGE

10. What is the purpose of the passage?

    (A) To analyze a phenomenon
    (B) To argue against conventional wisdom
    (C) To justify a decision
    (D) To describe a historical event

11. What is the purpose of lines 14–16 ("Originally . . . globe")?

    (A) To define current usage of a phrase
    (B) To address a likely reader objection
    (C) To use primary source evidence
    (D) To explain the root of a concept

12. As used in line 34, "integral" most closely means

    (A) essential.
    (B) economic.
    (C) geographic.
    (D) capitalist.

13. The author suggests that, in general, customers who use overnight delivery services are primarily concerned with

    (A) cost.
    (B) reliability.
    (C) holiday incentives.
    (D) fashion choices.

14. Which option gives the best evidence for the answer to the previous question?

    (A) Lines 4–8 ("Black Friday . . . movement")
    (B) Lines 27–32 ("Making sure . . . customer")
    (C) Lines 38–42 ("*When* it . . . bear")
    (D) Lines 59–62 ("It is . . . destination")

15. It is reasonable to infer that the author's attitude toward the process of logistical distribution is

    (A) skeptical.
    (B) positive.
    (C) neutral.
    (D) bellicose.

16. Which option gives the best evidence for the answer to the previous question?

    (A) Lines 8–11 ("Some people . . . Amazon.com")
    (B) Lines 18–21 ("Major . . . procurement")
    (C) Lines 62–67 ("Each time . . . sojourn")
    (D) Lines 72–75 ("Billions . . . behold")

17. Figure 1 provides the most direct support for which of the following statements in the passage?

    (A) Lines 1–4 ("Each year . . . traditions")
    (B) Lines 22–27 ("Other . . . establishment")
    (C) Lines 49–52 ("This massive . . . hours")
    (D) Lines 80–82 ("And if . . . increase")

18. Figure 2 is most helpful in explaining which action mentioned in the passage?

    (A) Lines 43–45 ("Product . . . center")
    (B) Lines 45–49 ("If it is . . . before")
    (C) Lines 62–64 ("Each time . . . employee")
    (D) Lines 69–72 ("companies . . . pipelines")

19. According to Figures 1 and 2, the relationship between the worldwide business to consumer sales and the worldwide number of digital consumers can best be described as

    (A) inversely related.
    (B) positively correlated.
    (C) exponentially related.
    (D) negatively related.

GO ON TO THE NEXT PAGE

Questions 20–28 are based on the passage and supplementary material that follow.

A nurse practitioner shares information about treatments for antimicrobials. Written in 2016.

Antimicrobials, commonly known as antibiotics, have been around in different forms for thousands of years. It is believed
line that the ancient Egyptians and Greeks were
(5) some of the first societies to use garlic and other spices for medicinal purposes to help boost the strength and endurance of their workers and soldiers. While the use of spices as antimicrobials is still a practice within
(10) Traditional Chinese Medicine, the utilization of pharmaceutical antimicrobials is more widespread in Western culture.

The past few decades have seen an explosion in antibiotic use as scientists
(15) continue to develop and release new medicines for bacterial, viral, and fungal infections. Antibiotics prescribed by doctors today are so advanced that they are able to target the action mechanisms of certain
(20) microorganisms. For example, one class of antibiotics targets cell wall synthesis of the microorganism, while another class inhibits protein synthesis. Targeting different mechanisms of action will either completely
(25) kill the microorganism or slow its growth. If the antibiotic kills the microorganism, it is classified as a bactericidal drug, while if it only slows the growth, it is considered bacteriostatic. Both categories of drugs have
(30) their advantages and disadvantages.

Bacteriostatic antibiotics are often prescribed to patients who have an intact immune system that can assist in killing the microorganism causing the infection.
(35) Allowing the innate immune system to

do some of the work decreases the length of time the patient needs to be on the antibiotic, which can help eliminate some of the unwanted side effects. Bactericidal
(40) drugs are prescribed when the patient may be immunocompromised (i.e., the natural immune system is not functioning properly) and cannot fight off the infection. Depending on the severity and type of
(45) infection, a doctor may select a narrow or broad-spectrum bactericidal drug. Narrow spectrum drugs are better for the patient as they only kill the microorganism causing the infection via a specific mechanism of
(50) action. This differs from broad-spectrum drugs as they kill the microorganism and any other cell with the same type of mechanism of action. This often causes serious and unpleasant side effects for the patient, such
(55) as superinfections and a wipeout of the body's natural flora barrier.

Both doctors and patients want to avoid complications from antibiotics, which is why doctors will often collect a sample
(60) of the microorganism from the patient in order to perform a culture and sensitivity test. This test helps to identify the specific microorganism causing the infection as well as the best antibiotic for treatment.
(65) Lab technicians are able to pinpoint the best antibiotic by measuring the "zone of inhibition" on the microorganism growth plate. The zone with the largest diameter typically signifies that it will be the best
(70) at fighting the infection. Prescribing an antibiotic that tests positive for the inhibition of growth or completely stops the growth of the microorganism will hopefully help the patient heal faster and experience
(75) fewer side effects.

GO ON TO THE NEXT PAGE

As the use of antibiotics continues to increase, there is growing concern within the healthcare community about the development of antibiotic resistant (80) microorganisms. Microorganisms that cause infections are able to gain resistance when their DNA spontaneously mutates, or when they receive DNA from another microorganism via conjugation. Once the (85) microorganism has secured the needed DNA sequence, many common antibiotics become ineffective in fighting the infection. The most common example of this is MRSA (methicillin-resistant *staphylococcus* (90) *aureus*), which has become a frequent hospital-acquired infection for many sick patients. MRSA is very difficult to fight and requires the use of very potent antibiotic treatments, such as IV vancomycin, for full (95) body infections. To help prevent these types of infections, the healthcare community is trying to better educate patients on proper use of antibiotics.

When patients receive a prescription (100) for an antibiotic from their pharmacy, they also receive instructions on how to properly complete the antibiotic regimen. Instructions include taking the entire prescription, even if the patient feels better half-way (105) through the regimen, as well as taking the correct dosage of the medication (e.g., do not double a dose). These instructions are important to follow because patients do not want to provide an optimal environment for (110) microorganisms to thrive. By following these simple instructions, patients will help to decrease antibiotic-resistant infections.

Antibiotic Tested	*E. coli* Zone of Inhibition	*S. aureus* Zone of Inhibition
Vancomycin	0 mm	20 mm
Ciprofloxacin	17 mm	16 mm
Amoxicillin	10 mm	15 mm

Zone of Inhibition measurements to determine the effectiveness of certain antibiotics against the microorganisms E. coli *and* S. aureus.

20. The passage as a whole most strongly suggests that medical professionals

(A) should push for more stringent licensure requirements for first responders.

(B) must educate patients on how to properly diagnose bacteriological infections.

(C) can improve their bedside manner if they recognize the common fears of the sick.

(D) need to consider how treatments will impact people other than the patient.

21. What is the primary function of the sentence in lines 29–30 ("Both categories . . . disadvantages")?

(A) To define a couple of major concepts

(B) To give examples in support of a claim

(C) To provide a transition to the following paragraph

(D) To state the thesis of the essay

GO ON TO THE NEXT PAGE

22. It is reasonable to infer from the passage that a bacteriostatic medicine and a bactericidal medicine would be optimally used on patients in which of the following respective situations?

(A) Relatively healthy, relatively ill
(B) Generally unhealthy, generally healthy
(C) Internally sick, externally sick
(D) Physically ill, mentally ill

23. Which of the following is a major concern of the passage's author?

(A) That doctors will lose the capacity to treat bacterial infections
(B) That patients will overdose on their antibiotic prescriptions
(C) That MRSA will lose its prominence in the medical community
(D) That Western medicine will not be open to alternative approaches

24. Which option gives the best evidence for the answer to the previous question?

(A) Lines 8–12 ("While the . . . culture")
(B) Lines 76–80 ("As the use . . . microorganisms")
(C) Lines 88–92 ("The most . . . patients")
(D) Lines 102–107 ("Instructions . . . dose")

25. As used in line 53, "serious" most closely means

(A) severe.
(B) thoughtful.
(C) genuine.
(D) quiet.

26. As used in line 82, "spontaneously" most closely means

(A) impulsively.
(B) extemporaneously.
(C) randomly.
(D) deliberately.

27. The information in the figure would most likely result from a medical practitioner doing which of the following actions mentioned in the passage?

(A) "Use garlic and other spices for medicinal purposes" (lines 5–6)
(B) "Develop and release new medicines" (lines 15–16)
(C) "Perform a culture and sensitivity test" (lines 61–62)
(D) "Better educate patients on proper use of antibiotics" (lines 97–98)

28. Based on the information in the passage and on the figure, which of these antibiotics would be most helpful in treating someone with an *E. coli* infection, assuming the patient was not allergic to any antibiotics and had no other illnesses besides the *E. coli* infection?

(A) Vancomycin
(B) Ciprofloxacin
(C) Amoxicillin
(D) Staphylococcus

GO ON TO THE NEXT PAGE

Questions 29–38 are based on the passage that follows.

Passage 1 is the beginning of Benjamin Franklin's 1771 autobiography. Passage 2 includes the opening of another autobiography published much later, in 1901, that of Booker T. Washington.

Passage 1

Dear son: I have ever had pleasure in obtaining any little anecdotes of my ancestors. You may remember the inquiries
Line I made among the remains of my relations
(5) when you were with me in England, and the journey I undertook for that purpose. Imagining it may be equally agreeable to you to know the circumstances of my life, many of which you are yet unacquainted
(10) with, and expecting the enjoyment of a week's uninterrupted leisure in my present country retirement, I sit down to write them for you. To which I have besides some other inducements. Having emerged from the
(15) poverty and obscurity in which I was born and bred, to a state of affluence and some degree of reputation in the world, and having gone so far through life with a considerable share of felicity, the conducing means I made
(20) use of, which with the blessing of God so well succeeded, my posterity may like to know, as they may find some of them suitable to their own situations, and therefore fit to be imitated.
(25) That felicity, when I reflected on it, has induced me sometimes to say, that were it offered to my choice, I should have no objection to a repetition of the same life from its beginning, only asking the advantages
(30) authors have in a second edition to correct some faults of the first. So I might, besides correcting the faults, change some sinister

accidents and events of it for others more favourable. But though this were denied,
(35) I should still accept the offer. Since such a repetition is not to be expected, the next thing most like living one's life over again seems to be a recollection of that life, and to make that recollection as durable as possible
(40) by putting it down in writing.

Passage 2

I was born a slave on a plantation in Franklin County, Virginia. I am not quite sure of the exact place or exact date of my birth, but at any rate I suspect I must have
(45) been born somewhere and at some time. As nearly as I have been able to learn, I was born near a cross-roads post-office called Hale's Ford, and the year was 1858 or 1859. I do not know the month or the day. The
(50) earliest impressions I can now recall are of the plantation and the slave quarters—the latter being the part of the plantation where the slaves had their cabins.
My life had its beginning in the midst
(55) of the most miserable, desolate, and discouraging surroundings. This was so, however, not because my owners were especially cruel, for they were not, as compared with many others. I was born in a
(60) typical log cabin, about fourteen by sixteen feet square. In this cabin I lived with my mother and a brother and sister till after the Civil War, when we were all declared free.
Of my ancestry I know almost nothing.
(65) In the slave quarters, and even later, I heard whispered conversations among the coloured people of the tortures which the slaves, including, no doubt, my ancestors on my mother's side, suffered in the middle
(70) passage of the slave ship while being conveyed from Africa to America. I have been

GO ON TO THE NEXT PAGE

unsuccessful in securing any information
that would throw any accurate light upon the
history of my family beyond my mother. She,
(75) I remember, had a half-brother and a half-
sister. In the days of slavery not very much
attention was given to family history and
family records—that is, black family records.
My mother, I suppose, attracted the attention
(80) of a purchaser who was afterward my owner
and hers. Her addition to the slave family
attracted about as much attention as the
purchase of a new horse or cow. Of my father
I know even less than of my mother. I do not
(85) even know his name. I have heard reports to
the effect that he was a white man who lived
on one of the near-by plantations. Whoever
he was, I never heard of his taking the least
interest in me or providing in any way for my
(90) rearing. But I do not find especial fault with
him. He was simply another unfortunate
victim of the institution which the Nation
unhappily had engrafted upon it at that time.

29. The tone of Passage 1 is best described as

   (A) abstract.
   (B) personal.
   (C) serious.
   (D) melancholy.

30. It is reasonable to conclude from Passage 1 that
    Franklin's personal financial situation

   (A) was as strong later in his life as it was when
       he was young.
   (B) worsened as he advanced in years.
   (C) had a random pattern of booms and busts
       over his life.
   (D) improved greatly over his lifetime.

31. Which option gives the best evidence for the
    answer to the previous question?

   (A) Lines 7–13 ("Imagining . . . for you")
   (B) Lines 14–17 ("Having emerged . . . world")
   (C) Lines 27–31 ("I should . . . first")
   (D) Lines 35–40 ("Since . . . writing")

32. As used in line 22, "suitable" most closely means

   (A) historical.
   (B) memorable.
   (C) applicable.
   (D) delightful.

33. Washington's most likely purpose in lines 41–53
    is best described as

   (A) to lament his increased senility.
   (B) to express his true identity.
   (C) to critique his familial relations.
   (D) to underscore his rootlessness.

34. As used in line 72, "securing" most closely means

   (A) reading.
   (B) obtaining.
   (C) creating.
   (D) safeguarding.

35. The source of information Washington primarily
    draws upon for the information in lines 64–93 is

   (A) publications.
   (B) hearsay.
   (C) statistics.
   (D) scholarship.

GO ON TO THE NEXT PAGE

36. The passages suggest that something that Washington was more likely to feel than Franklin was

   (A) unhappiness with societal conditions.
   (B) disappointment in his father's conduct.
   (C) curiosity about his heritage.
   (D) an interest in recording his thoughts for posterity.

37. It is reasonable to conclude that Booker T. Washington would very much like to have had the opportunity to do which of the following things that Benjamin Franklin spoke about in Passage 1?

   (A) Obtain anecdotes about his ancestors
   (B) Take time to write a memoir
   (C) Have a relationship with his children
   (D) Relive his life

38. Which option gives the best evidence for the answer to the previous question?

   (A) Lines 49–53 ("The earliest . . . cabins")
   (B) Lines 59–63 ("I was . . . free")
   (C) Lines 71–74 ("I have . . . mother")
   (D) Lines 91–93 ("He was . . . time")

Questions 39–47 are based on the passage that follows.

The Death of Physics—a scientist presents information on recent developments in physics. Written in 2015.

At the turn of the nineteenth century, a prominent physicist stated that physics as a field of study was finished due to the belief
Line that everything about the physical world
(5) had already been discovered. Newtonian Mechanics had held sway for over two hundred years and our understanding of the atom had not advanced much beyond the concepts of the ancient Greeks. The view of
(10) a static universe was the accepted construct and humanity's ignorance was a kind of simple bliss and arrogance.

   This all changed soon after the turn of the next century. A German patent clerk, Albert
(15) Einstein, turned Newtonian Mechanics on its head and developed the Theory of Relativity and the notion of space-time. In the 1920s, women studying photographic plates of various star systems took measurements that
(20) Edwin Hubble used to demonstrate that the universe is not static at all, but is expanding in all directions, no matter where you might be; this became known as Hubble's Law. Hubble's constant—the rate at which the
(25) universe is expanding—is currently estimated to be 21 km/s per one million light-years from Earth. This ushered in the notion of the Big Bang as the singular beginning of an expanding space-time and everything in it.
(30) As years went by, the precision of measuring the age of the Universe since the Big Bang kept evolving to a current estimate of 13.2 billion years. Arno Penzias and Robert Wilson provided additional evidence for this view
(35) of cosmology when an antenna they were

GO ON TO THE NEXT PAGE

adjusting in the 1960s detected a small amount of radiation from every direction in space.

(40) Scientists also began to explore the world of the very small, and the field of quantum mechanics was hatched. From a world of fundamental particles that included only protons, neutrons, and electrons, a never-ending march toward more fundamental (45) building blocks ensued, and now quarks, leptons, bosons, gravitons, etc. have become the particles that physicists use to try to make sense out of the nano-world. The recent discovery (2015) of the Higgs Boson (50) at the Large Hadron Collider in Europe created much excitement in the scientific community. This particle and the Higgs Field are responsible for giving every substance its mass and had been elusive since Peter Higgs (55) postulated their existence in 1964.

Where will this process end? Each time we cause particles to collide at ever-increasing energies, new constituents are created and investigated. It is as if we continue to peel (60) back the layers of an onion only to find more layers that invite exploration. In the modern era, the field of String Theory has been posited, theorizing that the vibrations of tiny string-like mechanisms provide the building (65) blocks of all particles. From String Theory, the idea of Multiple Universes has been proposed and evidence of this mind-blowing idea was reported in late 2015.

Now scientists insist that the "visible" (70) universe only contains about 30% of what is really out there, and the concepts of dark matter and dark energy are invoked to explain the motions of various large bodies that permeate our universe. We are 120 years (75) beyond the time when physics was declared dead to any new inquiries. Now, the steady

arrival of new and exciting perspectives and data from more precise and powerful instruments and machines launch new (80) explorations on a monthly basis. There is nothing dead about the field of physics, and I would claim it has never been more alive.

39. What is the principal claim of the passage?

(A) Dark matter and dark energy have become the primary focus for modern physicists.
(B) Rather than remaining static, physics is continuing to evolve just as it has in the past.
(C) The contributions of Peter Higgs to science exceed those of Albert Einstein.
(D) After many years of ignorant theorizing, physicists have finally uncovered the ultimate truth of the universe.

40. The author suggests that as physics has advanced, its theories are often

(A) practically applicable.
(B) ethically offensive.
(C) historically consistent.
(D) more counterintuitive.

41. Which option gives the best evidence for the answer to the previous question?

(A) Lines 5–9 ("Newtonian . . . Greeks")
(B) Lines 30–33 ("As years . . . years")
(C) Lines 48–52 ("The recent . . . community")
(D) Lines 65–68 ("From String . . . 2015")

GO ON TO THE NEXT PAGE

42. As used in line 10, "construct" most closely means

    (A) building.
    (B) observation.
    (C) theory.
    (D) astronomy.

43. As used in line 28, "singular" most closely means

    (A) odd.
    (B) unattached.
    (C) definitive.
    (D) lonely.

44. According to the passage, when did the scientific consensus most likely shift from an understanding of the universe as being static to being expansive?

    (A) Approximately 1800
    (B) The early 1900s
    (C) The late 1900s
    (D) 2015

45. Which option gives the best evidence for the answer to the previous question?

    (A) Lines 1–9 ("At the turn . . . Greeks")
    (B) Lines 13–23 ("This all . . . Law")
    (C) Lines 33–38 ("Arno . . . in space")
    (D) Lines 48–55 ("The recent . . . 1964")

46. What is the purpose of the sentence in lines 59–61 ("It is as if . . . invite exploration")?

    (A) To use an analogy to illustrate a concept
    (B) To describe the latest scientific evidence
    (C) To make connections between physics and biology
    (D) To express dismay at the state of modern science

47. It is reasonable to infer that the author's primary interest in physics is its potential to

    (A) provide practical inventions for everyday consumer use.
    (B) give a military advantage to those empowered with its findings.
    (C) advance medical science so that new cures for illness can be discovered.
    (D) help us understand the nature of the universe.

STOP

If there is still time remaining, you may review your answers.

WRITING AND LANGUAGE TEST

35 MINUTES, 44 QUESTIONS

> **Directions:** The passages below are each accompanied by several questions, some of which refer to an underlined portion in the passage and some of which refer to the passage as a whole. For some questions, determine how the expression of ideas can be improved. For other questions, determine the best sentence structure, usage, or punctuation given the context. A passage or question may have an accompanying graphic that you will need to consider as you choose the best answer.
>
> Choose the best answer to each question, considering what will optimize the writing quality and make the writing follow the conventions of standard written English. Some questions have a "NO CHANGE" option that you can pick if you believe the best choice is to leave the underlined portion as is.

Questions 1–11 are based on the following passage and supplementary material.

Read to Succeed

Reading is an enriching activity that is well worth making part of ❶ ones regular habits. Starting from an early age, children who read for pleasure encounter many new words and concepts that expand their minds. ❷ Although images are frequently used in society today, words, unlike images, require using one's mind to understand them, ponder their meaning, and ❸ to considering whether they are communicating something true or false. Studies have shown that reading more correlates with greater comprehension, cognitive development, and writing abilities. Those who read for fun more often have higher writing scores—in fact, those who

1. (A) NO CHANGE
   (B) one
   (C) one's
   (D) ones'

2. (A) NO CHANGE
   (B) Since
   (C) Because
   (D) In addition,

3. (A) NO CHANGE
   (B) consider
   (C) considered
   (D) considering

GO ON TO THE NEXT PAGE

**Average Writing Scores by Frequency
of Reading for Fun**

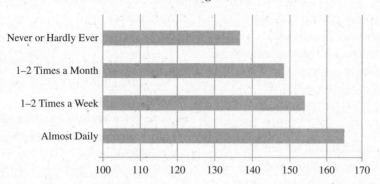

Note: Writing scores range from 0–300, and students surveyed nationwide.

Source: U.S. Department of Education, National Center for Education Statistics

read almost daily for fun outperform those who never or hardly ever read by approximately ❹ 10 points on national writing tests. This translates into higher levels of academic achievement, such as higher test scores in math, science, civics, and history.

In addition to improving one's intellectual abilities, the habit of reading has an occupational and financial payoff. ❺ Sixty-three percent of employers rate reading comprehension as being very important. There is a strong correlation between poor reading skills and unemployment, lower wages, and fewer opportunities for advancement. Those who can effectively read lengthy, complex, abstract texts, synthesize

4. Which of the following is supported by the data in the accompanying chart?

(A) NO CHANGE
(B) 30
(C) 60
(D) 120

5. The author is considering removing the underlined sentence from the passage. Should it be kept or removed?

(A) Kept, because it provides specific details in support of the previous sentence
(B) Kept, because it elaborates on salary details that result from avid reading
(C) Removed, because it repeats information already expressed in the passage
(D) Removed, because it provides far more detail than necessary to make the argument

GO ON TO THE NEXT PAGE

information, and make complex inferences **⑥** are more than three times as likely to find reading to be an enjoyable pastime. Among those who have jobs in management or in business, financial, professional, and related sectors, more than 60 percent have a high reading ability, whereas only 18 percent read at a basic level.

Beyond developing one's intellectual abilities and being financially rewarding, consider how reading opens whole new worlds! It enables one to learn from the experiences of literally thousands of other people—to benefit from their insights and to avoid their mistakes. It gives access to some of the greatest minds and ideas throughout history. Reading also stimulates the **⑦** imagination to identify with a hero in a story, consider what it would have been like to be at some historical event, or to form a picture of what one could accomplish in life.

Given how reading can benefit an individual, it is not surprising, then, that readers have positive effects on society. **⑧** Them who read literature are more than twice as likely to volunteer or do charity work and more than three times as likely to go to museums, attend plays or concerts, and create art as those who do not. Good readers are even more likely to play sports, attend sporting events, or do outdoor activities. **⑨** On the other hand, prisoners tend to have significantly worse reading skills than others.

6. Which of the following would provide the most specific and relevant elaboration to conclude this sentence?

(A) NO CHANGE
(B) are 2.5 times as likely as those with a basic reading ability to earn $850 or more per week.
(C) are twice as likely as those who do not read to spend over $100 a year on books and periodicals.
(D) are demonstrably more effective at remembering not just the broad ideas of what they read, but the finer details.

7. (A) NO CHANGE
(B) imagination: to identify with a hero in a story, to
(C) imagination; to identify with a hero in a story, to
(D) imagination, to identify with a hero in a story to

8. (A) NO CHANGE
(B) Them whom
(C) Those who
(D) Those whom

9. (A) NO CHANGE
(B) Therefore,
(C) Moreover,
(D) Thus,

GO ON TO THE NEXT PAGE

10 More or less, when one considers both the nature of the activity itself as well as the statistics, reading makes a big difference in life. **11** Enriching one's life, and community is well worth regularly delving into great books.

10. Which option best expresses that the author is confident in his point of view?

(A) NO CHANGE
(B) Dubitably,
(C) While there are merits to both sides of the issue,
(D) Clearly,

11. (A) NO CHANGE
(B) Enriching one's life and community, is well worth regularly delving into great books.
(C) Enriching one's life and community is well worth regularly delving into great books.
(D) Enriching one's life and community; is well worth regularly delving into great books.

GO ON TO THE NEXT PAGE

Questions 12–22 are based on the following passage.

Pluto

"My very educated mother just served us nine pizzas" is **12** a sentence, that may not mean much to young students anymore. However, to people of an older generation this sentence is almost universally recognized as a mnemonic device used to aid children in remembering the planets of our solar system. The sentence has changed recently, not because serving nine pizzas is against school lunch health standards, **13** but because the planets themselves have changed.

In 2006, **14** despite public outcries and complaints, scientists reclassified Pluto, effectively removing "pizzas" from the well-known memory aid. Pluto, discovered in 1930, had long been viewed as the adorable kid brother of the solar system, significantly **15** smallest than the older siblings and tagging along at the back of the line. That ended when several other similar sized planets were discovered in Pluto's orbit. The discovery of these smaller planets **16** were the beginning of Pluto's demise.

The issue with these smaller celestial objects was whether they could really be classified as planets. Many scientists wanted all of the smaller objects to be planets so that Pluto could remain one as well; **17** however, this proved to be impractical, as it would have resulted in objects smaller than our moon being planets. The International Astronomical Union, an organization

12. (A) NO CHANGE
    (B) a sentence that may not, mean much to young students anymore.
    (C) a sentence that, may not mean much, to young students anymore.
    (D) a sentence that may not mean much to young students anymore.

13. (A) NO CHANGE
    (B) and since
    (C) for a result
    (D) and

14. (A) NO CHANGE
    (B) despite public outcries,
    (C) even though there were complaints by members of the public,
    (D) OMIT the underlined portion.

15. (A) NO CHANGE
    (B) smallest then
    (C) smaller than
    (D) smaller then

16. (A) NO CHANGE
    (B) was
    (C) are
    (D) is

17. (A) NO CHANGE
    (B) as a result,
    (C) what is more,
    (D) consequently,

GO ON TO THE NEXT PAGE

that long has been in charge of classifying and naming celestial bodies, set about to solve the problem by clearly defining what a planet is. ⑱ Their goal was to give the criteria for what makes something a planet. Their proposal held that objects that were in orbit around the sun (but not around another planet) ⑲ were quite large and had a resulting large amount of gravitation, could be considered planets. Unfortunately, Pluto didn't meet these stipulations.

While Pluto is in orbit around the sun and has become nearly round, it isn't big ⑳ enough, and therefore doesn't have enough gravity, to clear its orbit. This is proved by the fact that many of those other small planet-like objects have been discovered in Pluto's orbit. Together, these objects now make up what has been named the Kuiper belt. They have each been classified as

18. The author is considering removing the underlined sentence. Should it be kept or removed?

(A) Kept, because it clarifies the goal of the Astronomical Union
(B) Kept, because it gives details on what constitutes a planet
(C) Deleted, because it repeats the idea of the previous sentence
(D) Deleted, because it contradicts information presented elsewhere in the passage

19. Which of the following options for the underlined portion would best elaborate on the topic of the sentence with the most specific detail?

(A) NO CHANGE
(B) were constituted of a great deal of mass and matter, and possessed sufficient gravitational pull to have a significant impact on their surroundings,
(C) had enough mass to become nearly round due to pressure, and had enough gravity to clear their orbit of any other bodies,
(D) had a tremendously large amount of mass, while enough gravity to be quite noticeable,

20. (A) NO CHANGE
(B) enough and therefore, doesn't have enough gravity, to clear its orbit.
(C) enough and therefore doesn't have enough gravity to clear, its orbit.
(D) enough, and, therefore, doesn't have enough gravity, to clear its orbit.

GO ON TO THE NEXT PAGE

dwarf planets, meaning that they meet most, but not all, of the qualifications of a full-sized planet. **㉑** <u>Because</u> most of the world has come to accept that Pluto is no longer a planet, some people remain stubbornly attached to their older, nostalgic views of the solar system. **㉒** <u>It is truly a shame that people cannot give up their old-fashioned views on what constitutes a planet.</u>

21. (A) NO CHANGE
    (B) While
    (C) Since
    (D) And

22. Which of the following would provide the most effective conclusion to the passage, tying it back to the introduction?

    (A) NO CHANGE
    (B) The significance of the advances in astronomical research cannot be understated.
    (C) While Pluto may have lost its planetary recognition, Mars and Jupiter continue to be recognized as planets.
    (D) After all, saying "my very educated mother just served us nothing" doesn't have quite the same ring to it.

GO ON TO THE NEXT PAGE

Questions 23–33 are based on the following passage.

Birth Order

Siblings are something most of us take for granted. ❷❸ We don't tend to spend a whole lot of time analyzing the people with whom we were raised—we are used to their personality quirks and we've adapted to deal with them. However, many of those traits that we take for granted in our siblings could be very different ❷❹ based on just one thing: birth order. Birth order is a very complex theory with lots of ins and outs. But when we boil it down to the basics, we can find personality traits ❷❺ which applies specifically to each of the positions in the family.

Firstborn children are leaders. They spend their early years getting lots of attention from their parents, and then they grow up ❷❻ being responsible for their younger siblings. These are the people who are perfectionists. They become the best at whatever they do. Firstborn children become CEOs, lawyers, doctors, astronauts, and politicians. They excel in leadership positions. ❷❼ In contrast, most of the presidents of the United States have been firstborn men or only

23. The author is considering inserting the following sentence at this point in the passage:

"Siblings are defined as those people to whom one is related as brothers and sisters."

Should this insertion be made?

(A) Yes, because it provides detailed examples in support of a claim.

(B) Yes, because it gives insight into the author's personal views.

(C) No, because it simply defines a widely understood term.

(D) No, because it is unrelated to the topic of the passage.

24. (A) NO CHANGE

(B) based on just one thing birth order.

(C) based, on just one thing: birth order.

(D) based on just one thing; birth order.

25. (A) NO CHANGE

(B) with apply

(C) that applies

(D) that apply

26. The author is considering removing the underlined portion of the sentence. Should it be kept or removed?

(A) Kept, because it gives statistical evidence

(B) Kept, because it provides a helpful elaboration

(C) Removed, because it is irrelevant to the topic of the sentence

(D) Removed, because it interrupts the author's line of reasoning

27. (A) NO CHANGE

(B) To object,

(C) In fact,

(D) On the other hand,

GO ON TO THE NEXT PAGE

children (only children are like firstborn children times ten). Firstborn children, though, may suffer from conditions like hypertension, as they have a hard time relaxing and letting go.

[1] A middle child can be any child born between the first and the last. [2] Middle children are very hard to pin down. [3] They often go through life feeling like they don't quite **28** fit in with their families. [4] They suffer from "middle child syndrome," which means they are overlooked or squeezed in the middle. [5] If a family is going to leave a kid at the rest stop on vacation, it is going to be the middle child. [6] This results in the middle child having a large group of friends outside the family; they are very social. [7] Many diplomats are middle children, since these people spend their childhood resolving fights within their families. **29**

This brings us to the youngest child. The youngest is often very charismatic. He or she grows up being the center of attention—fortunately, the youngest loves to entertain. **30** Entertainment is something that is quite popular with most modern-day consumers. Youngest children are free thinkers. They are artistic and creative as well. However, the youngest child doesn't have the drive that the oldest has, and can sometimes lose **31** there way in life.

28. (A) NO CHANGE
    (B) fit on
    (C) fits with
    (D) fits in to

29. The author is considering adding the following sentence to the previous paragraph:

    "Middle children are also mediators."

    Where would it most logically be placed?

    (A) Before sentence 1
    (B) Before sentence 3
    (C) Before sentence 5
    (D) Before sentence 7

30. Which of the following choices provides the most relevant and detailed elaboration of the previous sentence?

    (A) NO CHANGE
    (B) The youngest child may be significantly younger than his or her oldest sibling, particularly if his or her parents remarried.
    (C) The oldest child, to elaborate, will likely have a "take-charge" personality.
    (D) Many famous comedians, actors, and musicians are the youngest in their families.

31. (A) NO CHANGE
    (B) their
    (C) they're
    (D) his or her

GO ON TO THE NEXT PAGE

32 Birth order isn't a one-size-fits-all theory, there are many loopholes and exceptions. People can change, if they want to, through hard work. **33** Nevertheless, it can be helpful to understand the factors that influence personalities, and birth order helps a little.

32. (A) NO CHANGE
    (B) Birth order isn't a one-size-fits-all theory; there are many loopholes and exceptions.
    (C) Birth order, isn't a one-size-fits-all theory—there are many loopholes and exceptions.
    (D) Birth order, isn't a one-size-fits-all theory, there are many loopholes and exceptions.

33. (A) NO CHANGE
    (B) As a result,
    (C) Due to this,
    (D) Continuing,

GO ON TO THE NEXT PAGE

Questions 34–44 are based on the following passage and supplementary material.

Hermey Is Onto Something

{1}

In the 1964 Christmas classic "Rudolph, the Red-Nosed Reindeer," Hermey is a misfit elf who hopes to give up toy-making in order to practice dentistry. As a child, the only thing more appealing to me than being Santa's elf would have been to be Rudolph himself. **34** <u>A lifelong protester of bath time teeth brushing nail</u> clipping, and anything concerning strict routine hygiene, I simply could not understand the elf who would forgo the joys of Santa's workshop for a chance to play in somebody's disgusting mouth. **35** <u>On the one hand he had an amiable, loyal nature. Even though this was the case, Hermey appalled me.</u>

{2}

I recited this **36** <u>childhood memory from the early part of my life</u> to my first college roommate. Tim had just earned admission into Indiana University's School of Dentistry. After living in a single dorm room through undergraduate, I had found his apartment listed under the enticing entry "Looking for One Roommate, Cheap Rent for the Quiet and Introverted," and **37** <u>accepted</u> the adventure of graduate school and a roommate who preferred books to parties. Dental students, Tim explained, **38** <u>have many</u> reasons for pursuing the occupation.

34. (A) NO CHANGE
    (B) A lifelong protester of bath time teeth brushing, nail
    (C) A lifelong protester of bath time, teeth brushing nail
    (D) A lifelong protester of bath time, teeth brushing, nail

35. Which of the following options provides the best combined version of the two underlined sentences?

    (A) While it is truly the case that he has a nature that is loyal and amiable, he nevertheless appalled me.
    (B) Even though he had an amiable, loyal nature, I could not help but be appalled by Hermey.
    (C) Despite his amiable, loyal nature, Hermey appalled me.
    (D) Because of his amiable, loyal nature, I was appalled by Hermey.

36. (A) NO CHANGE
    (B) childhood memory
    (C) memory from my time period as a child
    (D) childhood memory and recollection

37. (A) NO CHANGE
    (B) excepted
    (C) inspected
    (D) expected

38. (A) NO CHANGE
    (B) have much
    (C) had much
    (D) has many

GO ON TO THE NEXT PAGE

{3}

Besides having great hand dexterity and steadiness, dentists also tend to be personable and interested in helping others maintain their health and self-confidence. Tim, while appropriately interested in diagnosing and treating ❸❾ patients problems with their teeth and gums, demonstrated real passion for repairing teeth and aiding in cosmetic dental concerns. An accident involving stairs and a hardwood floor had left Tim missing a front tooth from the age of seven until seventeen. He understood firsthand how being ashamed of your dental health can ❹⓿ effect your whole demeanor. His goal, he boasted, would be to ensure no other middle school kid would go ten years without cracking a smile.

{4}

While Tim's intentions are admirable, I found, with a little research, that there are several other reasons for becoming a dentist. In 2015, average estimates of a general dentist's annual salary for dentists ❹❶ with over six years experience approached $250,000. In fact, their expected

39. (A) NO CHANGE
    (B) patient's
    (C) patients'
    (D) those of patients

40. (A) NO CHANGE
    (B) effects
    (C) affects
    (D) affect

41. Which of the following statements is most consistent with the information in the supplementary graph?

    (A) NO CHANGE
    (B) with over six years experience approached $150,000.
    (C) with four to six years experience ranged between $200,000 and $250,000.
    (D) fresh out of dental school were less than $60,000.

2015 Annual Salaries for Healthcare Positions (in thousands of U.S. Dollars)

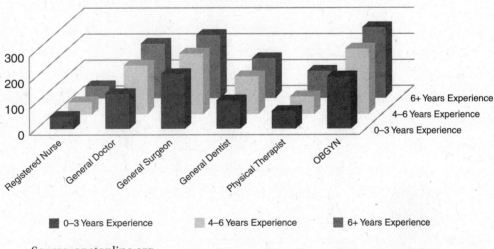

Source: onetonline.org

GO ON TO THE NEXT PAGE

salaries **42** <u>come close to those of general doctors.</u> The career prospects are equally impressive, and continuing to grow. Certainly, dentists complete a rigorous curriculum—after undergraduate, they go on to earn a doctorate in dental school, complete licensing standards, and sometimes work a 2–4 year residency—but the intense training pays off in job security and a rewarding income. **43** <u>However,</u> many dentists work in dental offices or start their own practice and enjoy normal 9 A.M. to 5 P.M., weekday hours. Even those who choose to work a more unconventional schedule find the compensation well worth their time.

{5}

Hermey, detestable as he was to my five-year-old self, might have been onto something after all. **44**

42. Which of the following properly uses information from the supplementary graph to provide logical support to the author's argument?

(A) NO CHANGE
(B) approximate those of OBGYNs.
(C) exceed those of general surgeons.
(D) roughly equal those of registered nurses.

43. (A) NO CHANGE
(B) Moreover,
(C) In contrast,
(D) Consequently,

44. The author wishes to insert the following sentence as a stand-alone paragraph in the passage.

"Anyway," he smirked, "the College of Toy-making is stingy with financial aid."

Before what paragraph would it most logically be placed?
(A) Paragraph 1
(B) Paragraph 2
(C) Paragraph 3
(D) Paragraph 5

STOP

If there is still time remaining, you may review your answers.

MATH TEST (NO CALCULATOR)

25 MINUTES, 17 QUESTIONS

Directions: For questions 1–13, solve each problem and choose the best answer from the given options. Fill in the corresponding oval on the answer sheet. For questions 14–17, solve the problem and fill in the answer on the answer sheet grid. Please use any space in the test booklet to work out your answers.

Notes:

- You **CANNOT** use a calculator on this section.
- All variables and expressions represent real numbers unless indicated otherwise.
- All figures are drawn to scale unless indicated otherwise.
- All figures are in a plane unless indicated otherwise.
- Unless indicated otherwise, the domain of a given function is the set of all real numbers x for which the function has real values.

Radius of a circle = r

Area of a circle = πr^2

Circumference of a circle = $2\pi r$

Area of a rectangle = length × width = lw

Area of a triangle = $\frac{1}{2}$ × base × height = $\frac{1}{2} bh$

Pythagorean theorem: $a^2 + b^2 = c^2$

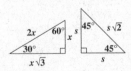

Special right triangles: 30-60-90 and 45-45-90

Volume of a box = length × width × height = lwh

Volume of a cylinder = $\pi r^2 h$

Volume of a sphere = $\frac{4}{3} \pi r^3$

Volume of a cone = $\frac{1}{3} \pi r^2 h$

Volume of a pyramid =

$\frac{1}{3}$ × length × width × height = $\frac{1}{3} lwh$

GO ON TO THE NEXT PAGE

KEY FACTS:

- A circle has 360 degrees.
- There are 2π radians in a circle.
- There are 180 degrees in a triangle.

1. What is the value of x in the following equation?

$$3x + 2 = \frac{4}{3}x$$

(A) $-\frac{6}{5}$

(B) $-\frac{2}{3}$

(C) $\frac{1}{4}$

(D) $\frac{5}{6}$

2. What are the solution(s) to the following equation?

$$5x^2 - 15x + 10 = 0$$

(A) 0

(B) 1, 2

(C) 1, 4

(D) 2, 5

3. A typist has already typed 3,500 words of a document. How many total words, $W(t)$, of the document will he have typed if he can type 70 words per minute and types for an additional t minutes?

(A) $W(t) = 3,500t$

(B) $W(t) = 70t - 3,500$

(C) $W(t) = 3,500t + 70$

(D) $W(t) = 3,500 + 70t$

4. $6a^2 + 8ab - 4ac$ is equivalent to which of the following expressions?

(A) $a(3a + 4b + 2c)$

(B) $2a(3a + 4b - 2c)$

(C) $4a(a + b - 2c)$

(D) $2a(3a - 4b + 2c)$

5. What represents the range of x-values in this inequality?

$$-3(x + 4) > 2x$$

(A) $x < -\frac{12}{5}$

(B) $x \leq -\frac{1}{3}$

(C) $x > \frac{7}{8}$

(D) $x \geq 3\frac{1}{2}$

6. The expression $\left(\frac{2}{3}x + 1\right)\left(\frac{3}{4}x - 1\right) = ?$

(A) $\frac{1}{6}x^2 - \frac{1}{3}x + 1$

(B) $\frac{1}{4}x^2 + \frac{1}{12}x - 4$

(C) $\frac{1}{2}x^2 + \frac{1}{12}x - 1$

(D) $x^2 + \frac{1}{4}x - 1$

7. At what x-values does the function $y = x(x - 5)(x + 2)$ intersect the x-axis?

(A) -10

(B) 0, 3, 12

(C) 2, -5

(D) 0, 5, -2

GO ON TO THE NEXT PAGE

8. At what point in the *xy*-plane will the functions $y = 4x - 3$ and $y = -\frac{1}{2}x + 2$ intersect?

(A) $\left(2, -\frac{2}{3}\right)$

(B) $\left(-\frac{3}{4}, \frac{5}{6}\right)$

(C) $\left(\frac{10}{9}, \frac{13}{9}\right)$

(D) $\left(1, \frac{3}{7}\right)$

9. The function *f* is given by $f(x) = 2 - |x - 4|$. For what value of *x* does the function *f* achieve its maximum value?

(A) 2
(B) 4
(C) 5
(D) 6

10. When $x > 0$, which of these expressions is equivalent to $\dfrac{1}{\frac{1}{2x}} + \dfrac{3}{\frac{6}{4x}}$?

(A) $4x$
(B) $7x$
(C) $\frac{1}{2}x - 4$
(D) $x^2 - 12$

11. If $\left(x^2\right)^{\frac{1}{5}} + \sqrt[5]{32x^2} = ax^{\frac{2}{5}}$ for all values of *x*, what is the value of *a*?

(A) 0
(B) 3
(C) 5
(D) 16

12. The value of money is affected by the inflation rate—the higher the inflation rate, the less valuable money will become over time. The rate of inflation is calculated using the formula below, in which CPI represents the consumer price index, a measure of the average of a typical basket of consumer goods and services (where goods and services are weighted relative to how often they are purchased by a normal consumer):

$$\frac{\text{This Year's CPI} - \text{Last Year's CPI}}{\text{Last Year's CPI}} \times 100$$

The current rate of inflation would *definitely* be zero if the CPI a year ago equaled which of the following?

(A) The CPI a year from now
(B) This year's CPI
(C) Zero
(D) 100

13. What is the *x*-coordinate of the minimum of the parabola with the equation $y + 17 = 6x^2 + 12x$?

(A) −1
(B) 0
(C) 2
(D) 3

GO ON TO THE NEXT PAGE

Grid-in Response Directions

In questions 14–17, first solve the problem, and then enter your answer on the grid provided on the answer sheet. The instructions for entering your answers follow.

- First, write your answer in the boxes at the top of the grid.
- Second, grid your answer in the columns below the boxes.
- Use the fraction bar in the first row or the decimal point in the second row to enter fractions and decimals.

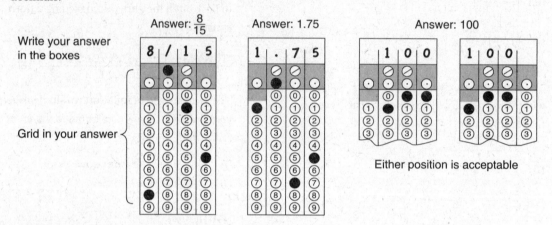

Write your answer in the boxes

Grid in your answer

Answer: $\frac{8}{15}$ Answer: 1.75   Answer: 100

Either position is acceptable

- Grid only one space in each column.
- Entering the answer in the boxes is recommended as an aid in gridding but is not required.
- The machine scoring your exam can read only what you grid, so you **must grid-in your answers correctly to get credit**.
- If a question has more than one correct answer, grid-in only one of them.
- The grid does not have a minus sign; so no answer can be negative.
- A mixed number *must* be converted to an improper fraction or a decimal before it is gridded.

  Enter $1\frac{1}{4}$ as 5/4 or 1.25; the machine will interpret 11/4 as $\frac{11}{4}$ and mark it wrong.

- **All decimals must be entered as accurately as possible.** Here are three acceptable ways of gridding

$$\frac{3}{11} = 0.272727 \ldots$$

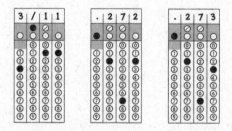

- Note that rounding to .273 is acceptable because you are using the full grid, but you would receive **no credit** for .3 or .27, because they are less accurate.

GO ON TO THE NEXT PAGE

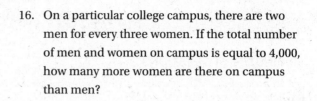
14.

In the isosceles trapezoid above, what is the measure of the smallest interior angle?

15. Given that (x, y) is a solution to the following system of equations, what is the sum of x and y?

$$2x - y = 3$$
$$4y = 6x$$

16. On a particular college campus, there are two men for every three women. If the total number of men and women on campus is equal to 4,000, how many more women are there on campus than men?

17. Given that $x \neq 0$, find the value of

$$\left(\frac{2x^4 + 3(2x^2)^2}{x^4} \right)^2.$$

STOP

If there is still time remaining, you may review your answers.

PRACTICE TEST 1

MATH TEST (WITH CALCULATOR)

45 MINUTES, 31 QUESTIONS

Directions: For questions 1–27, solve each problem and choose the best answer from the given options. Fill in the corresponding oval on the answer sheet. For questions 28–31, solve the problem and fill in the answer on the answer sheet grid. Please use any space in the test booklet to work out your answers.

Notes:

- You CAN use a calculator on this section.
- All variables and expressions represent real numbers unless indicated otherwise.
- All figures are drawn to scale unless indicated otherwise.
- All figures are in a plane unless indicated otherwise.
- Unless indicated otherwise, the domain of a given function is the set of all real numbers x for which the function has real values.

Radius of a circle $= r$

Area of a circle $= \pi r^2$

Circumference of a circle $= 2\pi r$

Area of a rectangle = **length** × **width** = lw

Area of a triangle $= \dfrac{1}{2} \times$ **base** $\times$ **height** $= \dfrac{1}{2}\,bh$

Pythagorean theorem: $a^2 + b^2 = c^2$

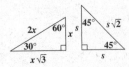

Special right triangles: 30-60-90 and 45-45-90

Volume of a box = **length** × **width** × **height** = lwh

Volume of a cylinder $= \pi r^2 h$

Volume of a sphere $= \dfrac{4}{3}\,\pi r^3$

Volume of a cone $= \dfrac{1}{3}\,\pi r^2 h$

Volume of a pyramid =

$\dfrac{1}{3} \times$ **length** $\times$ **width** $\times$ **height** $= \dfrac{1}{3}\,lwh$

GO ON TO THE NEXT PAGE

KEY FACTS:

- **A circle has 360 degrees.**
- **There are 2π radians in a circle.**
- **There are 180 degrees in a triangle.**

1. A roller coaster requires riders to be at least 48 inches tall. Given that there are approximately 2.54 centimeters in an inch, how tall must a rider be to the nearest whole *centimeter* to ride the roller coaster?

   (A) 96
   (B) 122
   (C) 148
   (D) 190

2. A bus is traveling at a constant rate of 50 miles per hour. At this rate, how far will the bus travel in $3\frac{1}{4}$ hours?

   (A) 150 miles
   (B) 160 miles
   (C) 162.5 miles
   (D) 175.5 miles

3. Which of the following expressions is equivalent to $7 - 2(y - 1)$?

   (A) $9 - 2y$
   (B) $5 - 2y$
   (C) $6 - 2y$
   (D) $4 + 2y$

4. Which of the following is a solution to the equation below?

   $$(x - 3)^2 - 81 = 0$$

   (A) 12
   (B) 11
   (C) 9
   (D) 8

Questions 5–7 refer to the following information and table.

The table below gives the results of a survey of a randomly selected sample of 400 individuals who are 15 and 16 years old. Each respondent selected the method of electronic communication that he or she used the most.

Primary Method of Electronic Communication

	Texting	E-mail	Video Chatting	Other	Total
15-year-olds	110	20	40	30	200
16-year-olds	85	45	30	40	200
Total	195	x	70	70	400

5. The table omits the value for x in the bottom row. Based on the structure of the table, what is the value of x?

   (A) 24
   (B) 38
   (C) 57
   (D) 65

6. The city of Springfield has 50,000 residents ages 15 and 16. Given that the sample in the table is representative of Springfield's residents, approximately how many 15- and 16-year-olds in Springfield would use video chatting as their primary method of electronic communication?

   (A) 3,100
   (B) 4,870
   (C) 8,750
   (D) 20,000

GO ON TO THE NEXT PAGE

PRACTICE TEST 1

7. What is the best estimation of the probability that a randomly selected 16-year-old from the sample would use texting as his or her primary method of electronic communication?

(A) 0.23

(B) 0.43

(C) 0.49

(D) 0.73

8. If $\frac{x}{4} = \frac{1}{2}$, then $\frac{4(x-3)}{(-12)}$ equals which of the following?

(A) $\frac{1}{16}$

(B) $\frac{1}{12}$

(C) $\frac{1}{6}$

(D) $\frac{1}{3}$

9. If the sale price on a coat is $72 and the original price of the coat was $90, what is the percent discount from this sale?

(A) 14%

(B) 20%

(C) 26%

(D) 80%

10.

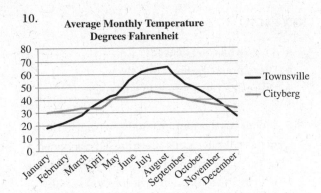

Average Monthly Temperature Degrees Fahrenheit

The average monthly temperatures for the cities of Townsville and Cityberg were recorded in the last calendar year. Based on the graph, which statement is true?

(A) The temperature on a randomly selected day in Townsville will be greater than the temperature on the same randomly selected day in Cityberg.

(B) The temperature on a randomly selected day in Cityberg will be greater than the temperature on the same randomly selected day in Townsville.

(C) The average monthly temperature in Townsville was greater than the average monthly temperature in Cityberg for the majority of the year.

(D) The average monthly temperature in Cityberg was greater than the average monthly temperature in Townsville for the majority of the year.

11. David has two quarters for every five dimes in his change dish, with no other coins present. If he has a total of $2 in coins in the dish, how many total coins does he have?

(A) 12

(B) 14

(C) 16

(D) 18

GO ON TO THE NEXT PAGE

12. A chef is making cookies from scratch. He requires a set period of time to gather the ingredients and to get everything set up to make the cookies. Then the chef needs a set period of time to make each individual cookie. If c represents the total number of cookies he is making and if t represents the total amount of time it takes to make c cookies, what is the meaning of the 20 in this equation: $t = 20 + 10c$?

(A) How much time it takes to make each individual cookie
(B) The fixed cost of the cookie ingredients
(C) The maximum number of cookies he can make in 10 minutes
(D) The amount of time it takes him to set things up prior to making a cookie

13. Jasmine has $100,000 in an investment portfolio, divided among only three categories: stocks, bonds, and cash. She has twice as much invested in stocks as she does in bonds. She also has three times as much invested in bonds as she has in cash. What percent of Jasmine's portfolio is invested in bonds?

(A) 22%
(B) 27%
(C) 30%
(D) 44%

Questions 14–15 refer to the following information and table.

A coffee shop recorded data on the types of beverages ordered by its patrons in a given month. Each patron visited only once during the month and purchased only one beverage. The four listed beverages are the only ones sold at this coffee shop.

	Cappuccino	Espresso	Latte	Americano	Total
Females under 18	230	125	325	170	850
Males under 18	170	185	240	220	815
Females age 18 and older	425	328	530	290	1,573
Males age 18 and older	350	429	477	313	1,569
Total	1,175	1,067	1,572	993	4,807

14. What (approximate) percentage of the drinks purchased at the coffee shop in the given month was espresso?

(A) 11%
(B) 17%
(C) 22%
(D) 36%

15. Assume that the sample in the month portrayed in the table is representative of the coffee shop's sales for an entire year. Based on these assumptions, if a female customer is selected at random, what is the approximate probability that she will purchase a latte?

(A) 0.35
(B) 0.41
(C) 0.46
(D) 0.53

GO ON TO THE NEXT PAGE

16. A line has the equation $y - 4x = 5$. What is the slope of a line that is perpendicular to this line?

(A) -4

(B) $-\dfrac{1}{4}$

(C) $\dfrac{5}{4}$

(D) 4

17. The formula for electric power, P, is $P = I \times V$, where I is the current and V is the voltage. The formula for voltage is $V = I \times R$, where I is also the current and R is the resistance. How will the power of a given current be affected if the resistance is doubled and the voltage is quadrupled?

(A) The power will be doubled.

(B) The power will be quadrupled.

(C) The power will be 8 times greater.

(D) The power will be 16 times greater.

18. **Average Number of Hours of Nightly Sleep**

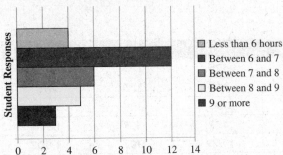

In the above histogram, the distribution of the number of hours of sleep per night as self-reported by 30 students is recorded. Which of the following values would be equal for the above set of values?

(A) Mean and median

(B) Mode and mean

(C) Median and mode

(D) Mean and range

19.

Monthly Expenses

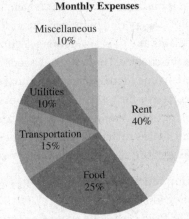

The percentages of Anita's monthly expenses are portrayed in the above chart. If Anita spent $600 on rent, what was the total of her other expenses for the month?

(A) $600

(B) $900

(C) $1,200

(D) $1,400

20. A wall's height is two-thirds that of its length. The entire wall will be painted. The paint costs $12 per gallon, and 1 gallon of paint covers 60 square feet. What expression gives the cost of the paint (assuming one can purchase partial and full gallons) to cover a wall that is L feet long?

(A) $\text{Cost} = L^2$

(B) $\text{Cost} = \dfrac{1}{5}L^2$

(C) $\text{Cost} = \dfrac{2}{15}L^2$

(D) $\text{Cost} = \dfrac{3}{64}L^2$

GO ON TO THE NEXT PAGE

21. Consider the function $f(x) = 2x - 3$. What is the range of the absolute value of this function?

    (A) $y < -3$
    (B) $y \leq 0$
    (C) $y \geq 0$
    (D) $y > 5$

22. An animal shelter can house only cats and dogs. Each dog requires 2 cups of food and 3 treats a day, while each cat requires 1 cup of food a day and 2 treats a day. If the shelter has available a total of 400 cups of food and 500 treats a day, what expressions portray the full scope of the number of c cats and d dogs the shelter could potentially house?

    (A) $2d - c \leq 400$ and $3d + c < 500$
    (B) $2d + c \leq 400$ and $3d + 2c \leq 500$
    (C) $4d + c < 400$ and $d + c < 500$
    (D) $2d + 2c \leq 400$ and $2d + 3c \leq 500$

23.

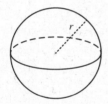

Which of the following expressions is equivalent to the diameter of the sphere portrayed above, with a radius of r and volume V?

    (A) $2\sqrt[3]{\dfrac{3V}{4\pi}}$

    (B) πr^3

    (C) $4\sqrt{\dfrac{2r^3}{3}}$

    (D) $\dfrac{4V^3}{3r^2}$

24. Caitlin opens a checking account that earns no interest to set aside spending money for vacations. Each month she puts the same dollar amount, $50, into the account. Unfortunately, she does not expect to be able to take a vacation at any point in the foreseeable future. Which of the following best describes the relationship between the number of months and the total amount of money in the account?

    (A) A linear relationship, with the line of the relationship having a negative slope
    (B) A linear relationship, with the line of the relationship having a positive slope
    (C) An exponentially increasing relationship
    (D) An inverse exponential relationship

25.

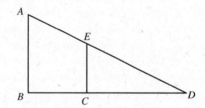

Note: Figure not drawn to scale

In the figure above, both angles ABC and ECD are 90 degrees. If the area of triangle ECD is 20 square inches, the length of EC is 4 inches, and the length of BC is 8 inches, what is the area of triangle ABD?

    (A) 32.4 square inches
    (B) 64.8 square inches
    (C) 320 square inches
    (D) 640 square inches

GO ON TO THE NEXT PAGE

26. Which of the following is an equivalent form of $\dfrac{(7x-7)(7x+7)}{7}$?

    (A) $x^2 - 1$

    (B) $49x^2 + 7$

    (C) $7(x^2 - 1)$

    (D) $\dfrac{(x^2 - 7)}{7}$

27.

Refrigerant ABC: Pressure in Pounds per Square Inch for a Given Temperature

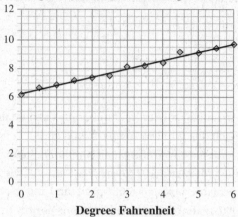

Degrees Fahrenheit

◇ Pressure in Pounds per Square Inch
— Linear (Pressure in Pounds per Square Inch)

A refrigerant manufacturer recorded the pressure associated with certain temperatures in a refrigerator using its new refrigerant, ABC. Which equation best approximates the best-fit line portrayed by the data in this graph, using P for pressure, T for temperature, and the same units as portrayed in the graph?

    (A) $P = 0.5T + 6.2$

    (B) $P = T + 6.2$

    (C) $P = 0.5T - 3$

    (D) $P = 7T + 5$

GO ON TO THE NEXT PAGE

Grid-in Response Directions

In questions 28–31, first solve the problem, and then enter your answer on the grid provided on the answer sheet. The instructions for entering your answers follow.

- First, write your answer in the boxes at the top of the grid.
- Second, grid your answer in the columns below the boxes.
- Use the fraction bar in the first row or the decimal point in the second row to enter fractions and decimals.

Answer: $\frac{8}{15}$ Answer: 1.75   Answer: 100

Write your answer in the boxes

Grid in your answer

Either position is acceptable

- Grid only one space in each column.
- Entering the answer in the boxes is recommended as an aid in gridding but is not required.
- The machine scoring your exam can read only what you grid, so you **must grid-in your answers correctly to get credit**.
- If a question has more than one correct answer, grid-in only one of them.
- The grid does not have a minus sign; so no answer can be negative.
- A mixed number *must* be converted to an improper fraction or a decimal before it is gridded.

  Enter $1\frac{1}{4}$ as 5/4 or 1.25; the machine will interpret 11/4 as $\frac{11}{4}$ and mark it wrong.

- **All decimals must be entered as accurately as possible.** Here are three acceptable ways of gridding:

$$\frac{3}{11} = 0.272727\ldots$$

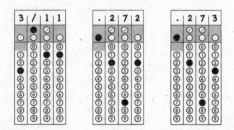

- Note that rounding to .273 is acceptable because you are using the full grid, but you would receive **no credit** for .3 or .27, because they are less accurate.

GO ON TO THE NEXT PAGE

28. A certain cube has edges of length L inches, surface area of A square inches, and volume of B cubic inches. For what value of L would $A = B$?

29. If (a, b) is a solution to the system of equations below, what is the value of a?

$$2a - \frac{1}{2}b = 4$$

$$3a + b = 6$$

A currency conversion store at an airport in New York City posts the following conversion rate table.

Currency Type	Currency per 1 U.S. Dollar
U.S. dollar	1.00
Euro	0.90
Indian rupee	68.01
South African rand	16.17
Japanese yen	116.36
Australian dollar	1.41

The conversion store charges 1 percent of the amount converted plus a $2 flat fee for each total transaction (including multiple-currency exchanges as long as they take place in a single visit to the store). The flat fee is assessed *in addition* to the 1 percent conversion fee.

30. Suppose a customer wanted to see the conversion rate, before doing a transaction or paying any associated fees, of U.S. dollars to Australian dollars. What is the conversion rate of U.S. dollars to 1 Australian Dollar to the nearest hundredth?

31. Andrew has come back to the United States from a trip to Asia and wishes to convert 700 Japanese yen and 900 Indian rupees. If he converts them to U.S. dollars at the airport currency store, how many U.S. dollars will he have from this conversion after the store transaction is complete to the nearest tenth of a dollar? (Ignore the dollar sign when gridding in your answer.)

If there is still time remaining, you may review your answers.

Reading Test

1. **D**	13. **B**	25. **A**	37. **A**
2. **A**	14. **C**	26. **C**	38. **C**
3. **B**	15. **B**	27. **C**	39. **B**
4. **A**	16. **D**	28. **B**	40. **D**
5. **C**	17. **D**	29. **B**	41. **D**
6. **B**	18. **D**	30. **D**	42. **C**
7. **C**	19. **B**	31. **B**	43. **C**
8. **D**	20. **D**	32. **C**	44. **B**
9. **B**	21. **C**	33. **D**	45. **B**
10. **A**	22. **A**	34. **B**	46. **A**
11. **D**	23. **A**	35. **B**	47. **D**
12. **A**	24. **B**	36. **A**	

Writing and Language Test

1. **C**	12. **D**	23. **C**	34. **D**
2. **A**	13. **A**	24. **A**	35. **C**
3. **B**	14. **B**	25. **D**	36. **B**
4. **B**	15. **C**	26. **B**	37. **A**
5. **A**	16. **B**	27. **C**	38. **A**
6. **B**	17. **A**	28. **A**	39. **C**
7. **B**	18. **C**	29. **D**	40. **D**
8. **C**	19. **C**	30. **D**	41. **B**
9. **A**	20. **A**	31. **D**	42. **A**
10. **D**	21. **B**	32. **B**	43. **B**
11. **C**	22. **D**	33. **A**	44. **C**

Math Test (No Calculator)

1. **A**	6. **C**	11. **B**	16. **800**
2. **B**	7. **D**	12. **B**	17. **196**
3. **D**	8. **C**	13. **A**	
4. **B**	9. **B**	14. **75**	
5. **A**	10. **A**	15. **15**	

ANSWER KEY
Practice Test 1

Math Test (With Calculator)

1. **B**	9. **B**	17. **C**	25. **B**
2. **C**	10. **C**	18. **C**	26. **C**
3. **A**	11. **B**	19. **B**	27. **A**
4. **A**	12. **D**	20. **C**	28. **6**
5. **D**	13. **C**	21. **C**	29. **2**
6. **C**	14. **C**	22. **B**	30. **0.71**
7. **B**	15. **A**	23. **A**	31. **17.1**
8. **D**	16. **B**	24. **B**	

Note: This table represents an estimate of how many questions you will need to answer correctly to achieve a certain score on the PSAT.

PSAT Section Score	PSAT Math— 48 Total Questions	PSAT Evidence-Based Reading and Writing 91 Total Questions	PSAT Section Score
760	48	91	760
710	45	86	710
660	43	79	660
610	38	71	610
560	34	63	560
510	28	53	510
460	24	43	460
410	18	30	410
360	13	19	360
310	8	12	310
260	4	6	260
210	2	3	210
160	0	0	160

ANSWER EXPLANATIONS

Reading Test

1. **(D)** In the passage, the workers are given menial, labor-intensive, unhygienic jobs. Nonetheless, they are thrilled to have the jobs. This is the passage's biggest contrast—that between "the attitudes of the workers and the true nature of their work." Choice (A) is flawed in that they never "take it easy." They are hard workers. Choice (B) is flawed in that the passage has nothing to do with "vegetarianism." Choice (C) is flawed in that even though the characters are immigrants, they make no mention of homesickness for their native land.

2. **(A)** The answer to this question is most apparent in lines 30–41 and 79–87. The two are absolutely thrilled about the prospect of work, and their attitude can best be described as one of "optimism." "Pessimism" and "resignation" are negative emotions that aren't applicable here. Similarly, though we might infer that this new work might bring the characters peace, there is nothing in the passage itself to suggest "peacefulness."

3. **(B)** In lines 4–7, the passage states that the boss had intended to hire another man but, upon finding Jurgis, decided that he would do instead. Really, it seems, *anyone* would do. This is most consistent with choice (B). Workers are "disposable"—they are *easily replaceable, used until they have nothing left and then discarded in favor of someone new.* "Skillful," "valuable," and "interesting" all convey much more respect for the employees than the supervisors actually possess.

4. **(A)** See the explanation for answer 3. Lines 4–7 state, "The boss had meant for him to enter, but had not said this, and so it was only when on his way out to hire another man that he came upon Jurgis." This best exemplifies the view of the workers as replaceable. Jurgis, another man, no matter who—anyone would do given enthusiasm for the unseemly nature of the occupation.

5. **(C)** Lines 17–24 describe Jurgis's job description. These lines "describe a character's professional tasks." We see nothing of personal motivation, as in choice (A). The major point of the paragraph is actually that Jurgis *has* a job and he is thrilled to do it, which makes choice (B) incorrect. These lines have nothing to do with the objection of the reader, as seen in choice (D).

6. **(B)** When handling these vocabulary questions, insert each option into the sentence to determine which is most apt in context. "All day long he was figuring to himself" means that he was *counting the money he was making*; he was "calculating" his earnings, as in choice (B). After you insert "believing," "assuming," and "doubting" into the sentence, it will be clear that none of these three provides a logical statement.

7. **(C)** When handling these vocabulary questions, substitute each choice into the sentence to determine which option is most logical in context. As in *power plants*, "plants" sometimes has a denotation of *factories*. Such is the case in this sentence, and choice (C) is the correct answer. "Vegetation" is the normal meaning for *plants*, but it is terribly illogical here. "Stations" and "houses" both have somewhat of a case for legitimacy in context, but "factories" is far superior given the production process occurring there.

8. **(D)** In lines 53–56, the passage mentions that Marija knew only the word "job," and even this word was very difficult for her to learn. Her English fluency, therefore, is "very limited." She has nothing of proficiency.

9. **(B)** See the explanation for question 8. Lines 53–56 state, "Marija had nothing to take with her save her two brawny arms and the word 'job,' laboriously learned; but with these, she had marched about Packingtown all day. . . ." *Laboriously* means "with difficulty." If she had difficulty learning one single, simple word, clearly her English was very basic.

10. **(A)** Eliminating the incorrect choices is probably easier than finding the correct answer immediately. Choice (B) can be eliminated since the passage makes no argument at all. Choice (C) can be eliminated since no decision was made. Choice (D) can be eliminated since this passage has nothing to do with history. Choice (A) is what remains, and it is our correct answer. The passage's purpose is to analyze the phenomenon of rapid package delivery and the logistics behind that process.

11. **(D)** Lines 14–16 are used to describe what the concept of "logistics" initially meant: it was a war term used to describe the delivery of ammunition. It is thus "explaining the root of a concept," as in choice (D). Choice (A) is flawed in that it defines *past*, not current, usage of a phrase. There is no likely reader objection, as in choice (B). To what would the reader possibly object? There is no primary source evidence provided, as in choice (C).

12. **(A)** When dealing with vocabulary questions, insert the options individually into the sentence to determine which is best given the context. "Essential" is the best answer, and it is the meaning normally associated with "integral." Prior knowledge of the word would have been quite helpful. These companies, the sentence is saying, have grown to be basic, fundamental parts of American society. "Economic," "geographic," and "capitalist" all fail to capture the author's desired meaning of how mainstream these companies have become.

13. **(B)** In lines 38–42, the author makes clear that customers are primarily concerned with "reliability." Customers are willing to pay "a premium price" for this "certainty," so it's reasonable to assume that reliability is most important. Choice (A) is incorrect because customers are actually paying *more* for this service. "Holiday incentives" and "fashion choices" are not mentioned in the passage.

14. **(C)** See the explanation to question 13 above. Lines 38–42 state, *"When it absolutely, positively has to be there overnight"* is the company's mantra and this idea "basically provides certainty of service for a premium price that consumers are willing to bear." If consumers are willing to pay more money for "certainty," or *reliability*, we can infer that this is something very important to them.

15. **(B)** The author mentions that logistics are "interesting" in line 60. Lines 72–75 mention that the process is "something to behold." She also speaks of how logistics keep people happy in line 80. Overall, the author's tone is therefore warm. She is appreciative and has a "positive" opinion of the concept, as seen in choice (B). The author is not "skeptical": she does not have doubts about logistics. It is not choice (C), as the author *does* take an opinion on the matter. "Bellicose" means "warlike." Choice (D), then, is not a viable option.

16. **(D)** See the explanation to question 15. Lines 72–75 state, "Billions of dollars have been invested in these types of service industries and the activity behind the scenes is something to behold." *Something to behold* is something that is interesting, perhaps even *fascinating*, to witness. This then best aligns with a "positive" opinion of the subject matter.

17. **(D)** Lines 80–82 state, "And if the recent past is any indication, consumer spending on e-commerce will only continue to increase." Figure 1 demonstrates the validity of this statement; notice how future projections in Figure 1 increase every year. Choice (D), then, is the correct answer.

18. **(D)** Lines 69–72 state, "companies in the business of logistics are constantly investing in new ways to handle the information and the items as they flow through the pipelines." As Figure 2 demonstrates that the number of digital buyers worldwide is expanding rapidly, it stands to reason that the current infrastructure will need to be updated and optimized to handle this additional strain on the system. Choice (D) is the correct answer. Choices (A), (B), and (C) all refer to concepts that Figure 2 fails to substantiate.

19. **(B)** Both the worldwide business to consumer sales and the worldwide number of digital consumers are increasing, and the relationship between the two is linear. Therefore, the answer is choice (B), "positively correlated." Choices (A) and (D) mean the same thing: as one variable increases, the other decreases. However, both the variables are increasing in this case. Choice (C), "exponentially related," is flawed in that the two are increasing linearly. If one variable were, for instance, the square or the cube of the other variable, then there would be an exponential relationship.

20. **(D)** The last two paragraphs analyze how improper usage of antibiotics can lead to the mutation and spread of drug-resistant infections. It stands to reason that a physician should not be overzealous in prescribing antibiotics, as there is a chance that one of these strains can mutate at any time. Physicians need not consider only the patient but, rather, society at large every time they prescribe antibiotics. The passage makes no reference at all to the topics of choices (A) and (C). Choice (B) is flawed in that physicians still must diagnose bacteriological infections; patients are not expected to provide their own medical care.

21. **(C)** Lines 29–30 mention "both categories of drugs," and the next paragraph then goes on to describe both categories. Thus, these lines serve to "provide a transition to the following paragraph." Choice (A) is flawed in that the lines do not "define a couple of major concepts" but, rather, only *refer* to them. In choice (B), no specific supporting examples are provided. In choice (D), these lines, although important, do not contain the thesis (main idea) of the passage.

22. **(A)** In lines 31–34, the passage states that "bacteriostatic antibiotics are often prescribed to patients who have an intact immune system." If a person's immune system is intact, it is fair to assume that that person is "relatively healthy," as described in choice (A). Choices (B), (C), and (D) all state that bacteriostatic antibiotics are used on people in various states of poor health, which is not the case.

23. **(A)** Lines 76–80 offer the best evidence of the author's initial reference to the risk of losing "the capacity to treat bacterial infections." In the closing lines, the author then advocates for various ways to promote proper usage of antibiotics so that infections do not mutate into untreatable strains. There is no reference to "overdose," as in choice (B). The passage does mention MRSA but makes no mention of it losing prominence, as stated in choice (C). The first paragraph speaks of alternative medicine in the Far East. However, it is not a major concern of the author that the Western world will not embrace these alternatives, as stated in choice (D).

24. **(B)** Lines 76–80 speak of "growing concern" about the "development of antibiotic resistant organisms," which would be organisms not susceptible to current medical treatments. This matches the question's requirements. Lines 8–12 speak of the use of spices, and the author makes no mention of an opinion on these. Lines 88–92 describe MRSA, which is a large problem in the medical community. However, the mention of MRSA, alone, does not constitute sufficient evidence for the question. Lines 102–107 merely mention instructions for taking antibiotics, which also doesn't entirely satisfy the question's requirement of "a major concern" for the author.

25. **(A)** In context, the use of "severe" "and unpleasant side effects" forms the most logical sentence. Side effects are never "thoughtful," "genuine," or "quiet."

26. **(C)** "Spontaneously" is used to describe actions that arise in a manner that is unplanned and without any prior indication of their occurrence. This definition is most consistent with "randomly." "Impulsively" is generally attributed to human action that occurs without prior thought. "Extemporaneously" is to speak or perform without prior planning, and "deliberately" means to do something with purpose or conviction.

27. **(C)** Lines 61–62 mention a "culture and sensitivity test," and the preceding lines define this test as one used to "identify the specific microorganism causing the infection as well as the best antibiotic for treatment." In lines 66–67, the author states that the primary determinant of these two is the "zone of inhibition." The figure shows the results of antibiotic testing on specific microorganisms and includes data on the zone of inhibition. Choice (C), then, is the best answer.

28. **(B)** Lines 68–70 state that the "zone with the largest diameter typically signifies that it will be the best at fighting infection." Under the *E. coli* column (second column), ciprofloxacin has the largest diameter at 17 mm. It would therefore be the most effective antibiotic in this particular instance, as in choice (B). Vancomycin would be the most effective medication against *S. aureus,* not against *E. coli.* Amoxicillin is the second-most effective. Not only is there no data on *Staphylococcus*, but also it is actually a bacterial strain and not an antibiotic.

29. **(B)** Benjamin Franklin is reflecting on his own life in a candid manner. He is addressing his son, and both the nature of Franklin's reflections and the concept of writing to one's son can only be described as "personal." The tone is open, revelatory—it is Franklin at his most *personal.* It is not "abstract"; Franklin is not speaking in a roundabout, symbolic way. The passage is perhaps "serious" in that it does not trivialize the task of describing a life, but "serious" is not as apt as "personal." It is not "melancholy"; the passage is more celebration than lamentation.

30. **(D)** In lines 14–17, Franklin describes being born into poverty and then achieving affluence. He entered the world poor but obtained wealth through his endeavors. This is most consistent with choice (D). Choices (B) and (C) imply at least some sort of financial hardship in adulthood, which was not the case. Choice (A) is flawed in that Franklin was not born wealthy.

31. **(B)** See the explanation for question 30. Lines 14–17 mention "having emerged from the poverty . . . to a state of affluence." This is evidence that Franklin's personal situation "improved greatly over his lifetime."

32. **(C)** When handling questions of vocabulary, insert the options into the sentence to determine which is most sensible in context. "Applicable" is the most logical option since "suitable" means "appropriate" or "apt" in this instance. "Historical," "memorable," and "delightful" all create sentences with different meanings.

33. **(D)** The vocabulary of the choices is perhaps the most difficult part of this question. "To underscore his rootlessness" is another way of saying *to emphasize the uncertainty of his background.* Choice (D) is the correct answer, as Washington is emphasizing that he really has very little idea about how he came into this world. Washington is not *complaining about his dementia,* as in choice (A), and choice (B) is flawed in that he is uncertain of his "true identity." Choice (C) is flawed in that Washington is not critical of his family; rather, he is critical of the system of slavery that led to the instability/absence of his familial relations.

34. **(B)** With vocabulary questions, substitute the options into the sentence to determine which is most logical. Based on the context, Washington *has been unable to acquire any information about his family.* "Obtaining," as in choice (B), is the proper word to signify *acquiring.* Choice (A) is flawed in that Washington has nothing to read; he has no information whatsoever. Choice (C) is flawed in that one does not go about "creating" a family history; the past cannot be altered, let alone *created.* "Safeguarding" means "protecting," and there is nothing to protect.

35. **(B)** Washington has acquired the little knowledge he has of his family through informal conversations and speculation. This is most evident in lines 85–87, where Washington states that he has "heard reports" about his family. This type of conjecture and secondary-witness testimonial is best represented as "hearsay." There were no "publications" of his family; he mentions nothing written at all. Similarly, there were no "statistics." Washington did not learn of his family through "scholarship," or academia; there was nothing to be studied.

36. **(A)** Washington was born a slave, and he makes mention of this dismal existence in lines 54–56. Franklin, however, was wealthy. Choice (A) is the correct answer as Washington experienced societal hardship and injustice while Franklin did not. Choice (B) is flawed in that Franklin does "not find fault with [his father]," as stated in lines 90–91. Choice (C) is flawed in that both men—not only Washington—remark of genealogical curiosity. Lines 34–40 mention Franklin's desire to record his thoughts for posterity, making choice (D) incorrect.

37. **(A)** In lines 1–3, Washington mentions "obtaining little anecdotes" about his ancestors. The consistent theme in Washington's passage is a thirst to know his roots. The ability to obtain such anecdotes would assist him in his quest for knowledge, so choice (A) is the correct answer. Choice (B) is flawed in that Washington is already writing a memoir. Washington makes no reference to children, as in choice (C), or to wishing to relive his life, as in choice (D).

38. **(C)** In lines 71–74, Washington states that he has "been unsuccessful in obtaining any information that would throw any accurate light upon the history of [his] family beyond [his] mother." Thus, he has searched in the past for familial anecdotes. To his dismay, however, none could be found. Choice (C) is the correct answer.

39. **(B)** The principal claim of the passage is that the field of physics is changing, developing, revolutionizing—new and fascinating physical discoveries occur regularly (as mentioned throughout the passage), despite the unnamed physicist's claim in the first paragraph that physics was dead. Choice (B) is the best answer. As far as the incorrect choices, dark matter and dark energy are mentioned only briefly. The passage makes no comparison regarding the relative value of the contributions of Higgs and Einstein. Choice (D) has a sentiment that is close, but "ignorant" is too strong a word. Additionally, the author never takes a blatant

critical stance against the physicists of the past. Moreover, the author states that physics is continuing to change all the time, so the "ultimate truth" is certainly something that is yet to be uncovered (and the passage leads one to believe that the concept of an *ultimate truth* is inconsistent with the nature of physical discoveries, as a whole).

40. **(D)** In lines 61-65, the author describes string theory, stating that the vibrations of "tiny strings" have led physicists to postulate about the nature of "multiple universes." That something tiny can lead to a hypothesis about something massive is quite paradoxical, as suggested by choice (D)—the correct answer. The author makes no mention of practical applicability, just as he makes no mention of ethics. Choice (C), "historically consistent," is the opposite of what the author is saying.

41. **(D)** See the explanation to question 40. That "multiple universes" (in all their unfathomable enormity) can come from the vibrations of "tiny strings" is certainly something *counterintuitive*. Choices (A), (B), and (C) all refer to ideas that are not consistent with something *counterintuitive*.

42. **(C)** On vocabulary questions, if there is any uncertainty, it is best to plug the options into the passage in place of the word. "Theory," in this case, makes far more sense than "building," "observation," or "astronomy." "Construct" isn't often used as a noun rather than a verb, but when it is, its meaning is generally *an idea or a theory*.

43. **(C)** In the context of the paragraph, "singular" refers to the type of beginning that the Big Bang was, making "definitive" most appropriate. Although the other words can stand in for "singular," they are not consistent with the context of the passage.

44. **(B)** The first paragraph describes a "static universe" as the general consensus of the 19th century in lines 9-12. Lines 13-23 then transition to a discussion of a shift in that consensus, particularly as a result of Hubble's discoveries. The author prefaces the mention of this discovery with lines 13-14, "This all changed soon after the turn of the next century." Choice (B), then, is the correct answer.

45. **(B)** See the explanation to question 44. Lines 13-23 reference the shift from static to expanding universe based on discoveries by Einstein and Hubble. In the first paragraph, the passage deals with the 19th century. "After the turn of the next century" must then refer to the beginning of the 20th century.

46. **(A)** In lines 59-61, the best indication that this is an analogy is provided by the words "it is as if. . . ." *As* indicates that this is a simile, which is a type of analogy. The author uses the image of peeling an onion to make clearer the concept of physics discoveries of late: peel a layer (discover something new) only to find that there are more layers (more discoveries yet to be found) beneath the layer just peeled. Choice (D) is incorrect in that the author is celebrating these discoveries rather than lamenting them. Choice (C) is flawed in that the onion is used metaphorically rather than literally biologically. Choice (B) is flawed in that no new evidence is being *described;* it is merely being compared metaphorically to something else.

47. **(D)** The author's primary purpose is the celebration of knowledge for knowledge's sake. He is thrilled that new physics discoveries carry us closer to understanding how the world works on a small scale and how the universe works on a larger scale. There is no mention of military application, consumer use, or medical science as described in choices (A), (B), and (C), respectively.

Writing and Language Test

1. **(C)** We need a possessive to illustrate the idea of the *regular habits of one*. Eliminate choices (A) and (B) as they forget apostrophes. Choice (D) reads as *reading habits of the ones*. It is plural, whereas we need singular. Choice (C) is the correct answer.

2. **(A)** A contrasting transition is required here. Essentially, the sentence is *images are used often in society, **but** words require more cognitive processing*. "Although" is the only option to achieve that contrast. Choices (B) and (C) express cause and effect, while choice (D) is acceptable when the passage is listing multiple things along the same thought process.

3. **(B)** The verb in this sentence must maintain concordance with "require using one's mind to. . . ." The *to* should signify that this must be an infinite verb. Choice (B), "consider," is infinitive. It is, therefore, the correct answer. Choice (C) is conjugated, choice (D) is a gerund, and choice (A) includes an incorrectly executed gerund.

4. **(B)** Analyze the chart for this question. We are comparing the writing scores of those who read for fun "almost daily" with the scores of those who read "never or hardly ever." The difference in points between these two groups is approximately 30.

5. **(A)** The underlined sentence directly builds on the claim in the previous sentence by using specific numerical evidence. Thus, it must be "kept, because it provides specific details in support of the previous sentence." Deleting the sentence sacrifices helpful information. It has nothing to do with "salary details."

6. **(B)** The previous sentence speaks of a strong connection between reading skills and career success. Our question requires a choice that is a "specific and relevant elaboration" on that previous sentence. Choice (A) refers to joy attained from reading, which is irrelevant. Choice (C) refers to consumer habits, which is irrelevant. Choice (D) refers to memory, which is irrelevant. Choice (B) is the only option that refers to career success.

7. **(B)** The independent clause is "reading also stimulates the imagination." The sentence best functions by using a colon and then listing the various ways it stimulates the imagination. Choice (B) does this perfectly. Choice (A) is a run-on sentence. Choice (C) incorrectly uses a semicolon; there must be a full sentence on both sides of the semicolon, but there isn't a full sentence after the semicolon here. Choice (D) incorrectly attaches a list to the independent clause.

8. **(C)** It would be more appropriate to say "those are more likely" rather than "them are more likely." Eliminate choices (A) and (B). Now rewrite the clause using *he* or *him*. It would be more appropriate to say *he reads literature*. Recall that *he* equals *who*, so choice (C) is the correct answer.

9. **(A)** The best option here is a contrasting transition. Essentially, *good readers are active, **but** bad readers tend to end up in prison*. This is a vast generalization, but that's the structure of the sentence! "On the other hand" is the only contrasting transition. "Therefore" and "thus" are cause-and-effect transitions. "Moreover" means "also."

10. **(D)** *Confidence* is the issue. "Clearly" is very confident; *it is obvious that it must be this way*, "clearly" indicates. "Dubitably" indicates strong doubt, which is the opposite of confidence. Choices (A) and (C) lack confidence in that neither really commits to an opinion; they are ambivalent and hesitant to make a judgment.

11. **(C)** Ultimately, this whole sentence is one independent clause that must not be interrupted by punctuation. There is only one subject and there is only one predicate, despite the sentence's length. Choices (A) and (B) add unnecessary commas. Choice (D) improperly employs a semicolon that requires a full sentence on both sides of the semicolon.

12. **(D)** Ultimately, unless a comma is required, avoid using one. Such is the case with this sentence, where everything reads perfectly without punctuation. Choices (A), (B), and (C) all interrupt the clause by inserting unnecessary commas.

13. **(A)** In this sentence, there is a pattern of, essentially, *not for* this *reason,* **but** for that *reason.* That "but" is necessary because it demonstrates the contrasting relationship that is apparent. "And since," "and," and "for a result" fail to capture that pattern of *not for this, but for that.*

14. **(B)** Choices (A), (B), and (C) all communicate the same message, but notice that choice (B) does it much more concisely without sacrificing meaning. Choice (D), "omit," leads to a grammatically correct sentence, but it ultimately deletes information that is relevant and productive.

15. **(C)** "Than" is used for comparisons, while "then" is used as a sequencing term. Eliminate Choices (B) and (D) since this is a comparison. When making comparisons, it is far better to use an *-er* word, like "smaller," rather than an *-est* word, like "smallest." Choice (C) is the correct answer.

16. **(B)** Notice the other verbs in this paragraph. They are in the past tense. So stay in the past tense to preserve parallelism. Eliminate choices (C) and (D) because they are in the present tense. The subject is "discovery," which is a singular noun that requires a singular verb. "Were" is a plural verb; eliminate it accordingly. "Was" is the best answer.

17. **(A)** Notice the relationship between the two clauses on each side of the semicolon: the second clause contrasts with the first clause. "However" is an appropriate contrasting transition. "As a result" and "consequently" both are used to express cause-and-effect relationships. "What is more" is another way of saying *additionally* or *also.*

18. **(C)** The previous sentence states, "[They] set about to solve the problem by clearly defining what a planet is." Notice that this communicates the *exact same* message as the underlined sentence. Therefore, the underlined portion should be "deleted, because it repeats the ideas of the previous sentence."

19. **(C)** The important part of this question is *specificity:* a choice is needed that provides the most relevant, logical, and "specific" information. Eliminate choices (A) and (D) for being far too general: they lack "specific" substance. Choice (B) manages to be lengthy and yet shallow at the same time. "A great deal of mass and matter" is the best example of this wordiness. Moreover, it still doesn't provide the specificity of choice (C), which wastes no words while still providing ample detail.

20. **(A)** The parenthetical element here was tricky to diagnose. Nonetheless, "and therefore doesn't have enough gravity" was the parenthetical element. If you remove it from the sentence, the clause still functions perfectly well. As a rule, a parenthetical element can be surrounded by two dashes or two commas to separate it from the rest of the sentence. Choice (B) uses the two commas but actually splits the parenthetical element into pieces. Choice (C) omits the first comma. Choice (D) has entirely too many commas *within* the parenthetical element, preventing continuity. Choice (A) is the best option.

21. **(B)** "While" expresses two things occurring simultaneously, which is the nature of this sentence. It also can function as a contrasting transition as it does here (but doesn't necessarily have to). Essentially, *most of the world accepts that Pluto isn't a planet,* **but, at the same time,** *some people stubbornly refuse to let Pluto go.* "Since" and "because" are cause-and-effect transitions, while "and" is a conjunction.

22. **(D)** Although all of the choices are relevant conclusions, only choice (D) manages to tie "back to the introduction," as the question requires.

23. **(C)** When deciding whether to include or delete a portion, we must decide first if that portion is relevant. Second, we must decide if the insertion repeats information that has already been stated or if it mentions information that can be readily inferred. In this case, the issue is with the second question: the reader already knows the definition of "sibling." The answer is choice (C).

24. **(A)** Choice (A) uses the colon perfectly as a lead-in for the term to be discussed. Choice (B) is a run-on sentence. Choice (C) places an unnecessary comma after "based." Choice (D) incorrectly employs a semicolon. Recall that a semicolon requires what would otherwise be a full sentence both before and after the semicolon. "Birth order" is not a full sentence.

25. **(D)** The subject of this clause is "personality traits," a plural noun that requires a plural verb. Eliminate choices (A) and (C) for using singular verbs. Choice (B) uses the word "with" improperly in this context. Thus choice (D) is the correct answer.

26. **(B)** Ultimately, if we were to delete the underlined portion, we would be removing information that is both relevant and productive. It provides a "helpful elaboration" in this sentence, and it contributes informative value to the passage. Choice (B) is the correct answer.

27. **(C)** Analyze the relationship between this sentence and the previous sentence. The first states that firstborn children "excel in leadership positions," and then the second gives an example to illustrate this. "In fact" is an ideal transition to provide an example, and choice (C) is the correct answer. Choices (A) and (D) both imply a contrasting relationship that is not apparent. Choice (B) speaks of an absent objection.

28. **(A)** The subject here is "they," a plural pronoun that requires a plural verb. Eliminate choices (C) and (D) for using singular verbs. "Fit in with" means to associate with successfully, whereas "fit on" indicates something else entirely. Choice (A) is much more effective than choice (B).

29. **(D)** The proposed insertion states that middle children are "mediators." Sentence 7 talks about mediating, which means resolving differences. Thus, it is most effective to place our insertion right before this sentence, as in choice (D).

30. **(D)** Read the previous sentence. We need to elaborate on the claim that the youngest child is an entertainer. Eliminate choice (A) for irrelevance. Eliminate choice (C) because it refers to the oldest child, not the youngest. Eliminate choice (B) for not mentioning entertaining. Choice (D), however, refers to youngest children as entertainers. It is, therefore, our best answer.

31. **(D)** This question requires a possessive pronoun to demonstrate the *youngest child's way in life.* Eliminate choices (A) and (C) for not being possessive pronouns. Choice (B), "their," must refer to *multiple people,* whereas the "youngest child" is *one person.* "His or her" is the best set of possessive pronouns for *one person* of indeterminate gender.

32. **(B)** Choice (A) is a *comma splice*. Choices (C) and (D) place unnecessary commas after "birth order." Choice (B)'s usage of a semicolon is ideal, especially since it has two independent clauses.

33. **(A)** It really is best to read this sentence along with the previous *two* sentences. This sentence *contrasts* with the previous idea of the paragraph that "birth order isn't a one-size-fits-all theory." Essentially this sentence says: *That may be true,* **but** *it is still useful.* The best substitute for *but* is "nevertheless." The other three choices fail to provide the contrasting relationship that the sentence requires.

34. **(D)** This is a list and requires commas between the items being listed. Choice (A) omits commas after the first two items. Choice (B) omits a comma after the first item, while choice (C) does not include a comma after the second item. Choice (D) includes all necessary commas.

35. **(C)** Choices (A) and (B) are simply excessively wordy versions of choice (C), which manages concision while maintaining the initial meaning. Choice (D) changes the initial contrasting relationship to one of cause and effect.

36. **(B)** All four choices communicate the exact same sentiment. However, choices (A), (C), and (D) are excessively wordy versions of choice (B), which is concise without sacrificing content.

37. **(A)** The sentence requires a word that signifies *to undertake* the adventure/*to embrace* the adventure. "Inspected" the adventure and "expected" the adventure do not communicate that meaning. "Excepted" means "excluded" and doesn't suit our purposes. "Accepted" is the best option.

38. **(A)** The first decision is whether to use "many" or "much." The sentence mentions "reasons," which are things that are easily countable. *Many reasons* is the better usage, so eliminate choices (B) and (C). Recall that we use "much" to describe things we cannot count. The subject is "dental students," which is a plural noun that requires a plural verb like "have." "Has" is a singular verb. Choice (A), then, is better than choice (D).

39. **(C)** A possessive is required that expresses the idea of *the problems of patients,* where *patients* is plural. Choice (A) isn't possessive. Choice (D) incorrectly uses both "those of" and "problems," which are illogical when combined. Choice (B) incorrectly expresses the problems of *one* patient. Choice (C) is the best answer.

40. **(D)** After the verb "can," an infinitive verb is required. Eliminate choices (B) and (C) because they are conjugated verbs. "Effect" is rarely used as a verb, but when it is, it means to bring about. "Affect" means "to influence." The sentence is much more logical with *influence,* so "affect" is the correct answer.

41. **(B)** Analyze the graph for this question. This is somewhat difficult to see with the added complexity of a third dimension, but general dentists with the dark gray bar (6+ years experience) have salaries that fall somewhere between 100 and 200 thousand dollars. This is consistent with choice (B) and directly contradicts choice (A). Choice (C)'s numbers are too large, while choice (D)'s number is far too small.

42. **(A)** Analyze the graph. General dentists' salaries are slightly below those of general doctors, so choice (A) is the correct answer. They are significantly less than those of OBGYNs and general surgeons, which eliminates choices (B) and (C), respectively. They far exceed those of nurses, which eliminates choice (D).

43. **(B)** Analyze the relationship between this sentence and the previous sentence. This sentence provides an additional reason for becoming a dentist (as referenced at the beginning of the paragraph), so "moreover" is the best choice. Choices (A) and (C) incorrectly assume a contrasting relationship, while choice (D) improperly states a cause-and-effect relationship.

44. **(C)** This quotation should follow paragraph 2, as choice (C) states. Essentially, this insertion is a reason to pursue dentistry rather than toy-making as offered by Tim. Tim supplies these reasons in paragraphs 3 and 4. None of the other choices offers a logical placement for the insertion.

Math Test (No Calculator)

1. **(A)** First, get all x-terms on one side by subtracting $3x$ from both sides. To combine the x-terms, we'll need a common denominator. So convert $3x$ to $\frac{9}{3}x$. After combining the x-terms, our equation becomes:

$$2 = -\frac{5}{3}x$$

Next, solve for x by dividing both sides by $-\frac{5}{3}$ (in other words, multiply both sides by $-\frac{3}{5}$):

$$-\frac{6}{5} = x$$

The answer is choice (A).

2. **(B)** First, factor out 5:

$$5(x^2 - 3x + 2) = 0$$

Dividing both sides by 5 leaves you with:

$$x^2 - 3x + 2 = 0$$

This can be factored as:

$$(x - 2)(x - 1) = 0$$

Set each factor to 0 to solve for possible x-values:

$$x - 2 = 0 \text{ so } x = 2$$
$$x - 1 = 0 \text{ so } x = 1$$

Therefore, the answer is choice (B). Alternatively, you could have used the quadratic formula to solve for possible x-values.

3. **(D)** The typist has already typed 3,500 words, so this will be a constant in the expression. The typist types 70 words per minute. So if he types for t minutes, he will type $70t$ more words. Therefore, the total number of words typed, $W(t)$, is given by the following expression:

$$W(t) = 3,500 + 70t$$

Choice (D) is correct.

4. **(B)** Factor out all common factors. $2a$ is a factor of all three terms, so it can be factored out:

$$2a(3a + 4b - 2c)$$

Alternatively, you could have redistributed the answer choices to eliminate choices (A), (C), and (D), which, respectively, equal, $3a^2 + 4ab + 2ac$, $4a^2 + 4ab - 8ac$, and $6a^2 - 8ab + 4ac$.

5. **(A)** First, isolate what's inside the parentheses by dividing both sides by -3. Remember to flip the inequality sign because you are dividing by a negative:

$$x + 4 < -\frac{2}{3}x$$

Next, get a common denominator for the x-terms:

$$\frac{3}{3}x + 4 < -\frac{2}{3}x$$

Then subtract the left-side x-term from both sides of the inequality to get all x-terms on the right side:

$$4 < -\frac{5}{3}x$$

Finally, divide both sides by $-\frac{5}{3}$, which is the same as multiplying both sides by $-\frac{3}{5}$. Again, remember to flip the inequality since we are multiplying by a negative number:

$$-\frac{12}{5} > x \text{ or } x < -\frac{12}{5}$$

The correct response is choice (A).

6. **(C)** Use FOIL to obtain this equation:

$$\frac{6}{12}x^2 - \frac{2}{3}x + \frac{3}{4}x - 1$$

The coefficient in front of the x^2 can be reduced, giving:

$$\frac{1}{2}x^2 - \frac{2}{3}x + \frac{3}{4}x - 1$$

To combine the x-terms, they need to have a common denominator:

$$\frac{1}{2}x^2 - \frac{8}{12}x + \frac{9}{12}x - 1$$

Combining these terms gives you:

$$\frac{1}{2}x^2 + \frac{1}{12}x - 1$$

Choice (C) is the answer.

7. **(D)** A function intersects the x-axis at its roots, where $y = 0$: this will occur when any of these three factors equals 0. Set each factor equal to 0 to determine the x-values:

$$x = 0$$
$$x - 5 = 0 \text{ so } x = 5$$
$$x + 2 = 0 \text{ so } x = -2$$

Therefore, the three x-values are 0, 5, and -2, which is choice (D).

8. **(C)** Notice that both functions give equations of lines. To find the point of intersection, we want to find the point (x, y) that is on both lines. Since (x, y) is on both lines, we can find this common x-value by setting the right sides of both equations equal to one another:

$$4x - 3 = -\frac{1}{2}x + 2$$

Combine like terms by adding $\frac{1}{2}x$ to both sides and by adding 3 to both sides:

$$\frac{9}{2}x = 5$$

Solve for x by dividing both sides by $\frac{9}{2}$ (in other words, multiply both sides by $\frac{2}{9}$):

$$x = \frac{10}{9}$$

This is enough to narrow it down to choice (C), but you could solve for y by plugging in $\frac{10}{9}$ for x in either equation:

$$y = 4\left(\frac{10}{9}\right) - 3 = \frac{40}{9} - 3 = \frac{40}{9} - \frac{27}{9} = \frac{13}{9}$$

9. **(B)** Notice that the function is 2 minus the absolute value of something. The absolute value of something must always be greater than or equal to 0. So either $f(x) = 2 - 0 = 2$ or $f(x)$ equals 2 minus some positive number. This second case, though, will result in a value that is less than 2. (Convince yourself of this. For instance, if the absolute value is 1, then $f(x) = 2 - 1 = 1$.) Therefore, the maximum value of f is 2. To find where this maximum will occur, we need to determine which x-values give $|x - 4| = 0$. This occurs when $x - 4 = 0$. Thus, $x = 4$, which is choice (B).

    Alternatively, you could have plugged in the potential x-values to determine which gives the maximum value for $f(x)$.

10. **(A)** Dividing by a fraction is the same as multiplying by its reciprocal: $\dfrac{1}{\frac{1}{2x}} = 1 \times \dfrac{2x}{1} = 2x$

    $$\frac{3}{\frac{6}{4x}} = 3 \times \frac{4x}{6} = \frac{12x}{6} = 2x$$

    Therefore:

    $$\frac{1}{\frac{1}{2x}} + \frac{3}{\frac{6}{4x}} = 2x + 2x = 4x$$

    Choice (A) is the correct answer.

11. **(B)** Let's try to simplify the left side of the equation a bit to get it in the same form as the right side. When an exponent is raised to another exponent, you multiply those exponents:

    $$\left(x^2\right)^{\frac{1}{5}} = x^{\frac{2}{5}}$$

    Also, $\sqrt[5]{32x^2}$ can be broken up into $\sqrt[5]{32} \times \sqrt[5]{x^2}$. Since $\sqrt[5]{32} = 2$, the expression can be further simplified:

    $$\sqrt[5]{32} \times \sqrt[5]{x^2} = 2x^{\frac{2}{5}}$$

    Therefore, the left side of the equation simplifies to:

    $$x^{\frac{2}{5}} + 2x^{\frac{2}{5}}$$

You can then combine like terms:

$$x^{\frac{2}{5}} + 2x^{\frac{2}{5}} = 3x^{\frac{2}{5}}$$

If $3x^{\frac{2}{5}} = ax^{\frac{2}{5}}$, then it follows from dividing both sides by $x^{\frac{2}{5}}$ that $a = 3$, which is choice (B).

12. **(B)** In order for the inflation rate, as given by this formula, to equal 0, the numerator of the fraction must equal 0. This will happen if the current year's CPI is equal to the last year's CPI, because subtracting a number from itself equals 0. This matches choice (B).

13. **(A)** First, get the equation in standard form by subtracting 17 from both sides:

$$y = 6x^2 + 12x - 17$$

When a parabola is in standard form, $y = ax^2 + bx + c$, the axis of symmetry is given by the equation $x = -\dfrac{b}{2a}$. Because the axis of symmetry passes through the vertex and this parabola opens up, the x-value that gives the axis of symmetry will also give the x-coordinate of the vertex. The y- and x-values of the vertex give the minimum value and its location on the parabola, respectively, so we want to know the x-value of the vertex to solve this problem.

In this case, $a = 6$ and $b = 12$, so:

$$x = -\frac{b}{2a} = -\frac{12}{2(6)} = -\frac{12}{12} = -1$$

This corresponds to choice (A).

Alternatively, you could have converted the equation to vertex form by completing the square to get:

$$y = 6(x + 1)^2 - 23.$$

Then the vertex is $(-1, -23)$, so $x = -1$.

GRID-IN QUESTIONS

14.

75 Isosceles trapezoids have two sets of congruent angles, and their interior angles add up to 360°. Therefore, we know:

$$360 = 105 + 105 + x + x$$

Combine like terms:

$$360 = 210 + 2x$$

Subtract 210 from both sides:

$$150 = 2x$$

Dividing by 2 tells you that $x = 75$. Therefore, the smallest interior angle is 75°.

15.

(grid-in answer: 1 5)

15 Solve the second equation for y to solve this system of equations using substitution:

$$y = \frac{6}{4}x = \frac{3}{2}x$$

Next, plug in $\frac{3}{2}x$ for y in the first equation:

$$2x - \frac{3}{2}x = 3$$

In order to combine the x-terms, you need a common denominator:

$$\frac{4}{2}x - \frac{3}{2}x = \frac{1}{2}x$$

So our equation becomes $\frac{1}{2}x = 3$. Dividing both sides by $\frac{1}{2}$ tells you that $x = 6$. Next, plug in 6 for x in the equation that you already solved for y:

$$y = \frac{3}{2}x = \frac{3}{2}(6) = \frac{18}{2} = 9$$

Since $x = 6$ and $y = 9$, their sum is $6 + 9 = 15$.

16.

(grid-in answer: 8 0 0)

800 This is a system of equations. If there are 2 men for every 3 women, the ratio is $\frac{m}{w} = \frac{2}{3}$. If there are a total of 4,000 students, $m + w = 4,000$. To solve this system of equations, solve the first equation for m. Then plug this value into the second equation using substitution. Solving for m gives:

$$m = \frac{2}{3}w$$

So the second equation becomes:

$$\frac{2}{3}w + w = 4,000$$

Combine like terms:

$$\frac{5}{3}w = 4,000$$

Dividing by $\frac{5}{3}$ (the same as multiplying by $\frac{3}{5}$) tells you that $w = 2,400$. To figure out how many more women there are than men, you need to know also how many men there are. Plug in 2,400 for w in the equation you already solved in terms of m. Then subtract the number of men from the number of women:

$$m = \frac{2}{3}w = \frac{2}{3}(2,400) = 1,600$$

$$w - m = 2,400 - 1,600 = 800$$

So there are 800 more women than men.

17.

	1	9	6

196 First, simplify the second term in the numerator:

$$3(2x^2)^2 = 3(4x^4) = 12x^4$$

So our entire expression becomes:

$$\left(\frac{2x^4 + 3(2x^2)^2}{x^4}\right)^2 = \left(\frac{2x^4 + 12x^4}{x^4}\right)^2$$

The x^4-terms of the numerator can be combined:

$$\left(\frac{2x^4 + 12x^4}{x^4}\right)^2 = \left(\frac{14x^4}{x^4}\right)^2$$

The x^4 in the numerator cancels with the x^4 in the denominator:

$$\left(\frac{14x^4}{x^4}\right)^2 = (14)^2 = 196$$

So the answer is 196.

Math Test (With Calculator)

1. **(B)** You can use the conversion given in the problem (2.54 centimeters per 1 inch) to cancel out the units you don't want (inches), leaving you with only the units that you do want (centimeters):

$$48\,\text{inches} \times \frac{2.54\,\text{centimeters}}{1\,\text{inch}} = 121.92\,\text{centimeters} \approx 122\,\text{centimeters}$$

Choice (B) is the correct answer.

2. **(C)** Recognize that $d = rt$, where d is distance, r is rate, and t is time. In this problem, $r = 50$ and $t = 3\frac{1}{4} = 3.25$. Use this information to solve for distance:

$$d = rt = 50 \times 3.25 = 162.5$$

The answer is choice (C).

Alternatively, you could have done dimensional analysis to cancel out the units you don't want, leaving you with only the units you do want (miles):

$$\frac{50\,\text{miles}}{1\,\text{hour}} \times 3.25\,\text{hours} = 162.5\,\text{miles}$$

3. **(A)** First, distribute the -2:

$$7 - 2(y - 1) = 7 - 2y + 2$$

Next, combine like terms:

$$7 - 2y + 2 = 9 - 2y$$

The answer is choice (A).

4. **(A)** First, use FOIL for the $(x - 3)^2$ term in the equation to obtain:

$$x^2 - 6x + 9 - 81 = 0$$

Then you can combine like terms:

$$x^2 - 6x - 72 = 0$$

This factors to:

$$(x - 12)(x + 6) = 0$$

Setting each term equal to 0 tells you that x can equal either 12 or –6. Only 12 is an option, so choice (A) is correct.

5. **(D)** Look at the bottom row. There are a total of 400 individuals. Each person selected the one type of communication that he or she prefers. So the first four numbers in the bottom row must add up to 400:

$$195 + x + 70 + 70 = 400$$

Combine like terms on the left side of the equation:

$$335 + x = 400$$

Subtract 335 from both sides to isolate x:

$$x = 65$$

The answer is choice (D).

Alternatively, you could have added the first two terms in the e-mail column to obtain x:

$$20 + 45 = 65.$$

6. **(C)** Because we are told that the information in the table is representative of the Springfield population, we expect that the fraction of 15- and 16-year-olds in the survey who prefer video chatting will be the fraction of 15- and 16-year-olds in Springfield who prefer video chatting. The fraction in the survey that prefers video chatting is:

$$\frac{70}{400} = 0.175$$

Multiplying this decimal by the number of 15- and 16-year-olds in Springfield gives the number of 15- and 16-year-olds in Springfield that we expect to prefer video chatting:

$$0.175 \times 50,000 = 8,750$$

Choice (C) is correct.

Alternatively, you could have set up a proportion, Let x denote the total number of 15- and 16-year-olds in Springfield who prefer video chatting. Since there are 50,000 15- and 16-year-old residents in Springfield, our proportion is:

$$\frac{70}{400} = \frac{x}{50,000}$$

By cross multiplying, we get:

$$3,500,000 = 400x$$

Dividing both sides by 400 gives:

$$x = 8,750$$

7. **(B)** To find any probability, divide the number of *successes* by the number of *chances*. In this case, the number of successes is the number of 16-year-olds who prefer texting, and the number of chances is the total number of 16-year-olds:

$$\frac{85}{200} = 0.425$$

This amount, 0.425, is approximately 0.43 as in choice (B).

8. **(D)** First, solve for x by cross multiplying:

$$2x = 4$$

Dividing by 2 tells you that $x = 2$. Next, plug in 2 for x in the expression:

$$\frac{4(2-3)}{-12} = \frac{4(-1)}{-12} = \frac{-4}{-12} = \frac{1}{3}$$

The answer is choice (D).

9. **(B)** This question is asking you what percent the discount is of 90. First, you need to know what the discount is, which you can get by subtracting the new price from the original price: $90 - 72 = 18$. Then, you can figure out what percentage 18 is of 90 by setting up a proportion, recognizing that 90 represents 100% of the quantity:

$$\frac{x}{100} = \frac{18}{90}$$

Next, cross multiply:

$$90x = 1800$$

Dividing by 90 yields $x = 20$. So $18 is 20% of $90, which is choice (B).

As an alternative to this approach, you could plug the values from the problem into this formula for a percentage change:

$$\% \text{ Change} = 100 \times \frac{(\text{New Value} - \text{Old Value})}{(\text{Old Value})}$$

10. **(C)** From the graph, we can tell that the average monthly temperature in Townsville is greater than that in Cityberg for April, May, June, July, August, September, October, and November, or eight months. Therefore, choice (C) is correct. Choices (A) and (B) are incorrect because the graph doesn't tell us anything about the temperature on any random day. Choice (D) is incorrect because the average temperature in Cityberg is greater only in January, February, March, and December.

11. **(B)** For this problem, you need to create a system of equations. First, having two quarters for every five dimes means that the ratio of quarters to dimes is:

$$\frac{q}{d} = \frac{2}{5}$$

Next, we need to come up with an expression that represents the value of the coins. Because quarters are worth 25 cents, the number of cents David has from q quarters will be $25q$. Similarly, the number of cents he has from d dimes will be $10d$. Because these expressions are in cents, we need the amount of money he has also to be in cents. There are 100 cents in 1 dollar, so David has 200 cents. Therefore:

$$25q + 10d = 200$$

Since $\frac{q}{d} = \frac{2}{5}$, we have:

$$q = \frac{2}{5}d$$

Next, plug this fraction in for q in the second equation:

$$25\left(\frac{2}{5}d\right)+10d=200$$

Combine the d-terms:

$$20d=200 \rightarrow d=10$$

Thus, there are 10 dimes. Plug 10 in for d in the equation that expresses q in terms of d:

$$q=\frac{2}{5}d \rightarrow q=\frac{2}{5}\times10=4$$

Thus, there are four quarters and ten dimes, giving David 14 coins total, which is choice (B).

12. **(D)** In this equation, the 20 is a constant. Therefore, this is a constant amount of time required that isn't dependent on the number of cookies the chef makes. Therefore, this is the amount of time he requires to get the ingredients and set things up, which matches choice (D).

13. **(C)** Create a system of equations. First, you know that Jasmine has \$100,000 invested among the 3 categories. So if s, b, and c represent the amount of money in stocks, bonds, and cash, respectively, then the investments can be shown as:

$$s+b+c=100,000$$

She has invested twice as much in stocks as in bonds, so $s=2b$.

She has invested three times as much in bonds as in cash, so $b=3c$.

The question asks how much money is invested in bonds, so we want to get s and c in terms of b. Plug these expressions into the first equation, and solve for b. The second equation is already solved for s in terms of b, but we need to solve the third equation for c in terms of b:

$$\frac{1}{3}b=c$$

Next, plug these expressions in for s and c in the first equation:

$$s+b+c=2b+b+\frac{1}{3}b=100,000$$

You can combine like terms to get:

$$\frac{10}{3}b=100,000$$

Divide both sides by $\frac{10}{3}$ to get $b = 30,000$. The question asks what percent is invested in bonds, so find what fraction 30,000 is of 100,000 and then multiply that number by 100%:

$$\frac{30,000}{100,000}\times100\%=30\%$$

Choice (C) is the answer.

Alternatively, you can figure out the ratio of the investments:

Cash : Bonds : Stocks $= 1 : 3 : 6$

The total of the numbers in this ratio is $1 + 3 + 6 = 10$.

Therefore, as fractions of the whole, the investments are $\frac{1}{10}$, $\frac{3}{10}$, and $\frac{6}{10}$.

The bonds are $\frac{3}{10}$, which translates to 30%.

14. **(C)** 4,807 beverages were purchased, and 1,067 of them were espresso. Therefore, the percentage of beverages that is espresso is represented by the following expression:

$$\frac{1,067}{4,807} \times 100\% = 22.2\%$$

The answer is choice (C).

15. **(A)** If the sample is representative of the sales for a year, then we would expect the proportion of females who purchased a latte during the year to be the same as the proportion of females who purchased a latte in the sample. In the sample, there were 850 females under 18 and 1,573 females 18 and over for a total of 2,423 females. Also, 325 females under 18 and 530 females 18 and over purchased lattes, for a total of 855 lattes purchased by females in the sample. Therefore, the probability that a randomly selected female would purchase a latte is given by the following fraction:

$$\frac{855}{2,423} = 0.3529$$

Choice (A) is the answer.

16. **(B)** First, get this line in slope-intercept form so that you can easily identify the slope. You can do so by adding $4x$ to both sides to get:

$$y = 4x + 5$$

The slope of this line is 4. The slope of a line perpendicular to this one will have a slope that is the negative reciprocal, $-\frac{1}{4}$, which matches choice (B).

17. **(C)** First, you need to get the power equation in terms of just resistance and voltage so that you can tell how changing these two quantities will change the power. Therefore, we need to get rid of current by solving for it in the second equation and plugging this expression into the power formula.

Since $V = IR$, then $I = \frac{V}{R}$. Now, plug this in for current in the power equation:

$$P = IV = \frac{V}{R}V = \frac{V^2}{R}$$

The problem states that resistance is doubled and voltage is quadrupled, so fill in these coefficients:

$$P = \frac{V^2}{R} = \frac{(4V)^2}{2R} = \frac{16V^2}{2R} = 8\frac{V^2}{R}$$

Therefore, you can see that power has been multiplied 8 times, which is choice (C).

18. **(C)** In this problem, the mean can't easily be figured out because we can't sum together all of the responses without knowing the actual numerical responses. (We know only the range of hours for each student.) The mode is between 6 and 7 hours since this was the most frequent response (12 students chose this range). The median in a series of 30 terms is found by arranging the terms from smallest to largest and then taking the average of the 15th and 16th terms. In this case, the 15th and 16th terms are both between 6 and 7 hours, so the median is between 6 and 7 hours. Thus, the median and mode are the same, which is choice (C).

19. **(B)** Anita's $600 rent represented 40% of her expenses, while 60% of her expenses were spent on everything else. We want to figure out what this 60% was, so we can set up a proportion:

$$\frac{x}{60} = \frac{600}{40}$$

Next, cross multiply:

$$40x = 36,000$$

Divide both sides by 40 to determine that $x = 900$. Therefore, Anita spent $900 on everything else, which is choice (B).

20. **(C)** First, you need to come up with an expression for the area of the wall. Then recognize that paint will cost $12 for every 60 square feet (paint costs $12 per gallon and 1 gallon covers 60 square feet).

You know that $W = \frac{2}{3}L$ and $A = LW$ since the wall is a rectangle. Plugging in $\frac{2}{3}L$ for W gives $A = L\left(\frac{2}{3}L\right) = \frac{2}{3}L^2$.

Multiplying the cost/area by the area will cancel out the area and leave you with cost:

$$\left(\frac{2}{3}L^2 \, \text{ft}^2\right)\left(\frac{12}{60\,\text{ft}^2}\right) = \frac{24}{180}L^2 = \frac{2}{15}L^2$$

The answer is choice (C).

21. **(C)** This question is asking you to determine the range of the following function:

$$g(x) = |2x - 3|$$

Because the entire function is inside an absolute value symbol, $g(x)$, which is the range, cannot be negative. Therefore, the answer is choice (C).

22. **(B)** First, let's come up with an expression to represent the amount of food consumed each day. Each dog consumes 2 cups, so d dogs consume $2d$ cups of food daily. Each cat consumes 1 cup of food per day, so c cats will consume c cups of food daily. Together, the dogs and cats consume $2d + c$ cups of food every day. The shelter has 400 cups of food, so $2d + c$ cannot exceed 400. This can be represented by the following inequality:

$$2d + c \leq 400$$

Similarly, each dog needs 3 treats daily, so d dogs eat $3d$ treats each day. Cats eat 2 treats daily, so c cats need $2c$ treats daily. The shelter has 500 treats available every day, so $3d + 2c$ cannot exceed 500:

$$3d + 2c \leq 500$$

These two equations match choice (B).

23. **(A)** The volume of a sphere is given by the formula $V = \frac{4}{3}\pi r^3$. The diameter is twice the radius, so we can solve for the radius and multiply by 2. To solve for r, first divide both sides by $\frac{4}{3}\pi$:

$$\frac{3V}{4\pi} = r^3$$

To solve for r, take the cube root of both sides:

$$\sqrt[3]{\frac{3V}{4\pi}} = r$$

Multiply this by 2 to get an expression for the diameter:

$$d = 2\sqrt[3]{\frac{3V}{4\pi}}$$

Choice (A) is the correct answer.

24. **(B)** Each month, Caitlin adds $50, so the function will have a constant slope of 50. Because the slope is constant, the function is linear. The slope is positive 50, so the answer is choice (B). We know that the slope will be positive because the two variables are directly proportional: as time goes on, the amount of money in the account increases.

25. **(B)** Triangle *ECD* has an area of 20 square inches and a height of 4 inches. We can plug this information into the formula for the area of a triangle ($A = \frac{1}{2}bh$) to obtain the base of the triangle, *CD*:

$$20 = \frac{1}{2}b(4) = 2b$$

Divide both sides by 2 to get that base $CD = 10$ inches. Therefore, the base of triangle *ABD*, which is side *BD*, is $8 + 10 = 18$ inches. Next, we need to find the height of triangle *ABD*. We can utilize the fact that these are similar triangles to set up a proportion:

$$\frac{AB}{4} = \frac{18}{10}$$

Cross multiply:

$$10AB = 72$$

Dividing by 10 tells you that $AB = 7.2$ inches. Plug in 7.2 for the height and plug in 18 for the base in the area equation:

$$A = \frac{1}{2}(18)(7.2) = 64.8$$

The area of triangle *ABD* is 64.8 square inches, which is choice (B).

26. **(C)** First, you can factor a 7 out of both factors of the numerator:

$$\frac{7(x-1) \times 7(x+1)}{7}$$

One 7 in the numerator will cancel out with the 7 in the denominator, leaving you with:

$$7(x-1)(x+1)$$

Next, use FOIL for the terms in the parentheses to get:

$$7(x^2 - 1)$$

The answer is choice (C).

27. **(A)** The y-intercept of the function is somewhere between positive 6 and 8, so we can eliminate choices (C) and (D). Next, find the slope. You can use any 2 points on the line of best fit, such as the endpoints:

$$m = \frac{y_2 - y_1}{x_2 - x_1} = \frac{9.6 - 6.5}{6 - 0} = \frac{3.1}{6} \approx 0.5$$

So the answer is choice (A). The line has a slope of 0.5 and a y-intercept of 6.2.

28.

6 A cube has 6 sides, so its surface area is given by the formula $SA = 6L^2$. The volume of a cube is given by the formula $V = L^3$. Set these two equations equal to one another:

$$6L^2 = L^3$$

You can divide both sides by L^2 to obtain $6 = L$.

29.

2 Multiply the first equation by 2. Then add the two equations together to get rid of b:

$$4a - b = 8$$
$$+\underline{(3a + b = 6)}$$
$$7a = 14$$

Dividing both sides by 7 tells you that $a = 2$.

30.

0.71 The fees in this case are extra information that we don't even need because the customer wants to know what the conversion rate is without taking fees into account. We know the conversion rate of 1 U.S. dollar (USD) to Australian dollars (AUD):

$$1\,\text{USD} = 1.41\,\text{AUD}$$

We want to know how many U.S. dollars a person would get for 1 Australian dollar, so divide both sides by 1.41:

$$0.709\,\text{USD} = 1\,\text{AUD}$$

When rounded to the nearest hundredth, the answer is 0.71.

31.

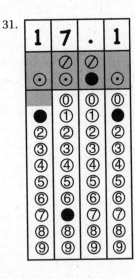

17.1 First, recognize that the store takes 1%, or 0.01 of the amount converted, leaving 99%, or 0.99, of the amount you started with. Therefore, instead of converting 700 Japanese yen, you're converting $0.99(700) = 693$ yen, and instead of converting 900 Indian rupees, you're converting $0.99(900) = 891$ rupees.

Next, use the conversions to cancel out the units you don't want (yen and rupees) to leave you with the unit that you do want (USD):

$$693\,\text{yen} \times \frac{1\,\text{USD}}{116.36\,\text{yen}} = 5.96\,\text{USD}$$

$$891\,\text{rupees} \times \frac{1\,\text{USD}}{68.01\,\text{rupees}} = 13.10\,\text{USD}$$

Add these together to get $5.96 + 13.10 = 19.06$. However, the store charges a $2 flat fee, so Andrew would end up with $19.06 - 2 = 17.06$. When rounded to the nearest tenth of a dollar, we get 17.1.

ANSWER SHEET
Practice Test 2

Reading Test

1. Ⓐ Ⓑ Ⓒ Ⓓ
2. Ⓐ Ⓑ Ⓒ Ⓓ
3. Ⓐ Ⓑ Ⓒ Ⓓ
4. Ⓐ Ⓑ Ⓒ Ⓓ
5. Ⓐ Ⓑ Ⓒ Ⓓ
6. Ⓐ Ⓑ Ⓒ Ⓓ
7. Ⓐ Ⓑ Ⓒ Ⓓ
8. Ⓐ Ⓑ Ⓒ Ⓓ
9. Ⓐ Ⓑ Ⓒ Ⓓ
10. Ⓐ Ⓑ Ⓒ Ⓓ
11. Ⓐ Ⓑ Ⓒ Ⓓ
12. Ⓐ Ⓑ Ⓒ Ⓓ

13. Ⓐ Ⓑ Ⓒ Ⓓ
14. Ⓐ Ⓑ Ⓒ Ⓓ
15. Ⓐ Ⓑ Ⓒ Ⓓ
16. Ⓐ Ⓑ Ⓒ Ⓓ
17. Ⓐ Ⓑ Ⓒ Ⓓ
18. Ⓐ Ⓑ Ⓒ Ⓓ
19. Ⓐ Ⓑ Ⓒ Ⓓ
20. Ⓐ Ⓑ Ⓒ Ⓓ
21. Ⓐ Ⓑ Ⓒ Ⓓ
22. Ⓐ Ⓑ Ⓒ Ⓓ
23. Ⓐ Ⓑ Ⓒ Ⓓ
24. Ⓐ Ⓑ Ⓒ Ⓓ

25. Ⓐ Ⓑ Ⓒ Ⓓ
26. Ⓐ Ⓑ Ⓒ Ⓓ
27. Ⓐ Ⓑ Ⓒ Ⓓ
28. Ⓐ Ⓑ Ⓒ Ⓓ
29. Ⓐ Ⓑ Ⓒ Ⓓ
30. Ⓐ Ⓑ Ⓒ Ⓓ
31. Ⓐ Ⓑ Ⓒ Ⓓ
32. Ⓐ Ⓑ Ⓒ Ⓓ
33. Ⓐ Ⓑ Ⓒ Ⓓ
34. Ⓐ Ⓑ Ⓒ Ⓓ
35. Ⓐ Ⓑ Ⓒ Ⓓ
36. Ⓐ Ⓑ Ⓒ Ⓓ

37. Ⓐ Ⓑ Ⓒ Ⓓ
38. Ⓐ Ⓑ Ⓒ Ⓓ
39. Ⓐ Ⓑ Ⓒ Ⓓ
40. Ⓐ Ⓑ Ⓒ Ⓓ
41. Ⓐ Ⓑ Ⓒ Ⓓ
42. Ⓐ Ⓑ Ⓒ Ⓓ
43. Ⓐ Ⓑ Ⓒ Ⓓ
44. Ⓐ Ⓑ Ⓒ Ⓓ
45. Ⓐ Ⓑ Ⓒ Ⓓ
46. Ⓐ Ⓑ Ⓒ Ⓓ
47. Ⓐ Ⓑ Ⓒ Ⓓ

Writing and Language Test

1. Ⓐ Ⓑ Ⓒ Ⓓ
2. Ⓐ Ⓑ Ⓒ Ⓓ
3. Ⓐ Ⓑ Ⓒ Ⓓ
4. Ⓐ Ⓑ Ⓒ Ⓓ
5. Ⓐ Ⓑ Ⓒ Ⓓ
6. Ⓐ Ⓑ Ⓒ Ⓓ
7. Ⓐ Ⓑ Ⓒ Ⓓ
8. Ⓐ Ⓑ Ⓒ Ⓓ
9. Ⓐ Ⓑ Ⓒ Ⓓ
10. Ⓐ Ⓑ Ⓒ Ⓓ
11. Ⓐ Ⓑ Ⓒ Ⓓ

12. Ⓐ Ⓑ Ⓒ Ⓓ
13. Ⓐ Ⓑ Ⓒ Ⓓ
14. Ⓐ Ⓑ Ⓒ Ⓓ
15. Ⓐ Ⓑ Ⓒ Ⓓ
16. Ⓐ Ⓑ Ⓒ Ⓓ
17. Ⓐ Ⓑ Ⓒ Ⓓ
18. Ⓐ Ⓑ Ⓒ Ⓓ
19. Ⓐ Ⓑ Ⓒ Ⓓ
20. Ⓐ Ⓑ Ⓒ Ⓓ
21. Ⓐ Ⓑ Ⓒ Ⓓ
22. Ⓐ Ⓑ Ⓒ Ⓓ

23. Ⓐ Ⓑ Ⓒ Ⓓ
24. Ⓐ Ⓑ Ⓒ Ⓓ
25. Ⓐ Ⓑ Ⓒ Ⓓ
26. Ⓐ Ⓑ Ⓒ Ⓓ
27. Ⓐ Ⓑ Ⓒ Ⓓ
28. Ⓐ Ⓑ Ⓒ Ⓓ
29. Ⓐ Ⓑ Ⓒ Ⓓ
30. Ⓐ Ⓑ Ⓒ Ⓓ
31. Ⓐ Ⓑ Ⓒ Ⓓ
32. Ⓐ Ⓑ Ⓒ Ⓓ
33. Ⓐ Ⓑ Ⓒ Ⓓ

34. Ⓐ Ⓑ Ⓒ Ⓓ
35. Ⓐ Ⓑ Ⓒ Ⓓ
36. Ⓐ Ⓑ Ⓒ Ⓓ
37. Ⓐ Ⓑ Ⓒ Ⓓ
38. Ⓐ Ⓑ Ⓒ Ⓓ
39. Ⓐ Ⓑ Ⓒ Ⓓ
40. Ⓐ Ⓑ Ⓒ Ⓓ
41. Ⓐ Ⓑ Ⓒ Ⓓ
42. Ⓐ Ⓑ Ⓒ Ⓓ
43. Ⓐ Ⓑ Ⓒ Ⓓ
44. Ⓐ Ⓑ Ⓒ Ⓓ

ANSWER SHEET
Practice Test 2

Math Test (No Calculator)

1. Ⓐ Ⓑ Ⓒ Ⓓ
2. Ⓐ Ⓑ Ⓒ Ⓓ
3. Ⓐ Ⓑ Ⓒ Ⓓ
4. Ⓐ Ⓑ Ⓒ Ⓓ

5. Ⓐ Ⓑ Ⓒ Ⓓ
6. Ⓐ Ⓑ Ⓒ Ⓓ
7. Ⓐ Ⓑ Ⓒ Ⓓ
8. Ⓐ Ⓑ Ⓒ Ⓓ

9. Ⓐ Ⓑ Ⓒ Ⓓ
10. Ⓐ Ⓑ Ⓒ Ⓓ
11. Ⓐ Ⓑ Ⓒ Ⓓ
12. Ⓐ Ⓑ Ⓒ Ⓓ

13. Ⓐ Ⓑ Ⓒ Ⓓ

14.

15.

16.

17.

Math Test (With Calculator)

1. Ⓐ Ⓑ Ⓒ Ⓓ
2. Ⓐ Ⓑ Ⓒ Ⓓ
3. Ⓐ Ⓑ Ⓒ Ⓓ
4. Ⓐ Ⓑ Ⓒ Ⓓ
5. Ⓐ Ⓑ Ⓒ Ⓓ
6. Ⓐ Ⓑ Ⓒ Ⓓ
7. Ⓐ Ⓑ Ⓒ Ⓓ

8. Ⓐ Ⓑ Ⓒ Ⓓ
9. Ⓐ Ⓑ Ⓒ Ⓓ
10. Ⓐ Ⓑ Ⓒ Ⓓ
11. Ⓐ Ⓑ Ⓒ Ⓓ
12. Ⓐ Ⓑ Ⓒ Ⓓ
13. Ⓐ Ⓑ Ⓒ Ⓓ
14. Ⓐ Ⓑ Ⓒ Ⓓ

15. Ⓐ Ⓑ Ⓒ Ⓓ
16. Ⓐ Ⓑ Ⓒ Ⓓ
17. Ⓐ Ⓑ Ⓒ Ⓓ
18. Ⓐ Ⓑ Ⓒ Ⓓ
19. Ⓐ Ⓑ Ⓒ Ⓓ
20. Ⓐ Ⓑ Ⓒ Ⓓ
21. Ⓐ Ⓑ Ⓒ Ⓓ

22. Ⓐ Ⓑ Ⓒ Ⓓ
23. Ⓐ Ⓑ Ⓒ Ⓓ
24. Ⓐ Ⓑ Ⓒ Ⓓ
25. Ⓐ Ⓑ Ⓒ Ⓓ
26. Ⓐ Ⓑ Ⓒ Ⓓ
27. Ⓐ Ⓑ Ⓒ Ⓓ

28.

29.

30.

31.

Practice Test 2

READING TEST

60 MINUTES, 47 QUESTIONS

Directions: Each passage or pair of passages is accompanied by several questions. After reading the passage(s), choose the best answer to each question based on what is indicated explicitly or implicitly in the passage(s) or in the associated graphics.

Questions 1–10 are based on the following excerpt.

The following passage is taken from the 1852 novel, The Blithedale Romance. *Mr. Coverdale, an idealistic young man, who has recently moved onto a utopian communal farm, is recovering from a fever. He is attended first by Hollingsworth, a philanthropist, and second by Zenobia, a beautiful wealthy resident of the farm.*

Happy the man that has such a man beside him when he comes to die! And unless a friend like Hollingsworth be at hand—as

Line most probably there will not—he had better
(5) make up his mind to die alone. How many men, I wonder, does one meet with, in a lifetime, whom he would choose for his death-bed companion? At the crisis of my fever, I besought Hollingsworth to let nobody else
(10) enter the room, but continually to make me sensible of his own presence, by a grasp of the hand, a word, a prayer, if he thought good to utter it; and that then he should be the witness to how courageously I would encounter
(15) the worst. It still impresses me as almost a

matter of regret, that I did not die then, when I had tolerably made up my mind to do it; for Hollingsworth would have gone with me to the hither verge of life, and have sent his
(20) friendly and hopeful accents far over on the other side, while I should be treading the unknown path. Now, were I to send for him, he would hardly come to my besdside, nor should I depart the easier for his presence.
(25) "You are not going to die, this time," said he, gravely smiling. "You know nothing about sickness, and think your case a great deal more desperate than it is."

"Death should take me while I am in the
(30) mood," replied I, with a little of my customary levity.

"Have you nothing to do in life," asked Hollingsworth, "that you fancy yourself so ready to leave it?"
(35) "Nothing," answer I; "nothing, that I know of, unless to make pretty verses, and play a part, with Zenobia and the rest of the amateurs, in our pastoral. It seems but an unsubstantial sort of business, as viewed through a
(40) mist of fever. But, dear Hollingsworth, your own vocation is evidently to be a priest, and

GO ON TO THE NEXT PAGE

to spend your days and nights in helping your fellow-creatures to draw peaceful dying breaths."

(45)   "And by which of my qualities," inquired he, "can you suppose me fitted for this awful ministry?"

"By your tenderness," I said. "It seems to me the reflection of God's own love."

(50)   "And you call me tender!" repeated Hollingsworth, thoughtfully. "I should rather say that the most marked trait in my character is an inflexible severity of purpose. Mortal man has no right to be so inflexible as it is my (55) nature and necessity to be."

"I do not believe it," I replied.

But, in due time, I remembered what he said.

Probably, as Hollingsworth suggested, (60) my disorder was never so serious as, in my ignorance of such matters, I was inclined to consider it. After so much tragical preparation, it was positively rather mortifying to find myself on the mending hand.

(65)   All other members of the Community showed me kindness according to the full measure of their capacity. Zenobia brought me my gruel, every day, made by her own hands; and whenever I seemed inclined to (70) converse, would sit by my bed-side, and talk with so much vivacity as to add several gratuitous throbs to my pulse. Her poor little stories and tracts never half did justice to her intellect. It was only the lack of a fitter ave-(75) nue that drove her to seek development in literature. She was made (among a thousand other things that she might have been) for a stump-oratress. I recognized no severe culture in Zenobia; her mind was full of weeds. (80) It startled me, sometimes, in my state of moral as well as bodily faint-heartedness, to observe the hardihood of her philosophy. She made no scruple of oversetting all human institutions, and scattering them as with a

(85) breeze from her fan. A female reformer, in her attacks upon society, has an instinctive sense of where the life lies, and is inclined to aim directly at that spot. Especially the relation between the sexes is naturally among (90) the earliest to attract her notice. Zenobia was truly a magnificent woman.

1. The point of view from which the passage is told is

    (A) first person.
    (B) third person.
    (C) objective.
    (D) omniscient.

2. Based on the passage as a whole, the narrator can best be characterized as

    (A) calmly resolute.
    (B) completely morbid.
    (C) overly dramatic.
    (D) patiently optimistic.

3. Which choice provides the best evidence for the answer to the previous question?

    (A) Lines 25–28 ("You are . . . it is")
    (B) Lines 45–47 ("And by . . . ministry")
    (C) Lines 65–67 ("All other . . . capacity")
    (D) Lines 74–76 ("It was . . . literature")

4. As used in line 43, "draw" most nearly means

    (A) inhale.
    (B) provoke.
    (C) infer.
    (D) sketch.

5. What best describes the figure of speech used by the narrator in lines 62–64 ("After . . . hand")?

    (A) Metaphor
    (B) Understatement
    (C) Personification
    (D) Irony

GO ON TO THE NEXT PAGE

6. What is the most likely reason that the author has capitalized the word "Community" in line 65?

(A) To be consistent with common cultural practices in the writing of the 1800s
(B) To label it as a formal proper noun since it likely refers to an idealistic commune
(C) To demonstrate the narrator's unusual passion for large urban developments
(D) To distinguish it from other municipalities discussed earlier in the passage

7. In the narrator's view, what was the major factor that drove Zenobia into her primary intellectual pursuit?

(A) Significant natural talent
(B) Her desire to shock her contemporaries
(C) Religious zeal
(D) A scarcity of opportunities

8. Which choice provides the best evidence for the answer to the previous question?

(A) Lines 67–69 ("Zenobia . . . hands")
(B) Lines 74–76 ("It was . . . literature")
(C) Lines 80–82 ("It . . . philosophy")
(D) Lines 82–85 ("She . . . fan")

9. As used in line 78, "severe" most nearly means

(A) dangerous.
(B) intense.
(C) uncomfortable.
(D) fertile.

10. Based on lines 82–90, what aspect of society is Zenobia most eager to reform?

(A) Xenophobic universities
(B) Widespread economic corruption
(C) Antiquated gender roles
(D) Environmental negligence

Questions 11–19 are based on the following passage.

The following passage is adapted from a speech delivered on June 26, 1963, by President John F. Kennedy. The speech was given in the Western-controlled part of Berlin in Germany during the Cold War between the United States and the Soviet Union.

I am proud to come to this city as the guest of your distinguished Mayor, who has symbolized throughout the world the fighting
Line spirit of West Berlin. And I am proud to visit
(5) the Federal Republic with your distinguished Chancellor who for so many years has committed Germany to democracy and freedom and progress, and to come here in the company of my fellow American, General
(10) Clay, who has been in this city during its great moments of crisis and will come again if ever needed.

Two thousand years ago the proudest boast was "civis Romanus sum." ("I am a
(15) citizen of Rome.") Today, in the world of freedom, the proudest boast is "Ich bin ein Berliner." ("I am a citizen of Berlin.")

I appreciate my interpreter translating my German!
(20) There are many people in the world who really don't understand, or say they don't, what is the great issue between the free world and the Communist world. Let them come to Berlin. There are some who say that
(25) communism is the wave of the future. Let them come to Berlin. And there are some who say in Europe and elsewhere we can work with the Communists. Let them come to Berlin. And there are even a few who say that it is true that
(30) communism is an evil system, but it permits us to make economic progress. Lass' sie nach Berlin kommen. Let them come to Berlin.

GO ON TO THE NEXT PAGE

Freedom has many difficulties and democracy is not perfect, but we have never
(35) had to put a wall up to keep our people in, to prevent them from leaving us. I want to say, on behalf of my countrymen, who live many miles away on the other side of the Atlantic, who are far distant from you, that they take the greatest
(40) pride that they have been able to share with you, even from a distance, the story of the last 18 years. I know of no town, no city, that has been besieged for 18 years that still lives with the vitality and the force, and the hope and
(45) the determination of the city of West Berlin. While the wall is the most obvious and vivid demonstration of the failures of the Communist system, for all the world to see, we take no satisfaction in it, for it is, as your
(50) Mayor has said, an offense not only against history but an offense against humanity, separating families, dividing husbands and wives and brothers and sisters, and dividing a people who wish to be joined together.
(55) What is true of this city is true of Germany— real, lasting peace in Europe can never be assured as long as one German out of four is denied the elementary right of free men, and that is to make a free choice. In 18 years
(60) of peace and good faith, this generation of Germans has earned the right to be free, including the right to unite their families and their nation in lasting peace, with good will to all people. You live in a defended island of free-
(65) dom, but your life is part of the main. So let me ask you as I close, to lift your eyes beyond the dangers of today, to the hopes of tomorrow, beyond the freedom merely of this city of Berlin, or your country of Germany, to the
(70) advance of freedom everywhere, beyond the wall to the day of peace with justice, beyond yourselves and ourselves to all mankind.

Freedom is indivisible, and when one man is enslaved, all are not free. When all are free,
(75) then we can look forward to that day when this city will be joined as one and this country and this great Continent of Europe in a peaceful and hopeful globe. When that day finally comes, as it will, the people of West Berlin can
(80) take sober satisfaction in the fact that they were in the front lines for almost two decades.

All free men, wherever they may live, are citizens of Berlin, and, therefore, as a free man, I take pride in the words "Ich bin ein Berliner."

11. The primary purpose of the passage is to

(A) express hostility.
(B) recount history.
(C) demonstrate solidarity.
(D) explain policy specifics.

12. As used in lines 8–9, the phrase "in the company of" most closely means

(A) joined by.
(B) in a business venture.
(C) under the orders of.
(D) at the request of.

13. The fourth paragraph, lines 20–32, can best be described as

(A) considering historical objections to a modern way of thinking.
(B) predicting the future course of events with specific observational evidence.
(C) encouraging the mass immigration of foreigners into a major city.
(D) addressing different thoughts about an idea with a common solution.

14. It can be reasonably inferred that President Kennedy considers the people of West Berlin to be best described as

(A) admirably resolute.
(B) security-conscious.
(C) emotionally distant.
(D) unusually anxious.

GO ON TO THE NEXT PAGE

15. Which option gives the best evidence for the answer to the previous question?

(A) Lines 28–31 ("And there . . . progress")
(B) Lines 33–36 ("Freedom . . . leaving us")
(C) Lines 36–41 ("I want . . . distance")
(D) Lines 42–45 ("I know . . . Berlin")

16. President Kennedy suggests that the people of East and West Berlin are most likely interested in which of the following?

(A) Initial interaction
(B) Visiting military allies
(C) Reunification
(D) Emulating ancient empires

17. Which option gives the best evidence for the answer to the previous question?

(A) Lines 13–17 ("Two . . . Berlin")
(B) Lines 36–42 ("I want to . . . years")
(C) Lines 49–54 ("for it is . . . together")
(D) Lines 78–81 ("When that . . . decades")

18. As used in line 66, the word "close" most closely means

(A) shut.
(B) finish.
(C) clasp.
(D) approach.

19. An unstated assumption of the paragraph in lines 73–81 is that

(A) if one person is enslaved, no one is free.
(B) financial independence is a key to true freedom.
(C) free people are inherently interested in peace.
(D) Berliners will continue to take the preeminent role in expanding freedom worldwide.

Questions 20–28 are based on the following passage.

This passage is adapted from a 2012 article on blackletter typeface.

The familiar, somewhat calligraphic anachronism that today we often refer to as "Old English" did not emerge until the 12th
Line century, around the time of the extinction of
(5) the Old English language. The Old English script or, more accurately, blackletter, is in reality not even English but evolved in medieval universities along the Franco-German border as an efficient alternative to both the
(10) highly variable "insular" scripts of England and Ireland, and the consistent though cumbersome Carolingian minuscule of Christian monasteries.

In 1454, Johannes Gutenberg carved an
(15) unusually ornamental blackletter script called "textualis" for his much-celebrated movable type printing press and a year later used the font to print his 42-line Bible. Compared with their Carolingian anteced-
(20) ents, the letters of textualis are distinct for their height, narrowness, and sharp angularity. The style enjoyed a brief period of popularity in the late 15th century but was crippled by an overabundance of labyrin-
(25) thine derivatives; such as the "littera textualis formata" used for ornamental books and the cursive "littera textualis currens" used for glosses. Although textualis was rarely used in printing after Gutenberg, the revolution-
(30) ary scale of his innovation firmly established blackletter—particularly the Schwabacher and Fraktur varieties—as the preferred script for printed texts throughout Europe.

As the immediate successor of textualis,
(35) the Schwabacher style strove for increased readability with significant reductions to

GO ON TO THE NEXT PAGE

capital embellishment and a smoother, more curvaceous form invocative of handwriting. Though Schwabacher is sometimes associ-
(40) ated with the Italian humanist writings of the early 16th century, it saw substantial use throughout all of Europe and was only partially deposed by Fraktur in the late 1700s. Schwabacher continued to appear in printed
(45) texts as a secondary typeface into the 20th century.

By far the most familiar blackletter style, Fraktur originated at the end of the 15th century through a commission of the Holy
(50) Roman Emperor Maximilian I; by the end of the 16th, it was the most widely used type-face in Europe. Though far less calligraphic than textualis, Fraktur is nonetheless more intricate than Schwabacher and combines
(55) the soft readability of the latter with the bold regality of the former. By the 18th century, Fraktur had achieved such ubiquity that it became colloquially synonymous with the blackletter style.

(60) Predictably, the cosmopolitan classicists of the 18th century began to prefer the mar-ginalized Antiqua scripts of prior centuries, which, being modeled after ancient Roman letterforms, eschewed medieval ornamen-
(65) tation altogether. Antiqua's subversion of blackletter began gradually, appearing pri-marily in scientific texts (which valued read-ability over appearance), while literature and newspapers adhered to more aesthetic styles.
(70) By the start of the 20th century, the majority of the Western world had accepted Antiqua typefaces as the standard font, but blacklet-ter remained disproportionately common in German-speaking nations.

(75) A lethal blow was dealt to blackletter when, on January 3, 1941, Nazi chancellery Martin Borrmann issued the *Schrifterlass* decree to all of Germany's public offices,

which described Schwabacher, Fraktur, and
(80) all other forms of blackletter as Judenlettern, or "Jewish letters," and prohibited their use in future printing. It remains to this day unclear what connection the Nazi party saw between the Jewish people and blackletter.
(85) Interestingly, however, it is understood that subsequent Nazi biblioclasms sometimes targeted texts based not only on their content but also their typeface. Blackletter made a brief return following the war but was soon
(90) abandoned by a German nation eager to modernize and reinvent its international image.

20. The overall purpose of this passage is

(A) to distinguish between the Old English typeface and the Old English language.
(B) to investigate the origin of blackletter typeface.
(C) to educate readers about the history and evolution of blackletter.
(D) to demonstrate the value of blackletter typefaces.

21. As used in lines 24–25, "labyrinthine" most nearly means

(A) mazelike.
(B) possessing many right angles.
(C) complex.
(D) menacing.

22. Based on the information in the passage, the primary advantage of the Fraktur variety of blackletter was that

(A) it was widespread throughout Europe.
(B) it balanced elegance with functionalism.
(C) it had the support of Maximilian I.
(D) it derived from ancient Roman letterforms.

GO ON TO THE NEXT PAGE

23. Which choice provides the best evidence for the answer to the previous question?

   (A) Lines 28–33 ("Although . . . Europe")
   (B) Lines 47–52 ("By far . . . Europe")
   (C) Lines 52–56 ("Though . . . former")
   (D) Lines 56–59 ("By the . . . style")

24. Apart from ease of readability, why else might the classicists of the 18th century have preferred using Antiqua typefaces to blackletter?

   (A) Using Antiqua typefaces prevented lay people from understanding the classicists' texts.
   (B) It distinguished the classicists' texts from those printed in the middle ages.
   (C) It was a faster and more efficient way to write in longhand.
   (D) It associated the classicist movement with the learning of ancient Rome and the classical period.

25. Which choice provides the best evidence for the answer to the previous question?

   (A) Lines 44–46 ("Schwabacher . . . century")
   (B) Lines 56–69 ("By the . . . styles")
   (C) Lines 60–65 ("Predictably . . . altogether")
   (D) Lines 70–74 ("By the start . . . nations")

26. The main purpose of including the *Schrifterlass* decree in the passage is to

   (A) show how typefaces have influenced modern history.
   (B) imply that blackletter was never very popular outside of Germany.
   (C) illustrate hypocrisy in a Nazi policy.
   (D) account for the final demise of blackletter.

27. The passage suggests that the most significant problem with the insular scripts was what?

   (A) They lacked consistency in their letterforms.
   (B) They were elaborate and time consuming.
   (C) They were isolated in England and Ireland.
   (D) They were used only in Christian monasteries.

28. As used in line 75, the word "lethal" most nearly means

   (A) mortal.
   (B) deadly.
   (C) final.
   (D) venomous.

Questions 29–37 are based on the following passages and chart.

These passages are adapted from the articles written in 2013 about invasive plants.

Passage 1

Today many of the most common and recognizable plants in our arboreal ecosystems are nonnative to North America. If you take
Line a walk through the woods almost anywhere
(5) in the temperate U.S., you'll probably come across clusters of honeysuckle, dandelions, bobbing water lilies, and dense patches of ivy. Despite their pervasiveness, none of these plants developed here naturally, but
(10) were introduced by human activity.

Some nonnative plants are introduced to new territories accidentally via interregional soil and food trade. Accidental introduction of nonnative organisms can often have
(15) negative and unforeseen consequences. For

GO ON TO THE NEXT PAGE

example, the Asian chestnut blight fungus was unexpectedly brought to the United States through the trade of plants; this fungus nearly wiped out the entire American chest-
(20) nut population, harming many animals that depend on chestnuts for food.

Many other species, however, have been purposefully spread within the U.S. for a wide range of beneficial uses: stock feed, ero-
(25) sion control, reforestation, and, most commonly of all, ornamental plants in gardens and parks. Intentional cultivation of nonnative invasive plants is generally far more beneficial than accidental introduction, although
(30) there are exceptions. For example, melaleuca trees were brought to the Florida Everglades from Australia; developers thought these trees would help dry up vast swampy areas, enabling residential and commercial con-
(35) struction. Unfortunately, the trees spread widely and covered up large swaths of the Everglades, displacing native plants. Florida has had to spend a great deal of money to remove these invasive trees.
(40) Although introduced animal species often become invasive in new ecosystems because of a lack of natural predation, it is difficult even for botanists to predict which exotic plants will flourish in a novel environment.
(45) Some plants require continuous human intervention and cannot spread independently into the wild. Others—honeysuckle, dandelions, water lilies, and ivy included—languish in domestication for a number of
(50) years and then suddenly naturalize, at which point they often become invasive.

Passage 2

For the past fifty years, it has been the conventional credence of ecologists and

biologists alike that invasive, nonnative plant
(55) species are, without exception, detrimental to the host ecosystem. However, recent studies at Penn State University indicate that the eradication of invasive plants—specifically fruit-bearing shrubs—can do more harm
(60) than good for the native animal populations.

After conducting studies in urban, rural, and forested environments, researchers found that an area's abundance of honeysuckle can function as a direct predictor
(65) of the number and diversity of birds living within a particular region. Having developed a mutualist relationship, native species of birds throughout the Midwest rely on honeysuckle fruit as a staple food source in the
(70) fall. Simultaneously, honeysuckle benefits by being spread to new regions when its seeds are eaten and subsequently dispersed by the birds.

Though common protocol would dictate
(75) that an invasive species like honeysuckle be removed from areas where it becomes dominant, these new findings demonstrate that such action would likely strike a significant blow to native bird populations. What's
(80) more, areas that today are abundant in honeysuckle typically host 30 to 40 percent more birds than these same regions did 30 years ago, indicating a long-term change for the better. Although some invasive species
(85) do cause tremendous and irreparable damage to their ecosystems, environments are not static. Environments change, develop, and adapt to transitions, whether they be natural or humanmade. We must learn to be
(90) more discriminating in our eradication of invasive plants from those areas where they have become an integral part of the greater ecosystem.

GO ON TO THE NEXT PAGE

Galapagos Visitors*

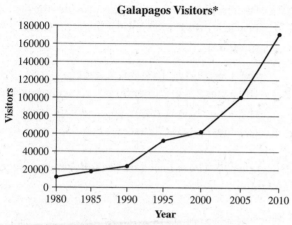

The Galapagos Islands have been isolated from human habitation until relatively recently.
*http://www.galapagos.org/conservation/tourism-growth/

29. Which of the following, if true, would most undermine the author's argument in lines 27–30 ("Intentional . . . exceptions")?

(A) A historical investigation into the origins of invasive plants that demonstrates that the majority were introduced by accident

(B) A global statistical analysis that demonstrates the net harmful effects from purposefully introduced invasive plant species

(C) A genetic analysis that establishes that invasive plant species share several fundamental characteristics in their DNA

(D) Discovery of three instances of invasive plant introduction that had a beneficial impact on the surrounding environments

30. As used in line 42, "predation" most nearly means

(A) placing events earlier in a sequence.

(B) habitats suitable for species development.

(C) plants appropriate for animal consumption.

(D) preying of one animal on others.

31. What is the primary function of lines 52–56 ("For the . . . ecosystem") in the first paragraph of Passage 2?

(A) To establish the narrator's scholarly authority in this field of study

(B) To state the principal argument of the passage

(C) To summarize a common understanding that is subsequently refuted

(D) To contrast the work of ecologists with those of biologists

32. Which of the following situations would be most similar to that discussed in lines 66–73 ("Having . . . birds")?

(A) Large whale species consume krill at higher latitudes.

(B) The male gorilla does not help with infants but does help defend against predators.

(C) Oxpecker birds eat predatory insects off the backs of zebras.

(D) Humans consume crabs they fish from the ocean.

33. As used in line 90, "discriminating" most nearly means

(A) biased.

(B) intolerant.

(C) tasteful.

(D) selective.

GO ON TO THE NEXT PAGE

34. The respective approaches to the discussion of invasive plants by Passage 1 and Passage 2 are

   (A) positive and negative.
   (B) pessimistic and optimistic.
   (C) broad and focused.
   (D) argumentative and analytical.

35. Passage 1 and Passage 2 agree that

   (A) intentionally introduced invasive plants have the potential to have a positive impact.
   (B) invasive plants are, without exception, harmful to the natural environment.
   (C) honeysuckle is the most well-known of the invasive plant species.
   (D) the negative consequences of invasive plants can be ameliorated through government intervention.

36. Based on the passages and the chart, what will be the most likely consequence of tourism with respect to invasive plants in the Galapagos in the future?

   (A) Due to an increase in humanity's awareness of the Galapagos, it is more likely that a desire for environmental stewardship of the islands will grow.
   (B) Due to an increase in economic activity as a result of tourism, the inhabitants of the Galapagos will have more money with which to combat unwanted plant species.
   (C) Due to an increase in human contact, it is likely that the number of nonnative organisms introduced by accident will increase.
   (D) Due to an increase in hotel construction as a consequence of tourism, intentional cultivation of invasive species will grow.

37. Which choice in the passages provides the best evidence for the answer to the previous question?

   (A) Lines 8–13 ("Despite . . . trade")
   (B) Lines 27–30 ("Intentional . . . exceptions")
   (C) Lines 40–44 ("Although . . . environment")
   (D) Lines 79–84 ("What's . . . better")

Questions 38–47 are based on the following passage and table.

Color Photography

   We tend to think of color photography as a profoundly modern innovation, belonging to an era no earlier than the 1950s. Although it
Line is true that it was not until the mid-twentieth
(5) century that compact devices like the Kodak Kodachrome and Polaroid instant camera made color photography widely available to the American public, the first known color photograph was developed about one hun-
(10) dred years prior, in the early 1840s.
   Pioneers of color photography such as American intellectual Levi Hill and renowned French physicist A. E. Becquerel were hampered in their efforts by a fidelity to the
(15) then-popular daguerreotype method, which slowly imprints a direct-positive image onto a metal plate treated with light-sensitive iodine and bromine crystals. Colloquially, these photographs were known as "tintypes."
(20) Color variants of this method—such as Hill's toilsome "heliochromy"—often took several days to develop and yielded only dim images with colors that faded rapidly when exposed to direct light.
(25)   A new approach was required before color photography could emerge as a truly viable artistic and documentary medium. Such an approach was theorized just ten years later. While Hill's and Becquerel's labors had

GO ON TO THE NEXT PAGE

emphasized the search for a novel, chamele-
onic compound to assume any spectral
wavelength shown upon it, Scottish physicist
James Clerk Maxwell used as his model the
color sensitivity of the human eye.

(35)   We are able to perceive colors because of
specialized photoreceptor cells lining our
retinas called "cones." Generally, humans
possess three types of cone cells, each of
which produces a distinct, transmembrane
(40) photopsin protein. Depending on the particular chromophore compound associated
with the cell's photopsins, the cone will have
a peak absorbance of electromagnetic radiation
at wavelengths of 420–440 nm, 534–545
(45) nm, or 564–580 nm. On the visible spectrum,
these peaks correspond to the colors red,
green, and blue, respectively. The brain's
integration of photons absorbed by these
three types of cones allows us to perceive col-
(50) ored light with wavelengths between roughly
400 and 700 nanometers, which comprises
the entire visible spectrum. Because of this
mechanism, humans are said to possess
"trichromatic vision."

(55)   In light of this phenomenon, Maxwell
noted that any hue of visible light could be
reproduced by a specific combination of
three colors. Thus, three black-and-white
transparencies of a single scene taken
(60) through red, blue, and green filters will, when
projected as a composite image, reproduce
with impressive accuracy the original, full-color
subject. Problems remained, however,
when it came time to develop these nega-
(65) tives onto paper in that the dyes used by
photographers were ineffective in expressing
certain colors, particularly those comprised
of lower wavelengths. By trial and error, it
was discovered by Becquerel and German
(70) chemist Hermann Vogel that the addition of

dyes made of aniline—an aromatic amine—
and chlorophyll to photographic emulsions
helped to reflect the reds and yellows that
previous dyes had simply absorbed.

(75)   Into the early 20th century, color cameras
themselves remained somewhat unwieldy;
this owed largely to the logistical complexi-
ties of exposing three separate, individually
filtered plates on the same subject. One
(80) design used a system of prisms and mirrors to split the lens image through three
internal filters, which in turn exposed three
plates simultaneously. A more compact and
less delicate device designed by German
(85) photographer Adolf Miethe simply included
a rotating filter disk, which allowed three
photographs to be taken in rapid succession.
From 1909 to 1915, Miethe's design was used
by his Russian protégé, Sergei Prokudin-
(90) Gorsky, in a project appointed to him by Czar
Nicholas II to document visually the history,
culture, and modernization of the Russian
Empire. His extensive and compelling work
in the Russian provinces constitutes the
(95) first major series of color photojournalism.
However, whenever a moving object was
included in the frame—particularly water—
the shortcomings of Miethe's design became
obvious. The consecutive exposure of plates,
(100) however swift, would always leave some
room for visual conflict between the three
images.

The issues of both convenience and syn-
chronous exposure were eventually solved
(105) by two professional, classical musicians—
Leopold Mannes and Leopold Godowsky,
Jr.—working recreationally for the Eastman
Kodak Company. Together they designed a
film that consisted of three separate emul-
(110) sion layers mounted on a single flexible
base, each of which captured and individu-

GO ON TO THE NEXT PAGE

ally filtered the lens image. Their design was marketed by Kodak under the name "Kodachrome" and was the first system to
(115) make the use of color film widely available to lay photographers.

Electromagnetic Waves and Their Wavelengths

Wave Type	Wavelength in Meters
Gamma	1×10^{-11}
X-ray	1×10^{-9}
Ultraviolet	2×10^{-8}
Infrared	1×10^{-6}
Radio	1.0

38. The passage outlines the evolution of the color photography process from being

(A) time consuming and unmanageable to efficient and compact.
(B) an object of widespread interest to a mere curiosity by elites.
(C) the province of artists to the focus of musicians.
(D) a modern innovation to a widespread convenience.

39. The evidence used in the essay is primarily comprised of

(A) esoteric psychological analysis.
(B) chemical and physical description.
(C) scientific and historical anecdotes.
(D) cross-cultural comparative study.

40. The passage suggests that which of the following kept Hill and Becquerel from further innovations in color photographic technology?

(A) A lack of scientific training
(B) Cultural bias toward Euro-American philosophy
(C) A failure to understand past successes
(D) Loyalty to a widespread approach

41. Which choice provides the best evidence for the answer to the previous question?

(A) Lines 11–13 ("Pioneers . . . French")
(B) Lines 14–15 ("hampered . . . method")
(C) Lines 20–24 ("Color . . . light")
(D) Lines 32–34 ("Scottish . . . eye")

42. As used in line 61, "composite" most nearly means

(A) crafted.
(B) visual.
(C) combined.
(D) quality.

43. As used in line 76, "unwieldy" most nearly means

(A) unsightly.
(B) cumbersome.
(C) expensive.
(D) precise.

GO ON TO THE NEXT PAGE

44. The passage suggests that Maxwell was able to make a scientific breakthrough in photographic technology by shifting his focus from

   (A) chemistry to biology.
   (B) anthropology to astronomy.
   (C) physics to mathematics.
   (D) artistry to geometry.

45. Based on lines 83–102, it can be logically inferred that a Miethe-designed camera could most successfully photograph a river under what weather conditions?

   (A) At high noon on a summer day with a light breeze
   (B) On a rainy, blustery day with mild flooding
   (C) On a freezing, windless day
   (D) It will capture any form of water with equally low quality

46. Based on the information in the passage and in the table, light visible to humans would have wavelengths between which two types of waves?

   (A) Gamma and X-rays
   (B) X-rays and ultraviolet
   (C) Ultraviolet and infrared
   (D) Infrared and radio

47. The originators of the Kodachrome film process are best described as

   (A) serendipitous tinkerers.
   (B) scholarly thinkers.
   (C) scientific masterminds.
   (D) mathematical prodigies.

STOP

If there is still time remaining, you may review your answers.

WRITING AND LANGUAGE TEST

35 MINUTES, 44 QUESTIONS

> **Directions:** The passages below are each accompanied by several questions, some of which refer to an underlined portion in the passage and some of which refer to the passage as a whole. For some questions, determine how the expression of ideas can be improved. For other questions, determine the best sentence structure, usage, or punctuation given the context. A passage or question may have an accompanying graphic that you will need to consider as you choose the best answer.
>
> Choose the best answer to each question, considering what will optimize the writing quality and make the writing follow the conventions of standard written English. Some questions have a "NO CHANGE" option that you can pick if you believe the best choice is to leave the underlined portion as is.

Questions 1-11 are based on the following passage.

Matter-Antimatter Asymmetry

It can be described as one of the greatest mysteries of modern physics. In a universe that **①** tends universally, as it were toward net neutrality, the apparently asymmetrical distribution of the baryon charge is a **②** singular and tantalizing puzzle. Atoms—and thus, matter, which composes the visible universe—possess a positive baryon charge equivalent to the number of protons and neutrons contained within the nucleus. Following physicist Carl D. Anderson's 1932 gamma ray **③** experiment which demonstrated the existence of antimatter, scientists anticipated the discovery of negatively charged baryon antimatter throughout the universe in quantities that would precisely counterbalance

1. (A) NO CHANGE
   (B) tends—universally, as it were toward net
   (C) tends—universally as it were, toward net
   (D) tends—universally, as it were—toward net

2. Which choice best expresses the mysterious nature of the asymmetrical distribution of the baryon charge?

   (A) NO CHANGE
   (B) large mystery.
   (C) interesting and fascinating dilemma.
   (D) unparalleled opportunity for knowledge.

3. (A) NO CHANGE
   (B) experiment, which demonstrated the existence of antimatter, scientists
   (C) experiment; which demonstrated the existence of antimatter, scientists
   (D) experiment which demonstrated the existence of antimatter scientists

GO ON TO THE NEXT PAGE

the positive baryon charge of matter. That discovery, thus far, has not been **4** <u>unfound.</u>

At odds with the Standard Model of physics, collision and radiation studies of antimatter **5** <u>has consistently confounded</u> scientists' efforts to reconcile the baryon asymmetry. In fact, the known universe appears to be dominated by up to 0.01 times more matter than antimatter. **6** <u>Since this is such an influential quantity,</u> such a discrepancy could soon prove to be a silver bullet for both the standard model and general relativity, whose tenets are entrenched in our understanding of everything from the interaction of subatomic particles **7** <u>to the big bang theory of cosmology.</u>

Physicists at UBC and TRIUMF have proposed scenarios in which the baryon asymmetry is resolved through the antimatter potentially extant in the dark matter regions of space. Dark matter— **8** <u>unobserved material inferred to exist by its quantifiable gravitational effect on visible galaxies</u>—is estimated to comprise roughly

4. Which choice would conclude the paragraph most consistently with the information in the passage as a whole?

(A) NO CHANGE
(B) surprising.
(C) forthcoming.
(D) acknowledged.

5. (A) NO CHANGE
(B) have consistently confided
(C) had consistently confided
(D) have consistently confounded

6. Which choice would provide the most logical connection between the previous sentence and the current sentence?

(A) NO CHANGE
(B) Though it may initially seem insignificant,
(C) Given the paucity of scientific consensus,
(D) Assuming that scientists are willing to disregard their instrumentation,

7. (A) NO CHANGE
(B) and the Big Bang theory of cosmology.
(C) and the cosmological theoretical foundations of the Big Bang.
(D) but the Big Bang theory of cosmology in contrast.

8. Should the underlined portion of the sentence be deleted, with the punctuation adjusted accordingly?

(A) Yes, because it digresses from the primary focus of the paragraph.
(B) Yes, because it is an illogical transition between the beginning and end of the sentence.
(C) No, because without this, the passage would contain no clarification about the amount of dark matter in the universe.
(D) No, because it clarifies a specialized term for nonscientist readers.

GO ON TO THE NEXT PAGE

23% of the universe by density. Visible atoms, **9** meanwhile, constitute less than 5%. The UBC and TRIUMF theories are hampered, however, by the inherent difficulties of studying the composition of dark matter. Currently, the most promising methods involve searching the sky for the spontaneous decay of protons, which—rarely, it must be acknowledged—may signify an atom's collision with a negative baryon dark matter particle.

Meanwhile, a research team at Fermilab known as the DZero Collaboration recently announced observations of matter-antimatter asymmetries on a scale never seen before. Prior to the DZero study, baryon asymmetry and similar CP violations **10** has been observed in laboratory settings only in much smaller—and thus, less helpful—orders of magnitude. This more substantial muon-antimuon asymmetry constitutes the first opportunity for the physicists to study a recurring anomaly of both charge conjugation and parity inversion in a controlled environment. The findings at Fermilab are at once unsettling in that they will soon necessitate a considerable reforming of our understanding of particle physics **11** but titillating in that they may well lead to a more sophisticated and penetrating understanding not only of particle asymmetry but of the nature and origin of the universe itself.

9. (A) NO CHANGE
    (B) as a result,
    (C) due to this fact,
    (D) precisely,

10. (A) NO CHANGE
    (B) have been observed
    (C) had been observed
    (D) is being observed

11. (A) NO CHANGE
    (B) and
    (C) moreover
    (D) for

Questions 12–22 are based on the following passage.

Glassmaking

Have **⑫** you ever noticed something strange about the glass in the windows of old buildings? Look closely, and you'll see that their surfaces, though smooth, have easily discernible inconsistencies in width, especially near the edges. As you look through the glass, you'll see that, like a correctional lens, these imperfections distort the images that pass through them. **⑬** Well into the 19th century, glass windows were often made using a technique called "glassblowing." Glassblowing is a very ancient craft, the earliest known instances **⑭** in which date back to more than 5,000 years ago in Egypt and Eastern Mesopotamia.

[1] Though a skilled glassblower can create remarkable (and almost perfectly symmetrical) items like vases, cups, and globes, the process of making a flat pane of glass can be particularly tricky. [2] **⑮** Traditionally, a bowl-shaped glob of molten glass was flattened into a disk using centrifugal force and then cut to the proper shape and size. [3] However, the viscosity of liquid glass is such that, as spinning progresses, the perimeter of the disk becomes much thicker than the center. [4] In these glass factories, glass is poured slowly into the center of a steel table and allowed to spread under the influence of gravity. [5] Panes created using this technique are usually identifiable for their bulbous centers and wavy surface **⑯** texture, additionally they are often very fragile, as the edges joining with

12. The author is considering changing the second-person "you" to the third-person "one" throughout the passage. Should the writer make this change?

(A) Yes, because it would make the essay more formal.
(B) Yes, because it would be consistent with general grammatical practices.
(C) No, because the essay would lose the sense of directly addressing the reader.
(D) No, because it would take away the primary focus of the essay on glassblowing.

13. (A) NO CHANGE
(B) Well, into the 19th century glass
(C) Well into the 19th century glass
(D) Well, into the 19th century, glass

14. (A) NO CHANGE
(B) in that
(C) for which
(D) of which

15. What is the best placement of the underlined word in its sentence?

(A) NO CHANGE
(B) before "glob"
(C) before "flattened"
(D) before "proper"

16. (A) NO CHANGE
(B) texture; additionally, they are often very fragile, as
(C) texture. Additionally they are often very fragile as
(D) texture additionally, they are often very fragile, as

GO ON TO THE NEXT PAGE

the window frame are typically narrower than the pane's body. **⑰**

Today we can produce even very large sheets of glass of nearly uniform thickness using the "float glass" process invented by Sir Alastair Pilkington in the mid-1950s. As the name implies, this technique **⑱** <u>involve floated molten glass on a bath of molten tin.</u> The atmospheric composition within a float furnace must be strictly regulated to prevent the tin from oxidizing. As glass enters the bath, its specific gravity and immiscibility with tin **⑲** <u>causes it to form</u> a continuous ribbon with perfectly smooth surfaces on both sides and an even width throughout. The glass is then gradually cooled until it can be lifted from the tin bath. Typically, its temperature at this time is around 1,100°C. The tin, meanwhile— **⑳** <u>given its relatively high atomic number</u>—remains in a fully molten state. The entire process is inexpensive, reliable, and **㉑** <u>relatively cheap</u> when compared to the laborious task of hand-spinning paned glass. However, a very close look can reveal imperfection even in this modern technique. If the glass is cooled **㉒** <u>to quickly</u>—as is sometimes the case in large-scale industrial production—the ribbon will absorb trace amounts of tin, leaving behind a faint haze on one side of the finished pane.

17. Where is the most logical placement of this sentence in the preceding paragraph?

"A reverse problem emerged in the industrial glassmaking procedures of the early 20th century."

(A) Before sentence [1]
(B) Before sentence [3]
(C) Before sentence [4]
(D) Before sentence [5]

18. (A) NO CHANGE
(B) involve floating molted glass with a bath of molted tin.
(C) involves floated molted glass on a bath of molted tin.
(D) involves floating molten glass on a bath of molten tin.

19. (A) NO CHANGE
(B) causes them to form
(C) cause them to form
(D) cause it to form

20. Which choice would best support the claim made in this sentence, given the information in the paragraph?

(A) NO CHANGE
(B) having a melting point of only 232°C
(C) with its unique molecular structure
(D) provided its atomic mass of approximately 118 units

21. The writer wants to complete this description of the process with a third phrase that will contrast this process with what follows in the sentence. What choice best accomplishes the writer's goal?

(A) NO CHANGE
(B) consistently dependable
(C) remarkably fast
(D) painstakingly challenging

22. (A) NO CHANGE
(B) too quickly
(C) to quick
(D) two quick

GO ON TO THE NEXT PAGE

Questions 23–33 are based on the following passage and supplementary material.

Electoral College

The United States is the only country in the world to use an Electoral College system to elect its chief executive. Each state has a certain number of electors based on **[23]** their number of senators and representatives. If a candidate wins the majority of the electoral votes, currently 270, **[24]** he or she wins the election. It is high time that America shifts from this undemocratic, elitist system to one in which the president is selected by a simple majority of the popular votes.

[25] Why do Americans allow a system that doesn't permit minority groups in society to have their say? Yet this is something that has happened five times in American history. John Quincy Adams, Rutherford B. Hayes, Benjamin Harrison, George W. Bush, and Donald Trump were all elected by a majority of the Electoral College while losing to another candidate in the popular vote. **[26]** The other presidential victors won both a majority of the electoral college and the most popular votes out of any of the candidates. Can you imagine voting for the student council president only to find that the winner did not actually receive the most votes? There would be outrage throughout the school.

23. (A) NO CHANGE
 (B) their numbers
 (C) its number
 (D) our number

24. (A) NO CHANGE
 (B) they win
 (C) they would have won
 (D) he or she won

25. Which choice would best introduce the paragraph?

 (A) NO CHANGE
 (B) Does it make any sense that our country has only elected male presidents with a female not even earning a major party nomination?
 (C) Why should Americans elect presidents who, in retrospect, do not measure up to our country's ideals?
 (D) How can our country call itself a democracy if it can allow someone to become president who did not win the popular vote?

26. The writer is considering deleting the underlined sentence. Should the sentence be kept or deleted?

 (A) Kept, because it specifies the mechanics of the American political process.
 (B) Kept, because it clarifies how the majority of American presidents have been elected.
 (C) Deleted, because it unnecessarily repeats implicit information from earlier in the paragraph.
 (D) Deleted, because it is not factually supported by the general claims made elsewhere in the passage.

GO ON TO THE NEXT PAGE

The Electoral College should not stay in place simply because it is something that **㉗** has been done for many years.

If the United States were to shift to a majority vote **㉘** system the way, the presidential candidates campaign for office would fundamentally change. Right now, candidates have little reason to bother campaigning in states that typically go strongly for one of the political parties. There is little logic in a Republican trying to win New York or a Democrat trying to win Texas. Instead, candidates focus their energies on **㉙** "swing states" like Florida and Ohio, which are relatively balanced along party lines. A Floridian or Ohioan will currently receive far more candidate visits and attention than a New Yorker or a Texan. **㉚** Ohio has a smaller population relative to Texas, although Ohio does have a greater population density than Texas. This would ensure that all U.S. citizens have an equal voice not just in theory but in reality.

The Electoral College served its purpose in years past when smaller states were concerned that larger states would **㉛** usurp their authority. Now that the union of states is firmly established after the

27. (A) NO CHANGE
    (B) had been done
    (C) had to be done
    (D) have been done

28. (A) NO CHANGE
    (B) system the way the presidential candidates campaign, for
    (C) system the way the presidential, candidates campaign for
    (D) system, the way the presidential candidates campaign for

29. (A) NO CHANGE
    (B) "swing states," like Florida and Ohio which
    (C) "swing states," like Florida and Ohio, which
    (D) "swing states" like Florida, and Ohio which

30. Which sentence would best strengthen the argument of the paragraph by transitioning between the previous and the following sentences?

    (A) NO CHANGE
    (B) If the Electoral College were abolished in favor of a majority vote system, candidates would have a much stronger incentive to campaign nationwide.
    (C) It is inherently unjust that candidates want to spend their time campaigning in places where they will inevitably emerge victorious while ignoring states with undecided voters.
    (D) Nationwide polls indicate that the average voters in states from high to low Electoral College representation uniformly agree that the time has come for a seismic shift in the political landscape.

31. (A) NO CHANGE
    (B) invade
    (C) touch
    (D) decline

GO ON TO THE NEXT PAGE

Civil War and after over two centuries of continuity, **32** it is time to abandon this relic of the past so that everyone in the United States has an equal voice.

33

State*	Estimated 2008 Population	Electoral votes in 2008
Alaska	686,000	3
California	36,757,000	55
Delaware	873,000	3
Ohio	11,486,000	20
Texas	24,327,000	34

*Source: *http://www.fairvote.org/assets/Uploads/npv/2008votersperelector.pdf*

32. Which choice would best reassert the fundamental claim of the passage?

(A) NO CHANGE
(B) our country needs to look with optimism rather than pessimism toward the future.
(C) we must look past our history, acknowledge our mistakes, and move to a more enlightened tomorrow.
(D) the time has come for justice for all peoples of the United States to become not just a dream but a reality.

33. Based on the argument in the passage as a whole and the information in the table, citizens in which state would have the greatest disincentive to abolish the Electoral College?

(A) Alaska
(B) California
(C) Delaware
(D) Ohio

GO ON TO THE NEXT PAGE

Questions 34–44 are based on the following passage.

The Lay of Hildebrand

Most English speakers are at least partially familiar with *Beowulf*, one of the oldest known examples of Anglo-Saxon literature. The poem's renown is bolstered **34** not only by its importance to the medieval epic form with also by its contribution to the evolution of the English language. Some controversy surrounds the exact age of the surviving manuscript, but most scholars place it between 900 and 1100 C.E. But for all its fame, it is somewhat surprising that, by comparison, another poem of equal age and perhaps even greater linguistic import is virtually unknown to the English-speaking world. **35**

An alliterative heroic verse like *Beowulf*, "The Lay of Hildebrand" is a genuine puzzle of medieval poetry, and **36** researchers still find the exact meaning of the poem to be quite a mystery. The "Lay" consists of a mere sixty-eight lines, written on two pages of parchment that were preserved in the first and last leaves of a theological codex. Although the manuscript may but slightly predate *Beowulf*, the narrative itself is almost **37** certainly the most ancient, and its form strongly retains and reflects the form of the early Saxonic oral tradition.

34. (A) NO CHANGE
    (B) not only by its importance to the medieval epic form but also
    (C) not only by its importance to the medieval epic form and also
    (D) not only by its importance to the medieval epic form since also

35. Suppose the author is going to write an essay discussing the poem *Beowulf*. Based on the information in this passage, what would most likely be the tone of the *Beowulf* essay?

    (A) Positive and appreciative
    (B) Dismissive and skeptical
    (C) Dogmatic and firm
    (D) Neutral and disinterested

36. Which choice would best support the claim in the first part of this sentence?

    (A) NO CHANGE
    (B) has striking similarities to the poem *Beowulf* because it repeats similar sounds at the beginnings of words.
    (C) scholarship has probably not revealed half of its significance with respect to the Germanic origins of English.
    (D) scholars are on a continual quest to decipher the symbolism of the poem, much like past researchers decoded the Rosetta Stone.

37. (A) NO CHANGE
    (B) certain to be the most ancient of the two,
    (C) certainly the ancient,
    (D) certainly the more ancient,

GO ON TO THE NEXT PAGE

[1] Penned together in Carolingian minuscule by two separate scribes, it consists of a bizarre blend of Old High German and Old Saxon grammar and vocabulary. [2] (Incidentally, the "Lay" is also the oldest extant Germanic poem.) [3] Theories aimed at resolving this mystery have ranged from **38** its dismissal as a poorly wrought translation to the insinuation that it is a window into a critical point of transition at which English was beginning to emerge from German. **39**

Whatever the case may be, even a superficial study of the text is a truly rewarding experience for any enthusiast of **40** neither English or German literature and language. It tells a story every bit as harrowing as *Beowulf*, and, to some minds, more **41** poetic, Hildebrand, a German long cast out from his kingdom, returns home in the service of an Asian army to overthrow his enemy. Unknowingly, he is **42** welcomed into a duel with the opposing army's champion, his only son. Although he learns of the irony prior to combat, he cannot convince his son of his identity and is forced to fight.

38. Which choice would provide the most sensible contrast with the latter part of the sentence?

(A) NO CHANGE
(B) the realization of its fundamental role in literary history
(C) its unequivocal demonstration as an outright forgery
(D) the presence of English and German linguistic roots

39. Where is the most logical placement of this sentence in the previous paragraph?

"From a linguistic standpoint, the 'Lay' is endlessly fascinating."

(A) Before sentence [1]
(B) Before sentence [2]
(C) Before sentence [3]
(D) After sentence [3]

40. (A) NO CHANGE
(B) neither English nor German
(C) either English nor German
(D) either English or German

41. (A) NO CHANGE
(B) poetic; Hildebrand a
(C) poetic; Hildebrand, a
(D) poetic Hildebrand, a

42. (A) NO CHANGE
(B) thrust
(C) made
(D) murdered

GO ON TO THE NEXT PAGE

Regrettably, because of the second **43** scribe's large and unwieldy penmanship, the poem's last ten lines or so would not fit on the parchment leaf and are thus lost to history. We are instead left with the compellingly **44** conclusive ending (roughly translated): "The white wood rang / Grimly as they hacked each other's shields / Until the linden slats grew lean and splintered / Broken by blades. . . ."

43. (A) NO CHANGE
    (B) scribe's large and unwieldy penmanship, the poems
    (C) scribes large and unwieldy penmanship the poems
    (D) scribe's large and unwieldy penmanship the poem's

44. Which word best describes the ending of the poem?
    (A) NO CHANGE
    (B) shocking
    (C) ecstatic
    (D) ambiguous

STOP

If there is still time remaining, you may review your answers.

MATH TEST (NO CALCULATOR)

25 MINUTES, 17 QUESTIONS

Directions: For questions 1–13, solve each problem and choose the best answer from the given options. Fill in the corresponding oval on your answer document. For questions 14–17, solve the problem and fill in the answer on the answer sheet grid. Please use any space in the test booklet to work out your answers.

Notes:

- You **CANNOT** use a calculator on this section.
- All variables and expressions represent real numbers unless indicated otherwise.
- All figures are drawn to scale unless indicated otherwise.
- All figures are in a plane unless indicated otherwise.
- Unless indicated otherwise, the domain of a given function is the set of all real numbers x for which the function has real values.

Radius of a circle = r
Area of a circle = πr^2
Circumference of a circle = $2\pi r$

Area of a rectangle = length × width = lw

Area of a triangle = $\frac{1}{2}$ × base × height = $\frac{1}{2} bh$

Pythagorean theorem: $a^2 + b^2 = c^2$

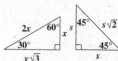

Special right triangles: 30-60-90 and 45-45-90

Volume of a box = length × width × height = lwh

Volume of a cylinder = $\pi r^2 h$

Volume of a sphere = $\frac{4}{3} \pi r^3$

Volume of a cone = $\frac{1}{3} \pi r^2 h$

Volume of a pyramid =
$\frac{1}{3}$ × length × width × height = $\frac{1}{3} lwh$

GO ON TO THE NEXT PAGE

KEY FACTS:

- **A circle has 360 degrees.**
- **There are 2π radians in a circle.**
- **There are 180 degrees in a triangle.**

1. $\dfrac{m^{\frac{5}{2}}}{m^{\frac{1}{2}}}=?$

   (A) m

   (B) m^2

   (C) m^4

   (D) $m^{\frac{1}{5}}$

2. A function never intersects the *y*-axis. Which of the following could be an equation of the function?

   (A) $y=2x-5$

   (B) $y=4$

   (C) $x=36$

   (D) $y=x$

3. A pastry chef has a recipe that calls for 3 tablespoons of vanilla extract for a cake. The chef has misplaced his tablespoon and has only a teaspoon available—there are 3 teaspoons for each tablespoon. If the chef is making a total of two cakes, how many teaspoons of vanilla extract should he use?

   (A) 3

   (B) 6

   (C) 12

   (D) 18

4. If $\dfrac{1}{4}a+\dfrac{1}{3}b=2$, what is the value of $3a+4b$?

   (A) 4

   (B) 18

   (C) 24

   (D) 36

5. $3a-3(b-a)$ can also be expressed as:

   (A) $2a-3b$

   (B) $3a^2-3ab$

   (C) $-b+a$

   (D) $3(2a-b)$

6. The following equations could all have the constant *k* equal zero and have a defined solution EXCEPT:

   (A) $kx=0$

   (B) $3=k-x$

   (C) $4k+x=7$

   (D) $\dfrac{2}{k}=x$

7. *A* and *B* are related by this system of equations:

   $$\frac{2}{3}A+\frac{3}{5}B=4$$

   $$2B=\frac{10}{9}A$$

   What is the value of *B*?

   (A) $\dfrac{1}{6}$

   (B) $\dfrac{2}{3}$

   (C) $\dfrac{20}{9}$

   (D) $\dfrac{40}{7}$

8. Which of the following equations properly expresses the functional relationship given by this expression?

   "Take an input variable and divide it by 4; then subtract 5 from the result."

   (A) $f(x)=\dfrac{x-5}{4}$

   (B) $f(x)=\dfrac{x}{4}-5$

   (C) $f(x)=5-\dfrac{x}{4}$

   (D) $f(x)=\dfrac{5-x}{4}$

GO ON TO THE NEXT PAGE

PRACTICE TEST 2

9.

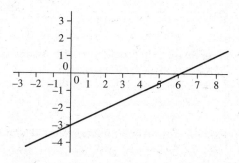

Which equation expresses the relationship between x and y shown in the graph above?

(A) $y = \frac{1}{2}x - 3$

(B) $y = 3x - 3$

(C) $y = 2x + 6$

(D) $y = -\frac{2}{3}x + 6$

10. In the equation below, F stands for gravitational force, m_1 and m_2 stand for the masses of two different objects, G is a constant, and d stands for the distance between the two objects. (Note that mass and distance must have positive values.)

$$F = \frac{G \times m_1 \times m_2}{d^2}$$

What would most minimize the gravitational force between objects 1 and 2?

(A) Minimize d

(B) Maximize m_1 and m_2

(C) Minimize $m_1 \times m_2$ and maximize d

(D) Maximize d, m_1, and m_2

11. How many real solution(s) does this system of equations have?

$$y = 2x - 5$$
$$y = 2x^2 + 4$$

(A) 0

(B) 1

(C) 2

(D) 3

12.

n	Pattern
1	1
2	$1 + 3$
3	$1 + 3 + 5$
4	$1 + 3 + 5 + 7$
5	$1 + 3 + 5 + 7 + 9$

The table above gives the values of a sum of the first n numbers, starting with 1. Which of the following is a correct statement about n?

(A) The product of n and its corresponding sum decreases as n increases.

(B) The difference between each additional value of n and the previous value of n is increasing exponentially.

(C) The sum of the first n odd numbers equals the square of n.

(D) The sum of the first n numbers is comprised solely of prime numbers.

13. If $-16 - 6x + x^2 = x^2 - abx - 8b$, where a and b are constants, what is the value of a?

(A) -6

(B) -2

(C) 3

(D) 5

GO ON TO THE NEXT PAGE

Grid-in Response Directions

In questions 14–17, first solve the problem, and then enter your answer on the grid provided on the answer sheet. The instructions for entering your answers follow.

- First, write your answer in the boxes at the top of the grid.
- Second, grid your answer in the columns below the boxes.
- Use the fraction bar in the first row or the decimal point in the second row to enter fractions and decimals.

Answer: $\frac{8}{15}$ Answer: 1.75   Answer: 100

Write your answer in the boxes

Grid in your answer

Either position is acceptable

- Grid only one space in each column.
- Entering the answer in the boxes is recommended as an aid in gridding but is not required.
- The machine scoring your exam can read only what you grid, so you **must grid-in your answers correctly to get credit.**
- If a question has more than one correct answer, grid-in only one of them.
- The grid does not have a minus sign; so no answer can be negative.
- A mixed number *must* be converted to an improper fraction or a decimal before it is gridded.

    Enter $1\frac{1}{4}$ as $\frac{5}{4}$ or 1.25; the machine will interpret 11/4 as $\frac{11}{4}$ and mark it wrong.

- **All decimals must be entered as accurately as possible.** Here are three acceptable ways of gridding

$$\frac{3}{11} = 0.272727\ldots$$

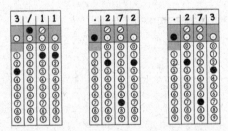

- Note that rounding to .273 is acceptable because you are using the full grid, but you would receive **no credit** for .3 or .27, because they are less accurate.

GO ON TO THE NEXT PAGE

14. Solve for x in the equation below:

$$4x - y = \frac{1}{2}x - y + 7$$

16. Consider the following system of equations with variables A and B and constant integers X and Y:

$$A + 2B = 4$$
$$XA + YB = 4X$$

By what number must the sum of X and Y be divisible in order for the two equations to have infinitely many solutions?

15. If $f(x) = 7x + 3$ and $g(x) = 2x^2$, what is the value of $f(g(1))$?

17. If a circle has the equation $(x - 4)^2 + (y - 3)^2 = 36$, what is the shortest straight-line distance from the center of the circle to the origin?

STOP

If there is still time remaining, you may review your answers.

MATH TEST (WITH CALCULATOR)

45 MINUTES, 31 QUESTIONS

Directions: For questions 1–27, solve each problem and choose the best answer from the given options. Fill in the corresponding oval on the answer sheet. For questions 28–31, solve the problem and fill in the answer on the answer sheet grid. Please use any space in the test booklet to work out your answers.

Notes:
- You CAN use a calculator on this section.
- All variables and expressions represent real numbers unless indicated otherwise.
- All figures are drawn to scale unless indicated otherwise.
- All figures are in a plane unless indicated otherwise.
- Unless indicated otherwise, the domain of a given function is the set of all real numbers x for which the function has real values.

Radius of a circle = r
Area of a circle = πr^2
Circumference of a circle = $2\pi r$

Area of a rectangle = length × width = lw

Area of a triangle = $\frac{1}{2}$ × base × height = $\frac{1}{2} bh$

Pythagorean theorem: $a^2 + b^2 = c^2$

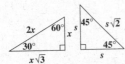

Special right triangles: 30-60-90 and 45-45-90

Volume of a box = length × width × height = lwh

Volume of a cylinder = $\pi r^2 h$

Volume of a sphere = $\frac{4}{3} \pi r^3$

Volume of a cone = $\frac{1}{3}\pi r^2 h$

Volume of a pyramid =
$\frac{1}{3}$ × length × width × height = $\frac{1}{3} lwh$

GO ON TO THE NEXT PAGE

PRACTICE TEST 2

KEY FACTS:

- A circle has 360 degrees.
- There are 2π radians in a circle.
- There are 180 degrees in a triangle.

1. Andrew's sports car has a speedometer that shows a maximum value of 180 miles per hour. Given that there are approximately 1.61 kilometers in one mile, what would be the maximum value of his speedometer (to the nearest whole number) if it were listed in kilometers per hour?

(A) $112 \, \frac{km}{hr}$

(B) $208 \, \frac{km}{hr}$

(C) $290 \, \frac{km}{hr}$

(D) $314 \, \frac{km}{hr}$

2. A recipe that will yield 6 cupcakes calls for 4 eggs, 3 cups of flour, and 6 cups of sugar. If someone wishes to make 15 cupcakes, how many cups of flour should he or she use?

(A) 6
(B) 7.5
(C) 12.5
(D) 13

Questions 3–4 refer to the following information and graph.

The Asian carp has experienced a rapid growth by displacing other fish in the Mississippi River. A researcher gathered three yearly samples from a 500-meter length of the Upper Mississippi River to determine the population trend of the fish over a decade.

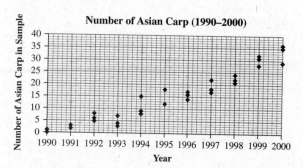

3. What is the approximate slope of the best-fit line of the data in the graph, expressed as $\frac{\text{change in carp}}{\text{change in year}}$?

(A) 3.3
(B) 4.8
(C) 5.7
(D) 7.6

4. If the number of carp continues to grow at the same rate, what value comes closest to the likely number of carp in the sample in the year 2015?

(A) 52
(B) 83
(C) 129
(D) 172

GO ON TO THE NEXT PAGE

5. Solve for x in the equation below:

$$7 + 2(x-3) = -3(x+1) - 4$$

(A) $-\dfrac{8}{5}$

(B) -1

(C) $\dfrac{3}{8}$

(D) 3

6. $(x^2 + 3x^2)^3 = ?$

(A) $3x^{12x}$

(B) $27x^5$

(C) $28x^6$

(D) $64x^6$

7. $4x^n + x^{4n} =$

(A) $5x^{5n}$

(B) $x^n(4 + x^{3n})$

(C) $5x^{4n^2}$

(D) $4x^n(1 + x^{3n})$

Questions 8–10 refer to the following information and graph.

The following questions refer to the information in the table below. A company has four different stores at four different locations throughout a large city. The company gathered data on the initial prices, sale prices, and respective quantities sold of a particular item.

Store	Price Before Sale	Quantity Sold Before Sale	Sale Price	Quantity Sold During Sale
Store A	$12.50	350	$11.00	400
Store B	$13.25	260	$10.00	520
Store C	$11.75	550	$9.50	625
Store D	$14.00	220	$10.25	460

8. Look at how many of the particular item Stores A and B sold at the presale price. What is the arithmetic mean of this set of values to the nearest tenth?

(A) 8.1

(B) 9.7

(C) 10.5

(D) 12.8

9. If a line were graphed using the quantity sold in Store D as the x-value and the price from Store D as the y-value, what would be closest to the y-intercept of the line?

(A) 12.2

(B) 14.4

(C) 17.4

(D) 20.8

10. Which of the following would be the most helpful piece of information to have about the data collected for the table in order to ensure comprehensive and accurate results?

(A) Prices at other retailers, such as restaurants

(B) A calculation of what the prices would be with twice as large a sale

(C) A survey of store managers about employee motivation

(D) If sales tax is included in the prices

11. If n represents m percent of x, how could the value of n be calculated?

(A) $n = \dfrac{mx}{100}$

(B) $n = 0.1mx$

(C) $n = \dfrac{100}{mx}$

(D) $n = 100mx$

GO ON TO THE NEXT PAGE

12. Bob deposits x dollars into his savings account on January 1, 2015, and the account grows at a constant annual rate of 3%, compounded annually. Assuming that Bob makes no deposits or withdrawals and that there are no account fees or other charges, what will be the amount of dollars in his account on January 1, 2017?

    (A) $0.06x$
    (B) $1.06x$
    (C) $1.0609x$
    (D) $1.092727x$

13. What are the possible values of b in the system of equations below?

$$b = 2a + 1$$
$$b + 2 = a^2$$

    (A) $-3, -7$
    (B) $-1, 7$
    (C) $3, -1$
    (D) $3, 7$

14. $2(a - 4b)(3 + b^3) = ?$

    (A) $2ab^3 - 24b$
    (B) $2ab + 6a - 4b^2 - 12b$
    (C) $2ab^3 + 4a - 6b^4 - 24b$
    (D) $2ab^3 + 6a - 8b^4 - 24b$

15. A librarian works at a constant pace, simultaneously shelving exactly 200 books in an hour and exactly 20 movies in an hour, and shelving only books and movies. If the librarian works for a total of T hours, which expression shows the total number of items (books and movies) that the librarian shelves during that time?

    (A) $220T$
    (B) $20T + 200$
    (C) $220T + 440$
    (D) $200T - 20$

Questions 16–18 refer to the following tables.

The tables below show an investor's percentage allocation in a portfolio. The first table shows the summary of investment types in the portfolio in the year 2000. The second table shows the summary of investment types in the portfolio in the year 2020.

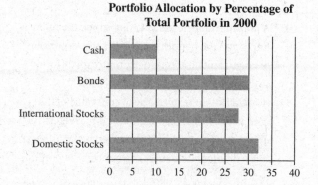

Portfolio Allocation by Percentage of Total Portfolio in 2000

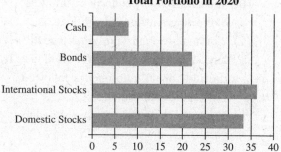

Portfolio Allocation by Percentage of Total Portfolio in 2020

16. If the total value of the investment portfolio in 2000 was $80,000 and the total value of it in 2020 was $200,000, by approximately how much did the amount invested in bonds increase from 2000 to 2020?

    (A) $8,000
    (B) $14,000
    (C) $20,000
    (D) $28,000

GO ON TO THE NEXT PAGE

17. Use the portfolio valuations from the years given in the preceding question. If the overall portfolio is growing at a linear rate, what should the value of the portfolio be in 2030?

(A) $180,000
(B) $260,000
(C) $340,000
(D) $580,000

18. A portfolio analyst wants to determine the relative impact on the performance of the stock portfolio of large-capitalization stocks, mid-capitalization stocks, and small-capitalization stocks. (Capitalization refers to the overall value of the company.) Based on the information given in the charts, how can you best characterize the impact of these different categories of stocks on the portfolio?

(A) There are more large-capitalization stocks than the other two types combined.
(B) There are roughly equivalent amounts of the different stock categories.
(C) The small-capitalization stocks are the largest percent of the portfolio, followed by the mid-capitalization stocks, followed by the large-capitalization stocks.
(D) Not enough information is provided to come to a conclusion.

19. Pam is going to watch a movie on her television at home. She is going to watch the movie as it was shown in movie theaters in its original aspect ratio of 1.85:1 length:height. Her television has an aspect ratio of 4:3 and a length of 48 inches. If the movie takes up the entire length of her television screen, how many inches of screen height, to the nearest whole inch, will NOT be used on her TV screen to show the movie?

(A) 10
(B) 16
(C) 22
(D) 44

20. If an amusement park worker measures 3 riders as being 48 inches, 56 inches, and 40 inches tall and the margin of error of each of the worker's measurements is ±2 inches, what is the possible range of the sum of the riders' actual heights in inches?

(A) $48 \leq$ total height ≤ 144
(B) $42 \leq$ total height ≤ 150
(C) $138 \leq$ total height ≤ 150
(D) $158 \leq$ total height ≤ 180

21. Given that x and n are numbers greater than 1, which of the following expressions would have the greatest overall increase in y values between x values from 2 to 100?

(A) $y = nx + 3$
(B) $y = -nx + 3$
(C) $y = x^n + 3$
(D) $y = x^{-n} + 3$

22. A new spaceship tourism company wishes to design a spacecraft that will allow its passengers to reenter Earth's atmosphere comfortably without losing consciousness. The physicians with whom the company consulted advised the company employees that healthy humans can survive up to $9g$ of force and lose consciousness at $5g$ of force. Which expression gives the range of g-force values, g, that the company's engineers should ensure the spacecraft can provide during reentry?

(A) $g < 5$
(B) $g > 5$
(C) $5 < g < 9$
(D) $g > 9$

GO ON TO THE NEXT PAGE

PRACTICE TEST 2

23. College football programs are permitted to pay a maximum of 1 head coach, 9 assistant coaches, and 2 graduate assistant coaches. If ABC University wishes to have at least 1 coach for every 4 players, which of the following systems of inequalities expresses the total number of coaches, C, and total number of players, P, possible?

(A) $C = 12$ and $P \leq 4C$
(B) $C \leq 12$ and $P \leq 4C$
(C) $C \leq 10$ and $P \leq 3C$
(D) $C = 1$ and $P \leq 4$

24. The final velocity of a given object is given by the following formula:

Final velocity =
Initial velocity + Acceleration × Time

If a ball has an initial velocity of $4\,\dfrac{m}{s}$ and a constant acceleration of $6\,\dfrac{m}{s^2}$ which inequality shows the range of times, T, that will cause the final velocity to have a value of at least $22\,\dfrac{m}{s}$?

(A) $T \geq 3$ seconds
(B) $T \geq 8$ seconds
(C) 3 seconds $\leq T \leq 5$ seconds
(D) 6 seconds $\leq T \leq 22$ seconds

25. The approximate relationship between Kelvin (K) and degrees Celsius (C) is given by this equation:

$$K = 273 + C$$

The freezing point of water is 0 degrees Celsius, and the boiling point of water is 100 degrees Celsius. What are the approximate freezing and boiling points of water in Kelvin?

(A) Freezing: 0; boiling: 100
(B) Freezing: −273; boiling: −173
(C) Freezing: 273; boiling: 373
(D) Freezing: 473; boiling: 573

26. A particular black hole has a density of $1.0 \times 10^6\,\dfrac{kg}{m^3}$. A physicist is conducting a thought experiment in which she would like to approximate how much she would weigh if she had the density of a black hole rather than her current weight of 150 pounds, assuming her volume remained the same. Given that her overall body density is approximately $990\,\dfrac{kg}{m^3}$ and that there are approximately 2.2 pounds in a kilogram, approximately how many pounds would she weigh in her thought experiment?

(A) 2,178
(B) 151,500
(C) 990,000,000
(D) 2,178,000,000

27. John is taking a rowboat both up and down a 16 km length of a river. A constant current of $1\,\dfrac{km}{hr}$ makes his trip downstream faster than his trip upstream since he is moving with the current downstream and fighting against the current when traveling upstream. If a round-trip journey took him a total of 4 hours and if he rowed at a constant pace the whole time, what is the rate in $\dfrac{km}{hr}$, to the nearest tenth, at which John is rowing independent of the current?

(A) 7.3
(B) 8.1
(C) 8.9
(D) 9.7

GO ON TO THE NEXT PAGE

PRACTICE TEST 2

Grid-in Response Directions

In questions 28–31, first solve the problem, and then enter your answer on the grid provided on the answer sheet. The instructions for entering your answers follow.

- First, write your answer in the boxes at the top of the grid.
- Second, grid your answer in the columns below the boxes.
- Use the fraction bar in the first row or the decimal point in the second row to enter fractions and decimals.

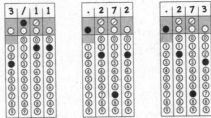

Write your answer in the boxes

Answer: $\frac{8}{15}$ Answer: 1.75   Answer: 100

Grid in your answer

Either position is acceptable

- Grid only one space in each column.
- Entering the answer in the boxes is recommended as an aid in gridding but is not required.
- The machine scoring your exam can read only what you grid, so you **must grid-in your answers correctly to get credit**.
- If a question has more than one correct answer, grid-in only one of them.
- The grid does not have a minus sign; so no answer can be negative.
- A mixed number *must* be converted to an improper fraction or a decimal before it is gridded.

  Enter $1\frac{1}{4}$ as $\frac{5}{4}$ or 1.25; the machine will interpret 11/4 as $\frac{11}{4}$ and mark it wrong.

- **All decimals must be entered as accurately as possible.** Here are three acceptable ways of gridding

$$\frac{3}{11} = 0.272727\ldots$$

- Note that rounding to .273 is acceptable because you are using the full grid, but you would receive **no credit** for .3 or .27, because they are less accurate.

GO ON TO THE NEXT PAGE

PRACTICE TEST 2

28. A high school is going to have its prom and is evaluating two different D.J.s—D.J. A and D.J. B. The first one, D.J. A, has a $300 rental fee and charges $150 per hour. The second one, D.J. B, has a $200 rental fee and charges $175 per hour. After how many hours of performing will the cost for both D.J.s be the same?

29. Marcus completely filled his truck's 14-gallon gas tank. The computer at the gas pump indicates that Marcus spent $34 in this transaction; the price per gallon was $3. How many gallons of gas did Marcus have in his tank before he started to fill it?

30. A lamp business uses the following equations to express supply and demand as a function of price and quantity for its lamps:

Supply: Price = 30 − Quantity

Demand: Price = 10 + 3 × Quantity

How many lamps does the business need to sell in order for the supply of lamps to equal the demand for lamps exactly, i.e., for the supply and demand to be at equilibrium?

31. What is the value of the smallest side in a right triangle with a hypotenuse of 8 and angles of 30 and 60 degrees?

STOP

If there is still time remaining, you may review your answers.

ANSWER KEY
Practice Test 2

Reading Test

1.	A	13.	D	25.	C	37.	A
2.	C	14.	A	26.	D	38.	A
3.	A	15.	D	27.	A	39.	C
4.	A	16.	C	28.	C	40.	D
5.	D	17.	C	29.	B	41.	B
6.	B	18.	B	30.	D	42.	C
7.	D	19.	C	31.	C	43.	B
8.	B	20.	C	32.	C	44.	A
9.	B	21.	C	33.	D	45.	C
10.	C	22.	B	34.	C	46.	C
11.	C	23.	C	35.	A	47.	A
12.	A	24.	D	36.	C		

Writing and Language Test

1.	D	12.	C	23.	C	34.	B
2.	A	13.	A	24.	A	35.	A
3.	B	14.	D	25.	D	36.	C
4.	C	15.	A	26.	C	37.	D
5.	D	16.	B	27.	A	38.	A
6.	B	17.	C	28.	D	39.	A
7.	A	18.	D	29.	C	40.	D
8.	D	19.	D	30.	B	41.	C
9.	A	20.	B	31.	A	42.	B
10.	C	21.	C	32.	A	43.	A
11.	B	22.	B	33.	A	44.	D

Math Test (No Calculator)

1.	B	6.	D	11.	A	16.	3
2.	C	7.	C	12.	C	17.	5
3.	D	8.	B	13.	C		
4.	C	9.	A	14.	2		
5.	D	10.	C	15.	17		

ANSWER KEY
Practice Test 2

Math Test (With Calculator)

1. **C**	9. **C**	17. **B**	25. **C**
2. **B**	10. **D**	18. **D**	26. **B**
3. **A**	11. **A**	19. **A**	27. **B**
4. **B**	12. **C**	20. **C**	28. **4**
5. **A**	13. **B**	21. **C**	29. **2.66 or**
6. **D**	14. **D**	22. **A**	**2.67**
7. **B**	15. **A**	23. **B**	30. **5**
8. **D**	16. **C**	24. **A**	31. **4**

Note: This table represents an estimate of how many questions you will need to answer correctly to achieve a certain score on the PSAT.

PSAT Section Score	PSAT Math (48 Total Questions)	PSAT Evidence-Based Reading and Writing (91 Total Questions)	PSAT Section Score
760	48	91	760
710	45	86	710
660	43	79	660
610	38	71	610
560	34	63	560
510	28	53	510
460	24	43	460
410	18	30	410
360	13	19	360
310	8	12	310
260	4	6	260
210	2	3	210
160	0	0	160

ANSWER EXPLANATIONS

Reading Test

1. **(A)** The passage uses the word "I" throughout, making the point of view first person since the passage is told from the viewpoint of the narrator. A third-person perspective would be from a more neutral, objective viewpoint. The narrator is certainly not objective, given his extreme focus on his own pain and suffering. The narrator is also not omniscient, given his lack of insight into the feelings and thoughts of others.

2. **(C)** The narrator focuses melodramatically on his own sickness and mortality throughout the passage. He is so dramatic that Hollingsworth, his purported friend, grows weary of listening to his many protests—see lines 25–28 in particular for this. The narrator's negativity contradicts being "calmly resolute" or "patiently optimistic," and his negativity is far too mild to be considered "completely morbid."

3. **(A)** Lines 25–28 give direct evidence to support the idea that the narrator is overly dramatic. The other options provide no such evidence.

4. **(A)** The sentence refers to drawing breaths, so "inhale" is the best choice. Breathing is not directly associated with provoking, inferring, or sketching.

5. **(D)** "Irony" means to have something be the opposite of what one would expect. The fact that Coverdale has prepared so much for death yet now finds himself recovering from his illness presents a situational irony. The statement is neither metaphor nor personification, because the situation is clearly expressed. The figure of speech is not an understatement, because if anything, Coverdale has a consistent tendency toward overstatement.

6. **(B)** The introduction to the passage states that Coverdale has moved to a "utopian communal farm." It is this commune to which the word "Community" refers. No evidence is provided in the passage that writers of the 1800s consistently wrote in this manner, as listed in choice (A). Choice (C) is incorrect because nothing indicates that the narrator is interested in larger urban developments. In fact, he has chosen to move to a farming community. Finally, the passage does not mention any other cities (municipalities), making choice (D) incorrect.

7. **(D)** Lines 72–76 indicate that Coverdale believes that Zenobia pursued literature because there was a lack of a "fitter avenue" and that her literary works did not do justice to her intellect. So her intellectual pursuit of literature was primarily a result of a lack of opportunities. Choices (A) and (B) both describe characteristics that would apply to her mindset, but these characteristics would not hold her back. Although Zenobia has passion and zeal for her beliefs, no evidence is provided to indicate that her zeal is religious in nature. Even if it were, religious zeal would not hold her back from her goals.

8. **(B)** Lines 74–76 best illustrate that a scarcity of opportunities led Zenobia to her primary intellectual pursuit of literature. Choice (A) refers to Zenobia's helpfulness toward the narrator. Choice (C) talks about her strength of mind. Choice (D) mentions her passion for reform.

9. **(B)** Rather than being intensely focused on a single intellectual area, Zenobia has a mind "full of weeds" that would cause her to have more diverse thoughts. Choice (A) is a valid definition of "severe" but does not describe this situation. Choices (C) and (D) are not valid definitions of "severe."

10. **(C)** Zenobia is most interested in the "relation between the sexes" when it comes to social reform. So she is most interested in reforming antiquated gender roles. No evidence is given that her primary reform objective is to change universities that are hostile toward foreigners as listed in choice (A), problems with economic fairness as described in choice (B), or destruction of the environment as shown in choice (D).

11. **(C)** The quote, "I am a citizen of Berlin," most directly demonstrates that Kennedy is expressing that the United States is standing shoulder-to-shoulder with its allies in Germany, making this a clear demonstration of solidarity. The other options fail to capture the primary purpose of the passage.

12. **(A)** Kennedy is recognizing the presence of General Claw with him, making "joined by" the correct option. There is no evidence to support the ideas that Kennedy and Clay were in a business venture, as in choice (B), or that Clay ordered him to come there, as in choice (C). Choice (D), "At the request of," is not an acceptable rephrasing of "in the company of."

13. **(D)** The repetition of the sentence, "Let them come to Berlin," shows that Kennedy believes that the common solution to different misconceptions about Berlin is for people to actually come there and see it for themselves. Choice (A) is incorrect because the objections addressed are not primarily historical. Choice (B) is incorrect because the commentary is on the present, not the future. Choice (C) is incorrect because Kennedy is not encouraging such an immigration—just that Berliners observe what is happening.

14. **(A)** Lines 42–45 give direct evidence in support of this when Kennedy states, "I know of no town, no city, that has been besieged for 18 years that still lives with the vitality and the force, and the hope and the determination of the city of West Berlin." He admires them for their exceptionality at being determined and resolute in the face of adversity. The other choices are not supported by evidence in the passage.

15. **(D)** Lines 42–45 best support the idea that Kennedy admires the people of West Berlin for their excellent resolve. The other line selections do not provide direct evidence of this idea.

16. **(C)** Lines 49–54 provide evidence to support this idea, focusing on how families have been divided because of the division of the city and that the people wish to be joined together again. Choice (A) is incorrect because the people of these cities have already had initial interactions since many of them are family. Choice (B) is incorrect because the people want to visit family, not military allies. Choice (D) is incorrect because there is no evidence to support that they wish to be like an ancient empire.

17. **(C)** Lines 49–54 give evidence to support the idea that Berliners wish to be reunited. The other selections do not provide such support.

18. **(B)** Kennedy's speech is coming to an end, so "close" most closely means "finish" in this context. The other options provide alternative meanings of "close" that do not apply in this sentence.

19. **(C)** The second sentence of this paragraph suggests that once all people become free, then there will be peace throughout the world. This assumes that free people will seek to be peaceful—it is possible that free people may want to seek out conflict with one another. Choice (A) is directly suggested, choice (B) is not mentioned, and choice (C) makes too great a leap as far as what Kennedy thinks the impact of Berliners will be in the future.

20. **(C)** The passage as a whole progresses chronologically. It discusses the origins of blackletter typeface centuries ago. It then elaborates on the evolution of this typeface throughout the centuries until the modern day, giving readers a basic education about blackletter. The other choices are all too narrow in their emphasis.

21. **(C)** In this case, the word "labyrinthine" is used to describe highly ornate works, like ornamental books and glosses. These works would be very complex by nature. Choices (A) and (B) are too literal, and choice (D) is too negative.

22. **(B)** This can be seen in the paragraph from lines 52–59. The author discusses both the intricacy and readability of Fraktur, making this typeface a balance of elegance and functionalism. The other options give accurate descriptions of Fraktur but do not clearly mention advantages of this form of blackletter.

23. **(C)** These lines best support the claim that Fraktur lettering balanced elegance with functionalism. The other choices establish that Fraktur was widespread but do not explain what advantages caused it to have this popularity.

24. **(D)** Lines 60–65 refer to the modeling of the letterforms on ancient Roman scripts. So it is highly plausible that the classicists of the 18th century wished to connect to the culture of ancient Rome. Although the other options may be true aspects of this lettering, they do not relate to its classical origins.

25. **(C)** Lines 60–65 give direct evidence in support of the idea that classicists preferred Antiqua over blackletter because it associated the classicist movement with the learning of ancient Rome and the classical period. The other options are not directly related to the answer to the previous question.

26. **(D)** The last paragraph begins by citing the "lethal blow" that was dealt to blackletter as a result of the *Schrifterlass* decree, meaning that the wide use of blackletter came to an end. Choice (A) is too vague and broad. Choice (B) is not supported by the text since blackletter previously enjoyed widespread popularity. Choice (C) is incorrect because the Nazi approach to this ban is more absurdly nonsensical than hypocritical since what these letters had to do with Judaism is unclear.

27. **(A)** Lines 5–11 refer to the insular scripts as being highly "variable." This means that people handwrote the scripts in a variety of ways, making them difficult to read. Choice (B) is incorrect since only the Carolingian minuscule is mentioned as cumbersome. Choice (C) is incorrect, because the passage does not support the notion that these scripts were limited to England and Ireland. Choice (D) is incorrect because the passage does not support that these scripts were used only in monasteries.

28. **(C)** "Final" makes the most sense here. The historical events described in this paragraph did not completely eliminate blackletter but did make its use much more of a rarity. Since "lethal" is describing the demise of a language and not a living thing, saying that the word means "mortal," "deadly," or "venomous" makes no sense.

29. **(B)** The author argues in these lines that intentional cultivation of nonnative plants is usually a good thing. A global analysis demonstrating that nonnative plants are typically harmful when introduced would therefore undermine—weaken—this argument. Choice (A) is not correct because knowing that most invasive plants were introduced by accident would not give information about their relative benefit. Choice (C) is incorrect because

it, too, would not give any facts about how harmful the plants were to their surroundings. Choice (D) is not correct because this would be too small a sample size to make such a sweeping claim.

30. **(D)** A lack of natural predators best accounts for why an introduced animal species becomes invasive. If no other animals eat it, the introduced species will have few obstacles to its spread. Choice (A) draws an incorrect definition based on the word "roots." Choice (B) incorrectly labels the environments as inhospitable. Choice (C) is the opposite of what would help animals flourish since the context says "lack of natural predation."

31. **(C)** The author immediately contradicts this statement in the following sentence. The general purpose of placing the sentence from lines 52–56 in the passage is to give a general summary of what many people think about this issue and then to use the entire passage to show why most people are incorrect about this topic. Choice (A) is incorrect because this text only indirectly establishes the author's authority. Choice (B) is not right because the thesis of the passage comes in the sentence that follows. Choice (D) is incorrect because ecologists and biologists are in agreement according to this sentence.

32. **(C)** Lines 66–73 describe a "mutualist" relationship, in which the species help one another. This is most similar to the oxpecker birds eating the predatory insects off the backs of zebras. The oxpeckers are gaining food, and the zebras are being cleaned. Choices (A) and (D) involve relationships beneficial to only one of the species. Choice (B) does not establish a reciprocal relationship with another species.

33. **(D)** "Discriminating" typically has a negative connotation that people associate with prejudice. However, in this context, the author is asserting that we need to be more careful and "selective" when picking which invasive plants to keep and which ones to exterminate. Choices (A) and (B) can apply to discriminating in other contexts. Choice (C) applies only to the quality of art, food, music, and so on.

34. **(C)** The first passage discusses invasive plants in general, while the second passage focuses much more in depth on how getting rid of invasive plants can do more harm than good to native animal species. Choice (A) is incorrect because neither passage is clearly positive or negative. Choice (B) is incorrect because Passage 1 is more neutral than pessimistic. Choice (D) is also incorrect because Passage 1 is more analytical than argumentative.

35. **(A)** Both agree that invasive plants can be potentially helpful. This can be seen in lines 22–24 of Passage 1 in which the author states that these plants have been spread for a wide range of "beneficial uses." In lines 79–84 of Passage 2, the author states that the invasive plants have caused a long-term change for the better. Neither author would agree with choice (B). Both agree that honeysuckle is a type of invasive plant, but neither asserts it is the most well-known variety, making choice (C) incorrect. Choice (D) is also incorrect since Passage 2 does not mention any potential benefits from government intervention.

36. **(C)** Lines 11–13 of Passage 1 indicate that some nonnative plants are introduced to new environments through accidental human contact. With an increase in human visitation, the Galapagos Islands will likely experience more accidental introduction of plants. Choice (A) is incorrect because the information does not suggest that an increase in human interaction leads to an overall improvement in conservation efforts. Although Passage 1 mentions using funding to fight the negative consequences of invasive plants,

information is not provided to support the notion that an increase in tourism will result in enough money to outweigh the negative consequences of increased human activity. Therefore, choice (B) is incorrect. Choice (D) is not right because the information does not support the notion that humans will consistently seek to introduce invasive species purposefully into new environments.

37. **(A)** Lines 8–13 best support the idea that an increase in human contact will lead to more accidental introduction of plant species. Choice (B) focuses on the benefits of intentionally introducing invasive plants. Choice (C) mentions the difficulty in predicting the consequences of plant introduction. Choice (D) mentions only one type of invasive plant.

38. **(A)** The last two paragraphs focus on this evolution. Color photography went from being "unwieldy" and unable to capture moving objects well to having instantaneous Polaroid photos. Choice (B) describes the opposite of the development of photography since over time, color photography became an object of widespread interest. While the creation of Kodachrome was made by musicians, it is too much of a stretch to say that photography in general became the focus of musicians. Therefore, choice (C) is not correct. Choice (D) is incorrect since the primary emphasis of the passage is on the shift in the size and usefulness of camera technology.

39. **(C)** An anecdote is a short and interesting story about something. The author uses scientific and historical anecdotes, sharing stories about the early pioneers of color photography up to modern Kodak researchers. Very little in the passage analyzes the thoughts of people (psychological analysis) as described in choice (A). Choice (B) is incorrect since chemical and physical description is a minor part of the essay. Choice (D) is incorrect since the essay focuses on the development of technology, not on the comparison of cultures.

40. **(D)** Line 14 mentions the scientists' "fidelity" (loyalty) to the then-popular daguerreotype method, which impeded the progress of Hill and Becquerel. Choice (A) is incorrect since the two had solid backgrounds in science. Choice (B) is incorrect since the passage does not mention that cultural bias played any role. Choice (C) is incorrect because the scientists' understanding of past successes likely made them less likely to think for themselves.

41. **(B)** Lines 11–15 provide the best evidence that Hill and Becquerel were hindered in their research by their loyalty to a widespread approach. Choice (A) merely states that the scientists were leaders in their field. Choice (C) refers to inferior methods of the past. Choice (D) refers to Maxwell, who came after Hill and Becquerel.

42. **(C)** Maxwell used black-and-white transparencies taken through red, blue, and green filters to show a combined image that had colors. The image cannot be characterized as "crafted" since it is a photograph, not a humanmade painting or craft. Therefore, choice (A) is incorrect. Although the image is certainly visual and may be of quality, as listed in choices (B) and (D), the primary meaning conveyed is that the image is a combined whole.

43. **(B)** "Unwieldy" most nearly means "cumbersome" (difficult to manipulate) in this context. The color cameras of the time are described as having multiple prisms and mirrors to make an image, which would be far from user friendly. Although the cameras could be "unsightly" or "expensive," as listed in choices (A) and (C), the description that follows focuses on the complexity of the cameras. Choice (D), "precise," is incorrect because the cameras had not reached a technological level where they could reasonably be labeled as such.

44. **(A)** The third paragraph reports how Hill's and Becquerel's chemistry-based approach toward color photography was ultimately unsuccessful. It also reports that Maxwell was able to make progress by focusing on how the human eye—a biological organ—perceives colors. The other options do not accurately describe this transition.

45. **(C)** Lines 96–99 state that the major shortcoming of Miethe's design was its inability to photograph moving objects properly because it needed a long exposure time. If an object was relatively stable, as objects would likely be on a freezing, windless day, Miethe's design would be more successful. Choices (A) and (B) do not work due to the presence of wind. Choice (D) is incorrect because frozen water could be more clearly photographed than moving water.

46. **(C)** Lines 47–52 state that humans are able to see wavelengths between 400 and 700 nanometers. A nanometer is 1×10^{-9} meters. So the visible wavelengths fall between the ultraviolet and infrared wavelengths.

47. **(A)** The last paragraph describes Mannes and Godowsky as casual tinkerers (as opposed to dedicated researchers) working "recreationally" and who had backgrounds in music rather than science. Thus, their discovery can best be described as "serendipitous," i.e., a fortunate finding by chance. The other options all focus on particular fields of study, which was not the case for Mannes and Godowsky with respect to their photographic research.

Writing and Language Test

1. **(D)** This is the only option that sets off the parenthetical phrase with the same sort of punctuation on either side, i.e., a dash. Commas can also set up parenthetical phrases, but a comma must be placed both before and after the phrase.

2. **(A)** By calling it a "singular" puzzle, the author expresses the remarkable nature of this puzzle. The word "tantalizing" indicates that this puzzle is extremely interesting yet challenging to solve. The other options do not express this same intensity.

3. **(B)** The sentence can still function as a complete sentence without the phrase "which demonstrated the existence of antimatter." So the phrase should be surrounded by commas to set it aside. Choice (A) does not have a necessary pause before the phrase. Choice (C) does not have the necessary completed sentence before the semicolon. Choice (D) has no pauses whatsoever.

4. **(C)** The passage as a whole indicates that a clear answer to this scientific dilemma has not been found nor is an answer expected in the near future. Hence, "forthcoming" makes the most sense. "Unfound" and "surprising" are the opposite of what is needed. "Acknowledged" indicates the solution may have been discovered but not yet recognized.

5. **(D)** The subject of this sentence is "studies," which is plural and requires the word "have." Additionally, this is something that has gone on from the past up to the present day. So using "have confounded" is logical. The word "confounded" means "confused," while the word "confided" means "shared a secret."

6. **(B)** The numerical amount of 0.01 times does not initially seem like a very large number, so choice (B) gives a helpful introductory connection in the current sentence. Choice (A) states that 0.01 is a larger quantity than it actually is. Choice (C) is incorrect because "paucity," which means "a lack of," contradicts the well-founded scientific observations mentioned. Choice (D) involves scientists ignoring their own observations.

7. **(A)** A phrase that starts with "from . . ." can be appropriately joined with "to . . . ." Joining "from . . ." with an "and" or with a "but" does not work in this context.

8. **(D)** Unless someone has studied physics, it is unlikely that he or she will be familiar with the term "dark matter." Thus, providing a scientific definition for the term before proceeding further is helpful. Choice (C) is incorrect because this phrase does not clarify the quantity of dark matter.

9. **(A)** "Meanwhile" provides a logical contrast between the relatively large percentage of dark matter and the relatively small percentage of visible atoms. None of the other options provides a logical contrast.

10. **(C)** This is an event that takes place *prior* to another event in the past, so "had" is needed. Choices (A) and (B) are in the past perfect tense, and choice (D) is in the present progressive tense.

11. **(B)** When using the phrase "at once . . . ," one needs to use "and" to transition to the second item in the list. Why? Since these two things exist "at once," the word "and" is an appropriate way to join them to one another.

12. **(C)** Changing from "you" to "one" would be especially problematic in the first paragraph, where the author focuses on engaging the reader's interest in glassmaking. Choice (D) is incorrect because changing from "you" to "one" would in no way shift the focus away from glassblowing.

13. **(A)** "Well" is used similar to the word "far" in this context, stating that this is for a great duration of time into the 19th century. A comma is needed after "century" to separate the dependent introductory phrase from the independent clause that follows. Choices (B) and (D) break up the phrase "well into." Choice (C) has none of the necessary pauses.

14. **(D)** "Of which" is the correct idiomatic usage of a preposition with "which" in this context. The author is trying to say that "this is the earliest known example *of this*."

15. **(A)** "Traditionally" should be left where it is since it provides an overall introduction to the way glass used to be made. Choice (B) would change the meaning of "bowl-shaped glob," choice (C) would limit the "tradition" to the flattening process, and choice (D) would limit the "tradition" to the shaping and sizing of the glass.

16. **(B)** The semicolon provides a needed break between the two independent clauses. The comma after "additionally" gives an appropriate pause separating the transition from the complete sentence that follows. Choices (A) and (D) are both run-on sentences. Choice (C) lacks the necessary comma after the introductory word "Additionally."

17. **(C)** Placing the sentence before sentence [4] breaks the paragraph into two halves. The first half focuses on older glassmaking procedures. The second half focuses on later ones.

18. **(D)** "Technique" is a singular subject, so the verb should be "involves." Choice (D) also uses the correct forms of "floating" and "molten" to describe the glass—"molted" does not work as a word in this context. Choices (A) and (B) have plural verbs, and choice (C) uses "molted" instead of "molten."

19. **(D)** The compound subject of "specific gravity and immiscibility with tin" demands a plural verb, hence "cause" works. In addition, the "it" is correct since the pronoun refers to the singular "glass."

20. **(B)** The sentence is stating that tin remains a liquid in the 1,100°C bath. So a statement about tin's melting point explains why tin reacts this way. Choices (A), (C), and (D) provide irrelevant facts about tin.

21. **(C)** Doing something "remarkably fast" is the best contrast with "laborious" since "laborious" means "involving a great deal of work." Choices (A) and (B) repeat ideas already mentioned in the sentence. Choice (D) does not provide the needed contrast with the second part of the sentence.

22. **(B)** When comparing amounts and sizes of things, "too" is the correct spelling. "Two" is a number, and "to" serves to connect words.

23. **(C)** "Its" refers to each singular state taken on its own, not as part of a group. The other options do not have number agreement with the context already established.

24. **(A)** The candidate would be a singular man or woman, so "he or she" is correct. "Won" is used when there is a plural subject and the phrase is in the past tense.

25. **(D)** The paragraph goes on to explain that a candidate winning the electoral college vote but not the popular vote does NOT occur frequently but, in the eyes of the author, is still a problematic occurrence. Choice (D) therefore best introduces the paragraph. Choices (A), (B), and (C) focus on political concerns but not on the ones discussed in this essay.

26. **(C)** Earlier in the paragraph, the author mentions that the winning candidate did not win the popular vote four times in U.S. history. It is reasonable to infer that the other times, the winning candidate *did* win the popular vote. Leaving this sentence in the paragraph is just wordy. Choice (D) is not correct because there is nothing in the passage that contradicts this information.

27. **(A)** The passage indicates that the Electoral College is still in place up to the present day. So "has been" is appropriate because it uses the singular past perfect tense, unlike the other options.

28. **(D)** Placing just one comma after "system" provides a break between the dependent introductory clause and the independent clause that follows. Moreover, it maintains the logic of keeping the phrase "the way the presidential candidates campaign" together as a unified whole, unlike choice (A).

29. **(C)** This choice uses commas to set off the examples of swing states. The sentence would still function as a complete sentence without this phrase, so the phrase can be set aside.

30. **(B)** The previous sentence explains that voters in swing states receive far more attention than voters in states that are more uniformly one party. Choice (B) would therefore connect to the concluding sentence that points out that a majority vote system would ensure that voters everywhere would have an equal say. Choice (A) focuses on irrelevant population density. Choice (C) describes the opposite of what occurs. Choice (D) does not provide a logical transition from the previous sentence.

31. **(A)** "Usurp" means to "seize power," usually inappropriately. This is the best word to convey the fears that the smaller states had. The larger states are not literally going to "invade." To "touch" or "decline" authority would pose no threat to the power of smaller states.

32. **(A)** The passage focuses on the need to abandon the Electoral College, which would be the "relic" mentioned in this choice, in favor of a majority vote system. Choices (B), (C), and (D) are too vague.

33. **(A)** According to the data in the table, citizens of Alaska have a greater per capita voice in the Electoral College than do citizens of the other states listed. Since Alaskan citizens have more say under the current system, they would not have a very strong incentive to abolish it.

34. **(B)** In this context, the phrase "not only . . ." should be followed by the transition "but also." No comma needs to come between these two phrases unless the phrases being compared are also complete sentences. "With," "and," and "since" are not accepted connections to "not only."

35. **(A)** The author would like "Lay" to achieve the same recognition that *Beowulf* does. The argument is not that *Beowulf* should receive less recognition than "Lay" but that "Lay" is worthy of the same sort of recognition as *Beowulf*. Thus, the author's tone would most likely be positive and appreciative. Choices (B) and (C) are too negative, and choice D is too dispassionate.

36. **(C)** This choice gives the most specific justification as to why scholars do not yet fully understand this poem. The other choices are rather vague.

37. **(D)** This option does not have unnecessary wording and also provides a needed pause before the second part of the sentence. It also provides an appropriate comparison between the two things by using the word "more." The word "most" is incorrect because it is used to compare three or more things. Choice (C) does not provide a comparison since it lacks any comparative words.

38. **(A)** This choice provides a contrast that appropriately focuses on the linguistic elements, with the possibilities ranging from something of poor quality to something of monumental significance. The other choices do not provide theories that would help explain the mystery of the origins of the "Lay."

39. **(A)** Placing this sentence at the beginning of the paragraph introduces the overall topic of the paragraph, namely what is interesting linguistically about the poem. If the sentence is not placed in this position, the paragraph would begin without a clarification of its subject.

40. **(D)** The author is arguing that a study of the text *would* be interesting to certain people. So saying "either" and its counterpart "or" makes sense.

41. **(C)** The semicolon is a softer linkage between two complete ideas than is a period. The idea after the semicolon clarifies why the "Lay" is potentially as interesting as and more poetic than *Beowulf*. The comma sets off a clarifying phrase. Choices (A) and (D) lead to run-on sentences, and choice (B) lacks a comma.

42. **(B)** "Thrust" indicates that Hildebrand was forced into the duel against his will, which was most certainly the case given that he was unwillingly fighting his son. Choices (A) and (C) are too mild in representing what happened. Choice (D) is incorrect because Hildebrand was likely not murdered *prior* to the duel.

43. **(A)** An apostrophe before the "s" is needed to show that the singular "scribe" possesses the penmanship and also to show that the "poem" possesses the "lines." A comma is also needed after "penmanship" to indicate the end of the parenthetical phrase.

44. **(D)** The transliterated passage presented in the text shows that there is not a clear ending to the story, making "ambiguous" the best option. The other choices indicate much more decisive outcomes.

Math Test (No Calculator)

1. **(B)**

$$\frac{m^{\frac{5}{2}}}{m^{\frac{1}{2}}} \rightarrow \text{Factor out an } m^{\frac{1}{2}} \text{ on the top} \rightarrow \frac{m^{\frac{1}{2}}m^2}{m^{\frac{1}{2}}} \rightarrow$$

Cancel the $m^{\frac{1}{2}}$ from the top and bottom $\rightarrow m^2$

2. **(C)** $x = 36$ does not have a y-intercept since it runs parallel to the y-axis. Therefore, this equation never intersects the y-axis. Here is a graph of $x = 36$:

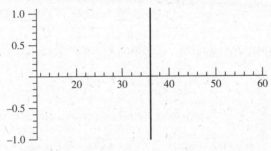

All of the other choices intersect the y-axis one time since they have a y-value when $x = 0$.

3. **(D)** There are 3 teaspoons in each tablespoon. So multiply $3 \times 3 \times 2$ to get the 18 total teaspoons needed for the 2 cakes.

4. **(C)** To format the equation like $3a + 4b$, multiply the entire equation by 12:

$$\frac{1}{4}a + \frac{1}{3}b = 2 \rightarrow \text{multiply by } 12 \rightarrow 3a + 4b = 24$$

Since there are two variables with just one equation, you need to do some sort of manipulation like this because a and b cannot be solved for individually without having another intersecting equation.

5. **(D)** Expand the expression and factor:

$$3a - 3(b - a) \rightarrow 3a - 3b + 3a \rightarrow 6a - 3b \rightarrow \text{factor} \rightarrow 3(2a - b)$$

6. **(D)** $\frac{2}{k} = x$ is undefined if $k = 0$. Dividing by 0 results in an undefined solution. All of the other equations have a solution for x when $k = 0$.

7. **(C)** Use substitution to solve for B.

$$2B = \frac{10}{9}A \rightarrow A = \frac{9}{5}B$$

Plug this into the other equation:

$$\frac{2}{3}A + \frac{3}{5}B = 4 \rightarrow \frac{2}{3}\left(\frac{9}{5}B\right) + \frac{3}{5}B = \frac{18}{15}B + \frac{9}{15}B = \frac{27}{15}B = 4$$

$$B = \frac{60}{27} = \frac{20}{9}$$

8. **(B)** When you are told, "Take an input variable," that refers to x. Then divide the x by 4 and subtract 5 from this, which gives the function $f(x) = \frac{x}{4} - 5$.

9. **(A)** This line has a y-intercept of -3 since that is where the line intersects the y-axis. You can calculate the slope using points on the line, $(0, -3)$ and $(6, 0)$:

$$\text{Slope} = \frac{\text{Rise}}{\text{Run}} = \frac{y_2 - y_1}{x_2 - x_1} = \frac{-3 - 0}{0 - 6} = \frac{1}{2}$$

Putting this in slope-intercept form ($y = mx + b$) results in the equation of the line:

$$y = \frac{1}{2}x - 3$$

10. **(C)** To minimize the overall gravitational force, the value of the numerator should be as small as possible and the value of the denominator should be as large as possible. Out of the possible answers, choice (C), would best accomplish this. It would make the value of $m_1 \times m_2$ as small as possible and make the denominator d^2 as large as possible.

11. **(A)** Set the two equations equal to each other. Express the result as a quadratic equation:

$$2x - 5 = 2x^2 + 4 \rightarrow 2x^2 - 2x + 9 = 0$$

Plug these values for a, b, and c into the quadratic equation. The only solutions are imaginary:

$$\frac{-b \pm \sqrt{b^2 - 4ac}}{2a} = \frac{2 \pm \sqrt{4 - 4 \times 18}}{2 \times 2} = \frac{2 \pm i\sqrt{68}}{4}$$

12. **(C)** Rewrite the table by calculating the actual sums:

n	Pattern	Sum
1	1	1
2	$1 + 3$	4
3	$1 + 3 + 5$	9
4	$1 + 3 + 5 + 7$	16
5	$1 + 3 + 5 + 7 + 9$	25

Each value in the "Sum" column is the corresponding value of n squared:

$$1 = 1^2 \,;\, 4 = 2^2 \,;\, 9 = 3^2 \,;\, 16 = 4^2 \,;\, 25 = 5^2$$

13. **(C)** The different terms on the two sides of the equation equal each other. So $-16 = -8b$, $-6x = -abx$, and $x^2 = x^2$. Why? This occurs because the constants must equal each other, the terms with an x must equal each other, and the terms with an x^2 must equal one another. Since $-16 = -8b$, $b = 2$. Plug in 2 for b in the second equation and cancel out the $-x$ to solve for a:

$$-6x = -abx \rightarrow 6 = a \cdot 2 \rightarrow a = 3$$

GRID-IN QUESTIONS

14.

Grid answer: **2**

2 Cancel out the y-terms on each side, and solve for x:

$$4x - y = \frac{1}{2}x - y + 7 \rightarrow 4x = \frac{1}{2}x + 7 \rightarrow 3.5x = 7 \rightarrow x = 2$$

15.

Grid answer: **17**

17 Work inside out by first solving for $g(1)$:

$$g(x) = 2x^2 \rightarrow g(1) = 2(1)^2 = 2.$$

Then put 2 in for x in the $f(x)$:

$$f(x) = 7x + 3 \rightarrow f(2) = 7(2) + 3 = 17$$

16.

Grid answer: **3**

3 There will be infinitely many solutions if the two equations are multiples of the same equation. The coefficients of the A and B terms in $A + 2B = 4$ add up to 3 since they are 1 and 2. Since $XA + YB = 4X$ is divisible by 4 on the right-hand side as is the other equation, the sum of X and Y must also be divisible by 3 in order for the two equations to be multiples of one another. To replicate the structure of the first equation, Y must equal $2X$ so that the two equations will be multiples of one another. To see this with greater clarity, consider this example:

$$A + 2B = 4$$
$$XA + YB = 4X$$

If the second equation had $X = 2$ and $Y = 4$, the equation would be twice the first equation: $2A + 4B = 8$. This equation is simply a multiple of the first one, making them essentially identical. As a result, there are infinitely many solutions since the equations overlap each other when graphed.

17.

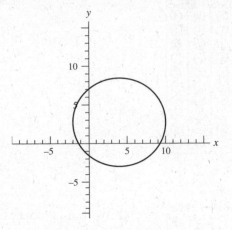

5 Based on the general equation of a circle, $(x - h)^2 + (y - k)^2 = r^2$, the center point is (h, k). For this circle, the center point is $(4, 3)$. This point is a distance of 5 from the origin, which has the coordinates $(0, 0)$. The graph of the circle is as follows:

You can calculate the shortest straight-line distance by using the distance formula or, even easier, recognizing that these numbers form a Pythagorean triple: 3-4-5. Recognizing that this is a Pythagorean triple will save you the time and trouble of calculating the distance using the distance formula.

Math Test (With Calculator)

1. **(C)** Multiply 180 by 1.61 to get the maximum value of the speedometer in kilometers per hour:

$$180\frac{\text{miles}}{\text{hr}} \times 1.61\frac{\text{km}}{\text{mile}} \to \text{the miles cancel} \to (180 \times 1.61)\frac{\text{km}}{\text{hr}} \approx 290\frac{\text{km}}{\text{hr}}$$

2. **(B)** Set up a proportion to solve for the unknown number of cups of flour.

Use the ratio 6 cupcakes to 3 cups of flour $\to \dfrac{6}{3} = \dfrac{15}{x} \to x = 7.5$

3. **(A)** Some approximate points that would be on the best-fit line are $(1990, 0)$ and $(1996, 18)$.

Calculate the approximate slope: $\dfrac{18 - 0}{1996 - 1990} = 3$, which comes closest to choice (A).

You can also visualize this by drawing the approximate best-fit line on the graph:

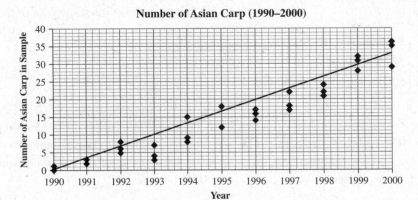

Number of Asian Carp (1990–2000)

4. **(B)** In the 10-year period shown in the graph, the number of carp has increased by approximately 35. After 15 more years of growth, there will be approximately 1.5 times the amount of growth that occurred during the 10-year period. To find the approximate total number of carp in 2015, calculate $35 + (1.5 \times 35) = 87.5$. This value is closest to choice (B). Since the calculation is an approximation, having a little variance in the answer is acceptable.

5. **(A)** Start by distributing the 2 through the parentheses on the left and the 3 through the parentheses on the right:

$$7 + 2(x - 3) = -3(x + 1) - 4$$
$$7 + 2x - 6 = -3x - 3 - 4$$

Simplify and solve for x:

$$1 + 2x = -3x - 7 \rightarrow$$
$$5x = -8 \rightarrow$$
$$x = -\frac{8}{5}$$

6. **(D)** Simplify by combining the like terms within the parentheses:

$$(x^2 + 3x^2)^3 = (4x^2)^3$$

Next cube both the 4 and the x^2:

$$(4x^2)^3 \rightarrow (4^3)(x^2)^3 \rightarrow 64x^6$$

7. **(B)** Factor an x^n out of the expression to get the answer:

$$4x^n + x^{4n} = x^n(4 + x^{3n})$$

You cannot combine x^n and x^{4n} into one term because they are not raised to the same power.

8. **(D)** The arithmetic mean is the average. Solve this problem using a weighted average. In other words, calculate the average by factoring in the relative amounts sold of the item by each store.

Store	Price Before Sale	Quantity Sold Before Sale	Sale Price	Quantity Sold After Sale
Store A	$12.50	350	$11.00	400
Store B	$13.25	260	$10.00	520
Store C	$11.75	550	$9.50	625
Store D	$14.00	220	$10.25	460

Store A sold 350 items for $12.50 each, and Store B sold 260 items for $13.25 each. The total number of items sold is $350 + 260$. You can compute the average as follows:

$$\frac{\text{Total income}}{\text{Total number of items sold}} = \frac{(12.50 \times 350) + (13.25 \times 260)}{(350 + 260)} \approx 12.8$$

9. **(C)** Calculate the slope of the line:

$$\text{Slope} = \frac{\text{Rise}}{\text{Run}} = \frac{y_2 - y_1}{x_2 - x_1} = \frac{14 - 10.25}{220 - 460} = -0.015625$$

Then create an equation for the line in slope-intercept form ($y = mx + b$) and solve for the y-intercept:

$$y = -0.015625x + b$$

Substitute a set of values from Store D to solve for b:

$$14 = (-0.015625 \times 220) + b \rightarrow b \approx 17.4$$

10. **(D)** The table does not specify whether or not sales tax is included in the given prices. If it is, the impact on the sales may be less pronounced than if sales tax is not included since consumers will still have to pay money in tax even if the item is on sale. The other choices would give irrelevant information. Choice (A) is incorrect because the prices at other retailers would not help determine the impact of sales at these stores. Choice (B) is incorrect because conducting a calculation will not give concrete information that will help you make a better prediction. Choice (C) is incorrect because no clear connection exists between employee motivation and the impact that these specific discounts would have on sales.

11. **(A)** The formula for calculating a percentage is $\frac{\text{Part}}{\text{Whole}} \times 100 = \text{Percentage}$.

So m represents the overall percentage, n represents the part, and x represents the whole. Plugging these values into the original equation gives:

$$\frac{\text{Part}}{\text{Whole}} \times 100 = \text{Percentage} \rightarrow$$

$$\frac{n}{x} \times 100 = m \rightarrow$$

$$n = \frac{mx}{100}$$

Alternatively, you can rephrase the question using concrete numbers:

"*If 10 represents 50 percent of 20, how can we calculate the value of 10?*" The only solution that gives the correct answer is choice (A):

$$\frac{\text{Part}}{\text{Whole}} \times 100 = \text{Percentage} \rightarrow$$

$$\frac{10}{20} \times 100 = 50 \rightarrow$$

$$10 = \frac{50 \times 20}{100}$$

This equation is in the same format as the equation shown in choice (A):

$$n = \frac{mx}{100}$$

12. **(C)** To determine a 3% increase on an original amount of x, add 3% to the original amount:

$$x + 0.03x = 1.03x$$

You can save time if you recognize that you can simply multiply x by 1.03 to determine the total of x plus 3% interest. The amount in the account is compounded twice. So multiply x by 1.03 twice:

$$x \cdot 1.03 \cdot 1.03 = 1.0609x$$

13. **(B)** Use substitution to solve for a:

$$b = 2a + 1 \text{ and } b + 2 = a^2 \rightarrow (2a+1) + 2 = a^2$$
$$2a + 3 = a^2 \rightarrow$$
$$a^2 - 2a - 3 = 0 \rightarrow (a-3)(a+1) = 0$$

When $a = 3$, $b = 7$, and when $a = -1$, $b = -1$.

14. **(D)** Use FOIL to calculate the product of the terms in parentheses:

$$2(a - 4b)(3 + b^3) = 2(3a + ab^3 - 12b - 4b^4) = 6a + 2ab^3 - 24b - 8b^4$$

Rearrange the values to put them in the order shown in the choices:

$$2ab^3 + 6a - 8b^4 - 24b$$

15. **(A)** For each hour the librarian works, he or she shelves a total of 220 items. Therefore, the total number of items shelved during T hours is $220 \times T$. The other answer choices have constants either added or subtracted to the term multiplied by T. These answer choices would illogically mean that the librarian could shelve or remove items without spending any time at all doing so.

16. **(C)** Bonds represented 30% of the 2000 portfolio and 22% of the 2020 portfolio. You can find the increase in bonds by subtracting the 2000 bond amount from the 2020 bond amount:

$$(0.22 \times 200,000) - (0.3 \times 80,000) = 20,000$$

17. **(B)** Based on the numbers in the previous question, the portfolio is increasing by $60,000 every 10 years. You add $60,000 to the 2020 value of $200,000 to get $260,000. Alternatively, you could calculate the slope of increase. However, noticing this simple pattern will save you time.

18. **(D)** The tables give information only about the allocation of international and domestic stocks. They do not contain any information about the allocation of large-capitalization stocks, mid-capitalization stocks, and small-capitalization stocks. So not enough information is provided to reach a conclusion.

19. **(A)** The height of Pam's television is 36 inches since 48:36 reduces to her screen ratio of 4:3. You can determine how many inches of height the movie image will take up on Pam's TV by setting up a ratio: $\frac{1}{1.85} = \frac{x}{48} \rightarrow x \approx 26$. Now subtract the height of the movie from the height of the TV screen to determine how many inches of screen height will NOT be used: $36 - 26 = 10$.

20. **(C)** Since there are three separate measurements that are each off by up to 2 units, you can determine the range of possible values by adding all the individual measurements together and then including a range of plus or minus 6:

$$48 + 56 + 40 = 144$$
$$144 + 6 = 150$$
$$144 - 6 = 138$$

Choice (C) shows the correct range.

21. **(C)** Try plugging in some sample values, like 2 and 100, for x and assume n is a constant like 3 to see how the equations behave:

Equation	Substitute $x=2$ and $n=3$	Value when $x=2$ and $n=3$	Substitute $x=100$ and $n=3$	Value when $x=100$ and $n=3$
A. $y=nx+3$	$y=3\times2+3$	9	$y=3\times100+3$	303
B. $y=-nx+3$	$y=-3\times2+3$	-3	$y=-3\times100+3$	-297
C. $y=x^n+3$	$y=2^3+3$	11	$y=100^3+3$	1,000,003
D. $y=x^{-n}+3$	$y=2^{-3}+3$	$3\frac{1}{8}$	$y=100^{-3}+3$	3.000001

Choice (C) clearly has the greatest overall increase, going from 11 to 1,000,003.

Alternatively, you can simply realize that a number greater than 1 to a power more than 1 will be greater than the other possibilities.

22. **(A)** Since the company does not want the passengers to lose consciousness, the passengers must not experience g forces equal to or greater than 5. The only possible range of g-values is $g < 5$, in which all the g-values are less than 5.

23. **(B)** The programs are permitted a maximum of 12 coaches. So C must be equal to or less than 12. Choice (B) is the only option with this statement. All of the other options do not allow for the full range of possible values for the number of coaches. Moreover, the number of players will be limited by the number of coaches if the university is to maintain a ratio of a maximum of 4 players per coach. By making the number of players less than or equal to 4 times the number of coaches, $P \le 4C$, the university will ensure that it has at least 1 coach for every 4 players.

24. **(A)** Plug the given values into the equation:

$$\text{Final velocity} = \text{Initial velocity} + \text{Acceleration} \times \text{Time}$$

$$\text{Initial velocity} = 4\frac{\text{m}}{\text{s}}$$

$$\text{Acceleration} = 6\frac{\text{m}}{\text{s}^2}$$

$$\text{Final velocity} = 22\frac{\text{m}}{\text{s}}$$

The final velocity must be *at least* $22\frac{\text{m}}{\text{s}}$. Set up the inequality so that the result for the final velocity could exceed $22\frac{\text{m}}{\text{s}}$:

$$22 \le 4 + 6T$$
$$18 \le 6T$$
$$3 \le T$$

25. **(C)** Plug the freezing point of water in degrees C into the equation:

$$K = 273 + C$$
$$K = 273 + 0 = 273$$

Choice (C) is the only option that has 273 for the freezing point. You can also plug in 100 for the boiling point in degrees C. You will get 373 as the result.

26. **(B)** Divide $1.0 \times 10^6 \dfrac{\text{kg}}{\text{m}^3}$ by $990 \dfrac{\text{kg}}{\text{m}^3}$ to determine by what multiple her weight will increase. Her weight will be 1,010 times greater. Then multiply 1,010 by 150 pounds to get 151,500 pounds.

27. **(B)** Use the formula Distance = Rate × Time to make your calculations. The distance is 16 km for the journey in either direction. The rates, however, are different. The rate going upstream is $1 \dfrac{\text{km}}{\text{hr}}$ less than the rate at which John is actually rowing because he is going against the current. The rate going downstream is $1 \dfrac{\text{km}}{\text{hr}}$ more than the rate at which he is actually rowing because he is going with the current. If x is the rate at which John is rowing, the time, u, to go upstream is:

$$d = ru \rightarrow 16 = (x-1)u \rightarrow u = \frac{16}{x-1}$$

The time going downstream, t, can be calculated in a similar way:

$$d = rt \rightarrow 16 = (x+1)t \rightarrow t = \frac{16}{x+1}$$

Since the total time of the journey is 4 hours, combine these two expressions together into one equation:

$$\frac{16}{x-1} + \frac{16}{x+1} = 4$$

Then solve for x:

$$\frac{16}{x-1} + \frac{16}{x+1} = 4 \rightarrow \frac{16(x+1)}{(x-1)(x+1)} + \frac{16(x-1)}{(x+1)(x-1)} = 4 \rightarrow$$

$$\frac{16(x+1) + 16(x-1)}{x^2 - 1} = 4 \rightarrow \frac{16x + 16 + 16x - 16}{x^2 - 1} = 4 \rightarrow$$

$$\frac{32x}{x^2 - 1} = 4 \rightarrow 32x = 4x^2 - 4 \rightarrow 4x^2 - 32x - 4 = 0 \rightarrow x^2 - 8x - 1 = 0$$

Use the quadratic formula to solve:

$$\frac{-b \pm \sqrt{b^2 - 4ac}}{2a} \rightarrow \frac{8 \pm \sqrt{(-8)^2 - 4 \cdot 1 \cdot (-1)}}{2 \cdot 1} = \frac{8 \pm \sqrt{68}}{2} = \frac{8 \pm 2\sqrt{17}}{2} = 4 \pm \sqrt{17}$$

You get two solutions. However, you can use only $4 + \sqrt{17}$ since velocity cannot be negative.

The value of $4 + \sqrt{17}$ is approximately 8.1.

28.

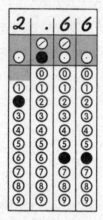

4 Set up equations expressing the total costs for each D.J., where T represents time:

$$\text{D.J. A's cost: } 300 + 150T$$
$$\text{D.J. B's cost: } 200 + 175T$$

Set the equations equal to one another, and solve for time:

$$300 + 150T = 200 + 175T \rightarrow 100 = 25T \rightarrow T = 4$$

29.

2.66 or 2.67 Marcus purchased $34 of gas at $3 a gallon. You can determine how many gallons of gas he purchased:

$$\frac{34}{3} = 11.33\overline{3}$$

Then subtract 11.333 from the total capacity of the tank:

$$14 - 11.333 \approx 2.67$$

You can answer 2.66 or 2.67—the PSAT will be fine if you round up or round down. Just be sure to fill out all the spots in the grid.

30.

5 Since the supply and demand are at equilibrium, set the two expressions equal to one another and solve for the number of lamps:

$$30 - \text{Quantity} = 10 + 3 \times \text{Quantity}$$
$$20 = 4 \times \text{Quantity}$$
$$5 = \text{Quantity}$$

31.

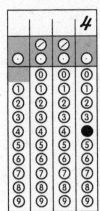

4 You can see what the side lengths are of this particular triangle in the drawing below:

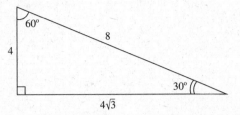

You can easily calculate these side lengths because this is a 30-60-90 triangle. So the side lengths can be expressed as x, $\sqrt{3}x$, and $2x$. (This formula is provided at the beginning of the math section.) The hypotenuse of 8 equals $2x$, and the shortest side equals x. Do the calculations to find the length of the shortest side:

$$8 = 2x$$
$$x = 4$$

Alternatively, you can just recognize that ratio of the smallest side to the hypotenuse in a 30-60-90 triangle is 1:2. So the value of the smallest side in a right triangle with a hypotenuse of 8 is 4.

Appendix

Appendix:
After the PSAT

Now that you have prepared for the PSAT, what comes next in terms of the National Merit Scholarship program and your future testing?

When Should I Receive My PSAT Test Results?

PSAT results from the October test date are typically available in mid-December. Be sure to get access to your online score report so that you can review questions you missed and the correct answers. You can find your score report at *www.psat.org/myscore*.

If you forget your online access information, your guidance counselor should be able to help you figure out how to log in.

Some schools also have the hard copies of the test booklets that you used for the PSAT. If so, be sure to ask your school for these so you can use them for future practice.

How Does National Merit Recognition Work?

Each year, about 1.6 million juniors take the PSAT. Out of those 1.6 million students, these are the numbers that receive some sort of recognition:

- **COMMENDED STUDENTS:** About 34,000 top PSAT scorers (approximately the 97th–98th percentile of test takers) receive letters of commendation.
- **NATIONAL MERIT SEMIFINALISTS:** About 16,000 students (approximately the 99th percentile, or the top 1 percent of all test takers)

  - Commended students and semifinalists are notified of their status in the September after taking the PSAT.

- **NATIONAL MERIT FINALISTS:** About 15,000 of the National Merit Semifinalists are named National Merit Finalists by meeting the program requirements (including maintaining high academic standing, confirming their PSAT performance with ACT or SAT scores, and being recommended by their high school principal).

  - National Merit Finalists learn of their status in February of their senior year.

- **NATIONAL MERIT SCHOLARS:** About 7,500 of National Merit Finalists are awarded National Merit Scholarships, ranging from one-time payments of $2,500 to recurring awards depending on the scholarship. (Approximately one-half of 1 percent of PSAT test takers earn a National Merit Scholarship.)

  - National Merit Scholars learn of their status between March and June of their senior year.
  - To earn the National Merit Scholarship, students are evaluated on their test scores, academic record, school recommendation, personal essay, and other factors.[1]

[1]*www.nationalmerit.org*

What if I Was Unable to Take the PSAT Because I Was Sick or Something Unusual Happened at the Test Site That Affected the Test Administration?

You should write to the National Merit Scholarship Program and explain your situation as soon as possible. Notify them by November 15 about any testing irregularities. Notify them by April 1 about the need for an alternate entry. Mail requests to the following address:

National Merit Scholarship Corporation
Attn: Scholarship Administration
1560 Sherman Avenue, Suite 200
Evanston, IL 60201-4897

It is advisable to confirm this mailing address at *www.nationalmerit.org*.

How Can I Use My Official PSAT Score Report to Help Me?

You can access your PSAT score online at *www.psat.org/myscore*. Among the key things to check out:

YOUR NMSC SELECTION INDEX: This number determines your eligibility for the National Merit Scholarship competition and is calculated by doubling your scores from the Reading, Writing/Language, and Math section scores. (Each section has a maximum score of 38, so the maximum selection index score is twice the sum of these three section scores—228.)

- To be selected as a National Merit Semifinalist, you will typically need a National Merit selection index of around 218. National Merit Scholarships are allocated on the basis of state representation, and the cutoff scores can be different depending on the state in which you reside. If you live in Massachusetts, for example, you may need a selection index of as high as 223. If you live in Wyoming, you may only need a selection index of 212.

QUESTION-LEVEL FEEDBACK: Evaluate which questions you answered correctly and which questions you missed.

- Take advantage of the online resources that allow you to review the actual test questions and answer explanations. This is the best possible diagnostic tool you can use, since you can carefully analyze what gave you difficulty on the PSAT, which is a preview of the SAT.
- As you review the questions you missed, look for patterns in what gave you difficulty:
- Did you have trouble with timing, either finishing too quickly and making careless errors or taking too much time and not attempting later questions?
- Should you focus your future practice on certain types of questions or material, such as grammar concepts, math concepts, or styles of reading passages?
- Did you have trouble with endurance during the test? Did your performance diminish as time went on? Do you need to do a better job getting enough rest in the days leading up to the test?

When Should I Take the SAT?

The SAT is used for college admissions purposes, and your performance on the PSAT will give you a great indication of how you will perform on the SAT. The SAT is offered several times during the year, typically during these months:

- March
- May
- June
- August
- October
- November
- December

You can register for the SAT by going to *www.collegeboard.org*. You should take the SAT at a time that works well with your schedule, and it is fine to take it at least two to three times if need be. Colleges will consider the best score you provide, and some will even "superscore"—i.e., take the best score from each section of the test.

Should I Take the ACT?

All colleges will accept either the SAT or the ACT for college admissions purposes, so you will likely want to try the ACT at least once. If you are a faster test taker and you are good at science, the ACT may be a particularly good fit for you—there is a science reasoning section on the ACT, and the ACT has more questions than the SAT to finish in the given amount of time. Fortunately, the ACT and SAT cover many of the same grammar and math concepts, so by preparing for one test, you are essentially preparing for the other.

Index

square, completing the, 350
standard deviation, 342–343
statistics, 342–346
   confidence interval, 343–344
   margin of error, 344
   mean/median/mode, 339–341
   range and standard deviation, 342–343
stress, handling, 4–5
style and tone questions, 219–220
subject, sentence, 225
subject-verb agreement questions, 238
subordination/coordination questions, 227
substitution, to solve a system of
     equations, 315
subtraction, of fractions, 322
sum of cubes, 348
support questions, 203–204
synthetic division, 353
systems of equations, solving, 317–321

T
tables, two-way, 332
tangent, 362
test accommodations, 4
test booklet, writing on the, 78, 80,
     200–201
thesis statements, 202
time, getting extra, 4
time/rate/distance problems, 318–321
timing strategies

   with math sections, 382–383, 396–397,
     428
   with reading passages, 77, 79
   with writing and language section, 200
tone, questions focusing on style and,
     219–220
topic sentences, 202
transitional words, 213
transitions, questions about, 213–216
triangle(s)
   area of a, 370
   right, 362, 370
trigonometry, 362–365
two-way tables, 332

U
undefined functions, 350
underlined portion (in test questions), 228
underlining, 78, 80, 200
underthinking, 382
"unfair" questions, 384
unfamiliar concepts, dealing with, 393–395
unit conversion problems, 391–392
unnecessary-punctuation questions,
     250–251
usage rules, in writing and language
     section, 199

V
variables

directly vs. inversely proportional, 337
   in systems of equations, 318
variation, direct vs. inverse, 337
verb, agreement of, with subject, 238
verb use questions, 230–232
volume formulas, 370

W
word meaning
   commonly confused words, 239–241
   and context, 217
   literal vs. intended meaning, 229
word-meaning questions, 81–82
word problems, translating, into algebraic
     expressions, 385–386
writing and language section, 199–279
   advanced drills, 281–309
   conventions of usage questions, 235–244
   idea development questions, 202–211
   practice exercises, 252–277
   preparing for, beyond this book, 279
   punctuation questions, 244–252
   scope of, 199
   strategies to use in, 200–201
   structure of, 199
   troubleshooting with, 278
writing on the test booklet, 78, 80, 200–201

Z
zeros (of a function), 357–358